About the Authors

MICHAEL CORRIGAN BCL (NUI) is a partner in the Dublin firm of solicitors, Corrigan and Corrigan. He graduated from University College Dublin in 1985 and qualified as a solicitor in 1989. He specialises in all areas of insurance-related litigation. He has lectured widely and has had many articles on insurance law published both in Ireland and abroad.

JOHN A. CAMPBELL MA (TCD) DIP EL (NUI) DIP ARB LAW (DIT) is a member of the Legal Department of AGF Irish Life Holdings Plc, having joined its subsidiary company, Church & General, in 1990. He graduated from the Law School, Trinity College in 1984 and qualified as a solicitor in 1988. He is a tutor on the Litigation module of the Law Society's Professional Course for Solicitors' Apprentices.

A Casebook of
Irish Insurance Law

Michael Corrigan
and
John A. Campbell

Oak Tree Press
Dublin

28/5/02

Oak Tree Press
Merrion Building
Lower Merrion Street, Dublin 2

© 1995 Michael Corrigan, John A. Campbell

A catalogue record of this book is
available from the British Library.

ISBN 1-872853-30-7 paperback
ISBN 1-872853-31-5 hardback

Cover Design: Mark Loughran

Printed in Ireland by Colour Books Ltd.

This book is dedicated to the memory of

*The Hon. Mr Justice Niall St John McCarthy
and his wife, Barbara*

and

James J. Sheehan

Contents

Acknowledgements

The publishers and authors would like to thank the following for generously allowing the reproduction of copyright material:

The Incorporated Council of Law Reporting for Ireland for *The Irish Reports*; The Round Hall Press for the *Irish Law Reports Monthly* and the *Irish Law Times Reports*; the Irish Jurist for the *Irish Jurist Reports*; and the Chief Justice and the President of the High Court for the unreported judgments of the Supreme Court and High Court.

Table of Statutes

Table of Cases

Note: References in bold indicate extracts from judgments

Introduction

Irish lawyers are well served by the wealth of legal texts, journals and reports available to them. Few fields of Irish Law remain unexplored and uncharted. Surprisingly, insurance law is such a field. It undoubtedly requires a comprehensive analysis, comparison and criticism that only a detailed academic work can deliver. This is especially so now, as in recent years the Irish Courts have shown themselves quite prepared to depart from established foreign precedent and develop their own independent jurisprudence. It is our hope that this casebook, in bringing together for the first time all the important Irish cases on insurance law, will be seen as a significant first step and encouragement to those more qualified than ourselves to undertake such an academic treatment. While such a work is awaited, this book should serve as a practical reference text and guide for everyone involved in the Irish insurance community, whether they be insurance agents, brokers, insurers, adjusters, assessors or lawyers.

As with any casebook, the cases included in this volume are left very much to speak for themselves. We have identified clearly those cases from which only extracts have been reproduced or which have been edited for ease of reference and clarity of expression. Those seeking to examine the details of a specific case may consider it appropriate to seek out the original text. In the introduction to each chapter, it has been our intention to place each case in the context of the general principles with which it deals and in context with the other cases in each of the chapters. We have deliberately kept the instructions general and simple in an attempt to avoid any unnecessary legal "jargon".

It was clear when preparing this book that there were significant areas of insurance law for which Irish authorities did not exist, most notably relating to the inception and provision of indemnity and the settlement of claims. This is undoubtedly as a consequence of the arbitration process in the resolution of disputes between insurers and their insureds. Unlike Great Britain the arbitration clause in Irish insurance contracts is generally all-embracing and not merely restricted to disputes where policy indemnity has been confirmed. Because of this significance and importance to Irish insurance law, we have devoted an entire chapter to it and its particular characteristics in insurance disputes.

In researching and preparing this book we have learnt a lot, not only in relation to the cases themselves but also from observing the manner in which the Irish courts have dealt with the problems raised in the cases. It was interesting to discover that the humane and practical approach adopted by the Irish judiciary has been present in the earliest of insurance cases coming before the Irish courts. As far back as the eighteenth century, the Irish judiciary have been quick to protect those who did not share the expertise and skill of the large corporation. In so doing they have shared the historical mistrust that Irish people display towards insurance companies, a mistrust well illustrated in the second act of Seán O'Casey's *The Shadow of a Gunman*, where a most concerned Mrs Grigson, worried at her husband's continued well-being, enquires of the hapless Seamus Shields:

> Mrs G.:   Do the Insurance Companies pay if a man is shot after curfew?
>
> S.S.:   Well now, that's a thing I couldn't say, Mrs Grigson.
>
> Mrs G.:   Isn't he a terrible man to be takin' such risks, an' not knowin' what'll happen to him. He knows them societies only want an excuse to do people out of their money....

With the voluntary adoption in 1989, in conjunction with the Insurance Act of that year, of quite strict "Codes of Practice for Life and Non-Life Insurance", and the appointment of an Insurance Ombudsman, Irish insurers have shown themselves quite prepared to honour obligations they assume to their policy-holders. There remains, however, the very real danger from those who seek to take advantage of, and abuse, the doctrine of "utmost good faith" and the trust that supports any contract of insurance. Insurers and the judiciary alike must therefore be vigilant to prevent and discourage such abuse in order to preserve the integrity of the contract of insurance. A careful balance must be kept and it is hoped that this book, by adding and contributing to a greater understanding of many of the principles of law involved, will help that process.

Each of us is responsible for the preparation of individual chapters. John A. Campbell's are Chapters 1, 2, 6, 10, 11 and 14. Michael Corrigan's are Chapters 3, 4, 5, 7, 8, 9, 12, 13 and 15. Responsibility is of course shared jointly.

Finally, we would ask fellow practitioners to advise us on any cases they might learn of that ought to be included in future editions. It would be our intention that this text will be updated and improved for the benefit of all.

We would like to acknowledge the support and assistance of all those who have contributed to the publication of this book and in particular: —

Our colleagues in Corrigan and Corrigan and in the legal department at Burlington House together with Rory Brady BL, Niamh Cronin, Frank Duggan BL, Kieran Fleck BL, Paul Gallagher SC, Malcolm Hughes, Peter M. Keane BL, Lyndon McCann BL, Laura Morrisey, John Murphy BL, Caeva O'Callaghan, Gerry O'Connor.

The personnel in the libraries of University College Dublin, Trinity College Dublin, the Society of Kings Inns and the Incorporated Law Society, and finally all our friends and colleagues in the insurance industry in Ireland.

Michael Corrigan
John A. Campbell

"A Policy ought be so framed that he who runs can read. It ought be so framed with such deliberate care, that no form of expression by which the party assured can be caught on the one hand, or by which the Company can be cheated on the other, shall be found on the face of it, and nothing should be wanting in it the absence of which may lead to such result."

Lord St Leonards
Anderson v. *Fitzgerald*
1853

CHAPTER 1

The Nature of the Contract

The essential nature of the contract of insurance has been the subject of regular judicial consideration. The leading Irish authority is *International Commercial Bank* v. *Insurance Corporation of Ireland (1990)* which concerned a loan made to a Swiss company to buy a hotel in Greece. Unfortunately for all concerned, Greek Law did not permit foreign ownership of either Greek land or shares in Greek companies. Three issues fell to be considered by Blayney J. in the High Court.

The first of these issues was the question as to whether the credit guarantee insurance agreement between the bank and ICI was a contract of insurance or one of guarantee. The second issue was whether the insurance brokers who arranged the agreement were acting as agents of the bank. ICI's claim for a complete indemnity from a re-insurance company (Meadows) was the third issue considered.

The High Court decision on this third issue was unsuccessfully appealed to the Supreme Court. The case is an interesting illustration of the way in which several related issues may arise out of the one business transaction.

One of the fundamental and distinguishing ingredients of the contract of insurance is that it is a contract of *uberrimae fidei* or *utmost good faith* as between the parties. This requirement imposes a duty on a party to disclose relevant (or material) facts within their knowledge to the other party in order that any decision made in relation to the contract is a fully informed one.

It is clear from *Murphy* v. *PMPA* (1978) that a corresponding obligation of confidentiality or a duty of non-disclosure is imposed on the part of the insurer in respect of information disclosed by the policy holder in such circumstances. In this case a Garda inspector was unsuccessful when he sought information from an insurance company on one of its policy holders.

International Commercial Bank plc *v*. Insurance Corporation of Ireland plc and Meadows Indemnity Company Ltd. (third party)
[1991] I.L.R.M. 726
The High Court

BLAYNEY J: In this action the plaintiff (to which I shall refer as the bank) claims against the defendant (to which I shall refer as ICI) the sum of 11.5 million Swiss Francs, together with interest, the principal and interest now being the equivalent of IR£6,237,040. This sum is alleged to be due under a credit guarantee insurance agreement entered into between ICI and the bank on 9 February 1984 whereby ICI agreed to indemnify the bank in the event of default being made by Amaxa SA (to which I shall refer as Amaxa), a Swiss registered company, in the repayment of a loan of 11.5 million Swiss Francs made to it by the bank. In the event of the bank's claim being successful, ICI claims against the third party (to which I shall refer as Meadows) a complete indemnity by virtue of re-insurance entered into between ICI and Meadows.

As between the bank and ICI the first issue that has to be considered is whether the credit guarantee insurance agreement was a contract of insurance or a contract of guarantee. ICI's case is that it was a contract of insurance, that there was non-disclosure by the bank of a material fact; that this made the agreement avoidable, and that it has been avoided by ICI. On the other hand, if the agreement was a contract of guarantee, since such a contract does not require *uberrima fides,* non-disclosure of a material fact would not affect its validity and the agreement would be binding on ICI.

A further issue arises as to the agency of the brokers who arranged the credit guarantee insurance agreement. ICI contends that they were the agents of the bank, and as it is on non-disclosure by them, and not by any servant of the bank, that ICI relies, proof of their agency is a crucial part of ICI's case, and this is contested by the bank.

As between ICI and Meadows, in the event of the bank's claim succeeding, ICI claims a complete indemnity from Meadows. This is resisted by Meadows on the grounds that it was fundamental to their agreeing to re-insure that ICI had obtained adequate collateral to secure their liability as insurers; that it was ICI's responsibility to obtain that collateral and that they had not done so. In addition they say that certain matters that were very material to the re-insurance risk being underwritten by Meadows were not disclosed by ICI and that they are accordingly entitled to avoid the contract of re-insurance.

Most of the basic facts are not in dispute and are as follows. The bank agreed to lend to Amaxa the sum of 11.5 million Swiss Francs on the terms of a loan agreement entered into between the parties in London on 9 February 1984. On the same date, ICI, in consideration of the bank making the said loan to Amaxa, undertook that, in the event of Amaxa failing to pay the bank any sum or sums due for payment in accordance with the loan agreement, it would irrevocably and unconditionally indemnify the bank for 100% of the amount of such sum or sums. The said indemnity was granted to the bank by ICI by way of a credit guarantee insurance agreement in writing for a period of seven years, subject to an annual premium of 201,250 Swiss Francs payable by Amaxa. ICI re-insured the entire risk of the said credit guarantee insurance with Meadows.

The bank duly lent 11.5 million Swiss Francs to Amaxa pursuant to the loan agreement. In 1987 Amaxa made default in making the payments due and the principal and all arrears of interest thereupon became payable. These were not paid by Amaxa. The bank thereupon called on ICI, pursuant to the terms of its credit guarantee insurance agreement to pay what was due and on ICI failing to pay the present proceedings were issued, and subsequently Meadows was brought in by ICI as a third party.

Amaxa is owned by two Greek nationals, Chrysostomos Kazantzis (to whom I shall refer as Mr Kazantzis) and his brother Gregory. Their father, Alexander Kazantzis was, at the time of the loan, the principal shareholder in a family company, the Kazantzis Hotel and Tourist Enterprise Co., which owned the Kerkira Golf Hotel in Corfu. Mr Kazantzis wished to buy out his father's interest in the family company and it was for this purpose that the loan was required.

Mr Kazantzis began his search for the necessary finance in the middle of 1983. He started by contacting a Mr Roy Fenn, who carried on business in the city of London, and he in turn contacted Mr John Gibbs who had at one time been a Lloyds' broker and had then engaged in a number of other businesses. Mr Gibbs put Mr Kazantzis in touch with the firm of Lloyds' brokers, Eberli and Shorter, but they were unable to assist. Mr Gibbs then contacted Mr Alfred Francis who had also retired from a career in the City, and was carrying on business on his own account part of which consisted in introducing prospective clients to banks.

The security being offered by Mr Kazantzis was the hotel in Corfu. Mr Francis turned this down. He took the view that no bank would be prepared to lend on such security but he suggested that a lending institution he was acquainted with might be prepared to make a loan on the security of a credit guarantee insurance agreement. Mr Francis had a copy of a set of conditions appropriate to such a type of insurance which he knew would be acceptable to the lending institution he had in mind which was a firm registered in Switzerland called Omni Commerce.

Mr Gibbs then attempted to obtain this type of insurance cover. He got in touch with Mr Jacobson, the President of Frank B. Hall of New Jersey, an American firm of insurance brokers, and Mr Jacobson tried to find an insurance company in the United States to underwrite the insurance but was unsuccessful. Frank B. Hall had an English subsidiary, Leslie and Godwin, one of the directors of which was Mr Robin McMillan. Mr McMillan took on the job of placing the insurance and got in touch with Mr John Grace, the general manager of ICI in London. They had a meeting in Mr Grace's office on 27 September 1983. Mr McMillan was offering what was known as a bouquet of insurance, i.e., insurance for different risks in respect of the Kerkira Golf Hotel, one of them being a form of credit guarantee insurance.

Following this meeting Mr McMillan sent Mr Grace what is known in insurance circles as a slip. This is a proposal made by a broker to an underwriter asking him to quote a premium for a particular insurance and to indicate what percentage of the risk he would be prepared to take. This slip was stamped by the Re-Insurance Corporation Guernsey (to which I shall refer as RCG) an insurance company set up by ICI in Guernsey, and by Meadows. This indicated an interest on the part of both these companies in quoting for the insurance. The slip had been brought to Guernsey by Mr Grace when he went there on 12 October for a board meeting of Meadows the following day. Mr Grace was a consultant to Meadows and in that capacity attended its board meetings. Mr Grace discussed the contents of the slip with Mr Michael Savage who managed the day to day affairs of Meadows and also with Mr Mascarella, the vice-president and general manager of Meadows who was the person responsible for taking the ultimate decisions as to what risks to underwrite.

Meadows had been incorporated in Guernsey in 1976 by Gould, an American company in the electronics business. It was set up as a captive insurance company, i.e., a company doing no business other than with its parent. In 1983 its business was managed by Channel Island Insurance Consultants Ltd of which Mr Michael Savage was the company secretary. He was also a director and the secretary of Meadows. Throughout 1983 and the part of 1984 with which this case is concerned, Mr Savage had charge of the management of Meadows but it was not part of his function to take any of the underwriting decisions. In 1978 or 1979 Meadows had begun writing a limited amount of business for companies other than its parent. One of the companies with which Meadows did re-insurance business was ICI and this had begun about 1979. Mr Grace and Mr Savage had been acquainted since then.

The slip was stamped by both RCG and Meadows on 17 October 1983. Mr Savage was the chief executive of RCG as well as being a director and the secretary of Meadows. And Mr Grace was a director of RCG in addition to being general manager of ICI in London.

It then emerged that the period of insurance proposed by the slip, which was three years, was too short. Mr McMillan required seven years rather than three. RCG was unable to underwrite a policy of that length so Mr Grace proposed to Mr Savage that Meadows should take the entire risk. Mr Savage consulted Mr Mascarella and having got the necessary authority from him he agreed that Meadows would issue a credit guarantee insurance policy for seven years. As an indication of Meadows' willingness to do this Mr Savage, on 20 October 1983, signed a copy of the credit guarantee insurance conditions which it was proposed to incorporate in the agreement.

Mr Mascarella stated in evidence that what he believed he had authorised Mr Savage to do was not to have Meadows as the direct insurer but simply as the re-insurer, with ICI as the direct insurer. He said he presumed all along, because of Meadows' previous relations with ICI, that insofar as Meadows was concerned what was involved from the beginning was re-insurance and not insurance. But I am satisfied that Mr Savage honestly believed that he had been authorised firstly, to insure directly half of the risk, and then the entire risk; however, as a subsequent development brought an alteration in the situation which made it immaterial whether he was correct in his belief of not, it is not necessary to decide if he was. If I had had to decide the issue, I would have been more inclined to accept Mr Savage's evidence rather than Mr Mascarella's which was largely based on presumptions.

The lending institution which was considering making the loan in October

1983 was not prepared to accept Meadows as the insurer because its capital was not sufficiently big, and it became necessary then to find another company to effect the insurance, with Meadows acting as the re-insurer. Mr McMillan agreed in the course of his cross-examination that what this meant was that he had to look for a fronting company, i.e., a company that would accept the primary risk but would be wholly indemnified by Meadows as the re-insurer. He approached Mr Grace with the request that ICI would front the transaction and, after some hesitation, Mr Grace agreed. This was about 7 November 1983. There was then a period in which nothing happened. Mr Grace said he thought the proposal had died a death. He had been away in January 1984 and when he came back to his office on 2 February 1984 he found that a meeting had been arranged with the bank on that day or the following day.

What had happened in the meantime was that Mr Francis on 23 January 1984 had spoken on the telephone about the transaction to Mr Pierce Phipps, the deputy general manager of the bank, who was in charge of their corporate finance department. Mr Francis followed his telephone call up immediately by writing to Mr Phipps on the same day and sending him a copy of the documentation which he had prepared when the loan was to have been made by Omni-Commerce.

From this point on matters moved very rapidly. At Mr Phipps' request a meeting with Mr Kazantzis was arranged. This took pace a few days after 23 January 1984. In addition to Mr Phipps and Mr Kazantzis, it was attended by Mr Francis, Mr Gibbs and Mr Mark Landale, a manager in the bank's corporate finance department. The purpose of the meeting was for Mr Phipps to become acquainted with Mr Kazantzis; to have Mr Kazantzis explain the deal to Mr Phipps and finally for Mr Phipps to obtain from Mr Kazantzis such additional information as he required.

The bank then sought references in respect of Amaxa and Mr Kazantzis from Swiss, German and English banks, and asked their solicitors, Norton Rose, to check that Amaxa was properly constituted under Swiss law. They also asked their solicitors to prepare the documentation which would be required to give effect to the transaction.

Two meetings were held before the loan agreement was signed on 9 February 1984, the first being referred to in evidence as the principals' meeting and the second, the lawyers' meeting. Nothing of significance was said or done at either of them so it is not necessary to give a detailed account of either. Present at the principals' meeting were Mr Kazantzis, Mr McMillan (who had to leave early), Mr Phipps and Mr Grace, and at the lawyers' meeting, Mr Grace, Miss Olwen Jones of Norton Rose, and Mr Mark Landale. At the principals' meeting Mr Grace stated that ICI wanted to enter into the credit guarantee insurance agreement in Guernsey. Mr Phipps said that he had no objection to this as long as it was ICI who was entering into the agreement. At the lawyers' meeting Miss Jones asked that Mr Grace's authority to sign the agreement be confirmed by a resolution of the board of ICI. Mr Grace took offence at this suggestion and would have refused to enter into the agreement if the request was insisted on. It was not.

The loan agreement was executed in the offices of the bank on 9 February 1984. The credit guarantee insurance agreement was executed in Guernsey by Mr Savage on the following day acting under an express written authority from Mr Grace. It was common case that both agreements were validly executed.

The loan was drawn down by Amaxa on 14 February 1984. During the first three years of the loan only interest was payable. These payments were met. The first instalment of principal, 1,045,455 Swiss Francs became due on 17 February 1987. It was not paid. This constituted an event of default under clause 10 of the loan agreement and entitled the bank to call in the entire loan of 11.5 million Swiss Francs which they did on 5 May 1987. On the same day the bank sought payment from ICI. ICI failed to pay and these proceedings were commenced by summary summons on 1 September 1987.

There is another aspect of the facts to which it is now necessary to turn. It figured very largely in the amended defence delivered by ICI and, while not expressly abandoned, it was considerably attenuated in counsel's closing submissions. From an early stage in the transaction it was intended that ICI would be given security by Mr Kazantzis which they could call on if they had to pay under the credit guarantee insurance. In a letter of 25 November 1983 from Mr Kazantzis to Mr Gibbs, Mr Kazantzis had said "the insurance company will have to be secured". And in a telex sent by Mr Grace to Omni-Commerce on 5 December 1983 Mr Grace confirmed that ICI, once they had received satisfactory security from the client, would be willing to guarantee the loan agreement. ICI alleged in their defence that various representations had been made to Mr Grace by the bank, its servants and agents in regard to the nature of the security and its value. In reply to a notice for particulars ICI alleged that the representations had been made by Mr McMillan and Mr Francis, and also by Mr Kazantzis. I am satisfied on the evidence that neither Mr McMillan nor Mr Francis made any representations to Mr Grace in regard to what security would be available to ICI. They were aware that Mr Grace intended to obtain security and that Mr Kazantsis was willing to offer the Kerkira Golf Hotel as security but they did not make any representation to him in regard to it. Any representations made by Mr Kazantzis would be irrelevant as it is clear that he was never the agent of the bank. And it was not suggested that any representations were ever made by Mr Phipps or Mr Landale. I am satisfied that ICI's allegations in regard to representations having been made to Mr Grace have not been substantiated.

I now turn to counsel's submissions on the issue between the bank and ICI and I propose to start with the submission made on behalf of ICI as it seems to me that the onus of proof was on ICI to show that the credit guarantee insurance agreement, which is *prima facie* a valid and enforceable agreement, is not binding on ICI. It is not my intention to set out the submissions of either side in full but merely to highlight in abbreviated form those which directly relate to the issues I have to determine.

On behalf of ICI Mr Cooke submitted that the credit guarantee insurance agreement was a contract of insurance and so a contract *uberrimae fidei*. The bank had a positive duty to disclose to ICI all facts material to the risk. And this duty extended not merely to facts of which they were aware, but also to facts of which they ought to have been aware. They failed in this duty. It is recited in the loan agreement that the purpose of the loan was to acquire a "100% interest in the Kerkira Golf Hotel in Corfu, Greece". And one of the events of default in clause 10 is the failure of Amaxa to apply the loan exclusively for this purpose. But the bank knew or ought to have known that the loan could not lawfully be applied for this purpose in Greece. This was established by the evidence of the two Greek lawyers called on behalf of ICI and Meadows. At worst it was doubtful in Greek law if the loan could be applied to the stated purpose. The bank impliedly represented to ICI that the stated purpose was lawful. Alternatively they failed to disclose to ICI that it was unlawful or that there was a doubt as to its legality. This gave ICI the right to avoid the contract. Mr Cooke further submitted that it was clear from the evidence of Mr Scarsbrook that he and Mr McMillan were aware of a problem in regard to a foreign company owning land in Greece. Leslie and Godwin were the bank's agents and accordingly the bank were deemed to have any knowledge that they had. What Leslie and Godwin knew was clearly material and so the bank had a positive duty to disclose it to ICI. And while Leslie and Godwin were initially agents for Mr Kazantzis and Amaxa, when the bank obtained the insurance they were the agents of the bank also.

Finally Mr Cooke submitted that the contract between the bank and ICI was a contract of insurance and not a contract of guarantee. It was treated by all parties as such and was entered into in consideration of a premium being paid.

On behalf of the bank Mr Shanley directed his submissions principally to two issues: firstly, whether the contract between the bank and ICI was a contract of insurance or a contract of guarantee and secondly whether Leslie and Godwin were the agents of the bank in the matter of procuring the insurance. On the first issue he referred to four distinguishing features between a guarantee and a contract of insurance set out in paragraph 809 of volume 25 of *Halsbury* and submitted that in the present case three of the four features indicative of a guarantee were present:

(1) That the surety had been approached by the debtor;
(2) That the surety was in as good as position as the creditor to assess the risk, and
(3) That the surety promised to pay the original debt and the interest accrued.

As to the duty of disclosure, if it was held that the contract was one of insurance, he submitted that there could be no duty to disclose something of which a person had no knowledge. It was clear on the evidence that none of the employees of the bank had any knowledge of any problem in regard to the purpose to which the loan was to be applied, accordingly they could not have been at fault. And as to the claim that Leslie and Godwin were agents of the bank, he submitted that they were from the beginning and remained exclusively the agents of Amaxa and Mr Kazantzis to obtain on their behalf a credit guarantee insurance which would be acceptable to the bank. He pointed out that Leslie and Godwin's commission was paid by Amaxa as also was the premium in respect of the insurance. If the bank had no knowledge of any problem, and Leslie and Godwin were not their agents, there could not have been any breach of the duty to disclose.

What distinguishes a contract of insurance from a contract of guarantee has been considered in a number of cases. The statement of the law to which most frequent reference is made is that contained in the judgment of Romer

L.J. in *Seaton* v. *Heath*[1] It is quite a lengthy passage but it seems to me that I should quote it in full at 792–793:

> "There are some contracts in which our courts of law and equity require what is called *uberrima fides* to be shewn by the person obtaining them; and, as that phrase is short and convenient, I will continue to use it. Of these, ordinary contracts of marine, fire and life insurance are examples, and in each of them the person desiring to be insured must, in setting forth the risk to be insured against, not conceal any material fact affecting the risk known to him. On the other hand, ordinary contracts of guarantee are not amongst those requiring *uberrima fides* on the part of the creditor towards the surety; and mere non communication to the surety by the creditor of facts known to him affecting the risk to be undertaken by the surety will not vitiate the contract, unless there be fraud or misrepresentation, and misrepresentation undoubtedly might be made by concealment. But the difference between these two classes of contract does not depend upon any essential difference between the word 'insurance' and the word 'guarantee'. There is no magic in the use of those words. The words, to a great extent, have the same meaning and effect; and many contracts, like the one in the case before us, may with equal propriety be called contracts of insurance or contracts of guarantee. Whether the contract be one requiring *uberrima fides* or not must depend upon its substantial character and how it came to be effected. There is no hard and fast line to be drawn between contracts of insurance and contracts of guarantee for the purpose for which I am now considering them; and certainly the rule as to contracts of insurance is not limited, as contended, to the three forms of marine, life and fire insurance: see the observations of Jessel M.R. in *London Assurance* v. *Mansel*.[2] Now when contracts of insurance are considered it will be seen that, speaking generally, they have in common several features in their character and the way they are effected which distinguish them from ordinary contracts of guarantee. Contracts of insurance are generally matters of speculation, where the person desiring to be insured has means of knowledge as to the risk, and the insurer has not the means or not the same means. The insured generally puts the risk before the insurer as a business transaction, and the insurer on the risk stated fixes a proper price to remunerate him for the risk to be undertaken; and the insurer engages to pay the loss incurred by the insured in the event of ₎certain specified contingencies occurring. On the other hand, in general, contracts of guarantee are between persons who occupy, or ultimately assume, the positions of creditor, debtor, and surety, and thereby the surety becomes bound to pay the debt or make good the default of the debtor. In general, the creditor does not himself go to the surety or represent, or explain to the surety, the risk to be run. The surety often takes the position from motives of friendship to the debtor, and generally not as the result of any direct bargaining between him and the creditor, or in consideration of any remuneration passing to him from the creditor. The risk undertaken is generally known to the surety, and the circumstances generally point to the view that as between the creditor and surety it was contemplated and intended that the surety should take upon himself to ascertain exactly what

---

[1] [1899] 1 QB 782.
[2] (1879) 11Ch.D. 363.

risk he was taking upon himself. In all the reported cases of guarantees that I have been able to find, in which it has been held that the party guaranteed owed no duty to the guarantor as to disclosure of material facts, the contracts, when examined, are found to have in substance, though of course not in every detail, the characteristics which distinguish contracts of guarantee from contracts of insurance as above stated by me."

Applying the considerations set out in that passage to the credit guarantee insurance agreement, the view I take is that the contract was not one which required *uberrima fides* on the part of the bank. In my opinion the contract was in substance a guarantee rather than a contract of insurance. I consider this as the only conclusion that can be reached if one looks at the substantial character of the contract and how it came to be effected — the two elements on which depends whether it is a contract requiring *uberrima fides*.

I start with the manner in which the agreement came to be effected. It is clear that it was procured by Amaxa, through Mr Kazantzis, as a security which would be acceptable to the bank and on which the bank would be prepared to make the loan. Furthermore, the agreement of ICI and Meadows to act as insurer and re-insurer respectively, had been procured in principle long before the bank was approached to make the loan. Mr Grace agreed to front the transaction, as he put it, about 7 November 1983, whereas the bank did not come into the picture until 23 January 1984. ICI's agreement to enter into the credit guarantee insurance was presented to the bank as the security for the loan. There was no question of the bank agreeing to make the loan and then deciding to insure against the risk of its not being repaid. The credit guarantee insurance was already in place in principle before the bank was approached to make the loan. The insurance was procured by Amaxa as a security for the bank and was not procured by the bank to protect itself against loss, which would be the normal object of a contract of insurance. And it is of course clear that the bank did not make any proposal for insurance to ICI, which would be the normal way of effecting a policy of insurance. So the situation was similar to that found in regard to guarantees where the creditor does not himself go to the surety. The only difference between what happened here and what normally happens in regard to guarantees is that ICI were being paid a premium by Amaxa for guaranteeing the loan, whereas in most guarantees the surety acts voluntarily, but in my opinion that does not alter the substance of the transaction.

I turn now to the substantial character of the contract. In my opinion the manner in which it is expressed and its effect are much closer to a guarantee than to a contract of insurance.

The first three clauses of the agreement are as follows:

"To: International Commercial Bank plc (the lender)

In consideration of your granting a loan of Swiss Francs 11,500,000 according to the loan agreement made on the ____ between the lender and Amaxa AG (the borrower) (the loan agreement) we, the undersigned, hereinafter referred to as the "indemnifier" declare;

In the event of the borrower failing to pay the lender any sum or sums (including, without limitation, sums due by reason of acceleration or otherwise) due for payment in accordance with the above mentioned loan agreement, the indemnifier undertakes irrevocably and unconditionally to indemnify the lender for 100% of the amount of such sum or sums.

Upon any such failure by the borrower to pay as aforesaid, the lender shall be entitled to make a claim hereunder in respect of the amount in default and the indemnifier shall pay to the lender 100% of such amount in default and interest accrued, within 30 days from the date of such claim being made."

It is interesting to compare these clauses with the first part of a precedent for a guarantee in volume 9 of *Butterworth's Encyclopaedia of Forms and Precedents* (fourth edition 1968) at p. 785:

"In consideration of your having at our request agreed to advance to D ... sums of money not exceeding at any time the sum of £___ which he may require during the period of ___ years from the ___ day ___ of ___.

We the undersigned hereby guarantee to you the repayment by the said D of all sums advanced by you to him as aforesaid with interest at the rate of _% per annum subject as hereinafter mentioned that is to say

1. Notice in writing of any default on the part of the said D is to be given by you to us, and within _ days from its receipt payment shall be made by us of all sums then due from us under this guarantee."

While there are differences in wording between the two, the effect of both is identical. In consideration of the creditor making the loan to the principal debtor the guarantor agrees that in the event of the default of the principal debtor payment shall be made by the guarantor within a certain time of all moneys due.

In addition to this similarity, the agreement contains two clauses which are appropriate only to a guarantee:

"1. This document shall provide a continuing indemnity and shall remain in full force and effect until all monies now or hereafter payable by the borrower under the loan agreement have been paid or satisfied in full and is in addition to and not in substitution for and shall not be prejudiced or affected by any other security or guarantee now or hereafter held by the lender for the payment of such monies.

2. The indemnifier shall not be exonerated in its liability under this document and such liability shall not be lessened or impaired by any time, indulgence or relief given by the lender to the borrower or by any amendment of or supplement to the loan agreement, or by the taking, variation, compromise, or renewal or release of or refusal or neglect to perfect or enforce any right, remedies or securities against the borrower or any other person or by anything done or omitted which but for this provision might operate to exonerate the indemnifier."

It is significant also that the consideration expressed in the agreement is the granting of the loan, which is the standard consideration in contracts of guarantee. There is no reference to the premium. This is only referred to in the cover note dated 9 February 1984 and sent by ICI to the bank. It states that the form of the insurance is "wording as attached", this being a reference to the actual agreement where the premium is not mentioned. And of course the bank was under no liability to pay the premium. So insofar as the bank was concerned, their making the loan was the consideration for the credit guarantee insurance.

That the contract was not one of insurance is to my mind confirmed by applying another of the tests proposed by Romer L.J. In the course of the passage cited he said:

> "Contracts of insurance are generally matters of speculation...."

Did the bank have means of knowledge as to the risk while ICI did not or did not have the same means? I don't think so. ICI had been dealing with the matter since it was presented to Mr Grace by Mr McMillan on 27 September 1983. Mr Grace had met Mr Kazantzis and had had ample time to consider the prospects of Amaxa being able to repay the loan. At worst it seems to me that ICI was in just as good a position as the bank to evaluate the risk. There is certainly nothing to suggest that the bank was in a better position.

Of the reported cases, that which comes closest to the present is *In re Denton's Estate, Licenses Insurance Corporation and Guarantee Fund Ltd.* v. *Denton,*[3] and on appeal.[4] The owner of a public house mortgaged it to a bank for £4,000. The mortgage contained a joint and several covenant by the mortgagor and surety to pay the principal and interest, the liability of the surety being limited to £1,000. The mortgage contained a covenant by the mortgagor to insure the mortgage debt with the plaintiff company in the name of the bank. Pursuant to this covenant an insurance was effected with the plaintiff company whereby it agreed that if the mortgagor made default the plaintiff company would pay the principal and interest. The mortgagor did make default. The plaintiff company paid the mortgage debt, interest and costs amounting in all to nearly £5,000. They realised £4,000 from the security. The surety had died and the action was brought against his personal representative. It was held by Swinfen Eady J. that the contract between the plaintiff company and the bank was one of suretyship and not of insurance. He said in his judgment at p. 678:

> "It was contended that the corporation was not in the position of sureties strictly and properly so called. I am not satisfied that this contention is well founded. The policy contains a recital of a proposal for guaranteeing the said mortgage debt and interest, and then it provides that if the insured shall become entitled to sell the mortgaged property — that is, if the mortgagor shall make default in payment on demand of the principal money and interest — the corporation will, after six months' notice, pay the principal money and interest to the mortgagee. In other words, if the principal does not pay, the corporation will pay."

---

[3] [1903] 2 Ch 670.
[4] [1904] 2 Ch 178.

Swinfen Eady J. held that the plaintiff company and the surety were co-sureties and that in view of the surety's liability being limited, the plaintiff company could only recover the proportion for which the surety was responsible. This was reversed on appeal, the Court of Appeal holding that the plaintiff company were guarantors to the bank of both the mortgagor and the surety, and that accordingly the plaintiff company was entitled to recover from the surety's personal representative the full £1,000 that the surety would have been liable to pay to the bank. But all three judges agreed with Swinfen Eady J.'s interpretation of the policy of insurance. Vaughan Williams L.J. said at p. 188:

> "No doubt the form is that of a policy of insurance; but I think there is nothing in the form of contract between the bank and the corporation being that of a policy of insurance to prevent the contract being one of guarantee."

Stirling L.J. said in his judgment at p. 192:

> "Swinfen Eady J. held that the instrument of 7 March 1900, was not merely an insurance against loss, and in that respect I agree with him."

And Cozens-Hardy L.J. said in his judgment at p. 195:

> "Now, on the construction of this document, I agree with Swinfen Eady J. that it was not an insurance against loss, but was a guarantee of the mortgage debt, and I adopt the reasoning contained in his very careful judgment on this point."

In that case the contract was held to be one of suretyship notwithstanding that it was in the form of a policy of insurance and had been issued on the basis of a proposal in writing which was made the basis of the contract of insurance. In the present case it seems to me that the grounds for holding the contract to be one of suretyship are stronger. There was no proposal in writing to ICI and the credit guarantee insurance is not in the form of a policy. Furthermore the agreement was drafted by the bank's solicitor and not by ICI. And the reasoning of Swinfen Eady J. is equally applicable. He said that the essence of the policy came down to this:

> "If the principal does not pay, the corporation will pay."

That is also the essence of the credit guarantee insurance.

It was common case that if the agreement was held to be a contract of guarantee, the requirement of *uberrima fides* would not arise, and that accordingly non-disclosure of a material fact would not be an answer to the claim. It is not necessary accordingly to refer to any authorities in support of this proposition. My finding that the credit guarantee insurance agreement was a guarantee and not a contract of insurance is sufficient to determine the bank's claim against ICI but it seems to me that I should nonetheless go on to express briefly my views on what the position would have been if I had come to the conclusion that the credit guarantee insurance agreement was simply a contract of insurance. This involves considering the contention that Leslie and Godwin were the agents of the bank in obtaining the insurance so that the bank were affected by non-disclosure on their part. I consider that this contention is not well founded for two main reasons.

Firstly, the insurance was not procured on behalf of the bank but on behalf of Amaxa. So Leslie and Godwin were their agents. Furthermore, the insurance had been procured before the bank was approached to make the loan. ICI had agreed in principle to grant the insurance to whatever bank was prepared to make the loan. So the work of Leslie and Godwin in obtaining the insurance had been completed before the bank came on the scene. Because of this Leslie and Godwin could not in my opinion have been the bank's agents.

The second reason is that for the bank to have been affected by Leslie and Godwin's non-disclosure of knowledge they had, that knowledge would have had to be acquired by Leslie and Godwin while acting as the bank's agents to procure the insurance. In my opinion the law is correctly stated at para. 811 of *McGillivray and Parkington on Insurance Law* (7th edition):

> "It is not all knowledge in the possession of an agent to effect an insurance which is imputed to and affects the assured, but only that which the agent acquired in the course of his agency while preparing to effect the particular insurance, so that the assured would not be deemed to know things which the agent had heard about earlier in connection with other insurances."

If Leslie and Godwin were the bank's agents, they could only have been such after 23 January 1984, and there was no evidence that the knowledge which Mr Scarsbrook [of Leslie and Godwin] had as to there being a problem in regard to a foreign company acquiring Greek land was acquired by him after that date.

I am of opinion accordingly that even if the credit guarantee insurance was a contract of insurance and not a contract of guarantee, ICI was not entitled to avoid the agreement and is liable to the bank for the full amount due under the contract.

In these circumstances it is necessary to consider ICI's claim against Meadows. And what has to be determined here is whether there are grounds on which Meadows is entitled to be released from the contract of re-insurance which it clearly entered into by signing on 30 January 1984 the relevant slip sent to it by Leslie and Godwin. So the onus of proof is on Meadows to attempt to establish such grounds.

It is necessary to start with a brief account of how Meadows came to enter into the contract of re-insurance. Mr Grace went to Guernsey to attend a meeting of the board of Meadows on 13 October. While there, either on the evening before the meeting, or after it had taken place, he spoke to Mr Mascarella and Mr Savage about the opportunity to underwrite a credit guarantee insurance. He had with him a slip from Leslie and Godwin setting out the details. This slip was stamped by Mr Savage on behalf of RCG and Meadows on 17 October 1983 indicating the interest of these two companies in writing the insurance. Initially the period of insurance was to have been three years, but this was altered to seven years and as RCG was unable to write a policy for that period it had to drop out. Meadows then apparently agreed that it would underwrite the insurance on its own. I say apparently because Mr Mascarella's evidence was that he believed that what was involved was re-insurance and not direct insurance. As matters turned out, it is immaterial which it was. As an indication of Meadows' apparent willing-ness to be the sole insurer, Mr Savage signed the credit guarantee conditions which were to be the basis of the insurance. But the lending institution which at that time was going to make the loan to Amaxa refused to accept Meadows as the insurer and in these circumstances Mr Grace, at the request of Mr McMillan, agreed that ICI would be the insurer with Meadows as the re-insurer. Such was the position on 7 November 1983 and when the bank came into the picture in January 1984.

In setting out this brief account of how the re-insurance agreement came into being, I have deliberately omitted to refer to one element n the trans-action because it is of such importance that I consider it more appropriate that it should be dealt with separately. This is the matter of the security to be provided by Amaxa as collateral for the risk being underwritten by ICI. Mr Grace said in his evidence that from the start he was looking for collateral. He also said that collateral must have been promised to Mr Savage as otherwise he would not have written the business. And Mr Mascarella said that Mr Grace, at the meeting in Guernsey on 12 and 13 October, said that the financial guarantee would be supported by the value of the buildings which was equal to twice the amount of the insurance they would be writing. Mr Mascarella also said that the question of collateral was very important to him; it was the basis for his agreeing in principle to take the insurance.

That collateral was being offered by Amaxa and Mr Kazantzis was clear. When the loan was to have been made by Omni-Commerce, one of the documents which Mr Kazantzis and his brother were going to execute was an assignment of the Kerkira Golf Hotel to ICI in the event of their having to make any payment under the policy. At the time the bank agreed to make the loan this had been altered and the security was to be the shares in the company which owned the hotel. On 2 February 1984, Mr Lampros T. Frangos, Mr Kazantzis' lawyer in Greece, wrote to Mr McMillan sending him a number of documents relating to the shares. These included a consignment agreement to be executed between ICI and Mr Kazantzis which made it clear that ICI were to have the existing shares and all future shares in A. Kazantzis SA as security for the risk they were underwriting. This letter and the enclosures were given by Mr McMillan to Mr Grace and passed on by him to Mr Savage.

I am satisfied on this documentary evidence, and also on the evidence of Mr Grace, Mr Savage and Mr Mascarella, that it was the intention of all the parties to the credit guarantee insurance agreement that ICI's undertaking to indemnify the bank should be secured by the shares in A. Kazantzis SA, the company which owned the Kerkira Golf Hotel. But it is common case that it was not so secured. Both ICI and Meadows agree that the purported security was wholly ineffective. As a result ICI had no security for its liability under the credit guarantee insurance.

It is because of the absence of such security that Meadows says that it is not bound by the contract of re-insurance. It is also submitted that the con-tract is void because of a failure on the part of ICI to disclose to Meadows facts which were material to the risk.

On the question of the absence of security, two separate submissions are made: firstly, that Mr Grace represented to Meadows that the risk being insured by ICI was a secured risk; that Meadows was induced to enter into the contract by such representation, and that as the representation was false, Meadows is entitled to rescind the contract; secondly, that it was a fundamental term of the contract between ICI and Meadows that security should be in place, and that the breach of that term released Meadows from its agreement.

Both of these submissions have considerable substance in them, but I prefer to approach the issue in a slightly different way. It seems to me that the answer to the question of whether Meadows is bound by the contract of re-insurance is to be found by examining the nature of that contract. What did Meadows agree to re-insure? What was the risk being accepted by ICI for which Meadows undertook ultimate liability? It seems to me that the risk was the failure of Amaxa to repay the loan, such risk, or rather the possible loss arising from it, being secured by the entire equity in Kazantzis SA. It was clearly part of ICI's agreement with Amaxa that the risk it was undertaking would be secured. And this was known to Meadows. So both ICI and Meadows knew that the risk being undertaken by ICI was to be secured. And it was this risk, a secured risk, that Meadows agreed to re-insure. It did not agree to re-insure a risk for which there was no security, and since it now turns out that there was no security for the risk, Meadows agreement to re-insure is inoperative. It was an agreement to re-insure a risk which was secured; it was not an agreement to re-insure an unsecured risk. Accordingly, it did not extend to cover ICI as matters turned out. For this reason ICI's claim against Meadows fails.

Mr Cooke [for ICI] submitted very strongly that ICI should not have to bear responsibility as they were only fronting for Meadows. He said they had agreed to be the insurer merely to facilitate Meadows who were not acceptable to Omni-Commerce, and that it was really Meadows who were undertaking the insurance as was evidenced by the fact that they got the entire of the premium. I am not prepared to accept this submission. Mr David Forrest, an experienced underwriter at Lloyds, whose evidence I accept, said that the word "fronting" was just jargon; that the fact that one insurance company was fronting for another did not alter the relationship between the insurer and the re-insurer. So ICI was the insurer, with all the responsibilities that that involved, and Meadows was the re-insurer.

One of the responsibilities was to see that the risk being undertaken by ICI was secured. Mr Forrest said that where collateral is being given by the insured, it is an inseparable part of the consideration received by the undertaker, the collateral and premium going together to form the premium package. He found it astonishing that no steps were taken independently to review and approve the collateral, and he considered it was very wrong to rely upon a letter written by a solicitor acting for a party other than the underwriter. I agree entirely with his views. It is difficult to understand the extraordinarily casual manner in which the matter was treated by Mr Grace. He took no steps whatever in regard to the collateral. He left it all to Mr Savage. He claimed that ICI's interests were being looked after by Mr Savage, but all Mr Savage had been instructed to do was to sign in Guernsey the necessary documents to give effect to the credit guarantee insurance agreement. I accept his evidence that he did not believe he had to do anything and did not understand he had to do anything, in regard to checking the security. So the position is that Mr Grace did not check the security himself, and did not instruct Mr Savage to check it either. The consequence was that there was no security and this was due to Mr Grace's default.

Having come to the conclusion that Meadows is not liable to ICI because it never agreed to re-insure an unsecured risk, it is not necessary for me to consider the further submission that the contract of re-insurance was void for non-disclosure.

I dismiss the claim of ICI against Meadows and grant the bank a decree on its claim against ICI....

Unreported, 31 July 1992
The Supreme Court

McCARTHY J. (FINLAY C.J. AND O'FLAHERTY J. CONCURRING): International Commercial Bank Plc (ICB) lent 11.5 million Swiss Francs to Amaxa SA.; the Insurance Corporation of Ireland Plc (ICI) contracted to indemnify ICB against default by Amaxa. The Meadows Indemnity Company Limited (Meadows) contracted to indemnify ICI if ICI had to indemnify ICB. Amaxa defaulted; ICB sued ICI who sued Meadows; ICB recovered against ICI and that matter is over; ICI failed against Meadows and appeals. ICB is now the Hong Kong and Shanghai Banking Corporation and ICI, for the purpose of this case, is Icarom Plc.

It was a fairly routine financial operation, a loan guaranteed by one insurer who accepted the security offered and committed itself to making the same security available to the next insurer. The security offered was a luxury Hotel on the island of Corfu in Greece. That security was to be implemented by the transfer of shares in the company owning the Hotel; the share certificates were held to the account of ICI, but they were far from being a security. They did not represent 100% of the shareholding, they were less than 50%. More injuriously they could not lawfully be transferred to a non-Greek National; the land on which the Hotel stood could not be lawfully transferred to a foreign company. The shares in Kazantzis SA were worthless. Neither ICI nor Meadows had adequately investigated the true value of the security. The issue is — who bears the loss?

I have summarised the events which are set out in helpful detail in the judgment of Blayney J. in the High Court. These facts as found by him are not challenged. The essential nature of the ICI appeal, the claim between ICB and ICI having been settled, is, as set out in the written submission:

> "ICI submits the finding of the High Court that the agreement between ICI and Meadows was one of re-insurance was inconsistent with the finding that the contract between ICB and ICI was one of guarantee and not one of insurance. If the ICB/ICI contract was one of guarantee, the ICI/Meadows contract must be one of counter-guarantee or counter-indemnity."

In short, the arrangements between ICB, ICI and Meadows were made back-to-back.

It is convenient to cite from the critical and, in part, much criticised, extract from the judgment of Blayney J:

"I am satisfied on this documentary evidence, and also on the evidence of Mr Grace, Mr Savage and Mr Mascarella that it was the intention of all the parties to the Credit Guarantee Insurance Agreement that ICI's undertaking to indemnify the bank should be secured by the shares in A. Kazantzis SA, the company which owned the Kerkira Golf Hotel. But it is common case that it was not so secured. Both ICI and Meadows agree that the purported security was wholly ineffective. As a result ICI had no security for its liability under the credit guarantee insurance.

It is because of the absence of such security that Meadows says that it is not bound by the contract of re-insurance. It is also submitted that the contract is void because of a failure on the part of ICI to disclose to Meadows facts which were material to the risk.

On the question of the absence of security, two separate submissions are made: firstly, that Mr Grace represented to Meadows that the risk being insured by ICI was a secured risk; that Meadows was induced to enter into the contract by such representation, and that as the representation was false, Meadows is entitled to rescind the contract; secondly, that it was a fundamental term of the contract between ICI and Meadows that security should be in place, and that the breach of that term released Meadows from its agreement.

Both of these submissions have considerable substance in them, but I prefer to approach the issue in a slightly different way. It seems to me that the answer to the question of whether Meadows is bound by the contract of re-insurance is to be found by examining the nature of that contract. What did Meadows agree to re-insure? What was the risk being accepted by ICI for which Meadows undertook ultimate liability? It seems to me that the risk was the failure of Amaxa to repay the loan, such risk, or rather the possible loss arising from it, being secured by the entire equity in Kazantzis SA. It was clearly part of ICI's agreement with Amaxa that the risk it was undertaking would be secured. And this was known to Meadows. So both ICI and Meadows knew that the risk being undertaken by ICI was to be secured. And it was this risk, a secured risk, that Meadows agreed to re-insure. It did not agree to re-insure a risk for which there was no security, and since it now turns out that there was no security for the risk, Meadows agreement to re-insure is inoperative. (This word was the subject of considerable criticism). It was an agreement to re-insure a risk which was secured; it was not an agreement to re-insure an unsecured risk. Accordingly, it did not extend to cover ICI as matters turned out. For this reason ICI's claim against Meadows fails."

ICI argues that the arrangements being back-to-back the nature of the contract between ICI and Meadows cannot have been different from that between ICB and ICI. Either the agreement and the contract between ICI and Meadows were both in the nature of contracts of insurance or else they were both in the nature of contracts of guarantee. This may be so, but it does not advance the ICI case against Meadows any further. It overlooks the reality — whether one calls it a guarantee or a re-insurance contract, the reality was that Meadows would pay in respect of a loss for which ICI were liable under their agreement with ICB, if, and only if, the risk — default by Amaxa — was secured in the manner contemplated, by the shares in Kazantzis. In terms, Meadows agreed to re-insure what it believed to be a risk undertaken under a contract of insurance. It was not a contract of insurance but one of guarantee and certain legal consequences flowed from that. The trial Judge is correct in saying that, in terms, Meadows agreed to re-insure but did not agree to re-insure a risk for which there was no security; the reality, of course, was that Meadows agreed to insure ICI in respect of a loss that might be sustained under what in fact was a contract of guarantee, but the agreement to insure was in respect of a secured risk under that contract. The risk was not secured; therefore, there was nothing upon which the contract of insurance could operate — "Meadows agreement to re-insure was inoperative".

As Mr Isaacs QC said in the oral submissions, it doesn't matter what you call the contract or the arrangement; it is the reality that must be seen. The reality was, as I have said, that Meadows would pay in respect of the loss if, and only if , the risk was secured. It was not secured; Meadows refused to pay; Meadows was right. I would dismiss the appeal.

Inspector John Murphy *v.* P.M.P.A. Insurance Company
[1978] I.L.R.M. 25
The High Court

DOYLE J: Part IV of the Road Traffic Act 1961 provides for the compulsory insurance of mechanically propelled vehicles. Included in Part IV of the Act is s.75 which empowers the Minister for Local Government to make regulations dealing *inter alia* with the issue by vehicle insurers of certificates of insurance, the keeping of certain records relating to vehicle insurance and the giving of information when required by members of the Garda Síochána and officers of the Minister. The section also provides that a person who contravenes a regulation under the section which is declared to be a penal regulation shall be guilty of an offence. The Minister in exercise of the powers so conferred on him by s.75 made certain regulations known as the Road Traffic (Compulsory Insurance) Regulations 1962 S.I. No. 14 of 1962.

Art. 7 of the Regulations provides that when an approved policy of insurance is issued to a person the insurer shall issue to such person a certificate of insurance. Every certificate of insurance is required by this article to be in the form in the second schedule to the Regulations and to state the particulars of the policy which are required in the said form to be specified. The form of certificate in the second schedule sets out the particulars which are to be incorporated and they comprise:

1. The name and address of the person to whom the policy of insurance has been issued
2. The period of cover
3. Limitations as to use
4. Persons or classes of persons whose liability is covered
5. Vehicles or classes of vehicles the use of which is covered and

6. Drivers or classes of drivers whose driving is covered.

Art. 9(8) requires the insurer to keep in respect of each approved policy of insurance issued by him a record of:

(a) the particulars and other matters required to be stated on a certificate of insurance relating to such policy or guarantee.

(b) the issue of any such certificate.

(c) the loss, destruction, obliteration or defacement of any such certificate until twelve months have elapsed from the expiry of the period of cover of the policy.

It is provided at art.9(1) as follows:

> "The records required to be kept under these regulations shall be kept by the insurer
>
> (1) At premises in the state in the possession or control of the insurer at which he carries on the business of insurer.
>
> (2) An insurer shall on request admit a member of the Garda Síochána or a duly authorised officer of the Minister to the premises in which records required to be kept under these regulations are kept at any time while such premises are open to business and any such records shall be submitted to the member or officer for his inspection and he shall be permitted to inspect the records and make copies thereof.
>
> (3) An insurer shall furnish to a member of the Garda Síochána or a duly authorised officer of the Minister any information in relation to any approved policy of insurance issued by him which such member or officer shall require."

Art. 9(5) provides that "records required to be kept under these regulations" means the documents and other records required in pursuance of arts. 7 and 8 of these regulations to be retained or kept for twelve months by an insurer and, for the purposes of being considered in this case, relate to the certificate of insurance referred to at art. 7 of the regulations.

Art. 10 provides that art. 9 of the regulations shall be a penal regulation for the purposes of s.75 of the Act hereinbefore referred to.

P.M.P.A. Insurance Co. Ltd. ... "the insurers" is a company licensed to carry on the business of motor-car insurance in the state. It had issued to one, Michael J. Mellon, a member of the Garda Síochána, an approved policy of insurance pursuant to the provisions of the Road Traffic Act 1961. On 27 September 1976 one, Inspector John Murphy ... "the complainant" called to the place of business of the insurers ... and sought information relating to the insurance policy of the said Michael J. Mellon. It appears that the employee of the insurers who dealt with the complainant's request was unwilling to furnish the information sought until he should receive authorisation from a superior officer. On the following day the insurers through their senior assistant manager Mr F. Giles wrote to the complainant in the following terms:

"...

Dear Mr Murphy,

With reference to your recent visit to our office in which you required certain information regarding our above insured we would ask you to forward in writing complete details of your request when the matter will have our full attention.

Yours faithfully
F. Giles
Senior Assistant Manager."

On 28 September 1976 the complainant wrote to the insurers in the following terms:

"....
Dear Sir,
Re: Michael J. Mellon....
      Further to my visit to your offices on 27 instant and letter dated 27 September, 1976 signed by Mr F. Giles received here on this date I am to request that you be good enough to supply me with the following information concerning the above-named and the insurance held by him
      (a) copy of Mr Mellon's certificate of insurance
      (b) copies of all applications, proposals, statements and other documents made by Mr Mellon for the purpose of obtaining insurance since he first became insured with your company
      (c) a statement indicating if he was covered by insurance in respect of motor-car 8309 ZA on the 24/9/76 and remains so covered.
      Mr Giles ... is already in possession of all the information relating to the reason why this information is sought. Please note in particular Mr Mellon's date of birth and any driving licences he may have mentioned when applying for his insurance. I would appreciate an early reply as a matter of urgency.

Yours faithfully,
J. Murphy,
Inspector."

The last mentioned letter does not appear to have elicited a reply and on 11 October 1976 the complainant called to the insurers' offices where he had a discussion with the manager Mr Hughes and he repeated his request for the information sought in the letter of 28 September. Mr Hughes stated that he had read the letter but that the company was taking legal advice upon the matter so as to satisfy themselves whether the information was such as the insurers were required by law to give. The information was not furnished then or subsequently.
      ... [A]t the sitting of the District Court held at 3 Morgan Place on 15 March 1977 the complainant ... charged the insurers ... for failing on a demand being made of it by a member of the Garda Síochána in pursuance of the provisions of the Road Traffic (Compulsory Insurance) Regulations 1962 art. 9 made under the Road Traffic Act 1961 to furnish all information in relation to an approved policy of insurance issued by it to one Michael J. Mellon contrary to the Road Traffic (Compulsory Insurance) Regulations 1962 art. 9 made under the Road Traffic Act 1961 s.75. The matter appears to have been extensively argued before the District Justice. It was contended on behalf of the insurers that they owed a duty to their insured to treat as confidential information which might be supplied to them by their insured for

the purpose of obtaining insurance cover. It was further contended that the information which the insurers were obliged to give under art. 9 was information contained in or relating to the records which the insurers were bound pursuant to the provisions of the Regulations to keep. They claimed that the information required to be made available by art. 9 did not include information which the insurers were not obliged by statute to keep and which were contained in the insurers' private records. Therefore they said that the insurers were not obliged to divulge all the information demanded by the complainant's letter of 28 September 1976 or all the information relating to their insured which might be in their possession. The complainant submitted that the insurers were obliged under the provisions of the regulations to disclose any information which they had in their possession when requested by a member of the Garda Síochána or other authorised person. The District Justice reserved his decision and subsequently convicted the insurers and fined them the sum of £5.

The contract of insurance entered into between the insurers of the one part and Mr Michael Mellon of the other part was a contract *uberrimae fidei*, that is to say it was a contract based upon the exercise of the utmost good faith by each party. Mr Mellon for his part was under an obligation to disclose to the insurers every material circumstance which might influence the judgment of the insurers in fixing the premium or indeed in deciding whether or not they would take on the risk. It is clear that such disclosure might involve matters of a very personal and private character so far as Mr Mellon was concerned, for instance the topic of his health. Concealment or non-disclosure of such matters by Mr Mellon might well entitle the insurers to avoid the contract if they were subsequently to discover the fact of such concealment or non-disclosure. It seems to follow that the insurers for their part contracted an obligation of confidentiality in respect of such personal information furnished by their insured in the course of negotiating the insurance contract, more particularly when the information involved disclosures which might in particular circumstances lead to the detriment of the person seeking insurance. The insurance contract therefore set up a particular relationship between the insurers and their insured Mr Mellon. The complainant nevertheless contends that the effect of art. 9 is to grant him what must be regarded as an exceptional privilege, that is to obtain the information which he sought despite the fact that it was clothed with a cloak of confidentiality. To this extent the obligation under art. 9 to furnish the information sought, if obligation it be, appears to constitute an encroachment to a greater or lesser degree on natural liberty or natural rights. It seems to me therefore that any such encroachment, if it be intended, must be manifested with reasonable clearness. A further requirement in my opinion is that the encroachment to be justified must be demonstrated to fall within the general spirit and scope of the enactment. It has to be determined therefore whether the "information" referred to in art. 9(3) relates to the documentation and records referred to in the other sub-articles of art. 9 and refers and relates to them solely or whether it bears the much wider interpretation contended for by the complainant which presumably would include the proposal form which forms the basis of the insurance policy and which commonly is recited to form part of and to be read with the terms of the policy and other documents of a more or less private nature such as medical reports or information of that character. If the matter is left uncertain or is to be gathered by mere doubtful inference then the narrower construction must prevail.

... I have come to the conclusion that the contract between the insurers and their insured was one *uberrimae fidei;* it carried a corresponding obligation of confidentiality on the part of the insurers because of the special relationship which the contract set up between themselves and their insured. It must also be taken into account that in the special circumstances of this contract the disclosure sought by the complainant may operate to the detriment of the insured Mr Mellon because of his particular status as a member of the Garda Síochána, in which force the complainant occupies a position of authority. To give effect to the regulation in the present case would entail an encroachment on the natural rights of the insured Mr Mellon and also in my view conflict with the obligation springing from a natural right which lies upon the insurers. Reading sub-article 3 therefore as it must be read in the context of the whole of art. 9 and the other sub-articles therein comprised and indeed in the light of the Road Traffic Compulsory Regulations as a whole, I conclude that it does not manifest with reasonable clearness an intention to invade or limit or restrict the natural rights in question in this case. It follows that the offence with which the insurers were charged has not been made out and I answer the query of the District Justice by finding that the defendant insurers ought to have been acquitted.

CHAPTER 2

Indemnity

Broadly speaking, policies of insurance may be divided into two categories: those which are Contracts of Indemnity and those which are not. Life Insurance and Personal Accident Policies are not Contracts of Indemnity, as the amounts due under such policies become payable upon the happening of specified events such as a death or accident. This type of insurance is to be contrasted with property, liability and motor policies where the concept of indemnity is one of the central elements of the contract between the insurance company and the insured. In consideration of the premium paid by the latter, the insurance company will indemnify the insured in relation to a claim properly arising under the policy.

The nature of the indemnity has been judicially considered on several occasions. An early example is the judgment of Pennefather B. in *Vance* v. *Forster* (1841).

It is clear from *Phoenix Assurance Company Limited* v. *Four Courts Hotel Company Limited* (1935) that the company's liability to provide an indemnity is dependent upon the insured paying the premium.

What then is meant by the indemnity? Firstly, a loss must have been suffered by the insured. This is an essential prerequisite as the purpose of the policy is to restore the insured to the position which he enjoyed before the occurrence of the incident giving rise to the claim.

Secondly, the amount of the indemnity will not automatically equal the sum insured under the policy. This sum simply represents the upper limit of the company's exposure in the event of a successful claim and the insured will not be entitled to recover more than the actual sum insured. *Brodigan* v. *The Imperial Livestock & General Insurance Company Limited* (1927) is an interesting examination of the nature of the indemnity policy.

Thirdly, the company is only liable for the actual loss suffered by the insured. The basis on which the loss is assessed and calculated is therefore of considerable importance and had recently been considered by the Supreme Court in *St Alban's Investment Company* v. *Sun Alliance and London Insurance Limited and Provincial Insurance*

Company Limited (1983), a case which concerned a fire policy.

In *Andrews* v. *the Patriotic Assurance Company of Ireland* (1886) the extent of an insurer's indemnity to an insured (landlord) was not reduced solely because a third party (tenant) has also insured his own interest in the same subject matter under another policy.

Phoenix Assurance Company Limited *v.*
Four Courts Hotel Limited
[1935] I.R. 628
The High Court

HANNA J: The question which comes up for decision on this appeal arises upon the construction of a contract entered into between the parties, which is of great importance to them, but is somewhat ambiguous and difficult to construe. This contract, as it stands, was ancillary to two contracts of insurance for fire and consequential loss and is in the following terms:—

> "In consideration of a discount of 5 (five) per cent. off the net premium for the policies, we hereby undertake to continue the insurance under the above numbered policies for a period of three years, and to pay the premiums annually in advance, it being understood that during the currency of this agreement the sums insured may be proportionally reduced to correspond with any reduction in value.
>
> This agreement shall be held to apply to any policy or policies issued within the period covered by the agreement in substitution for any of the above numbered policies
>
> Date 25th Oct., 1929.
>
> (Signed) Four Courts Hotel Co. Ltd.
> Henry Kilbey
> Mang. Director."

A memorandum of this agreement was endorsed on each of the two policies. The agreement was carried out for the first year and also for the second year — the Hotel Company paying the premiums in advance and obtaining a reduction of 5 per cent. thereon, in return. In the third year, however, the Hotel Company declined to continue the insurance or pay the premiums, and, in consequence, this action has been brought to recover the premiums due for the third year.

... I am clearly of opinion that [the Plaintiff] is not entitled to recover the amount of the premiums "whether under the contract or as damages for the breach thereof". This seems to me to be clear from the cases cited on behalf of the defendants which in my opinion, establish the proposition that where no risk is incurred by an Insurance Company under a policy of insurance no premium is payable and any premiums paid thereunder must be returned. In this case no risk was undertaken by the Insurance Company for the year in question because the Hotel Company refused to continue the policies. Hence the Insurance Company cannot recover the premiums....

O'BYRNE J: ... What are the rights of the parties in law? On behalf of the Hotel Company a very old case has been cited, *Tyrie* v. *Fletcher*,[1] decided in 1777. That case, however, has never been overruled or questioned and is cited in modern text books of authority. In that case Lord Mansfield said (at p. 668):—

> "This case is stript of every authority. There is no case or practice in point; and, therefore, we must argue from the general principles applicable to all policies of insurance. And I take it, there are two general rules established, applicable to this question: the first is, that where the risk has not been run, whether its not having been run was owing to the fault, pleasure, or will of the insured, or to any other cause, the premiums shall be returned: because a policy of insurance is a contract of indemnity. The underwriter receives a premium for running the risk of indemnifying the insured, and whatever cause it be owing to, if he does not run the risk, the consideration, for which the premium or money was put into his hands, fails, and therefore he ought to return it."

This quotation is entirely applicable to the present case. And the effect of applying it is that, as no risk was undertaken, the Insurance Company would be bound to return the premiums for the third year, even if they had been paid. Therefore, *a fortiori*, the Insurance Company are not entitled to sue for and recover premiums in respect of a year during which they undertook no risk....

The Supreme Court

KENNEDY C.J: ... The law governing fire insurance is simply the law governing all written contracts and is not to be complicated by introducing the law governing marine insurance which is now largely a matter of statutory regulation. Nevertheless counsel did seek to enlighten us by reference to that branch of law.

We must, then, approach this case as one of contract between the two parties and, as in every other case of contract, the first question to be determined is what the parties agreed to do, and that is to be ascertained from the documents before us....

... The effect of the modifying agreement [of 1929] is, in my opinion, an agreement on the part of the insured to renew the policy in each of the three subsequent years by payment of the premium less by five per cent in respect of each year, and, after payment of the reduced premium in respect of such year, to indemnify the Insured against the loss specified during that year. If the premium were not paid in respect of any of the three yearly periods, the Insurance Company was not to be obliged to indemnify the Hotel Company, nor could the Insurance Company be required to accept any subsequent tender of the amount of the premium either reduced by the discount or at all.

Now, the Hotel Company failed to tender, at or before the agreed date, the amount of the premium in respect of the third yearly period. The Insurance Company was, therefore, released from the obligation to indemnify the Hotel

---

[1] 2 Cowp. 666.

Company during that period which expired on the 29th of September, 1932, and no claim to indemnity has arisen. The indemnity was expressly conditional on payment of the premium in advance on or before the agreed date in each of the three years. There is no doubt that the Insurance Company, having been induced to accept the reduced premium in each of two years, was entitled to expect the third payment in due course and would be entitled to recover damages in respect of breach of contract.... The Insurance Company claims simply to be paid the amount of the premium as if the risk had been undertaken which, on the express terms of the contract, was definitely not the case. In my opinion, the claim put in that way, and the plaintiff's refusal to put it otherwise, is not sustainable in law or equity.

I am therefore, of opinion that the appeal must be dismissed....

FITZGIBBON J: ...After a careful examination of the policy itself, and of the memoranda and the "agreement" of October 25th, 1929, and having listened with attention to the very clear and concise argument of Serjeant Sullivan, I have come to the conclusion that the contract entered into by the defendants did not create a liability on the part of the defendants to pay a liquidated sum upon a named date ... [I]n my opinion the true contract between the parties was that the defendants would tender a premium on the 29th of September in the years 1930 and 1931, and would apply for a renewal which the plaintiffs might have refused if they chose to do so, but, if they elected to grant it, they would have been bound to allow them discount of 5 per cent on the amount of the premium.

I can find nothing in the policies or the agreement which binds the plaintiffs to grant a renewal even if the defendants should tender the premium on the appointed day, and the suggestion of Serjeant Sullivan that this is in fact a contract of insurance for a term of three years at a rate of premium payable by instalments is manifestly impossible of acceptance. The results of such an interpretation, even if the wording of the contract admitted of it, would be absurd. Suppose the subject-matter of the policy were destroyed by fire in the first or second year, is the insured to continue to pay the remaining premiums, and upon what property does the risk attach? It is, in my opinion, quite impossible to treat this as a contract on the part of the insured to pay three premiums on three named dates, in consideration of a reduction of 5 per cent upon the net amount of each premium, irrespective of what may have happened to the property insured during the three years covered by the premiums. Yet that is, in substance, the contract for which the plaintiffs contend. Furthermore, the amount of each premium cannot be ascertained until the new policy, or the renewal of the existing policy, is about to be taken out, for the amount of the premium depends upon the sum insured, and that sum " may be reduced to correspond with any reduction in value". The agreement upon which he relied was thus stated by Serjeant Sullivan:— "This is an agreement to insure for three years, and if the premium is tendered I couldn't reject it." I can find nothing in the policy or the agreement which supports this construction of the language used....

We have been referred to several cases upon the law of marine insurance in which it was held that where a premium for insurance had actually been paid it might be recovered as money paid without consideration where the risk had not actually attached, and it was contended that because the plaintiffs in the present case had never been under any liability to indemnify the defendants they could not sue for the premium. Hanna J. appears to have based his decision, in part at least, upon this ground. With all respect to his view, I am unable to see the bearing of the marine insurance cases upon the present one. I think it will found that in every case in which the assured was held entitled to a return of a premium already paid by him the decision of the Court proceeded upon the ground that the risk against which the insurance had been effected was a severable one, and that if the vessel had never set out upon the voyage there was no consideration for the premium. But in all these cases the premium had been paid, and the assured was seeking a return of the whole or a part upon the ground that the risk had never commenced.... But it was never held that this principle applied to a time policy, such as the policy of insurance against fire in the present case; and in *Loraine* v. *Thomlinson*[2] and *Tyrie* v. *Fletcher*,[3] where the policy was a time and not a voyage policy, it was held that there could be no apportionment, and therefore no return, of the whole or part of the premium.

... If I were of opinion that the insurance in the present case was for three years, and that the gross amount payable was calculated and payable by annual instalments, I should follow *Loraine* v. *Thomlinson*[4] and *Tyrie* v. *Fletcher*[5] where it was held that on a policy for a period the premium cannot be apportioned, nor can any part of it be recovered, once the risk has attached, but holding, as I do, that there is not, and never was, in the present case any contract by the plaintiffs to insure the defendants for three years, they cannot recover the premium upon the contract, and their remedy is confined to an action against the defendants for damages for breach of their contract to tender a premium on or before September 29th, 1931, and to request them to renew their policy of insurance for a third period of one year from that date.

The terms of the contract in the present case exclude the application of the principle which governed the decisions in *Loraine* v. *Thomlinson*[6] and *Tyrie* v. *Fletcher*,[7] upon which the plaintiffs rely, while the decisions upon voyage policies, cited on behalf of the defendants, are irrelevant in a case which turns upon a policy covering a period of time....

MURNAGHAN J: ... In the indorsement on the Civil Bill the claim for the premium is founded solely upon the agreement, dated 25th October, 1929. The Judge of the Circuit Court held that this agreement did not bind the plaintiffs to accept a renewal if offered by the defendants, and that consequently the premium could not be sued for. In his opinion a claim for damages for breach of the agreement to renew might be well founded, but, as the plaintiffs refused to accept any amendment of the Civil Bill claiming

---

[2] 2 Doug. 585.
[3] 2 Cowp. 666.
[4] 2 Doug. 585.
[5] 2 Cowp. 666.
[6] 2 Doug. 585.
[7] 2 Cowp. 666.

damages, he dismissed the action.

In the High Court Mr Justice Hanna held that the plaintiffs were under no obligation to renew the insurance, and he held that, inasmuch as no risk attached during the year 1931/32, the plaintiffs could not recover the premium for that year, although he held that damages might be recovered for breach of the agreement to renew. Mr Justice O'Byrne held that, even if the plaintiffs were bound to accept a renewal, which was a matter of doubt, as no renewal had been sought, no risk attached during the year 1931/32, and that no premium in respect of that year could be recovered.

At the hearing of this appeal Mr Serjeant Sullivan for the plaintiffs asked us to take a different view of the arrangement which had been arrived at. He asked us to hold that the policy of insurance was for a definite period of three years, and that there could be no question of annual renewal either on the part of the plaintiffs or defendants. He contended that the premium was due as a simple debt under a contract for three years.

The combined effect of the agreement [of 25 October 1929], as it is called, and the memorandum endorsed on the policy ["A discount of 5 per cent of the net premium on this policy is allowed in consideration of the insured having undertaken to continue the insurance for a period of three years from 29th September 1929 and to pay the premium annually in advance..."] is to make a contract, but there is ground for ambiguity in the language which has been used. The phrase "in consideration of the insured having undertaken to continue the insurance for a period of three years", may justly be said to be an unhappy phrase in the case of a definite agreement for three years. The contract between the parties should, however, be construed as incorporating so much of the original policy as can reasonably be made part of the contract: *Home Insurance Company of New York* v. *Victoria-Montreal Fire Insurance Company*[8] in the Privy Council.

On the whole it does seem to me that the endorsement or memorandum attached to the policy indicates an agreement on the part of the insurance company to enter into a policy extending over three years, and binding themselves in this way. I do not see why a mere agreement to renew entered into by the defendants should be sought to be made part of the policy.

But even if it be accepted that the contract made by the insurance company was for a term of three years, the point has been taken that this contract has also embodied a condition making the liability of the insurance company depend upon payment of the premium annually in advance. As no premium was paid in advance in respect of the year 1931/32, the plaintiffs incurred no liability for the year as they would have done if the policy had been for a definite term of three years without any such condition. It has been determined that if there be an insurance of a ship for a definite period — 12 months — at the rate of so much per month — once the risk has attached there can be no apportionment, even if the risk cease at the end of two months: *Loraine* v. *Thomlinson*;[9] but here the position is not the same, as, in substance, the company making the insurance assumes no liability for each

---

[8] [1907] AC 59.
[9] 2 Doug. 585.

successive year unless the annual premium has been paid in advance.

On the construction of the agreement entered into in the present case it appears to me clear that the plaintiffs did not unconditionally assume liability in respect of the third year. It has not been disputed that under general principles of the law of insurance where the risk has never begun the premium is not recoverable. What has been contended for is that the risk for the entire period has attached and that there can be no apportionment of the premium. Mr Serjeant Sullivan cited the case of *International Correspondence School, Ltd.* v. *Ayres*[10] in support of his contention. In that case a lengthy course of instruction was to be paid for in instalments, and it was held that the plaintiffs were entitled to recover the instalments as they fell due even if the defendant refused to continue the course. As a mere matter of construction, however, that case is distinguishable, as there was no condition that the instruction would be given only if the instalments were paid in advance.

It would be competent to the plaintiff company to make an agreement assuming liability for the entire period even if the premium was not paid in advance, but that is far from the agreement entered into. On the facts of the case, by reason of the condition, the plaintiffs did not assume liability for the year 1931/32, and they are not entitled to recover the premium.

Vance *v.* Forster, Whittaker and Johnson
(1841) Ir. Cir. Rep. 47
Assize Court

Headnote:
Assumpsit on a policy of assurance against fire....

The premises in question consisted of a cotton mill, and the machinery thereof.... [T]he Assurance Company contracted and agreed with the plaintiff in the manner following, viz.: "That we the said directors will, in case, during the continuance of this policy, the property hereinbefore described, or any part thereof, shall be burned, destroyed, or damaged by fire, pay or reinstate, or make good to the said assurer ... all such loss or damage as the said assured shall suffer or sustain by such fire, not exceeding in the whole the sum of £3,500.... It appeared that the building and premises ... had been totally consumed by fire, and the only questions between the parties were, the amount of the loss sustained upon the machinery, and the mode in which such loss was to be estimated.

After the trial had been in part proceeded with, it was (in accordance with the suggestion of the Court) consented by the parties that the case should be referred to three of the persons who had been impanelled as jurors....

PENNEFATHER B addressed the referees in manner following, viz.: The loss upon the buildings is not disputed, therefore, to the extent of the sum insured upon them, there is no question; these two items remain, viz. the sum of £400 insured on "millwright work", and the sum of £2,300 on what is called "clock-

---

[10] 106 L.T. 845.

makers' work". On these two items the question which you are about to
determine arises. It has been properly stated that a policy of assurance is a
contract of indemnity; and although the assured may name such sum on
which to pay a premium, as the Assurance Company shall agree to, yet the
nomination of and assent to such sum will not conclude the company as to the
amount of the sum payable in case of loss: in such case the assured will not,
under any circumstances, recover more than the sum named in the policy;
and he will not recover so much unless he proves that he sustained damage to
the amount of that sum, and in every case, where the amount of the damage
falls short of the sum named in the policy, the amount of the sum payable by
the Assurance Company will be commensurate with the damage. You are now
to inquire into and ascertain the actual damage which the plaintiff has sustained in relation to those portions of the assured premises which are covered
by the sum of £400 and £2,300: to arrive at a proper conclusion thereupon,
you are to take into account the state of the plaintiff's mill as it was at the
time of the fire, which you will ascertain from the evidence produced before
you; and you will then take into your consideration the first cost of the
machinery which has been consumed, and the state or condition of the
machinery of the mill immediately before the fire took place. It is said, on the
one side, that (in estimating the plaintiff's loss), it would not be unfair to take
the value of new machinery as a standard: on the other side it is contended
that a certain rateable deduction ought to be made from the price of new
machinery, and that the balance is the sum at which the plaintiff's loss ought
to be estimated. These may be propositions not undeserving of your
consideration, but are not, in my mind, the tests by which you are to arrive at
a conclusion upon the matters now before you. It is impossible to lay down
any fixed rule, or to say that a third or fourth is to be deducted, as a
difference of value, between old and new machinery, because that would be to
exclude from your consideration the actual state and serviceable order of the
machinery at the time of the fire: you are to see in what state and condition
the machinery was at the time of the fire, and what it would cost to replace
that machinery: you may try what it would cost to replace it with new
machinery, taking into account the entire expense of new machinery; and if
you resort to that mode, you are then to inquire whether the mill would be
better, and how much better, with new machinery, than it was with the
machinery standing therein at the time of the fire, and the difference in value
should be deducted from the expense of the new machinery. The plaintiff (to
the amount of the sums insured) must be borne harmless as to his loss; and I
think that the expense of the carriage of the machinery from the place where
it is to be purchased, to the mill, and of setting it up so as to put the insured
premises in *statu quo*, ought to form a part of the plaintiff's compensation. By
the terms of the policy the Company had the option of putting the premises in
their former state, and it was proper in them to reserve that option for the
purpose of protecting themselves against fraud and excessive demands; but if
they do not choose to exercise that option, but say, "we will repay you the
amount of the loss", then that amount is to be ascertained by estimating the
cost of restoring the premises to the state they were in at the time of the fire,
by which they were destroyed. It may be difficult to ascertain the cost of
restoring the mill exactly to its former state; but I think it might fairly be

done by estimating the amount of the sum which it would cost to set up new machinery in the plaintiff's mill, and then deducting from that sum, the difference in value between such new machinery when erected, and the old machinery when destroyed. In this manner I think that the actual loss sustained by the plaintiff could be ascertained; but there is no particular standard or rule by which the difference in value between old and new machinery is to be estimated. You are to estimate the loss actually sustained by the plaintiff, and although I have suggested one way in which, as I think, this loss may be estimated, yet other modes or ways of estimating it may occur to your minds: at the same time it is to be borne in mind that, in point of law, the plaintiff is entitled to be indemnified for his actual loss only....

Brodigan v. The Imperial Live Stock and General Insurance Co., Ltd.
(1927) 61 I.L.T.R. 193
The High Court

JOHNSTON J: This is an application to stay the action on the ground that the policy of insurance in respect of which the action is brought contains a condition that arbitration shall be a condition precedent before any liability under the policy arises. The plenary summons claims £250 alleged to be owing by the defendants to the plaintiff on foot of a blood-stock policy, dated Aug. 17, 1926, by which the defendants insured the life of the plaintiff's filly, "Midships Vis", in that sum. The filly died on Oct. 30, 1926, and the plenary summons was issued on March 12, 1927.

The insurance originated in a "proposal for insurance of animals", dated Aug. 16, 1926, addressed to Messrs Coyle & Co. (Brokers), Ltd., as follows:— "Please effect insurance on my behalf of the animal specified hereunder for a period of twelve months, against death from natural causes, fire, accidents or the act of God, as well as from destruction necessary in the interests of humanity during that period and including special risk of ... (sea transit, operation or other special risk is not included unless specially mentioned)." The particulars set out in the proposal contained the following statements:— "Full value, £1,000. Amount to be insured, £250. Premium, £16 5s. 0d." There was then a declaration by the plaintiff that the information given in the proposal was in every respect true and correct, and that the proposal should be the basis of the contract between the plaintiff and the company. A certificate by a veterinary surgeon stated that in his opinion the animal was "in good health and fit for insurance for the amount shown." The following conditions of insurance formed part of the proposal:—

> "1. All policies cover risk of death from disease, accident, fire or lightning, as well as from the necessity of destruction in the interests of humanity. Note:— In comparing rates regard should be had to the conditions of policies. Fire and lightning risks and disease, such as farcy or glanders, are frequently excluded by others."

On the back of the proposal were set out the "general ratings for each £100. Smaller or larger amounts in proportion." The animal to be insured

came under "Class 5 — Foals, one to five months old", and the rating was £6
10s. per cent for twelve months.

The policy, which was dated Aug. 17, 1926, contained this statement on its
face:— "Bloodstock Managers for Ireland: Irish Bloodstock Agency, Coyle &
Co. (Brokers), Ltd." It was recited that the plaintiff was "desirous of effecting
an insurance on the life of the dark bay filly, 'Midships Vis' ... during the
period 17th day of August, 1926, to midnight 16th day of August, 1927, for
the sum of £250", and that the plaintiff had furnished certain particulars, the
truth of which he had guaranteed. The following was the operative part of the
policy:—

> "The company hereby agrees (subject to the conditions printed in the margin
> hereof, which are deemed to be incorporated herein and form part of the
> policy) to indemnify the assured against the loss sustained through the
> death of any animal/s insured hereunder ... but not exceeding the sum in-
> sured hereby on such animal/s (and *pro rata* only with any other subsisting
> insurances, and less any sum recovered from any third parties) during the
> above-mentioned period from natural causes, fire or accidents, arising or
> occurring during the said period (sea risk, foaling or castration, and death
> consequent upon inoculation or operation without the previous consent of the
> company excepted)...."

It was further provided that the insurance was not to "cover loss" occasioned
through an animal becoming unfit or incapable of fulfilling the functions or
duties for which it was kept or employed. The arbitration clause was as
follows:—

> "It is a condition precedent to any liability of the company to make any pay-
> ment under this policy that if any difference shall arise between the com-
> pany and the assured, it shall be referred to two arbitrators, one to be
> nominated by each party, with power to such arbitrators to appoint an
> Umpire or Oversman, and unless and until an award has been made no legal
> proceedings shall be commenced. All liability under this policy shall cease
> and determine unless arbitration proceedings or competent judicial proceed-
> ings to establish liability shall have been commenced by the assured or his
> representatives within twelve months after the date of the death of any
> animal insured hereunder."

The conditions in the margin provided that the assured should "furnish to
the company all particulars as to the illness or accident and death in such
form and such other information as the company may require."

When the filly died the assured wrote to the company claiming the full
amount of the insurance, and the company asked for "some definite information as to the value of your foal." The assured wrote on Dec. 6 pointing out
that he had before insurance sent a full pedigree of the animal and that it
was the company itself that had fixed the figure at £250:— "You issued a
policy covering this amount and accepted premiums on same. I may say at
once that I will not accept one penny less than above figure." After some further correspondence the plenary summons was issued, and then the present
motion was instituted to stay the action on the ground that all disputes

should be referred to arbitration before any right of action could arise.

It is argued on behalf of the plaintiff, with a great deal of persuasiveness, that no "difference" has arisen or could arise between the parties once the insurance company was satisfied that the animal had died as a result of one of the causes contemplated by the policy. In the case of an insurance against fire there can be different degrees of destruction, and the insurer's liability is limited by the actual loss that the insured had incurred. But, notwithstanding the famous protest of Mark Twain, that the report of his death had been grossly exaggerated, there can be no degrees as regards death. Under such circumstances it is contended that the insurance was one on the life of the animal; that the policy was a valued policy on such life, and that the interest of the plaintiff and the amount payable by the company have been agreed upon and are fixed by the contract. But when I turn to the actual phraseology of the policy itself, it is hard to see how such a contention can be sustained. The recital is that the assured "is desirous of effecting an insurance" on the life of the filly for the sum of £250, and the company agrees to "indemnify the assured against the loss sustained through the death" of the animal, "but not exceeding the sum insured hereby."

The maximum is further limited by this clause:— "And *pro rata* only with any other subsisting insurances, and less any sum recovered from any third parties." This clause brings in the principle of contribution and subrogation, which are the invariable accompaniment of indemnity. Indeed, in *Castellain* v. *Preston*,[11] Bowen, L.J., said that subrogation, in regard to insurance matters, "is part of the law of indemnity." If Brodigan had sold the animal and it had died within the twelve months from some cause within the contemplation of the policy, would the assured have been entitled to have claimed the policy monies? I think not. The policy actually provides for such a contingency in the following clause:—

> "The company will continue the risk under this policy for the same amount and on the same terms and conditions should the property or interest be transferred by sale or otherwise during the currency of this policy, provided always that written notice of such transfer be received by and the transfer be approved by the company."

Neither in the correspondence nor in the policy itself has the company made any admission as to the value of the filly, and no evidence as to its value was asked for. The two certificates that were demanded deal only with the health of the animal and its fitness (presumably as a consequence) for insurance. I find it impossible to think that the company cannot now call upon the assured to give them reasonable particulars of the amount of the loss sustained by him through the death. It seems to me that the use of the word "indemnify", coupled with the other circumstances, renders the plaintiff's point unarguable. Mr Campbell [for the assured] suggests that it is impossible now to supply any information as to the value of the animal; but the very same difficulty arises in the case of a house and its contents which have been totally destroyed by fire. I have no doubt that the correspondence, the

---

[11] 11 Q.B.D. 380, at p. 403.

proposal and the terms of the policy will form an element — possibly a decisive element —in the calculation of the loss by the arbitrators, but I cannot hold in favour of the assured that they must necessarily be regarded as the sole element.

It is contended further, on behalf of the assured, that the actual agreement between the parties was one for the issue of a valued policy, and that the plaintiff is entitled to have the present policy rectified in order to carry out that agreement. There is no doubt that if the plaintiff can show any sort of grounds for rectification, this Court must allow the action to proceed, but I can see no ground for such a claim. I can find no evidence of an agreement between the parties that a valued rather than an indemnity policy should be issued. In his first letter the plaintiff said:— "I enclose full pedigree of above filly.... It is value for £1,000 on its breeding, but I want to know what insurance would cost for 12 months against accident or death for, say, £500. It is a good strong filly and can be examined by a V.S." In their replying letter the company says:— "I regret we would not be able to insure an animal of this breeding for so much as £500, the utmost amount we would be prepared to insure being £250, and we would want a veterinary surgeon's certificate as to its fitness." The proposal signed by the assured says:— "Please effect insurance on my behalf on the animal specified hereunder for a period of twelve calendar months against death from natural causes, fire, accidents, or the act of God...." This was addressed to insurance brokers, who were to "effect the insurance" for the plaintiff. The plaintiff, if he had read the "conditions of insurance" set out in the proposal, would have had his attention drawn to the fact that there were many companies which insured live stock and that there were more than one form of policy in use in respect thereof. Condition 5 is as follows:— "Any insurance required will be arranged with company or underwriters where best value can be obtained, having regard to security, wording of policy, liberality of benefits and reputation for claims settlements." Condition 6, in my opinion, suggests very strongly that an indemnity insurance was contemplated in this proposal:— "On payment of transfer fee of 2s. 6d. insurance will generally be changed from one animal to another, subject to veterinary certificate, or, on request, insurance will be transferred to a new owner." It is further provided in the proposal that that document should be "the basis of the contract" between the assured and the company. The policy itself sets out that "the said assured hath supplied certain particulars the truth of which he hereby warrants for the purpose of this insurance." On Aug. 16, the plaintiff wrote to the brokers saying:— "Herewith I enclose cheque £16 5s., insurance 'Midships Vis' for twelve months from date, with veterinary and independent certificate attached (for £250)"; and, in reply, the brokers say:— "I am obliged by instructions for insurance herein. I have with pleasure arranged as required and I hope that you will approve the attached document." "The attached document" — the policy — contained on its face the following note:— "Please examine this policy and conditions. If incorrect, return to the Irish Bloodstock Agency, 7 Anglesea Street, Dublin." The plaintiff received the policy and kept it, and there was no further communication between the parties until the animal was at the point of death, a little over two months later.

There is nothing in the correspondence suggesting that the plaintiff expected a valued policy to be issued to him, and so far as the proposal, taken as a whole, is concerned it suggests the issue of an indemnity policy. Even, however, if this were not so, I find it difficult to see how any Court could alter a contract with reference to the terms of the negotiations which preceded it. If the plaintiff is right in his view of what took place, it seems to me that the conclusion to be arrived at is that the parties were never *ad idem* and that there was no contract at all.

The ordinary contract of insurance contained in a marine or fire policy is a contract of indemnity: *Castellain* v. *Preston*.[12] If such policies were to be regarded as valued policies,[13] then (as Bowen, L.J., said in that case) the contract of insurance would not be a contract against loss, "but might become a speculation for gain." I think that the reasoning in *Castellain* v. *Preston*[14] applies with equal force in the case of policies for the insurance of live stock. In conclusion, I may add that in all cases of which I am aware in which something of the nature of rectification took place, some kind of antecedent arrangement or contract binding upon both parties was proved, such as the customary "slip" in the case of marine insurances: *Ionides* v. *Pacific Fire Insurance Co.;*[15] *Cory* v. *Patton*.[16]

I must make an order staying the action pending the taking place of the arbitration and the costs of both parties will be reserved.

St Alban's Investment Company v. Sun Alliance & London Insurance Limited and Provincial Insurance Company Limited
[1983] I.R. 363
The High Court

McWILLIAM J. : The plaintiffs' claim arises out of associated contracts of insurance entered into by the plaintiffs with the defendants in respect of property situate at Maxwell Street, Glasgow. The property was purchased by the plaintiffs in May, 1977 (with other adjoining property) for approximately £25,000. A purchase price of £15,000 approximately has been apportioned on the property with which this case is concerned. Mr O'Hara, the proprietor of the plaintiffs, had substantial interests in two companies in Scotland; one of them, Cohar Distributors Ltd., conducted a retail furniture and carpet business and had premises close to the property which was purchased in 1977. The property was probably built in or about the beginning of the century and was constructed of sandstone.

Having purchased the property, the plaintiffs employed Atlantic Insurance Brokers (hereinafter called Atlantic) to arrange to have it insured against fire risks. Atlantic approached the second defendant (Provincial Insurance) with whom property owned by Cohar Distributors and by Mr

---

[12] 11 Q.B.D. 380.
[13] [where the amount recoverable is fixed by the policy]
[14] 11 Q.B.D. 380.
[15] L.R. 6 Q.B. 674, L.R. 7 Q.B. 517.
[16] L.R. 7 Q.B. 304

O'Hara's other company in Scotland had been insured. Atlantic sought cover for £30,000 to allow for inflation as Mr O'Hara stated in evidence. The approach to Provincial Insurance appears to have been made by telephone. A letter dated the 24th May, 1977, and written to Atlantic by Provincial Insurance included the following passages:— "We refer to our telephone conversation on 12.05.77 and confirm we are holding cover for fire perils only in the sum of £30,000 the building situate at 85, Maxwell Street, Glasgow" and — after requiring the acceptance of certain terms relating to the circumstance that the building was unoccupied — "3. The floor area of the building is about 4,000 square feet, so that the total floor area is some 20,000 square feet. The present sum insured of £30,000 therefore affords a rebuilding cover of £1.50 per square foot. A realistic figure should be fixed; but please note that, whilst the building remains unoccupied, our maximum acceptance would be £50,000, so that we should expect you to find co-insurers for the balance above this amount."

Atlantic then approached the first defendant (Sun Alliance) and, by letter dated the 23rd June, 1977, Sun Alliance wrote to Atlantic as follows:— "Dear Sirs, Fire Proposal ... St Albans Investment Company Limited, 69, Highfield Road, Rathgar. With reference to your recent conversation with our Mr Murphy regarding the premises No. 85, Maxwell Street, Glasgow, we confirm holding cover for a sum of £250,000 for fire perils only. We understand the premises will shortly be occupied and we will then arrange to have the risk surveyed. As soon as our surveyor's report is available we will contact you again."

During June and July, Mr O'Hara consulted (through Cohar Distributors and his other Scottish company) architects and quantity surveyors for the preparation of plans for converting part of the premises into a public house and the preparation of the necessary documents for an application for a liquor licence. Whether he expected to be able to complete this conversion or not, it is clear that Mr O'Hara had it in mind at that time.

Before any policy was issued and before any further step had been taken, the property was destroyed by fire on the 15th August, 1977; the fire started in some adjoining premises. A short time later policies were issued by the defendant insurers in what has been described as the standard policy form. This form provides for payment to the insured of the value of the property at the time of the happening of its destruction, with an option to the insurer to reinstate the property. Evidence has been given that, where the reinstatement of property is required by an insured, the policy will contain what is described as a "reinstatement clause". No such clause was contained in these policies.

As a result of the fire, the building had to be taken down at considerable cost, which was between £8,000 and £15,000 — apparently the latter figure included the cost of taking down adjoining premises. There was no clear evidence as to this and I would estimate the cost of demolishing the plaintiffs' property at £9,000. The evidence of the value of the site after demolition was also unsatisfactory, and I estimate it at £20,000.

The defendant insurers deny that they insured the premises on the basis of rebuilding or reinstating them, and evidence was given that such cover was not sought and that the policies which were issued after the fire were in accordance with the original agreement between the parties. The defendants explain the reference to rebuilding in the letter of the 24th May, 1977, as an indication to Atlantic that, in the case of partial damage, a clause as to general average would apply and that, in the case of partial destruction, the insured would only recover such proportion of the cost of repair as the total sum insured would bear to the cost of rebuilding the entire premises if totally destroyed. They claim, therefore, that they are only liable to compensate the plaintiffs on the basis of the market value of the premises at the time of the fire, less the value of the site after deducting the cost of demolition. They rely very strongly on the fact that the plaintiffs placed their insurance through a broker, who should have been fully aware that an agreement to indemnify the cost of rebuilding would require a reinstatement clause in the policy, and who should have been fully aware of the application of general-average provisions. Mr Considine, the member of Atlantic who conducted the transaction, agreed that the provision of a reinstatement clause is outside the standard form and that it is rare to give such cover in regard to old buildings.

The plaintiffs claim to be entitled to the full sum of £300,000 as the cost of rebuilding is considerably more than that sum.

I am satisfied that, originally, Mr O'Hara proposed to insure on the basis of being compensated for loss in accordance with the value of the property. It is not suggested that he knew anything about general average himself, although his companies had a number of other policies of fire insurance. He stated that the figure of £300,000 was suggested to him, presumably by Atlantic, and that he would not have thought of it himself.

It was very strongly urged on behalf of the defendant insurers that, as the insurance was effected by an insurance broker on behalf of the plaintiffs, and as that broker was fully conversant with the position about reinstatement clauses, the negotiations must be presumed to have been conducted on the basis of that knowledge. It was also urged that, in the insurance business, the word "rebuilding" is not a term with any significance and that, if rebuilding cover is required, the word "reinstatement" is appropriate so that the word "rebuilding" cannot mean reinstatement. The first proposition seems to be reasonable, but I cannot see any justification for saying that "rebuilding" does not mean what it says, although the insurance practice may be of assistance in ascertaining what was in the mind of the insurers.

In deciding what the parties intended, it is clear that Mr O'Hara, in naming the sum of £300,000 in the first instance, was insuring himself against the loss of the cost price or value of the property. When he got the letter from Provincial Insurance in May, 1977, he accepted the sum of £300,000 recommended by Atlantic and did not then consider whether £300,000 would be his entitlement or not. From this, I conclude that, at this time, the question of reinstatement or rebuilding was not considered by him at all. This is borne out by the fact that, after the fire and after the issue of the policies, neither the plaintiffs nor their agents raised any question about reinstatement or rebuilding although minor errors in the policies were noted and pointed out. This being so, I am of opinion that there was no agreement by the parties as to reinstatement or rebuilding and that the plaintiffs are only entitled to be indemnified for their loss and are not entitled to recover on the basis of an agreement for reinstatement.

I have been referred to a number of cases from which it appears that, according to the circumstances, the indemnity may be calculated in various ways. First, and this is strongly urged by the defendant insurers, the indemnity may be calculated on the basis of the market value of the premises at the time of the fire. Secondly, and also urged by the defendants, the indemnity may be calculated on the basis of the cost of similar premises, if such are available. Thirdly, the indemnity may be calculated on the basis of the cost of erecting modern premises which would provide the same facilities as the premises destroyed. Lastly, and this is strongly urged on behalf of the plaintiffs, the indemnity may be based on the cost of rebuilding premises similar to those destroyed.

To take the last proposition first, I am of opinion that, unless there are very special circumstances — as was the case in *Reynolds* v. *Phoenix Assurance Co. Ltd.*[17] — there can be no commercial justification for erecting a sandstone building, which would be identical to one built at the beginning of the century, at an estimated current cost of something in the region of £500,000.

On the evidence before me, I am of opinion that there are no premises available which are suitable, as to location and convenience, for the purposes for which the plaintiffs purchased the premises destroyed, although the evidence tendered as to value may be relevant otherwise.

Mr O'Hara stated that he purchased the premises because they were convenient to his other business premises and could be used, in part, in conjunction with the other premises, and that he also intended to reconstruct part of the ground floor for the purposes of a licensed premises with a discothèque on the first floor. That he seriously considered the licensed-premises venture is borne out by estimates, for the conversion, which he obtained from architects and quantity surveyors. There was a conflict of evidence as to the suitability of the location for new licensed premises but I am not concerned to decide whether such a business, if commenced, would necessarily have been financially successful or not. What does appear to be relevant is whether the plaintiffs intend to proceed with similar plans or to rebuild the premises in any form if compensation on this basis is awarded. This Mr O'Hara has refused to state; from which I conclude that there are no special circumstances, as in *Harbutts* v. *Wayne Tank Co.*,[18] which make it necessary to have any building on this site, although, by reason of the fire, he has lost the opportunity of putting into effect the plans which he was considering. In this connection, the cost of putting up a modern building was not considered by either party although one witness stated that the original building was not listed for preservation and that the area was not a conservation area. From this I assume that a different type of building may be constructed.

With regard to the value of the premises, the one thing that is quite clear is that the purchase price of £15,000 was wholly unrealistic and that the plaintiffs got a quite exceptional bargain. The valuations given in evidence were widely divergent; they ranged from £35,000 — through £45,000 — to £130,000. Although the defendant insurers laid considerable emphasis on the

---

[17] [1978] 2 Lloyds Rep 440.
[18] [1970] 1 Q.B. 447.

injustice of the plaintiffs making a substantial profit in relation to the original purchase, that is not relevant in itself because the purchase was made at a bargain price and the profit arose from that transaction and only indirectly on the insurance money which may be paid.

In all the circumstances, I estimate the value of the property at £65,000, from which must be deducted the value of the site less the cost of demolition. This results in a figure of £54,000.

The Supreme Court

O'HIGGINS C.J.: ... In these proceedings the plaintiffs claim that each of the two defendants, to the extent of its share of the sum for which the property was insured, is bound to indemnify on the basis of the cost of rebuilding or reinstating the property which was destroyed. This claim is put forward on alternative grounds.

In the first place the plaintiffs contend that the insurance effected by Mr Considine with each defendant was on the basis of a rebuilding cover and with the intention that the policy which would issue would contain a reinstatement clause. The plaintiffs contend that this was the clear intention of all the parties at the time that the original insurance was effected. Alternatively, the plaintiffs submit that, even if the correct cover is that contained in the standard fire policy which was issued by each defendant, such cover (on the facts and circumstances of this case) extended to the cost of rebuilding.

The first of these alternative submissions was put forward strongly in the High Court. It rested on the evidence of Mr Considine and on the contents of the letter from Provincial Insurance in which the defendant advised a realistic insurance figure for rebuilding. Mr Considine stated that he made Sun Alliance aware of the contents of that letter; and he argued that Sun Alliance and Provincial Insurance must have been aware that he was seeking cover on a rebuilding basis. He admitted that such requirement was not expressly mentioned by him and that the insertion of such a clause in a fire policy was rare. Both Sun Alliance and Provincial Insurance adduced evidence that cover of the kind suggested would never have been contemplated by them, particularly in the case of an old building such as the one owned by the plaintiffs. Mr Justice McWilliam decided that issue against the plaintiffs in the following terms:—

> "In deciding what the parties intended, it is clear that Mr O'Hara, in naming the sum of £30,000 in the first instance, was insuring himself against the loss of the cost price or value of the property. When he got the letter from Provincial Insurance in May, he accepted the sum of £300,000 recommended by Atlantic and did not then consider whether £300,000 would be his entitlement or not. From this, I conclude that, at this time, the question of reinstatement or rebuilding was not considered by him at all. This is borne out by the fact that, after the fire and after the issue of the policies, neither the plaintiffs nor their agents raised any question about reinstatement or rebuilding although minor errors in the policies were noted and pointed out. This being so, I am of opinion that there was no agreement by the parties as to reinstatement or rebuilding and that the plaintiffs are only entitled to be

indemnified for their loss and are not entitled to recover on the basis of an
agreement for reinstatement."

On this appeal the plaintiffs submit that the learned trial judge's conclusion and finding in this respect was wrong and that he should have held
that both defendants were liable for reinstatement cover to the extent of the
sums insured on the basis of an express contract to that effect. I do not agree.
I have considered very carefully all the evidence which was before the learned
judge and I have come to the conclusion that his decision on this aspect of the
case was fully justified on the evidence and was correct. Mr O'Hara entrusted
the arrangement of the insurance cover to an experienced firm of insurance
brokers. Mr Considine, the principal of that firm did not expressly specify
reinstatement cover. It was established that such cover is not normal cover
and is unusual, at the very least, in the case of old and unoccupied buildings.
On the evidence, I can see no basis on which a term of such special
significance should have been implied and, in my view, the learned trial judge
was correct in refusing to so hold.

The alternative submission made on behalf of the plaintiffs, in support of
a claim based on the costs of rebuilding, was to the effect that it was only in
this manner, on the facts of this case, that the plaintiffs could be indemnified. The trial judge rejected this submission and proceeded to assess the
loss on the basis of market value. Clearly he was influenced in this direction
by his recollection of Mr O'Hara's evidence with regard to an intention to
rebuild. The following extract from the judgment indicates the manner in
which the judge approached this issue:—

> "There was a conflict of evidence as to the suitability of the location for new
> licensed premises but I am not concerned to decide whether such a business,
> if commenced, would necessarily have been financially successful or not.
> What does appear to be relevant is whether the plaintiffs intend to proceed
> with similar plans or to rebuild the premises in any form if compensation on
> this basis is awarded. This Mr O'Hara has refused to state, from which I
> conclude that there are no special circumstances, as in *Harbutts* v. *Wayne
> Tank Co.*[19] which make it necessary to have any building on this site,
> although, by reason of the fire, he has lost the opportunity of putting into
> effect the plans which he was considering."

In that passage, in so far as he refers to the evidence of Mr O'Hara, I
think the judge's recollection is at fault. I have read the transcript of this
evidence with care and I cannot see any basis for the comment that Mr
O'Hara had refused to state whether he intended to rebuild. Indeed, as I read
his evidence, I formed the contrary impression; not only did he deal with the
matter fully in his direct evidence but he also maintained a view during the
course of his cross-examinations that he always had the intention to rebuild.
In particular, I would refer to the transcript at p. 28 of volume 2, (commencing with Q. 255) where Mr O'Hara was asked a number of questions on
this topic. In his answers he made it clear that it was always his, or rather

---

[19] [1970] 1 Q.B. 447.

the plaintiffs' intention, to rebuild on the site. What would be built depended on the cost, the financial resources available and, in particular, the amount of compensation which he would obtain. He made it clear that, in this respect, the £300,000 for which the destroyed property had been insured was critical. He denied suggestions that he would be unable to rebuild if the cost exceeded that sum — even if it went as high as £1 million. He asserted that he would do so if he got the insurance money.

In fact, Mr O'Hara complained in his evidence that the defendant insurers had failed to honour an undertaking as to rebuilding which, he understood, was conveyed to him by the loss adjusters (McLaren, Dick & Co. Ltd.) by letter of the 20th September, 1977. That firm of loss adjusters acted for the defendant insurers and at one stage were willing, apparently, to act also for the plaintiffs. The letter to which Mr O'Hara referred was addressed to the plaintiffs and was in the following terms:—

> "We refer to our recent telephone conversation with Mr O'Hara and confirm that although in terms of the policy insurers have the option to insist that the proceeds of the policy be applied in the reinstatement of the property, so far as possible, this option is rarely exercised and primarily the decision as to whether or not to rebuild rests with you. If, for example, you do not consider it necessary to rebuild the property on the existing site, you may prefer to base your claim on the diminution in market value of the site due to the fire damage. Alternatively, if you require to have this accommodation reconstructed at this location, you are entitled to base your claim on the cost of reconstruction less a reasonable allowance for the improvement which would result from having a new building instead of the old structure."

Mr O'Hara complained that, following that letter, he asked on a number of occasions for information as to what kind of a building he would be allowed to reconstruct, in other words, he wished to know how much money would be made available to him to enable reconstruction or rebuilding to take place. His complaint was that he had not received any satisfaction in this respect and that he had been offered merely compensation on the basis of market value, and so he had initiated these proceedings. Therefore, I must conclude that, in relation to the disclosure of an intention to rebuild, the trial judge, in delivering his judgment, either did not appreciate or did not correctly recall the evidence of Mr O'Hara. However, that does not necessarily mean that the conclusion which the judge reached was erroneous.

I now turn to what I consider to be the correct conclusion on the facts of this case but, before doing so, I think some general principles which are applicable should be stated.

The standard fire policies which were issued by the defendant insurers were described as "unvalued policies" — see Ivamy on General Principles of Insurance Law (4th ed. p. 466). This means that the amount of the insurance specified in the policies does not necessarily represent the amount of the indemnity. The position was put thus in the last century in an Irish case: I quote from the judgment of Pennefather B. in *Vance* v. *Forster*[20] at p. 50 of the report:—

> "It has been truly stated that a policy of insurance is a contract of indemnity, and that while the insured may name any sum he likes as the sum for which he will pay a premium, he does not, by so proposing that sum, nor does the company by accepting the risk, conclude themselves as to the amount which the plaintiff is to recover in consequence of the loss — because, although the plaintiff cannot recover beyond the sum insured on each particular item of insurance, he cannot recover even that sum unless he proves that he has sustained damage, and then he will recover a sum commensurate to the loss which he has sustained...."

Of course, the sum for which the property is insured has considerable relevance, in the event of partial loss, under the modern *pro rata* average clause. However, where there has been total destruction of the property, the average clause does not apply and the amount recoverable depends on what is established as a full indemnity. At this stage I think it is well to remind the parties that this form of insurance is about indemnity — nothing less and nothing more. Let me do so in the words of Brett L.J. who, in *Castlellain* v. *Preston*,[21] said at p. 386 of the report:—

> "In order to give my opinion upon this case, I feel obliged to revert to the very foundation of every rule which has been promulgated and acted on by the Courts with regard to insurance law. The very foundation, in my opinion, of every rule which has been applied to insurance law is this, namely, that the contract of insurance contained in a marine or fire policy is a contract of indemnity, and of indemnity only, and that this contract means that the assured, in case of a loss against which the policy has been made, shall be fully indemnified, but shall never be more than fully indemnified. That is the fundamental principle of insurance, and if ever a proposition is brought forward which is at variance with it, that is to say, which either will prevent the assured from obtaining a full indemnity, or which will give to the assured more than a full indemnity, that proposition must certainly be wrong."

What is the position in this case? Mr O'Hara, through the plaintiffs, bought a property for a trifling sum. In this respect he was either very lucky or he displayed considerable business acumen. The property which he bought was ideally situated in a developing area. It provided convenient and suitable storage and other accommodation for his existing business in an adjoining building and, in particular, its ground and first floors were suitable for conversion into a public bar and discothèque. That he intended this conversion was fully accepted by the trial judge. It was not in dispute that he had engaged architects and surveyors to draw up plans for the structural alterations entailed and that he had employed a firm of lawyers to proceed with the application for an intoxicating liquor licence. This property, ideally suited for

---

[20] (1841) Ir. Cir. Rep. 47. See p. 29 of this book.
[21] (1883) 11 Q.B.D. 380.

the purposes which he had in mind, was totally destroyed by fire. What then was his loss?

If the building which was destroyed could have been replaced by another, similarly situated, with more or less the same convenience and possibilities, then his loss could be measured by the cost of acquiring such other building — with due regard being paid to the value of the vacant site less the cost of demolition of the destroyed building. But, as the judge found, there was no such other building available. Various other premises had been suggested but none was in any way similar or suitable or could fairly be regarded as a replacement for that which had been destroyed. Could a notional market value compensate for the loss? I do not think so. The premises were not on the market; they were bought as an investment for development and not for resale. In my view, the assessment of a notional figure, based on a hypothetical sale, could not meet what the plaintiffs have lost by the destruction of the one building which suited their particular requirements and plans. If these requirements are to be met and the plans are to proceed, another building on the same site must be provided.

In this respect this case is very similar to *Reynolds* v. *Phoenix Assurance Co. Ltd.*[22] In that case the insured bought an old maltings for a trifling sum of £16,000. They immediately insured it for £18,000 in order to cover the purchase price plus an addition for the cost of acquisition. They planned to use the premises as a grain store and later, with the installation of extra machinery, for the making of animal feeding stuffs. The insurance was later increased to £500,000 and, finally, to a figure of £628,000 to cover the building and machinery against fire. The risk was accepted by four insurance companies, with the defendant company issuing the policy as the leading company. The policy was a standard fire policy. The premises were almost completely destroyed by fire and the question of proper compensation became the subject of litigation. On the facts, Forbes J. rejected the insured's contention that they had contracted on a reinstatement basis; nevertheless, he held that the cost of reinstatement still remained a possible means of measuring the loss, even though prior agreement to that effect could not be found in the contract. He was of the view (p. 453) that "where the owner is not inevitably to be dispossessed [*from the site*] the market is not an ineluctable solution, and the commercial logic of the market is not the necessary criterion" when considering the loss. In such circumstances he held that the test should be that stated by O'Connor L.J. in *Murphy* v. *Wexford County Council*[23] at p. 240 of the report:—

> "Would he [*the owner*], for any reason that would appeal to an ordinary man in his position, rebuild it if he got replacement damages, or is his claim for such damages a mere pretence?"

Accordingly, holding that the insured did have a genuine intention to rebuild if given the insurance monies, Forbes J. concluded (p. 453) by deciding the issue before him in the following terms:—

---

[22] [1978] 2 Lloyd's Rep. 440.
[23] [1921] 2 I.R. 230.

"The upshot is that I am satisfied that the plaintiffs do have the genuine intention to reinstate if given the insurance money; that this is not a mere eccentricity but arises from the fact, as I find, that they will not be properly indemnified unless they are given the means to reinstate the building substantially as it was before the fire but with appropriate economies in the use of materials."

Another case which was referred to in argument was *Carrick Furniture House* v. *General Accident.*[24] It appears to me that the same reasoning was adopted in that case, with the result that the insured was held entitled to the replacement cost.

I cannot see why a different conclusion should be reached in this case. The building which was destroyed was required as an adjunct to Mr O'Hara's existing business and was an essential feature of his plans for the future. Alternative accommodation, equally suitable, was not available. On the evidence, in my view, it was not open to conclude that Mr O'Hara had any intention other than to rebuild. Of course, this depended on the agreement of the defendant insurers in that the payment of sufficient compensation was essential. The letter from the loss adjusters (McLaren, Dick & Co. Ltd.) dated the 20th September, 1977, a short time after the fire, indicated clearly a point of view which coincided with what Mr O'Hara has in mind. This was to the effect that he could rebuild if he wished to do so. It is apparent that this letter was not acted upon in the sense that there was no follow-up. Subsequent exchanges between the parties ended with Mr O'Hara being offered accommodation based on a hypothetical market value and so this litigation ensued.

I have come to the conclusion that the indemnity to which the plaintiffs are entitled can only be secured by rebuilding on the site a suitable building. Obviously, an exact replacement of what was there is neither possible nor necessary. However, some building providing the essential accommodation which is required should be constructed. At the trial, evidence was given by Mr Dobson (of the firm of Doig & Smith, quantity surveyors, Glasgow) that the construction on the site of a warehouse-type building providing appropriate accommodation would have cost £256,935 in the year 1977. This would have involved the use of concrete blocks instead of sandstone which, in any event, would not have been available. There was also evidence suggesting higher figures for a substitute building. All figures given in relation to 1977 or 1978 would, as a result of inflation, require to be almost doubled to meet the present-day situation. As the trial judge did not consider rebuilding as the basis for indemnity, this evidence was not pronounced upon by him and, as a result, there was no finding as to the type and cost of a suitable substitute building. In addition, any new building would involve the application of the betterment principle and an appropriate allowance would have to be made in respect of new materials for old. It seems to me that this aspect of the case now requires a further hearing in the High Court.

Accordingly, I would direct that this action be remitted to the High Court to find the cost of constructing, within a reasonable period after the fire, a

---

[24] 1977 S.C. 308.

suitable replacement building on the site; such a finding should include an allowance for betterment.

In my view, in failing to concede and agree that the plaintiffs were entitled to rebuild in the sense of constructing on the site a suitable replacement, the defendant insurers have been in breach of their contracts. Accordingly, they are liable to the plaintiffs in damages. It would seem to me that these damages should correspond to the increase in the cost of constructing the building today, compared with the cost in 1977. It may be also that there are other headings of damages which can be established. Accordingly, I would direct that, in addition, the High Court be directed to enquire into and determine what damages should be awarded to the plaintiffs.

I would allow this appeal and would discharge the order made in the High Court.

GRIFFIN J: ... The case made on behalf of the plaintiffs in all the negotiations which took place before proceedings were instituted, in the pleadings, and on the hearing in the High Court, was that the contract of insurance effected in each case included what is known as a reinstatement clause or memorandum, in which event the policy holder would be entitled to be paid the cost of reinstating the damaged or destroyed building up to the limit of the sum insured. Cover of this nature is not included in a standard fire-insurance policy. The evidence established that cover of this kind is not given unless it is expressly sought by the proposer for insurance; and that, because of its age and because it was unoccupied, it would be most unusual for an insurance company to grant cover of this kind in the case of a building such as that owned by the plaintiffs. Even if the defendant insurers had been asked to grant reinstatement cover, the officials of both companies were quite adamant that they would not have provided it. Mr Considine, the plaintiffs' insurance broker, accepted that the insurers had not been asked to provide such cover, and that this was solely due to an omission on his part.

The learned trial judge held that there was no agreement to grant re-instatement cover, and I agree with the Chief Justice that, on the facts, the trial judge was fully justified in so holding. Indeed, in view of the evidence given at the trial, it is difficult to see how he could have come to any other conclusion.

However, the plaintiffs claim that, even if there was no reinstatement clause in the contract, they are entitled under the terms of the policy to the cost of rebuilding the premises, as that is the only way, they allege, in which they can be paid the value of the property.

Under the policies issued respectively by Sun Alliance and Provincial Insurance, each defendant agreed that, if the property insured or any part of such property should be destroyed or damaged by fire (inter alia), each de-fendant would pay to the plaintiffs the value of the property at the time of the happening of its destruction or the amount of such damage (or, at its option, reinstate or replace such property or any part thereof) subject to a limit of £250,000 in the case of Sun Alliance, and to a limit of £50,000 in the case of Provincial Insurance. Each of these two policies was a standard fire insurance policy.

It is well settled for upwards of one hundred years that such a policy is a contract of indemnity under which an insured may recover his actual loss, not exceeding the maximum amount specified in the policy. What is generally regarded as the authoritative statement of the right of an insured to be indemnified under such a policy is that of Brett L.J. in *Castellain* v. *Preston*[25] (at p. 386 of the report), which statement has been quoted by the Chief Justice in his judgment. In the case of such a policy, therefore, what the insurer agrees to do is to indemnify the insured in respect of loss or damage caused by fire, and the insured is entitled to be paid his actual loss — no more and no less. The net issue in this appeal is the basis on which the amount of that loss is to be ascertained. The plaintiffs claim that they can be compensated properly only by the cost of rebuilding, whilst the defendant insurers say that, on the facts of the case, the correct basis should be that of market value at the time of the destruction of the premises.

... What Mr O'Hara had in mind at the time of the purchase was that he would endeavour to obtain a public-house licence for portion of the ground floor being approximately 1,500 square feet in area, and that he would have a discothèque on the first floor immediately over the public house. He instructed an architect to prepare a plan for the alterations and the architect obtained from a quantity surveyor a preliminary estimate of the likely cost of the alterations. Before any further steps had been taken, the premises, still vacant, were destroyed by fire on the 15th August, 1977. As the portion that remained after the fire was dangerous, it was demolished at a cost of £9,000 shortly thereafter; the site then became, and has remained at all times, a vacant derelict site.

What is the loss that was suffered by the plaintiffs as a result of the fire? As Sir James Campbell C. said in *Murphy* v. *Wexford County Council*[26] at pp. 233–4 of the report:—

> "... the principle to be applied in such a case is that of restitution, or restitutio in integrum, as it is called, but I cannot agree that this principle is necessarily or even generally only consistent with restoration or reinstatement. It means ... that the law will endeavour, so far as money can do it, to place the injured person in the same position as if the contract had been performed, or before the occurrence of the tort...."

That case was one of malicious damage, but the principle is the same. In *Munnelly* v. *Calcon Ltd.*[27] in which the plaintiffs' premises had been demolished as a result of the wrongful act of the defendants, Mr Justice Henchy put the matter thus at p. 399 of the report:—

> "I do not consider that reinstatement damages, which may vastly exceed damages based on diminished value, are to be awarded as a prima facie right or, even if they are, that the plaintiff's intention as to reinstatement should be the determining factor. I do not think the authorities establish that there is a prima facie right to this measure of damages in any given case. In my view, the particular measure of damages allowed should be objectively

---

[25] (1883) 11 Q.B.D. 380.
[26] [1921] 2 I.R. 230.
[27] [1978] I.R. 387.

chosen by the court as being that which is best calculated, in all the circumstances of the particular case, to put the plaintiff fairly and reasonably in the
position in which he was before the damage occurred, so far as a pecuniary
award can do so."

And at p. 400 he said:—

"... a court, in endeavouring to award a sum which will be both compensatory
and reasonable, will be called on to give consideration, with emphasis
varying from case to case, to matters such as the nature of the property, the
plaintiff's relation to it, the nature of the wrongful act causing the damage,
the conduct of the parties subsequent to the wrongful act, and the pecuniary,
economic or other relevant implications or consequences of reinstatement
damages as compared with diminished-value damages."

The plaintiffs claim that the loss should be evaluated by reference to the
cost of reinstatement or, alternatively, by an equivalent modern replacement;
the defendant insurers claim that the amount could best be ascertained by
reference to the value of the premises at the time of the fire. In support of
their claim that the loss should be ascertained by reference to the cost of
reinstatement, the plaintiffs rely on *Reynolds* v. *Phoenix Assurance Co. Ltd.*[28]
In that case the insured purchased old maltings (measuring 300' x 80') for
£16,000 in the summer of 1972 for use as a grain store, and for the milling of
grain and other materials in the production of animal feeding stuffs. The
premises were destroyed by fire in November, 1973, at which time they were
insured for over £600,000. On the facts of that case, Forbes J. held that the
insured were entitled to be compensated on the basis of reinstatement in the
sum of £246,883 (together with certain architects' and surveyors' fees) which
he held was sufficient, on the evidence he heard and accepted, to put the
insured in the position in which they would have been had the insurers not
refused to pay under the contract. The plaintiffs say that that case is on all
fours with the instant case and that they should be compensated on the same
basis.

The learned trial judge took a different view. He evaluated the loss by
reference to the value of the premises at the date of the fire, in respect of
which he had been given valuations ranging from £35,000 to £130,000. In
arriving at this conclusion, the trial judge said in the course of his judgment:— "What does appear to be relevant is whether the plaintiffs intend to
proceed with similar plans or to rebuild the premises in any form if
compensation on this basis is awarded. This Mr O'Hara has refused to state;
from which I conclude that there are no special circumstances, as in *Harbutts* v. *Wayne Tank Co.*,[29] which make it necessary to have any building on
this site, although, by reason of the fire, he has lost the opportunity of putting
into effect the plans which he was considering." Counsel for the plaintiffs says
that in that passage, the judge was wrong and that he erred on the facts as
Mr O'Hara, in the course of his evidence (at volume 2 of the transcript at QQ.

---

[28] [1978] 2 Lloyd's Rep. 440.
[29] [1970] 1 Q.B. 477.

255–282) had said that he did intend to rebuild, although he was uncertain as to whether he would build the same building or a smaller one. This Mr O'Hara undoubtedly said at the hearing; but the learned trial judge, who had heard and seen all the witnesses and had the opportunity of evaluating their evidence, had abundant evidence of the refusal of Mr O'Hara from a period commencing shortly after the fire right up to the time of the trial (some four and a half years) to state what his intentions were in relation to rebuilding. It appears to me that it was that refusal to which the judge was referring and, therefore, it is necessary to consider the evidence in relation to the attitude of Mr O'Hara and the stand which he adopted in his negotiations and discussions with the representatives of the defendant insurers and with the loss adjusters retained by them.

Immediately after the fire, Sun Alliance retained a firm of loss adjusters (Messrs McLaren, Dick & Co. Ltd.) as is usual in such cases. When Mr Andrews of that firm went to examine the premises within a day or two after the fire, he met Mr O'Hara and told him who and what he was. Mr O'Hara asked whether it was possible that the firm would act for him also; on being told (somewhat surprisingly to me) that it was, he engaged them to act on his behalf also (vol. 2 – Q.59). On the 20th September, 1977 Mr Andrews wrote to Mr O'Hara advising him of his rights under the policy and of the options open to him and the alternative ways in which he could base his claim. This letter was in terms which, in my view, clearly made it one written to Mr O'Hara by the loss adjusters not as agents for the defendant insurers but as the plaintiffs' adjusters. Unfortunately, Mr O'Hara does not seem to have heeded their advice: instead, he acquired a number of text-books on fire insurance and some articles written in professional periodicals on the principle of indemnity. From his reading of that material he concluded that, as he was insured for £250,000, he was entitled to that sum and not a penny less, and that he was entitled to settlement on a rebuilding basis regardless of whether he rebuilt or not: see the transcript of evidence at pp. 22, 23, 28 of book 4. That was a misconception by him of the law on the question.

In my view, the correct legal position is stated in the joint judgment of Kitto, Taylor and Owen JJ. in the High Court of Australia in *British Traders Insurance Co. Ltd v. Monson.*[30] At pp. 92-3 of the report of that case they said:—

> "It is far too late to doubt that by the common understanding of business men and lawyers alike the nature of such a policy controls its obligation, implying conclusively that its statement of the amount which the insurer promises to pay merely fixes the maximum amount which in any event he may have to pay, and having as its sole purpose, and therefore imposing as its only obligation, the indemnification of the insured, up to the amount of the insurance against loss from the accepted risk."

The stand which Mr O'Hara took then was the one he maintained at all times thereafter. In one sense it was consistent that he should maintain it, because he and his advisors maintained at all times (not only in the pleadings

---

[30] (1964) III C.L.R. 86.

and in the particulars furnished but to the end of the hearing in the High Court) that the policies included a reinstatement clause or memorandum. From October, 1977, onwards, he called to the offices of Sun Alliance in Glasgow and in Dublin on numerous occasions. On most of those occasions he was armed with his textbooks and articles, and he quoted liberally from them. Until the early part of 1978 he dealt in Dublin with Mr Colgan, a senior claims official. In his dealings with Mr Colgan, the attitude of Mr O'Hara was and remained that he wanted £250,000 regardless of what he contemplated doing with the premises; that he would give no indication as to what his intentions were in regard to rebuilding; and that it was no concern whatsoever of Sun Alliance, nor were they entitled to inquire, what he did with the proceeds of the claim (vol. 4 – QQ. 254–6). At the end of 1977 he retained a firm of loss adjusters (Messrs Sidney Balcombe & Sons Ltd.) on behalf of the plaintiffs; thereafter he was advised by Mr Grewcock of that firm. In May, 1978, an offer of £41,5000 was made by the defendants' loss adjusters to Mr Grewcock, and this offer was refused.

Mr O'Hara continued to call to the Dublin office of Sun Alliance and, on the 21st June, 1978, an important meeting took place in their offices in Dublin; it was attended by Mr O'Hara, Mr Grewcock, and Mr Rigby (the claims superintendent of Sun Alliance). In respect of that meeting, Mr Rigby in his evidence (vol. 4 – Q. 466) said:— "Mr O'Hara on behalf of St Alban's had taken no steps, as far as I knew, with regard to rebuilding, would not tell me whether he intended to rebuild, and would not tell me how much he had purchased the property for, would not tell me what he thought to be the market value." Mr Rigby was requested to write to Mr Grewcock setting out the position of Sun Alliance and their proposals; this he did by letter dated the 27th June, 1978. In that letter he set out the respective positions taken by the plaintiffs and Sun Alliance on the applicability of reinstatement conditions, he referred to the provisions of the policy in regard to the cover granted to the plaintiffs and to the view of Sun Alliance that their liability would be met by the payment of a sum based on the value of the property at the time of fire — while appreciating, nevertheless, that other factors might have to be taken into consideration. The letter then contained the following passage:— "On the basis of the foregoing, therefore, our loss adjusters submitted an offer in the sum of £41,500 which has been rejected. You are aware from recent discussions that we are amenable to reviewing this figure if it is shown to be inadequate. Insured is not prepared to discuss settlement based on the foregoing principles, but solely requests payment of the sum insured (£250,000). We are not prepared to accept — and as a matter of public policy would not be entitled to accept — that payment of the sum insured represents indemnity. Indeed, to date *insured refuses to advise us whether it is his intention to rebuild the property or not.*" I have added the emphasis.

That letter was written to the plaintiffs' consultant, Mr Grewcock, who had been present at the meeting of the 21st June, 1978. The allegation in that letter of the refusal of Mr O'Hara to state his intentions was not refuted at any time. There was no evidence, nor was there any suggestion made at the trial, that Sun Alliance had been informed, at any time prior to the hearing of the action, of any intention of Mr O'Hara to rebuild. Significantly, Mr Grewcock was not called as a witness at the trial.

If Mr O'Hara had a genuine intention to rebuild, I can see no reason whatsoever why he should have repeatedly refused so to inform Sun Alliance as that would have been highly material information which would have enabled them to assess properly the amount which would give a true indemnity to the plaintiffs. It is inconceivable that any business man would attempt to reinstate these buildings at an estimated cost of about £1,000,000. It is equally inconceivable that, in times of inflation and constantly escalating building costs, no steps should have been taken by Mr O'Hara, if he intended to rebuild, to make preparations and, if necessary, to arrange for the erection of a modern purpose-built building which would be suitable to his needs at a cost, according to the evidence of some £256,000 — bearing in mind that Mr O'Hara's evidence was that he was aware that if the old buildings had not been destroyed, it would have required an expenditure of between £100,000 and £150,000 to alter the old buildings so as to make them suitable for his purposes. No plans or specifications of any kind were prepared, nor was a bill of quantities drawn up for any proposed building; the site was just left lying derelict up to the time of the trial and, indeed, to the time of the appeal. Further, there was evidence that since the fire Mr O'Hara has purchased for £16,000 another warehouse of approximately 6,000 square feet. A quantity surveyor did give evidence of the cost of erecting a replacement building at 1977 prices, but he was requested to prepare his bill only days before the trial, as was the valuer who gave evidence of the value of the premises.

In my opinion, the learned trial judge was quite justified in holding that Mr O'Hara had refused to state, at a time when he might reasonably have been expected to do so, whether he intended to rebuild, and that the judge was justified in drawing the inference that the plaintiffs had not formed a genuine intention to rebuild.

In my view *Reynolds* v. *Phoenix Assurance Co. Ltd.*[31] is clearly distinguishable from this case. In that case, the judge having heard and seen both insured in the witness box, had no hesitation in accepting their evidence; he found that the insured's solicitors made it clear throughout the correspondence that the insured's intention was to rebuild; that the insured did have the genuine intention to reinstate; that the maltings were ideally suitable for use in connection with the insureds' business without any alteration or additional expenditure on their part, apart from the provision of necessary machinery; and that, in the lengthy negotiations and correspondence which took place in the months following the fire, the insurers had accepted that, so long as the insured intended to reinstate, the true measure of indemnity was the cost of reinstatement which, they agreed, was £243,000.

Evidence of the value of the premises in this case was given by three valuers. On behalf of the defendant insurers two valuers valued the premises at £35,000 and £50,000 respectively; on behalf of the plaintiffs, one valuer assessed their value at £130,000. However, the plaintiffs' valuer had been asked to make his valuation only a few days before the trial, being four and a half years after the premises had been demolished. The learned trial judge fixed £65,000 as being the value of the premises at the date of the fire; in my

---

[31] [1978] 2 Lloyd's Rep. 440.

judgment he was justified in so holding and I would uphold this finding. On the hearing of this appeal it was agreed that the site value should be taken to be £10,000. In the result, the plaintiffs are entitled to the sum of £64,000 when the amended site value is taken into account. Accordingly, in respect of the 14 grounds of appeal, the plaintiffs fail save in respect of damages which should be increased by £10,000 by reason of the value of the site....

HEDERMAN J: ... The plaintiffs' claim is based on two alternative grounds. First, the plaintiffs contend that the insurances effected by Mr Considine with the defendant insurers were made on the basis that the policies which would issue would contain a reinstatement clause for rebuilding the premises. Alternatively, the plaintiffs claim that, if the cover is that contained in the standard fire policy which was issued by each defendant, that cover, in the circumstances of this case, extended to the cost of rebuilding the premises at No. 85 Maxwell Street.

At the hearing in the High Court, the trial judge accepted evidence that this type of cover is not given in cases of standard fire insurance policies. The insurance broker who acted on behalf of the plaintiffs, Mr Considine, was aware of this and was aware of the fact that it would be most unusual to obtain reinstatement cover in the case of old buildings, or unoccupied buildings, because of the inherent dangers attached to such buildings with regard to the risk of fire. Mr Considine accepted that he did not ask the defendant insurers to provide reinstatement cover. I agree with the Chief Justice and Mr Justice Griffin that the trial judge was correct in holding that reinstatement cover was not provided by these insurance policies.

Therefore, policies, which were agreed to be standard fire-insurance policies, only provided indemnity cover to the plaintiffs, that is to say, cover under which the plaintiffs were entitled to receive from the defendant insurers a sum that was the equivalent of what the plaintiffs had actually lost. The dispute in this case is concerned with how best, by an award of damages, can the plaintiffs be put fairly and reasonably into the position they occupied before the fire took place.

The plaintiffs' case is that the Court can only do so by awarding them the costs of rebuilding the premises; while the defendants say that, in the circumstances of this case, it should be done by reference to the market value of the premises at the time of the fire.

As this was a policy of indemnity, the plaintiffs could not recover the cost of rebuilding unless they had a genuine intention of rebuilding and it would have been reasonable for them to do so. In the course of his judgment, the trial judge said:— "From this, I conclude that, at this time, the question of reinstatement or rebuilding was not considered by him at all. This is borne out by the fact that, after the fire and after the issue of the policies, neither the plaintiffs nor their agents raised any question about reinstatement or rebuilding although minor errors in the policies were noted and pointed out." Further, the learned trial judge stated:— "What does appear to be relevant is whether the plaintiffs intend to proceed with similar plans or to rebuild the premises in any form if compensation on this basis is awarded. This Mr O'Hara has refused to state; from which I conclude that there are no special circumstances, as in *Harbutts* v. *Wayne Tank Co.*,[32] which make it necessary to have any building on this site, although, by reason of the fire, he has lost the opportunity of putting into effect the plans which he was considering."

Counsel for the plaintiffs takes issue with that finding because Mr O'Hara said in evidence that he did intend to rebuild, if he got the insurance money. The trial judge appears not to have accepted that evidence having regard to all the other evidence, which indicated that Mr O'Hara had refused at all times to tell the defendant insurers whether he intended to rebuild or not. Mr O'Hara went further in indicating to the defendant insurers that it was none of their business whether he intended to rebuild or not....

In my opinion, the trial judge was justified in holding that Mr O'Hara did not have the intention to rebuild. When the trial judge referred to the refusal of Mr O'Hara to state if he intended to rebuild, in my view the judge was referring to this evidence. This is further demonstrated by the words used, which are identical with those used by Mr Rigley [sic] of Sun Alliance in his letter of the 27th June, 1978, to the plaintiffs' loss adjuster, Mr Grewcock.

In *Munnelly* v. *Calcon Ltd.*[33] Mr Justice Henchy said at p. 399 of the report:—

> "In my view, the particular measure of damages allowed should be objectively chosen by the court as being that which is best calculated, in all circumstances of the particular case, to put the plaintiff fairly and reasonably in the position in which he was before the damage occurred, so far as a pecuniary award can do so."

In my view the trial judge was justified in taking market value as the measure of damages necessary to put the plaintiffs fairly and reasonably in the position they would have occupied had the fire not occurred.

Indeed, while the plaintiffs always claimed the loss of rebuilding, which their quantity surveyor estimated at a sum close to £300,00 (including architects' fees etc.), Mr O'Hara and his advisors seem to have overlooked the fact that from any such sum there would have to be deducted the cost of converting the old premises, which on the evidence, would have been between £100,000 and £150,000, and an allowance for betterment, which would seem from the decided cases to be usually between 25 and 33 per cent. Therefore, if Mr O'Hara had intended to rebuild or had rebuilt, in my view the deductions from the sum of £300,000 would have reduced the sum claimed to a sum not appreciably greater that the sum awarded in this case.

With the adjustment for the site which was agreed at the hearing, the plaintiffs are entitled to recover an additional £10,000 but, on my findings, I agree with Mr Justice Griffin that the plaintiffs do not succeed on any ground of appeal other than damages....

---

[32] [1970] 1 Q.B. 447.
[33] [1978] I.R. 387.

Andrews and Others *v.* The Patriotic Assurance Company of Ireland (No. 2)[*]
(1886) 18 L.R.I. 355
Exchequer Division

PALLES C.B: The question upon the demurrer to the first defence is, whether the amount recoverable under a fire policy effected by the landlord of a house is liable, under the usual average conditions, to be rateably reduced by reason of another insurance effected upon the same house by a tenant, bound by his covenant to repair, but not bound to insure, where the sum received under the latter policy has not been, in fact, applied towards the re-instatement of the insured premises.

The question depends upon the meaning of the words *"the same property"* in the condition. Is it the structure of the house? for if it be the defence is good; or is it the estate of the insured in the house? as if so the demurrer should be allowed.

In construing the policy we ought not to assume the ordinary and *prima facie* meaning of the words to be "the same structure", and then endeavour to ascertain whether there is enough to justify us in arriving at the conclusion that the words were used in some other or secondary sense. We ought, in the first instance, to take the instrument as a whole, and, from the consideration of that whole, endeavour to ascertain the meaning of the words in question as they occur in the particular clause.

The only material fact extrinsic to the words of the instrument itself which we are entitled to use in construing the document appears to be that the persons who were assured — the plaintiffs — were not absolutely entitled to the house, but had, previous to the policy, leased it to one Guy, a tenant by a lease, which contains a covenant by the tenant to repair, but not a covenant to insure.

Now, what is the contract? The principal clause is, that if the property shall be destroyed or damaged by fire, the funds of the Company shall pay or make good all such loss or damage, not exceeding in the whole the sum assured. In terms, then, this is a contract to reinstate or repair *in specie*, or to pay the full sum, within the sum assured, that such reinstatement or repair may cost. However, notwithstanding these words, the meaning and intention of the parties to such a contract is now practically settled to be, not to pay the actual amount of the loss of or damage to the premises, but to indemnify *the assured* from the loss, or, in other words, to pay the amount of the loss or damage to his interest in the premises. This is forcibly put by Brett, L.J., in *Castellain* v. *Preston*.[34] "The very foundation, in my opinion," says the Lord Justice, "of every rule which has been applied to insurance law is this, ... that the contract of insurance contained in a marine or fire policy is a contract of indemnity, and of indemnity only, and that this contract means that the assured, in case of a loss against which the policy has been made, shall be fully indemnified, but shall never be more than fully indemnified. That is the

---

[*] Extract; a further extract from the judgment appears in Chapter 3 at p.67.
[34] 11 Q.B.D. 380, 386.

fundamental principle of insurance, and if ever a proposition is brought forward which is at variance with it ... that proposition must certainly be wrong." How is such a principle to be worked out? Not by the application of the laws against wagering. Those laws have no operation by way of qualifying contract; they may render particular contracts void, but they cannot alter them. Effect, therefore, can be given to the principle in question only by construing the contract in reference to it; and, so construing the words contained in this document, the fact that the interest of the assured in the property is limited and not absolute, in itself affords strong reasons for reading, if, indeed, it does not coerce us to read, the words "the same property" as the property of the assured in the thing described in the policy, and not the thing itself. The word "property" is, in our jurisprudence capable of bearing the one meaning or the other; it is a question of construction upon the entire instrument in which of these two senses it is used.

Again, the expression to be construed is not "property" *simpliciter*, but "*the same* property". The same as what? Is it the same *as is above described*, or the same *as is above assured*? Having regard to the object of the contract, I entertain no doubt that the latter is the true meaning. What, then, is the property assured? The expression is not a very accurate one; but once it is determined that the amount contracted to be paid is the value, not of the thing described but of the interest of the assured in that thing, it follows that the risk contracted to be borne is damage, not to the thing described but to the interest of the assured in that thing, or in other words, that the thing assured is not the described property but the interest of the assured in that property.

Again, this contract for insurance is to endure so long, and so long only, as the insured shall pay and the Company shall accept a certain stipulated annual sum. This sum we must take to be the estimated one which will pay the Company for the risk they have undertaken, and the risk is, in the body of the policy, expressed to be dependant upon a single contingency, viz. the property being damaged by fire.

Now, this contract being made, "subject to the conditions set forth hereafter, which are to be taken as part of this policy", what would you expect to find in such conditions? You would expect provisions relating to the conduct of the assured and of those over whom he had control, provisions affecting or possibly making void the policy in case of fraud in its making or procurement, or in the event of circumstances which increase the actual risk above that which was contemplated and paid for; and perhaps clauses giving effect to the principle I have mentioned, and providing against anything more than a complete indemnity being recovered by the assured. But *prima facie* you would not expect to find in such provisions any condition making void the policy, or reducing the sum recoverable, by reason of the act of a third party, over whom the assured had not control: unless such act would involve the reinstatement of the premises, or an indemnity against the risk insured against being received by the assured from some source other than that provided by the policy. Such a condition would leave one contingency uncovered as to the whole or part of the amount insured. It would reduce the contract from one of full indemnity, and would render the Company free from liability in an event apparently covered by their premium. It would introduce into the contract the element which the law struggles to exclude from contracts of this description — the element of wagering. To say that if your premises are burned, the amount you shall be paid shall depend, not solely upon the amount of injury you sustain, but upon the contingency of a third party having or not having, without your consent or against your will, done, or abstained from doing, some act which you cannot prevent and which will not benefit you is, in its essence, a wager.

I am not clear that, in the case of a limited owner, every clause in this policy would not be satisfied by construing the word "property" wherever it occurs, as meaning the estate or interest of the assured in the premises. Although, in such a clause as the 7th, "property" might *prima facie* mean the thing assured, the contract would be equally satisfied by holding that it meant the estate or interest, because the things could not be destroyed without the estate or interest being destroyed at the same time; and I am not clear that the same reasoning that, I think, drives us to read the word "property" in the body of the policy as "estate or interest in the property" might not equally apply to those clauses. But I do not think it necessary to go into that question. I will assume that, in several places in these conditions, the word "property" is used as signifying the thing, and not the estate in that thing; and, reading it in that way, I hold that, although the construction which we put upon this document involves reading the same word in two different senses in two different parts of the instrument, we are driven to that for the purpose of giving effect to the primary object of this contract of insurance, holding that it shall be an indemnity against loss by fire, and preventing it being what otherwise it would be — a mere wager as to the result of a fire.

That is my opinion upon the construction of the policy alone, and without deriving any assistance from the numerous cases which have been referred to during the argument, basing my opinion solely upon the ground that the essence of a contract of fire insurance is a contract for indemnity....

[Counsel for the insurance company] then says that in the present case the risks are not distinct; but in order to make anything of this argument, he must be prepared to go the full length, and to satisfy us that the risks of both Companies in the present case are the same identical risk; and if he succeeds in doing that, I admit the defence would be good.

But are the risks the same? The contract of the Patriotic Company is to indemnify the Misses Andrews from loss and damage by fire. The amount of that loss and damage would be determined in the ordinary way, by ascertaining the amount that their estate and interest in the premises were injured; and, as they had the benefit of a covenant by their tenant to keep in repair, which would involve an obligation to rebuild, the defendants here (if they paid them the full amount of the loss that they had sustained) would have been entitled, by way of subrogation, to stand in their place as against the tenant, and sustain the same action, and recover the same amount from him as the plaintiffs here would have been entitled to recover, if the amount had not been paid by the Insurance Company. But the risk insured against by the Guardian Company was, *prima facie* at least, a wholly different risk. They contracted to pay to the tenant the damage that he sustained — that is, the damage that his estate and interest sustained, including his liability under his covenant to his landlords. How can these two risks be called the same? I heard no logical argument to show that the risks were the same; but the course adopted by the learned counsel was to tell us there was a long series of authorities that established that the risks were the same; and he asked us to follow that series of authorities without inquiring into their origin, or satisfying us that there was anything in the law of this country to render them applicable to this country....

[A]nd it is, in my view, a necessary part of our decision of this case, that there is no law in this country which entitles the landlord of a house destroyed by fire to insist, in the absence of express contract, on the money received by his tenant from an Insurance Company being specifically applied to the reinstatement of the premises. In my opinion the remedy of the landlord in this country is a remedy *in personam* against the tenant upon his covenant to repair, and is nothing more. He has no specific right, such as the landlord in England has, under the statute....

On the whole, then, I am of opinion that where you are dealing with a policy of insurance effected by the tenant of a house, the word "property" in the average condition must, in order to effectuate the intention of the parties, be read in the sense of estate or interest of the assured person in the subject-matter specifically described in the policy....

CHAPTER 3

Subrogation

The doctrine of subrogation has its roots in the principle of indemnity; and while it is very much a product of the common law, arising automatically in the insurance contract, almost all modern policies make specific provision for it. Essentially, it is the right of an insurer which has discharged its obligations to an insured to be put in the place of the insured so that it can take advantage of any rights available to the insured to diminish or discharge the loss for which the insured has been indemnified.

That the insurer upon indemnifying the insured acquires such rights is a fundamental principle of insurance, ensuring that the insured receives no more than a full indemnity and does not profit from being so insured.

Subrogation is not an area of law that has given rise to frequent disputes in Ireland, though those cases that do exist illustrate well the core principles of the doctrine.

Because an insurer acquires the rights of recovery originally available to its insured, upon fully indemnifying the insured, that insurer cannot avoid its contractual liabilities to the insured simply because the insured has such rights of recourse. Equally, a third party against whom a possible right of action exists cannot avoid liability on the ground that the insured has already been indemnified, or will be indemnified by its insurer. This latter point arose in the case of *The Ballymagauran Co-operative Agricultural and Dairy Society Limited* v. *The County Councils of Cavan and Leitrim* (1915) where it was held that the existence of a policy of insurance did not prevent a claim being brought by the co-operative against the local authorities. This was endorsed in the more recent case of *Doyle* v. *Wicklow County Council* (1974) in which the Supreme Court refused to reduce the amount of a malicious injury claim to take account of sums already received by the applicant from his insurance company. Both cases acknowledged the insurer's entitlements so to proceed under subrogation.

That an insurer is entitled, under the doctrine to any such rights available to its insured which will diminish its loss and in respect of

[57]

which the insured has been indemnified is clear. However, the right so vested is not absolute and as regards losses in respect of which no indemnity has been received, as for instance due to under-insurance, the insured's rights take precedence. This was adverted to, and endorsed, by the Master of the Rolls in the case of *Driscoll* v. *Driscoll* (1918).

As the right of subrogation can be a very valuable one for an insurer, the insurer is entitled to expect that it will not be unduly prejudiced in its exercise of that right by the actions of the insured. Equally, an insurer must be wary in the exercise of its rights not to harm or prejudice in any way any remaining rights of the insured. No Irish case appears to exist illustrating this principle. However, in an 1886 case, the Patriotic Assurance Company of Ireland sought to withhold payment to its insured because it alleged the insured had failed properly to exercise a possible right of recovery against a third party. The Chief Barron, while suggesting a right of refusal to pay could exist, held that there was no merit in the company's submissions; *Andrews and Others* v. *The Patriotic Assurance Company of Ireland* (1886).

The Ballymagauran Co-operative Agricultural and Dairy Society Limited *v.* The County Councils of Cavan and Leitrim*
[1915] 2 I.R. 85
Court of Appeal

O'BRIEN L.C: The question involved in the present appeal is undoubtedly one of great practical importance. It arises on a case stated by Lord Justice Holmes sitting as judge of assize in respect of a claim for malicious injury. The counties immediately interested are Cavan and Leitrim, but the decision will affect every county in Ireland, hence the necessity of very careful consideration of every point that has been raised in the course of the arguments.

The claimants were the proprietors of the Ballymagauran creamery, whose premises were maliciously destroyed by fire on the 23rd March, 1914.

The learned Lord Justice found that they would be entitled to compensation from the two counties in the sum of £70, apportioned between them at the rate of £52 10s. to one, and £17 10s to the other, subject to the legal question raised, which, if decided in their favour, would relieve them from all liability.

It appears that the appellants were insured under a policy which contained no clause or stipulation relieving the insurers from liability in the case of loss by malicious burning. It was admitted that the insurance company was quite solvent.

---

* Extract.

The judge was of opinion, to use his own language, that "it would be curious if a company which had received a premium for indemnifying the applicants against loss by fire should be relieved from its obligations by enforcing compensation from the ratepayers," and he intimated that he would feel himself obliged to dismiss the application, but being asked by the applicants to state a case he consented to do so, and stated the present case for the opinion of this Court.

No question was raised as to the liability of the insurance company to pay, and the case is free from any practical difficulty caused by any considerations of this kind.

The terse manner in which Lord Justice Holmes put his view goes to the root of the problem to be solved. The only case in which the matter previously arose, so far as we know, was one before Lord O'Brien C.J., sitting as judge of assize in Belfast, where he held that the actual payment of the insurance did not prevent recovery of compensation under the section: *Jones* v. *Belfast Corporation*.[1] The report does not show, however, that the case was argued very keenly, nor does the Lord Chief Justice give any reason for his opinion, but it undoubtedly represents the view which was held by the Bench and Bar largely during the many years the statute was in force, although the contrary opinion expressed by Lord Justice Holmes, and which must be dealt with in the present case, was frequently mooted.

It is singular that it only comes up for considered decision after so many years; but I do not think any inference can be fairly drawn one way or the other from this.

Passing for the moment from the important question raised by Mr Henry on behalf of the counties as to the technical effect of the words of sect. 135, one matter stands out clearly, namely, that the Legislature, for reasons which we must assume to be right, has thought fit to cast upon absolutely innocent ratepayers the liability to make good damage sustained by one of them arising from the criminal act of persons for whose conduct no one of these ratepayers is in any sense morally responsible. It is not that the baronies or counties are insurers of property maliciously destroyed in their district; but although they are not placed in the position of trespassers, as was done by earlier statutes, they are made liable in a statutory procedure to compensate for the loss inflicted on innocent owners of property by the acts of wrongdoers. Whether the counties could themselves insure against a liability of this kind need not be considered, but it certainly seems to me that they cannot be deemed as, directly in any event, having an interest in a policy of assurance which a ratepayer for his own additional protection may take out; and, speaking with all respect, it does not occur to me that the act of the insurance company in endeavouring to obtain compensation from the county in the name of the injured person can be looked at as a relieving of the insurance company from its obligations. The obligation of the county is a direct primary liability to the person injured; the obligation of the company one of indemnity, not to the community but to the individual; and to my mind at any rate the problem presents itself rather in this form, that it would be singular if the

[1] 32 I.L.T.R. 32.

prudent act of the ratepayer in insuring for his own benefit was to relieve the county from the primary obligation which is placed upon it to pay compensation.

The practice of insuring, in cities at any rate, property against loss caused by malicious injury, be it fire or any other wanton or unlawful method of destruction, is now very general; and if the view which is presented to us by the counties in this case is correct in law, the result would be that the large body of property owners insuring against malicious damage would really be only insuring in the interest of others who are in no sense in privity with the contract of insurance at the time it is made.

It appears to me that the liability is primarily on the county, and not primarily on the insurance company. If it were primarily on the insurance company, then, of course, there would be great force on broad grounds of justice in the contention of the county.

While this represents to my mind the general position of affairs, it does not follow that Mr Henry's argument is wrong; but if it be the true light in which to approach the section, one must be on one's guard against a contention that prima facie seems erroneous.

Put shortly, the argument is that as compensation for loss is the basis of the section, the person injured cannot receive more than compensation for the loss, but that he ought not to receive anything if he could be, or has been, compensated from some other source, in this case the policy of insurance. Mr Henry, for the appellants, admits that under the law as it stood before 1836, when the proceeding was by action, the question of the existence of the policy could not be taken into consideration, but he says that the abolition of the action, which was based on the fiction that the innocent ratepayers were in the shoes of the trespassers, coupled with the peculiar words of the section, makes a cardinal difference.

Of course it is not a question of the ratepayer ultimately getting paid twice over, and — as in the case of *Mason* v. *Sainsbury*,[2] to which I will afterwards more fully refer, and in other cases — the proceedings are taken in the name of the insured person, but ultimately the money if recovered will go in ease of the insurers, whose contract is only a contract of indemnity.

The first important case which was relied on is *Mason* v. *Sainsbury*.[3] That was a proceeding, in the name of the person whose property had been destroyed, to recover compensation under 1 Geo. 1, c. 5, sect. 6[4]. The insurance company having already paid compensation on their insurance, the proceeding of course was one taken for the benefit of the company. It was held that the existence of the policy could not be taken into consideration in assessing compensation; but this distinction is sought to be drawn by counsel, that it cannot be an authority where the proceeding is founded, not on the basis of an action for trespass, where the amount of compensation may conceivably be larger than the damage to the property, but on statutory

---

[2] 3 Dougl. 61.

[3] *Ibid.*

[4] An Act for preventing journalists and riotous assemblies, and for the more speedy and effectual punishing of the rioters.

proceedings where mere compensation for the injury or damage is to be given, limited by the qualifying words "ought to receive".

Now although a great deal of the argument at the Bar, and some of the reasons given for the decision, dealt with the proceeding as one placing the hundred for civil purposes in the place of the trespassers, the principle of the case is not, when we come to deal with subsequent developments, necessarily limited to cases of actions involving trespass as their foundation.

The county is not placed in the position of a trespasser — no doubt all the money which could be recovered from a trespasser cannot be recovered from it — but the right arises by reason of a trespass having been committed, a wrongful act involving the destruction of the property, and to the extent of some compensation the county, in lieu of the wrongdoer, is made liable. Their liability is not so extensive as the liability of the wrongdoer, but it covers some of the liability, a liability which could not come into existence, but for the wrongful act by reason of which innocent persons are made legally accountable in damages. When the old action was abolished by section 139, and the new proceedings, equally based on the doing of a wrongful act and compensation by innocent persons were substituted, I should have thought, apart from authority, that so far from there being a different principle involved, the principle would be the same, although the amount to be recovered might probably be less.

In point of fact a reference to another case which is in the same volume of Douglas' reports, the *London Assurance Company* v. *Sainsbury*,[5] shows that in assessing damages under the statute of George 1,[6] the juries assessed on the basis of actual loss and nothing else; that, however, though useful to be noted, does not settle the law.

The next case to be referred to is the case of *Clarke* v. *The Inhabitants of the Hundred of Blything*.[7] This was a case of malicious burning under 9 Geo. 1, c. 22 s.7,[8] which requires that the hundred shall make satisfaction and amends to every person for the damage that he shall have sustained by the setting fire to any stack by any offender against that Act. *Mason* v. *Sainsbury*[9] was applied in that case, and without any such distinction as is sought to be made in the present instance, but it is only fair to say that the *Blything* Case was decided on a note of *Mason* v. *Sainsbury*,[10] and not on the judgment as reported in Douglas; but the arguments of counsel on behalf of the defendants were the same as the arguments here, although the words of the section are different. Abbot C.J. had no doubt about what the decision should be. In that case the Chief Justice referred to the policy of the law, the object of which was to aid in the bringing of offenders to justice, and we can see the

---

[5] 3 Dougl. 245.
[6] "An Act for preventing journalists and riotous assemblies, and for the more speedy and effectual punishing the rioters".
[7] 2 B. & C. 254.
[8] "An Act for the more effectual punishing of wicked and evil-disposed persons going armed in disguise and doing injuries and violences to the persons and properties of his majesty's subjects".
[9] 3 Dougl. 61.
[10] *Ibid.*

same policy in the latter part of section 137 of the Grand Jury Act.

The next case, which is nearly always cited in connexion with *Mason* v. *Sainsbury*,[11] and which has received approval from the House of Lords in *Simpson* v. *Thompson*,[12] is the case of *Yates* v. *Whyte*.[13] In that case, speaking of *Mason* v. *Sainsbury*,[14] Chief Justice Tindal treats the case simply as one establishing that recovery upon contract with the insurers is no bar to a claim for damages against a wrongdoer, quoting Lord Mansfield in *Mason* v. *Sainsbury*,[15]

> "Though the office paid without suit, this must be considered as without prejudice; and it is, to all intents, as if it had never been paid. The question comes to this: Can the owner of the house having insured it, come against the hundred under this Act? Who is first liable? If the hundred be first liable, still it makes no difference. If the insurers be first liable, then payment by them is satisfaction, and the hundred is not liable. But the contrary is evident, from the nature of the contract of insurance. It is an *indemnity*."

Mr Justice Vaughan says: "We every day see the insured put in the place of the insurer. And in *Clarke* v. *The Hundred of Blything*,[16] the authority of *Mason* v. *Sainsbury*[17] was expressly recognised by Lord Tenterden."

Mr Justice Vaughan, quoting *Mason* v. *Sainsbury*,[18] omits the latter part of Lord Mansfield's judgment, in which he mentions the fact that the Act put the hundred in the place of the trespassers; but it is clear to my mind that he treats it as a case simply where the insurer, after he has discharged his liability on his contract of indemnity, stands in the place of the insured. As I have said already, the statute may not give to the insurer all the remedies that would be given against the trespassers, but it does to some extent cast the liability arising from the trespass on a person who is not a trespasser, and the form of the proceeding cannot obscure the substance. The learned judge brackets with *Mason* v. *Sainsbury*[19] the case of *Randal* v. *Cockran*,[20] which was merely a case of placing the insurers in the position of the insured with regard to the proceeds of certain captures made under letters of reprisal.

Once we look at it from the point of view of a primary liability on the county, and only a contract of indemnity with the person who suffers damage, there does not seem to me to be any real difficulty in the case.

---

[11] 3 Dougl. 61.
[12] 3 A.C. 279.
[13] 4 Bing. N.C. 272.
[14] 3 Dougl. 61.
[15] *Ibid.*
[16] 2 B. & C. 254.
[17] 3 Dougl. 61.
[18] *Ibid.*
[19] *Ibid.*
[20] 1 Ves. Sen. 98.

Lord Blackburn in the case of *Simpson* v. *Thompson*,[21] speaking of *Mason* v. *Sainsbury*,[22] says (p. 293):

> "The right of the underwriters could not arise in those cases by relation back to the passing of the property at the time of the loss, for there was no such passing of the property. It could only arise, and did only arise, from the fact that underwriters had paid an indemnity, and so were subrogated for the person whom they had indemnified in his personal rights from the time of the payment of the indemnity."

This seems to me to place *Mason* v. *Sainsbury*[23] and *Yates* v. *Whyte*,[24] as laying down a general proposition not controlled by the extent to which damages could be recovered from the innocent party in respect of the wrongful act, nor by the form of procedure.

On the assumption that the cases of *Mason* v. *Sainsbury*[25] and *Yates* v. *Whyte*,[26] did not proceed upon the narrow ground suggested at the Bar, of course they, and all cases following them, are clear authority in favour of the view which was taken by the Lord Chief Justice in *Jones* v. *Belfast Corporation*.[27] The fact that the insurance company clearly cannot make a claim under the Grand Jury Act in their own name, does not seem to me to help the contention of the county.

If the case is looked at from the point of view that I think it must be, the word "ought" in the section cannot have the force or be read in the sense contended for. Whether he is insured or whether he is not insured, it appears to me that the person injured ought to receive such compensation as is reasonable in respect of the damage done to the property, and whether he can put it in his own pocket or whether, arising from other principles of law, he must pay it to the insurance company, it is none the less a sum which he ought to receive, being the person injured.

I do not think that we get any help whatsoever from sect. 106, and I am not at all to be taken as assenting to the proposition which was thrown out at the Bar that the amount of an accident policy should be taken into consideration on a claim under that section. I express no opinion on it, though I certainly have one.

It is better to take section 135, as it must be taken, in conjunction with section 137, 139 and 140, and construe it accordingly.

Cases under Lord Campbell's Act were strongly pressed on us. The Legislature has deemed it right to abolish with regard to insurance the distinction drawn as to compensation in the case where the plaintiff was maimed for life, and useless for work, and the case where the accident caused death. The Grand Jury Act, in the way I regard it, has a public policy behind it, one quite

---

[21] 3 A.C. 279.
[22] 3 Dougl. 61.
[23] *Ibid.*
[24] 4 Bing. N.C. 272.
[25] 3 Dougl. 61.
[26] 4 Bing. N.C. 272.
[27] (1898) 32 I.L.T.R. 32.

different from that which underlies Lord Campbell's Act, and I should be violating that policy if I applied those cases to the Grand Jury Act.

Joseph Doyle v. The Council of the County of Wicklow*
[1974] I.R. 55
The Supreme Court

FITZGERALD C.J: I agree with the judgment about to be delivered by Mr Justice Griffin.

WALSH J: I agree with the judgment ... read by Mr Justice Griffin. I wish, however, to add one qualification in respect of the portion of it which deals with the question of insurance.

A policy of fire insurance is a policy of indemnity only. Therefore, the fact that an applicant is the holder of a policy of fire insurance is not a matter to be taken into account when he brings an application for damages for malicious injury. The vast majority of such policies contain a clause giving the insurance company a right to subrogate, and to bring the claim in their own name. However, it is possible (though the cases may be few) to have a policy of fire insurance which expressly excludes the right of subrogation. In such a case, an insurance company would not be entitled to bring a claim in the name of the applicant. If a County Council wishes to challenge the right of an insurance company to proceed in the name of an applicant under a claim of subrogation, and the matter has been put in issue, then questions may be asked with reference to the nature of the policy of insurance and the policy itself would be both relevant and admissible in evidence.

BUDD J: I agree with the judgment of Mr Justice Griffin.

HENCHY J: I also agree with that judgment.

GRIFFIN J: ... With regard to the second question, posed in the Case Stated [(i) Can an applicant recover for malicious damage in respect of which he has been paid by an insurer, and (ii) do the Malicious Injuries Acts, 1836, 1857 etc. entitle an insurer, where the policy so provides to maintain an application for compensation in the name of the policy-holder for the purpose of recovering moneys paid to the policy-holder pursuant to the said contract of insurance?], counsel for the respondents contend that they are entitled to investigate whether the applicant was insured against damage by fire and they submit that, if he was, he is not entitled to recover compensation from the respondents under the Criminal Injury code. They submit that if the applicant is insured against loss, and has been paid, he would be getting unjust enrichment if he were entitled to recover from the respondents, for the net

---

* Extract.

result would be that he would be paid twice for the same loss. Alternatively, they say that, while the proceedings have been brought in the name of the insured, this is effectively a claim on behalf of the insurance company to whom the premises damaged did not "belong" within the meaning of s. 135 of the Grand Jury (Ireland) Act, 1836; and that, accordingly, the insurance company is not entitled to recover compensation. This argument ignores the basis of a policy of fire insurance, which is simply a contract of indemnity. In my opinion, it is beyond question that all claims of the insured arising out of any ground of legal responsibility vest in the insurer by subrogation. The value of all benefits received by the insured from claims which have been satisfied before payment under the policy ought to be deducted from the indemnity at the time of payment; equally, after the insurers have paid the insured under the policy, they have an equity in respect of all the insured's unsatisfied claims. When the insured person receives any benefits from such claims he must account to the insurers therefor and repay to them anything which he receives beyond a complete indemnity. The right of an insured plaintiff to proceed against the wrongdoer for the benefit of the insurers was recognised early: see *Mason* v. *Sainsbury*[28]. In that case it was contended that the insurers should not be entitled to recover in an action, brought in the plaintiff's name, because they had received the insurance premium and were entitled to no more — whether a loss occurred or not. This argument was rejected by the court, Lord Mansfield saying at p.64: "The office paid without suit, not in ease of the hundred and not as co-obligors, but without prejudice. It is, to all intents, as if it had not been paid ... I am satisfied that it is to be considered as if the insurers had not paid a farthing." — See also *Castellain* v. *Preston*.[29]

Quite apart from principle, there is ample judicial authority against the proposition propounded by the respondents. In *Jones* v. *Belfast Corporation*,[30] Sir Peter O'Brien L.C.J., without giving reasons, stated that the law was quite clear on the point at issue and awarded compensation notwithstanding the fact that the premises damaged by fire were fully covered by insurance and that the insurance money had actually been paid to the owner. In *Ballymagauran Co-operative Agricultural and Dairy Society Limited* v. *The County Councils of Cavan and Leitrim*,[31] it was held by the Court of Appeal in Ireland, upon an application for compensation under the criminal injury code, that the fact that the premises damaged were insured against fire cannot be taken into consideration when assessing the amount of compensation to be recovered from the County by the owner of the premises. O'Brien L.C. said at p. 92:—

"The practice of insuring, in cities at any rate, property against loss caused by malicious injury, be it fire or any other wanton or unlawful method of destruction, is now very general; and if the view which is presented to us by the counties in this case is correct in law, the result would be that the large

---

[28] (1782) 3 Doug. K.B. 61.
[29] (1883) 11 Q.B.D. 380, 388.
[30] (1897) 32 I.L.T.R. 32.
[31] [1915] 2 I.R. 85. At p. 58 of this book.

body of property owners insuring against malicious damage would really be only insuring in the interest of others who are in no sense in privity with the contract of insurance at the time it is made. It appears to me that the liability is primarily on the county, and not primarily on the insurance company. If it were primarily on the insurance company, then, of course, there would be great force on broad grounds of justice in the contention of the county."

Palles C.B. said at p. 100:—

"I am of opinion that as held in *Mason* v. *Sainsbury*[32] as regards England, so also in Ireland, although the hundred, barony, or county is not criminally responsible, it is for civil purposes put in the place of the wrongdoers, and the primary liability is on the hundred, barony, or county, from which it follows that as between it and the person whose property is damaged his insurer and himself are one."

In my opinion, the *Ballymagauran Case*[33] was correctly decided so it is irrelevant whether the applicant in the present case had insured against the risk of damage by fire or otherwise, or whether or not he had already been paid on foot of his policy of insurance. If he had already been paid on foot of the policy of insurance he, as the insured, must account to the insurers for any benefit he receives from his claim for compensation against the respondents....

In Re Driscoll, Deceased.
Driscoll v. Driscoll*
[1918] 1 I.R. 152
Chancery Division

O'CONNOR M.R: ... I now come to the claim of the Insurance Company. That is based on the right of subrogation, and the contention of the company is that whatever sum is recovered by the insured must go to recoup the Company the amount paid on foot of the policy, irrespective of the consideration whether the insured has been fully indemnified against the loss sustained. This is met by the insured's contention that until he is fully indemnified he is not bound to contribute anything to the Company. I have no doubt that this latter view is correct. A contract of insurance against fire is only a contract of indemnity, and I think that the foundation of the doctrine of subrogation is to be found in the principle that no man should be paid twice over in compensation for the same loss. The corollary to this is that a contract of indemnity against loss should not have the effect of preventing the insured from being paid once in full. I do not think that this can be disputed. The law seems to be well settled,

---

[32] (1782) 3 Doug. K.B. 61.
[33] [1915] 2 I.R. 85. At p. 58 of this book.
* Extract.

and is recognised in the leading textbooks, and is fully borne out by the cases cited by Mr Meredith: *Darrell* v. *Tibbitts*[34] and *Castellain* v. *Preston*.[35]

Andrews and Others *v.* The Patriotic Assurance Company of Ireland[*]
(1886) 18 L.R.I. 355
Exchequer Division

PALLES C.B: ... I now come to the demurrer to the second defence, which raises a much smaller question, but still one which the defendants are entitled to have decided. I have stated that the tenant here held under a lease containing a covenant to repair; and that, in my opinion, according to the well-settled law, the defendants here, upon paying the landlords the amount of the loss sustained, would have been entitled to stand in their stead against the tenant, and to recover from him the amount which the landlords would have been entitled to recover by an action upon the covenant to repair. That is the origin of this second plea, which I need not occupy public time by reading. The gravamen of the allegation contained in it is, that the plaintiffs did not sue their tenant upon the covenant to repair, and that since the occurrence of the fire the tenant had become bankrupt, and therefore the defendants, if they now paid the amount of the claim, would not be able to recover over any part of it against the tenant. It is admitted inferentially by the pleadings that the defendants had notice of this fire, and of the plaintiff's claim, within fifteen days after it occurred. It is not alleged in the plea that the defendants requested the plaintiffs to sue the tenant, nor that they applied to the plaintiffs for liberty to use their names in suing the tenant, either without making any provision for payment, or upon payment. On the contrary, it appears tolerably plainly, upon the whole defence, that the Company from the commencement repudiated their liability to anything more than a nominal sum, as recoverable under this policy. The contract of the defendants was to pay; the right of the defendants was, upon payment, to sue either in the name of the plaintiffs, or in equity in their own names. They broke their contract by not paying, and thereby failed to acquire the status of having a right themselves to institute independent proceedings, until a period arrived when, by reason of the bankruptcy of the tenant, such proceedings would be ineffectual. Their equity is, that although they broke their contract, they are entitled to say to the landlords, "You were bound to sue your tenant for our benefit, though we did not ask you to do so, and though we repudiated our liability"; and they are to do this, though probably the very object of effecting this policy of insurance was to prevent the landlords being driven to the necessity of such a suit.

There is no law which says that a mere omission to sue the tenant is to constitute a defence for the Insurance Company. Nothing is alleged in this

---

[34] 5 Q.B.D. 560.
[35] 11 Q.B.D. 380
[*] Extract; a further extract from the judgment appears in Chapter 2 at p. 53.

plea in the way of action upon the part of the plaintiffs. All that is complained of is the mere omission, or laches. Serjeant Hemphill, in arguing the case, used the word "acquiescence", a word which, according to my view may involve a great deal more than mere omission. That word, however, is not used in the plea. There nothing more is relied upon than mere omission to sue, and that is called in the plea an act of negligence, which is said to excuse the defendants here.

... [T]o apply the doctrine I have referred to to the present case, I take the original contract of insurance. By that contract the Insurance Company acquired no right to have any property whatever applied to their indemnification. They would have had the ordinary right, by way of subrogation, to stand in the place of the original creditors; but if they do not think fit to avail themselves of that right of subrogation, by payment, and then suing, I hold that the mere omission on the part of the landlord to sue the tenant is no answer to the landlord's claim....

CHAPTER 4

Contribution

The doctrine of contribution is also a natural extension and corollary of the principle of indemnity. It arises in circumstances where an insured's loss is seemingly covered by more than one policy of insurance. Its purpose is again to ensure that an insured is not over-indemnified, seeking payment from more than one source. Where such double insurance exists an insured is entitled to claim against either or both insurers until the insured is fully indemnified. Should the insured claim against just one insurer, that insurer is then entitled under subrogation to seek a pro rata contribution from the other insurer, that contribution ultimately depending on the exact nature and extent of each of the policies involved.

A number of requirements must be satisfied before an insurer can successfully obtain contribution.

Firstly, the policies of insurance involved must be indemnity policies, as opposed to policies that pay a fixed sum irrespective of the loss, such as life assurance or personal accident policies.

Secondly, the subject matter of the insurances must be the same. This is essentially a question of fact involving an examination of the loss that has occurred and a determination as to whether the policies involved cover that loss. In the case, *Hibernian Insurance Plc* v. *Eagle Star Insurance Plc and Guardian Royal Exchange Plc* (1987), Mr Justice Costello having reviewed all the evidence held that Hibernian was not entitled to obtain contribution from GRE, as GRE's policy did not cover the circumstances of the loss. Eagle Star, however, on the facts was obliged so to contribute as valid cover did apply, the subject matter of the insurances being the same.

Thirdly, not only must the insured be the same, but the interest of the insured and the risk assumed by the insurers must also be the same. This was not examined in any detail in the *Hibernian* case, the submissions on either side apparently relating only to whether the policies covered the loss in question. In *Zürich Insurance Company Limited* v. *Shield Insurance Company Limited* (1988), Zürich sought to recover from Shield its outlays in respect of sums paid by it to discharge its liabilities under a motor policy issued to its insured, Quinnsworth and its employees, in respect of injuries caused by one such employee to a co-employee in a road traffic accident. Shield was Quinnsworth's employer's liability insurer and its policy would have provided indemnity to Quinnsworth in respect of the injured employee's claim against it. The Supreme Court held that because the interests insured and the risks assumed by each insurer were different, and in any event Quinnsworth was held to be entitled to seek full reimbursement from the negligent employee, Zürich was not entitled to obtain contribution from Shield. Had it been otherwise, in theory, Quinnsworth could have obtained full indemnity from Shield in respect of its liability and then have sought recovery from its negligent employee, he being indemnified by Zürich, thereby being double indemnified in respect of the same loss.

Similarly, there is the requirement that the legal interest in the subject matter insured must also be the same. In *Andrews and Others v. Patriotic Assurance Company of Ireland* (1886)[*] and more recently in *In re Kelly's Carpetdrome Limited* (1985), while the same subject matter was insured the policies covered the different interests of a landlord and a tenant in the same premises. In *Andrews* the tenant had already received monies from his insurers but had not applied them to rebuilding the damaged premises. The landlord's insurers sought to refuse payment of any monies to the landlord on the basis that a full indemnity in respect of the premises had already been paid, albeit from a different source. In *Kelly's* a pro rata contribution clause existed in the landlord's policy. His insurers sought to limit their liability to 50 per cent of the loss; the balance presumably to be obtained from the tenant's insurers on whose policy the interest of the landlord was noted. In both cases it was held that because the interest of each insured was different, contribution, properly so called, did not arise. The landlord's insurers could not therefore evade their responsibility to their insured. In theory it was open in both cases for the landlords' insurers, having discharged the sums due to their insureds to seek recovery under subrogation from the tenants, and thus their insurers. The reality though in both cases was that the right of recovery was worthless, hence insurers' attempts to limit their own initial exposure.

---

[*] The relevant part of this judgment appears in Chapter 2 at p. 53.

Hibernian Insurance Plc. *v.* Eagle Star Insurance Plc & Guardian Royal Exchange Assurance Plc
Unreported, 17 February 1987
The High Court

COSTELLO J: The deceased Robert Gent was employed as a Workshop Manager by Dublin Road Motors (Dundalk) Ltd. when he was killed in an accident which occurred on the 18th May, 1981. He was driving a red Alpine car owned by Talbot (Ireland) Ltd. The accident involved a collision with another car, whose driver, James Townsend, sued Dublin Road Motors, Talbot, and Mr Gent's widow and personal representative.

Prior to the accident, Mrs Gent (now Mrs McGuigan) had entered into a contract of insurance in respect of a Hillman Imp car which she then owned with Hibernian Insurance Plc the plaintiffs herein. Mr Gent was a named driver on the policy. On the morning of the accident Mr Gent arranged that the red Alpine would be put on his wife's policy. As a result the Hibernian became liable to indemnify Mrs Gent in respect of the claim made against her by Mr Townsend. The Hibernian settled Mr Townsend's claim for a very large sum and in these proceedings claim a contribution in respect of the settled claim: firstly, against Eagle Star Insurance Plc, who had in May, 1981 entered into a contract of insurance with Talbot (the owners of the red Alpine) and secondly against Guardian Royal Exchange Assurance Plc who at that time had entered into [a] contract of insurance with Dublin Road Motors (Mr Gent's employers) in respect of, inter alia, vehicles in their custody or control.

The Eagle Star policy covered any motor vehicle the property of Talbot, and any driver of a car the property of Talbot which was being driven with Talbot's permission. The issue in the Hibernian claim against Talbot is whether at the time of the accident Mr Gent was driving the red Alpine with their consent.

The Guardian Royal Exchange's policy was a policy of indemnity in respect of any vehicle "in the custody or control" of Dublin Road Motors. Mr Gent was a named driver on the policy when using such a vehicle for social, domestic and pleasure purposes. The issue in the Hibernian claim against the Guardian Royal Exchange is whether the red Alpine was in the custody or under the control of Dublin Road Motors at the time of the accident.

I can give the reasons for my conclusions briefly as they depend on findings of fact. These findings depend on how I resolve the strongly conflicting evidence in the case; in particular whether I accept the evidence of Mr Wallace, the General Manager of Dublin Road Motors, where it differs from that of witnesses from Talbot, in particular Mr Kenny and Mr Cunningham. I have concluded that I should prefer Mr Wallace's evidence, partly because I found him more convincing, and partly because his evidence is corroborated in important respects by the contemporary records and is consistent with the probabilities of the case. (I should add, that, I think Mrs McGuigan's recollection on important aspects of this case is not accurate — which is perfectly understandable in the light of the tragic events in which she was involved.)

I hold:—

1) [T]here was no question that the red Alpine was borrowed for the pur-

pose of demonstrating it by a potential customer whose interest in the model had been stimulated by a white Alpine on which the deceased had been working prior to the accident.

2) In April 1981 the deceased had approached Mr Wallace for a loan of a car with an automatic transmission which he could lend to Canadian friends (Mr and Mrs O'Driscoll) who were to visit him and his wife in the following May. Mr Wallace agreed to do so if such a car was in the company's possession when the O'Driscolls arrived.

3) There was no suitable car available in Dublin Road Motors as the O'Driscoll visit was approaching. Mr Wallace agreed with Mr Gent's suggestion that he (Mr Gent) should approach Talbot with a view to getting a loan of a car from Talbot for the O'Driscolls but he made it clear that Mr Gent would have to make his own arrangements to have it insured.

4) The car was delivered on Friday, 15th May. Mr Wallace agreed a few days earlier that during the period of its loan a replacement car, a blue Alpine, then in the possession of Dublin Road Motors would be given to Talbot. He agreed to this to facilitate the transaction which the deceased had arranged with Talbot. The red Alpine was not in fact required for the business of Dublin Road Motors and was not used for it. It was taken away by the deceased, and used by him and his wife on the weekend of the 16th–17th May, and by the deceased alone on the 18th May, the day of the accident.

5) On the morning of the 18th May the deceased telephoned the local office of the Hibernian to add the red Alpine to his wife's policy and the names of Mr and Mrs O'Driscoll as named drivers on his wife's policy (in respect of whom he had earlier obtained signed forms for this purpose). An extra premium of £30 was later paid by Mrs McGuigan.

6) At no time was the red Alpine in the *custody* of Dublin Road Motors or under its *control*. It was in the custody and control of the deceased, but he was not acting as their agents when he took possession of it — he obtained it for his own private purposes, unconnected with the Company's business.

7) It follows that as the Guardian Royal Exchange was only liable under this policy in respect of vehicles owned by or under the control or custody of Dublin Road Motors that they are under no liability in respect of Mr Townsend's claim. It further follows that the claim by the Hibernian against them for a contribution fails.

I now turn to the claim by the Hibernian against the Eagle Star.

The first condition of Eagle Star's liability under their policy with Talbot was that the vehicle involved in an accident which gave rise to a third-party claim was a vehicle the property of or under the control or in the custody of Talbot. As the red Alpine which the deceased was driving was the property of Talbot the terms of the first condition were met.

But the policy only covered third-party claims if the vehicle was being driven with Talbot's permission, and so if the deceased was driving with

Talbot's permission when the accident occurred Eagle Star are liable to contribute half the claim arising out of Mr Townsend's accident.

In relation to this claim I make the following findings:

1) The negotiations which lent [sic] to the loan of the red Alpine were conducted by the deceased and Talbot's representatives, and not by Mr Wallace and those representatives.

2) I think it is unlikely that the deceased informed either Mr Cunningham or Mr Kenny or Mr Grimes that he was proposing to lend the red Alpine to his Canadian friends. I think that Talbot's representatives lent it to the deceased as a courtesy car, that is one which would be used by the employees of Dublin Road Motors for showing it to prospective purchasers.

3) The arrangement was a casual and an informal one. There was no express limitation placed by Talbot's representatives on how the car was to be used by the employees of Dublin Road Motors. The evidence satisfies me that Talbot's representatives must have been aware that when courtesy cars are lent to dealers that employees of the dealers not only use them to demonstrate them to potential customers, but also use them for their own private purposes. I cannot imply into the permission granted a term that when employees are using courtesy cars for private purposes such use would be limited in any particular way.

4) At the time of the accident the car was being driven by the deceased for private purposes, that is he was driving it to Dublin to meet his Canadian friends when they arrived at Dublin airport. In my view when the accident happened the deceased was driving within the terms of the permission which had been granted by Talbot for the use of the car.

I conclude therefore that the Hibernian is entitled to claim fifty per cent contribution against the Eagle Star in respect of the sums paid to Mr Townsend arising out of the accident of the 18th May, 1981.

Zürich Insurance Company *v.*
Shield Insurance Company Limited
[1988] I.R. 174
The High Court

GANNON J: The plaintiff and the defendant are both insurance companies with which Quinnsworth Ltd. had contracts for indemnity against liability for damages for injury by accident to Martin Sinnott. The plaintiff's liability derives from a motor insurance policy in respect of negligent driving of Quinnsworth's motor car in which Martin Sinnott was a passenger. The defendant's liability derives from an employers' liability policy in respect of injury by accident to an employee arising out of and in the course of employment with Quinnsworth Ltd. which was the employer of Martin Sinnott.

On the 20th September, 1976, Martin Sinnott an employee of

Quinnsworth Ltd. was travelling as a passenger in a motor car the property of Quinnsworth, which was being driven by Edward Durning who was also an employee of Quinnsworth Ltd. On that date Martin Sinnott sustained severe personal injuries when the motor car was involved in a collision with a bus, the property of C.I.E. In an action by Martin Sinnott against C.I.E., Quinnsworth Ltd. and Edward Durning for damages for injuries and loss sustained by the negligent driving of the motor car and of the bus Martin Sinnott obtained final judgment for £569,640 and costs. In final judgment the claim against C.I.E., the owners of the bus, was dismissed and the entire liability was placed on Edward Durning from whom Quinnsworth Ltd. was held entitled to indemnity for the full amount awarded, and a claim by Edward Durning for indemnity by or contribution from Quinnsworth Ltd. was rejected.

The plaintiff undertook by its motor policy to provide indemnity against liability at law for damages for bodily injury to any person arising out of an accident caused by or in connection with any private type motor car, the property of any of the group of companies therein described as the insured. Although not one of the companies named in the policy, Quinnsworth Ltd. was one of such companies. By that policy the like indemnity was provided by the plaintiff for the driver of every such motor car driving with the authority of one of the insured companies. Under the terms of the plaintiff's motor policy it was liable to discharge the judgment obtained by Martin Sinnott and so indemnify against their liability at law both Quinnsworth Ltd. and Edward Durning. The defendant undertook by its employers' liability policy to provide indemnity to "Quinnsworth Limited and/or associated and subsidiary companies" against liability to pay compensation for injury by accident or disease sustained by any employee in the immediate service of the insured arising out of and in the course of his employment by the insured in the business of supermarket-grocery and provisions.

In these proceedings the plaintiff claims that the liability at law for damages for injury by accident to Martin Sinnott is a liability for which the defendant, under the employers' liability policy, must provide indemnity to Quinnsworth. The plaintiff seeks a declaration that it is entitled to a 50% contribution from the defendant of the amount paid on foot of the award to Martin Sinnott and for an order for payment by the defendant of such contribution.

It is an accepted principle of law that a claimant who has recovered full satisfaction in damages from one party cannot also recover the same or any part of that claim from another party equally liable for the same damage. There may not be double satisfaction merely because there is double indemnity. A corollary of this principle is that as between those persons who are liable in damages to compensate the same claimant upon the same cause of action the one who discharges the liability in full is entitled in equity by subrogation to recover from the others a contribution of the proportions of what he has paid commensurate with the liability of such others to the same claimant. The basis for the claim by the plaintiff herein against the defendant is the right of subrogation which the plaintiff claims to have to enable it recover from the defendant on foot of Quinnsworth's policy with the defendant a contribution of a proportionate part, namely 50%, of the amount paid by the plaintiff on behalf of Quinnsworth to Martin Sinnott on foot of Quinnsworth's policy with the plaintiff. The defendant denies that the injury to Martin Sinnott was caused by an accident arising out of and in the course of his employment with Quinnsworth in its business of supermarket-grocery and provisions. It also contends that the right to contribution as sought by the plaintiff is not available save where the indemnity afforded by both policies is in respect of the same risk, the insured in each policy is the same person, and the interest of the insured in the risk against which the indemnity is obtained is the same in each case.

The disputed question of fact, relating the incident and injury to Martin Sinnott to his employment with Quinnsworth, was tried by me on oral evidence. From the evidence given to me by Mr McHugh, Mr Kutner, and Edward Durning, I am convinced that Martin Sinnott, consistently with the duties of his employment with Quinnsworth, could not have declined to travel in the car being driven by Edward Durning. His employment with Quinnsworth required that Martin Sinnott not only would obey the express instructions of his superiors in the same employment but also would co-ordinate the discharge by him of his duties of employment with the performance by such fellow employees in the discharge by them of their duties of their employment with Quinnsworth Ltd. The circumstances of the particular journey and the necessity of co-ordination with Messrs Kutner and Durning were such that Quinnsworth required Martin Sinnott to travel in that car for that journey and that Martin Sinnott did so because it was a particular requirement of his employment with Quinnsworth. At the conclusion of the oral evidence and the legal submissions in relation thereto I concluded as a necessary inference that Martin Sinnott's injuries caused by the negligent driving by Edward Durning of the car were sustained by Martin Sinnott while in the immediate service of Quinnsworth Ltd. and were caused by accident arising out of and in the course of his employment with Quinnsworth Ltd.

Upon such finding it followed that Quinnsworth had the benefit of double indemnity by two policies of insurance. The legal principle applicable to such circumstances is stated by Lord Mansfield in *Godin et al.* v. *London Assurance Company*[1] as follows:—

> "Before the introduction of wagering policies, it was, upon principles of convenience, very wisely established, that a man should not recover more than he had lost. Insurance was considered as an indemnity only, in case of a loss: and therefore the satisfaction ought not to exceed the loss. This rule was calculated to prevent fraud; lest the temptation of gain should occasion unfair and wilful losses.
>
> If the insured is to receive but one satisfaction, natural justice says that the several insurers shall all of them contribute pro rata, to satisfy that loss against which they have all insured.
>
> No particular cases are to be found, upon this head: or, at least, none have been cited by the counsel on either side.
>
> Where a man makes a double insurance of the same thing, in such a manner that he can clearly recover, against several insurers in distinct

---

[1] (1758) 1 Burr. 489 at 492.

policies, a double satisfaction, "the law certainly says that he ought not to recover doubly for the same loss, but be content with one single satisfaction for
it." And if the same man really and for his own proper account insures the
same goods doubly, though both insurances be not made in his own name,
but one or both of them in the name of another person, yet that is just the
same thing: for the same person is to have the benefit of both policies. And if
the whole should be recovered from one, he ought to stand in the place of the
insured, to receive contribution from the other, who was equally liable to pay
the whole."

Before concluding his judgment in that case Lord Mansfield emphasised
that a double insurance is where the same man is to receive two sums instead
of one, or the same sum twice over, for the same loss by reason of his having
made two insurances; but where two persons insure two different interests
each to the whole value this is not within the idea of double insurance.

In the circumstances of double insurance the insurer by whom the claim is
discharged in full has an equitable right to require contribution from the
other insurers so that the payment is borne fairly by all (*North British and
Mercantile Insurance Company* v. *London, Liverpool and Globe Insurance
Company*[2]). But an insurer who has made payment to the insured under the
policy of indemnity is entitled to the benefit of all rights of the insured in
respect of the loss for which indemnity was provided, including the right of
action against the tortfeasor who has caused the loss. Thus by subrogation
the insurer may in the name of the insured recover from the tortfeasor the
loss of the insured for which the insurer provided indemnity under the policy.
Because the purpose of such right of subrogation is to enable the insurer
obtain the benefit of any means whereby the loss or damage may be or may
have been diminished this right of subrogation is not limited to pursuing an
existing cause of action. (See *Castellain* v. *Preston*[3]). Because of the emphasis
placed upon this latter aspect I think it desirable to quote from the judgment
of Brett L.J. in that case at p. 388 of the report where he says:—

"In order to apply the doctrine of subrogation, it seems to me that the full
and absolute meaning of the word must be used, that is to say, the insurer
must be placed in the position of the assured. Now it seems to me that in
order to carry out the fundamental rule of insurance law, this doctrine of
subrogation must be carried to the extent which I am now about to endeavour to express, namely, that as between the underwriter and the
assured the underwriter is entitled to the advantage of every right of the
assured, whether such right consists in contract, fulfilled or unfulfilled, or in
remedy for tort capable of being insisted on or already insisted on, or in any
other right, whether by way of condition or otherwise, legal or equitable,
which can be, or has been exercised or has accrued, and whether such right
could or could not be enforced by the insurer in the name of the assured by
the exercise or acquiring of which right or condition the loss against which
the assured is insured, can be, or has been diminished."

[2] (1877) 5 Ch. D. 569.
[3] (1883) 11 Q.B.D. 380.

At pp. 389 and 390 of the report Brett L.J. goes on to say:—

"And I go further and hold that if a right of action in the assured has been satisfied, and the loss has been thereby diminished, then, although there never was nor could be any right of action into which the insurer could be subrogated, it would be contrary to the doctrine of subrogation to say that the loss is not to be diminished as between the assured and the insurer by reason of the satisfaction of that right."

The defendant accepts the principle of contribution between two insurers equally liable to provide the same indemnity for the same risk to the one insured. But it contends that the risk of liability for which indemnity is given is not the same under the two policies and the interest of the insured is not the same. The nature and purpose of the equitable relief which is sought by the plaintiff in this claim is to give equality of remedy to both where the rights of both are equal. The defendant submits that the right to contribution applies only where the insurances are obtained by the one insured having the same rights under both policies and does not apply where different persons are insured in respect of different interests.

The policy which the plaintiff issued is a policy in respect of which there are a number of insureds both named and unnamed and of these Quinnsworth is one. They are all companies. A limited liability company as owner of a car cannot incur liability as user of the car except on the principle of vicarious liability for the driver. As such owners they necessarily had to procure insurance cover against the risks of the driving of their vehicle by whatever driver, and not merely against their risk of vicarious liability. Section 56 of the Road Traffic Act, 1961, prohibits the driving of the car by the driver unless there be an approved policy of insurance with a vehicle insurer whereby the driver or some other person who would be liable for injury caused by the negligent driving would be insured against all sums without limit. The motor policy taken out by Quinnsworth, *inter alia,* with the plaintiff is such a policy as is required to comply with s. 56 of the Road Traffic Act, 1961. By that policy the plaintiff provides insurance for all sums without limit for injury caused by the negligent driving of Edward Durning who happened to be the driver on the occasion. No duty of care or otherwise owed by the owner of the car, even though the employer of the passenger, to the passenger came within the ambit of the cover or indemnity afforded by the plaintiff's policy other than the vicarious responsibility for the driving by the driver. The owner whose liability is vicarious only would be entitled in all cases of negligent driving to full indemnity by the driver. The liability of the plaintiff under its policy with Quinnsworth Ltd. is to satisfy all claims against the driver for the negligent driving of Quinnsworth's car. This liability extends also to satisfying all claims against the negligent driver by Quinnsworth for indemnity against its vicarious liability to an insured person. The indemnity provided by the plaintiff's insurance in respect of injury to persons from negligent driving on the part of the driver and given to the driver in its policy is a risk which would exist regardless of whether the driver was or was not an employee of the owner of the car. The duty of the driver, the breach of which constitutes the risk for which cover or indemnity is given by the plaintiff's insurance policy, is not a duty owed to the owner as

his employer. It is a duty owed to the public in general and to the passenger
in the car in particular. It is a duty in respect of the driving of the car and not
in respect of any other duty as an employee of the owner.

The employers' indemnity policy which the defendant issued to Quinnsworth Ltd. is cover against the liability which Quinnsworth might incur to an
employee, including Martin Sinnott, for injury to him by accident arising out
of and in the course of his employment of the nature specified in the schedule
to the policy. Quinnsworth Ltd. is the named insured, although other subsidiary or associated companies could qualify, but the cover is related only to
the business of supermarket-groceries and provisions. The defendant's policy
does not afford cover to any servant or agent of Quinnsworth or other person
for injury for which such servant or agent or other person would be liable to
any employee of Quinnsworth. That is to say the policy does not include as an
insured any person for whose actions Quinnsworth Ltd., the insured, would
be liable vicariously. The employer of Martin Sinnott owed to him a duty of
care for his safety in the performance of the duties imposed on him by his
employment. The duty of Quinnsworth as such employer included the obligation to consider all risks of harm to Martin Sinnott in the course of his employment which would be reasonably foreseeable. For breach of such duties
Quinnsworth, although a limited liability company and not an individual,
would be directly and personally liable to Martin Sinnott at common law.
There could be cases of breach of such duty involving an element of vicarious
liability for breach by a fellow employee of his duty of care to Sinnott in the
employment. There could be many cases giving rise to the liability of Quinnsworth at common law as employer for injury to an employee arising out of
and in the [course] of his employment for which no recourse for indemnity on
the basis of vicarious liability would be available to Quinnsworth as
employer.

By the issue of its policy the defendant assumed risk for paying by way of
indemnity on behalf of Quinnsworth sums without limit for which Quinnsworth might be held liable at common law or under specified statutes for injury to Martin Sinnott by accident arising out of and in the course of his
employment. By the issuing of the motor policy the plaintiff assumed risk for
paying by way of indemnity on behalf of Quinnsworth and on behalf of
Edward Durning sums without limit for which Edward Durning might be
held liable for injury to Martin Sinnott in respect of the negligent driving of
Quinnsworth's car. If, and insofar as, Quinnsworth might be held liable
vicariously for injury to Martin Sinnott in respect of the negligent driving of
their car by Edward Durning, Quinnsworth would be entitled to full indemnity from Edward Durning whose liability would have to be discharged by the
plaintiff under its policy. Although Quinnsworth is the insured under both
policies, the interest of Quinnsworth is not the same under both policies.
Neither are the risks of affording indemnity assumed by the plaintiff and the
defendant under their respective policies the same in nature or circumstances
even though they could arise upon the happening of the same event. The
plaintiff under its policy with Quinnsworth must indemnify Edward Durning,
and insofar as it indemnifies Quinnsworth it is entitled by subrogation to
have recourse to Edward Durning. The defendant under its policy with
Quinnsworth has no obligation to indemnify Edward Durning, and is obliged

to indemnify Quinnsworth without regard to any question of liability to Martin Sinnott on the part of Edward Durning. If Quinnsworth had called upon the defendant to indemnify it against its liability to Martin Sinnott the defendant would be entitled to claim by subrogation in Quinnsworth's name from Edward Durning the amount for which Quinnsworth might be held liable to Martin Sinnott. As such claim would rest solely upon the negligence of Edward Durning in the driving of Quinnsworth's car Edward Durning could require the plaintiff under its policy with Quinnsworth to discharge such claim by the defendant. In such circumstances the plaintiff as insurer of Edward Durning could not withhold payment to the defendant of the entire amount which Quinnsworth would have been held liable to pay to Martin Sinnott by reason of their vicarious liability for Edward Durning's negligent driving.

The nature of the wrongful act of Edward Durning, namely the negligent driving of Quinnsworth's car, is such that whether Quinnsworth calls upon the plaintiff or upon the defendant to indemnify it for its vicarious liability the end result would be that Edward Durning could be held liable to recoup to Quinnsworth or to its insurers or either of them the amount paid to Martin Sinnott. The proceedings already concluded in the action by Martin Sinnott against C.I.E., Quinnsworth, and Edward Durning involved a determination of the right of Quinnsworth to have recourse to Edward Durning for indemnity and have disposed of any claim by Edward Durning for contribution or indemnity by Quinnsworth. The effect of the final judgement in those proceedings is that whatever payments have been made to Martin Sinnott by Quinnsworth, or by Quinnsworth's insurers, whether by the plaintiff or by the defendant or by both, may be recouped by recourse by subrogation to Edward Durning. Consequently, even if the plaintiff was to obtain the relief claimed herein the effect thereof would be to enable the defendant by subrogation to have recourse to Edward Durning for the 50% claimed and paid. But any such claim would have to be met by the plaintiff under its policy as insurer of Edward Durning and consequently the 50% which it now seeks to recover from the defendant would have to be repaid by it to the defendant.

In my opinion the plaintiff is not entitled in law to the relief claimed or to the order sought. I am further of opinion that if the plaintiff was entitled to the relief and order the defendant nevertheless would be entitled in law upon the principles set out in *Castellain* v. *Preston*[4] to recover from the plaintiff ultimately whatever sums the plaintiff could in these proceedings recover from the defendant.

The Supreme Court

Finlay C.J: I have read in draft the judgment which Mr Justice McCarthy has prepared and I agree with it.

Henchy J: I also agree with it.

---

[4] (1883) 11 Q.B.D. 380.

Griffin J: I also agree.

Hederman J: I agree.

McCarthy J: The facts in this matter are fully set out in the judgment of Gannon J. in the High Court. The sole factual issue decided in that court was that Martin Sinnott's injuries were caused by accident arising of and in the course of his employment with Quinnsworth. The plaintiff does not challenge any inference of fact duly made by the trial judge but the defendant, by its own notice of appeal, challenges the finding that Martin Sinnott was injured in an accident arising out of his employment.

On the basis of the finding as stated, Gannon J., in a reserved judgment, examined the nature of the cover provided to Quinnsworth by each of the insurers, the plaintiff in a motor insurance policy and the defendant in an employers' liability policy: he concluded that, since the entire liability for the accident was placed on Edward Durning from whom Quinnsworth were entitled to indemnity for the full amount awarded, and Durning's claim for indemnity by or contribution from Quinnsworth was rejected, it followed that, whatever line of approach one took, the end result was that the plaintiff must pay all the damages and costs. Since I agree with that conclusion, and it does not rest upon the inference as to the accident arising out of Sinnott's employment, I express no view upon the latter finding, the nature of which is clearly open to review by this Court of appeal.

So far as relevant, the plaintiff's policy reads:—

> "Section 1
> Liability to third parties
> (1) Indemnity to the insured
> > a) The company will indemnify the insured against liability at law for damages and claimant's costs and expenses and all costs and expenses incurred with its written consent in respect of death of or bodily injury to any person and damage to property where such death injury or damage arises out of an accident caused by or in connection with any motor car described in Endorsement Number 1.
> (2) Indemnity to other persons
> > The company will within the terms of subsection (1) indemnify (a) any person driving any motor car described in the Endorsement Number 1 on the insured's order or with the insured's permission.
> Exceptions to Section 1
> The company shall not be liable
> > d) in respect of death or bodily injury to any person arising out of and in the course of such person's employment by the person claiming to be indemnified under this section.
> *Avoidance of Certain Terms and Right of Recovery.*
> Nothing in this policy or any endorsement thereon shall affect the right of any person indemnified by this policy or of any other person to recover an amount under or by virtue of the provisions of the law of any territory in which the policy operates relating to the insurance of liability to third parties. BUT the insured shall repay to the company all sums paid by the

company which the company would not have been liable to pay but for the provisions of such law."

The defendant's policy provided for indemnity by it of Quinnsworth in respect of any liability to pay compensation for injury by accident arising out of and in the course of his employment by the insurer to any employee in the immediate service of the insured.

Martin Sinnott was in the immediate service of the insured and was found by the judge to have sustained personal injury by accident arising out of and in the course of his employment by the insured; that insured (Quinnsworth) was liable to pay compensation for such injury and, therefore, entitled to be indemnified by the defendant in respect of such compensation, in this instance at common law.

Clearly, on these established facts and with the inference drawn by the trial judge, Quinnsworth enjoyed a double indemnity. Where there is double indemnity, and one insurer pays the full amount, ordinarily, he is entitled to recover contribution from the other insurer; where there are but two, then fifty per cent. The *locus classicus* of this part of insurance law is *North British and Mercantile Insurance Company* v. *London, Liverpool and Globe Insurance Company.*[5] The facts, so far as relevant, were as follows:—

B. & Co. Wharfingers had by policies of insurance insured against loss or damage by fire in certain sums grain and seed the assured's own interest, or on commission, for which they were responsible. Part of the grain stored in the warehouses of B. & Co. belonged to R. & Co., merchants, and by the usage of the trade B. & Co., as warehousemen, were responsible to R. & Co. for any loss or damage to the grain by fire. R. & Co. had insured their grain by fire policies with other insurance companies. A fire destroyed a quantity of the grain so stored by R. & Co. with B. & Co. B. & Co. were paid in full by the several insurance companies and suit was instituted to determine the liability of the insurance companies *inter se.* It was held that B. & Co. were primarily liable for the loss, but being indemnified by their insurers, the latter was ultimately liable, and the companies with whom R. & Co. were insured were not liable to the companies to contribute to the loss.

Mellish L.J. at p. 583 — in seeking to apply the principle of subrogation — said:—

> "Where different persons insure the same property in respect of their different rights they may be divided into two classes. It may be that the interest of the two between them makes up the whole property, as in the case of a tenant for life and remainderman. Then if each insures, although they may use words apparently insuring the whole property, yet they would recover from their respective insurance companies the value of their own interests, and of course those values added together would make up value of the whole property. Therefore it would not be a case either of subrogation or contribution, because the loss would be divided between the two companies in proportion to the interests which the respective persons assured had in the property. But then there may be cases where, although two different persons insured in respect of different rights, each of them can recover the

---

[5] (1877) 5 Ch.D. 569.

whole, as in the case of a mortgagor and mortgagee. But wherever that is the case it will necessarily follow that one of these two has a remedy over and against the other, because the same property cannot in value belong at the same time to two different persons ... [b]ut yet it must be that if each recover the full value of the property from their respective offices with whom they insure, one office must have a remedy against the other. I think whenever that is the case the company which has insured the person who has the remedy over succeeds to his right of remedy over, and then it is a case of subrogation."

Both parties to this appeal have relied upon the *North British* case in support of their arguments. Mr Hickey says that once there is double indemnity then the equitable right to sharing or contribution is an absolute principle of insurance law; Mr Quirke says the key lies in the right of subrogation and the extent to which it can be enforced. In my view, the right to contribution does not apply where different persons are insured in respect of different interests — the example taken by Melish L.J. of the tenant for life and remainderman is in point but that is not the type of difference that exists in the instant case where the difference is essentially in the nature of the policy; insurance companies do not lose the right to contribution because one policy extends to a far greater variety of risks than another; so long as both policies cover the risk arising out of which the claim has been made. When one turns to subrogation, however, in my judgment, the plaintiff faces an insuperable barrier. In the course of argument, Mr Hickey conceded that if his contention was upheld, the end result could be that Durning would be personally liable to indemnify one or other of the insurers, at least to 50% of the amount in question. Happily, the employees of Quinnsworth, and indeed, any other employees including those of insurance companies, who drive company cars and give lifts in the course of work to fellow employees, are not faced with such dire consequences. Accepting as I do, the principles enunciated by Brett L.J. in *Castellain* v. *Preston*[6] cited by Gannon J. in his judgment, the pursuit of the subrogation claim by the plaintiff through Quinnsworth against Durning inexorably leads to Durning's liability to satisfy *all* claims without the benefit of any indemnity directly from Quinnsworth. Durning enjoys no benefit from the defendant's cover given to Quinnsworth — that is the nub of the contribution issue.

The plaintiff advanced an argument based upon the construction of that part of the policy which I have quoted and, particularly, in exception (d); that exception which, on its face, would exclude cover in respect of Sinnott's injuries is in clear breach of the prohibited conditions provisions of the Road Traffic Act, 1961, but its effect is avoided by the immediate subsequent provision, by reason of which, perhaps, Quinnsworth may be liable to the Zürich, upon which question I express no view. Suffice it to say that in my judgment it has nothing to do with this case which concerns rights of subrogation and the question of contribution between insurers.

I share the view of the learned trial judge that, however one approaches the alleged right of contribution, the end result must be that Edward Durning

---

[6] (1883) 11 Q.B.D. 380.

must pay and his only right to indemnity lies against the plaintiff; in the result, one happily in accordance with common sense, this action ends where it began as a Road Traffic Act case covered by motor insurance.

I would dismiss the appeal.

In the Matter of Kelly's Carpetdrome Limited and in the Matter of the Companies Acts — 1963 and 1983
Unreported, 14 April 1985
The High Court

Barrington J: This is an application for a direction on a point of insurance law arising in the liquidation of the above-named Kelly's Carpetdrome Limited.

The Applicant is the liquidator of Kelly's Carpetdrome Limited and the Respondent is the Royal Insurance (U.K.) Limited acting on behalf of themselves and other co-insurers who provided indemnity for the liquidator in certain circumstances.

Kelly's Carpetdrome Limited was ordered to be wound up, and the Applicant was appointed official liquidator, on the 28th of July, 1981.

The Applicant is a member of the well known accountancy firm of Messrs Coopers and Lybrand and, on his appointment, became a beneficiary of certain insurance cover which arises on foot of an agreement between that firm and the Respondents. This policy of insurance is known as insolvency insurance and provides automatic cover to members of the firm of Coopers and Lybrand when appointed as either liquidators or receivers over companies. This form of insurance was designed to be of particular assistance to accountants who take up the position of liquidators of companies and provides a form of blanket insurance cover in respect of their activities, and the property over which they were appointed, once the insurers are notified.

By Order of Mr Justice Costello dated the 23rd day of April 1982 it was declared that the businesses carried on by Kelly's Carpetdrome Limited and by another company, Monck Properties Limited, constituted a single business enterprise and that all the assets, undertakings and liabilities of Monck Properties Limited fell to be aggregated with those of Messrs Kelly's Carpetdrome Limited in the winding up of the latter company. The liquidator duly notified the Respondents of the making of the said aggregation Order of the 23rd of April 1982. and the assets which formerly belonged to the said Monck Properties Limited thereupon obtained the benefit of cover under the liquidator's said insolvency policy with the Respondents.

Among the assets of Monck Properties Limited were certain premises at 345, 347, 349 and 355 North Circular Road, Dublin. On the 14th of June, 1982 these premises were destroyed by fire.

The parties are agreed that the damage done to the premises came to some £585,000. The Respondents agree that the premises were on the date in question covered by the insolvency policy but claim that their liability is limited to 50% of the damage done in the circumstances hereinafter appearing. They have accordingly paid the liquidator the sum of £292,500 and the present dispute concerns the other £292,500, being, the balance of the said sum of £585,000.

Both parties agree that the insurance effected by the liquidator with the Respondents was subject to the Respondents' standard terms and conditions which (at clause 8) contained the following provision —

> "If at the time of the destruction or damage to any property hereby insured there be any other insurance effected by or on behalf of the insured covering any of the property destroyed or damaged, the liability of the company hereunder shall be limited to its rateable proportion of such destruction or damage."

The Respondents claim that there was another insurance "effected by or on behalf of the insured", and that, in the circumstances, the Respondents are entitled to limit their liability under the insolvency policy to 50% of the loss.

This claim of the Respondents arises in the circumstances set out below.

By agreement dated the 28th day of January, 1981, the said Monck Properties Limited let to a third company, Messrs Kelly's Carpet Drive-in Limited, the said premises at 345, 347, 349 and 355 North Circular Road for a term of two years and nine months from the 8th day of December, 1980.

Under the terms of the said letting agreement the said Messrs Kelly's Carpet Drive-in Limited were obliged to repair the said premises, but were not under any express obligation to insure them. Indeed, under clause 2 paragraph (i) of the letting agreement the tenant covenanted —

> "That he shall not do or suffer to be done anything which may render the landlord liable to pay in respect of premises or the building in which the same are situate or any part thereof more than the present rate of premium for insurance against fire on residential premises or which may make void or voidable any policy for such insurance."

It does not appear that, at the date of the fire, Messrs Monck Properties Limited had any insurance of the kind contemplated by the above covenant. But it does appear that the said Messrs Kelly's Carpet Drive-in Limited took out fire insurance in respect of the said premises with Lloyds Underwriters and others for a period of twelve months commencing on the 18th day of August 1981. In the normal course this cover would have been effective on the date of the fire on the 14th of June 1982. It is not clear whether Messrs Lloyds ever issued a formal policy but there is no doubt that they purported to give insurance cover to Messrs Kelly's Carpet Drive-in Limited in respect of fire and that they "noted" the interest of Messrs Monck Properties Limited in the premises.

The Respondents' case is that the insurance taken out by Messrs Kelly's Carpet Drive-in Limited was insurance effected "by or on behalf of" Messrs Monck Properties Limited and that as by virtue of the said aggregation Order of the High Court of the 23rd of April, 1982, Messrs Monck Properties Limited was declared to be one enterprise with Messrs Kelly's Carpetdrome Limited and the assets and liabilities of the two companies aggregated, the said insurance cover should be regarded as insurance cover taken out "by or on behalf of" Messrs Kelly's Carpetdrome Limited. In these circumstances the

Respondents claim that the situation is caught by clause 8 of their standard conditions and that they are, accordingly, entitled to limit their liability under the insolvency policy.

After the fire it would appear that the liquidator first purported to formulate a claim under the Lloyds policy. Insurance Brokers acting for Lloyds admitted by letter dated the 20th of July 1982, that the interest of Monck Properties Limited had been "noted on the policy". They added, however, that the nature of Messrs Monck's interest in the property had not been disclosed to the underwriters who were unaware that Messrs Monck Properties Limited owned the premises and that Messrs Kelly's Carpet Drive-in Limited were merely tenants. Later Messrs Lloyds repudiated liability on foot of the policy and claimed that it was void ab initio. It is not clear on what grounds Messrs Lloyds made this claim, but the liquidator clearly fears that Messrs Lloyds' claim to repudiate may be well founded and has shown no enthusiasm for pursuing the claim against Messrs Lloyds any further. The Respondents, however say that the liquidator should at least exhaust his remedies against Messrs Lloyds before asking them to indemnify him in respect of the second moiety of the damage.

The liquidator, on the other hand, says that the only policy governing the loss suffered by him is the insolvency policy effected by his firm with the Respondents. No other policy, he submits, was effected by him, or on his behalf, to protect his estate from the loss of damage by fire. Likewise, he submits that his position, or that of Kelly's Carpetdrome Limited, or that of Monck Properties Limited, cannot be worsened by the act of the tenant of Monck Properties Limited in taking out insurance to protect its own interest and having the interest of the landlord noted on the policy. Likewise, he submits that the action of the tenant of Monck Properties Limited in purporting to take out insurance with Messrs Lloyds Underwriters cannot have the effect of forcing the liquidator to bring against Messrs Lloyds a claim in which he has no faith instead of relying on the perfectly valid policy which his firm admittedly has with the Respondents.

The fundamental principle of insurance law is that the policyholder is indemnified against specified losses but is never allowed to make a profit out of the happening of the event insured against. For that reason the policyholder cannot improve his position by taking out a second policy with another company against the same risk because, should the risk insured against materialise, the amount recoverable under each policy will abate proportionately and the total amount recoverable by the policyholder will be the same.

Clauses such as clause 8 in the Respondents' standard conditions are designed to deal with this principle of double insurance. But, the liquidator submits, the present case is not a case of double insurance because the estate of the tenant and the estate of the landlord are different. The relevant principle in the present case is not that of double insurance but of subrogation. If the Respondents compensate the liquidator in full under the terms of the insolvency policy they will be entitled to the benefit of any claim which the liquidator may have against Messrs Kelly's Drive-in Carpetdrome Limited and through them against Messrs Lloyds Underwriters.

Messrs Monck Properties Limited and Messrs Kelly's Carpetdrome Drive-in Limited had interests in the same property but their estates in the property were quite different. The landlord was entitled to receive his rent and his interest consisted of the reversion expectant on the determination of the tenancy. The tenant was entitled to enjoyment and occupation of the premises subject to the terms and conditions of the tenancy agreement.

The issues and facts are very similar to those dealt with by Chief Baron Palles in the case of *Andrews and ors.* v. *The Patriotic Assurance Company of Ireland* (No. 2).[7] In that case the plaintiff was the owner of a house which he had leased to a tenant. The lease contained a covenant on the part of the tenant to repair but did not contain a covenant to insure. The landlord insured the premises with the defendant company in the sum of £1,000 and the tenant also insured them with another company in the sum of £1,100.

The landlord's policy with the defendant company was subject to an average condition very similar to condition number 8 in the Respondents' standard terms and conditions in the present case. The wording of the condition was as follows: —

> "If at the time of any loss or damage by fire happening to any property hereby insured there be any other subsisting insurance or insurances, whether effected by the insured or by any other person covering the same property, this Company shall not be liable to pay or contribute more than its rateable proportion of such loss or damage."

The premises were destroyed by fire and the tenant was paid, on foot of his policy, the sum of £625, but did not apply this sum in reinstating the premises. Subsequently he became bankrupt.

The landlord claimed against the defendants on foot of his policy. The defendants denied liability except in the sum of £62, which they admitted to be due as their apportionment of the loss, and relied firstly upon the average condition quoted above, and secondly upon the plaintiff's neglect in failing to compel the tenant to repair the premises out of the insurance moneys recovered by him.

Chief Baron Palles held, on demurrer, that neither defence could be sustained.

The Chief Baron held that the case was not one of double insurance and that the clause quoted had no application because while both policies applied to the same house, the estate of the landlord and the estate of the tenant in the house were different. Therefore, the risks assumed by the two insurance companies were different. In a passage which appears at page 365 of his Judgment the Chief Baron discusses the question of whether the risks assumed by the two insurance companies are the same —

> "But are the risks the same? The contract of the Patriotic Company is to indemnify the Misses Andrews from loss and damage by fire. The amount of that loss and damage would be determined in the ordinary way, by ascertaining the amount that their estate and interest in the premises were injured; and, as they had the benefit of a covenant by their tenant to keep in repair, which would involve an obligation to rebuild, the defendants here (if

---

[7] (1886) 18 L.R.I. 355. See Chapter 2 (p. 53) and Chapter 3 (p. 67).

they paid them the full amount of the loss that they had sustained) would have been entitled, by way of subrogation, to stand in their place, as against the tenant, and sustain the same action, and recover the same amount from him as the plaintiffs here would have been entitled to recover, if the amount had not been paid by the Insurance Company. But the risk insured against by the Guardian Company was, prima facie at least, a wholly different risk. They contracted to pay to the tenant the damage that he sustained — that is, the damage that his estate and interest sustained, including his liability under his covenant to his landlords. How can these two risks be called the same? I heard no logical argument to show that the risks were the same...."

The Chief Baron also rejected the plea that the landlords were, in ease of the defendant Insurance Company, obliged to sue the tenant to repair the premises. On the contrary, the obligation of the defendant Insurance Company was to indemnify the landlords against their loss whereupon they would become entitled, by subrogation, to any claim which the landlords might have against the tenant. At page 369 of his Judgment, Chief Baron Palles says —

"The contract of the defendants was to pay; the right of the defendants was, upon payment, to sue either in the name of the plaintiffs, or in equity in their own names. They broke their contract by not paying, and thereby failed to acquire the status of having a right themselves to institute independent proceedings, until a period arrived when, by reason of the bankruptcy of the tenant, such proceedings would be ineffective."

It appears to me that the present case is on all fours with the case of *Andrews and ors.* v. *The Patriotic Assurance Company of Ireland*,[8] the only possible distinction — if it is a distinction — being that the interest of Monck Properties Limited was "noted" by Lloyds Underwriters. We do not know the circumstances in which this interest came to be "noted" or whether Monck Properties were or were not aware of the fact that their interest had been "noted" on their tenant's policy. Even if they were, the noting of their interest could only be regarded as a means of ensuring that the tenant complied with his repairing covenant by applying any moneys recovered from his Insurance Company to the repair of the premises. Such a provision cannot, in my opinion, affect the liquidator's rights against his own insurers. However, these insurers will, upon indemnifying the liquidator in respect of his loss, be entitled, by subrogation, to any rights which the liquidator may have against the tenant or its insurers.

It accordingly appears to me that the Respondent Insurance Companies are obliged to discharge in full the loss and damages sustained by the official liquidator arising from the fire which took place on the 14th of June 1982 at 345, 347, 349 and 355 North Circular Road, Dublin.

---

[8] (1886) 18 L.R.I. 355. See Chapter 2 (p. 53) and Chapter 3 (p. 67).

CHAPTER 5

Insurable Interest

It has long been an essential requirement of any policy of insurance that the insured have an "insurable interest" in the subject matter of the insurance. This requirement relates to both life and non-life policies of insurance, but, because of their natures, different considerations apply to each. At its simplest the concept of insurable interest is easily understood. However, considerable confusion can arise in its application to any given set of circumstances. In essence it demands that an insured have both an economic interest and a proximate legal relationship to the subject matter insured. The courts in Ireland have always adopted a broad, somewhat "liberal" approach to these requirements, regarding the principle as primarily technical in nature, and have therefore been loath to find against an insured solely on the basis of lack of insurable interest. A good example is to be found in the short case of *James and Others* v. *The Royal Insurance Company* (1875). It is interesting to note that in those cases in which insurable interest is an issue it has generally only been raised by insurers as one of a number of defences and seldom as a defence in itself.

The requirement of insurable interest as it is known today has its origins in a number of different principles. Firstly, in the concept of indemnity, whereby it is stated that if the insured has no interest in the subject matter of the insurance he can suffer no loss and therefore has nothing in respect of which he can be indemnified. Secondly, and more importantly, it has its roots in the legislature's long-standing abhorrence of gambling and wagering contracts; if the insured has no interest he is essentially wagering on the occurrence and outcome of a specified event in which he is not directly involved. This is something the legislature would not tolerate — hence the passing by it of numerous statutes prohibiting wagering, both in general terms and specifically relating to insurance. The distinction between insurable interest as required by the nature of the indemnity policy and as required by statute, can be significant. If the insured lacks the interest as required by the nature of the policy, the policy is simply voidable, so that if the insurer does not rely on its absence the insured can still recover. However, if the interest is absent and is required by statute, the policy is illegal and is null and void, irrespective of the wishes of the parties to the contract. Because the consequences are so serious in such circumstances, it is not surprising that most of the Irish cases on the subject are devoted to determining the exact scope and application of the legislation to particular contracts of insurance. For example in *Keith* v. *The Protection Marine Insurance Company of Paris* (1882) Baron Fitzgerald in the Court of Exchequer held that the Marine Insurance Act, 1745, had no application in Ireland.

Similarly, other cases have dealt with the scope and application of the most significant statute on insurable interest — the Life Assurance Act, 1774, its application being extended to Ireland by the Life Assurance (Ireland) Act, 1886.

In *Brady and Others* v. *The Irish Land Commission* (1920) O'Connor M.R. suggested in passing that it was doubtful that the 1774 Act applied to fire policies. This was examined in closer detail in *Church and General Insurance Company* v. *Connolly and McLoughlin* (1981) when Mr Justice Costello held that not only did the 1774 Act not apply to fire insurance but that its application to Ireland was restricted solely to policies of life insurance. In contrast, in the earlier decision of Mr Justice Henchy in the Supreme Court in *Motor Insurers Bureau of Ireland* v. *P.M.P.A. Insurance* (1979), the court seemed to proceed and take for granted that the 1774 Act was of more general application, but did not examine the subject in the detail of Mr Justice Costello. In that case, the Supreme Court held that the insurance of a motor vehicle is insurance of "goods", and therefore falls within Section 4 of the 1774 Act which removes such "goods" from the ambit of the Act. The requirement to have an insurable interest was, however, still necessary and arose by virtue of the policy being one of indemnity. It was, therefore, unenforceable until such time as an insurable interest was acquired. In *O'Leary* v. *The Irish National Insurance Company Limited* (1958), Mr Justice Budd again emphasised the importance of insurable interest in policies of motor insurance, but did not investigate the origins of the principle. He also proceeded on a similar basis in *Coen* v. *Employers Liability Assurance Corporation Limited* (1962), where the issue of insurable interest arose in a dispute as to whether proceedings should be stayed and referred to arbitration.

The House of Lords in its decision in *Macaura* v. *The Northern Assurance Company Limited* (1925) adopted a very rigid and uncompromising approach to the requirement of insurable interest (while not strictly an Irish case for the purposes of this publication, this case does have its roots in Northern Ireland). There the obligation arose by virtue of the nature of the policy being one of indemnity, with only passing reference being made to the statutory requirements. It was held that the insured — even though he was the sole shareholder and creditor of the company which owned the subject matter of the insurance — could not enforce the policy of insurance for lack of interest. In very similar circumstances Mr Justice Lynch in *P.J. Carrigan Ltd and P.J. Carrigan* v. *Norwich Union Fire Society Limited (No. 2)* (1987) held that the insured did indeed have an insurable interest in a destroyed house, in that while he was not the actual owner, it being in the name of a limited company, he ultimately had a significant beneficial interest in the house, thereby entitling him to claim under the policy.

Before moving on, it is surprising to note that in none of the cases that have come before the Irish courts has reference been made to the applicable Gaming and Lotteries Act, 1956, which renders void every gambling or wagering contract which is what a contract of insurance is if there is no insurable interest. This is obviously something that will have to be addressed by the courts in the future.

The law relating to insurable interest and life policies is somewhat more straightforward and less technical in its operation. Here the relevant statutes play a far more significant role than with non-life policies. The most important legislation is again the Life Assurance Act, 1774. In the very early case, *The British Commercial Insurance Company* v. *Magee* (1834), the Irish Exchequer Chamber held that life policies which were wanting of an insurable interest were not void at Common Law but were so void because of the demand of the 1774 Act that an insurable interest be present. As the 1774 Act had not then been applied to Ireland, the policies in question were upheld and found to be valid. Essentially the 1774 Act as applied to Ireland by the Life Assurance (Ireland) Act, 1886, demands that a person claiming on a life policy must show:

- That the person on whose behalf the policy was made does indeed have an insurable interest in the life insured;

- That the policy is expressly made on behalf of the person for whom was it indeed made; and

- That the sum claimed is no greater than the amount of the claimant's interest.

The apparent strictness of the Act has been tempered somewhat in Ireland by a number of statutes, namely the Assurance Companies Act, 1909, and the Insurance Act, 1936. Both these Statutes expanded significantly the categories of persons who could be regarded as having an insurable interest in the life of another. Now almost all close relatives can be said to have an interest in the person whose life is covered by insurance. At Common Law this had been restricted almost to persons only having an interest in their own life and that of their spouse.

Both statutes were the subject of litigation in the cases of *O'Brien* v. *The Irish National Insurance Company Limited* (1932) and *Gallagher & McPartland* v. *The Industrial Life Assurance Amalgamated Company Limited* (1946). Both cases involved the question of the legality of policies taken out by either a brother or sister of the deceased and an examination of the extent of their interest in that person. In both, the legality of the policies was upheld. The legality of a number of policies was again raised in the decision of the Supreme Court in *Wall* v. *The New Ireland Assurance Company Limited* (1962). It was so raised in a most interesting manner when the New Ireland sought, amongst other issues, to refuse to refund premiums paid by them on a number of policies taken out by a son on his mother. They alleged that the policies were void for want of insurable interest, and also that the son's motive in taking out the policies was less than bona fide. They were successful, with the court holding that the policies were indeed void and that, by virtue of the manner in which they were proposed, the premiums did not have to be repaid.

By and large, however, it is rare for insurers to raise the issue of insurable interest to avoid their contractual obligations. It is primarily a technical requirement and, in the absence of significant substantive reasons for relying on it as a defence, it is unlikely that an insurer would obtain a sympathetic hearing and so succeed in invoking it before an Irish court.

James and Others *v.* The Royal Insurance Company
(1875) 9 I.L.T.R. 194
Court of Common Pleas

LAWSON J: This is an action on a common policy of fire insurance. The answer to the action is simply that Evans had not, at the time alleged, any interest in the subject matter insured [namely certain fixtures and furniture in premises situated in the city of Limerick]. The only question is, has he any interest in the matter insured to entitle him to bring an action? ... This Evans entered into partnership under a verbal agreement with Johnston, whose trade assignee in bankruptcy he was, which agreement was afterwards to be turned into a deed. On the faith of that agreement he got into possession of certain premises. The place was mortgaged to one McCormick, whose sanction was required before Evans could enter. McCormick attached a condition to the giving of possession, saying, "I have always been in the habit of having it insured; you must insure, or I will not allow you to go into possession." If Evans had not insured, would he not be open to an action by McCormick, who would recover whatever the value was? He, therefore, enters into possession, not alone as a bailee, but under a contract to insure the goods and fixtures, on being allowed to enter and use and occupy the premises; and this contract he carries out. He is now told that he has no insurable interest. But, unless we were prepared to overrule *Marks* v. *Hamilton*[1] — and even apart from that case — we should hold that the plaintiff had an insurable interest.

KEOGH AND MORRIS, JJ., CONCURRED.

Keith v. The Protection Marine Insurance Company of Paris[*]
(1882) 10 L.R.I. 51
Exchequer Division

FITZGERALD B: ... This is an action on a policy of insurance, alleged to have been effected on account of the Plaintiff by Roxburgh, Currie, and Company, for £250 on the freight, advances, stores, and outfit of and in a ship called the "Minnie Knapp", of which the Plaintiff was then, and during the continuance of the risk, owner, at and from Glenarm in the county of Antrim to Newcastle in the United Kingdom, and alleging the total loss of the vessel on her voyage, and during the continuance of the risk. The Defendants plead that the ship was at the time of the making of the policy, and during the voyage and continuance of the risk, a British ship, that the policy was an English policy made in England, and that the said ship belonged to a British subject. The defence then avers that the policy contained a clause providing that the premises insured were warranted free from all average and without benefit of salvage, and also contained a clause providing that no further proof of interest than the policy should be required. The Plaintiff replies that the policy was and is a French policy, made between the Plaintiff, who was at the time of its making domiciled, and is still domiciled, in Ireland, and the Defendants, who are a French Company, having their principal office in Paris, and that the said policy was made in Ireland, and that the said ship was registered in Ireland. To this reply the Defendants have demurred.

The pleadings are peculiar; but I think we must assume that the policy, which contained the clauses mentioned in the Defendant's defence, was made in Ireland, but that the vessel belonged to a British subject.

It would seem to me that the introduction into the policy of the clauses mentioned makes the policy a wager policy, but this would not have been a valid objection to it at common law. This, I apprehend, whatever doubt might have been entertained with respect to the matter, is to be considered now as the law: it is so laid down by Parke B., in delivering the judgment of the Exchequer Chamber in *Dalby* v. *The India and London Life Assurance Company*[2]: at p. 387, he says,

> "Policies of insurance against fire and against marine risks are both properly contracts of indemnity, the insurer engaging to make good within certain limited amounts the losses sustained by the assured in their buildings, ships

---

[1] 21 L.J. Ex. 109.
[*] Extract.
[2] 15 C.B. 365.

and effects. Policies on maritime risks were afterwards used improperly, and made mere wagers on the happening of those perils. This practice was limited by the Marine Insurance Act, 1745,[3] and put an end to in all except a few cases. But at common law before this statute, with respect to maritime risks, and the Life Assurance Act, 1774,[4] as to insurance on lives, it is perfectly clear that all contracts for wager-policies and wagers which were not contrary to the policy of the law were legal contracts; and so it is stated by the Court in *Cousins* v. *Nantes*[5] to have been solemnly determined in the case of *Lucena* v. *Crawford*,[6] without even a difference of opinion among all the Judges. To the like effect was the decision of the Court of Error in Ireland, before all the Judges except three, in *The British Insurance Co.* v. *Magee*,[7] that the insurance was legal at common law."

The two first cases mentioned by the learned Judge are cases of marine insurance; the third, as well as the case before him, were cases of life insurance. The contract, therefore, in this case would have been legal at common law.

However, the English ante-Union statute referred to, Marine Insurance Act, 1745,[8] never expressly re-enacted by the Parliament of Ireland, did enact "that from and after the 1st day of August, 1746, no assurance or assurances shall be made by any person or persons, bodies corporate or politic, on any ship or ships belonging to his Majesty, or any of his subjects, or any goods, merchandises or effects laden or to be laden on board of any such ship or ships, interest or no interest, or without further proof of interest than the policy, or by way of gaming or wagering, or without benefit of salvage to the assurer, and that any such assurance shall be null and void to all intents and purposes."

It seems to me that if this statute was or is binding on the Irish subjects of the sovereign, the policy or contract before us is void.

It is well known that at the time of passing this Act, and for a long time after, there did exist an Act of the English Parliament, but never re-enacted by the Irish Parliament, the statute [Dependency of Ireland on Great Britain, Act 1719[9]], which did expressly declare and enact "that the King's Majesty, by and with the advice and consent of the Lords Spiritual and Temporal and Commons of Great Britain in Parliament assembled had, hath, and of right ought to have, full power and authority to make laws and statutes of sufficient force and validity to bind the kingdom and people of Ireland".

Even if this statute were still in force, and actually binding on the Irish subjects of the sovereign, it would be necessary to show that the intention of the sovereign to bind Ireland was expressed, or could be collected by necessary implication. I confess it does not appear to me that any such intention can be collected from the language of the Marine Insurance Act, 1745. No

---

[3] 19 Geo. 2, c. 37.
[4] 14 Geo. 3, c. 48.
[5] 3 Taunt. 315.
[6] 2 Bos. & P. 324; 2 N.R. 269.
[7] Cooke & Alcock 182.
[8] 19 Geo. 2, c. 37.
[9] 6. Geo. 1. c. 5.

doubt it relates as was said, to any ship or ships belonging to any of His Majesty's subjects; but the policies avoided are policies made by any person or persons, bodies corporate or politic, with nothing to show that this includes policies made in Ireland. I do not think that even if the Act [Dependency of Ireland on Great Britain, Act 1719[10]] were still existing, and binding on Irish subjects, that the Marine Insurance Act, 1745, could be held binding on Irish subjects.

But it is also well known that by the English statute [An Act to repeal an Act made in the sixth year of the reign of his Majesty King George the fifth, entitled, An Act for the better securing the Dependency of the Kingdom of Ireland upon the Crown of Great Britain[11]], that Act [An Act for the better securing the dependency of the kingdom of Ireland upon the Crown of Great Britain[12]] was repealed; and further, by the statute [An Act for removing and preventing all doubts which have arisen, or might arise, concerning the exclusive rights of the Parliament and courts of Ireland, in matters of legislation and judicature, and for preventing any writ of error or appeal from any of his majesty's courts in that kingdom from being received, heard and adjudged, in any of his majesty's courts in the kingdom of Great Britain[13]], also an English Act, it was declared and enacted "that the right claimed by the people of Ireland to be bound only by laws enacted by His Majesty and the Parliament of that kingdom in all cases whatever, shall be, and it is hereby declared to be established and ascertained for ever, and shall at no time hereafter be questioned or questionable." Even, therefore, if the Marine Insurance Act 1745 had purported to extend to Ireland, it never could be binding on the Irish subjects of the sovereign, unless re-enacted by the Parliament of Ireland or of the United Kingdom.

However, in the argument of this case, a statute of the Irish Parliament passed at the time that the right mentioned in the [Irish Appeals Act, 1783[14]], and recognised by that Act, was being claimed by the Irish people, was referred to as in effect re-enacting that statute. It is the Irish statute [An Act for extending certain of the provisions contained in an act, instituted, and act confirming all the statutes made in England[15]], by which it is enacted, in sect. 1, "That all statutes heretofore made in England or Great Britain for the purpose of settling and assuring forfeited estates in this kingdom, and also all private statutes made in England or Great Britain, under which any lands, tenements or hereditaments in this kingdom, or any estate or interest therein, are or is held or claimed, or which any way concern the title thereto, or any evidence respecting the same, *and also* all such clauses and provisions contained in any statute made in England or Great Britain *concerning commerce, as import* to impose equal *restraints* on the subjects of England and Ireland, or of Great Britain and Ireland, and to entitle them to *equal benefits*; *and also* all *such* clauses and provisions contained in any statutes

---

[10] 6. Geo. 1. c. 5.
[11] 22 Geo. 3 c. 53.
[12] 6 Geo. 1 c. 5.
[13] 23 Geo. 3 c. 28.
[14] 23 Geo. 3.
[15] 21 & 22 Geo. 3 c. 48.

made as aforesaid as equally concerning the seamen of England and Ireland, or of Great Britain and Ireland, save so far as the same have been altered or repealed, shall be accepted, used and executed in this kingdom according to the present tenor thereof, respectively." It was argued that the provisions of the Marine Insurance Act, 1745 are within this enactment, as provisions concerning commerce having the equality mentioned.

Now, in the first place, it seems to me very clear that this enactment relates only to English Acts importing to bind Irish subjects, in which respect it differs from a distinct section, the 3rd of the same statute, relating to other English statutes having no relation to the present question. If therefore, I be right in thinking that the statute [Marine Insurance Act, 1745[16]] does not import to bind Ireland, that statute would not be within the enactment. But, in the next place, I am quite satisfied that the statute [Marine Insurance Act, 1745[17]] is not a statute concerning commerce within the meaning of the enactment. it purports to impose no restraints, nor to give any privileges of trade to the subjects of the one kingdom or the other.

I am of opinion that the covenant before us is not avoided by the statute relied on, inasmuch as such statute is not of force in Ireland, and that, being legal at common law, the demurrer ought to be overruled.

Brady and Others *v.* The Irish Land Commission
[1921] 1 I.R. 56
Chancery Division

O'CONNOR M.R: This action raises a question of very great importance to the defendants, the Irish Land Commission. It has been brought to try the right of the plaintiffs as successors in title of the owner of a demesne which was sold by him to the Land Commission, repurchased under the provisions of the Irish Land Act, 1903, to moneys recovered under a policy of fire insurance of a unique character, and in a form specially designed for the purpose of securing an annuity payable to the Commission in repayment of an advance with interest of the purchase-money made out of the Land Purchase Fund.

[The demesne of Bailieborough Castle, in the County of Cavan, and certain tenanted lands were in the ownership of Mr William Cochrane, who in the year 1910 received a proposal from the Land Commission to purchase from him the entire estate for the sum of £5,757, of which £5,212 was to be advanced from the Land Purchase Fund, and the balance, £545, was to be lodged in cash with the Land Commission by the vendor. This proposal contained a proviso that the vendor should enter into an undertaking to repurchase the demesne for the sum of £2,464 of which £1,919 was to be advanced by the Land Commission, and the balance, £545 (the sum already mentioned), was to be lodged in cash by the vendor, and to effect a policy of insurance against damage by fire on the dwelling-house and offices in the form and with a company approved of by the Land Commission for the sum of £1,540 in the name of the Commission for a term of sixty-eight and a half

---

[16] 19 Geo. 2 c. 37.
[17] *Ibid.*

years, with all premiums fully paid up and compounded for in advance, and to enter into such contract as the Land Commission might require, to observe the terms of the policy, and to constitute the Commission his attorneys for the purpose of obtaining payment of any moneys which might become payable on foot of the policy, and to lodge it, together with the power of attorney, with the Land Commission.]

The purpose to be served by the policy is obvious. The advance for the repurchase with interest was to be repaid by an annuity secured on property, a substantial portion of which was of a perishable nature, and liable to be destroyed by fire. Against this contingency the purchaser was to insure at his own expense; and of course he was insuring not merely for the protection of the Land Commission, but for his own, he being vitally interested in the preservation of the insured property. The interest of the purchaser in the policy was recognised by the provision that he was to give a power of attorney to the Land Commission to recover any moneys payable under the policy. If he was to have no interest in the policy, this provision would be unmeaning.

But the distinguishing feature of the policy was to be a single premium policy covering the risks for a long term of years. But whose risk was it intended to cover? Certainly not the risk of the Land Commission alone, because the person to pay the annuity was as much interested in preserving the property out of which it was to be paid as the person to receive it. And, if the purchasing owner was to have an interest in the policy, was the interest to be his only, and not to devolve on his successors in title? This was certainly not the intention, because his ownership was bound in the ordinary course to devolve on some other person during the currency of the annuity. Obviously the insurance was to be effected to insure the property, no matter in whose ownership it was, during the term of sixty-eight and a half years. The payment down of a lump sum as a composition for the premiums, which in the ordinary course would be payable from year to year on a policy renewable from year to year, could have no other meaning. In order to make such a policy effective, according to the intent, it could not have been taken out in the name of the purchasing owner. If it was, it would have insured him, and him only. It would not have insured his successors in title, because under the established principles governing fire insurance policies they only insure the interest of the assured in the subject-matter, fire policies being mere personal contracts enforceable by persons who at the date of the contract and at the date of the loss have an interest in the subject-matter. That being so, it was necessary in the case of the policy in question to have it taken out in the name of an assured whose interest would presumably continue during the whole of the term, viz., the Land Commission, entitled to receive the annuity during the whole term of the policy, and destined to receive it without any transmission of interest, save in the case of redemption — a contingency with which I will deal later on.

No doubt there was another reason for taking out the policy in the name of the Land Commission. It was advisable, for the greater security of the Land Commission, that the moneys payable under the policy should be receivable by them; but this was merely a matter of precaution, the first reason I have mentioned going to the root of the matter. This was the first stage of the transaction, and it indicates the intention of the parties. I will deal later on with the question whether the intention was lawfully and effectively carried out.

The policy was subject to the usual conditions, but attached to and incorporated with it is a memorandum providing, inter alia, that the company should not be at liberty to require the Land Commission to show at any time that its interest in the premises or property amounted to or was commensurate with the extent of the loss or injury which might have at any time accrued, and that the company undertook to pay or make good to the Commission all such loss or injury to an amount not exceeding the sum insured, irrespective of the interests involved. I emphasise the word "interests", as indicating that more than the interest of the Land Commission was in the minds of the parties; but I will come back to this proviso presently....

[... There was also a contemporaneous indenture made between Cochrane, the purchaser, and the Land Commission, which recited the purchase, and that it was one of the terms of the advance of the purchase-money that the purchaser should effect a policy of insurance against fire in the mansion-house and offices in the sum of £1,540 in the name of the Commission; such policy to cover the term of sixty-eight and a half years from the date thereof by the payment of one premium. It then recited that the policy had been effected, and by the indenture the purchaser covenanted with the Land Commission not to do any act which would avoid the policy, and appointed the Commission, their agents and servants, to be the true and lawful attorneys of the purchaser and his successors in title in his and their name and names, and in his and their behalf on every occasion on which the premises should be damaged by fire, to enter upon and take possession of the insured premises, and to do all things necessary and proper for obtaining payment of any moneys which should become payable on foot of the policy, and for the observance and performance of the several conditions of the policy. This document was also attached to and incorporated with the policy....]

Now, it is to be observed that the power of attorney given by this indenture is not in accordance with the clause contained in the proposal to purchase, which was to constitute the Land Commission the attorney of the purchaser for the purpose of obtaining payment of the moneys payable on foot of the policy. The power given was only to enter on the lands and to perform certain conditions of the policy. There was no need for a power of attorney to obtain payment, because the policy was in the name of the Commission, and they were legally entitled to sue on it. Reliance was placed by counsel for the Land Commission on the form of the power of attorney actually given, as not indicating any interest in any person except the person named as the assured. This is no doubt so, but still I think that the agreement in the proposal to purchase pointed at interest in the purchaser in the contemplated policy, and gives a complexion to the entire transaction. I also draw attention to the power of attorney, which purports to be on behalf of the principals, successors in title, but merely for the purpose of showing that they were contemplated to have an interest in the policy. I must now refer to the memorandum attached to the policy relieving the Land Commission from the obligation to show an interest in the subject-matter to the extent of the loss. It was contended on behalf of the Land Commission that this made the policy a wager policy to all intents and purposes, and that the policy moneys were to be held by them for their own exclusive benefit, irrespective of the interests involved. See what this might lead to. A claim might not arise under the policy until the last half year of the term of the annuity. The Land Commission would at that time have been repaid all but an insignificant part of the advance with interest, and would in addition get the policy moneys — in fact, would be paid twice over. This was certainly not the intention of the parties. It must be remembered that the transaction was one carried out by a public department, whose duty it was to aid land purchase by advances of public money, and to secure the repayment of the advances. Security was the only legitimate object, and not a profit out of a gamble. The only intelligible meaning of the transaction is that the Land Commission was to receive the money, and to apply it according to all the interests concerned. The first and paramount interest should be that of the Land Commission, but when that interest was served there came the interest of the owner for the time being of the lands. There is, indeed, no such trust expressly declared, but it is implied by the nature of the transaction — res ipsa loquitur. It is a question of fact in each case what was the interest which it was intended to cover by the policy; was it intended to cover only the interest of the person effecting the policy, or his and another interest? (See judgment of Bowen L.J. in *Castellain* v. *Preston*[18]). We are not troubled in this case with any question arising under [The Life Assurance Act, 1774] even assuming that this Act applies to fire insurance policies in Ireland, which is doubtful. The validity of the policy has not been questioned by the Land Commission, nor could it be, because the Land Commission has been paid on foot of it, and has now possession of the money. The question of fact is determined in the plaintiff's favour by the nature of the transaction, and particularly by the attached memorandum and indenture, which showed the joint interest of the Commission and the purchaser.

If the Land Commission was the only party entitled to the benefit of the policy, the result would be that it would be entitled to repayment of the full amount of the advance, and also the full amount of the policy. This, it seems to me, would be in excess of their statutory duty, which was merely to secure repayment of the advance made out of the Land Purchase Fund.

On the 15th July, 1915, Cochrane conveyed all his estate and interest in the premises to the plaintiffs, and the annuity payable to the Land Commission has been discharged by them to date. On the 21st November, 1918, the main portion of the insured premises was destroyed by fire, and £1,200 has been received by the Land Commission on foot of the policy.

Stripping the case of all the immaterial surroundings which are mentioned in the pleadings, the question for decision is whether the plaintiffs have any interests or rights in the policy money. The Land Commission has set out the defence that the plaintiffs have no rights or interest whatsoever, and claim the right to appropriate the moneys, and to continue to receive the annuity. They base their defence on two grounds: (1) that Cochrane, the original purchaser, had no interest in the policy; (2) that if he had, that interest did not rest in the plaintiffs as his successors in title. I have already

---

[18] 11 Q.B.D. 380 at p. 398.

shown that the nature of the transaction necessarily involved a joint interest in the policy in the original owner, Cochrane, and the Land Commission.

But then comes the question: did the interest of Cochrane pass to the plaintiffs as his successors in title?

[... The 5th condition of the policy was as follows:— "This policy shall cease to be in force as to any property hereby insured upon the interest therein passing from him otherwise than by will or operation of law, unless notice thereof be given to the corporation, and the insurance be declared to be continued to his successor in interest by a memorandum made on the policy by or on behalf of the corporation, and the expression 'insured' herein shall include every successor in interest to whom the insurance be so declared to be or is otherwise continued....]

The exception made in the case of the passing of an interest by will or operation of law is in effect a declaration that the policy shall continue in force for the benefit of the person to whom the property the subject-matter of the policy had passed by operation of law, this being a case excepted from the clause providing for the cesser of the policy. But this is expressly declared by the final words: "Insured herein shall include every such successor in interest to whom the insurance be so declared to be or is otherwise continued." In other words, the "insured" is a person coming within the exception of the case described as the passing of an interest by operation of law.

I will now consider condition 5 specially with reference to the present case. I cannot conceive any passing of interest from the Land Commission except by operation of law, and that in only one way, by the redemption of the annuity during its currency. The owner of the property would on redemption acquire all the interest of the Land Commission, and become the "insured" within the meaning of the policy — a result accomplished by its terms, and in complete accord with the equity of the transaction. This, to my mind, is convincing proof that the parties, including the insurance company, intended, as they must necessarily have, that the owner for the time being was to have an interest in the policy. The right of redemption is a legal incident of a Land Commission annuity, to be carried out by operation of law, which, under the conditions of the policy, makes the redeeming owner "the insured". But it is not merely the original purchaser who has the right to redeem. His successors in title have the same right to acquire the interest of the Land Commission in the property by redemption — an operation of law. And if the original owner becomes the insured by redeeming, so must every subsequent owner who redeems.

It follows from this that on redemption the Land Commission should hand over the policy to the redeeming owner for the time being. Why should the Land Commission keep it? There would no longer be any risk to cover. It may be objected that this reasoning fails in the present case because there has as yet been no redemption, and the operation of law referred to in the condition would not take place until redemption had been accomplished. There is some force in this, but it is met by the answer that before redemption there is at least an inchoate interest in each successive owner who has a right to redeem in a policy such as we have here — a policy co-extensive with the terms of the annuity. This inchoate interest distinguishes the present case from those in which successors in title have been held to have no interest in policies effected by their predecessors. A purchaser has no interest in the policy of his vendor, because at the date of the policy he is not merely a stranger to it, but to the property insured. A remainderman has no interest in the policy of the tenant for life, because he has no interest in the estate for life. But it could not be said that a vendor who, after the contract for sale had, at the request of the purchaser, and with money supplied by the latter, effected a policy in his own name, could refuse to recognise any right of the purchaser in it. Nor could it be said that a tenant for life who, under the terms of the settlement, was bound to insure a mansion-house could put the moneys recovered under a fire policy into his own pocket.

No doubt as between mortgagor and mortgagee, if one of them effects a policy on the subject-matter of the mortgage, the other has no interest in it, and cannot claim the benefit of it apart from special contract. The reason of this is that the mortgagor or mortgagee in whose name the policy is effected is the only person who is privy to it, and the other is a stranger. But that cannot apply to a policy to which all three parties are privy, being made so by the incorporation of the indenture between the owner and the Land Commission with the policy. The original owner, therefore, had an interest in the policy, but only so long as he continued to be the owner. The Land Commission, as the nominal assured, would be a trustee of that interest, and I think that the document demonstrate that it was intended that the trust should continue for the owners' successors in title, who are expressly mentioned in the incorporated indenture. The power of attorney given on behalf of successors in title was in law inoperative, but it clearly indicated the intention that they should stand in the same position towards the policy as the original owner.

It may be said that even if that were so the original owner did not assign his interest in the policy to the plaintiffs, his successors in title, but I do not think that any express assignment was necessary, because the Land Purchase Act gave them, as I have pointed out, the right to redeem the annuity — the right to acquire the interest of the Land Commission by an operation of law, and so become the "insured" in the strict technical meaning of the policy. This I have described as an inchoate right which brings the plaintiffs into privity with the policy, and enables them to claim the benefit of it.

As against this, it was argued that the policy was a wager policy under the clause in the memorandum. It is not necessary to go into the question whether a wager policy of fire insurance is not void, or to comment on the making of a wager by a great public department; but I will say this, that unless I am coerced by the language of the policy, I am not to construe it as a wager. I do not interpret the memorandum as making the policy an interest or no interest policy. The only object of the memorandum was to make the amount payable independent of the separate loss of the Land Commission, which might only be trifling, while a serious loss might accrue to the owner. The words "irrespective of the interests involved" show that the policy was intended to cover other interests than that of the Land Commission; in fact, that it "involved" other interests, although the whole amount was to be paid to the Land Commission. Indeed, the incorporated documents showed what the other interests were. But the idea of a wager policy is contradicted by the policy itself. The rights of the Commission to indemnity and subrogation are specially provided for by the conditions. These rights are foreign to a wager transaction. Undoubtedly the insurance company are entitled under the policy in question to the usual rights of indemnity and subrogation; and if the Land Commission are entitled to appropriate the policy money, and do so, and still continue to recover the annuity, they will become liable to repay the amount to the insurance company. But I hold that they cannot do so. I wonder have the accountants of the Land Commission considered to what credit the policy money should be carried if it is, as they contend, a wager policy. It seems to me that to be accurate they should open a betting account. In truth, they are not entitled to keep the money. They are not entitled to recover anything more than the annuity. That is the only thing owing to them out of the transaction. Everything above that belongs to the owner of the estate.

As I have already mentioned, there are special circumstances detailed in the pleadings, but it is unnecessary to deal with these, having regard to the view I take. I am of opinion that the plaintiffs are entitled to the benefit of the policy. They are entitled to have the policy moneys applied in reinstating the buildings or reimbursing the plaintiffs, who are reinstating them, or in having them applied towards the redemption of the annuity.

The plaintiffs having succeeded, are entitled to the costs of the action, to be paid by the defendants, although it cannot be said that the Land Commission acted in any way perversely or unreasonably. The form of policy is unique, and the position was somewhat obscure. This action will settle their rights, and they will know how to deal with future cases arising out of the same form of policy.

In the Matter of the Arbitration Act, 1954
Church and General Insurance Co.
v. Connolly and McLoughlin[*]
Unreported, 7 May 1981
The High Court

COSTELLO J: ...The Plaintiffs' submissions on this part of the case can be summarised as follows. The arbitrator found that the insurable interest of the Defendants in the premises was that of a tenant at will. But he also found that they were entitled to be indemnified not only in respect of the damage sustained to this insurable interest but also in respect of loss and damage caused to the interests of the owners in fee of the premises. This determination was incorrect, the Plaintiffs submit. As part of their argument my attention was drawn by the Plaintiffs to a proposition of law contained in Halsbury's *Laws of England* Fourth (Hailsham) Edition, Volume 25 at paragraph 641 dealing with insurances taken out for the benefit of several interests which reads as follows:

> "Warehousemen and other bailees effect policies which will enure for the benefit of their bailors and similar insurances are effected by mortgagors or

---

[*] Extract. The remainder of this judgment — in which the facts are contained — appears at p. 448 in Chapter 11.

mortgagees, tenants for life or remaindermen, lessors or lessees and a company, its contractors and subcontractors, for the benefit of other persons interested in the same property. Insurances of this latter kind may be made in the performance of some contract or in the discharge of some duty, although this is not necessary.... All that is required to make the insurance effective is what *at the time of insuring it is his* (i.e. the person effecting the insurance) *intention (was) to cover their interests as well as his own....* If the requisite intention is established, the insurance is a valid insurance enuring for the benefit of all persons interested".

The Plaintiffs say that that part of the statement which I have underlined is incorrect. They refer to *Hepburn* v. *A. Tomlinson (Hauliers) Ltd.*[19] and claim that this establishes that a unilateral intent on the part of one person to a contract of insurance to confer a benefit on an unnamed third party will not suffice to confer such a benefit, that extrinsic evidence on this point should not be permitted, and that the intention to confer a benefit on the owner of an insurable interest other than that of the insured must be gleaned from the policy itself. Applying this principle (and not the proposition of law in Halsbury which I have quoted) the Plaintiffs say that I should look at the terms of the policy, that it is apparent from these that there was no intention to benefit anyone but the Bandon Youth Club, and that as there was no intention to benefit the fee simple owner it follows, it is claimed, that there is an error of law on the face of this award. I was referred to an Australian authority, *British Traders Insurance Co. Ltd.* v. *Honson*[20] as an example of a case in which the tenants under a lease for one year could only recover in respect of the actual loss sustained by them.

To succeed on this submission the Plaintiffs must not only establish that the arbitrator made an error of law but that this error appears on the face of the award. An error in law on the face of the award means

> "that you can find in the award or a document actually incorporated thereto, as for instance a note appended by the arbitrator stating the reasons for his judgment, some legal proposition which is the basis of the award and which you can then say is erroneous" [per Lord Dunedin, *Champsey Bhara and Co.* v *Jivraj Alloo Spinning and Weaving Co.*[21]]

In examining the determination made by the arbitrator I can find no error of law on its face. He found that the Defendant had an insurable interest in the property as tenants at will, that they are entitled to be indemnified under the policy by the Company, and that such indemnity should cover not only the loss and damage they suffered to their limited interest but also the loss and damage caused to the owners in fee of the premises.

The law permits a person with a limited interest in a property to insure not only his interest but the interests which others may have in the same property, and what the arbitrator has found in this case is that the

---

[19] [1966] 1 All E.R. 418.
[20] (1964) 111 C.L.R. 86.
[21] [1923] A.C. 480 at p. 487.

Defendants have done what the law permits them to do. There seems to be nothing erroneous therefore on the face of this award. To discover error the Plaintiffs must go behind the award and show that the arbitrator received and considered evidence which, on the basis of the *Hepburn* decision, he should not have received and considered. But I cannot go behind the award for the purpose of deciding that it is bad on its face. Alternatively the Plaintiffs must argue that the only basis in law on which the arbitrator could decide the issue before him was that laid down in the *Hepburn* case, and that as the policy cannot be construed as showing an intention to benefit the fee simple owner the award is bad in law and this error appears on its face. But even if I am entitled to look at the policy for the purpose of ascertaining whether the award is bad on its face (and the Defendants argue that I cannot) and even if I were to hold that the arbitrator can only seek the parties' intention from the policy and must not receive evidence of the insured's intention at the time the contract was made (and it is not necessary for me to reach final decisions on these points) I am not prepared to hold that the arbitrator *must* be in error in holding that there was an intention to benefit the fee simple owner in this case. Having regard to the very large sum insured it seems to me that it would have been open to him to reach such a conclusion. If this is so then I could not hold that there is an error of law on the face of this award.

I now come to the second "misconduct" argument under section 38 and to the suggestion that the arbitrator's award should be set aside because it has the effect of enforcing an illegal contract. In support of their view that it is "misconduct" of an arbitrator to make an award which enforces an illegal contract the Plaintiffs refer to *David Taylor Ltd* v. *Barnett*,[22] a case which related to the sale of Irish stewed steak at a price above the price fixed by law. A dispute, arising from non-delivery, was referred to arbitration. A motion to set aside the arbitrator's award was brought claiming (a) that the award was bad on its face and (b) that the arbitrator was guilty of misconduct in that he had failed to take into account the illegality of the contract. The seller failed on the first point, but succeeded on the second. It is of significance to note that it appears from the judgment of Singleton L.J. that the illegality of the contract was brought to the notice of the arbitrator (p. 846). The Plaintiffs' argument on the principle established by this case is based on the Life Assurance Act, 1774[23] and they submit (a) the provisions of this Act apply to fire insurance; (b) they were applied in this country by the Life Assurance Act, 1866; (c) the 1774 Act[24] makes it unlawful to enter into a policy of fire insurance without inserting the names of all persons interested in the policy. In the present case the name of the fee simple owner was not inserted on this policy. The arbitrator's award, it is submitted, has the effect of enforcing an illegal contract, and should therefore be set aside.

To consider this argument I must first examine the 1774 Act.[25] It is

---

[22] [1953] 1 All E.R. 843.
[23] 14 Geo. 3, c. 48.
[24] *Ibid.*
[25] *Ibid.*

entitled an "Act for regulating insurances upon Lives, and for prohibiting all such Insurances, except in cases where the persons insuring shall have an Interest in the Life or Death of the Persons insured". It would seem from this that it was intended that the Act should only apply to life assurance and that it has nothing to do with fire insurance. However, the Act has a preamble which recites that "whereas it hath been found by experience that the making of insurances on lives *or other events* where the assured shall have no interest hath introduced a mischievous kind of gaming" and section 2 of the Act provides that

> "It shall not be lawful to make any policy or policies on the life or lives of any person or persons, *or other event or events* without inserting in such policy or policies the person's or persons' name or names interested therein, or for whose benefit, or on whose account such policy is so made or underwrote".

The Company says that the words in the section I have underlined, *"or other event or events"*, mean that it is not lawful to effect a policy of insurance either on the life of any person, or other event unless the names of persons interested therein are inserted on it, and that the "other events" referred to include policies of fire insurance. But the problems of construction which this case presents are not exhausted by the 1774 Act.[26] The 1774 Act[27] was applied to this country by the Life Assurance Act, 1886. This was entitled "An Act to amend the Law relating to Life Assurances in Ireland" and having recited the title of the 1774 Act[28] to which I have already referred it provided in two short sections as follows:

> "1. From and after the commencement of this Act the Provisions of the said recited Act shall extend to Ireland.
>
> 2. This Act shall commence and take effect from and after the first day of November in the year one thousand eight hundred and sixty six, and shall apply to all Policies of Insurance upon lives entered into upon and after that date."

It will become immediately apparent that in the construction of these two Acts two problems of some magnitude arise. The first is: does the 1774 Act[29] apply to fire insurance policies? The second is: even if the 1774 Act[30] is to be so construed did section 2 of the 1866 Act apply to this country only those provisions of the earlier Act which related to life assurance policies.

Before giving my decision on these points there is a preliminary point of importance to which I should advert. Had the Plaintiffs advanced the illegality argument before the arbitrator had rejected it I do not see how it could be said that the arbitrator was guilty of misconduct on doing so. The present case is very different to the *Barnett* Case in which the illegality of the con-

---

[26] 14 Geo. 3, c. 48.
[27] *Ibid.*
[28] *Ibid.*
[29] *Ibid.*
[30] *Ibid.*

tract was perfectly clear and the arbitrator chose to ignore it after it was drawn to his attention. In the present case the statutory prohibition is far from clear and I do not consider that an arbitrator could be said to be guilty of misconduct merely because he interpreted an ambiguous statutory provision in a manner which I might consider erroneous. As pointed out in Russell on "Arbitration", 19th Edition, at p. 476, it is not misconduct for an arbitrator to make a mistake of law. But in fact the situation in this case is that the points now made on the Acts of 1774[31] and 1866 were never advanced before the arbitrator. How then can I hold him guilty of misconduct? I do not think I can and it seems to me that all the submissions made as to the misconduct of the arbitrator must fail.

But that does not finally dispose of the arguments based on the Acts of 1774[32] and 1866 because in my view if the attention of the court is drawn to an arbitration award whose enforcement would be contrary to public policy the court might well consider that it should in the exercise of its discretion remit the award even though the point had not been raised before the arbitrator. And so it seems to me that I should consider the arguments I have just summarised and reach a conclusion firstly on the application of the 1774 Act to fire insurance policies on buildings and secondly as to the application of the 1774 Act[33] to this country.

MacGillivray on "Insurance Law", Sixth Edition paragraph 144, asserts that the 1774 Act[34] applies to insurances on buildings and finds support for this view from *In Re King decd.*[35] But the passage referred to (a passage from the judgment from Lord Denning, M.R.) seems to me to be clearly obiter, and, strange as it may seem, it has not been finally or authoritatively decided in England that the 1774 Act[36] applies as MacGillivray suggests. Ivamy on "Fire and Motor Insurance" (1973 Edition) holds a view contrary to that of the editors of the latest edition of MacGillivray and states that the right of an insured who has a limited interest only in houses and buildings to cover the interests of other persons as well as his own is not affected by the 1774 Act[37] (see pp. 177 to 181). The latest editor of Halsbury's *Laws of England* (see Fourth (Hailsham) edition, Volume 25, paragraph 633, footnote 9) agrees with him. Ivamy points out (1) that the statute in practice has never been treated as applicable to fire insurance and although questions on the lawfulness of fire policies have frequently been raised no court has suggested that the 1774 Act[38] applied, the judicial silence on the point is, it is suggested, significant; (2) that the mischief which the statute was intended to remedy did not at the time of its passing exist in connection with fire insurance; (3) the amount recoverable by the insured under a policy of life insurance is calculated on a different basis to that recoverable on a policy of fire insurance, and if the

---

[31] 14 Geo. 3, c. 48.
[32] *Ibid.*
[33] *Ibid.*
[34] *Ibid.*
[35] [1963] Ch. 459, at p. 685.
[36] 14 Geo. 3, c. 48.
[37] *Ibid.*
[38] *Ibid.*

same construction is applied to the latter type of policy as to the former this would mean that a policy of fire insurance would not be regarded as a contract of indemnity — a conclusion contrary to all the authorities on the subject.

I find the arguments advanced by Ivamy persuasive and it seems to me that the 1774 Act should not be construed as applying to fire insurance policies on buildings. But even if they did the Plaintiffs must show that they were applied in this country by the Act of 1866. MacGillivray suggests that this was the effect of the 1866 Act (see: paragraph 30 of the sixth edition), but I do not interpret the Act in this same sense. The is entitled "An Act to amend the Law relating to Life Insurances in Ireland" and makes no references to amending the law relating to other forms of insurances. Although section 1 applied the provision of the 1774 Act to this country section 2 provided that after the commencement date the 1774 Act "shall apply to all Policies of Insurance upon lives entered into upon and after that date". It made no provision that the Act was to apply to any other type of policies of insurance after that date. And so I conclude that the 1774 Act only applies in this country to policies of life insurance. It follows therefore that there was nothing unlawful in the manner in which the policy was entered into by the parties on 8th April 1975, that it would not be contrary to public policy to enforce it and that the Plaintiffs illegality argument fails.

Finally, the Plaintiffs have urged (but this, it should be said, was not pressed with any great vigour) that the award cannot stand because there cannot be a finding that the insured had only a limited interest in the premises (see answer to question 3) and a finding that they are entitled to the full indemnity (see answer to question (1)). But, as I have already indicated, there is nothing inconsistent with such a finding as the limited owner is, if he takes the right steps, entitled to obtain the indemnity which the arbitrator has found the insured is entitled to in the present case.

In the result, I will dismiss the Plaintiffs' claim in these proceedings.

The Motor Insurance Bureau of Ireland *v.* P.M.P.A. Insurance Company Ltd.
[1981] I.R. 142
The Supreme Court

HENCHY J: In October, 1969, Peter Flynn was travelling as a passenger in a motor car driven by his brother at Kinnegad in the county of Westmeath. The car collided with another car and he suffered serious injuries. He sued Patrick J. Mahon, the driver of the other car, and Fr Mackin who, he claimed, was the owner of the other car. In subsequent proceedings in the High Court it was held that the negligence of Mr Mahon was the sole cause of the accident. It was also held in the High Court, and in this Court on appeal, that Fr Mackin was not the owner of the other car and so the case against him was dismissed. Judgment was given against Mr Mahon for the sum of £44,904 and costs.

Unfortunately, Mr Mahon was not covered by insurance in respect of the car (JLI 859) that he had been driving at the time of the accident. As appears from the report of the appeal taken to this Court (*Flynn* v. *Mackin*[39]). JLI 859 was a new car which Mr Mahon, a garage owner, was delivering to Fr Mackin. Fr Mackin had agreed with Mr Mahon that, in return for an old car plus £250, Mr Mahon would let him have a new Vauxhall Viva car. Mr Mahon did not have a new Vauxhall Viva in stock, but he arranged to get one from a firm called Athlone Motors; the one which he got was JLI 859. Having been told what the number of the new car was to be, Fr Mackin arranged to have the insurance on his old car transferred to the new car. The insurers of the old car were the respondent insurers and, prior to the time of the accident, they had issued a certificate of insurance in respect of JLI 859 in favour of Fr Mackin. When the accident took place, Mr Mahon was driving JLI 859 from Athlone Motors to Kinnegad for the purpose of delivering it to Fr Mackin.

For the reasons given by this Court in *Flynn* v. *Mackin*,[40] it was held that the agreement between Fr Mackin and Mr Mahon was only an agreement to barter or exchange goods; that it did not constitute an agreement for the sale to Fr Mackin of the car JLI 859; that even if it did, it would have been only an agreement for the sale of future goods, and that JLI 859 had not been appropriated to the contract; and that, accordingly, the property in JLI 859 had not become vested in Fr Mackin. Since Fr Mackin was not the owner, he had no insurable interest in the car JLI 859 at the time of the accident, and, as Mr Mahon was not his servant or agent, there could be no question of making Fr Mackin liable personally (or the respondent insurers under the policy) for the judgment given against Mr Mahon. That judgment could be executed only against Mr Mahon; but unfortunately, he had no insurance covering his driving and he was unable to satisfy the amount of Flynn's judgment.

Because the judgment creditor, Mr Flynn, has not been able to recover the amount of his judgment from the judgment debtor, Mr Mahon, a dispute has arisen between the appellant Bureau and the respondent insurers as to which of them should bear the cost of satisfying the judgment. The dispute has arisen in this way. Mr Flynn's judgment was satisfied by the appellant Bureau pursuant to an agreement dated the 30th December, 1964, and made between the Minister for Local Government and the appellant. The appellant now seeks to recover from the respondent the sum so paid in satisfaction of the judgment and does so pursuant to the terms of an agreement (the domestic agreement) dated the 16th December, 1966, and made between the appellant Bureau of the one part and, of the other part, each of those insurance companies (including the respondent insurers) and members of the underwriting syndicates at Lloyds who transact the business of compulsory motor-vehicle insurance in the Republic of Ireland. In that domestic agreement it is provided that, if judgment is obtained against any person in respect of a Road Traffic Act liability and the appellant Bureau satisfies that judgment, the appellant shall be entitled to recover from "the insurer concerned" the sum paid to satisfy the judgment.

The judgment obtained by Peter Flynn is in the category to which those

---

[39] [1974] I.R. 101.
[40] *Ibid.*

provisions of the domestic agreement refer. It is the contention of the respondent insurers that they do not fall within the expression "the insurer concerned" as it is used in the domestic agreement and that, accordingly, they are not obliged to repay the appellant. The appellant disagrees and says that, in the agreed (or established) circumstances of this case, the respondent insurers should be held to come within the true ambit of the expression "the insurer concerned". The domestic agreement contains a provision that such a dispute may be sent to arbitration. The parties to this appeal have had recourse to that provision. They chose an arbitrator and invested him with the powers of an arbitrator under the Arbitration Act, 1954. The arbitrator found that the respondent insurers were "the insurer concerned" but he stated his award in the form of a special case under s. 35 of the Arbitration Act, 1954, for the decision of the High Court.

In the High Court the judge differed from the arbitrator and held that the respondent insurers were not "the insurer concerned". The judge was of the opinion that an insurance company could be "the insurer concerned" only if, at the date of the accident, it is providing insurance in respect of the liability of the user or some other person who would be liable for injury to person caused by the negligent use of the vehicle at the time by the user; he held that the insured must either be the user of the vehicle or have an interest in the vehicle and that the respondent insurers, not being in either category, were not "the insurer concerned". It is from that decision that this appeal has been taken by the appellant.

It is agreed that the result of this appeal will depend on the answer to a pure question of law, *viz.*, are the respondent insurers "the insurer concerned" in the sense in which the expression is used in the domestic agreement?

The domestic agreement, as its recitals show, was entered into for the purpose of implementing (in accordance with the articles of association of the appellant Bureau) the agreement of the 30th December, 1964, between the Minister for Local Government and the appellant Bureau. That agreement imposed, in certain circumstances, liability on the appellant for injury to person such as is required to be covered by an approved policy of insurance under s. 56 of the Road Traffic Act, 1961. One of the primary purposes of the domestic agreement is to enable the appellant to transfer that liability to an individual insurer in certain circumstances, if the individual insurer was "the insurer concerned".

It is common ground that, under the domestic agreement, the respondent insurers are liable to pay the appellant the sum claimed, if the respondents are captured by the definition of "the insurer concerned" in the domestic agreement. That definition commences with the following general statement:—

> "The insurer concerned means the insurer who at the time of the accident which gave rise to the Road Traffic Act liability was providing any insurance against such liability in respect of the vehicle arising out of the use of which the liability of the judgment debtor was incurred...."

Even if the definition stopped there, I think it would have to be held that the respondent insurers are captured by it because, at the time of the accident, they were providing (within the limitations of the policy) insurance against Road Traffic Act liability in respect of the car JLI 859.

Consider the position that had arisen. By mutual agreement, Fr Mackin's insurance in respect of his old car had been terminated. That contract of insurance had come to an end, so that the old car was uninsured against Road Traffic Act liability. Instead, a new or varied contract of insurance had been made whereby the respondent insurers had agreed with Fr Mackin that they would insure him against Road Traffic Act liability in respect of the car JLI 859 on the same terms as they had given in the defunct insurance in respect of the old car. Therefore, at the time of the accident there was a valid subsisting insurance of JLI 859. In fact, as the arbitrator has found, the respondent insurers had issued to Fr Mackin a certificate of insurance in respect of that insurance. Because it was an indemnity insurance, and because it is of the essence of an indemnity insurance that the insured cannot claim a benefit under the indemnity unless he has an insurable interest arising out of the event in question, it must be held that the then current policy of insurance in respect of the car JLI 859 was subject to an implied term that the indemnity under the policy could not be claimed until the insured acquired an insurable interest in that car.

Since an insurance of a motor vehicle is an insurance of "goods" within the meaning of s. 4 of the Life Assurance Act, 1774, and is, therefore, excluded from the requirement in that Act that the insured must have an insurable interest at the time entering into the contract (see *Williams* v. *Baltic Insurance Association of London Ltd.*[41]), the fact that Fr Mackin had no insurable interest in JLI 859 when he entered into the contract did not make the insurance illegal.

It is true that at the time of the accident the insurance was ineffective, for want of insurable interest under the policy, to provide cover against Road Traffic Act liability; but that is a different thing from saying that the respondent insurers were not "providing any insurance" against Road Traffic Act liability at the time of the accident. They *were* providing such insurance, but the right of the insured to claim indemnity under it was in abeyance, or suspended, until he acquired an insurable interest in the vehicle in question. It is to be noted that the definition speaks of "providing any insurance" and not of "providing any insurance which is currently effective to give cover" or the like. Indeed, the definition clause goes on to provide expressly that, in certain specified cases, insurers will come within the definition of "the insurer concerned" notwithstanding that the insurance in question could not be providing cover which is currently valid — for example, where the policy had become void, or was void ab initio.

The decision of this Court in *Motor Insurers' Bureau of Ireland* v. *Eclipse Motor Policies at Lloyds*[42] is an example of a case where the insurer was held to be "the insurer concerned" notwithstanding that cover under the policy had been suspended. The essential facts were these. The insured had taken out an approved policy under the Road Traffic Act with the insurer, the insured

---

[41] [1924] 2 K.B. 282.
[42] Unreported. Supreme Court 23/5/73.

failed to pay the full amount of the premium and, when payment was requested, his wife (as his agent) requested that the policy be allowed to lapse.

At the time of the accident giving rise to the judgment debt, the insurer, in
compliance with that request, had suspended the insurance so that there was
no cover under the policy. The insurer had also arranged that the amount of
the premium which the insured might have reclaimed as a result of the suspension of the insurance would be held in credit against the renewal of the
policy. As the policy had not been cancelled but only suspended, it was held
that the insurer was "the insurer concerned" because there had been an existing policy of insurance against the Road Traffic Act liability and so the
insurer could be said to have been providing insurance against that liability.

Here the case for deeming the respondent insurers to be "the insurer concerned" is, if anything, more cogent. They had issued a policy of insurance
against Road Traffic Act liability to the insured Fr Mackin, in respect of the
vehicle in question. Insurance cover against that liability was not effective at
the time of the accident because it was an implied term that, before the insured could acquire any right of indemnity under the policy, he must first
acquire an insurable interest in the vehicle in question; and he had not done
so. But, no less than in the *Eclipse Case*[43] there was a valid policy in existence
and its operation as an indemnity against Road Traffic Act liability was but
suspended pending the acquisition by the insured of an insurable interest.
Subject to that suspension, the policy was a valid subsisting policy. Unlike the
Eclipse Case,[44] the activation of the insured's right of indemnity under the
policy did not require to be negotiated or agreed. All the insured had to do in
order to get the full benefit of that indemnity was the unilateral act of acquiring ownership of the vehicle.

Therefore, I find it impossible to hold that at the time of the accident the
respondent insurers were not "providing any insurance" against Road Traffic
Act liability in respect of the vehicle in question.

Any lingering doubt one might harbour about the correctness of that conclusion seems to me to be dispelled by another provision of the definition
clause in the domestic agreement. It stipulates that:—

> "An insurer is concerned within the meaning of this agreement notwith-
> standing that ... (ii) some term, description, limitation, exception or condi-
> tion (whether express or implied) of the insurance or of the proposal form on
> which it is based expressly or by implication excludes the insurer's liability
> whether generally or in the particular circumstances in which the judgment
> debtor's liability was incurred".

That clarification or extension of the general definition of "the insurer
concerned" seems to me to envisage circumstances such as those of this case.
As I have pointed out (and as was noted by this Court at p. 108 of the report
of *Flynn* v. *Mackin*[45]), at the time of the accident the insurance against Road
Traffic Act liability had been transferred by Fr Mackin to the car JLI 859.

---

[43] Unreported. Supreme Court 23/5/73.
[44] *Ibid.*
[45] [1974] I.R. 101.

However, that insurance, by necessary implication, contained the proviso that, before Fr Mackin could claim any benefit under the policy, he would have acquired an insurable interest in JLI 859. As he had not done so, there resulted an exclusion of the insurer's liability under the policy. The implied proviso resulting in that exclusion comes within the description of "some term, description, limitation, exception or condition (whether express or implied) of the insurance" which "excludes the insurer's liability ... in the particular circumstances in which the judgment debtor's liability was incurred." It clearly follows, therefore, from that particular part of the definition clause that the respondent insurers are "the insurer concerned".

Accordingly, I would allow this appeal and restore the finding of the arbitrator that the respondent insurers are "the insurer concerned" under the domestic agreement in respect of the judgment debt in question.

KENNY J (DISSENTING): The facts from which this dispute arises have been dealt with fully in the judgment of Mr Justice Walsh in *Flynn* v. *Mackin*[46] and by the High Court judge in this case so I need not repeat them in detail. For the purposes of this appeal they are:—

1. The property in the car JLI 859 never passed to Fr Mackin.
2. He never had ownership, possession, custody or control of it.
3. He had a policy of motor insurance against Road Traffic Act liability with the respondent insurers in respect of another car.
4. Shortly before the accident he had arranged with them that the cover given by the policy mentioned at No. 3, *supra*, would be transferred to the car JLI 859.
5. At the time of the accident on the 25th October, 1969, Mr Mahon was the owner of the car JLI 859 and was driving it; he was not insured in respect of it and was not driving it as the servant, or with the consent, of Fr Mackin.
6. Judgment was subsequently recovered by the injured person against Mr Mahon (but not against Fr Mackin) for personal injuries arising out of the accident.

The dispute now before us arises out of the interpretation of an agreement of the 16th December, 1966, between the appellant Bureau and the companies and syndicates carrying on motor insurance business in the Republic of Ireland (including the respondent insurers). That agreement has been referred to as "the domestic agreement". Section 78 of the Road Traffic Act, 1961, prevented any company or syndicate from carrying on motor insurance business in the Republic unless they were members of the appellant Bureau and had undertaken that they would deal with third-party claims in respect of mechanically propelled vehicles insured by them on terms similar to those from time to time agreed between the Minister for the Environment and the Bureau. The domestic agreement expressed the way in which the obligations arising out of the agreement with the Minister were to be shared out between the insurance companies and the syndicates.

The net question in dispute is whether the respondent insurers are "the

---

[46] [1974] I.R. 101.

insurer concerned" as that expression is defined in the domestic agreement. That definition, so far as relevant, reads:—

> "'The insurer concerned' means the insurer who at the time of the accident which gave rise to the Road Traffic Act liability was providing any insurance against such liability in respect of the vehicle arising out of the use of which the liability of the judgment debtor was incurred. An insurer is concerned within the meaning of this agreement notwithstanding that ... (iii) the judgment debtor was in unauthorised possession of the vehicle arising out of the use of which the liability of the judgment debtor was incurred."

That definition contains the term "Road Traffic Act liability" which is defined in the domestic agreement in these words:—

> "'Road Traffic Act liability' means such liability for injury to person ... as is required to be covered by an approved policy of insurance under section 56 of the Act." "The Act" is defined as meaning the Road Traffic Act, 1961.

Section 56 of the Road Traffic Act, 1961, so far as relevant, provides that a person shall not use in a public place a mechanically propelled vehicle unless a vehicle insurer would be liable for injury caused by the negligent use of the vehicle by a person using it, or there is in force at the time of the accident a policy of insurance whereby he, or some other person who would be liable for injury caused by the negligent use of the vehicle, is insured against all sums which the person using the vehicle or some other person would become liable to pay to any person as damages or costs on account of injury to persons or property caused by the negligent use of the vehicle at that time by the person using it. The reference to the liability of another person is to s. 118 of the Act of 1961 under which a person who uses a motor vehicle with the consent of the owner is deemed to be using it as the servant of the owner, with the result that the owner and his insurance company have to pay claims arising from the user's liability to third persons.

Undoubtedly, an insurance policy which had been issued by the respondent insurers in connection with the vehicle JLI 859 was in existence when the accident happened; but the person insured under that policy (Fr Mackin) was not liable in respect of the injuries caused by the accident. He had no Road Traffic Act liability in respect of vehicle JLI 859 until he became the owner of it or had possession of it. The respondent insurers were not providing insurance against the Road Traffic Act liability of Mr Mahon when he was driving it, and he was not Fr Mackin's servant or agent. The fact that there is a policy in force in relation to a car at the time of an accident does not mean that the insurance company which issued the policy is automatically "the insurer concerned" as that term is defined by the domestic agreement. The policy must be one which provides insurance to the insured, or those using the vehicle with his consent, against Road Traffic Act liability. Fr Mackin had no Road Traffic Act liability in respect of the car JLI 859 at the time of the accident. I should add that Mr Mahon was not in unauthorised possession of that car at the time of the accident as he was then the owner of it. It seems to me that "such liability" in the definition in the domestic agreement refers to Road Traffic Act liability and that at the time of the accident the respondent insurers were not providing insurance against that liability in respect of the car.

Counsel for the appellant Bureau placed strong reliance on the decision of this Court in *Motor Insurers' Bureau of Ireland* v. *Eclipse Motor Policies at Lloyds.*[47] In that case an owner of a motor bicycle had taken out a policy of motor insurance which, because of non-payment of the premium, was subsequently suspended but was not cancelled. The question was whether the insurance syndicate were "the insurer concerned" within the meaning of the domestic agreement. There was no issue in that case as to whether the policy provided insurance against the owner's Road Traffic Act liability because it undoubtedly did. The question was whether the fact that the policy was not in force at the time of the accident had the effect that the syndicate were not "the insurer concerned". The language used by any judge must always be related to, and interpreted by reference to the problem which he is dealing with; a sentence in his judgment which seems to be of wider application is not to be read as a statement of general principle unless the judge is attempting to state one. The whole of Mr Justice Walsh's judgment relates to the facts which he was dealing with; it does not lay down any general proposition.

In my opinion, the respondent insurers were not "the insurer concerned" for the purposes of the domestic agreement and the answer to question (f) in the arbitrator's award should be "No". As the arbitrator gave the costs of the reference to the appellant Bureau because it succeeded before him, I would refer the Case back to him to amend his award as to costs. I would give the costs in the High Court and in this Court to the respondent insurers.

PARKE J: I have had the opportunity of reading the judgment of Mr Justice Henchy with which I am in complete agreement. The facts are so fully set out in that judgment that I will confine myself to referring only to such of them as appear to be essential to resolve the issue which arises.

The issue to be decided is whether the respondent insurers are "the insurer concerned" within the meaning of the agreement dated the 16th December, 1966, (the domestic agreement) so as to make them liable to recoup the appellant Bureau for the sum expended by the Bureau in satisfying the judgment recovered by the plaintiff in *Flynn* v. *Mackin.*[48]

The expression "the insurer concerned" is defined by clause 4(a) of the domestic agreement. The definition commences with the following statement:

> "'The insurer concerned' means the insurer who at the time of the accident which gave rise to the Road Traffic Act liability was providing any insurance against such liability in respect of the vehicle arising out of the use of which the liability of the judgment debtor was incurred...."

The clause goes on to provide that an insurer "is concerned" notwithstanding that (inter alia):—

> "(ii) some term, description, limitation, exception or condition (whether express or implied) of the insurance or of the proposal form on which it is

---

[47] Unreported. Supreme Court 23/5/1973.
[48] [1974] I.R. 101.

based expressly or by implication excludes the insurer's liability whether generally or in the particular circumstances in which the judgment debtor's liability was incurred."

No other portion of the definition clause appears to be relevant. Having regard to that definition, I consider the salient facts to be:—

1. The respondent insurers issued to Fr Mackin, prior to the accident, a certificate of insurance against Road Traffic Act liability in respect of motor car JLI 859; that insurance was neither cancelled nor suspended by the respondents.
2. Motor car JLI 859 was the vehicle arising out of the use of which the judgment debtor's liability was incurred.
3. At the time of the accident, no property in the car had passed to Fr Mackin and, therefore, he had no insurable interest in the car at the time.

The respondent insurers rely upon the foregoing circumstances to relieve them of liability. They contended that, as Fr Mackin was without an insurable interest and could not have claimed indemnity under the policy, they are excluded from the scope of the definition of "the insurer concerned" contained in the domestic agreement. I do not consider that contention to be correct.

The opening statement of the definition which I have quoted says in express terms that the insurer concerned is one who, at the time of the accident, was providing insurance against Road Traffic Act liability in respect of the relevant vehicle. That is not qualified by any reference to any exclusion arising because of a disability on the part of the insured person to claim the benefit of the indemnity. The definition could have been so qualified by a later provision in the clause; not only was that not done but sub-clause (ii) —which I have also quoted — seems to make it clear that the insurer is still captured by the definition even if for some reason the insured person cannot claim indemnity. It might well have been designed to cover (inter alia) just such a case as the present one.

This view seems to be amply supported by the decision of this Court in *Motor Insurers' Bureau of Ireland* v. *Eclipse Motor Policies at Lloyds.*[49] In that case the insurers, at the request of the insured person's agent, suspended his policy so that, when a claim for Road Traffic liability arose, there was no insurance cover available to the policy holder. As in the present case, it was contended that in such circumstances the insurance company was excluded from the definition of "the insurer concerned" but that submission was rejected by Mr Justice Walsh who, in the course of his judgment, said:—

> "However, the particular wording of the domestic agreement does not so confine the phrase. Inasmuch as there was a policy of insurance in being in respect of this liability though not in force at the time, the insurers can be said in a general way to have been providing insurance against such liability as distinct from the more particular requirements of the Road Traffic Act."

It seems to me that in the context the words "though not in force" used by

---

[49] Unreported. Supreme Court 23/5/73.

Mr Justice Walsh may be equated to the expression "not enforceable" which would be apt in the present case.

Therefore, I would allow the appeal and affirm the arbitrator's finding that the respondent insurers are "the insurer concerned" within the meaning of the domestic agreement in respect of the judgment debtor's liability.

O'Leary *v.* The Irish National Insurance Company Ltd.
[1958] Ir. Jur. Rep. 1
The High Court

BUDD J: On the 21st November 1955 the plaintiff was travelling in her husband's motor car which was proceeding down the main street of Bandon. A motor car driven by one Andrew Murphy at a very fast rate of speed narrowly avoided colliding with the car in which the plaintiff was seated. She was at the time pregnant, and stated in her evidence that she got a terrible shock and felt wretched after the accident. She was later taken ill and delivered of a dead child. Dr Callanan who attended her stated that the condition of her foetus indicated that it would have been dead around the time of the incident. The inference, he said was that the death occurred as the result of the fright which the plaintiff sustained. The plaintiff was ill for some time afterwards and was put to expense in connection with medical attention and her stay in a nursing home. The defendants, the Irish National Insurance Co. Ltd., took up the attitude at the hearing that they were not much concerned with the circumstances of the accident, as they denied liability to the plaintiff on grounds which I shall deal with later. No evidence was therefore presented on behalf of the defendants in connection with the actual incident and its results to the plaintiff. On the facts as they were proved before me I am satisfied that the plaintiff suffered injury and damage as a result of the negligent driving of the motor car driven by Andrew Murphy but the real question I have to determine is as to whether or not the defendants are liable to pay to the plaintiff the damages that she has sustained.

The plaintiff first issued a civil bill against Andrew Murphy the driver of the car. Her solicitors were apparently unable to serve that civil bill and later an application was made to the Circuit Court for liberty to institute proceedings against the present defendants as insurers of the motor car in question in lieu of against the driver, pursuant to sub-section (I)(d) of section 78 of the Road Traffic Act, 1933. The order made by the learned Circuit Court Judge dated the 2nd October, 1956, however, ordered that the Irish National Insurance Co. Ltd. be added as defendants in the proceedings. Having been served with the civil bill they duly entered a defence and the first plea therein is a denial that the Company were the insurers of Andrew Murphy on the date of the accident or on any other date. The action came on for hearing in the Circuit Court and by order dated the 27th February, 1957 Andrew Murphy was struck out as defendant and the proceedings as against the Irish National Insurance Co. Ltd. were dismissed with costs. From so much of that order as dismissed the proceedings against the present defendants the plaintiff appealed.

In the course of the hearing certain evidence was given relating to the ownership of the car involved in the incident, a Skoda, registration No. ZK 3265 and I find as a fact that it was the property of the driver Andrew Murphy.

Prior to the incident giving rise to the plaintiff's illness with its sad results for her, Stephen Murphy, father of Andrew Murphy had taken out a policy of insurance with the defendants, the Irish National Insurance Co. Ltd., which on the face of it indemnified him and any person driving with his consent against third party claims arising out of the driving of the vehicle described in the schedule to the policy, which was the Skoda motor car involved in the incident. But Stephen Murphy, as I find, never owned that motor car and in effect attempted to enter into a contract of insurance insuring himself against third party claims arising in respect of the driving of a motor car which he did not own. He never even drove the car himself but he stated in his evidence that his son Andrew always drove the car with his consent.

The policy in question, No. 9/184883, ran for the period of a year from the 12th September 1955 and was thus current at the time of the incident. It follows the general lines of a third party motor policy. The proposal and declaration of Stephen Murphy are deemed to be incorporated therein and in the proposal form Stephen Murphy is described as the owner of the Skoda motor car ZK 3265, also described in the schedule to the policy, wherein the horse power and the date of manufacture of the care are also set out. Under the terms of the policy the defendant company agree to indemnify the insured against all sums which he or his personal representatives shall become liable to pay to any person (other than certain excepted persons of whom the plaintiff is not one) by way of damages or costs on account of injury to person or property occasioned by, through or in connection with any vehicle described in the schedule. At the date of the incident the Skoda car was the only car mentioned in the schedule. Subject to the limitations of the indemnity granted by the policy to the insured and its terms, the defendant company also agreed to indemnify any driver described in such schedule subject to certain provisos not relevant to consider. Under the heading "Description of Drivers" in the schedule there appears *inter alia*: "(b) Any person who is driving on the Insured's order or with his consent the vehicle bearing the Index Mark and Registration number stated above".

The defendants relied in the first instance on two technical points relating to matters of procedure. They contend that the learned Circuit Court Judge had no jurisdiction to add the Irish National Insurance Co. Ltd. as defendants under the provisions of section 78 (1) (d) of the Road Traffic Act, 1933, and that his order was consequently a nullity because, in the first place there was no proper evidence before the Court that the driver of the car was not in Ireland at the time of the application, and, secondly, because the section does not empower the Court to add or join a defendant as was done in this case but only to give leave to a claimant to institute proceedings against the vehicle insurer in lieu of the owner or driver as the case may be. With regard to the first point I am against the defendants' contention because it seems to me that the learned Judge might on the evidence before him have based his order on another ground provided for in the section namely that the driver could not be served with the process. The second contention is in my view technically correct. Since however the defendants entered a defence to the proceedings and appeared and defended the proceedings both before the Circuit Court and before me it seems possible that a further difficult question of estoppel may arise and I prefer accordingly to base my judgment on what I regard as a more substantial ground.

Apart from the technical point the first submission that the defendants made was that they never insured Andrew Murphy and as a consequence they contended that they were never liable to indemnify him in respect of claims by third parties, including the plaintiff, either at common law or by virtue of the provisions of the Road Traffic Act, 1933. In common parlance they were never "on risk". They say that the only basis on which they could be made liable would be if there existed a valid contract of insurance under which they were bound to indemnify Andrew Murphy in respect of the plaintiff's claim. The plaintiff on the other hand contends that a valid policy was issued to Stephen Murphy by the defendant company and under its terms the driving of Andrew Murphy was covered as a person driving with the insured person's consent. It was submitted that the extension clause provides for the indemnity and cover of a person driving the scheduled car against third party claims when driving with the "insured's" consent and not with the "owner's" consent. It was argued that even though Stephen Murphy was not the owner of the car the policy was nevertheless issued to him and a premium paid thereunder, and, that, since Andrew Murphy was driving with his consent the car mentioned in the schedule, his driving of that car was legally covered under the terms of the contract. The argument must come to this, that, if a person takes out the policy purporting to cover the driving by himself or by others with his permission of a certain car which he does not own, that fact being unknown to the insurers, such other person in so driving that car with his consent is entitled in law to be indemnified under the terms of the policy and therefore that a person in the position of the plaintiff here is entitled to recover against the insurers direct under the provisions of the Road Traffic Act, 1933, section 78.

Section 78 of the Road Traffic Act, 1933, has undoubtedly altered the law by allowing an injured third party to proceed directly against the insurers or indemnifiers of the owner or driver of a motor car liable to the third party. Moreover, the insurer is not entitled to plead any invalidity of the policy arising out of the fraud, misrepresentation of false statement to which the claimant was not party or privy , which, if a misdemeanour under the Act, was not the subject of a prosecution and conviction. It is also, however, apparent from the wording of the section that the third party, therein referred to as the claimant, can only recover, as one would in all common sense suppose, against a person bound to indemnify the owner or driver respectively against whom the claim in the first instance arises. The latter portion of sub-section (1) (d) of section 78 provides that in the proceedings permitted to be taken against the vehicle insurers the claimant is to be entitled to recover therein from the vehicle insurers any sum which he would be entitled to recover from the owner or driver "the payment of which the insurer ... has insured". I omit reference to vehicle guarantors for clarity sake. The question then is, was Andrew Murphy insured under the policy against the claims of

third parties, including the plaintiff, arising out of his driving of the motor car in question?

The cardinal fact to be borne in mind in connection with the issues I am dealing with is that Stephen Murphy, the person supposedly in contractual relationship with the defendant Company, was not the owner, and never was the owner, of the Skoda motor car mentioned in the policy, which was at all relevant times the property of his son Andrew Murphy. I have in the first instance to determine what effect had these facts on the validity of the policy and the existence of any contract of insurance and indemnity on the part of the defendants. The House of Lords decision in *Rogerson* v. *Scottish Automobile and General Insurance Co. Ltd.*[50] seems to me very relevant in principle to the point at issue although the facts are not quite the same. The defendant company contracted under a policy of insurance to indemnify the plaintiff against all sums which he should become liable to pay for bodily injury caused to any person by a motor car described in the schedule to the policy. The policy also provided that the insurance should cover the liability of the insured in respect of the use by him of any motor car being used instead of the insured car. He purchased a new car in part exchange. Before any transfer of insurance was arranged he met with an accident while driving the new car, causing injury to a third party who brought an action against him claiming damages. The defendants repudiated liability and the plaintiff thereupon instituted proceedings against them claiming a declaration that they were bound to indemnify him. The plaintiff's contention was that the motor he was using was one covered by the words in the policy "any car ... being used instead of the insured car" and that an accident caused by it was an accident the liability in respect of which was covered by the policy. "That" said Lord Buckmaster in the course of his speech, agreed with by the other learned Law Lords sitting, "is not my view of the matter. To me this policy depends upon the hypothesis that there is in fact an insured car. When once the car which is the subject matter of this policy is sold, the owner's rights in respect of it cease and the policy so far as the car is concerned is at an end." Admittedly there is a distinction on the facts in that, in the present case, instead of parting with the car mentioned in the policy, Stephen Murphy never owned the car, and furthermore the plaintiff's counsel contend that the extension clause relating to drivers driving with the consent of the insured provides them with a valid basis of claim.

The decisions in three other cases to which I am about to refer seem to me to clarify the law relative to the circumstance which I have to deal with in this case. Goddard J. (as he then was), had to deal, in *Tattersall* v. *Drysdale*,[51] *inter alia,* with the liability of insurers under an extension clause where the insured owner had parted with the motor car mentioned in the policy. The extension clause dealt with was one extending the indemnity to the assured against third party risks "whilst personally driving for private purposes any other private motor car ... not belonging to the assured in respect of which no indemnity is afforded the insured by any other insurance applying to such

---

[50] (1931) 146 L.T. 26.
[51] [1935] 2 K.B. 174 and [1935] All E.R. Rep. 112.

car", provided that the car insured by the policy should not be in use at the same time. The plaintiff traded in his motor car, covered by the policy containing the above extension clause, in exchange for a car to be supplied to him by a company of motor car dealers. He then obtained a loan of another car from a director of the company to whom he had traded in his own car pending the arrival of the new car. The borrowed car was covered by a policy issued to the director mentioned, one Mr Gilling, and also contained an extension clause indemnifying a person driving the insured car with the assured's permission provided that such person was not indemnified under any other policy. While driving that car the plaintiff was involved in an accident and damages were later recovered against him. The plaintiff sued one of the underwriters who had issued the latter policy to Mr Gilling, claiming a declaration that the underwriter was bound to indemnify him under the extension clause. One of the issues was as to whether or not the plaintiff's own policy was in force at the time having regard to the terms of the proviso in the policy sued on. Referring to *Rogerson's Case*,[52] Goddard J. said that the decisive factor, in his view, in the House of Lords' decision above referred to was that the subject matter of the insurance was the specified car and that as the assured had parted with it he no longer was interested in the policy. "The true view" he said "in my judgment, is that the policy insures the assured in respect of the ownership and user of a particular car, the premium being calculated, as was found in *Rogerson's Case*,[53] partly on value and partly on horse power. It gives the assured by the extension clause a privilege or further protection while using another car temporarily, but it is the scheduled car which is always the subject of the insurance". He went on to say that to construe the policy otherwise would be to hold in effect that two distinct insurances were granted, one in respect of the scheduled car, and another wholly irrespective of the ownership of any car. He concluded his observations by saying "It may be that a person who does not own a car can get a policy which would insure him against third party risks whenever he happens to be driving a car belonging to someone else; but the clause I am considering is expressly stated to be an extension clause, that is, extending the benefits of the policy and accordingly if the insured ceases to be interested in the subject matter of the insurance the extension falls with the rest of the policy". In the result he held that the plaintiff was not covered by his own policy and the learned judge then proceeded to consider the liability of the underwriter insuring Mr Gilling. An important issue as to the right of the plaintiff to sue under the extension clause in Mr Gilling's policy by virtue of the provisions of the English Road Traffic Act, 1930, section 36 subsection 4 was also dealt with but I am not concerned with that aspect of the case at the moment.

I now turn to deal with another decision of the same learned judge, now Lord Chief Justice of England, namely *Peters* v. *General Accident, Fire and Life Insurance Corporation, Ltd.*[54] The relevant facts of the case are these. A certain Mr Comber was the owner of an Austin van which was insured under

---

[52] [1931] 146 L.T. 26.
[53] *Ibid.*
[54] [1937] 4 All E.R. 628.

a policy issued by the defendants. Mr Comber sold his van to a Mr Pope. The entire purchase money was not paid but it was held that the property in the car passed to Mr Pope. Pope was involved in an accident with the plaintiff while driving the van and the plaintiff recovered damages against him. The plaintiff brought an action against the defendant insurance company under the provisions of section 10 of the English Road Traffic Act, 1934. That section, like section 78 of our own Act, provides for the recovery of damages from an insurer after judgment has been obtained against an insured person. It is to be noted that the right is given "notwithstanding that the insurer may be entitled to avoid or cancel or may have avoided or cancelled the policy". The policy itself was handed by Comber to Pope at the time of the sale. The policy contained an extension clause whereby the insurance company agreed to treat as the policy holder any person driving the van with the policy holder's permission. Following *Rogerson's Case*[55] and his own decision in *Tattersall* v. *Drysdale*[56] Goddard J. held that the policy had lapsed when Comber parted with the van. Dealing with the extension clause which the plaintiff claimed to be entitled to succeed under, on the basis that Pope was driving with Comber's permission, Goddard J. pointed out that he had held in *Tattersall's Case* that the extension clause went with the rest of the policy. Having referred to the terms of the extension clause in Comber's policy he went on to say that in order to bring himself within the English Road Traffic Act, 1934, section 10, the plaintiff must show that he had got judgment against an insured person. He had already held in *Tattersall* v. *Drysdale*[57] that people driving with the consent of the assured were, under the provisions of the English Road Traffic Act, 1930, persons insured under the policy because of the provisions of that Act providing that insurers were to indemnify the persons or class of persons mentioned in the policy. "Can it be said here", however, he proceeds, "by any stretch of the imagination that Mr Pope was driving by the order or with the permission of Mr Comber. It seems to me that it is quite impossible to say that. He bought the car. It was his own car and he was driving his own car, not by Mr Comber's permission and certainly not under his order". He accordingly held that when Comber sold the car his insurance on that car lapsed and that there was then no insurance and that it was quite impossible to say that a person who is driving his own car, which he had bought and the property in which was in him, was driving with the permission or on the order of the person who sold the car. Accordingly, the plaintiff failed to recover on either ground against the insurance company.

The cases so far dealt with are cases where the property in the car insured had been parted with and the policy had lapsed so that no insurance existed. Is there any difference in principle where the person alleged to be insured in fact never owned the car at all? If there is I find difficulty in seeing what it could be and I am entirely supported in that view by the decision of Branson J. in *Zürich General Accident Co.* v. *Buck*.[58] The relevant facts in that case

---

[55] (1931) 146 L.T. 26.
[56] [1935] 2 K.B. 174 and [1935] All E.R. Rep. 112.
[57] *Ibid.*
[58] [1939] 64 L.l.L.R. 115.

were these. One H.A. Buck advanced the purchase price of a motor van to his brother W.E. Buck. W.E. Buck then purchased a motor van for use in his business and drove it himself. A third party policy was taken out in the name of H.A. Buck. W.E. Buck while driving the van was involved in an accident. The insurance company later brought proceedings for a declaration that they were entitled to avoid the policy. Branson J. at p. 119 said "It is quite plain on the evidence that the van was the brother's van, was to be used in the brother's business and that H.A. Buck had nothing whatever to do with it. This is a third party risks policy and there is no way in which any third party injured by this vehicle, while it was being driven by W.E. Buck, could possibly have any claim against H.A. Buck, and therefore H.A. Buck had no insurable interest at all in the matter in respect of which this policy was issued. For that reason again, the policy is valueless."

From the cases to which I have referred it would seem to me that the following legal propositions can be deduced or logically follow. (1) When an insured person parts with a motor car, the subject matter of his policy of insurance, the policy is at an end and with it goes the indemnification provided for by the policy. (2) An extension clause purporting to insure the driving of the insured car by another person with the owner's consent falls with the rest of the policy. (3) If a person purports to take out a policy of insurance in respect of a certain car, of which he is not in fact the owner, it being represented or understood that he is the owner, no valid contract of insurance ever comes into operation for want of subject matter and lack of insurable interest and no extension clause can ever come into valid operation. (4) A person driving his own car requires no one's permission to drive it and consequently cannot be said to be driving with an insured person's consent so as to bring him within the indemnity of a policy containing an extension clause covering the driving of the scheduled car with the insured's permission. (5) The terms of the English Road Traffic Act, 1934, entitling a third party in certain circumstances to recover the amount of a judgment obtained against the driver of a car, apparently covered by a policy of insurance against the insurers direct, notwithstanding that the insurers may be entitled to avoid or cancel the policy, will not assist a third party to recover if in fact there has never been a valid contract of insurance in existence or if it has lapsed.

The decisions I have referred to are not of course binding upon me, but with respect, I agree with the reasoning underlying them and with the decisions themselves. Applying the principles which I have said I feel may be validly deduced from them it would seem to me in the first place that there never was any valid contract of insurance between Stephen Murphy and the defendant insurance company. It follows that the extension clause relied on never came into operation. Even if it had, the facts do not bring Andrew Murphy's driving on the date in question within the terms of the clause since he could not be said to have driven his own car with his father's permission within the meaning of the terms of the clause. Furthermore the terms of section 78 of the Road Traffic Act, preventing the insurers of a car from relying on the invalidity of a policy, as against a third party claiming directly against them, are of no more avail to the plaintiff here than were the somewhat similar words of the English Road Traffic Act of 1934 to the plaintiff in *Peters' Case*,[59] since there never was, in my view, any valid contract of insurance between Stephen Murphy and the defendant company and the defendant company were never insurers of the car or of the driver of the car within the meaning of the section. Accordingly the plaintiff fails in her claim against the defendant company and the proceedings must be dismissed.

There is one other matter which I must refer to before concluding my judgment in deference to the able argument of the defendant's counsel on the point. It was decided in *Vandepitte* v. *Preferred Accident Insurance Corporation of New York*[60] that the type of extension clause I have been dealing with conferred no rights on a person driving with the insured's permission unless there was an intention on the part of the insured to create a trust for such person or unless the insured was acting with the privity of such person so as to be contracting on his own behalf. The decision was one of the Privy Council on appeal from the Canadian courts and the provision of the English Road Traffic Act did not apply. Goddard J. in *Tattersall* v. *Drysdale*[61] held, however, that the effect of section 36 (4) of the English Road Traffic Act, 1930, was to confer a right of action on such a person against the insurers. That section provides that "notwithstanding anything in any enactment a person issuing a policy of insurance under this section shall be liable to indemnify the person or class of persons specified in the policy in respect of any liability which this policy purports to cover in the case of these persons or classes of persons". The enactment particularly referred to in the view of Goddard J. was the Life Assurance Act, 1774 dealing with insurable interest. Mr Fitzgerald says that since there is no similar enactment operating here such persons cannot recover against insurers unless they can show that there was an intention on the part of the insured to create a trust for them or unless the assured was acting with their privity and consent. The evidence he says does not show that Stephen Murphy acted with the required intent or with his son's consent. On the other hand it was held in *Williams* v. *Baltic Insurance Association of London Ltd.*,[62] as I follow the decision, that the Life Assurance Act, 1774 did not apply to a case of motor insurance. Furthermore, section 78 of the Road Traffic Act, 1933 may be said on its face to confer a right of action on third parties against insurance companies and it might be held to have the same effect as section 35 (4) of the English Act. I say no more than that the argument seems open. Mr Fitzgerald's contention involves far reaching results to persons seeking to assert third party claims against insurance companies. Having regard to the conclusion I have already come to it is unnecessary for me to express a view on that point and I prefer to leave this particular matter open for future argument and decision.

---

[59] [1937] 4 All E.R. 628.
[60] [1933] A.C. 70.
[61] [1935] 2 K.B. 174 and [1935] All E.R. Rep. 112.
[62] [1924] 2 K.B. 282.

Macaura v. The Northern Assurance Co., Ltd., and Others*
(1925) 59 I.L.T.R. 45
The House of Lords

BUCKMASTER L.J: My Lords, the appellant is the owner of the Killymoon estate in the County of Tyrone. The respondents are five insurance companies with whom at various dates in January and February of 1922, the appellant effected insurance against fire on timber and wood goods in the open situate on the Killymoon domain not within a hundred yards of any saw mill or any building in which wood working by power other than wind or water was carried on. Neither the amounts nor the exact language of the policies are material for the purposes of the present appeal, nor is the fact that the policies were really effected in the name of the appellant and the Governor and the Company of the Bank of Ireland, for the real questions that arise for determination are these: (1) Whether the appellant had any insurable interest in the goods the subject of the policies? and (2) Whether the respondents were in circumstances at liberty to raise the contention that he had no such interest in the manner in which it was raised in the course of these proceedings? The history of the matter can be stated in a few sentences. The appellant, upon whose estate the timber in question was originally standing, on the 30th day of December, 1919, assigned the whole of it to a company known as the Irish Canadian Saw Mills, Ltd., the amount to be paid for the timber felled and unfelled being £27,000, while a further £15,000 was to be paid for the cost incurred by the appellant in felling the timber that was then down. The total price paid was therefore £42,000, satisfied by the allotment to the appellant or his nominees of 42,000 fully paid £1 shares in the company; no further shares than these were ever issued. The company proceeded with the operations of cutting the timber, and by the end of August, 1921, it had all been felled and sawn up in the saw mills. In the course of these operations the appellant had become the creditor of the company for £19,000, and beyond this it is stated that the debts were trifling in amount. The timber when cut remained lying on the appellant's land, and on the 22nd of February, 1922, the greater part of it was destroyed by fire. The appellant accordingly claimed against the companies upon the policies and, on the 30th of May, 1922, in an answer sent on behalf of all the companies, it was stated that the companies must decline to accept liability for the loss of any timber within a hundred yards of the saw mill. The appellant and the Bank of Ireland accordingly instituted proceedings by issuing writs against each of the respondent companies, and each of the statements of claim delivered contained the following allegation:

> "3. The plaintiffs were at the date of the effecting of the said policy of insurance and at the time of the loss and damage hereinafter mentioned interested in the said timber to the amount so insured thereon as aforesaid."

On production of the policies all these actions must have been dismissed,

---

* Extract.

since each contained a clause referring all disputes to arbitration and making
the award of the arbitrator a condition precedent to any liability on the part
of the companies. Instead of pleading this as a defence to the actions the companies applied to stay the actions and refer the matters in dispute to arbitration, and on the 21st of July, 1922, an order was made to that effect. Upon the
hearing of the arbitration several charges of fraud and dishonesty were made
against the appellant, all of which failed, and upon the point initially raised
in the letter to which reference has been made the arbitrator decided in the
appellant's favour, but he held that in the circumstances the appellant had no
insurable interest in the timber, and this view has been supported in the
Court of King's Bench and in the Court of Appeal. The question as to the competency of the arbitrator to determine the dispute as to the insurable interest
of the plaintiff only arises if no such insurable interest can be recognised by
the law, and it is this point therefore that first arises for consideration. It
must, in my opinion, be admitted that at first sight the facts suggest that
there really was no person other than the plaintiff who was interested in the
preservation of the timber. It is true that the timber was owned by the Company, but practically the whole interest in the Company was owned by the
appellant. He would receive the benefit of any profit, and on him would fall
the burden of any loss. But the principles on which the decision of this case
rests must be independent of the extent of the interest he held. The appellant
could only insure either as a creditor or as a shareholder in the company. And
if he was not entitled in virtue of either of these rights he can acquire no
better position by reason of the fact that he held both characters. As a creditor his position appears to me quite incapable of supporting the claim. If his
contention were right it would follow that any person would be at liberty to
insure the furniture of his debtor, and no such claim has ever been recognised
by the Courts. It is true that ever since the case of *Godsall* v. *Boldero*,[63] where
a creditor of Mr Pitt was held entitled to effect an insurance upon his life, this
interest has always been recognised, but this depended as was said by Lord
Ellenborough, upon the means and probability of payment which the continuance of a debtor's life affords to his creditors and the probability of loss
which would result from his death. In the case of *Moran, Galloway & Co.* v.
Uzielli and others,[64] where a creditor for ships' necessaries was held entitled
to insure the ship, the decision expressly depended upon the fact that the
creditor had a right *in rem* against the vessel, and the learned Judge said
that "in so far as the plaintiffs' claim depends upon the fact that they were
ordinary unsecured creditors of the shipowners for an ordinary unsecured
debt, I am satisfied that it must fail. The probability that if the debtor's ship
should be lost he would be less able to pay his debts does not, in my judgment, give to the creditor any interest, legal or equitable, which is dependent
upon the safe arrival of the ship." This is, in my opinion, an accurate statement of the law, and the appellant therefore cannot establish his claim as
creditor. Turning now to his position as shareholder, this must be
independent of the extent of his share interest. If he were entitled to insure

---

[63] 9 East 72.
[64] [1905] 2 K.B. 555.

holding all the shares in the company, each shareholder would be equally entitled, if the shares were all in separate hands. Now, no shareholder has any right to any item of property owned by the company, for he has no legal or equitable interest therein. He is entitled to a share in the profits while the company continues to carry on business and a share in the distribution of the surplus assets when the company is wound up. If he were at liberty to effect an insurance against loss by fire of any item of the company's property, the extent of his insurable interest could only be measured by determining the extent to which his share in the ultimate distribution would be diminished by the loss of the asset — a calculation almost impossible to make. There is no means by which such an interest can be definitely measured, and no standard which can be fixed of the loss against which the contract of insurance could be regarded as an indemnity. This difficulty was realised by counsel for the appellant, who really based his case upon the contention that such a claim was recognised by authority and depended upon the proper application of the definition of insurable interest given by Lawrence, J., in *Lucena* v. *Cranford.*[65] I agree with the comment of Andrews, L.J., upon this case. I find equally with him a difficulty in understanding how a moral certainty can be so defined as to render it an essential part of a definite legal proposition. In the present case, though it might be regarded as a moral certainty that the appellant would suffer loss if the timber which constituted the sole asset of the company were destroyed by fire, this moral certainty becomes dissipated and lost if the asset be regarded as only one in an innumerable number of items in a company's assets and the shareholding interest be spread over a large number of individual shareholders. The authorities which have the closest relation to the present are those of *Paterson* v. *Harris,*[66] and *Wilson* v. *Jones.*[67] In the first of these cases a shareholder in a company that was established for the purpose of laying down a submarine cable between the United Kingdom and America, effected an insurance upon his interest in the cable. The shareholder's insurable interest in the cable does not appear to have been disputed and the real question, therefore, was never argued. In the case of *Wilson* v. *Jones,*[68] where another policy was effected by a shareholder in the same company, it was distinctly held that the policy was not upon the cable but upon the shareholder's interest in the adventure of the cable being successfully laid. It was attempted by the underwriters to limit the insurance to an interest in the cable itself, which would have lessened the risk, but it was held that this was not the true construction of the policy. It was not argued that, if it were, the shareholder had no interest to insure, but both Martin, B., in the Court of Exchequer, and Willes, J., in the Exchequer Chamber,[69] stated that the plaintiff had no direct interest in the cable as a shareholder in the company, and, so far as I can see, this consideration it was that assisted the Court in determining that the insurance was upon the adventure in which the shareholder had an interest and not upon the cable in which he had none.

---

[65] 2 Bos. & Pul. (N.R.) 269.
[66] 1B. & S. 336.
[67] L.R. 1 Ex. 193.
[68] *Ibid.*
[69] L.R. 2 Ex. 139.

There are no other cases that even approximately approach the present case, and, properly regarded, I think the case of *Wilson* v. *Jones*[70] is against and not in favour of the appellant's contention. Upon the merits of this dispute, therefore, the appellant must fail. Neither a simple creditor nor a shareholder in a company has any insurable interest in a particular asset which the company holds. Nor can his claim to insure be supported on the ground that he was a bailee of the timber, for in fact he owed no duty whatever to the company in respect of the safe custody of the goods; he had merely permitted their remaining upon his land....

SUMNER L.J: My Lords, this appeal relates to an insurance on goods against loss by fire. It is clear that the appellant had no insurable interest in the timber described. It was not his. It belonged to the Irish Canadian Saw Mills Co., Ltd., of Skibbereen, Co. Cork. He had no lien or security over it and, though it lay on his land by his permission, he had no responsibility to its owner for its safety, nor was it there under any contract that enabled him to hold it for his debt. He owned almost all the shares in the company, and the company owed him a good deal of money, but, neither as creditor nor as shareholder, could he insure the company's assets. The debt was not exposed to fire nor were the shares and the fact that he was virtually the company's only creditor, while the timber was its only asset, seems to me to make no difference. He stood in no "legal or equitable relation to" the timber at all. He had no "concern in" the subject insured. His relation was to the company, not to its goods, and after the fire he was directly prejudiced by the paucity of the company's assets, not by the fire. No authority has been produced for the proposition that the appellant had any insurable interest in the timber in any capacity, and the books are full of decisions and *dicta* that he had none. *Paterson* v. *Harris*[71] and *Wilson* v. *Jones*[72] are very special cases, and neither is in point here. In the former there was no plea traversing the allegation that the plaintiff had an insurable interest. The Court, construing the policy as one really expressed to be on the cable, dealt with the case as one in which interest was admitted therein, but its decision of the case after this admission of interest is not a decision that a shareholder as such has an insurable interest in a company's assets themselves. In the latter, where the policy described the subject matter of the insurance in a very obscure manner, it was held that the shareholder insured had an interest that he could insure in the profits of the adventure so described, but it was expressly stated that he had no such interest in his shares in the company....

---

[70] L.R. 1 Ex. 193.
[71] 1 B. & S. 336.
[72] L.R. 1 Ex. 193.

P.J. Carrigan Limited and P.J. Carrigan v. Norwich Union Fire Society Limited and Scottish Union and National Insurance Company Limited (No. 2)*
Unreported, 11 December 1987
The High Court

LYNCH J: This action has been brought by the Plaintiffs on foot of a policy of insurance called a Home Plus Policy No. 7867 x 12789. The policy was issued by the Defendants to one or other or both of the Plaintiffs and was signed on behalf of the Defendants on the 6th of November 1978.

The policy insured on a re-instatement basis the premises known as Glebe House, Rathcore, Enfield, Co. Meath (the Glebe) and its contents in respect of (inter alia) damage by fire. A fire occurred in the Glebe at or about 6 a.m. on Friday the 22nd of May 1981 and severely damaged the Glebe and destroyed and damaged much of its contents. At the date of the fire the Glebe was insured for a maximum sum of £110,000 and its contents for a maximum sum of £35,000. The cost of re-instatement of the Glebe in 1981/82 would have been about £80,000 and would now be about £100,000. The value of the contents destroyed was and is £24,900.

The main defence to this Action is that the claim is fraudulent because the Defendants allege that the house was deliberately set on fire by the second Plaintiff and/or persons acting in consort with him for the purpose of recovering the insurance money in respect thereof. The Defendants also relied on two other grounds of defence of a more technical nature, first, that the Glebe was used for the purposes of trade or business contrary to a condition of the policy and, secondly, that the Glebe and its contents were owned by the first Plaintiff P.J. Carrigan Limited (the Company) while the insured was the second Plaintiff who had no insurable interest in the property.

I shall deal with these two technical defences first. The plea that the operation of the policy was ousted by user of the Glebe for the purposes of trade or business was rightly abandoned in closing submissions by Counsel for the Defendants because there was really no evidence of such user as would have brought this exclusion clause into operation. The principal technical defence was therefore that the Glebe was owned by the Company but the insured was the second Plaintiff and that the second Plaintiff had not got an insurable interest in the Glebe so that the insurance was inoperative. The Plaintiffs in answer to this defence conceded that the Company was the owner of the Glebe but claimed that the Company was also the insured. The issues thus raised involve a consideration first of the ownership of the Company and its relationship, if any, with the second Plaintiff and secondly consideration of the circumstances of taking out the insurance and the subsequent operation thereof.

The company was incorporated on the 21st of July 1978. It has a share capital of £10,000 divided into 10,000 shares of one pound each. All of such shares as have been issued are according to the Company's register of

---

* Extract; the remainder of this judgment appears in Chapter 9 at p. 577.

shareholders owned by the second Plaintiff's brother Owen Carrigan and the latter's wife Kathleen Carrigan. Both Owen Carrigan and Kathleen Carrigan live at Belcoo, Enniskillen, Co. Fermanagh, where Owen Carrigan runs a garage business. Neither Owen Carrigan nor Kathleen Carrigan gave evidence in the trial of this Action before me notwithstanding that if they were the true beneficial owners of all the issued share capital of the Company they would have had the major if not the sole interest in a successful outcome of these proceedings.

The second Plaintiff comes from Belcoo, Enniskillen, aforesaid but he had been residing in the Dublin area for some 25 years at the time of the fire. The second Plaintiff is now residing in London where he is the manager of a public house. The Company has ceased to trade since in or about 1985 and the evidence before me did not disclose whether it now has any assets or not and in particular as to whether it has any interest in the Saggart garage premises hereinafter referred to but the probabilities are that it has in fact no property whatsoever.

The second Plaintiff stated in evidence that the Company bought the landlord's interest in a garage premises in Saggart, Co. Dublin, where he the second Plaintiff had carried on a garage business as tenant in the premises for some three to four years previously. The second Plaintiff also stated in evidence that he thereafter ran the garage business for his brother Owen Carrigan who with his wife Kathleen Carrigan were the sole owners of the Company and that he the second Plaintiff had no beneficial interest whatever in the Company but was secretary thereof. No documents to corroborate the purchase of the landlord's interest in the garage premises at Saggart by the Company were produced in evidence but the second Plaintiff stated that the purchase of this interest in those premises was financed by his brother Owen Carrigan alone. No explanation was given as to what became of the second Plaintiff's tenancy interest in the premises nor as to why the second Plaintiff should have abandoned his tenancy interest and the goodwill of the garage business which he had built up in the premises in Saggart apparently for no consideration whatever.

When the purchase of the Glebe was negotiated the contract dated the 11th of May 1978 was signed by the second Plaintiff as purchaser and he described himself therein as of Saggart, Co. Dublin where the garage premises are situate and not of Churchtown, Co. Dublin, where he stated in evidence that he lived with his wife and two children. On the 30th of May 1978 Lombard and Ulster Banking Ireland Limited (Lombard and Ulster) approved a loan to the second Plaintiff personally for £20,000 for the purposes of purchasing the Glebe. On the 15th of June 1978 Lombard and Ulster substituted the Company as the purchaser of the Glebe and the person or body approved for the loan of £20,000 but the second Plaintiff was a personal guarantor of the Company's liability for that loan as were also his brother Owen Carrigan and sister-in-law Kathleen Carrigan.

At the time of the purchase of the Glebe I am satisfied that matrimonial disputes and difficulties had arisen between the second Plaintiff and his wife and that was the reason why the conveyance of the Glebe was taken in the name of the Company which became the registered full owner of the Glebe on the 9th of May 1979 on Folio 12387F (formerly folio 6090F) of the register Co. Meath.

The insurance proposal form which is undated was signed by the second Plaintiff in person. It was completed with the assistance of Mr John Kilmurray of the Plaintiff's insurance brokers Messrs Murray Kilmurray and Company Limited. The proposal form first named the second Plaintiff as proposer. Then his name was crossed out and the Company name was written in as proposer. Then the word "Ltd." was crossed out from the Company name so as to restore the second Plaintiff as personal proposer. I accept the evidence of Mr John Kilmurray that he would not and did not cross out the word "Ltd." without the consent of the second Plaintiff and that such crossing out was on the express instructions of the second Plaintiff and insofar as the evidence of the second Plaintiff conflicts with this situation I reject it.

A letter was written dated the 18th October 1978 to the Defendants by Messrs Murray Kilmurray and Company Limited intimating the interest of Lombard and Ulster in the Glebe which was then being purchased and a change of the name of the proposed insured from that of the second Plaintiff to the Company.

I am satisfied that this letter was received by the Defendants but that the proposal form was received thereafter and therefore superseded the instructions in the letter of the 18th October 1978. It should be noted that the proposal form already includes in it a reference to the interest of Lombard and Ulster in the Glebe then under purchase and that it nominated the second Plaintiff as personal proposer and therefore as intended insured. I am also satisfied that the letter of the 18th October 1978 was destroyed by the Defendants in the ordinary course of their business and hence their inability to trace and produce the original of that letter for these proceedings. I find as a fact that the second Plaintiff is the proposer in the proposal form and the insured in the policy of insurance and the reference to the "other(s)" is to the interest of Lombard and Ulster and not the Company. This is borne out by the fact that the Second Plaintiff submitted two claim forms after the fire dated respectively the 28th of May and the 9th of June 1981 in each of which he is named as insured although in that of the 28th of May 1981 the Company's name was first inserted and again the word "Ltd." was crossed out thus restoring the second Plaintiff's name as the person insured. These forms are both signed by the second Plaintiff and in each of them he is twice described as the owner of the Glebe.

I find as a fact therefore that the second Plaintiff has had a substantial beneficial ownership in the Company and may indeed have been the sole beneficial owner thereof, Owen Carrigan and Kathleen Carrigan being trustees of the issued share capital for him. It is of course also significant that the name of the Company is as stated in the title to these proceedings and I reject the evidence of the second Plaintiff that his name was chosen for the name of the Company as a sort of joke.

Through the Company the second Plaintiff had a substantial if not the entire beneficial interest in the Glebe. The second Plaintiff arranged for the Glebe to be purchased in the Company's name in an effort to prevent his wife with whom he was then in dispute from getting any rights to the Glebe under the provisions of the Family Home Protection Act 1976. Because the Glebe had been purchased in the name of the Company the second Plaintiff hesitated as to whether he should put the insurance in the name of the Company but ultimately decided to put it in his own name and had the word "Ltd." crossed out so as not to complicate the payment of any moneys which might become payable under the policy to himself.

As I find that the second Plaintiff is the insured and had also a substantial if not the whole beneficial interest in the Glebe it follows that he had an insurable interest in the Glebe and in its contents and this technical defence of the Defendants fails. It should be noted however that my findings that the second Plaintiff is the insured and had an insurable interest in the Glebe involves a rejection of the Plaintiffs' case and of the second Plaintiff's evidence that the Company is the insured and was also the sole owner of the Glebe....

The British Insurance Company v. Magee
Cooke et al. 182
Exchequer Chamber

BUSH C. J: ... This writ of error has been brought to reverse the judgment of the Court of Exchequer, in an action of debt on a policy of Insurance for £500 upon a life, in which the declaration does not state, that the plaintiff below had any interest in the life insured, nor does the policy ... contain such a statement. The defendant below pleaded three pleas, insisting that the plaintiff had not any interest in the life insured, upon which pleas issue has been joined, and three other pleas, insisting that the plaintiff had not any interest to the amount of £500 at the time of executing the policy, or at the death of the life; and another plea stating, that the plaintiff was not damnified by the death to the extent of £500. To these last four pleas the plaintiff demurred generally, and the Court of Exchequer having allowed the demurrers, this writ of error is brought to reverse the judgment. The plaintiffs in error have not insisted in argument, that the pleas demurred to are good, on the contrary, the note in the paper books confines their case to an attack on the declaration, and accordingly they have only contended, that the declaration ought to be held bad on general demurrer, inasmuch as it does not allege that the plaintiff below had any interest in the life assured, in support of which they have relied on the case of *Godsal* v. *Boldero*[73] as deciding, that a policy on a life insurance is a mere contract of indemnity, upon which the plaintiff below can only recover to the extent of his loss sustained by the death of the life insured, therefore, that he must have an interest in that life. The counsel for the defendant in error, in the first place contended, that if it were necessary for the plaintiff to shew an interest, his interest sufficiently appeared upon the declaration and policy, and that it was not necessary to allege it more particularly, as from the nature of the policy it is to be implied; and secondly they argued, that an insurance on a life is a wagering policy, not

---

[73] 9 East 72.

falling within that class of cases, in which certain insurances might be condemned by the common law on the ground of policy or morals, and that in
Ireland no such statute has been enacted as the [Life Assurance Act, 1774[74]],
which in *England* has prohibited such insurances, unless in cases where the
party insuring has an interest. This latter argument has been encountered by
an allegation, that the insurance is illegal at common law independently of
statute, and that the [Life Assurance Act, 1774[75]] was merely declaratory of
the common law. However that has not been sustained, for no authority has
been cited, to shew that such an insurance has been held illegal, as being
against policy or morals, in any case decided in *England* before the statute;
and it is only necessary to look into the statute to be satisfied that it is not
declaratory, for it does not recite any existing doubt, or prevailing mistake as
to the law, but on the contrary recites "that making insurances on lives or
other events in which the assured shall have no interest, has been found by
experience to have introduced a mischievous kind of gaming"; and then
enacts, "that *from and after the passing* of this act, no insurance shall be
made in which the insured shall have no interest"; thus recognising the
frequency of the practice, and the necessity for preventing it *in future*. The
Court are, therefore, unanimously of opinion, that the judgment of the Court
of Exchequer must be affirmed, with reasonable costs.

O'Brien *v.* The Irish National Insurance Co., Ltd.
(1932) 66 I.L.T.R. 159
The Circuit Court

SEALY J: In this case, in my opinion, section 36 of the Assurance Companies
Act, 1909, comes to the plaintiff's relief. I believe she had quite a good expectation of having to pay for the expenses of her brother's death; and I do not
think the amount she insured for was unreasonable. Accordingly, on that
ground, the defence fails. Nor do I think there was any misrepresentation. I
do not think that the pain in her brother's shoulder was a thing the plaintiff
was under any obligation to disclose. The plaintiff must therefore have a
decree for the amount claimed, with costs.

Gallagher & McPartland *v.* The Industrial & Life Assurance
Amalgamated Company Limited
(1946) 80 I.L.T.R. 99
The High Court

DIXON J: The claim in this case is based on fraudulent misrepresentation.
Leaving aside for the moment the question of pleading, the suggested

---

[74] 14 Geo. III. C. 48.
[75] 14 Geo. III. C. 48 *Eng.*

fraudulent misrepresentation appears to resolve itself into two different matters — first of all the question of the amount which might become payable under the policies, and secondly, the question of the right, or power, of the plaintiff, McPartland, to take out a policy at all. The second suggestion would really relate to the legality of the policies in question; and it seems to me to be sufficiently covered by the endorsement on the Civil Bill.

Dealing first with the question of the amount, McPartland says (in detailing the discussion with the agent) that the Agent said to him: "You have a sister and you ought to have her insured" and McPartland replied "No, I never had anything to do with insurance, I have enough to do without it"; and then the Agent said "6d. a week would do you no harm", and he is suggested by McPartland to have also said that there would be £18 or £20 for McPartland at the end of it. After some further discussion, McPartland consented and a proposal form was filled in. When the amount was mentioned, there was also a discussion or some reference to the question of the bonus. Was there a definite representation as to the amount that would be paid apart from the question of any bonus under the policy? In cross-examination, McPartland admitted that he received the policy shortly afterwards and that he knew from then the amount it was for. Further, the sum assured is set out in the proposal form and it has not been suggested or proved that it was inserted at a later date. Yet, no question appears to have been raised with the Agent or, until now, with the Company, of any misrepresentation as to the amount nor is this matter referred to in the correspondence or pleaded in the Civil Bill. On the contrary, with the knowledge he then had, McPartland took out the second policy, three months later for the same amount and on the basis of a similar proposal form. In these circumstances, I am not satisfied that there was any misrepresentation, as to the benefit secured, operating on the mind of McPartland in respect of either policy.

On the other hand, I think the Agent did implicitly represent that the amount assured would be paid on the death of the life. Was this a misrepresentation fraudulently made by the Agent?

Before the 1909 Act it was not legal to take out a policy, as in this case, by a brother on the life of his sister because up to then he had no insurable interest in her life. The Act of 1909 altered the position to this extent that it made it legal for a policy to be effected on the life of *inter alios,* a sister, for the purpose of providing for funeral expenses, and that provision, in my view, implicitly conferred an insurable interest in the life of a sister. Sec. 50 (3) of the Act of 1936 — which makes this insurable interest express — can be regarded in either of two ways namely either as stating the law as it stood before or as extending it by excluding any question of the reality of the insurable interest if the statutory conditions applied. I do not think it is necessary to decide that question, although I regard Sec. 52 as applying the provisions of section 50 to the policies in this case. The former section clearly contemplates a policy which might have been invalid up to the date of the commencement of Part Five of the Act; and the words "in force" would then mean "in existence", in the sense of not having lapsed or ceased to exist, before the Act of 1936. In my view the Act of 1936 applies to these policies.

Both under Sec. 50 of the Act of 1936 and under Sec. 36 of the Act of 1909, there may be an insurable interest where the relationship exists and the

Policy is for funeral expenses. I have the evidence of Mr McPartland as to the form being filled up in his presence and signed by him and also the Proposal form itself, in which Question 10 (b) as to whether the money is to be applied for funeral expenses is answered "yes". McPartland did not say he was in ignorance of this fact; he only mentioned one question as to which any difficulty arose when the proposal was being signed and that was the question of the age of the Insured. That does not, however, exclude the possibility that the whole document was gone through and that he knew the contents of what he was signing. It was for him — if it was the fact — to exclude this possibility. I must, therefore, take the proposals signed by him as showing that he knew that. It may be that if I had not before me the proposals, I would have been more impressed by the evidence as to Mrs McGowan being in better circumstances than McPartland when the policies were taken out; but I have his own statement in the proposal forms as to his own belief that there was such a likelihood of his having to pay something in the way of funeral expenses as to give him an insurable interest. Now, if that is the position he was entitled to take out the policies and I do not see how I can hold that the agent misrepresented the position. I must therefore hold that there was not a fraudulent misrepresentation affecting the taking out of these policies.

The result of this case is unfortunate for the plaintiffs but it is in essence a case in which a risk was taken on both sides and the risk in this instance turned out unfortunately for the plaintiffs and proved to be a bad bargain for them. I must reverse the decree of the learned Circuit Judge and dismiss the action with costs in both Courts.

Wall and Wall v. The New Ireland Assurance Co. Ltd.*
[1965] I.R. 386
The Supreme Court

WALSH J. (Ó DÁLAIGH C.J., LAVERY J., KINGSMILL MOORE J., HAUGH J. ALL CONCURRING): ... Briefly stated, the case as it came before the President is concerned with ten policies of assurance upon the life of Ellen Wall, eight of which had been effected by her son, Mark Wall, the plaintiff and respondent, and two of which had been effected in the name of Ellen Wall upon her own life. They were all policies of industrial assurance. The first of these policies was effected on the 26th December, 1940, and the last on the 8th February, 1954. The purpose for which the eight policies were effected in each case was stated by Mark Wall to be for the funeral expenses which would be incurred by him in connection with the death of his mother. It was claimed by Mark Wall that all these policies, save the first policy, were illegal because in truth and in fact they were all, save the first one, merely gambling policies on his part to protect himself against the financial loss which had accrued to him on foot of the first policy by reason of the fact that the death of his mother had not taken place and which, in fact, did not take place until after the commencement of the proceedings. The other two assurance policies, namely,

---

* Extract.

those effected in the name of and upon the life of Ellen Wall, were effected upon the 20th March, 1950, and the 18th February, 1952, respectively. The said Ellen Wall, who joined with Mark Wall as co-plaintiff in the proceedings, in the statement of claim disclaimed any beneficial interest in either of these policies and Mark Wall claimed that the said two policies were effected by him and for his own benefit upon the life of the said Ellen Wall and to the knowledge of the said Ellen Wall and were also in the nature of gambling policies for the purpose of protecting his financial interests in the policies already referred to. The learned President found as a fact that the plaintiff's allegations were correct and that furthermore the true purpose for which these policies were effected by Mark Wall was not merely known to the servants and agents of the appellant Company at the time the policies were effected but that they in fact actively participated in and suggested the transactions to the said Mark Wall. It was also found as a fact that the servants and agents of the Company did not inform the appellant Company of their knowledge and indeed actively concealed from the Company the correct state of affairs and even, on occasion, when the Company began to query the necessity for the policies being taken out by Mark Wall, succeeded in misleading the Company to the point where the Company's doubts were set at rest and the policies issued. The two "own life" policies effected in the name of Mrs Wall were the result of a suggestion made to Mark Wall by one of the servants of the Company that they should be effected in the name of the mother as it was doubtful whether the appellant Company would accept any more proposals from Mark Wall, and it was on that basis that Mark Wall had the proposal forms signed by his mother who was apparently aware of the whole transaction. It appears to be quite clear that at least so far as these two policies were concerned Mark Wall was aware that the servants and agents of the Company were in fact misleading their own Company as to the true effect and intent of these policies.

The total of the amounts insured by the eight policies effected by Mark Wall in his own name was £411 14s. 0d. Sect. 50 of the Insurance Act of 1936, sub-s. 1 (a), includes the insuring of money to be paid for the reasonable expenses in connection with the death and funeral of a parent to be among the purposes for which industrial assurance companies may issue policies of industrial assurance (which would otherwise have been illegal by reason of s. 1 of the Life Assurance Act, 1774, as applied to Ireland by the Life Assurance Act of 1886). The learned President found as a fact that the sum of £411 14s. 0d. was grossly in excess of what could be considered as reasonably necessary to defray expenses in connection with the death and funeral of Mrs Wall and that in fact a reasonable amount would be between £125 and £140 although the actual cost to Mark Wall in connection with the death of his mother was £80. The first five of these policies assured an amount of £127 6s. 0d. The President held that the other three therefore failed to come within the protection afforded by s. 50 of the 1936 Act on the ground that the sums they assured were in excess of what was reasonably necessary to defray the funeral expenses. He also held that the last three of the five policies which amount to £127 6s. 0d. were illegal although the total sum assured was not greater than what he had held might reasonably be contemplated as necessary to defray the funeral expenses because the last three of those five policies had in fact been effected not to meet the funeral expenses but rather to insure Mark Wall against the financial loss he was going to suffer upon the first two policies by reason of his mother's longevity. The President therefore held that they were in truth and in fact gambling policies and not being genuine funeral expense policies did not fall within the protection afforded by s. 50 of the Act and were illegal by virtue of s. 1 of the Act of 1774.

The appellant's appeal was taken in respect of the President's decision condemning as illegal the last three of the five policies which total £127 6s. 0d. and against his decision condemning as illegal the two policies effected in the name of Mrs Wall upon her own life and against the decision of the President in holding that the plaintiff, Mark Wall, was entitled by virtue of s. 50. sub-s. 2, of the Act of 1936 to repayment of the premiums paid in respect of these policies which had been so condemned as illegal.

Having regard to the President's findings of fact in relation to the two policies effected in the name of Mrs Wall I have no doubt that in law these policies are rendered illegal by section 2 of the Act of 1774. That section makes it illegal to make any policy or policies "on the life or lives of any person or persons or other event or events without inserting in such policy or policies, the person's or persons' name or names interested therein or for whose use benefit or on whose account such policy is so made". The fact that Mrs Wall was not merely aware of it, but herself participated in the arrangement, does not affect the matter at all and in my view there is a clear authority for holding that these policies are void for illegality. To cite but a few cases, I refer to *Hodson* v. *Observer Life Assurance Society;*[76] *Evans* v. *Bignald;*[77] *Forgan* v. *Pearl Life Assurance Company.*[78] Furthermore, the illegality of those policies does not depend upon either the knowledge or ignorance, as the case may be, of the Company or its servants or agents of the facts which render the policies illegal. The question of such knowledge however does affect the right to recover the premiums paid on foot of these policies and that is a matter to which I will return at a later stage.

With regard to the policies effected by Mark Wall in his own name upon the life of his mother the position is somewhat more complex. Sect. 50, sub-s. 1 *(a)*, of the Act of 1936 speaks of — "the insuring of money to be paid for the reasonable expenses in connection with the death and funeral of...." As I have already said, the actual amount covered by the first five of these policies did not exceed what the President held one might contemplate as being a reasonable amount for funeral expenses. Therefore the policies not merely did not exceed that sum but purported to be for that purpose. It does not appear to me that an insurance company should, nor is it contended for by the respondents in this case, in the absence of knowledge on its own part be at the mercy of the secret and undisclosed intentions of the person effecting such a policy of insurance if, on the face of it, the transaction is legal. If, therefore, the plaintiff, Mark Wall, while ostensibly effecting these five policies for the purpose of funeral expenses had the secret intention of using three of them as

---

[76] (1857) 8 E. & B. 40.
[77] (1869) L.R. 4 Q.B. 622.
[78] (1907) 51 Sol. Jo. 230.

a form of insuring himself against financial loss on the first two policies, that fact or intention alone would not, even if proved to exist at the time, invalidate or render illegal the policy. On the other hand I am satisfied that if it can be proved not merely that the plaintiff had that intention but had communicated that intention to the Assurance Company or if the Company had actual or imputed knowledge of that intention at the time the policy was effected, the policy would, notwithstanding its ostensible purpose, be illegal. Therefore, so far as these policies are concerned the question of knowledge on the part of the appellant Company is of vital importance not merely on the question of the recoverability of the premiums of these policies if they are illegal but on the very question of illegality itself.

Section 75 of the Act of 1936 prohibits an industrial assurance company from employing any person who is not in the regular employment of such company, either part-time or whole-time, to procure or endeavour to procure any person to enter into a contract of industrial assurance with that or any other industrial assurance company. The agents who took part in the transactions above referred to were the servants of the Company in the whole-time employment of the Company and were in receipt of regular fixed remuneration and, in addition, received some form of bonus or premium for each new piece of business acquired for the Company. The instructions issued by the Company to these agents included, *inter alia,* one which stated that the proposal form must be clearly completed in ink giving as many particulars as possible to the questions set out thereon and that the answers to the questions on the proposal forms must be given by the proposer and, whenever possible, such answers to the questions indicated in the form should be in the handwriting of the proposer and that further, for his own protection, and in the interests of the Company, the agent should exercise the greatest care in seeing that the questions on the proposal forms were fully and accurately answered and where any doubt existed the agent should make independent enquiries to satisfy himself of the truth of the answers given by the proposer. In my view the relationship between the agent and Company was such that it was clearly the duty of the agent to communicate to the Company any knowledge on his part or information coming to his notice which impugned or threw doubt upon the accuracy or veracity of the answers to the questions on the proposal form and it appears to me that the authority given by the appellant Company to its agents was such that ordinarily the Company would be deemed to have notice of all such matters coming to the knowledge of the agents in the course of their employment as from the moment the Company would have received such notice from their agent if he had performed his duty and had taken such steps as he ought reasonably to have taken to communicate the facts or circumstances. The learned President in the course of his judgment stated that he was extremely doubtful whether in the circumstances of the case the knowledge of the agents could properly have been attributed to the Company but he did not consider it necessary to decide the point. For the reasons I have already given it is necessary for the purpose of this decision to decide the matter. I think the learned President was correct when he stated that the policies would never have come into existence but for the acts of the Company's own agents and that the Company would not have been ignorant of the circumstances which would render them illegal but for their agents' omission to inform them of the true facts.

So far as the last three of the five policies which made up the sum of £127 6s. 0d. were concerned it is clear on the facts as found by the President, and which are not in dispute, that Mark Wall falsely stated that the object of the insurance was for funeral expenses and that the agents of the Company not merely were aware of that but in fact had suggested that course to him. Similarly in the case of the policies taken out in the name of Mrs Wall upon her own life it was falsely stated by Mrs Wall that the policies were for her own benefit and this course was suggested by the Company's agents and these policies were effected in these circumstances with the knowledge and the active assistance of the beneficiary really intended, namely, Mark Wall. The learned President in dealing with this matter has stated that he thought it was right to say that he believed that "a charitable view of the evidence in this regard of the plaintiff and the Company's agent was also the correct view". He did not think that either the plaintiff or the Company's agents were conscious that what was being done could be construed as a fraud on anyone or in any sense. While I think it is true that neither the plaintiff nor the Company's agents intended to commit any fraud in the sense of intending to take money out of somebody's pocket or wrongfully deprive somebody of money, it seems to me to be beyond question on the facts found that the Company was induced by false statements and active concealment of facts to issue policies which to the knowledge of the plaintiff and the Company's agents it would not have done if it had known the true facts. In my view that is fraud.

It has been submitted on behalf of the appellants that the general rule which I have enunciated as to the occasions in which notice to the agent is deemed to be notice to the principal does not apply where the agent is himself a party or privy to the commission of fraud upon, or misfeasance against, the company and that in such event his knowledge of such fraud or misfeasance and of the facts and circumstances connected therewith is not to be imputed to the company and, secondly, that where the plaintiff knew that the agent intended to conceal the knowledge from the company, that such knowledge was not imputed to the company. In the 12th edition of Bowstead on Agency, Article 107, p. 243 this is stated to be the law. These are in fact alternative submissions. For the respondent it is submitted that, once it is established that the duty of the agent is such as has been established in this case, the general rule applies.

In support of the first proposition the appellants rely upon *Newsholme Bros.* v. *Road Transport and General Insurance Co.*;[79] *Houghton & Co.* v. *Nothard, Lowe and Wills*;[80] *and Re Hampshire Land Co.*;[81] and in the case of the second proposition they rely upon *Sharpe* v. *Foy*.[82] I agree with the views expressed in those cases so far as they deal with the question of imputed knowledge.

In my view the case where an agent is a party or privy to the commission

---

[79] [1929] 2 K.B. 356.
[80] [1928] A.C. 1.
[81] [1896] 2 Ch. 743, at p. 749.
[82] (1868) 17 W.R. 65.

of a fraud or of an act of deceit upon his principal is different from the one where the agent, though being neither a party nor privy to the commission of the fraud, is, nevertheless, aware of it but for the sake of his own interests does not reveal that situation to his principal. In the latter case the knowledge of the agent when he is under a duty to communicate such knowledge to his principal is deemed to be the knowledge of his principal even though in fact it has not been communicated to him. But in the former case I am of opinion that even when there is a similar duty on the part of the agent the fact that he is a party or privy to the commission of a fraud or misfeasance upon his principal precludes his knowledge from being imputed to his principal because his participation requires the suppression of his knowledge — a circumstance which is a negation of the basis of the general rule that the knowledge of the agent is to be imputed to the principal. It is to be noted that a similar exception is given statutory recognition in the Partnership Act, 1890, s. 16 of which provides as follows:— "Notice to any partner who habitually acts in the partnership business of any matter relating to partnership affairs operates as notice to the firm, except in the case of a fraud on the firm committed by or with the consent of that partner."

In my view the appellants in this case cannot have imputed to them the knowledge of their agents in respect of the true objects of the third, fourth and fifth policies which were effected by Mark Wall for the ostensible purpose of the funeral expenses in connection with the death of his mother and which the President found to be illegal. I am of opinion therefore that these three policies are not illegal as the Company had neither actual nor imputed knowledge at the time they were effected of the fact that the true purpose of the policies was not for such funeral expenses. That knowledge was known only to the respondent, Mark Wall, and to the Company's agents who participated with Mark Wall in deceiving the Company on this matter. For the purpose of advancing this deceit the Company's agents, if they are to be regarded as anybody's agents, could only be the agents of Mark Wall.

I turn now to consider the position of the two policies effected in the name of Mrs Wall upon her own life — which I have already adjudged to be illegal. The only question therefore is whether the plaintiff is entitled by virtue of the provisions of s. 53, sub-s. 2, of the Act of 1936 to recover the premiums. It has been established that he had paid the premiums. For the reasons already given in respect of the other three policies I am satisfied that knowledge cannot be imputed to the Company, that is to say, the knowledge of the true nature of these policies. Sect. 53, sub-s. 2, provides that where an industrial insurance company issued an illegal policy the company shall be liable to pay to the person entitled thereto a sum equal to the amount of the premiums paid on foot of the policy unless "such company proves that owing to a false representation on the part of the person who effected or the person who made the proposal for such policy, such company did not know that such policy was illegal or *ultra vires* such company." It is therefore quite clear that under this sub-section ignorance on the part of the company is not sufficient to enable it to resist repayment of premiums save in the circumstance of the special defence provided by that section when a false representation has been made on the part of the person who effected or who made the proposal for such policy. The section imposes upon the company the burden of proving that it was owing to a false representation on the part of such person that the company did not know that the policy was illegal or *ultra vires*. The learned President in his judgment held that the appellants had failed to discharge this onus of proof, namely, the onus of showing that their ignorance of the illegality of these policies was due to false representations made by the plaintiff. In view of the fact that he had expressly omitted to decide the question of imputed knowledge and coupled with the expression of his doubt as to whether such knowledge could in the circumstances be imputed to the Company, it would appear that the learned President's view on the failure of the Company to discharge the onus of proof was arrived at by an extremely rigid construction of the sub-section. He said:— "Nevertheless, it seems to me unrealistic to suggest that in all the circumstances the Company's ignorance was owing to the plaintiff's declarations: they were, no doubt, a contributing factor, but it appears to me that the real and effective cause is to be found in acts and omissions of the Company's own agents." When the doctrine or principle of imputed knowledge is left out of account on this reasoning, it seems to come down to saying that once there were any persons other than the person who made the false statement who had knowledge at the time the policies were effected of the falsity of the representations made the Company could never prove that their ignorance was due to the false representations because it could be said that it was also to some extent, if not equally, due to the failure of somebody else who in fact had a duty to tell them to so inform them. In my view the section cannot be construed as meaning that the Company must fail to discharge the onus of proof if it appears that there is some person from whom they might have expected to hear the information but who had failed to have given the information. Neither can it be read as if the Company were under an obligation to make all reasonable enquiries and must prove they had done so and still do not know. This section is already quite stringent in requiring the Company *(a)* to be able to prove the absence of actual and imputed knowledge and *(b)* that false representations had been made to them. It appears to me that it is sufficient if they can show *(a)* that they had neither actual nor imputed knowledge; *(b)* that the false representation was made, and *(c)* that they acted upon that. In my opinion on the facts of this case as found by the President the appellants did in law establish the onus laid upon them by the statute and the respondent was not entitled to judgment for the amount equal to the premiums paid on the foot of these policies. For these reasons I think that this appeal should be allowed.

CHAPTER 6

Policy Interpretation

Insurance policies are to be construed like any other written documents, and a series of rules governing their interpretation has evolved to assist the Courts in their task. These rules may be summarised in the following points:

- The intentions of the parties as gathered from the policy are to prevail;
- The words used are to be given their ordinary grammatical meaning. If, however, the wording of a clause is ambiguous and one reading produces a fairer result than the alternative, the reasonable interpretation should be adopted;
- Oral (or "parol") evidence may be introduced to ascertain the intention of the parties where the meaning of a clause is ambiguous;
- Any ambiguity is to be construed against the party using it. This is the *contra proferentem* rule;
- The commercial object of the contract as a whole is to be borne in mind when construing any particular word, phrase or clause and if necessary regard may be had to the entire policy.

All of the cases included in this chapter arise out of attempts by insurance companies to refuse indemnity in situations where policyholders had already paid their premiums and claims had been notified. It is essential that this background is not lost sight of when considering any bias in favour of the policyholder evident in the judgments.

The first four cases deal with fire policies. In *McDonnell* v. *Carr* (1833), the expiry date of a policy was established by reference to an examination of the entire contract.

Fitzgerald J.'s judgment in *Jameson* v. *Royal Insurance* (1873) is a neat example of the application of the second and third of the rules. Here a claim was resisted by the insurer on the grounds that the fire had been caused by the insured's own negligence. This interpretation was rejected unanimously by the four Judges of the Queen's Bench Division. Fitzgerald J. applied the *contra proferentem* rule. He also adopted the more grammatical construction of the clause in question.

Palles C.B.'s judgment in *Gorman* v. *The Hand in Hand Insurance Company* (1877) is an illustration of the judicial approach to the construction of exemption clauses in policies. Once the policyholder had established a prima facie claim, the onus was on the company to bring the case within the ambit of the exemption clause.

Gorman was cited by counsel but was not referred to by Palles C.B. in his judgment in *Walker* v *The London & Provincial Fire Insurance Company* (1888) which involved the interpretation of the phrase "occasioned by or in consequence of" incendiarism.

The next two cases arise from life policies. The policy in *Harvey* v. *Ocean Accident & Guarantee Corporation* (1904) contained a condition that it would not extend to death by suicide. The Court of Appeal found that there was a presumption against suicide justifying a finding of death by accident which enabled a claim under the policy to proceed.

To similar effect was *O'Hagan* v. *The Sunlife Insurance Company of Canada* (1932). Although *Harvey* was referred to by Counsel it was not cited in the judgment.

The application of the phrase "Riot or Civil Commotion" is considered in three cases.

In *Cooper* v. *General Accident & Life Assurance Corporation* (1922), a case involving a motor policy, the Plaintiff's car had been stolen in 1920. The case turned on the meaning of the phrase "loss or damage occasioned through riot or civil commotion within the land limits of Ireland".

The King's Bench Division held in favour of the plaintiff. In the leading judgment Moloney C.J. adopted the views of Palles C.B. in *Gorman* in relation to the onus of proof. The Court of Appeal in Southern Ireland also found for the Plaintiff. The High Court of Appeal for Ireland, however, ultimately found in favour of the defendant company.

Boggan v. *Motor Union Insurance Company* arose out of the theft of another insured car in 1920. The trial judge and a majority of the Court of Appeal in Southern Ireland held in favour of the policyholder. The phrase under consideration here related to "loss or damage arising during ... or in consequence of ... riot, civil commotion...."

An illustration of the principle as it applies in fire policies is provided by *Craig* v. *The Eagle Star and British Dominion Insurance Company* (1922).

General Omnibus Company Limited v. *London General Insurance Company Limited* (1932) concerned a motor policy described by the Chief Justice as an "ill-drawn document, stupid and unintelligible in many parts". One of the plaintiff company's buses had been involved in an accident. The High Court and, on appeal, the Supreme Court were faced with a three-pronged attempt to refuse indemnity.

Although they reached different conclusions as to whether the claims were out of time by reason of a three-month limitation period contained in the policy, the judges were unanimous in rejecting the insurer's other arguments *firstly*, that the overloading of the bus exempted it from liability and *secondly,* that it was not bound by the bus company's decision to settle the claims.

In Re Sweeney and Kennedy's Arbitration (1948) is a decision of a divisional High Court on the interpretation of a question and answer contained in a proposal form as to whether any of the policyholder's drivers were under twenty-one. All three arguments advanced by the company in seeking to repudiate liability were rejected by the Court. In doing so, the Court considered the meaning of the phrase contained in the form that "this Declaration shall be held to be promissory".

In *King* v. *Cornhill Insurance* (1992) the High Court held that a Mitsubishi Shogun was a "motor car". Its driving was therefore covered under a motor policy. The insurance company's attempt to refuse indemnity was fatally flawed by the inclusion in its own printed list of Private Motor Cars of the type of vehicle in question!

The Supreme Court considered the meaning of "injuries arising out of and in the course of employment" in *Buckley's Stores Limited and Buckley* v. *National Employers Mutual General Insurance Association Limited* (1977), a case of a road traffic accident where there were in existence two employer liability policies and one motor policy.

In *Rohan Construction Limited* v. *Insurance Corporation of Ireland* (1986) the Supreme Court reversed the decision of Keane J. that in the circumstances of the case a sub-contractor was not covered by its professional indemnity or public liability policies. The Supreme Court held that the plaintiff was covered by the professional indemnity policy.

A policy of marine insurance was the subject of judicial consideration in *Brady* v. *Irish National Insurance Company* (1986). The company's attempts to refuse indemnity were upheld by O'Hanlon J. on the basis that the use of cooking facilities was, in the circumstances of the case, an added risk outside the category for which cover had been provided. The policy holder's appeal from this decision was upheld by the Supreme Court (Griffin J. dissenting). The case is a good illustration of the special features of this category of insurance.

Dillon v. *McGovern* (1993) arose out of a contract to insure cattle. The case is an interesting example of the application of both the parol evidence rule and the *contra proferentem* principle. Geoghegan J. cited a passage of the judgment from *In Re: Sweeney and Kennedy's Arbitration*.

McDonnell *v.* Carr
(1833) Hayes & J. 256
The Court of Exchequer

Headnote:
A policy of insurance against fire [was] effected with the Atlas Insurance Company ... for a period commencing from the 25th of March, 1830, and ending on the 25th of March 1831....

Among the conditions of insurance endorsed on the policy, and referred to in the body of it, were the following: "No policy will be considered valid, for more than fifteen days after the expiration of the period limited therein, unless the premium and duty for the renewal of such policy shall have been paid within that time, and the printed form of office receipt given....

On the 31st of March, 1831, a fire took place, which consumed the premises. On the day after their destruction, the plaintiff tendered the premium for one year to the agent of the company, which he refused to accept. The trial took place before Jebb J., at the last assizes for the county of Cork, when the plaintiff was nonsuited, the Learned Judge being of the opinion that the period of insurance had already expired when the fire took place....

[Counsel for the Insurance Company argued that] [t]he obvious intention of both parties was, that the policy should exist during these fifteen days, not so as to secure the insured from loss happening during that time; but so that, upon the payment of the new premium, if the company chose to accept it, the expenses of another policy and stamp might be saved, and the former insurance kept up, Tarleton *v.* Staniforth.[1]

THE COURT[*]: It is true that the policy recites a proposal from the plaintiff to effect insurance for one year; but nevertheless, the agreement is, that if, "during the continuance of the policy", a fire should take place, the insurers would be answerable. The question then is, construing the whole policy together, when did it expire? There is nothing which could have originally limited the insurers to one year; and they have not limited themselves by the contract. We think that, looking to the policy and endorsement, the insurance has been actually effected for one year and fifteen days. The words of the policy in this case are materially different from those in *Tarleton* v. *Staniforth.*[2] No such saving would be effected, as that mentioned by the defendant's counsel. The stamp duty must be paid every year, and a new instrument is actually issued....

---

[1] 5 T.R. 695.
[*] Smith B. was absent
[2] 5 T.R. 695.

Jameson *v.* Royal Insurance Company
I.R. 7 C.L. 126
Queen's Bench

WHITESIDE C.J: With respect to the construction of the contract entered into by the Company with the Plaintiff in this case, we are of opinion that the true interpretation of it is that contended for by the Plaintiff....

As to the seventh defence

> ["That the stock in trade in the counts mentioned was damaged and destroyed by and through the carelessness, negligence, and improper conduct of the Plaintiffs and their servants in not making due and proper investigation of the strength and fitness of certain gearing, bolts, nuts, and other apparatus connected with the still, and in not having such gear, bolts, and nuts, and other apparatus, in safe and proper working order and condition, and in managing the fires usually employed in and about the still-house therein mentioned."]

the question raised upon it is of great importance. It is a plea that the parties by whom the insurance has been effected were guilty of negligence; that this negligence caused the loss which they have suffered, and that by reason of it the Company is exempt from liability under the policy. I find it stated in Bunyon on Fire Insurance,[3] that "it is firmly settled, that the insurers are still liable to make good the loss, that very negligence by which it has been occasioned being one of the principal risks to guard against which is the object of the insurers." We do not think that the case of *Austin* v. *Drewe*[4] establishes the proposition for which the Defendants' counsel contend, though an attempt appears to have been made to obtain for it the sanction and authority of the Court. The Chief Justice in that case declines to determine what he calls the "extreme questions" suggested in support of this view by the Solicitor-General. We, at all events, cannot sanction this defence.

O'BRIEN J: It may be remarked, that the seventh defence only avers that the loss was caused by negligence. It does not traverse the fact that the loss was occasioned by fire. With respect to the other defence demurred to, it appears to me that under the policy two things should concur in this case, in order to exempt the Company: first, that the still should be injured by the ordinary fire heat; and second, that the spirits should be in the still at the time of the damage. One of these conditions was wanting, for there is no statement here that the still was damaged by the ordinary fire heat.

FITZGERALD J: I concur in the judgment of the Court. The language of this instrument is capable of two constructions; but, inasmuch, as it is the language of the Defendants for the purpose of ensuring their own protection, I think we should give it the construction most favourable to the Plaintiffs, —

---

[3] p. 166.
[4] 2 Marshal, 130.

especially too, as it happens to be the more grammatical.

As to the seventh defence, it does not allege that the fire was occasioned by the negligence of the Plaintiffs; but it says that the loss was occasioned thereby. I think that where there is no allegation that the fire was caused by any wilful omission or misfeasance, the defence entirely fails, and is bad, even if it were not necessary to decide the other question. Negligence is no defence to an action on a policy of insurance, for the object of such a policy is to protect against negligence.

Gorman *v* The Hand in Hand Insurance Company[*]
I.R. 11 C.L. 224
Exchequer Division

PALLES, C.B: This case has been argued on showing cause against cross rules. The Defendant's rule is to enter a verdict for them pursuant to leave reserved, or to reduce the damages by £71, the value of hay of the crop of 1876, which was consumed by the fire; the Plaintiff's rule is to increase the damages by £35, the injury caused by the fire to agricultural machines....

The policy is not in its *terms* limited to damage by accidental fire: "the Society agrees (subject to the conditions indorsed, which are to be taken as part of the policy), that if the property described shall be destroyed or damaged by fire ... they will ... pay or make good *all* such loss and damage." The third indorsed condition provides that the policy shall not cover, *inter alia*, loss or damage caused by the act of an incendiary; and reading this condition, as we are bound to do, as part of the policy, the contract is that the Defendants shall be liable for loss by fire, provided it be not the act of an incendiary. When, therefore, it is once shown that the loss resulted from fire, the Plaintiff has established a *prima facie* case, and the onus is thrown upon the Defendants to prove that the act which caused the fire was within the proviso....

Walker *v.* The London and Provincial Insurance Company
(1888) 22 L.R.Ir. 572
Exchequer Division

PALLES C.B: This was an action upon a fire policy effected with the defendants upon certain goods in the dwelling-houses and shops No. 10 High-street, and 1 & 2 Edward-street, Portadown. The policy was subject to a condition that it did not cover "any loss or damage occasioned by, or in consequence of ... incendiarism." The three houses mentioned in the policy appear to have adjoined each other; and on the other side of one of them (No. 10) was a house No. 9 High-street, in which one Macaulay lived. It was admitted at the trial that Macaulay burned his house No. 9, and it was proved in the cross-examination of the plaintiff that the insured property was burned by

---

[*] Extract.

the fire spreading from Macaulay's house. At the trial the facts do not appear to have been in dispute. No question was left, or asked to be left to the jury. The verdict was entered for the plaintiff, and the question for us is whether the defendants are entitled to have it changed into a verdict for them.

This question resolves itself into two — First, whether the word "incendiarism" in the condition is limited to acts of incendiarism committed in the houses described in the policy, or some of them; secondly, whether, upon the facts as proved at the trial, and having regard to the course of that trial, we can say, as matter of law, that the loss or damage to the plaintiff's goods was occasioned by, or in consequence of, the wilful act of Macaulay.

I am of opinion that the word "incendiarism", as used in the condition in question, cannot be read in the limited sense which has been contended, but that it includes any act of incendiarism, wherever committed, which directly caused the loss or damage sued for. The risk insured against, as described in the body of the policy, includes all loss caused by fire, irrespective of the place where the fire originated. Thus, had the fire in Macaulay's house been accidental, the loss sued for would unquestionably have been within the risk, although the origin of the fire was outside houses mentioned in the policy. The condition operates as an exception out of the generality of the description of fire contained in the body of the policy, and excludes from the risk damage resulting from wilful, as distinguished from accidental, fires; and in my opinion the effect of the policy and condition does not, for the purpose in hand, materially differ from that which it would have been, if the body of the policy had limited the risk to damage "by fire, not being incendiarism". The locality of origin of fire in the body of the policy being thus immaterial to the contract, so also, in my opinion, ought to be the locality of origin of that particular description of fire — incendiarism — which, by the contract of the parties, is to be excepted out of the general description of fire in the body. This seems to me to be the natural, if not the necessary, construction of the document as a whole.

The principal argument for the plaintiff upon this question was that the words of the clause are doubtful or ambiguous; and it was said that as the language of the policy is the language of the defendants, the construction of it ought to be adopted which bore most strongly against them. It is unnecessary to discuss the cases which have been cited at each side upon this question, as, in my opinion, there is no doubt or ambiguity in the meaning of the instrument.

The second question presents to my mind more difficulty. The words are "loss or damage occasioned by, or in consequence of, incendiarism". I entertain no doubt that the words "occasioned by, or in consequence of", mean *directly* occasioned by, or the *direct* consequence of"; and that to establish that relation between the loss or damage sued for, and the act of Macaulay, which is necessary to bring the loss within the third condition, it is not sufficient to show that the incendiarism was the cause of the damage, in the sense *causa sine qua non*, or that but for the act of Macaulay the loss would not have happened. The mere fact that the fire spread from Macaulay's to and burned the plaintiff's house and goods does not, *per se* and irrespective of the question of causation, amount to a defence. Upon the other hand, there can be no doubt that although Macaulay (as in favour of the plaintiff, I assume him to have done) intended to burn his own house only, and not the adjoining one, yet the reasonable and probable (although, perhaps, to him unforeseen) consequences of his own acts are in law his wilful acts, as if they had actually been intended by him....

In each of the cases cited for the plaintiff, *Reynolds* v. *Accidental Insurance Co.*,[5] *Winspear* v. *Accident Insurance Co.*,[6] and *Lawrence* v. *Accidental Insurance Co.*,[7] there was evidence of a cause of death subsequent to the illness of the assured; and the decisions were that the death was to be attributed to the ultimate cause, and not to the primary or antecedent one — the illness — although in each of the cases that illness was a *sine qua non*; and that as the death would not have ensued without the operation of the second and independent cause, in law the death was to be attributed to that cause alone, as *causa causans*. So in the present case, if evidence had been given of any act which might, in law, have been deemed accidental, and which was subsequent to the felonious act of Macaulay, and without which the plaintiff's goods would not have been burned, those cases would have been in point. For instance, if it had been shown that a fireman, in removing goods from Macaulay's burning house, had accidentally thrown some portion of the burning material upon or near the plaintiff's premises, and so communicated the fire to them; and if it were shown that such accidental act of the fireman was not reasonably to have been anticipated as a result of the existence of a fire in Macaulay's house, then the cases cited by Mr McLaughlin would have been applicable. If then it had been left to the jury to determine whether the burning of the goods insured was a reasonable consequence of Macaulay's act, and had that question been answered in the affirmative, I should have been of opinion that the loss sued for was both "occasioned by", and was "in consequence of", Macaulay's act, within the meaning of the policy. It would have been "occasioned by" Macaulay's act, as the reasonable consequences of Macaulay's acts are, in law, to be deemed his acts. It would also have been "in consequence of" the act of Macaulay, as the thing that would, upon the assumption I have been proceeding, have been found to have been its reasonable consequence: so that the same result would have ensued from the consideration of either branch of the condition, and the defendants would, in that event, have been entitled to succeed. Neither party, however, asked that question to be left, nor was it left to the jury: and the question is, whether, having regard to the course of the trial, we must hold that the connection, by way of probable consequence, between Macaulay's act, and the loss sued for, was conceded by the plaintiff. Having given the matter the best consideration in my power, I am of opinion that we must hold that the plaintiff did concede this. He himself said, upon cross-examination, that his loss was caused by the spreading of the fire from Macaulay's house. Any other cause was not suggested, either by him or by any of his witnesses. As to the one cause mentioned by the plaintiff, it was in itself adequate to produce the result which, in fact, ensued. The circumstances under which that cause took effect

---

[5] 22 L.T. (N.S.) 820.
[6] 6 Q.B. Div. 42.
[7] 7 Q.B. Div. 216.

are not suggested to have been unusual or peculiar. We then have the case treated by the parties, not as involving matter of fact, but a question of law; and although there has been no actual reservation by the Judge, we must take the whole course of the trial as showing that the only matter in controversy was one of law, viz. The meaning of the word "incendiarism".

Upon these grounds, and being myself clearly of opinion that, had the questions been left to the jury they ought to have found that Macaulay's act was the direct cause of the loss sued for, I am coerced to hold that both the question suggested in the argument must be ruled in favour of the defendants, and that consequently the verdict must be entered for them.

DOWSE B. AND ANDREWS J. CONCURRED.

Harvey v. Ocean Accident and Guarantee Corporation
[1905] 2 I.R. 1
Court of Appeal

FITZGIBBON L.J: ... The award, so far as material, is in these terms — That the death was caused solely by drowning. That the assured died solely from the effects of bodily injury from an outward, external, and visible means or cause, but that no evidence was given by either party on which the arbitrator could find or determine at what particular part of the river, in what manner, under what circumstances, or from what immediate cause he became immersed in the river so as to be drowned, or on which he could find or determine, apart from any presumption of law that might exist, whether the cause of death was accident or one of the causes expected from the policy.

Suicide is, in this case, the only expected cause of which there is any evidence or suggestion.

He further awarded that proof of the death by drowning was given, but that no proof was given to the directors of the circumstances under which the drowning took place, from which the directors ought reasonably to have been satisfied that the death was caused by accident. If, on the true construction of the policy, the *onus* lay on the claimant to give such particulars of the drowning as ought reasonably to satisfy the directors that the drowning was caused by accident, he awarded that such particulars were not given, and that the claimant did not fulfil the condition of the policy so as to entitle him to recover on the same.

On these findings the arbitrator, under the Common Law Procedure Act, 1856, section 8 stated his award in the form of a special case for the opinion of the High Court, and from that opinion given in the King's Bench Division the present appeal is brought.

The reference to the Court is contained in the following words:

[1. Whether proof by said W.W. Harvey that said C.M. Harvey was found drowned in the River Lee, and that his death resulted solely from drowning, was a sufficient compliance with the terms and the conditions of the policy to entitle said W.W. Harvey to recover the amount assured, unless it was proved by the Corporation that the drowning resulted from one of the causes excepted by the policy?

2. Whether the *onus* lay on the said W.W. Harvey to give to the directors of the Corporation such particulars of the drowning of said C.M. Harvey, and the proximate cause thereof, as ought reasonably to satisfy the directors that the drowning was the result of accident?]

Beyond all doubt the answer to the second question must be in the affirmative, if we read it as a question of law applicable to the particulars supplied to the directors before the submission in this case; and though we have no jurisdiction to decide any question of fact, or to go beyond answering the questions which the arbitrator has submitted as part of his award to the High Court, I think he was right in holding that the newspaper cutting and the coroner's finding were not particulars sufficient to satisfy the directors, as reasonable men, that the drowning was caused by accident. But after the submission further evidence was produced for the first time, and further particulars were discovered, tending to explain the finding of the body where it was found, also tending to show the probability of accident, and to lessen the suspicion of suicide; and the first question is asked upon this altered state of facts. It is to be regretted that the arbitrator could not make up his mind upon the question of fact. It is suggested that he exceeded the reference in entering upon it at all, and the second question certainly seems to be immaterial if the arbitrator had authority to decide whether the policy should be paid or not. But the arbitrator has made it part of his award that he could not find, apart from any presumption of law, whether the cause of death was accident or suicide; and the first question is unintelligible to me, unless it means that we are to say whether there is any presumption of law which ought to turn the scale, as between accident and suicide, where there is evidence both ways.

I cannot say that, as the case stood before the arbitrator, the issue of accident or suicide was one which should have been withdrawn from a jury; or that a verdict either way could have been set aside as against the weight of evidence; or that, if the directors had declined to be satisfied with the evidence of the case presented to the arbitrator, they could have been compelled to pay. So far as the first question is at all intelligible to me as a question of law, I can only understand it as asking this — If a man is found drowned, and certainly drowned either by accident or by suicide, and there is no preponderance of evidence as to which of the two caused his death, is there any presumption against suicide which will justify a jury or an arbitrator in finding that the death was accidental and innocent, and not suicidal and criminal? In my opinion there clearly is such a presumption. I have no jurisdiction to decide the question whether there is a preponderance of evidence one way or the other in this case. If I had such jurisdiction, I should have little hesitation in finding that the assured fell by accident into the Lee, from the dangerous path which he was following by night on his way to the house of his sister, to whom he was going on her birthday, in the hope of inducing her to relieve his pecuniary embarrassments by cashing the cheque which was found in his pocket. *Trew's Case*[8] is a decision that death by drowning is death from an

---

[8] 6 H. & N. 839.

outward, external, or visible means or cause, and that death from such a cause is *prima facie* death by accident. Where it is proved that such a cause has produced death, and that the cause came into operation either from accident which is innocent, or from suicide which is criminal; if the tribunal of fact finds the evidence so equally balanced that there is precisely the same weight of evidence of accident as of design, if I was a judge charging a jury which had the exclusive jurisdiction to decide the fact, I would direct them, as matter of law, that the presumption against crime justified them in turning the scale to the side of accident. If the first question does not mean to ask whether such a direction would be right, I do not know what it means. Accordingly, I answer it in the affirmative....

LORD JUSTICE WALKER CONCURRED.

HOLMES L.J: Charles Harvey, who was the steward of the Queenstown Yacht Club, and the holder of a policy of assurance against accidental death from the Ocean Accident and Guarantee Corporation, Limited, was last seen alive on the 1st April, 1902, driving in a covered car in the city of Cork. On the 20th April his body, in an advanced state of decomposition, was found in the southern branch of the River Lee, beyond the western boundary of the borough. There was an inquest resulting in the verdict of "found drowned", and a copy of the newspaper report of the proceedings thereat was sent by William Harvey, brother and administrator of the deceased, to the directors of the Corporation, and afterwards there was some correspondence between their solicitors, in which, without an actual refusal on the part of the corporation to pay the assurance money, there was no admission of liability. Finally, on the suggestion of the solicitor for Mr Harvey, an arbitrator was agreed to, and the terms of reference were embodies in a deed, dated 30th May, 1903. By it Mr Lawrence, the arbitrator was to award and determine — (a) whether the deceased died solely from the effects of bodily injury, sustained by accident, from an outward, external, and visible means or cause within the meaning of the policy; and (b) whether proof satisfactory to the directors of the Corporation of the cause of the death of the deceased was given by the administrator within the meaning of the policy. The second of these questions is founded on a provision in the policy which requires as a condition precedent to payment that proof satisfactory to the directors should be given of the cause of death. I am at a loss to understand what object the parties had in view when they included in the same reference these two questions.

We are all agreed that what was required by the condition precedent was satisfactory proof of death by accident, but it was quite conceivable that the arbitrator might answer question (a) in the affirmative, and question (b) in the negative. What was the result intended in that event? No period is limited within which the proof is to be supplied. It is admitted that it would be in time if given before the claim is barred by the Statute of Limitations; and the intention may have been that if Mr Lawrence had found on the evidence before him that the death was accidental, this would have been accepted by the directors as satisfactory proof, even if no such proof had been previously given. The arbitrator is, perhaps, inferentially authorised to declare the legal consequences of his findings; but it is not part of our duty to say what would be the effect of answering the first question in the affirmative, and the second in the negative; and I am not to be understood as offering any opinion on this point.

The arbitration was proceeded with in due course, with the result that Mr Lawrence has stated the special case now under consideration pursuant to the Common Law Procedure Act, 1856, s. 8. He submits in this document two questions described as questions of law, but at the request of the parties he annexed his notes of the evidence of the witnesses examined before him, adding that the Court was to be at liberty to refer to the same, and draw such inferences of fact thereon as he ought to have done. This was not only a legal course to take, but in the circumstances proper and even necessary.

The first of Mr Lawrence's questions is neither relevant nor intelligible, unless it is considered in connexion with the evidence, and the special case is silent as to one or two material inferences of fact. It was proved beyond reasonable doubt that the deceased came from Queenstown, where he lived in the Yacht Club, to Cork between six and seven o'clock on the evening of the 1st April, that after a short delay at the railway station he drove through some streets of the city, and that about, or soon after, 8 o'clock he lost his life by drowning in the River Lee, at some point beyond the western borough boundary. The place in which he was first immersed in the water is a matter of speculation, but it is pretty certain that it was higher up the river than where the body was found on the 20th April, and that the corpse was carried down the stream for some distance by a flood on the 19th. That the death was the result of accident, or suicide, is beyond doubt. The case was conducted on this assumption; the evidence demonstrates it; and I assume that this was the view of the arbitrator. There was neither proof, nor attempted proof, that Mr Harvey had been suffering from illness, sleeplessness, despondency, or depression. The witnesses who had seen him shortly before his death had noticed nothing peculiar in his words or manner. The ground on which it is suggested that he may have taken his own life is anxiety arising from pecuniary difficulties. He had an annual income of £150, with free apartments and board as club steward, and another £100, arising from consular fees; but he had no property of any kind beyond a few shares in a shipping company, of the value of about £70. At the time of his death he owed about £1,200, consisting for the most part of debts of long standing. There is no one on whom money troubles sit more lightly than on a bachelor, with an income which his creditors cannot touch. This seems to have been the deceased's position; and I am not surprised that nothing was found in his papers or elsewhere indicating pecuniary pressure, except for a sum of £16, the price of a cigarette case. There is, however, no doubt that he was in urgent need of about £50 at the time of his death. He was in the habit of receiving club subscriptions and bar money, which it was his duty to account for to the committee, and on the day of his death he owed the club £59. The accounts, with the bank book, were laid before the committee monthly, and it was proved that in the week before Mr Harvey's disappearance he wrote up his books, with a view, presumably, to the April inspection of them, and that he seemed pleased with the result. He must, however, have known that, although he was allowed to retain some money against petty disbursements, the amount due by him was too great to pass the committee, and that some money would be required to keep him out of trouble. Still there was nothing to cause despair, or even perturbation. He had some good friends. On the Saturday before his death Mr Daly gave him "with pleasure" an acceptance for £40, to square his bank account. About the same time, he told Mr O'Grady that he wanted some money urgently, and he would have got it if Mrs O'Grady had not interfered. Indeed, notwithstanding the lady's intervention, Mr O'Grady would probably have yielded if he had been told the purpose for which the loan was needed, for he was Mr Harvey's security to the Yacht Club; but the deceased does not seem to have pressed the matter. He probably expected to get the money from another quarter, for he wrote to Mr Brennan requesting the loan of £50, and sending as security the certificate for the shares already mentioned. I infer that this letter was written on either the 30th or 31st March, as the reply was delivered in Queenstown on the 2nd April, enclosing a cheque for £50, and returning the certificate. The foregoing is the evidence relating to Mr Harvey's pecuniary circumstances, and I find therein nothing from which I can infer such anxiety of mind as would be likely to lead to suicide, while in the transaction with Mr Daly on Saturday, and in the letter to Mr Brennan on Sunday or Monday, there is evidence that he was not on those days contemplating self-destruction.

The incident or the cigarette case, when taken in connexion with Mr Allen's evidence, is immaterial, and need not be referred to; but there is another matter of great importance with which I must deal.

At the inquest no explanation was given of the body being found in the upper waters of the Lee. This circumstance indeed is as difficult to account for on the theory of suicide as of accident. I know no place affording better facilities for drowning than from Queenstown seaward; and why a man residing there should go to the city of Cork, and some distance beyond it, to look for water, is a mystery. The evidence at the arbitration gives a natural explanation of his being in the neighbourhood of the place where his body was found on the evening of his death. I have no reason to doubt the truthfulness or substantial accuracy of what was deposed to by Mrs Haynes. She was the sister of the deceased, and they were on friendly terms. She had made him a present of £300 in 1884; she had lent him £100 in 1897, still unpaid; and at different times £10, £15, and £35, for which he gave post-dated cheques, afterwards duly honoured. She lived in Cloughroe House, seven miles and a half from Cork, where he visited her from time to time, and where she gave him all save one of the sums mentioned. He always arrived after 8 p.m., and once he came so late that Mrs Haynes was in bed, and had to be roused by pebbles thrown against the window. I gather that he generally walked to her house, as he seems either to have stayed there for the night, or been driven back again in his sister's trap. There are two highroads from Cork to Cloughroe; but there is also, for part of the way, a public path through the fields along the south bank of the river — a portion of which is described as absolutely dangerous to anyone walking along it in the dark. On at least one occasion, and probably on more, he used this path in coming to Cloughroe House. The 1st April was Mrs Haynes' birthday, on which he was in the habit of writing to her, or paying her a visit; but no letter was received from him on the day of his death. Now, it is incredible to me that the deceased, who was in need of £50, who was refused money by Mr O'Grady, and who did not know whether Mr Brennan would give it, would not endeavour to obtain it from the sister who had assisted him on previous occasions. I, therefore, draw the inferences of fact that he came to Cork on the 1st April with the intention of seeing her; that he selected her birthday as favourable for his purpose; and that when he reached the Lee, west of the city, he was on his way to her house. I am assisted in coming to this conclusion by the circumstance that he had in his pocket a blank cheque which could be post-dated like the previous ones given to her. If I am right in this, it is, I think, much more probable that he accidentally fell into the river when walking in the dark on the dangerous part of the path, than that he threw himself in before he had completed his purpose.

The foregoing observations clear the way for the consideration of the questions submitted in the special case. The second gives no trouble. The *onus* lay on the claimant to give to the directors such particulars of the drowning, and the proximate cause thereof, as ought reasonably to satisfy them that the drowning was the result of accident; and as Mr Lawrence found as a fact that such satisfactory proof was not given before the arbitration, we are not at liberty to question this finding, even if we desired to do so. Moreover, we all concur in thinking that he was perfectly right in this conclusion.

The difficulty of the case is caused by the first question — Whether proof that Harvey was found drowned in the River Lee, and that his death resulted solely from drowning was a sufficient compliance with the terms and conditions of the policy to entitle the claimant to recover the amount assured, unless it was proved by the Corporation that death resulted from one of the causes excepted by the policy? If this is to be read without a reference to the facts proved, or any findings of fact thereon, it is a purely abstract question not arising in this case, and which I do not think could arise in any case. On the assumption I have made, the question becomes absurd. In all instances in which the circumstances that led to the death of a man found drowned become the subject of legal inquiry, something is known of the man himself, of when he was last seen, of the state of his mental and bodily health at that time, of the place where the body was found, and of other material matters. If the first question is intended to exclude all these things from the consideration of the Court, it ought not to be answered at all. We have declined to answer questions in cases stated by the Land Commission for which there was far more excuse. I am, however, sure that this was not the intention of Mr Lawrence — an experienced and careful lawyer. It is quite true that he has not decided any question of fact in connexion with the first question, but he gives the reason for this. There was, he says, no evidence on which, discarding mere conjecture, he could find at what point of the river, or from what cause, the deceased became immersed in the water, so as to be drowned. This accounts for his annexing to the case notes of the evidence, and for the provision that the Court is at liberty to draw such inferences of fact as the arbitrator ought to have done. Such a reservation is unusual, and would have been unmeaning if Mr Lawrence had himself found the facts; but being unable to do so, the case would have been incomplete without it. I have already stated the inferences I have drawn from the evidence; and if the first question is to be dealt with on the assumption that those inferences are incorporated in the case, it would follow that an affirmative answer ought to be given thereto.

But there is another, and perhaps a more satisfactory, ground for coming to the same conclusion. Let me refrain from drawing any inference of my own, and take up the neutral position assumed by the arbitrator. I presume that he had no doubt that the cause of death was either suicide or accident; but that he was unable to choose between them. A man in good health goes on the sea alone in a boat, and he is neither seen nor heard of until his body is washed ashore a week or two later. There is an absence of other evidence, and a legal tribunal, investigating a claim under a policy of assurance similar to Mr Harvey's, is in a state of absolute doubt as to the cause of death. In such a case is there any presumption of law in favour of accident as against any other cause of death? I think there is. The death can only be reasonably accounted for in one of two ways — immersion in the water by accident or design; and an innocent cause ought to be presumed as against what would be *prima facie* a crime. There is ample authority that the presumption against crime is applicable in a civil action. I have found no English case turning on suicide; but my brother, Lord Justice Walker, has called my attention to an American case, *Walcott* v. *American Life, &c.,* mentioned in the *addendum* to the last edition of Taylor on Evidence, page ccxxxviii, where it is stated that it has been held in a civil action (*e.g.* in an action on a policy of assurance), where there is no evidence as to its cause, that a death must be presumed to have been natural, and not to have been suicide, since suicide is a felony. This was the view of the Lord Chief Justice, and he would, I think, have answered the first question in the affirmative, if he had not drawn an inference of fact different from mine.

Cockburn, C.J., said, in *Trew* v. *Railway Passengers' Assurance Company*[9]:— "We ought not to give to these policies a construction which will defeat the protection of the assured in a large class of cases." To require affirmative evidence of accident in cases like the present would undoubtedly have this effect.

For the reasons I have stated, I answer the first question in the affirmative, and the second in the affirmative; but, as I have already said, I give no opinion as to the effect of these answers.

O'Hagan v. The Sun Life Insurance Company of Canada
[1932] I.R. 741
The High Court

O'BYRNE J: This is an action brought by the plaintiff as personal representative of Hugh Wilfred O'Hagan, deceased, to recover (a) a sum of £2,000 with bonus thereon, claimed to be payable under a policy of insurance, dated the 15th day of August, 1928, and entered into between the said Hugh Wilfred O'Hagan and the defendant Company, and (b) a sum of £2,000, claimed to be

---

[9] 6 H. & N. 839.

payable under the "Double Indemnity Accident Benefit" clause of the said policy....

The defendant Company have brought into Court the sum of £2,078 8s. 5d., which is admittedly sufficient to satisfy the plaintiff's claim under the first head, and no question arises with reference thereto.

By a clause of the said policy referred to as the "Double Indemnity Accident Benefit" clause it is provided that

"If the Company shall be furnished with due proof that the death of the assured resulted during the continuance of this policy, directly and independently of all other causes, from bodily injury received before attaining the age of sixty, and caused solely by external, violent and accidental means within ninety days of the date of sustaining such injury, the Company will pay, in addition to the sum assured set out on the first page of the policy, an amount equal to such sum assured (but not including bonus additions), payable at the same time and in the same manner as such sum assured. Exceptions:— This Double Indemnity Accident Benefit does not extend to or include homicide nor death resulting from self destruction, whether the assured be sane or insane, or any attempt thereat, nor death resulting from the taking of poison or the inhaling of gas, whether voluntarily or otherwise, nor death resulting from violation of the law by the assured, nor death resulting out of police duty in any military, naval or police organisation, nor death resulting from riot, insurrection, or war, or any act incident thereto, nor death resulting from participation, either as a passenger or otherwise, in aeronautics or submarine operations, nor death resulting directly or indirectly from bodily or mental infirmity or disease of any kind, poisoning or infection, other than infections occurring simultaneously with and in consequence of an accidental cut or wound, nor death from injuries of which there is no visible contusion or wound on the exterior of the body, drowning and internal injuries revealed by autopsy excepted."

It will be noted that the clause provides that the Company is to be furnished with due proof that the death resulted from such a cause as is contemplated therein. It is, however, admitted by counsel on behalf of the defendant Company that the Company is not entitled to act unreasonably, but is bound to act upon reasonable proof, and, accordingly, in determining the question in issue between the parties I am entitled to ask myself whether the evidence produced before me constitutes due proof that the death resulted from such cause.

For the proper determination of this case it is necessary to have regard to the history of Mr O'Hagan, as proved in evidence before me.

He was formerly employed as an Engineer by the Great Northern Railway Co. He married the plaintiff in October, 1913, and in the year 1914 he went to Peru where he entered into the employment of the Peruvian Corporation as Assistant Locomotive Superintendent. Mr O'Hagan and his wife lived in Peru until the year 1919, two children, both girls, having been born in the meantime. In August, 1919, they came to Ireland for a holiday, and returned to Peru in January, 1920, and subsequently a son was born in that country. In the year 1921 Mr O'Hagan was promoted to be Chief Locomotive Engineer at a salary of £1,500, which at the time of his death had been increased to the sum of £1,700. In the year 1926 Mr O'Hagan again came to Ireland with his wife and family for a holiday. He took a house at Monkstown, in County Dublin, and that house remained his property down to the date of his death. He returned to Peru in October, 1926, and Mrs O'Hagan and the children followed in 1927. In the year 1928 Mrs O'Hagan and the children came to this country for reasons of health, and occupied the house at Monkstown, and have since been living in this country. In June, 1930, Mr O'Hagan came home on leave and resided with his wife and family at Monkstown. On the 28th October, 1930, he left home to return to his employment in Peru. At this time one of his daughters had been sent to school to Mount Anville, and it was arranged that the other daughter should go there shortly afterwards. Mr O'Hagan was seen off from the North Wall by his wife and two children, the third child being at school, as above stated. It was feared that the two girls would be lonely at school if all the family went away at once, and, accordingly, it was arranged that Mrs O'Hagan and the boy should remain in this country until the following spring, when they were to join Mr O'Hagan in Peru. On the afternoon of 30th October, Mr O'Hagan left Liverpool in the R.M.S. "Orbita" bound for Peru, and was last seen alive on that vessel on the night of the 31st October. On each of the three days, 29th, 30th and 31st October, he wrote a letter home to his wife and, in addition, he sent two telegrams to her and one, on the 30th October, to his son to congratulate him on his birthday.

On the evening of the 31st October Mr O'Hagan dined at the table of the Chief Officer, Mr Langford, who gave evidence before me. Shortly afterwards he was seen walking up and down the First Class Promenade Deck, in conversation with Mr Sunnaway, a friend of his from Peru. Mr Sunnaway appears to have retired some time after 9 o'clock, and at half past 9 o'clock Mr O'Hagan was sitting on a chair on the First Class Promenade Deck, where he was seen by a steward named Rowbotham, who also gave evidence before me. Rowbotham states that there was nobody else on that deck at 9.30, and he (Rowbotham) thereupon retired to the pantry on that deck. He came out again on to the deck at 10 o'clock and walked right around the deck, but there was nobody on the deck at that time, the chair on which Mr O'Hagan had been sitting being then vacant. Mr O'Hagan was never seen again. When a steward went to call him the following morning he was not in his cabin and his bed has not been slept in. The steward thereupon gave the alarm, a search was instituted, but Mr O'Hagan could not be found. The first port of call, after leaving Liverpool, was not reached for some hours afterwards, and it is obvious that there was no means of leaving the ship in safety.

The weather conditions on the night of the 31st October as entered in the Log Book, were as follows:— "8 p.m. Light wind, cloudy, overcast and rainy weather. Midnight — Gentle breeze, moderate swell, cloudy and occasional drizzle."

Rowbotham in the course of his evidence stated that it was a "dirty evening", that it was raining part of the time, that there was a slight swell and some wind ahead blowing against the vessel.

It is admitted, and is obvious on the evidence, that Mr O'Hagan died some time during the night of the 31st October or morning of the 1st November, and what I have to consider is how and in what manner he met his death.

No evidence has been offered, nor has any suggestion been made that he met his death by means of violence offered to him by any person, and, having regard to the circumstances and to the fact that no noise or commotion was heard by the deck steward or anybody else on board, so far as has been ascertained, I do not think that any such theory is reasonably possible, and I, accordingly, dismiss it from my consideration.

It seems to me to have been established, beyond all doubt, that he left the vessel, alive or dead, sometime during the night of the 31st October. I have already ruled out the possibility of his death by violence. It was tentatively suggested that he may have died as the result of some seizure or heart attack. It seems to me unlikely that, if he had died in this way, his dead body could have got into the sea, but, in any event, the evidence before me establishes, to my satisfaction, that he was a man in perfect health and I accordingly reject, as highly improbable and unreasonable, the theory that he died in this way.

Accordingly, it seems to me that the only reasonable inference from the evidence is that he got into the water alive, and that he got there either by accident or in a deliberate attempt to take his own life; and what I really have to consider and determine is whether he committed suicide or died as a result of accidental drowning. In dealing with that question, it is necessary for me to bear in mind the fact that the onus of proof rests upon the plaintiff, and, in order to succeed in this action it is necessary for her to establish by satisfactory evidence that death did, in fact, result from accidental drowning.

On behalf of the Company strong reliance was placed upon the fact that, when last seen alive, Mr O'Hagan was in a position of safety, and the evidence of the Chief Officer would tend to suggest that an accidental fall from the ship was impossible. It does seem to me that the possibility of an accidental fall from the part of the First Class Promenade Deck on, which Mr O'Hagan was last seen alive, is highly unlikely, though not, in my opinion, impossible. I cannot, however, close my eyes to the possibility that sometime after half-past 9 o'clock Mr O'Hagan may have moved from that deck and gone on to some other deck, possibly even to the Second Class Promenade Deck. On the latter deck the possibility of an accidental fall into the sea is much greater. I accept completely the evidence of the Chief Officer that the vessel, built as it is, furnishes every reasonable and proper protection against accidental falling over, but, even accepting the evidence in this way, I am still of opinion that on a night such as this, a passenger, going to and leaning over the side of the boat, for the purpose of relieving nausea or for any other purpose, might accidentally fall over.

The improbability of Mr O'Hagan having committed suicide seems to me on the evidence to be greater than the improbability of his having fallen accidentally into the sea. He was a man in the prime of life and in excellent health. He had had a most successful career and was obviously interested in his work. He seems to have been held in the highest esteem by his employers. He had, so far as has been ascertained, no financial or business worries. He was happily married and seems, from his acts and from his letters, to have been devoted to his wife and family. It is clear that he felt lonely on going away, and I accept the evidence of Mr Langford that, on this night of the 31st October, he seemed somewhat dejected, which I attribute, as did Mr Langford, to his having just left his wife and family. His letters show the greatest love for his family, and it appears from the letter of the 30th October that he was looking forward to his wife joining him in Peru the following spring. In all these circumstances it seems to me that the improbability of his having committed suicide is so great that I cannot accept the suggestion, provided there is any other reasonable explanation of his death.

If the evidence in favour of accidental death on the one hand and suicide on the other were equal, I would be entitled, acting on the well recognised legal presumption against crime, to infer that the deceased died as a result of accident. In the circumstances of this case I do not think it is necessary for me to rely upon or have recourse to this presumption, as I have come to the conclusion that the balance of evidence is in favour of accidental drowning.

In these circumstances I have arrived at the conclusion that the plaintiff has discharged the onus of proof which rests upon her, and is entitled to recover under the foregoing clause of the policy.

Cooper *v.* The General Accident Fire and Life Assurance Corporation Ltd.
[1922] 2 I.R. 38
King's Bench Division

MOLONY C.J. [PIM AND GORDON J.J. BOTH CONCURRING]: On the 7th May, 1920, Captain Richard W. Cooper, of Ballinrea, Douglas, Co. Cork, insured his motor car with the defendant company, and, under the policy, the company undertook that, during the period covered by the policy, they would, subject to the exceptions, special provisions, and conditions contained therein, or endorsed thereon, indemnify the insured against the loss of or damage to the plaintiff's motor-car, by whatever cause such loss or damage might be occasioned. The exceptions to which the policy is stated to be subject are four in number, but the only one which is material to the present case provides against liability on the part of the company for "loss or damage occasioned through riot or civil commotion within the land limits of Ireland".

The motor-car was in Captain Cooper's garage in Ballinrea, which is between five and six miles from the City of Cork, when on the 28th October, 1920, between the hours of 7 p.m. and 8 p.m., the plaintiff heard what he thought was a car. He states in his evidence that he "went to the back door (from house into yard). I opened it. A voice said, 'Shut the door.' I opened it again. The voice again said, 'Shut that door.' A third time this happened. All I saw was an arm: it held what might have been a revolver, or else a stick. Shortly after, I saw car moving off." As the plaintiff heard a car started at the time when he saw a man's hand holding a revolver, or stick, we may infer that at least two persons were engaged in the theft.

The defendants have pleaded that they are protected from liability by reason of the exception to which I have referred, and that the loss which Captain Cooper undoubtedly sustained on the occasion by the disappearance of his car was loss or damage occasioned by riot or civil commotion. So far as the pleadings are concerned, that point is expressly pleaded in the defence, and evidence was given by Mr Patrick Riordan, who is a District Inspector, R.I.C., stationed in Cork, and whose district included Douglas, that in October five cars in his area were taken; one of these was the plaintiff's car, and two were from neighbours of the plaintiff. He also says that one car was taken from outside the Imperial Hotel in Cork, where it was left in the street during a children's party; and further on that "there is a state of guerrilla warfare in parts of Cork County and in the City of Cork," but that "this does not apply to Douglas or to five or six miles round." In answer to Mr Conner later in his evidence he says there was at least one gang of motor thieves operating in Macroom, which, however, was not in his district. On this evidence the defendants claim that they have brought the case within the exception.

There has been a good deal of argument at the Bar as regards the onus of proof. I think the onus of proving that the loss was occasioned by civil commotion rests on the defendants but even if that were not so, I should be inclined to hold that Mr Justice Moore was right in the decision at which he ultimately arrived. As regards the onus of proof, this case cannot be distinguished from *Gorman* v. *The Hand-in-Hand Insurance Co.*[10] There the company agreed, subject to the conditions, that if the property were destroyed by fire they would make good any such loss or damage; but one of the conditions was that the policy did not cover loss or damage caused by the act of an incendiary. There is there a general acceptance of liability for damages, and then a particular exception as regards loss or damage caused in a particular way, just as in the present case there is a particular exception as regards loss by civil riot or commotion. In that case the learned Chief Baron says:

> "The third endorsed condition provides that the policy shall not cover, inter alia, loss or damage caused by the act of an incendiary; and reading this condition as we are bound to do, as part of the policy, the contract is that the defendants shall be liable for loss by fire, provided it be not the act of an incendiary. When, therefore, it is once shown that the loss resulted from fire, the plaintiff has established a prima facie case, and the onus is thrown upon the defendants to prove that the act which caused the fire was within the proviso. The defence is not in any sense a traverse of an allegation comprised within the general averments of the complaint; it is plea in confession and avoidance, and the proof of it is upon the defendants."

That case has been considered in the case of *Hurst* v. *Evans*[11] where it was distinguished by Lush J. as not applicable to the facts and circumstances with which he was dealing. I am not concerned, in the present case, to decide whether the distinction is a sound one, but I may say in passing that I am inclined to doubt it.

In *Munro, Brice, & Co.* v. *War Risks Association*[12] the question on whom the onus of proof rested was again considered by Bailhache J., and that learned Judge in five propositions makes what I conceive to be a correct statement of the law, and he adopted the principles enunciated by the Chief Baron in *Gorman* v. *Hand-in-Hand Insurance Co.*[13] The onus is, therefore, on the

---

[10] I.R. 11 C.L. 224. See p. 144.
[11] [1917] 1 K.B. 352.
[12] [1918] 2 K.B. 78.
[13] I.R. 11 C.L. 224. See p. 144.

defendant of satisfying the Court that the loss we are dealing with in this case was occasioned by riot or civil commotion. Civil commotion has been defined by Lord Mansfield in these words: "I think a civil commotion is this — an insurrection of the people for general purposes, although it may not amount to a rebellion, where there is an usurped power. If you think it was such an insurrection of the people for the purpose of general mischief, though not amounting to a rebellion, but within the exceptions of the policy, you will find for the defendants." I cannot find that the case in which these words were used by Lord Mansfield is reported, but the definition will be found at page 167 of Bunyon on Fire Insurance, sixth edition, and it has been frequently quoted since the occasion on which it was uttered in connection with the destruction by fire of the house of Langdale in the Lord George Gordon Riots in 1780.

Now, in the present case there is, and was at the time of this theft, a good deal of disturbance amounting to civil commotion, and even to actual rebellion, in the City and County of Cork. A number of motor thefts have occurred and will occur in Cork, as well as in every other county. The facts deposed to by the plaintiff in this case establish a theft, and I am assuming in favour of the defendants that the evidence establishes the existence of civil commotion in the City and County of Cork. But a connection between civil commotion and the theft must be established, and established not by mere conjecture, but by inference from facts. In a case of a somewhat similar policy to the present one — *Winicofsky* v. *Army and Navy General Assurance Co.*[14] — Mr Justice Bray had to consider a claim on an insurance policy against burglary. The burglary was committed during an air-raid, when people were thinking more of protecting their lives than their property. During air-raids the number of burglaries had increased, and the insurance company sought to escape liability on the ground that the loss was "a loss occasioned by hostilities, or loot, sack, or pillage in connection therewith", the fact being that during an air-raid the insurer went to a shelter, and left his shop unattended. When he returned he found that the place had been broken into by burglars. Bray J. in his judgment says that "he could not agree that the burglary was a loss caused by hostilities, though, no doubt, the air-raid, which was an act of hostilities, produced a state of affairs which made things easier for the burglars." In the same way it is not established in this case that the theft was due to riot or civil commotion, although, no doubt, the state of the City and County of Cork made things easier for thieves, because, as we all know, in the present disturbed state of affairs property cannot receive the same protection from the police as it would have if the police were confined to their ordinary police duties. The onus of proof is, as I have said, on the defendants of bringing the case within the exception. They have failed to do so....

PIM J: I agree with my Lord's judgment ... It has ... been submitted that the only possible explanation of the theft is that the car was taken by hostile forces. If we drew such an inference, it might be correct; but, in my view, we

---

[14] 35 T.L.R. 283.

are certainly not coerced to such a conclusion, not even entitled to draw it. Thieves fish in troubled waters, and it is obvious that this car may have been taken by thieves with a view to theft, and nothing more.

We cannot eliminate every explanation other than the one which suggests the act of a hostile force. Consequently, I think Mr Murnaghan's contention must fail. If it fails, he is driven back to the argument concerning the onus of proof, on which point I am entirely in agreement with the judgment of my Lord.

The Court of Appeal in Southern Ireland

RONAN L.J: ... We are all agreed on what appears to me to be the only question of law in the case — that once the loss was established the burden rested on the defendants of proving that that loss was caused by riot or civil commotion. I say "caused" deliberately, as, in my opinion, the word "occasioned" means precisely the same thing as "caused".... The question in this case, therefore, resolves itself into this: Ought Mr Justice Moore to have been affirmatively satisfied on the evidence before him that this was a loss occasioned by civil commotion? It is only one step on Mr Murphy's way [for the company] to establish that civil commotion existed in the neighbourhood; his difficulty arises in establishing the next step, that the loss was thereby occasioned, and, in my judgment, he has not done so. We have heard a great deal of argument as to the balance of probabilities. Now, I have read the judgment of the Lord Chief Baron in *Gorman's Case*,[15] and from this and other decisions it is quite clear that unless there is a balance of probability in favour of a plaintiff asserting a proposition, it is the duty of the Judge to withdraw the case from the jury. The only effect of there being such a balance of probability in favour of the party asserting the proposition is that he is thereby entitled to have the question left to the jury; but it in no way decides how the jury ought to determine the question. What a judge has to do in such a case as the present is to ascertain whether, taking the evidence before him as a whole, he is satisfied as to the fact.... The evidence consists of statements of opinion by a police officer, statements of specific facts by him, facts not within his own knowledge, which, for the purpose of this judgment, I shall assume the Judge gave proper effect to, and the statements of the plaintiff himself. We have not a verbatim report of the evidence. We have not seen the witnesses or heard them. The Judge at the trial, no doubt, himself asked the witnesses questions. Matters must have arisen on which he satisfied himself as the case went on. He was in a much better position to judge of the weight of the evidence than we are. Accordingly, where a case is tried by a Judge, with or without a jury, and where the Court of Appeal has necessarily an imperfect record of it, we are slow to interfere with his findings of fact without clear grounds for so doing. The question here is purely one of fact, depending upon the weight of evidence and the weight of evidence alone. Four Judges have already arrived at the same conclusion of fact — Mr Justice

---

[15] I.R. 11 C.L. 224. See p. 145.

Moore and the three Judges of the appellate tribunal, who have concurred with his view. The House of Lords has repeatedly laid it down that when two separate Courts have agreed as to a question of fact, nothing but an overwhelming case would induce them to overrule that decision. In my opinion in this case the evidence shows only that the motor-car was stolen by two men who came there for that purpose; and it was perfectly open for the Judge on the evidence before him, according to the weight he attached to it, to arrive at the conclusion he did. Having regard to the fact that the King's Bench Division unanimously came to the same conclusion, this Court should not interfere with their decision. I may add that although I have not dealt with the authorities cited by Mr Conner, dealing with the principle of insurance law applicable to the case, I fully appreciate their force, and the argument which Mr Conner has based upon them.

O'CONNOR L.J: The first question involved in this case is one of law — namely on whom did the burden of proof rest? I am of opinion that once the insured person proved the theft or loss the onus lay on the insurance company of proving that the theft or loss came within the exception in the policy.

The second question is also one of law — namely, as to the construction of the words "occasioned by civil commotion". Now that there was civil commotion existing in this district at the time is beyond controversy, and it was so found by the learned Judge. In my judgment, as a matter of law, if this car was taken by insurrectionists and as part of the insurrectionary campaign, the loss to the plaintiff would have been occasioned by civil commotion. That, however, does not carry the defendants the whole way, because the burden of proof was on them, and when the case came before the learned Judge at the trial, who tried the case without a jury, he was not satisfied as a matter of fact that they had discharged the burden of proof resting on them. I confess that if I had been the Judge at the trial I would have drawn a different inference from the facts, and I am doubtful whether the learned Judge gave sufficient weight to the several matters which have been so ably pressed upon us by Mr Murphy. I shall summarise them. First, there was the fact to which I have adverted of the existence of civil commotion in the district, and the desire of the insurrectionists to obtain motor-cars for the purposes of the insurrection. Second, there was the time of the happening. It was at seven or eight o'clock of an October evening, an appropriate enough time for an insurrectionary gang carrying out their objects by force, but not one that would be chosen by ordinary motor thieves. Third, there was the occurrence in the district at about the same time of five motor thefts, two of which were from neighbours of the plaintiff. Fourth, there was the show of force on the occasion. Fifth, there was also the rarity of the crime of motor-stealing before these troubles arose. Speaking from my own experience in the Law Room of Dublin Castle during a period of four years, I never came across a single instance of this particular crime, though it may, no doubt, be said that once the forces of law and order are inoperative, thefts of every kind may occur more easily than before. The learned Judge at the trial, however, was not satisfied that the defendants had discharged the onus resting on them of proving that the loss was occasioned by civil commotion. The same conclusion was unanimously arrived at by the Judges in the King's Bench Division, including the Lord Chief Justice. My colleagues are of the same opinion, and I am not prepared to carry my opinion so far as to dissent from the judgment at which they have arrived....

The High Court of Appeal for Ireland

SIR JOHN ROSS C:... [T]he simple facts ... are not disputed. The car must have been taken for some purpose. Two theories are put forward. The plaintiff contends that it was an ordinary case of robbery, where the thief takes the car to sell it, or to keep it for his personal use. The defendants contend that the taking of the car must be considered in the light of the surrounding circumstances; that it is an incident in the working of an existing belligerent system, and that the purpose and intention of the takers are of the utmost importance. I cannot help thinking, with great respect to them all, that the attention of the learned Judges who have dealt with this case was too much occupied in considering the question of onus. A question of onus may be sometimes of immense importance, as for instance, in an action for damages for malicious prosecution, where the plaintiff must produce evidence to satisfy the Judge that it is inconsistent with the existence of reasonable and probable cause before he can get to the jury at all. But in a case of this kind, where the facts are not in dispute and where everything depends on the inferences to be drawn from the facts, there is little advantage in discussing the question of onus. The judicial mind derives a certain amount of comfort and satisfaction in arriving at a doubtful conclusion by throwing the onus argument into the scale. The truth is that the facts will support either of the two antagonistic conclusions. If to an equal degree, the question of onus is all-important, because if the facts are equally consistent with the two adverse conclusions, the party on whom the onus lies must fail.

The question here is one of a balance of probabilities, and the scale is to be turned by a correct conclusion founded on circumstantial evidence. "The question of onus of proof is not," says Bowen L.J. in *Abrath* v. *North-Eastern Railway Co.*,[16] "a rule to enable the jury to decide on the value of conflicting evidence." If the proper inference from the evidence is what is asserted by the plaintiff, the plaintiff succeeds; if it is that contended for by the defendants, the onus, if it is on them, is satisfied, and the defendants succeed. What is the meaning of "loss or damage occasioned through civil commotion occurring within the limits of Ireland"? We need not trouble to go back to Lord Mansfield's definition. Nobody can deny that at the time of this occurrence there existed civil commotion within the limits of Ireland. Some call this commotion war, others guerrilla warfare, others rebellion and insurrection, others use more condemnatory descriptions. We have nothing to do with the ethics of the movement, whether it is criminal or excusable. We find that it existed, that it was highly organised and was systematically worked against the then established Government of the land. It operated all over the country, and it is proved in this case to have been operating in the City of Cork.

---

[16] (1883) 11 Q.B.D. 440, at p. 456.

... The words of the exception must receive a reasonable construction. A reasonable construction seems to me to be, that if the car was taken by some persons for the purpose of being used in the civil commotion, or of assisting those who were furthering the civil commotion, that is sufficient to establish the exception. The District Inspector says that the combatants largely avail themselves of motors in their attacks on the police and military. In his area five cars were taken in the month of October. It is not suggested that these cars were taken by ordinary motor thieves....

I am not at all captivated by the suggestion that thieves fish in troubled waters. From what we know of the conditions of the present conflict, I should think it extremely unlikely that ordinary thieves would select these areas as a field for their operations; they would find it very difficult to either keep or dispose of the plunder.

... When we know that this irregular warfare was carried on by sudden concentration of large numbers of armed men on isolated barracks, we can well appreciate the value of such a motor-car as this for the purpose of carrying on hostilities. The facts speak for themselves. The car is to be taken from a military officer, who must be presumed to be a man of ordinary courage and nerve. It is not taken in the dead of the night, when the occupants of the house would be asleep. It is taken between 7 and 8 o'clock, on an October evening, boldly and openly, and not at a time that would be chosen by thieves. It is taken with a show of force, accompanied by peremptory commands, suggesting that though only two men are actually engaged, further force is immediately available. It is taken at a place that is within fifteen minutes' drive of the very centre of the movement. Several other cars have been taken in that very month for the purposes of the insurrectionary campaign.

The rarity of the crime of motor-stealing before the period of disorder is another element to be considered. The way in which the matter was handled gives one the idea that the operators were disciplined men, and belonged to a body equipped with an intelligence department. They knew who were in the house, and how to get the car out. Some of these elements by themselves may seem to be of little importance, but all taken together lead one irresistibly to the conclusion that this was no ordinary theft, but the work of the organisation that was operating through the country....

Mr Conner [for the plaintiff] in his very able argument now boldly contends that to make good the defendants' contention that the damage was occasioned by civil commotion, there must have been an actual disturbance or tumult on the premises, and that otherwise the civil commotion was not the immediate cause of the loss of the car, though it may have been the remote cause. This argument does not appear to have been pressed in the Courts below. At all events, it is not discussed in any of the judgments. He contends that there is no necessity for a balance of probabilities; that if the car was taken by a person engaged in civil commotion for the furtherance of the purposes of the commotion that makes no difference; it was not the direct cause of the loss. He insists that the proximate cause of the loss was the taking of the car by the two men, which amounted to a theft. If the car was proved to have been afterwards used by the insurrectionary body for attacks on the police or military, he contends it would make no difference. Even if the men who took it avowed that they required it for insurrectionary purposes, he says that would be irrelevant. The civil commotion may have been the cause that led to the theft of the car, but the Court, he insists, has no right to inquire into the causes of causes — the purpose is immaterial.

It cannot be disputed that in insurance cases you must only look to the proximate cause of the loss. A policy excludes death from fits; the insured in consequence of a fit falls across a railway and is killed by an engine, or falls into the water and is drowned. In both these cases the company is rightly held liable because the fit is not the proximate cause of the death in either case.

The way in which the matter presents itself, to my mind, is this. Civil commotion may manifest itself in various ways — in homicide, in arson, in tumult, in kidnapping, in ambushes, in forcible capture of war material, and such like. Each of these things when it occurs is an incident or a constituent element in the civil commotion: it goes to constitute the civil commotion that is manifesting itself in this form for the time being. It is not clear thinking to hold that the civil commotion is an entity by itself, and that these manifestations of its operation are something distinct from it. For the time being the particular manifestation constitutes a form of civil commotion itself.

It is a strong thing, no doubt, for the defendants to ask this Court to arrive at a conclusion different from that of seven learned and experienced Judges. If there were any dispute as to the credibility of the witnesses, if there were any doubt about any fact as distinguished from an inference to be drawn from proved facts, the finding of the Judge at the trial ought to outweigh the opinions of any appellate tribunal which has not had the witnesses before it. But in this case we have no reason for believing that every material fact was not set out in the Judge's report, and the sole question is as to the proper inference to be drawn from the facts. I cannot think that the House of Lords cases referred to by Ronan L.J. are really applicable to this case.

Lord Lindley says in *Montgomerie* v. *Wallace James*[17]: "I entirely concur in thinking that there is no law or settled practice in the House to prevent it from differing even from two concurrent findings of fact, if on careful consideration of the evidence this House comes to the conclusion that the findings are wrong." Lord Halsbury, in the same case, p. 75, uses these words: "But where no question arises as to truthfulness, and where the question is as to the proper inference to be drawn from truthful evidence, then the original tribunal is in no better position to decide than the Judges of the Appellate Court." These observations were approved and applied by Lord Dunedin in *Dominion Trust Co.* v. *New York Life Insurance Co.*[18] If the attention of Ronan L.J. had been called to these cases, the Court would have had the great advantage of his opinion on the proper inferences to be drawn from the facts. It is plain that if O'Connor L.J. had not been unduly affected by the weight of numbers, he would have drawn the inference that this was a loss occasioned by civil commotion.

While deeply conscious of our responsibility in overruling the decision of

---

[17] [1904] A.C. 73.
[18] [1919] A.C. 257

seven Judges of distinction, I cannot evade the duty of forming and expressing my own conclusion. I am of opinion that the damage was occasioned
through civil commotion, and, therefore, that the judgment of the trial Judge
should be set aside, that the order of the King's Bench Division should be
reversed, that the order of the Southern Ireland Court of Appeal should be
reversed, and judgment entered for the defendants with costs of all the
proceedings.

O'CONNOR M.R. CONCURRED.

ANDREWS L.J: ... The arguments advanced on behalf of the plaintiff in
support of his judgment may be briefly summarised.... In the first place, it is
alleged that the facts proved do not disclose the existence of any civil
commotion on or in the immediate vicinity of the plaintiff's premises from
which the motor-car was taken at the time of the occurrence, and that proof of
the existence of such civil commotion is a necessary condition of the
defendants' immunity from liability under the policy; secondly, that even if
the existence of civil commotion within the true meaning of that term as used
in the fourth exception in the policy was proved, there is no satisfactory
evidence that the loss sustained was occasioned thereby; thirdly, that the
onus of proving both these facts, and, accordingly, of bringing the case within
the fourth exception, lay upon the defendants, and that they failed to
discharge such onus....

1. It is apparent from a perusal of the learned Judge's notes of the trial
that if the existence of civil commotion on or in the immediate vicinity of the
plaintiff's premises at the time of the occurrence is an essential condition of
immunity from liability, the defendants must fail, as there is no such finding
by the learned Judge, and, further, no facts were proved from which any such
conclusion could have been arrived at. But, in my opinion, it is quite unnecessary for the defendants to prove the existence of such civil commotion at
such time and place. To support such a view it is necessary not only to read
into the fourth exception words which are not contained in it, but also to
delete from it the words, "occurring within the land limits of Ireland", which
immediately follow, and which qualify or define the civil commotion referred
to in the exception. If the loss was directly occasioned through civil
commotion, it is, in my opinion, wholly immaterial where or when such civil
commotion occurred, provided it was within the land limits of Ireland.

2. Assuming then that proof of civil commotion at the time and place of
the occurrence is unnecessary, is there any evidence or any sufficient evidence of civil commotion occurring within the land limits of Ireland causing
the loss?

The existence of civil commotion at the time of the occurrence in Cork
City, which was only between five and a half and six miles distant, is found as
a fact by Moore J., who had ample grounds for so finding upon the uncontradicted evidence of District Inspector Riordan, that a state of guerrilla
warfare existed in parts of Cork County and in the City of Cork. Is there,
then, evidence directly connecting such civil commotion with the loss of the
plaintiff's motor-car? It must at once be admitted that there is no coercive
evidence upon this point; but there is, in my opinion, ample evidence from
which such connection not only might but should be inferred....

... [T]he facts ... impel ... me to the almost irresistible conclusion that the car was taken by insurrectionists for unlawful purposes connected with the widespread civil commotion which at that time existed throughout the country.

But Mr Conner, for the plaintiff, argues that even if this be so, the court cannot have regard to any such purposes; and he cited to us several authorities in support of the proposition that in insurance law one can only have regard to the proximate as distinguished from the remote cause. This proposition is too well settled to admit of question: *Winspear* v. *The Accident Insurance Co. Ltd.*,[19] *Lawrence* v. *The Accident Insurance Co., Ltd*,[20] *Britain S.S. Co.* v. *King.*[21] But, in my judgment, there is a slight confusion of thought in applying the principle underlying these decisions to the present case. There is no question here as to proximate or remote causes. It is a common case that the cause of the loss was theft. The purpose for which the car was taken may be, and in the present case is, an important element in determining the true character of the theft, which, in my opinion, was an incident in the civil commotion; and it seems to me that to deny to the defendants the right of showing the purpose for which the car was stolen was an unlawful purpose connected with civil commotion, would in effect be to strike the fourth exception out of the policy. I cannot accede to this argument; and I, accordingly, hold that there is ample evidence that the loss of the plaintiff's car was occasioned through civil commotion.

3. Plaintiff's third contention, however, is that the onus of proving the facts to bring the case within the fourth exception lies upon the defendants, and that they have not discharged this onus, but, on the contrary, have left the case in such a state of doubt and uncertainty as to whether the taking of the car was the work of ordinary motor thieves or of insurrectionists, that he is entitled to a verdict.

I entirely agree with the contention that the onus lies upon the defendants of bringing the case within the fourth exception, once the plaintiff has proved, as he did, that the car was stolen. So far as this Court is concerned, we are bound by the case of *Gorman* v. *Hand-in-Hand Insurance Co.*,[22] which is indistinguishable in principle from the present case, and which, in my opinion, was rightly decided. If it conflicts with the decision of Lush J. in *Hurst* v. *Evans*,[23] I prefer the latter, as did Bailache J. in *Monro, Brice, & Co.* v. *War Risks Association, Ltd., and Others.*[24] But, holding as I do, that the onus is on the defendants, I am of opinion that in proving the facts, which they have done, and to which I have already made specific reference, the defendants have not left the case in what Hamilton L.J. called in *Fleet* v. *Johnston*[25] "a state of equilibrium", but, on the contrary, have discharged this

---

[19] 6 Q.B.D. 42.
[20] 7 Q.B.D. 216.
[21] [1921] 1 A.C. 99.
[22] I.R. 11 C.L. 224. See p. 145.
[23] [1917] 1 K.B. 352.
[24] [1918] 2 K.B. 78.
[25] 29 T.L.R., 207.

onus, and brought the case within the exception referred to....

Boggan *v.* Motor Union Insurance Co.
[1922] 2 I.R. 184
The Court of Appeal in Southern Ireland

RONAN L.J: ... The defendants called no evidence. Mr Battersby [for the defendants] contended that the case came within exception C of the exceptions stated in the policy, and that consequently the loss was not covered. He argued: (1) that the four armed men constituted a riot; (2) that the loss arose during the riot; (3) that the loss was occasioned by the riot; and (4) that the onus of showing that the loss was not occasioned by the riot lay on the insured, and that he had not discharged such onus. The Chief Justice says:—"With some hesitation I came to the conclusion that the case was one of theft, and that the mere fact of the theft having been committed by four armed men acting in concert did not make it a riot within the meaning of the policy. On Mr Battersby's argument, the policy would not cover any case of robbery which was committed by three or more men. I therefore gave judgment for the plaintiff."

Two questions arise in the case, and they arise on the policy. The policy provides that "the company will, subject to the terms, exceptions, and conditions contained herein or endorsed hereon, indemnify the insured against loss, damage, or liability as hereunder mentioned actually occurring during the period above set forth or during any period for which the company may accept payment for the renewal of this policy." The insurance included: (1) loss of or damage to any vehicle by accident; and (2) loss of or damage to any vehicle by "fire, burglary, housebreaking, or theft". Prima facie the case is within the latter clause, and the question is whether it is taken out of it by exception C of the exceptions. The words of that exception are: "Loss or damage arising during (unless it be proved by the insured that the loss or damage was not caused thereby) or in consequence of earthquake, war, invasion, riot, civil commotion, military or usurped power". The burden is on the defendants to prove that the case is within the main part of the clause; but once it was proved that the theft took place during or in consequence of a riot the burden would lie on the plaintiff to prove what is in the parenthesis, namely, that the loss or damage was not occasioned thereby.

... Policies of this kind have to be construed under some general rule of construction. Mr Justice Dodd has favoured me with a very full analysis of the authorities on this question; and he has called my attention to some American cases. American cases do not, of course, bind this court. If the view of the Judges here does not agree with the American judgments, it is their duty not to follow them; but, at the same time, great respect must be paid to the opinions of distinguished American Judges. In one of these American cases, *Spring Garden Insurance Co.* v. *Imperial Tobacco Co.*,[26] I find a very elaborate and careful judgment by Mr Justice Carroll. He says:

> "In the construction of policies the same rule obtains as does in the construction of other contracts, with the exception that a policy will be construed in favour of the insured so as not to defeat, without plain necessity, his claim to the indemnity which in taking the insurance it was his object to secure; and where the words are fairly susceptible of two interpretations, that which will sustain his claim and cover the loss must by preference be adopted. It may also be said that ambiguities and words, sentences, or clauses of doubtful meaning, will be construed against the insurer, and this for the reason, so often declared, that the companies themselves prepare the policies with great care and deliberation; and as the insured has no election except to accept them as prepared and presented to him, it is fair that they should be construed most strongly against the insurer and most liberally in favour of the insured, so that the purpose for which the insurance was obtained may be effectuated if this can be done without doing violence to the contract."

The language of the exception in the policy before us is very remarkable. It is not loss caused by riot or civil commotion. It is loss or damage arising "during" or "in consequence of" riot or civil commotion. To my mind these words point to the view that there is or has been a riot, as distinguished from the specific burglary, housebreaking, or theft. In the present case there was no such riot. The riot sought to be established consisted exclusively of the theft or robbery with violence.

... In dealing with this case we must consider whether the robbery occurred during a riot, or whether we must take clause 2 and exception C together, and read clause 2 as "loss or damage by burglary, housebreaking, or theft, except where such burglary, housebreaking, or theft constitutes a riot in law". That seems to me to be inconsistent with the policy as a whole. The meaning of the policy seems to be that if, while a riot is in progress, or, if there has been a riot, and in consequence of it, a theft takes place, the company is free; but the mere fact that the crime of theft itself contains elements of riot at law does not exclude the right of the insured under the policy. In that case every robbery for which on indictment the accused could technically be convicted also for riot would be outside the policy.

... The second question in the case is that of civil commotion. I have read the evidence, and it seems to me to establish clearly that there was no civil commotion. In his report the Chief Justice did not refer to civil commotion at all; and Mr Battersby, with that absolute fairness which always characterises him, told us that in the Court below he rested his case mainly on riot, but that he raised the point about civil commotion; and I have no doubt he did.

As to civil commotion, we have the advantage of the judgment of the Lord Chancellor (Sir John Ross) in *Cooper* v. *General Accident Assurance Corporation*.[27] He says:

---

[26] 136 American State Reports, 164.

"Two theories are put forward. The plaintiff contends that it was an ordinary case of robbery, where the thief takes the car to sell it, or to keep it for his personal use. The defendants contend that the taking of the car must be considered in the light of the surrounding circumstances; that it is an incident in the working of an existing belligerent system, and that the purpose and intention of the takers are of the utmost importance."

In the Court of Appeal in Southern Ireland O'Connor L.J. said: "In my judgment, as a matter of law, if this car was taken by insurrectionists and as part of the insurrectionary campaign, the loss to the plaintiff would have been caused by civil commotion." That view was confirmed in the High Court of Appeal by the Lord Chancellor, who, having stated that purpose and intention were of the utmost importance, goes on to say:

"I cannot help thinking, with great respect to them all, that the attention of the learned Judges who have dealt with this case was too much occupied in considering the question of onus. A question of onus may be sometimes of immense importance.... But in a case of this kind, where the facts are not in dispute, and where everything depends on the inferences to be drawn from the facts, there is little advantage in discussing the question of onus."

I confess I cannot understand these observations. They must, I think, as Mr Justice Dodd has suggested to me, be regarded as dicta. Lord Campbell reminds us, in *Attorney-General* v. *Dean and Canons of Windsor*,[28] that dicta are to be treated with respect, but followed only so far as agreeable to sound sense and prior authorities. Ross C. adds:

"The judicial mind derives a certain amount of comfort and satisfaction in arriving at a doubtful conclusion by throwing the onus argument into the scale. The truth is that the facts will support either of the two antagonistic conclusions — if to an equal degree, the question of onus is all-important, because if the facts are equally consistent with the two adverse conclusions, the party on whom the onus lies must fail. The question here is one of a balance of probabilities, and the scale is to be turned by a correct conclusion founded on circumstantial evidence."

But once the balance inclines to one side the question must be left to the jury; the fact must be proved, and the probability must be such as to satisfy the tribunal of fact.

On this branch of the case I will only say, speaking for myself, that my own knowledge of the state of the country, my knowledge of Wexford, being absolutely nil, I am unable to say whether it is more probable that these men took the car in order to sell it than that they captured it as part of an insurrectionary system. I cannot come to the conclusion that the Chief Justice was wrong in not being satisfied that the taking of the car was part of a belligerent system; and on this branch of the case I agree with his decision.

---

[27] [1922] 2 I.R. 38, at p.47. See p. 157 of this book.
[28] 8 H.L.C. at p. 392.

There is one other matter on which I should like to say a word. In judging a question of this kind in Ireland in the present day, probability depends largely upon the place where and the time when the incident happened. In a matter of this kind there is a loose way of talking. Everybody knowing anything about the country knows that different persons have different means of knowledge. The Lord Chancellor refers to the crime of motor-stealing before the period of disorder. There is not one scrap of evidence of that in *Cooper's Case*[29] or in this case. In the course of his judgment in *Cooper's Case*,[30] O'Connor L.J. says that while acting as law officer he never came across a single instance of motor-stealing; but, on the other hand, Mr Justice Dodd told us that at Green Street he had tried several such cases. If one Judge happens to have had some special experience, and another Judge happens not to have had that experience, is it seriously contended that the judgment of the Judge at the trial is to be reversed because of some Judge's personal knowledge of facts which were not brought before either of the Courts below? I really know nothing myself about Wexford. I do not read the newspapers carefully, or remember what I read; I have nothing to guide me in this case except the evidence on which the Chief Justice acted; and on that evidence I am not satisfied that the car was taken as part of an insurrectionary system.

For these reasons I am of opinion that the judgment of the Chief Justice should be affirmed.

O'CONNOR L.J: I regret that I am obliged to differ from my colleagues.... I am of opinion that the true meaning and scope of this policy is that where the arm of the ordinary law is paralysed by commotion, disturbance, or riot, the insurers are not liable for theft by armed men. Of course, I say nothing as to a theft or burglary effected by several armed men; there may be such, perhaps, without being a riot, because the terror populi might be absent.

Although I do not base my judgment on civil commotion, I wish to say one or two words on that question. There was a great deal of argument upon it, and some loose observations were made by witnesses to the effect that there was no civil commotion at the time. I wonder what those witnesses would designate civil commotion. No civil commotion at a time when the police had been forced from some of the outlying barracks! no civil commotion at a time when cars were being commandeered and receipts given for them! The ordinary burglar or thief does not give receipts for motor-cars. Matters had not, indeed, come to a head; martial law had not been proclaimed; but the outbreak of civil commotion and the proclamation of martial law do not usually synchronise. Civil commotion did prevail in Wexford when armed men gagged the driver of the car in question here and took it away. I am perfectly satisfied that there was civil commotion; but whether the occurrence was occasioned by it or not I express no opinion, though I should have had no doubt if I had been the Judge of first instance.

---

[29] [1922] 2 I.R. 38. See p. 157 of this book.
[30] *Ibid.*

In *Cooper's Case*[31] the King's Bench Division and Ronan L.J. came to the same conclusion as Moore J. The High Court of Appeal and I were of different opinion. This case seems to me to be stronger in favour of the insurance company than *Cooper's Case*.[32] For these reasons I think the appeal ought to be allowed.

DODD J.: The action comes before us on an application to set aside a verdict and judgment given by the Lord Chief Justice of Ireland, sitting without a jury, on Friday, the 25th of November, 1921....

The learned Chief Justice decided as a question of fact that the theft did not come within the exception "civil commotion", and as a question of law that the mere fact of the theft having been committed by four armed men did not make it "a riot" within the meaning of the policy. Both findings are challenged. The question for us is: are we to set aside either or both? The defendants called no evidence....

I do not, however, rest my judgment upon whether there was evidence upon which the culprits could have been convicted or not. That was not the ground of the Chief Justice's decision. It rests upon the construction of the contract.

The insurers have what they call a comprehensive policy. It is for common use in the United Kingdom, and was apparently made before the increased risks arising from the state of things in Ireland were taken into consideration. The insurance company are entitled to rely on that. But so also is the insured, and we must treat it as such. The insurers agree to indemnify the insurer for a Ford motor car for private hire against loss, damage, or liability by fire, burglary, housebreaking, or theft. If that clause stood alone, the company would be clearly liable. But then come what are called "exceptions". I leave out the parenthesis for a moment. "Except loss or damage arising during or in consequence of earthquake, war, invasion, riot, civil commotion, military or usurped power." It is not well to rely too strongly on the collocation of the words, merely on the word "riot" being interposed between "invasion" and "civil commotion". But it is of moment that it is an exception in a policy of insurance, something abnormal in the way of risk, as petrol on the premises in a fire policy, or the liability to fire in a flax mill, which leads to an increased premium. And apart from the mere order, it being included as a category of "earthquake, war, invasion, civil commotion, military or usurped power", does give a clue to the interpretation to be put upon the word. It has nothing to do with criminal law. The subtleties of lawyers, and the points that might be made either in the prosecution or defence of a man or men accused in a criminal court are entirely irrelevant. The word must find its meaning from the insurance standpoint of increased risk. It points to a condition of things in the body politic, some risk ejusdem generis with war, invasion, or civil commotion altering the normal risk — a tumultuous and violent disturbance of the peace in a local area — such as the Bristol riots, the Gordon riots, the Porteous riots, the Belfast riots, the Derry riots, the Bantry

---

[31] *Ibid.*
[32] *Ibid.*

riots; such a state of things as would lead, if prolonged, to a reading of the Riot Act analogous to the general disturbance by invasion, or war, or civil commotion, military and usurped power, but not intended to apply to what was merely an incident in an ordinary theft. It points to something aliunde the theft itself. And this is what the Chief Justice had in mind. Every word in the "exception" and the parenthesis confirms this interpretation — "arise during a riot", "in consequence of a riot", "occasioned thereby". All of these words point to a thief taking advantage of a state of riot to carry out an independent operation on his own behalf. Can it really be intended that if two armed men steal the car with threats and menaces, the insurance company must pay; if a third is added, the insured must bear the loss?

The contract must be construed as a whole, and on the facts of this particular case I am of opinion that what occurred was not within the contemplation of the parties a "riot"; or, if it can be brought within the word, the loss did not arise "during" or "in consequence of" the riot, nor was it "occasioned" thereby.

I desire to add that my decision is uninfluenced by any question as to the onus of proof. I have been influenced by the consideration that if the insured owners of motor cars are not protected against risk such as this the premiums have been flung away. All Mr Battersby has to do is to say the loss occurred in Ireland and ask for judgment.

I am therefore of opinion that the Chief Justice's ruling on this point also must be upheld, and that his judgment on the whole case be confirmed, and this application be dismissed with costs.

Craig *v* The Eagle Star and British Dominions Insurance Co. and Others
(1922) 56 I.L.T.R. 145
King's Bench Division

MOLONY L.C.J: Thomas Craig claimed as against the first mentioned company under a policy of insurance dated 24th January, 1919, whereby the company agreed to insure the claimant against loss or damage by fire to the extent of £23,500. He made similar claims against the English Insurance Co., Ltd., for £5,000, under a policy dated 4th June, 1920, and against the Drapers and General Insurance Co., Ltd., for £11,500 under two policies dated 4th February, 1918, and 5th May, 1920. The three claims arose out of a fire which occurred on the claimant's premises on the 17th August, 1920. The companies contended that they were not liable on the ground that the loss was caused or happened through civil commotion. In pursuance of a provision in each of the policies the dispute in each case was referred to arbitration, and by three several awards, all dated 5th May, 1922, the arbitrators found that the loss was not occasioned nor did it happen through civil commotion, and they awarded the claimant the full sum claimed under each of the policies, but agreed to state a special case ... and the question submitted was whether, upon the facts, the arbitrators were justified in finding that the sum awarded in each case was payable under the policy? It was contended on behalf of the respondents that the evidence proved that the loss occurred through civil commotion.... The definition of civil commotion has been extended somewhat in this country by the decision of the High Court of Appeal in the case of *Cooper* v. *The General Accident Fire and Life Assurance Corporation, Ltd*[33] .... The Lord Chancellor, in his judgment, referred to the fact that civil commotion may manifest itself in various ways — in homicide, in arson, in tumult, in kidnapping, in ambushing, in forcible capture of war material, and such like. Each of these things when it occurs is an incident or a constituent element in the civil commotion, it goes to constitute the civil commotion that is manifesting itself in this form for the time being. In the present case it appears from the evidence set forth in the cases stated that the drapery premises of the claimant were maliciously set fire to, and that in or about the same time the business premises of Mr John S. Melville, on the other side of the street, were also set on fire. The fires were clearly malicious, but there was no evidence as to who were the perpetrators of the crimes or how many persons may have participated in the criminal acts.... [E]ven if the crimes were ... committed by a number of persons in pursuance of an organised conspiracy, the case of the *London and Manchester Plate Glass Co.* v. *Heath*[34] shows that this would not be sufficient to amount in itself to a civil commotion. On the whole case I am of opinion that the arbitrators were amply justified in holding that the loss was not caused by, nor did it happen through, civil commotion, and that consequently the claimant is entitled to recover the sums secured by the different policies mentioned.

SAMUELS J. CONCURRED.

General Omnibus Company, Limited, *v.* London General Insurance Company, Limited
[1936] I.R. 596
The High Court

HANNA J: The facts that are relevant to this case are as follows:—

The plaintiffs insured, under a policy of insurance, dated July 11th, 1929, four buses in general terms in respect of accidents from April 4th, 1929, to April 4th, 1930. One of them met with a collision on September 14th, 1929, when running from Dublin to Maynooth, and on that occasion it was carrying at least ten persons in addition to its legitimate seating complement of thirty-four, for which it was originally licensed.

Now, I find as a fact that the bus ran into a turf cart and injured the driver, a man called Roche, and also a passenger in the bus, called Lynch, who was standing on the step of the bus alongside the driver's partition. Lynch seems to have been in this dangerous position in consequence of the

---

[33] [1922] 2 I.R. 38. See p.157 of this book
[34] [1913] 3 K.B. 421.

over-loading of the bus, and if he had been seated the accident to him would not have occurred.

Notice of the accident was given on the same day, or the next day, by the Bus Company to the Insurance Company, and on September 16th, a report of the facts was obtained from the driver, and on 16th December the Insurance Company wrote repudiating all liability, as the bus was carrying more passengers than it was entitled to carry, and, that being so, they did it at their own risk. Prior thereto Roche had issued a plenary summons against the Omnibus Company to recover damages, but the Insurance Company repudiated all liability and refused to defend. This action was remitted to the Circuit Court, and on June 20th, 1930, Roche recovered judgment for the sum of £31 7s. 11d., including costs of the proceedings, which, with the present plaintiffs' costs, amounting to £28 3s. 0d., makes a total of £59 10s. 11d. Lynch subsequently brought an action against the Bus Company who, on the advice of their counsel, and having regard to the facts proved in Roche's case, consented to judgment, on the case being opened in Court, for £650 damages and costs, taxed to £206 19s. 7d. This sum, in addition to £111 6s. 8d. the present plaintiffs' costs, makes in all £968 6s. 3d. The defendants, the Insurance Company, having refused to pay the amounts, the plaintiffs have now brought this action to recover these two sums amounting in all to £1,027 17s. 2d.

The defence as argued before me was as follows:—

That under the terms of the policy, exemption (e), no risk was undertaken by the Insurance Company in respect of passengers where the bus was overloaded; that, as regards both claims, they were out of time by reason of the fact that, under condition 5 of the policy, there is a limitation of three months from the date of the repudiation of liability by the Insurance Company within which the insured should make his claim; and thirdly that, as regards the claim in Lynch's case, the policy did not cover the insured in respect of the sum paid by way of compromise without the consent in writing of the Insurance Company under condition 2 endorsed on the policy.

The first defence depends upon the interpretation and construction of the exclusions or exceptions as stated in exemption (e). The policy starts by giving an indemnity in general terms and then imposing exceptions. The law is that the Insurance Company must bring their case clearly and unambiguously within the exception under which they claim benefit, and, if there is any ambiguity, it must be given against them on the principle *contra proferentes*. The general indemnity is in clause 4 in the following terms:—

> "Liability at law for compensation (including law costs awarded and taxed, or agreed, of any claimant) for death of, or bodily injury to, any person not being a passenger in, or driver of such vehicle...."

This, *prima facie,* covers Roche's case.

The same indemnity is given in the next sentence in respect of any person being a passenger travelling on a bus where the number of persons carried does not exceed 131 passengers in one accident or occurrence. *Prima facie,* this would cover Lynch's case.

This general indemnity is subject to the following exclusion:—

(e)   "Loss, damage and/or liability to the vehicle, caused or arising while such vehicle .... is conveying any load in excess of that for which it was constructed...."

We must read with this the schedule at the top of the policy and of the proposal, each of which sets out specifically and distributively the seating capacity of each bus. As the policy is drawn up in general form, which may apply to any class of motors, the word "load" must be construed with reference to the particular class of vehicle insured, and the test of the word in this policy is the capacity given in the schedule and in the proposal. As I have indicated, I find that this bus was carrying a load of passengers in excess of that for which it was licensed. This leaves only the question as to what subject-matter this clause applies. It has been argued before me that the words "loss, damage and/or liability to the vehicle" include not only loss or damage to the vehicle but also loss and liability in respect of passengers. If the Insurance Company intended such a limitation by the exemption they have not clearly expressed it and I cannot extend this exclusion beyond its ordinary meaning. I therefore confine it (the exclusion) to the breakdown of, or loss or damage to, the bus by any of the circumstances set out in the exclusion. This seems to me to give an intelligible meaning to the words. I think this view is strengthened by reference to the words qualifying loss or liability in the other exclusions.

On the second point, as to condition 5, this is claimed as one of the conditions precedent to the right of the insured to recover, and the relevant part is: "If a claim be not made within seven days after the accident or loss has occurred or, if made and rejected by the Company, an action or suit be not commenced within three months after such rejection...." Now, the first question arises herein, in respect of both Roche and Lynch, when did the loss occur in respect of which a claim was made and rejected by the Company? This will give us, in each case, a terminus from which to measure the three months. As regards the ordinary law, so far as the Statute of Limitations is concerned, time does not begin to run until the cause of action is complete, whether it be a debt or a tort, and that is the proper test in this case; equally, with the converse proposition, that there can be no repudiation or rejection by the Company within that condition, so as to start the three months' bar in their favour, until the insured either makes the claim in respect of a loss, or suffers a loss by being compellable to make a payment by process of law under a judgment, or has actually made a payment in respect of which he is to be saved harmless by the Company. In my view, the right under this policy for the insured to claim within the meaning of that condition does not arise until a loss to him has legally matured, and the limitation clause runs from the rejection of the claim in respect thereof.

The plenary summons in this case was issued on February 2nd, 1931, and so far as Roche's case is concerned it is barred by this clause.

Subject to the consideration of the third point the action in respect of Lynch's claim is in time.

The third point is that the sum claimed in Lynch's case was a compromise assessment of damages.

Counsel for the Insurance Company relies on condition 2 of the policy which reads:—

> "No admission, promise or payment shall be made by the insured without the written consent of the Company, which shall be entitled, if it so desires, to take over and conduct in the name of the insured the defence and settlement of any claim, or to prosecute in his name for its own benefit any claim or indemnity for damages or otherwise against any third party, and shall have full discretion in the conduct of any proceedings or in the settlement of any claim, and the insured shall give all information and assistance as the Company may require, failing which, benefit under this policy will be forfeited."

We can start with this, that it was not contended in this case that the settlement or the costs claimed in Lynch's action were incurred improvidently, unreasonably, or *mala fide*. In my opinion it is settled law that it is no bar to an indemnity that the liability has been arrived at by agreement or compromise which was not improvident, unreasonable, or *mala fide*. In the case of *Smith* v. *Compton*[35] and also in the Irish case *Caldbeck* v. *Boon*[36] it was decided that it was open to show that such a compromise was not unreasonable. The same principle is established in *Lord Newborough* v. *Schröder*.[37]

Finally, what is the effect of condition 2? It is concerned, in my opinion, with the taking over by the Insurance Company of the proceedings on behalf of the insured, and its intendment is that nothing is to be done by the insured to prejudice the main right of the insurer, so that, if the Insurance Company has to contest the case, the insured is not to make any "admission, promise, or payment without the written consent of the Company". I cannot accept the arguments *contra*, for this condition is quite inconsistent with the circumstances under which the insured has to defend his own action. I am further of opinion that an Insurance Company which refuses to take advantage of the right under that condition to take over the action, and repudiates liability on any ground, would be debarred from relying on such a condition as a condition precedent, and would be confined to such remedy, if any, as they had on its substance as a part of the contract. If, under such circumstances of repudiation, a payment or settlement could be proved improvident, unreasonable, or *mala fide,* the Insurance Company might rely on such rights as they had outside the condition. Reading condition 2 as a whole, I am satisfied that it must be read and interpreted as I have indicated, and that the compromise here was not an "admission, promise or payment" within the meaning of the condition or affected by its terms. The defendants, therefore, having failed to avail themselves of any of the rights under this condition, its terms became in my opinion irrelevant.

---

[35] 3 B. & Ad. 407.
[36] I.R. 7 C.L. 32.
[37] 7 C.B. 342, at pp. 398–9.

I must hold that the plaintiffs are entitled to recover the amount of £968 6s. 3d. paid in Lynch's case.

The Supreme Court

KENNEDY C.J: This is an appeal by the defendant Insurance Company from the judgment for £968 6s. 3d. and costs entered for the plaintiff Omnibus Company at the trial of the action by Hanna J.

... There is no dispute of fact in the case and the questions to be decided upon this appeal are entirely matters of interpretation of the document containing the contract of insurance. The policy is in many respects an ill-drawn document, stupid and unintelligible in many parts, due perhaps to amendments made from time to time by unskilled draftsmen in the form used by the Company so as to meet particular cases as they occurred, but the Court must take the document as it stands before it and do its best to interpret it and give effect to such interpretation.

The first and the main case of the Insurance Company rests upon the case as to over-loading founded upon the "exclusion" *(e)*. It is extraordinarily difficult to make sense of this clause not merely by reason of the use of that objectionable device of modern laziness "and/or", but also because of the difficulty of giving a sane meaning to the words "liability to the vehicle". One may speculate that, as was suggested, the expression "and/or liability" was an amendment subsequently inserted in the form but erroneously introduced before, instead of after, the words "the vehicle", or one may make other guesses at the explanation of the thing. The Court, however, has nothing to do with such speculations. We must take the contract as made between the parties and see whether upon any reasonable construction of the clause it operates to exclude the plaintiff Company from the benefit of the indemnity claimed. After careful consideration we are agreed, and Mr Justice Hanna also thought, that there is no plausible construction of the clause which will exclude the present claim by reason of the vehicle "conveying any load in excess of that for which it was constructed", especially so, having regard to the terms of the indemnity in respect of bodily injury to a person "being a passenger travelling in such vehicle", which liability is limited to 131 passengers in any one accident. I have nothing to add to the views expressed on this clause in the opinion about to be read by Mr Justice Murnaghan. In my opinion, the present claim is not within the terms of the matters excluded from the policy by reason of the fact that the vehicle was conveying a load in excess of 34 passengers.

The second clause to be considered is condition No. 2....[38] The Insurance Company relies upon the fact that James Lynch's action was settled by a payment made without the written consent of the Company as forfeiting the policy. In my opinion, having regard to the fact that, though formally urged by the plaintiff Company to undertake the conduct of the action, the Insurance

---

[38] Set out at p.177 above.

Company, having from the first and at all times repudiated the policy in reliance upon the exclusion to which I have just referred, cannot be heard, on the one hand, insisting that the policy was forfeited and repudiating all liability under it, and, at the same time, insisting that the Company must give a written consent in writing to any demand or payment made by the insured. There is no suggestion made that the compromise of Lynch's action was in any respect improvident or was *mala fide,* and I am of opinion for the reasons stated in the opinion about to be read by Mr Justice Murnaghan that Mr Justice Hanna was right in his decision that condition No. 2 is no answer to the present claim.

Considerable difficulty arises in the interpretation and application of condition No. 5 which is the last resort of the Insurance Company but which has been very strongly pressed. The problem is to determine as from what date the period of three months runs within which the plaintiff Company should bring an action to establish the claim to indemnity, failing which all benefit under the policy becomes forfeited and the liability of the Insurance Company ceases. I agree with Mr Justice Hanna that on no construction can the claim in respect of Roche's case be saved, but Mr Justice Hanna has held that this action to enforce the claim in Lynch's case has been commenced within the period of three months mentioned in the clause. He does so by holding that the claim could not be made until judgment was obtained by Lynch in respect of which the plaintiff Company could claim indemnity because the cause of action was not complete before such judgment. The judgment in Lynch's case was given on the 3rd of November, 1930, and, if Mr Justice Hanna's view of the clause is accepted, then the present action would have been brought within the period of three months, the originating summons having been issued on the second day of February, 1931, one day before the expiry of the period of three months on that calculation.

The one crucial question in my opinion is:— What is the meaning of the expression "claim made within seven days after the accident or loss has occurred"? It will be found on examining the headings of the indemnity granted by the policy, that both the words "accident" and "loss" have subject-matter therein as some of the subjects of indemnity are not matters arising from accident, *e.g.,* loss arising from burglary, loss arising from theft, etc., and, in my opinion, the word "loss" in the particular clause has reference to those headings of the indemnity provisions of the policy, and the present case would not in my opinion fall within that term but is covered by the word "accident". If that view be accepted, then it appears to me to be quite beyond doubt that the claim must be made within seven days after the accident in a case like the present and that, if so made and rejected, the claimant must institute his suit to establish his right to indemnity against the Insurance Company within three months after such rejection. For this purpose the cause of action was, in my opinion, complete when the Insurance Company rejected the claim and repudiated liability. Such an action was *Tinline* v. *White Cross Insurance Association, Limited.*[39]

---

[39] [1921] 3 K.B. 327.

The first rejection of the claim of the plaintiff Company was on the 16th of December, 1929, repeated and confirmed on the 18th of December, 1929, 28th of January, 1930, and 27th of June, 1930. It is true that at none of these dates had Lynch's claim been brought to a determination in a Court of Justice, but the plaintiff Company was well aware, having had advice at an early date, that it was not necessary to wait because it might, forthwith, as it announced its intention of doing, have instituted the action against the Insurance Company for a declaration of liability under the policy, and, if the only defence the Insurance Company could have presented would have been the defence under the exclusion clause *(e)* of the policy, the plaintiff Company must have succeeded in obtaining a declaration of the liability of the Insurance Company notwithstanding the exclusion clause, which must, in my opinion, have been held not to apply to the case. The plaintiff Company failed to take the threatened action within the time specified in the contract. The Company was bound by the terms of its contract, however rigid they may be, and, as I interpret the document, cannot succeed in the present action, the claim in which, in my opinion, became barred by the time limit imposed by condition No. 5.

In my opinion, therefore, differing on this point from the opinion of Mr Justice Hanna, the judgment in this action must be set aside and judgment entered for the Insurance Company with costs.

FITZGIBBON J: I do not propose to deal at any length with two of the defences pleaded by the appellants. All the members of the Court agree for reasons which are fully stated in the judgment which is about to be read by my Brother Murnaghan and to which I desire to add nothing that the exclusion of "loss, damage and/or liability *to the vehicle* caused or arising whilst such vehicle is engaged in racing, pace-making, in any reliability trial, speed testing (other than Police testing) or is conveying any load in excess of that for which it was constructed or arising outside the Irish Free State, or loss or damage and/or liability of *any kind* arising whilst any such vehicle is being driven by any person other than a competent licensed driver" does not apply to a claim such as that which arose in the circumstances of the present case, in which there was no "loss, damage and/or liability *to the vehicle*", whatever that may mean. The defendants, upon whom the onus rested, have failed to bring themselves within the words of the exclusion from a clear obligation under clauses 4 and 5 of the agreement to indemnify contained in the policy.

In my opinion also, if the defendants were bound, in the particular circumstances of this case, by the contract to indemnify the plaintiffs, they cannot rely upon the alleged non-compliance by the assured with the terms of clause 2 of the conditions endorsed upon and incorporated with the policy of assurance. From the earliest moment the defendants expressly repudiated all liability in respect of the accident which occurred on September 14th 1929. To each letter from the plaintiffs or their solicitor, giving information to the defendants or calling upon them to take up or to interest themselves in the defence of the claims threatened or the actions brought against the plaintiffs, the invariable reply was: we have repudiated all liability under the policy "and we are not prepared to deal with the matter *in any way whatever*." If they were not justified by the terms of their contract in taking up that attitude, they cannot now rely on the failure of the plaintiffs to consult them about the settlement of Lynch's claim. If ever there could be an express waiver by an insurer of all right to be consulted in the settlement by the assured of a claim against him, there is such a waiver on the facts of this case. The attitude that "We repudiate all liability on our part under the contract, but we hold you to act as if we had not done so, and we insist that you shall obey us in the conduct of an action for the result of which we deny all responsibility" is utterly untenable. In my opinion, there was an express waiver by the defendants of all right to be consulted about the conduct of the defence of the proceedings instituted by Lynch against the plaintiffs.

The third ground of defence is the only one which has caused any difficulty in my mind, and the doubt which I have is due only to the difference of opinion in this Court upon the question involved.

In my opinion condition No. 5 affords, in the circumstances of this case, a defence to the plaintiff's claim. The material words of that condition are as follows:

> "If a claim be not made within seven days after the accident or loss has occurred, or, if made and rejected by the company, an action or suit be not commenced within three months after such rejection, all benefit under this policy shall be forfeited and the Company will not be in any way liable thereunder."

In my opinion, the word "claim" in that condition can refer only to a claim under the policy by the assured against "the Company", which is defined to mean the defendants. It would make the policy worthless if the assured had no indemnity unless the third party formulated his claim within seven days after the accident in which he was injured, or if, having preferred his claim, and the Company, in exercise of their right to defend proceedings, having rejected it, he did not commence legal proceedings within three months from the date of such rejection. Therefore I am quite convinced that the "claim" referred to in condition 5 must be a claim by the assured under the policy. That *claim* must be made "within seven days after the accident or loss has occurred". It is a matter distinct from the "notice of accident" which must be given to the insurer "immediately upon the occurrence of such accident *or loss,* or in the event of any claim whatsoever", and in my opinion the claim to which the condition refers is an intimation by the assured that he intends to hold the insurer liable to indemnify him under the terms of the policy. There may be, and one can scarcely pretend to judicial ignorance that there are, accidents and losses in respect of which the insured, though he may give notice of them to the insurer, does not think it worth his while to claim an indemnity, because the 10 per cent bonus in case of "no claim" is worth more to him than the indemnity against the particular accident or loss, and there is actually in the policy under consideration a provision for a bonus allowance in the event of no *claim* within twelve months. In my opinion the plain object of the condition was to enable the insurer to know, in the case of any accident or loss of which he received notice, whether the assured claimed to be indemnified or not, so that he might investigate the matter and decide whether he would settle with the injured party or defend any proceedings, or, as happened in this case, repudiate liability altogether on the ground of a violation by the assured of the condition upon which an indemnity was guaranteed.

I cannot accept the construction of this clause which interprets the word "loss" as applicable to an adverse verdict, and would relieve the assured from making any "claim" until after a verdict had been recorded against him, on the ground that he had incurred no loss until the action had proceeded to judgment, and that no claim could be formulated until the liability had been reduced to monies numbered. Suppose the assured defends an action successfully, is he incapacitated from making a "claim" to be indemnified against the costs until he has failed to recover the party and party costs from his unsuccessful opponent, and has taxed the solicitor and client bill of his own attorney.

In truth I can find no place in this policy in which the word "loss" is not satisfied by its primary meaning of the physical disappearance or destruction of some article, except the exclusion in sub-clause (f) of *"loss of use* of such vehicle during repair or *any consequential loss* arising directly or indirectly from any accident, damage, injury *or loss"*. The condition No. 1 requiring "notice of any accident *or loss"* to be given in writing to the insurer "immediately upon the occurrence of such accident *or loss"* cannot mean that the assured may wait till an adverse verdict has been recorded against him before he gives notice to the Company, that he then has, under condition 5, seven days from the verdict to put in a claim in respect of it, although the Company may have, as they did here, repudiated all liability as soon as they were informed of the circumstances of the "accident" out of which the "loss" was supposed to have arisen.

There is no doubt that a person claiming a right to be indemnified under a policy of assurance can institute proceedings against the insurer if the latter repudiates liability to indemnify him in accordance with the terms of the policy, or claims that in the particular circumstances of the case the policy is inoperative, and that a declaration that such a right exists may be obtained before any verdict has been recovered against the party claiming it. In *Tinlin* v. *White Cross Insurance Association Limited,*[40] an insurance company repudiated liability to indemnify a motorist against whom several actions, some of which had been prosecuted to judgment, were pending. The assured instituted proceedings to obtain a declaration that he was entitled to indemnity against the result of the pending actions, and Bailhache J. held that he was entitled to the declaration sought, and where there is a *bona fide* dispute it is obviously to the advantage of both insurer and assured that their respective rights and liabilities should be ascertained, if possible, before, and not after, expensive litigation with third parties. In my opinion, the object and effect of condition 5 was to provide means for such an ascertainment in case of dispute.

The views of the parties cannot decide the question of construction, but any suggestion that the interpretation I have put upon the clause will occasion hardship in this particular case is obviated by the fact that the same

---

[40] [1921] 3 K.B. 327.

interpretation was put upon it by the plaintiffs, who had actually instructed their solicitor, very shortly after, and well within the prescribed period of three months of, the rejection of their claim to an indemnity by the defendants, to institute proceedings against the defendants to compel them to accept liability.

In my opinion judgment should have been given for the defendants....

MURNAGHAN J: It is not disputed that the claim for indemnity made under the policy in this action comes within the general indemnity against liability at law for compensation, which the plaintiff Company have incurred towards the claimant Roche, who was not a passenger, as well as towards Lynch, who was a passenger. It accordingly lies upon the defendants in accordance with the established rules of construction to bring the case within an exception. The defendants accordingly rely upon clause *(e)* under the heading "exclusions", viz.: "This policy does not cover or insure against ... loss, damage and/or liability to the vehicle caused or arising whilst such vehicle is engaged in racing, pace-making, in any reliability trial, speed-testing (other than Police testing), or is conveying any load in excess of that for which it was constructed or arising outside the Irish Free State, or loss or damage and/or liability of any kind arising whilst any such vehicle is being driven by any person other than a competent licensed driver."

On the question of fact the Judge at the trial has found that the vehicle was conveying a load in excess of that for which it was constructed, but it still remains to be established as a matter of construction that the subject-matter of the claim is "loss, damage and/or liability to the vehicle". These words are not very intelligible, but we cannot speculate as to what was intended, and a meaning must be given as reasonable as possible to the words used. In the clause "loss, damage and/or liability" is contrasted with "loss or damage and/or liability of any kind". If, in the present case, the bus had not been driven by a licensed driver, the exception would cover the case, but it is difficult to see how liability at law for damages arising out of negligence can be "loss, damage and/or liability to the vehicle". If the words "and/or liability" were transposed so that the clause *(e)* read:— "This policy does not cover or insure against ... loss or damage to the vehicle and/or liability caused or arising whilst such vehicle is conveying any load in excess of that for which it was constructed", there might be some ground for the defendants' argument. But it is impossible to make such a transposition which would alter the contract entered into, and in my opinion the words "to the vehicle" cannot be disassociated from the words preceding. In my opinion the defendants have failed to bring themselves within this exception.

The defendant Company rely also upon the endorsed condition No. 2 which reads as follows:

> "No admission, promise or payment shall be made by the insured without the written consent of the Company, which shall be entitled, if it so desires, to take over and conduct in the name of the insured the defence and settlement of any claim, or to prosecute in his name for its own benefit any claim or indemnity for damages or otherwise against any third party, and shall have full discretion in the conduct of any proceedings or in the settlement of

any claim, and the insured shall give all information and assistance as the Company may require, failing which benefit under this policy will be forfeited."

There is no dispute as to the facts which give rise to the question of construction involved in the application of this condition. The defendant Company at an early stage repudiated all liability, by reason of the overcrowding of the bus, in both Roche's claim and Lynch's claim. After Roche had succeeded in an action in the Circuit Court, Lynch's action came to a hearing in the High Court. The plaintiff Company, who were defending this action, gave every information to the Insurance Company from time to time, and again informed the Company that the case was in the list for trial. The Insurance Company adhered to their decision and refused to take any part in the proceedings. When the case was actually at trial before a Judge and jury, on the advice of senior counsel the action was compromised for the sum of £650 and costs. The contention of the defendant Company is that they are under no liability because, by reason of the settlement in Court, the insured made "an admission, promise or payment" within the meaning of condition 2. In my opinion the meaning of the condition is that the insured must not do anything which will prejudice the Insurance Company in conducting the defence of the action, if the company desires to take over the defence. In my opinion the clause has no application to a case such as the present where the Insurance Company has refused to take any part in defending the action, and it does not debar the insured from settling the case when it has come into Court for final determination. There is no suggestion that the compromise was unreasonable, and it must in many cases be a saving of considerable amount to avoid a protracted hearing in Court.

Another defence made by the defendant Company is that the action has not commenced in time. The endorsed condition 5 so far as material reads:— "If a claim be not made within seven days after the accident or loss has occurred or, if made and rejected by the Company, an action or suit be not commenced within three months after such rejection, all benefit under this policy shall be forfeited and the Company will not be in any way liable thereunder."

The accident giving rise to the claims brought by both Roche and Lynch occurred on 14th September, 1929. Notice of the accident was duly given, but, after the Insurance Company had investigated the claim, a letter of repudiation was written on 16th December, 1929. The judgment in Roche's claim was given in June, 1930, and the judgment in Lynch's claim was given on 3rd November, 1930. The summons in the action was issued on 2nd February, 1931.

With regard to many classes of claim for indemnity under the policy the right to the indemnity will arise immediately upon the occurrence of the accident. But in the case of an indemnity for liability at law, the question of liability is not ascertained at the date of the accident. It will frequently depend upon the view formed subsequently by a jury in an action for negligence. In such a case the subject-matter of the indemnity does not arise until the liability at law has been ascertained. In my opinion a claim under the policy in such a case i.e. a claim for indemnity against liability at law for compensation, can only properly be said to have arisen when the liability at law has been established. And, further, the claim for indemnity at law for compensation can only be said to have been repudiated when it is ascertained that the liability exists. The Insurance Company may prospectively give notification that they will repudiate any claim that may be made if liability is afterwards established, but this is not, properly speaking, a repudiation of a claim under the policy. An action in the ordinary way cannot be brought upon the policy for an indemnity which has not yet been established. I agree with the view taken by Mr Justice Hanna that the period of three months only begins to run from the date when liability at law has been established. The only action which the defendants suggest could have been taken is one for a declaration that, if the third party succeeded in establishing a case of liability at law, the Insurance Company would be bound by the contract of indemnity. I do not think that the clause can be interpreted to apply to such a proceeding — it deals with a claim which arises under the policy and not hypothetical claims which will arise only if the third party has been successful in his action against the insured.

In Re Sweeney and Kennedy's Arbitration
[1950] I.R. 85
The High Court

KINGSMILL MOORE J. DELIVERED THE JUDGEMENT OF THE COURT: On the 4th March, 1946, Denis Sweeney, being anxious to insure a motor lorry, his property, signed a proposal form for insurance which was furnished to him on behalf of a group of underwriters at Lloyds'. The form was printed and, apparently, adapted to be used in respect of any form of commercial vehicle from a delivery van to the heaviest form of tractor now using the roads. Sweeney had no say in the preparation or wording of the form which, when presented to him, was entirely the product of the underwriters. Various questions appeared on the form requesting information on matters which the underwriters desired to ascertain. Some related to the type of cover required, some to events in the past, some to the present state of affairs and one as to intended future usages. Question No. 9 ran as follows:— "Are any of your drivers under 21 years of age or with less than 12 months' driving experience?" To this Sweeney answered, "No", and the arbitrator has found as a fact that this answer correctly stated the facts on the day when the proposal form was signed. He has found further that at that date Sweeney had no intention of employing as a driver his son, Thomas, and by inference, that Sweeney had no intention of employing any driver under twenty-one.

On the 18th March, 1946, a policy issued in respect of the vehicle. By a recital the written proposal was deemed to be incorporated in the policy. It was from time to time renewed and a number of other vehicles of different kinds were subsequently brought within its provisions by different endorsement slips. This policy was in force at the time of the accident which gave rise to the present dispute.

From the month of June, 1946, to the month of February, 1947, Sweeney occasionally employed his son, Thomas, who was under 21, to drive one or other of his motor vehicles; from the 2nd February, 1947, Thomas was regularly so employed. On the 7th October, 1947, Thomas, then still under 21, but with over twelve months' experience, was in charge of one of the insured vehicles when a fatal accident occurred while the vehicle was being off-loaded. The dependants of the deceased man claimed damages against Sweeney who referred the claim to the underwriters, but the underwriters refused to accept liability. Thereupon, the dispute as to whether liability attached was submitted to arbitration, pursuant to the terms of the policy, and the learned arbitrator, having taken evidence and heard argument, found that the underwriters were bound to indemnify Sweeney against his liability (if any) to the dependants of the deceased man, but, on request, drew up his award in the form of a Special Case for our opinion as to whether he was right in so holding.

Mr Doyle, who appeared for the underwriters, argued first that the employment of a driver who was under 21 so fundamentally altered the character of the risk insured that the policy was automatically avoided. Question No. 9 and its answer showed, he said, that the underwriters based their calculations on the assumption that only drivers of maturity would be engaged, and if a driver under 21 years of age was employed the basis of this calculation went by the board and the subject of the insurance was radically altered. In support of this proposition he cited two cases: *Denison* v. *Modigliani*[41] and *Beauchamp* v. *National Mutual Indemnity Insurance Co. Ltd.*[42]

Denision v. *Modigliani*[43] was an unusual and extreme case. The owners of an ordinary merchant vessel had insured it as such. Subsequently, they desired to furnish it with guns and to provide it with a letter of marque which would convert it into a privateer entitled by international law to chase, capture, and take prize any enemy vessel. The underwriters, to whom this project was communicated, consented to guns being taken on board — for the guns could be used defensively to resist capture, and so might decrease the risk — but they definitely refused to allow the vessel to carry a letter of marque. Nevertheless, a letter of marque was obtained and, while carrying it, the vessel was captured by an enemy privateer. The owners of this vessel claimed against the underwriters. Lord Kenyon held that there was such an essential alteration of circumstances from the condition of the vessel at the time of the insurance as ought to discharge the underwriters unless it were done with their consent. Grose J. held that there was a direct departure from the nature of the contract, as understood between the parties. Even if no use were made of the letter of marque, it held out a temptation which was altogether repugnant to the nature of the contract entered into and contrary to the professed understanding of the contracting parties.

In *Beauchamp's Case*[44] the insured, as the Court found, had given a warranty that no explosives would be used in the work of demolishing a large mill. Explosives were used, with fatal results. Finlay J., having first decided

---

[41] (1794) 5 T.R. 380.
[42] [1937] 3 All E.R. 19.
[43] (1794) 5 T.R. 380.
[44] [1937] 3 All E.R. 19.

the issue as to whether there was or was not a warranty, went on to consider what would be the position apart form any question of warranty, and came to the conclusion that the company had only insured what he called a "non-explosive demolition", and that the risks involved in "explosive demolition" were so widely different that, even if there had been no warranty, the insurance would be avoided. To this conclusion he was slightly helped by evidence on behalf of the insurance company that it would not have entertained the risk of insuring a demolition where explosives were to be used. There is no finding before the Court that any evidence was given on behalf of the underwriters that they would have refused to insure Sweeney if they knew one of his drivers was under 21 and it has not been so suggested. I do not, however, stress this point. Whether a change in risk is so great as to avoid an insurance must always be a question of degree and a question of the opinion of the Court in the circumstances of the case. I can see a vast difference between the risks involved in insuring a merchantman and a privateer; a smaller, but still very substantial, difference between the risks involved in insuring an explosive and a non-explosive demolition; and a very exiguous difference between the risks of insuring when a driver is under or over 21. The law provides that licenses to drive motor vehicles may be given to persons of specified ages, the ages varying with the class of the vehicle; and when a person is driving a vehicle of the category which by his age he is entitled to drive there is, I think, some presumption that, as far as age reflects on competency, he is competent to drive it. Certainly, this would be an honest and reasonable view for an insured person to take in a case where he had not been expressly limited by the terms of the policy to the employment of drivers over 21 years of age. Certain categories of vehicles may not, by law, be driven by persons under 21 and, as the framework of the proposal form was apt to cover an application for insurance of such vehicles, he might reasonably consider that question No. 9 was designed to call attention to this fact. If insurers take a different view as to the proper age of drivers from the view of the law it is open to them — indeed, I would say, incumbent upon them — to make this clear by the insertion of specific provisions in the policy and not to attempt to secure their ends by a side wind. I hold there was no such alteration in the subject-matter of the insurance as would or could avoid the policy.

Mr Doyle's second argument was that Question No. 9 and its answer, taken by themselves, must in all the circumstances of the case be construed as amounting to a warranty that no driver aged under 21 years and with less than 12 months' experience would be employed during the currency of the policy. Question and answer, so far as grammar is concerned, deal only with the point of time when the answer is given; but Mr Doyle says that the question is meaningless unless it is construed as referring to the future and that by necessary intendment it must so refer. For this proposition he relied on the first point decided in *Beauchamp's Case*[45] which it is now necessary to examine a little more closely.

---

[45] [1937] 3 All E.R. 19.

Mr Beauchamp was a builder who had formed the project of demolishing — and, subsequently rebuilding — a large mill in Oldham. Before starting this work he took out a policy of insurance in respect of employees to be engaged in the work of demolishing this particular building. On the proposal form was the question, "Are any ... explosives ... used in your business?" to which the answer given was, "No". By the terms of the proposal form answers were made the basis of the contract. As already mentioned explosives were subsequently used, resulting in the death of three men. Finlay J. held that question and answer must be held to refer forward to the period of demolition. At p. 22 he gives his reasons as follows:—

> "It is necessary here to ascertain what was being insured and what was being referred to. The plaintiff, as I mentioned was a builder. He was a person who was not doing any other demolition work. This insurance was solely in respect of the one isolated demolition job, so to speak, at this Alexandra Mill, at Oldham, and it seems to me, therefore, that the proposal form must inevitably have reference to the future, because, though, in fact, the plaintiff was in business, he was not insuring anything with regard to his general business, but was insuring in respect only of this special job in the future. Accordingly, it seems to me that the whole of the proposal must be regarded as having reference to a future event, and when, in these circumstances, he is asked, 'Are any acids, gases, chemicals, explosives, or any other dangerous preparations used in your business,' that does not, of course, mean his present business of a builder: it means the business on which he is going to embark, the business of demolition. Accordingly, it seems to me that it does have the nature of a warranty or a condition."

This was a decision on special facts. An unusual work, not yet commenced, and out of the ordinary business of the insured, formed the sole subject of insurance. By its nature it might easily require the use of explosives, which are not ordinarily required in the business of building, as opposed to demolition. It appears, moreover, that both parties understood question and answer to refer to the future, though Mr Beauchamp was under the mistaken idea that he was to be at liberty to employ an independent person to use explosives. In construing a policy regard must always be had to the surrounding circumstances in order that the policy may be read as the parties intended it to be read: *Union Insurance Society of Canton Ltd.* v. *George Wills & Co.*[46] The circumstances in *Beauchamp's Case*[47] showed clearly that the question and answer, though apparently referring to the present, were intended to refer to the future, and the case is merely an example of the general rule that the ordinary meaning of words or the ordinary usage of grammar may give place to a special meaning or usage where the circumstances clearly, imperiously, and irresistibly so demand. I do not think the circumstances of the case with which we are dealing make any such demand and, by contrast

---

[46] [1916] 1 A.C. 281.
[47] [1937] 3 All E.R. 19.

with *Beauchamp's Case*,[48] would refer to the later and illuminating case of *Woolfall & Rimmer Ltd.* v. *Moyle*,[49] heard before the English Court of Appeal. The proposal form contained the question, "Are your machinery, plant and ways properly fenced and guarded, and otherwise in good order and condition?" and the declarations in the proposal form were made the basis of the contract. The plaintiffs answered the above question, "Yes", an answer which was true when made. Subsequently, an accident took place as a result of defect in scaffolding. It was contended for the underwriters that question and answer did not merely relate to the time when the proposal form was signed but extended to the future condition of the machinery, plant, and ways during the currency of the policy. Goddard L.J., at p. 76, said shortly:— "It is unarguable to maintain that that [i.e., the answer] refers to the future." The Master of the Rolls, at p. 70, deals fully with the point, saying:—

> "In my opinion, there is not a particle of justification for reading into that perfectly simple question any element of futurity whatsoever. The argument that the Court should read into it such an element was based, as I understood it, on the suggestion that the answer would be valueless from the underwriters' point of view unless that were done. I entirely disagree. The value of the question to the underwriters, as I construe it, is that it enables them to find out with what sort of person they are dealing, that is, whether or not he keeps his machinery, plant and ways properly fenced and guarded and otherwise in good order and condition. Obviously, if he were careless about that, so that at the time the question was answered his machinery, plant and ways were not in good order and condition, the risk would be of a different character. If the underwriters intended to refer to the future, it is most unfortunate that a printed document of this kind, tendered by Lloyds' underwriters to persons desiring to insure with them, should not be so expressed. Had they intended that this question should carry the meaning which they now suggest, nothing would have been easier than to say so. If they did not mean it, I am at a loss to understand how the point comes to be taken."

It seems to me that nearly every word in this passage is applicable to the case now before us. Here, also, the value to the underwriters of Question No. 9 was to find out with what sort of person they were dealing. Obviously, if Mr Sweeney habitually employed young and inexperienced drivers it was a matter to be taken into consideration. Here, also, if the underwriters intended to refer to the future it is most unfortunate that a printed document, tendered by Lloyds' underwriters to persons desiring to ensure with them, should not be so expressed. Here, also, had they intended that this question should carry the meaning which they now suggest, nothing would have been easier than to say so. Here, also, if they did not mean it, I am at a loss to see how the point comes to be taken.

---

[48] *Ibid.*
[49] [1942] 1 K.B. 66.

Finally, Mr Doyle contended that even if Question No. 9 and its answer, taken by themselves, were not clearly meant to refer to the future, as well as the present state of affairs, yet that last paragraph of the proposal form imported such a reference to the future. The last paragraph runs:— " I declare that the above statements and particulars are true, that the vehicles described are my property and in good condition, and I hereby agree that this declaration shall be held to be promissory, and so form the basis of the contract between me and the underwriters of the 'Eclipse' Policy, and I am willing to accept a Policy subject to the terms, exceptions, and conditions prescribed by the underwriters therein, and to pay a premium thereon." Mr Doyle relied particularly on the sentence; "I hereby agree that this shall be held to be promissory, and so form the basis of the contract...." In his contention the word, "promise", and its cognate words, must always refer to a future time. In this, I think, he is in error. The most usual meaning of the verb "to promise", is "to undertake to do or abstain from doing something in the future". But there is a well-recognised second usage in which "to promise" means "to assert confidently, to declare". Such an assertion refers to a future state of affairs, but it may also refer to the present, as in the phrase, "I promise you that it is so." It is true that the Oxford dictionary classes this latter usage as colloquial or archaic; but an archaism or two in an insurance policy will not give a lawyer familiar with their verbiage too violent a shock. Certain marine policies seem compounded of little else but archaisms.

Mr Kenny, for the insured, in an argument as logical as it was devastating, contended that the word, "promissory", was used in the second sense which I have mentioned. It signified a positive declaration, applicable alike to future, present, and past states of affairs, according to the wording of the particular question, and of such a nature as to constitute, not merely a representation, but a warranty, breach of which would, in insurance law, avoid liability. For this meaning, said Mr Kenny, the sentence provided its own dictionary. It did not end with the word, "promissory", but continued, "*and so shall form the basis of the contract.*" A sentence introduced by the words, "and so", must be either explanatory of, or a logical corollary of, the preceding word or words. Thus, the meaning of the word, "promissory" must be some meaning which made the declaration a basis of the contract. It raises a statement from the rank of a representation to that of a warranty: per Lord Blackburn in *Thomson* v. *Weems*;[50] *Dawsons Ltd.* v. *Bonnin.*[51] In the latter case, Viscount Cave says, at p. 432:— "... when a document consisting partly of statements of fact and partly of undertakings for the future is made the basis of a contract of insurance, this must (I think) mean that the document is to be the very foundation of the contract, so that if the statements of fact are untrue or the promissory statements are not carried out, the risk does not attach." It may be remarked, parenthetically, that in this passage Viscount Cave is using the word, "promissory", in the more usual meaning equivalent to "involving an undertaking as to the future". This is clear from the earlier words of the

---

[50] 9 App. Cas. 671 at p. 684.
[51] [1922] 2 A.C. 413.

sentence.

The interpretation so given by Mr Kenny to the word, "promissory", in the proposal form, though unusual, involves no violation of grammar or language. In this interpretation the word can be applied accurately and intelligibly to questions whether they refer to past, present, or future. If the question refers to the future the answer becomes a warranty as to the existence of a state of affairs in the future. Where the question is so couched as to refer to the present or the past, then the answer is a warranty that a certain state of affairs exists in the present or existed in the past. Mr Doyle's interpretation, on the other hand, not merely tortures language, but involves a person who has answered an apparently straightforward question as to the present or past in a concealed warranty as to the future. Such a carefully camouflaged method of extracting a future warranty would hardly commend itself to the Court, and I would be loth to attribute such an intention to the underwriters.

An attempt to apply Mr Doyle's interpretation to other questions (and, I think, he was forced to admit that if it applied to one it applied to all) reveals manifest absurdities. Take, for instance, Question 2:— "Have you or your driver during the past 5 years been convicted of any offence in connection with a motor vehicle?" To this the answer correctly given was, "No". If, as is argued, the subsequent provision that the declaration is to be promissory amounts to an undertaking that what was true for the past will remain true for the future, we arrive at the extraordinary position that Sweeney was undertaking that neither he nor any driver of his would in future be convicted of a motoring offence; and that if he or his driver subsequently was involved in a collision and was convicted of driving without due consideration the underwriters could repudiate liability for any claims arising out of such a collision. It does not seem likely that anyone would knowingly propose for such a nugatory insurance.

It would be easy to show similar absurdities which would be produced by the application of Mr Doyle's interpretation to other questions and answers. Indeed, it is difficult to see how any insurer could answer this vital question No. 9 without involving himself in difficulties. Mr Sweeney's answer of "No" was correct in fact; but according to the contention of the underwriters, this answer involved a promise never to employ a driver aged under 21 years or without twelve months' experience. Was Sweeney to safeguard himself by explaining that in certain circumstances he might be obliged, for a longer or shorter time, to employ a driver aged under 21? How far was he to elaborate the circumstances, which had not yet arisen and which might be difficult to foresee. I cannot conceive that an applicant for insurance who is asked a specific question is bound to do more than give a truthful answer to such questions or that there is any obligation to provide answers to questions which are not asked. In saying this I am not forgetting the over-riding obligation to make full disclosure of all facts clearly material to the risk, but as a qualification I would adopt the words of Lord Shaw in *Condogianis* v. *Guardian Assurance Co.*[52]:—

---

[52] [1921] 2 A.C. 125.

"In a contract of insurance it is a weighty fact that the questions are framed
by the insurer, and that if an answer is obtained to such a question which is
upon a fair construction a true answer, it is not open to the insuring company to maintain that the question was put in a sense different from or more
comprehensive than the proponent's answer covered. Where an ambiguity
exists, the contract must stand if an answer has been made to the question
in a fair and reasonable construction of that question. Otherwise the ambiguity would be a trap against which the insured would be protected by Courts
of law."

For the reasons given I am of opinion that Mr Kenny's interpretation of
the sentence, "this declaration shall be held to be promissory", is a correct
interpretation and that the interpretation urged by Mr Doyle is unsustainable. But, even if I am wrong in my conclusion that the interpretation is
reasonably free from doubt, the case must be decided against the underwriters if the words are ambiguous. The wording of the proposal form and the
policy was chosen by the underwriters who knew, or must be deemed to have
known, what matters were material to the risk and what information they
desired to obtain. They were at liberty to adopt any phraseology which they
desired. They could have provided clearly and expressly that no driver should
be employed who was under 21 years of age or had less than 12 months'
experience, and they could have done this by means of a special condition or
by an addition to the final proviso under the heading, "Description of
Drivers", in the policy. Indeed, they could have secured their object (if it was
their object) with perfect clarity in half a dozen ways. If, then, they choose to
adopt ambiguous words it seems to me good sense, as well as established law,
that those words should be interpreted in the sense which is adverse to the
persons who chose and introduced them: *Anderson* v. *Fitzgerald*,[53] per Lord St
Leonards, at p. 507; *Fowkes* v. *Manchester and London Life Assurance and
Loan Association*,[54] per Cockburn C.J. at p. 925, and per Blackburn J., at p.
929; *Fitton* v. *Accidental Death Insurance Co.*,[55] per Willes J., at p. 135.

Assuming, then, that the interpretation is not so clear as I think it is, and
that Mr Doyle's interpretation of the words may be as feasible as Mr Kenny's,
I must still decide against the underwriters who chose words raising such
ambiguity. I would like to associate myself with the opinion of Lord Greene
M.R. in *Woolfall & Rimmer Ltd.* v. *Moyle*,[56] at p. 73, where he says:—

"... if underwriters wish to limit by some qualification a risk which, *prima
facie,* they are undertaking in plain terms, they should make it perfectly
clear what that qualification is. They should, with the aid of competent
advice, make up their minds as to the qualifications they wish to impose and
should express their intention in language appropriate for achieving the
result desired. There is no justification for underwriters, who are carrying on
a widespread business and making use of printed forms, either failing to

---

[53] 4 H.L. Cas. 484.
[54] 3 B. & S. 917.
[55] 17 C.B. (N.S.) 122.
[56] [1942] 1 K.B. 66.

make up their minds what they mean, or, if they have made up their minds what they mean, failing to express it in suitable language. Any competent draughtsman could carry out the intention which [counsel] imputes to this document, and, if that was really intended, it ought to have been done."

This is but the latest expression of a sentiment which judge after judge has uttered for nearly a century. In *Anderson* v. *Fitzgerald*[57] Lord St Leonards says, at p. 510:—

"A policy ought to be so framed, that he who runs can read. It ought to be framed with such deliberate care, that no form of expression by which, on the one hand, the party assured can be caught, or by which, on the other hand, the company can be cheated, shall be found upon the face of it."

Lord Wright adopted this passage in *Provincial Insurance Co.* v. *Morgan*,[58] and in that case also Lord Russell of Killowen says, at p. 250:—

"For myself I think it is a matter of great regret that the printed forms which insurance companies prepare and offer for acceptance and signature by the insuring public should not state in clear and unambiguous terms the events upon the happening of which the insuring company will escape liability under the policy. The present case is a conspicuous example of an attempt to escape liability by placing upon words a meaning which, if intended by the insurance company, should have been put before the proposers in words admitting of no possible doubt";

and in *Glicksman* v. *Lancashire and General Assurance Co.*[59] Lord Atkinson says, at p. 144:— "I think it is a lamentable thing that insurance companies will abstain from shaping the questions they put to intending insurers — in clear and unambiguous language."

It is useless for me to attempt to add to the words of such great Judges, and I content myself with recording them once more and pointing out that the result of using ambiguous expressions is generally a decision against those who deal in such ambiguities.

King *v.* Cornhill Insurance Company Limited
[1993] 2 I.R. 43
The High Court

BLAYNEY J: This case concerns a single net issue which arises under a motor insurance policy taken out by the Plaintiff with the defendant company. One of its terms provides as follows:

"Section I   Driving other cars

---

[57] 4 H.L. Cas. 484.
[58] [1933] A.C. 240 at p. 255.
[59] [1927] A.C. 139.

Except where the insured is a firm, company or more than one person, we will in terms of Section A and C indemnify you while driving any motor car or motor cycle not belonging to you and not hired to you under a hire purchase agreement provided such motor car or motor cycle is being used within the "limitations as to use" specified in the current certificate of insurance issued with this policy. No indemnity is granted under this section if indemnity is afforded to you by any other insurance."

The issue which arises is whether a particular vehicle, owned by the plaintiff's father, which was involved in an accident on the 29th October 1988 while being driven by the plaintiff, is a "motor car" so that the driving was covered by the policy. If it is, it is common case that the clause entitles the Plaintiff to an indemnity. The defendant company contends that the vehicle is not a motor car, and has refused to indemnify the Plaintiff in respect of claims arising out of the accident. The Plaintiff contends that it is and in these proceedings claims a declaration that he is entitled to an indemnity under the policy. If the vehicle is a motor car, he is entitled to succeed. If it is not, his claim fails.

The vehicle in question is manufactured by Mitsubishi and its model name is "Shogun". It is commonly referred to as a Mitsubishi Shogun. A photograph put in evidence shows it to look like a large jeep. It has straight sides, and three doors — one at each side, and one at the rear which contains a large glass window. The "Shogun" was purchased by the Plaintiff's father in May 1988. At that time it had only three windows — one in each of the side doors, and one in the rear at the back. Two additional windows were added subsequently above each of the rear wheels replacing metal panels which had been there previously.

The Plaintiff's father is a farmer and he bought the "Shogun" for the purpose of his business. He has 45 acres of land and also owns a hotel. The "Shogun" was bought from Tractamotors Limited in Cavan. They had imported it from Northern Ireland and on importation it had been declared to be a goods vehicle. It was also bought as such. By being imported as a goods vehicle it had attracted a low rate of duty. When purchased by the Plaintiff's father the "Shogun" had no rear seat and this was still the position at the date of the accident. On that date the Plaintiff had with him in the "Shogun" his niece Julie Feeley, aged 14, who was sitting in the passenger seat in front, and his three children, aged six, five, and four months in the back. Two of his children and Julie Feeley were injured in the accident.

There is no definition of "motor car" in the Road Traffic Act 1961. Counsel for the Defendant Company submitted that it should be defined as being a "vehicle constructed primarily for the carriage of one or more passengers" which is one of the classes of vehicles in respect of which insurance cover for passengers is obligatory under s. 65 subsection 1 para. (a) of the Road Traffic Act 1961 and art. 6, sub-art., para. (b) of the Road Traffic (Compulsory Insurance) Regulations, 1962 (S.I. No. 14). He submitted that as the "Shogun" had no back seat it was not constructed primarily for the carriage of passengers and so was not a motor car.

In this context evidence was tendered by the Defendant Company, which was not disputed, that insurance companies will not give passenger cover in respect of a vehicle which has no seat behind the driver. Whether or not there are side windows in the back of a vehicle is not relevant. It is because of the absence of a seat behind the driver that passenger cover would be refused. There was also evidence, which again was not contested, that where a commercial vehicle is being insured, the policy will not include a clause permitting the insured to drive other motor cars.

The Plaintiff relied principally on the evidence of Richard Devlin, an insurance broker and consultant with 40 years' experience in insurance. He said that the "Shogun" is classified as a private motor car and in support of this he produced the printed list of private motor cars compiled by the Defendant Company, in which the "Shogun" is included. He produced as well similar printed lists compiled by four other Insurance Companies: the Norwich Union, the Sun Alliance, the Church and General, and the Hibernian, and the "Shogun" is also included in each of these.

On behalf of the defendant Mr Comyn submitted that the issue was whether the "Shogun" was a private motor car or a commercial vehicle and he contended that it was a commercial vehicle because, having no rear seat, an Insurance Company would not give passenger cover if they were insuring the vehicle itself. But the type of cover which an Insurance Company would be prepared to give is not the test. The test is whether the "Shogun" is correctly described as a motor car. And I accept the evidence of Mr Devlin on this point. He says that it is classified as such by the Defendant Company and four other Insurance Companies. It seems to me that that is very strong evidence that the "Shogun" should be taken to be a motor car. I would add that the principal witness called on behalf of the Defendant Company, Mr Sean Fitzgibbon, the senior underwriter and motor superintendent with the Defendant Company for the last eight years, accepted in cross-examination that the only thing that in his opinion prevented the "Shogun" from being a motor car was the absence of a rear seat. But in expressing that opinion I have no doubt that he was strongly influenced by the fact that in his view an insurance company would not give passenger cover when insuring the "Shogun".

The Defendant's case relied heavily on this fact. It was submitted that because passenger cover could not have been obtained for the "Shogun" that it could not have been the intention of the Defendant Company that the "Shogun" would come within the description of a "motor car" in the driving other cars clause in the Plaintiff's policy. But what the Defendant Company's intention was cannot be looked at independently of the words used in the clause. What the Court has to do is to ascertain the meaning of the clause by construing the words actually used in it. And I am satisfied on the evidence that the Mitsubishi "Shogun" does come within what the ordinary person would understand to be a motor car. I consider that the ordinary person would not be concerned with whether the vehicle had a back seat or not. If the vehicle looked like a motor car, it would be taken to be a motor car. And the photograph shows that it does look like a motor car.

For these reasons I consider that the Plaintiff has made out his case and I will make the declaration sought.

Buckley's Stores Limited and Patrick Buckley *v.* National Employers Mutual General Insurance Association Limited and Others
[1978] I.R. 351.
The Supreme Court

O'HIGGINS C.J. (KENNY AND PARKE J.J. CONCURRING): This is an appeal by the first defendant against the judgment of Mr Justice Hamilton delivered in this action on the 10th April, 1975, and the order made thereunder. In his judgment the learned trial judge held that the first defendant was liable to indemnify the first plaintiff in respect of certain High Court proceedings brought against the plaintiffs by Noreen Bourke and Kathleen Cronin. These High Court proceedings arose from a road accident which occurred on the 9th October, 1967. The learned trial judge held that the first defendant was so liable pursuant to an employer's-liability policy issued by the first defendant to the first plaintiff....

The following facts appear to be relevant in the consideration of this appeal. The first plaintiff is a company which was incorporated on the 20th February, 1958, and carried on the business of hardware, sawmilling, furnishers, undertakers, Calor Gas agents and haybarn erectors at Main Street, Millstreet in the county of Cork. Despite its somewhat confusing name, Millstreet is a town in the county of Cork; it is situate some 38 miles from Cork city. In connection with the said business the company had in operation an employer's-liability policy which was issued by the second defendant; this policy covered those employed by the company in the Millstreet business. The policy provided the usual indemnity against liability and damages arising from injury suffered by any such employee arising out of and in the course of such employment. The policy had been arranged by the company's brokers (O'Donnell's Insurance Ltd.) and only applied to those employees of the company who were engaged in the Millstreet business. The cover provided by this policy was in operation on the 9th October, 1967, when the accident occurred. On that date the company also had in operation a road-traffic policy issued by the third defendant; this policy covered, inter alia, the Triumph car which was involved in the accident.

It appears that some time prior to the date of the accident the company acquired premises in Academy Street in the city of Cork for the purpose of developing a departmental store in Cork city on similar lines to the business which was carried on in Millstreet. This new store was opened on the 5th October, 1967. Prior to the opening, a number of the company's employees in Millstreet had been working in the Academy Street premises for the purpose of preparing for the opening, and they assisted further in the early stages after the opening.

The company's brokers took out a further employers'-liability policy on behalf of the company in relation to the new business in Cork. This policy was taken out with the first defendant and provided for cover commencing on the 15th September, 1967, and extending to the 29th September, 1968. This policy was similar in terms to the policy taken out with the second defendant in respect of the Millstreet business. It provided an indemnity to the company against any liability for damages, etc., in respect of bodily injury which was suffered by an employee while so employed and which arose out of and in the course of such employment in the Cork business.

On the 9th October, 1967, the position was that the company has employer's-liability cover with the second defendant in respect of the company's employees at the Millstreet business, and a similar cover with the first defendant in respect of the company's employees at the Cork business. In addition, the company had motor-insurance cover with the third defendant in respect of the motor vehicles described and specified in the motor-insurance policy.

As to the Millstreet employees who were working in the Cork premises, it appears that these continued to be paid by the Millstreet business but the amount of such payments was subsequently reimbursed by the Cork business.

With regard to the two employees who were involved in the accident which led to these proceedings, it appears that the practice was for the second plaintiff to drive them each morning from Millstreet where they lived to the city of Cork where they were directed to work. The second plaintiff was a director of the company and he so drove the two girls in a Triumph car which was the property of the company and which was specifically covered by the motor policy taken out with the third defendant. For these two girls to get to the premises of the Cork business each morning, some form of transport was obviously required since they lived 38 miles away. The lift so provided by the second plaintiff met this requirement; however I do not understand from the transcript that these girls were under any contractual obligation so to travel to work.

On the morning of the accident the second plaintiff drove the company's Triumph car, with the two employees of the company as passengers, from Millstreet to Cork city. In the course of the journey the car was involved in a collision, which was due to the negligent driving of the second plaintiff; and both of the girl employees were injured.

One might have expected that this simple accident resulting in injury to two employees of a company which was well covered by employer's-liability insurance — involving, as it did, a motor vehicle which was fully insured for road-traffic and was driven by the company's authorised agent — would have led to no problems with regard to insurance cover. Unfortunately, this was not to be so. A long period of controversy and dispute ensued during which various steps were taken in an unrewarding effort to discover under which thimble lay the pea or, in other words, to ascertain which of the three insurance companies was on cover in respect to the liability involved as a result of the collision. The third defendant, maintaining that the two employees had received bodily injury arising out of and in the course of their employment because they were being driven in their employer's car to their place of work, asserted that the liability was covered by one or other of the employer's-liability policies. Accordingly, the third defendant relied on condition 3 of its own policy, which stated:—

"If at the time any claim arises under this policy there is any other existing insurance covering the same loss, damage or liability the company shall not be liable except under section III of this policy to pay or contribute more than its rateable proportion of any loss, damage, costs and/or expenses provided always that nothing in this condition shall impose on the company any liability from which but for this condition it would have been relieved under proviso (a) to the cover granted to persons driving the insured vehicle."

It was also pointed out on behalf of the third defendant that the extension to the cover in its motor policy to the driver of the insured's vehicle did not apply under its policy when the driver was entitled to be indemnified under any other policy.

At this stage, the two injured girls had initiated separate proceedings in the High Court in which they claimed damages against the second plaintiff, as the driver of the car in which they were injured. Whoever put forward these contentions on behalf of the third defendant, he ignored the fact that these two claims had been brought against the second plaintiff personally — and not against the company. In respect to the second plaintiff's liability for his own negligent driving, no possible cover existed under either of the two employer's-liability policies. However, in pursuance of the contention so put forward, the third defendant asserted that the two employees were being carried in the company car by reason of their employment and that the accident caused injuries which arose out of and in the course of such employment. Accordingly, the third defendant maintained that the liability involved in the accident was covered by one or other of the two employer's-liability policies. Therefore, in pursuance of the conditions mentioned in its own policy, the third defendant maintained that it should only meet 50% of the claim and that the other 50% should be met either by one of the two other insurance companies or by each of them contributing 25% of the claim. No agreement was reached with regard to this proposal, and so the plaintiffs sought arbitration under all three policies.

The second and third defendants agreed to the arbitration proposal, but the first defendant declined to have anything to do with such arbitration proceedings and maintained that its policy was with the company, and that no question or dispute had arisen with regard to such policy. The attitude of the first defendant was that the claims of the company's employees were road-accident claims against the second plaintiff personally, in relation to which the first defendant had no interest. While these arguments were proceeding, the two employees appear to have held their hands and, instead of pressing ahead with their actions against the second plaintiff, took no positive steps.

The late Mr John A. Costello was appointed arbitrator by all the parities who were willing to proceed to arbitration and he entered upon the arbitration. Since the first defendant declined to appear, the arbitration proceedings were adjourned. It appears that at this stage a new move was made with the obvious intention of involving the first defendant. The two employees, obviously at the suggestion of one or other interested party, applied to the High Court to add the company as a defendant, and this was done. The employees' claims were settled for £1,870 in respect of Kathleen Cronin and for £4,000 in respect of Noreen Bourke. Subsequently, the arbitration was resumed without the first defendant being present or taking any part. While this arbitration resulted in a finding that the second defendant was not liable but otherwise left the issue unresolved as between the first and second defendants, it does not appear to me that this award can now have any bearing on the issues involved in these proceedings in so far as they relate to the first defendant. Since the first defendant took no part in the arbitration proceedings and did not submit thereto, that defendant cannot be bound in any way by the findings of the arbitrator. In any event the arbitration did not result in a solution of the problems which had been raised.

Accordingly, the plaintiffs discharged the amounts due to the two injured employees and then commenced this action for the purpose of obtaining a court declaration as to what policy applied to the liability involved in the accident in question. The learned trial judge, having held that the two girls suffered bodily injury arising out of and in the course of their employment in the Cork business, decided that the first defendant was liable, and the first defendant has appealed against that decision. In my view, the first defendant is entitled to succeed.

I do not think it is necessary to consider in which business these girls were employed. In my view, the accident in which they were involved was not one arising out of and in the course of their employment. The question is whether these girls were under an obligation by the terms of their employment to travel in the vehicle in question. This was the test applied by Lord Denning M.R. and by Sachs L.J. to the construction of similar words in an employer's-liability policy in *Vandyke* v. *Fender.*[60] I respectfully agree with the views expressed by both those learned judges in their judgment in that case. As already indicated, I cannot find anything in the transcript which would indicate that the travelling in the car was anything more than a matter of mutual convenience. It is not in issue that the girls were in the car and were travelling to Cork because they were employees of the company. However, that does not mean that they were so travelling because they were obliged by the terms of their employment to do so. It appears to me to have been quite permissible for these girls, or for other employees from Millstreet, to travel in any vehicle of their choice provided, of course, they arrived in Cork at the premises of the Cork business in time to do their work.

Therefore, in my view, neither of the two employer's-liability policies applied to the accident in which these girls were involved. This being so, it seems to me that this case ought to end as it started. It started, and should end, as relating to a simple road accident covered by the usual motor policy issued by the third defendant. In my view, the third defendant is and always was liable to indemnify the first plaintiff in respect of the accident....

Rohan Construction Ltd and Rohan Group PLC *v.* Insurance Corporation of Ireland Ltd
[1986] I.L.R.M. 419
The High Court

KEANE J: In the year 1977 a company called Agrivest Ltd decided to become

---

[60] [1970] 2 Q.B. 292.

involved in what seemed at the time the promising market of selling molasses to farmers in the South West of Ireland. With this in view, they proposed to store the molasses in a tank to be specially constructed for the purpose in a dry dock which they occupied under a lease from the Limerick Harbour Commissioners. The storage tank was constructed by the first-named plaintiffs under their then title of Sitecast (Ireland) Ltd.

The project unfortunately proved disastrous for nearly everyone concerned. For reasons which I will discuss in a moment, large quantities of water percolated into the tank and Agrivest Ltd were unable to use it for the storage of molasses. They alleged that, as a result, they suffered serious financial losses and they accordingly instituted proceedings in which a number of parties, including the first-named plaintiffs, were ultimately joined. In these proceedings, the sum of £2.6 million damages was claimed by Agrivest Ltd and Co-operative Molasses Traders Ltd.

The plaintiffs were insured by the defendants under two Professional Indemnity Policies nos SP1420 and SP1425 and notified the defendants of the claim being made against them. Because of the relatively small Irish market in such insurance and the scale of the risks involved, it was customary in the insurance business to lay off such risks and, accordingly, the defendants had effected re-insurance under both these policies in London. The London underwriters adopted the position that it had not been established to their satisfaction that these policies did apply and inconclusive correspondence and discussions took place on this matter over a considerable period of time. During the course of these discussions, the Irish solicitor for the underwriters suggested that the risk in question might be covered by a Public Liability Policy which the plaintiffs also maintained with the defendants, but which was not reinsured with the underwriters.

The uncertainty as to the plaintiffs' insurance cover did not, of course, delay the progress of the action brought against the plaintiffs and the other parties who were alleged to have been responsible for the defects in the storage tank. The defendants, while maintaining that their liability or that of the reinsurers to indemnify the plaintiffs under any of the policies had not been established to their satisfaction, appointed a firm of engineers, Messrs Rooney McLoughlin and Associates, to investigate the allegations against the plaintiffs and prepare a report and also nominated senior counsel to appear on their behalf.

The report prepared by Messrs Rooney McLoughlin and Associates concluded that the work carried out by the plaintiffs had complied with the drawings and specifications and that the problems were caused by a failure in design. The consulting engineers responsible for the design, Messrs Ove Arup and Partners, and the consulting architects to the project, Messrs Frank Murphy and Partners, had also been joined in the proceedings. On the basis of Messrs Rooney McLoughlin's report, it seemed as though the plaintiffs had a reasonably good prospect of resisting the claim made against them. When the trial loomed nearer, however, as so often happens, matters became less clear-cut, particularly since it transpired that the consulting engineers retained by Agrivest Ltd, Messrs M.J. O'Connor and Associates, took a radically different view and were assigning a significantly greater part of the blame for what went wrong to the plaintiffs. It also was becoming obvious to all concerned, and their legal advisers, that, having regard to the complexity of the technical issues and the magnitude of the claim as to damages which had to be investigated, the case would probably be relatively lengthy. This gave an added stimulus to the eve of trial negotiations and ultimately the case was settled. The damages were scaled down to £735,000 and, of this, the plaintiffs agreed to pay £150,000, together with an appropriate proportion of the costs. The greater part of the damages was paid by Messrs Ove Arup and Partners, Messrs Frank Murphy and Partners also making a contribution. The defendants were aware of the plaintiffs' proposal to settle the proceedings, but reserved their position as to their liability under the respective policies. The defendants having failed to admit liability under these policies, the present proceedings were instituted in which the plaintiffs claim a declaration that the defendants are liable to indemnify them under one or other of these policies.

The first issue that arises for determination is as to whether the settlement effected by the plaintiffs was in the circumstances a reasonable and prudent compromise of the proceedings brought against them....

The plaintiffs carried out the works in question under a sub-contract with a firm called Fairclough Mulcahy Ltd....

... I am satisfied that the settlement entered into by the plaintiffs was reasonable and prudent in the circumstances. Indeed I would go further and say that, in the light of the evidence given in these proceedings, it would have been folly in the extreme for the plaintiffs to have rejected the advice of their lawyers and committed themselves, and the defendants whom they were hoping would indemnify them, to litigation which would be protracted, expensive and, from their point of view, at best uncertain in its outcome.

The second issue is as to whether the defendants are liable under either or both of the policies to which I have referred to indemnify the plaintiffs in respect of the agreed damages paid to them together with the proportion of the costs for which they agreed to be liable and their own costs.

It is clear that policies of insurance, such as those under consideration in the present case, are to be construed like other written instruments. In the present case, the primary task of the court is to ascertain their meaning by adopting the ordinary rules of construction. It is also clear that, if there is any ambiguity in the language used, it is to be construed more strongly against the party who prepared it, i.e. in most cases against the insurer. It is also clear that the words used must not be construed with extreme literalism, but with reasonable latitude, keeping always in view the principal object of the contract of insurance. (See *MacGillivray and Parkington on Insurance Law*, 7th ed., at p. 433 *et seq.*)

I shall deal first with the Professional Indemnity Policies. There were two of these, numbered SP 1240 and SP 1245. The principal difference between them was in the definition of activities and duties in respect of which cover was given. In SP 1240 they were defined as:

> "(1) Design, specification, supervision and/or the provision by the insured of advice or technical information.
> (2) The management of works under the direction of architects, engineers, surveyors, and/or project or contract managers.
> (3) Such additional activities as are stated under item 10 of the schedule.
> Item 10 of the schedule is:

'work normally undertaken by architects and consultants relative to building and civil engineering, structural engineering, mechanical engineering, electrical engineering, heating and ventilation engineering'."

The only difference in SP 1245 is that clause (2) is in the following terms:

"Management of projects, contracts or works, supervision, contract coordination, quantity surveying and procurement (of material, equipment, plant, material things and technical services) under the direction of architects, engineers, surveyors and/or project or contract managers."

It was not suggested on behalf of the plaintiffs that they were covered under any clause other than clause (2) in either policy.

An initial question arises in relation to the clause in the later policy (which being in wider terms was naturally relied on more strongly by the plaintiffs), i.e. as to whether the closing words "under the direction of architects, engineers, surveyors and/or project or contract managers" qualify all the words which precede them or simply the words which immediately precede them, i.e. "procurement (of material, equipment, etc...)". It seems to me more probable that they were intended to qualify all the preceding words, since in the earlier version of the clause they are undoubtedly intended to qualify the words "the management of works" and the words after "management" in the second clause seem to be merely an expansion or elaboration of the phrase "the management of works" in the earlier policy. That construction would seem to be somewhat less favourable from the plaintiffs' point of view, but whichever construction is adopted, I am satisfied that the plaintiffs are not entitled to be indemnified under either policy SP 1240 or SP 1245 in respect of their liability, if any, to the plaintiffs in the original proceedings.

If one takes the individual activities and duties which are covered by clause (2), it is obvious that liability in the present case did not arise under the headings "quantity surveying" and "procurement". Can it then be said that a potential liability arose in the relevant proceedings in respect of the "management of projects, contracts or works, supervision, contract coordination"? In this context, it is essential to bear in mind what the duties and activities of the plaintiffs actually were. They were sub-contractors, no more and no less. The allegation against them was not that they had failed in any professional or managerial skills which might reasonably have been expected of them, but rather that they had done their work badly. On the evidence of Mr O'Connor, this allegation would have been supported in two ways, first, by demonstrating that they had in certain respects deviated from the specification and, second, that they had failed to use their own judgment and commonsense as experienced sub-contractors by failing to draw the attention of the consultants on the project to the possible consequences of the design fault. No matter at what level of the hierarchy a person may be employed, he does not become a mere robot: whether he be a highly qualified engineer, a tradesman or even an unskilled labourer, he is expected, in addition to any specialist qualifications he may have, to use his own commonsense and experience in relation to the task he is doing. If it is alleged that he has failed to do so, that, of itself, does not amount to a claim that he has been negligent or in breach of contract in his "management", "supervision" or "co-ordination" of the relevant works.

I think that this conclusion is borne out by the wording of the policy taken as a whole. Its title — "Professional Indemnity Policy" — would not appear at first sight appropriate to a liability such as arose in the case of the plaintiffs in the present case. Moreover, under the heading "Litigation" one finds the following condition 2:

> The Corporation will not require the insured to dispute any claim unless a senior counsel (to be mutually agreed upon by the Corporation and the insured) advise that the same could be contested with a reasonable prospect of success by the insured and the insured consents to such claim being contested, such consent not to be reasonably withheld.
>
> In the event of any dispute arising between the insured and the Corporation as to what constitutes an unreasonable refusal to contest a claim at law, the President for the time being of the professional body of which the insured is a member shall nominate a referee to decide this point (only) and the decision of such referee shall be binding on both parties.

I think that this clause well illustrates what the intention of the parties was in entering into the policy. It is obvious that, in the case of persons in positions of individual professional and managerial responsibility, the effect of litigation on their reputations may from their point of view be an extremely important factor in determining whether a particular action should be compromised. The existence of such a clause in the policy demonstrates very clearly the kind of liability that was being insured against, and it is emphatically not the liability to which the plaintiffs were potentially subject in the relevant proceedings.

I next consider the Public Liability Policy which was dated 3 July 1973. This is headed "Public Liability Policy" and in its operative part provides as follows:

> The Corporation will indemnify the insured in respect of accidents happening on in or about any of the places specified in the schedule against all sums ... which the insured shall become legally liable to pay as compensation for
> (1) accidental bodily injury or disease to any person other than the persons hereinafter defined in the exceptions to this policy.
> (2) accidental loss of or damage to property other than the property hereinafter defined in the exceptions to this policy caused by or through
> (a) The fault or negligence of the insured or of any person in the service of the insured in the course of the said business
> (b) any defect in the premises ways works plant or machinery connected with or used in the said business.

Under the heading "Exceptions" the policy goes on to provide *inter alia* as follows:

> The indemnity expressed in this policy shall not apply to or include ...
> (2) liability assumed by the insured by agreement unless such liability would have attached to the insured notwithstanding such agreement...
> (8) liability in respect of injury or disease loss or damage caused by or in connection with or arising from ...
> (e) contracts imperfectly inefficiently or improperly fulfilled.

I mention paragraph 8 (e), because it was relied on by the defendants as excluding liability in the present case. I am satisfied, however, on the evidence that this clause was deleted in the original policy and, accordingly, it is unnecessary to consider it further.

Attention was directed during the course of the argument to the use of the expression "accidents" and cognate words in the operative part of the policy, Mr Liston SC submitting on behalf of the defendants that they were inappropriate to the type of liability which arose in the present case. Both Mr Liston SC and Mr McCann SC for the plaintiffs referred me to authorities cited in the relevant volumes of *Words and Phrases Judicially Defined* and *Stroud's Judicial Dictionary* on the meanings which the courts have from time to time attached to these expressions. Counsel accepted, however, that these decisions were of somewhat limited value in the context of the present case, turning as they usually did on the use of the words in life policies. The fact that the damage in the present case was caused by penetration of water into the tank over a period of time would not, I am inclined to think, deprive it of the character of an "accident", given that the damage in question was not intended or foreseen by the plaintiffs or anyone else and, accordingly, could properly be regarded as "accidental". I do not, however, find it necessary to express any concluded view on that aspect of the case, since it seems to me that clause (2) is conclusive in favour of the arguments advanced on behalf of the defendants.

It was submitted on behalf of the plaintiffs that this clause did not apply in the present case, since (a) the plaintiffs had entered into no contract with Agrivest Ltd or Molasses Co-operative Ltd, the plaintiffs in the original action and (b) their liability to the plaintiffs in those proceedings arose in tort and not in contract.

While this argument is superficially attractive, I am satisfied on consideration that it is fallacious. It was expressly provided that the indemnity was not to include "liability assumed ... by agreement". The plaintiffs unquestionably assumed liability in respect of any defective workmanship when they entered into the sub-contract on 8 December 1977 with Fairclough Mulcahy Ltd. It was as a result of entering into that agreement that they found themselves in a position of potential liability in the original proceedings, either as third parties brought in by the main contractors or as defendants in the event of the plaintiffs making a claim against them in negligence. The fact that from the plaintiffs' point of view a claim against them also lay in tort [is] in this context not material; the fact that the liability may also have existed in tort does not mean that it is any the less a "liability assumed by the insured by agreement" within the precise meaning of clause (2).

Nor do the words "unless such liability would have attached to the insured notwithstanding such agreement" avail the plaintiffs. They are plainly inappropriate to the circumstances of the present case where liability only arose because the plaintiffs had entered into the sub-contract. There may well be circumstances in which an insured may choose to enter into a specific agreement in respect of his potential liability to third-parties arising out of works he has engaged on and in such circumstances clause (2) may have no application, since the liability might have existed in any event irrespective of the agreement. That is not this case: it is again necessary to stress that had the plaintiffs not agreed to carry out these works they would never have been liable to anyone.

Again, I think that the heading of the policy is of some relevance; the parties in entering into a "Public Liability Policy" were unlikely to envisage an indemnity being provided in respect of what is, in a sense, the obverse of a "Public Liability", viz. a liability arising out of a private agreement. The weight to be attached to that is somewhat reduced by the deletion of the exceptions for "contracts imperfectly inefficiently or improperly fulfilled", and if there were no other features of the policy, the plaintiffs might have been entitled to cover, even though it is not a policy which one would have thought was intended to meet the risk they encountered in the present case. For the reasons I have given, however, I think that clause (2) of the exceptions is conclusive in excluding liability on the part of the defendants under the policy.

I should add that while both plaintiffs and the defendants laid stress on the attitudes adopted by the various parties concerned as to which policy, if any, the plaintiffs were insured under, I have not treated this as in any sense a material factor in arriving at these conclusions. Thus, it was suggested on behalf of the defendants that the plaintiffs had never seriously attached any significance to the Public Liability Policy, until the Irish solicitor for the re-insurers drew attention to it. Similarly, the plaintiffs contended that the attitude of the defendants at all stages was that, while they could not commit the reinsurers, they were inclined to the view that the plaintiffs were entitled to cover under the Professional Indemnity Policy. So far as the plaintiffs are concerned, however, in the absence of any claim based on estoppel, these considerations cannot avail them. In the end, the case depends on the intention of the parties as expressed in the two policies which I have had to construe and it is for that reason that the plaintiffs' claim must be dismissed.

[1988] I.L.R.M. 373
The Supreme Court

GRIFFIN J. (FINLAY C.J. AND HEDERMAN J. CONCURRING): The question for determination on this appeal is whether, under either or both of two policies of insurance effected by the plaintiffs with the defendants, the plaintiffs are entitled to be indemnified against the sum of £150,000 and costs which they agreed to pay to Agrivest Ltd ("Agrivest") and their contribution towards settlement of an action brought by Agrivest against them and two other defendants. In the High Court, the learned trial judge held that the defendants were not obliged to indemnify the plaintiffs under either policy and it is against that decision that this appeal has been brought by the plaintiffs.

The Policies

The period of insurance in respect of [Professional Indemnity Policy] SP1240 was from 6 May 1977 to 5 May 1978 inclusive and in respect of SP1245 from 1 May 1980 to 30 April 1981 inclusive. As the claim in this case was notified to the Insurers on 22 October 1980 it is agreed that the policy applicable at the material time was SP1245.

... It was a condition of the policy (under the heading "Litigation") that the defendants would not require the plaintiffs to dispute any claim unless a senior counsel (to be mutually agreed upon by the plaintiffs and the defendants) advised that a claim could be contested with a reasonable prospect of success by the plaintiffs and the plaintiffs consented to such claim being contested, such consent not to be unreasonably withheld. In view of the finding of the learned trial judge on the reasonableness of the settlement, the only live issue in this appeal is as to whether the negligent acts of the plaintiffs occurred in the conduct and execution of the activities and duties defined in the policy.

It is well settled that in construing the terms of a policy the cardinal rule is that the intention of the parties must prevail, but the intention is to be looked for on the face of the policy, including any documents incorporated therewith, in the words in which the parties themselves have chosen to express their meaning. The court must not speculate as to their intention, apart from their words, but may, if necessary, interpret the words by reference to the surrounding circumstances. The whole of the policy must be looked at, and not merely a particular clause. See *Ivamy on Insurance Law*, 5th Edn. (1986) at p. 333/334.

As to cl. 2, it seems quite clear that what is included in it is exclusive of the work referred to in cl. 1 and 3. It does not therefore include or cover work normally undertaken by architects and consultants by reason of the wording of item 10 of the schedule. Whereas cl. 2 in Policy No. SP 1240 provided only for one activity i.e. "the management of works" under the direction of architects etc., the relevant cl. 2, having regard to the punctuation, provides for five activities, viz.:

(1) Management of Projects, contracts or works,

(2) Supervision,

(3) Contract co-ordination,

(4) Quantity Surveying and

(5) Procurement of material, equipment etc.

This last activity is undoubtedly qualified by "under the direction of Architects, Engineers, Surveyors and/or Project or Contract Managers", but in the absence of punctuation after the bracket it is at least open to question whether those words also qualify the first four activities. However, for the purpose of this judgment, I am prepared to assume that all five activities were qualified by these words.

There was evidence on behalf of the plaintiffs that the role of a contractor in any building contract is to ensure that the contract work being done by them is properly managed, to provide a programming plan and procurement of materials, to co-ordinate with the other sub-contractors and with the consulting engineers, and to ensure that everything would happen as it should happen. This evidence was not challenged on cross-examination. Building contracts or sub-contracts which are *not* made on the printed conditions of contract approved by the Construction Industry Federation or alternatively by one of the professional bodies of architects or engineers, must be very rare nowadays. A standard condition in all these contracts is that the work should be completed by the contractor or sub-contractor in accordance with the directions and to the reasonable satisfaction of the architect or engineer as the case may be. It appears to me to be reasonable to assume, having regard to the wording of cl. 2, that the parties to this policy (and in particular the defendants who drafted the policy) had this fact in mind when the policy was being effected, and that the policy was, so to speak, tailored to meet the kind of projects or works which the plaintiffs undertake.

Of the activities specified in cl. 2, quantity surveying has no application to this case, and there would appear to be no evidence on which it could be said that the co-ordination of the contract on the part of the plaintiffs left anything to be desired. However, in my opinion, the provisions in relation to (a) the management of projects, contracts or works, (b) supervision, and (c) procurement of materials etc. in cl. 2 do apply to this case. It was part of the duty of the plaintiffs to ensure that the work was properly managed and supervised. That would include ensuring that there was adequate excavation so that the pipes could be laid at the correct level, that the joining of the pipes was properly done, that the concrete surround for the pipes would be uniformly 100 mm. in thickness, and that the variation in the quality of the concrete used could not have taken place. They also had a duty to ensure that proper materials were provided and, in relation to the quality of the concrete, there was a failure to procure materials. In my view, it does not matter whether the water penetrated the tank due to the manner in which the plaintiffs did the work, or to a design fault. In the latter event, it was the duty of the plaintiffs, as experienced contractors, to draw the attention of the consulting engineers to the alleged design fault and not to lay the pipes, make the joints and construct the concrete surround for the pipes in the manner in which they did.

The defendants allege that, even if cl. 2 does apply to the management and supervision of the works, the claim of the plaintiffs is still outside the scope of the policy as the claim is a mixed claim of negligence and breach of contract in the manner in which they constructed the works. They rely on what was stated by Devlin J. in *West Wake Price and Co.* v. *Ching*.[61] In that case a firm of accountants took out a policy of insurance to cover themselves against loss for any claim made against them in respect of àny act of neglect, default or error arising out of the conduct of their business as accountants. The policy contained a "Queen's Counsel" clause (similar to the litigation clause in the instant case). A dishonest clerk in the firm fraudulently converted sums of money belonging to two clients of the firm, and the firm was sued by the clients. The underwriters refused a request for indemnity under the policy and the firm sought a declaration that the claims formulated in the writs issued against them were claims based in negligence, and in consequence brought into operation the Queen's Counsel clause. Devlin J. held that in each action there was only one claim which was primarily in respect of fraud, and that to fall within the scope of the policy the character of the claim must not be a mixed one of fraud and negligence alone, and that accordingly the claim was outside the scope of the policy.

In my view, that case is to be distinguished from the instant case, in which the only claim against the plaintiffs by Agrivest was in negligence — they did not seek to claim against the plaintiffs, nor could they do so, in respect of the

---

[61] [1957] 1 W.L.R. 45.

construction of the work under the plaintiffs sub-contract with Fairclough. In any event, I find it difficult to see how the fact that the same act amounted to both a tort and a breach of contract could enable insurers to avoid liability under a Professional Indemnity Policy on the basis that it was a mixed claim — if that were the true legal position, such a policy would be of little avail to a professional man, such as a solicitor, accountant, architect, engineer, doctor, dentist etc., as the same act of negligence causing damage to the client is almost invariably a breach of contract also — see, for example *Finlay* v. *Murtagh*[62] a decision of this Court.... The premiums in respect of these policies are substantial — in the instant case, the premium payable in 1980 was £38,316, and, to put it in context, its value in July 1984, when the claim against the plaintiffs was settled for £150,000, was almost £70,000.

In my judgment, the plaintiffs are entitled to be indemnified by the defendants under the Professional Indemnity Policy in respect of the sums paid by them in discharge of the claim of Agrivest.

Public Liability Policy

There was also in force at the material time a Public Liability Policy. That Policy provided as follows:

> Subject to the terms exceptions and conditions contained herein or endorsed or otherwise expressed hereon The Corporation will indemnify the Insured in respect of accidents happening on in or about any of the Places specified in the Schedule against all sums but not exceeding the Limits of Indemnity specified in the Schedule which the Insured shall become legally liable to pay as compensation for
> (1) Accidental bodily injury or disease to any person other than the persons hereinafter defined in the Exceptions to this policy
> (2) Accidental loss of or damage to property other than the property hereinafter defined in the Exceptions to this Policy caused by or through
> (a) The fault or negligence of the Insured or of any person in the service of the Insured in the course of the [said] Business [of the Insured]
> (b) any defect in the premises ways, works, plant or machinery connected with or used in the said Business.

The exceptions to the Policy included one providing that

> The Indemnity expressed in this Policy shall not apply to or include
> (2) liability assumed by the Insured by Agreement unless such liability would have attached to the Insured notwithstanding such Agreement.

Before the policy can apply there must have been an "accident". "Accident" is not defined in the policy but it is an expression with which all lawyers and most laymen would be familiar, and in respect of which there was a great body of case law under the Workmen's Compensation Acts when they were in force. In *Fenton* v. *Thorley & Co. Ltd*,[63] Lord MacNaghten said at p. 448 that

---

[62] [1979] I.R. 249.
[63] [1903] A.C. 443.

the word "accident" is used in the [Workmen's Compensation] Act, "as plain men understand it" and "in the popular and ordinary sense of the word as denoting an unlooked-for mishap or an untoward event which is not expected or designed". Lord Lindley at p. 453 referred to it as "any unintended and unexpected occurrence which produces hurt or loss".

I have the greatest reservation as to whether what occurred in this case could be considered to be an "accident" within the definitions of Lord MacNaghten and Lord Lindley. However, like the learned trial judge, I do not consider that it is necessary to express any concluded view on the matter.

In the construction of this policy also the intention of the parties must prevail. In this regard, the statement of Lord Wilberforce in *Reardon Smith Line Ltd* v. *Yngvar Hansen-Tangen*[64] seems apposite. There he said:

> "When one speaks of the intention of the parties to the contract, one is speaking objectively — the parties cannot themselves give direct evidence of what their intention was — and what must be ascertained is what is to be taken as the intention which reasonable people would have had if placed in the situation of the parties. Similarly, when one is speaking of the aim, or object, or commercial purpose, one is speaking objectively of what reasonable persons would have had in mind in the situation of the parties ... what the court must do must be to place itself in thought in the same factual matrix as that in which the parties were."

In *Staffordshire Area Health Authority* v. *South Staffordshire Waterworks Co.*,[65] Lord Denning M.R. having quoted this excerpt from the speech of Lord Wilberforce said:

> "We are to put ourselves in the same position as the parties were in at the time they drew up the instrument, to sit in their chairs with our minds endowed with the same facts as theirs were, and envisage the future with the same degree of foresight as they did. So placed we have to ask ourselves: 'what were the circumstances in which the contract was made?'"

In the case of what is entitled a Public Liability Policy, would reasonable persons, in the situation of the parties, have in mind that under the policy the parties would expect that the events which took place in this case would be covered? In my opinion, they would not. The intention of the parties would, in my view, clearly appear to be that cover was intended for what the ordinary reasonable man would understand by an "accident" occurring in the course of the carrying out of the work for which the insured had contracted. Construing the documents as a whole, the policy would not appear to be one in which the policyholder is indemnified against any liability he might have to the person who employed him or with whom he has a contract. If this were so, such a policy would be construed as covering all defective work for which the policyholder had contracted, and the policy would enure for the benefit of such persons as, say, a building owner. The consequences would be that no-one could

---

[64] [1976] 3 All E.R. 570 at pp. 574-5.
[65] [1978] 3 All E.R. 769 at p. 775.

reasonably expect to get such a policy, and if he could succeed in obtaining such a policy, the premium would be so prohibitive that it would be uneconomical. In contrast to policy No. SP 1245, it would be straining the construction of this Public Liability Policy beyond normal limits to hold that the employer should get from the insured and that he in turn could recover from the insurers any loss sustained because the work was not carried out properly. In my opinion, the intention of the parties was *not* that this policy should apply to events such as occurred in this case.

I would accordingly hold that the plaintiffs are entitled to be indemnified by the defendants in respect of Policy No. SP 1245, but are not entitled to be indemnified under the Public Liability Policy, and, to that extent would allow this appeal.

Brady v. Irish National Insurance Co. Ltd
[1986] I.L.R.M. 669
The High Court

O'HANLON J: The facts are not in dispute in this case, and the issue to be determined between the parties concerns the proper interpretation to be placed on the terms of a contract of insurance made between them on 9 July 1982 whereby the defendant agreed to insure the plaintiff against loss of, or damage to, a motor cruiser called "Dutch Maid", and against liabilities to third parties arising out of user of the said vessel or the plaintiff's interest therein.

The plaintiff bought the vessel, in a second-hand condition, in the year 1982 with a view to using her as a Shannon cruiser, and to some extent for sailing on the canals. The insurance contract was based on a Proposal Form dated 21 June 1982, which contained the following questions and answers, *inter alia*:

> "18. Who undertakes repairs, overhauls, or alterations when necessary?
> *Answer:* Self if possible.
> 24. (a) Where will the vessel be laid-up? (State whether on mud berth, ashore or afloat?)
> *Answer*: Afloat canal or Shannon.
> (b) State the exact period the vessel will be laid-up e.g. 1 November to 31 March.
> *Answer:* November to April.
> (c) State nature of supervision during such period.
> *Answer:* Supervised mooring."

The proposal form contained the usual provision at the end, as follows:

> I warrant that the above statement and particulars are correct and complete. I agree that this proposal shall be the basis of the contract between me and the company.

Having used the cruiser on the Shannon during the Summer of 1982 the plaintiff proceeded to lay her up for the winter at Lowtown, on the canal between Dublin and the Shannon. Apparently a marina has been established at Lowtown, at an old C.I.E. Depot, and large numbers of boats are laid-up there for the winter, either afloat or on the hard. A friend of the plaintiff, called Eric Timon, also a boatowner, and a fellow-employee of the plaintiff in the E.S.B., was another to avail of these facilities, and his boat was laid-up on the hard immediately adjoining where the "Dutch Maid" was afloat.

Both men used the laying-up period to effect necessary works of maintenance and overhaul on their vessels, and co-operated with one another in doing so — to the extent that each had a key to the other's boat and was free to go on board whenever they visited Lowtown to check that all was well, and, at times, to carry out some work for the benefit of the other party. They usually travelled down from Dublin together at weekends, and would work away on the boats, each concentrating at times on his own task and at other times combining their energies to deal with one of the vessels. If one happened to go down without the other, as happened from time to time, that one would set to work on whichever vessel needed most attention for the time being. No one else had a key to either vessel save the two owners concerned.

On Sunday, 6 March 1982, the plaintiff went down on his own to Lowtown and did some work on his boat. Its equipment included a cooker and refrigerator operated by Calor gas, and a geyser located in the toilet area which was a source of hot water when required which was also fuelled by Calor gas. All three pieces of equipment were connected to a single cylinder. On the date referred to, the plaintiff knew that the geyser was giving trouble and he removed it to his car to bring it up to Dublin for servicing. Before doing so he disconnected the regulator which connected the three pieces of equipment to the gas cylinder, so that for the time being no gas was coming from the cylinder. There was a stop-cock attachment provided on the cooker and refrigerator which would enable the supply of gas to these fittings to be cut off, while allowing it to come through to other equipment, but no stop-cock was provided on the geyser, and when he disconnected it, the plaintiff left the connecting pipe hanging loose and open. He anticipated that he would have the geyser back in commission by the following weekend.

Next day, Monday, 7 [March], the plaintiff called in to Mr Timon's place of employment to have a chat with him, but was told that he was "out on a job". Had Mr Timon been there, the plaintiff says that he would, in the normal course of things have told him about such work as he had carried out on the Sunday, including the removal of the geyser from his own boat for servicing purposes. Having missed his friend on the Monday, he called again on Tuesday, to be told that Mr Timon was on leave. Unknown to the plaintiff, Mr Timon had made a late decision the previous evening to spend Tuesday down in Lowtown working on his boat. While there, as his own boat was on its side on the hard, he availed of the galley facilities on the plaintiff's boat, reconnected the regulator on the Calor gas cylinder, and unwittingly caused two very serious explosions which damaged the vessel extensively and caused injuries to Mr Timon and to two other men who were in the vicinity. Once he reconnected the regulator, put in a new cylinder, and attempted to light the cooker for a second time, gas had escaped from the open pipe which normally served the geyser and accumulated in the lower reaches of the vessel, and this was clearly the cause of the explosions which took place.

The outcome of this unfortunate occurrence was that the plaintiff's motor cruiser had to be regarded as a total loss, subject to an allowance for the salvage value of the hull, and he has had an intimation from the injured parties of their intention to claim damages against him for negligence.

In this situation the plaintiff has applied to the defendant, as his insurer, to indemnify him against the damage to his vessel, and to undertake responsibility for meeting any claims which may be established by the third parties, up to the limit of £100,000 referred to in the policy.

The defendant contends that in the circumstances of this case the obligation to provide such indemnity does not arise, by reason of certain clauses and conditions which are found in the policy. The particular provisions relied on are as follows:

(a) "Loss of or Damage to the Vessel" is dealt with specifically in the "Institute Yacht Clauses", which are incorporated as conditions of the policy, and clause 16 which deals specifically with the question of insurance cover in respect of damage by explosions, concludes with the words — "provided such loss or damage has not resulted from want of due diligence by the owners of the vessel, or by any of them, or by the managers, or by the assured".

(b) A further document which is also incorporated into the policy of insurance contains the following provision:

> "*Special Warranties*
> The insured hereby warrants that at the commencement of the period of indemnity and at all times during the period of indemnity, the insured vessel is and shall be —
> (i) Seaworthy or otherwise fit for the purpose and use intended, tight, staunch, strong, sound and in good condition.
> (ii) During the laid-up period, laid-up in a place of safety, dismantled, not fitted out or available for immediate use and not used for any purpose whatsoever other than dismantling, fitting out or customary overhauling."

The defendant says that the proper conclusion to be drawn from the evidence is that the plaintiff did not exercise due diligence and that it was this default on his part which caused the damage to the vessel; furthermore, that the vessel at the time of the explosion was not seaworthy or otherwise fit for the purpose and use intended, but was left in a dangerous condition by reason of the fact that a connection to the Calor gas system was left open and anyone reconnecting the regulator and operating the cooker or refrigerator without knowing that the geyser had been disconnected would cause a major gas leakage and create an immediate risk of an explosion of the type which occurred. Finally, the defendant claims that the plaintiff was in breach of clause (ii) of the Special Warranties Clause, in permitting the kitchen facilities to be used for cooking and other domestic purposes during the laid-up period.

Reference was made in the course of the argument, to two sections of the Marine Insurance Act 1906. For the plaintiff, Mr Whelehan SC referred to s. 18 of the Act, dealing with the obligation of the assured to make full disclosure, and in particular to the following words which appear in s. 18 (3) (b):

> "... The insurer is presumed to know matters of common notoriety or knowledge, and matters which an insurer in the ordinary course of his business, as such, ought to know...."

A good deal of evidence was tendered for the purpose of establishing that owners of boats of the type damaged in the explosion commonly lay them up for the Winter, either on the hard or afloat, and spend much of their spare time getting the boats ready for the new season; that it is common practice in such circumstances for the galley to be used while works of overhaul and refurbishing are in progress, and that this was well-known to the boat-owning fraternity and to their insurers — a "matter of common notoriety" to use the words of the Act. I am prepared to accept that there is and always has been a common practice of the type referred to.

Mr Butler SC, for the defendant, submitted that s. 18 of the Act was concerned only with the obligation of the assured to make full disclosure to the insurer before the contract was concluded, of every material circumstance known to the assured, and that there was no allegation made in the present case of any failure on the plaintiff's part to comply with this obligation. He, in turn, relied on the provisions of s. 33 of the Act, dealing with Warranties, and in particular on sub-s. (3) of that section, which provides as follows:

"A warranty, as above defined, is a condition which must be exactly complied with, whether it be material to the risk or not. If it be not so complied with, then, subject to any express provision in the policy, the insurer is discharged from liability as from the date of the breach of warranty, but without prejudice to any liability incurred by him before that date."

Dealing first with the defendant's contention that the damage to the vessel was caused by want of due diligence on the part of the plaintiff and that any claim based on clause 16 of the Institute Yacht Clauses was thereby defeated, it is necessary to consider the meaning and scope of that expression used in clause 16 — "want of due diligence".

The same expression is found in the Australian Sea Carriage of Goods Act 1923 and its meaning and effect were considered in the case of *Riverstone Meat Co. Ltd* v. *Lancashire Shipping Co. Ltd.*[66] Willmer L.J. said:

"The obligation now imposed is to exercise due diligence, not to see that due diligence has been exercised — still less is there any warranty that due diligence has been exercised. An obligation to exercise due diligence is to my mind indistinguishable from an obligation to exercise reasonable care — a concept not unfamiliar in English Law, and one to be sharply distinguished from the obligation, to which certain relationships give rise, to see that care is taken" (at p. 219).

In that case the Court of Appeal, upholding the decision of the trial judge, held that the shipowners had exercised due diligence to make their ship seaworthy by entrusting works of necessary repair to ship repairers of high repute, notwithstanding that the work was done negligently and caused the vessel to become unseaworthy in the course of a subsequent voyage.

I think that reference should also be made to the case of *Fraser* v. *B.N. Furman (Productions) Ltd,*[67] where the Court of Appeal in England considered

---

[66] [1960] 1 All E.R. 193.
[67] [1967] 3 All E.R. 57.

ιow it should interpret a condition in an employer's liability policy requiring the insured to "take reasonable precautions to prevent accidents and disease". Diplock L.J. said:

> "The first point to consider is the question of construction of that condition. It must be construed, of course, in the context of a policy of insurance against specified risks. The risks so specified, which are 'liability at law for damages', are liability for breach of statutory duty for which the owner or occupier of the factory would always be personally liable, negligence at common law of the employer, for which he would be personally liable, and also the negligence of his servants, for which he would be vicariously liable. Therefore, when one approaches the construction of the condition, one does so in this context and applies the rule that one does not construe a condition as repugnant to the commercial purpose of the contract.
>
> There are three considerations to be borne in mind on the wording of this condition. (i) It is the insured personally who must take reasonable precautions. Failure by an employee to do so, although the employer might be liable vicariously for the employee's negligence or breach of statutory duty, would not be a breach of the condition. That was established in, and was the *ratio decidendi* of *Woodfall & Rimmer Ltd* v. *Moyle & Anor.*[68] (ii) The obligation of the employer is to take precautions to prevent accidents. This means in my view to take measures to avert dangers which are likely to cause bodily injury to employees. (iii) The third work to be construed in this context is 'reasonable'. 'The insured shall take reasonable precautions to prevent accidents'. 'Reasonable' does not mean reasonable as between the employer and the employee. It means reasonable as between the insured and the insurer having regard to the commercial purpose of the contract, which is *inter alia* to indemnify the insured against liability for his (the insured's) personal negligence. That, too, is established by the case that I have cited. Obviously the condition cannot mean that the insured must take measures to avert dangers which he does not himself foresee, although the hypothetical reasonably careful employer would have foreseen them. That would be repugnant to the commercial purpose of the contract, for failure to foresee dangers is one of the commonest grounds of liability in negligence. What in my view is 'reasonable' as between the insured and the insurer, without being repugnant to the commercial object of the contract is that the insured should not deliberately court a danger the existence of which he recognised, by refraining from taking any measures to avert it. Equally the condition cannot mean that, where the insured recognises that there is a danger, the measure which he takes to avert it must be such as the hypothetical, reasonable employer, exercising due care and observing all the relevant provisions of the Factories Act 1961 would have taken. That, too, would be repugnant to the commercial purpose of the contract, for failure to take such measures is another ground of liability in negligence for breach of statutory duty.
>
> What in my judgment is reasonable as between the insured and the insurer, without being repugnant to the commercial purpose of the contract, is that the insured, where he does recognise a danger, should not deliberately

_____

[68] [1941] 3 All E.R. 304.

court it by taking measures which he himself knows are inadequate to avert it. In other words, it is not enough that the employer's omission to take any particular precautions to avoid accidents should be negligent; it must be at least reckless, i.e., made with actual recognition by the insured himself that a danger exists, not caring whether or not it is averted. The purpose of the condition is to ensure that the insured will not refrain from taking precautions which he knows ought to be taken because he is covered against loss by the policy (at p. 60)."

These statements of judicial opinion commend themselves to me and I propose to adopt them for the purpose of the present judgment. Clause 16 of the Institute Yacht Clauses purports to include cover for loss of or damage to the vessel "caused by the negligence of any person whatsoever".

When the plaintiff disconnected the geyser he recognised that he was leaving the gas connection in an unsealed condition and that it could be a possible source of danger. It was put to him that he should have given express warning to the other person who had a key to the boat and freedom of access to it at any time — Eric Timon — and/or that he should have placed a warning notice in a prominent position in the boat to ensure that the regulator would not be reconnected inadvertently while the pipe was open. He said in reply that he thought he had taken adequate precaution by disconnecting the regulator (thereby halting *pro tem.* the emission of gas from the cylinder) and locking up the boat; that he only envisaged leaving things in that condition for about a week; that in the meantime no one, other than himself and Mr Timon had a means of lawful access to the boat, and that they invariably went down together when visiting the boats, or each would notify the other when going alone — that was the first and only occasion that Mr Timon had gone on his own with no forewarning to the plaintiff. There was also the circumstance that the plaintiff made two efforts to contact Mr Timon during the two-day interval which elapsed between the disconnection of the gas pipe and the happening of the explosion.

I am of opinion that the plaintiff did not (to use the words of Diplock L.J.) "deliberately court a danger which he recognised by taking measures which he knew were inadequate to avert it". As between the plaintiff and Mr Timon there may well have been a want of reasonable care, but I think that as between the plaintiff and his insurers he exercised due diligence in doing what he himself believed to be more than adequate to avoid danger of injury to any person arising from the disconnection of the gas supply.

This finding is sufficient to dispose of the first limb of the defence to the claim put forward by the defendant, but it leaves for consideration the second ground of defence which relies on the alleged breach of warranty.

Looking at the overall purpose of this contract of insurance, my impression is that it was designed to provide cover for the insured against loss of or damage to the vessel, and against liabilities to third parties arising out of the ownership and use of the vessel, throughout the entire period of insurance, provided such loss or damage or third party claim was not attributable to a failure by the insured himself to keep the vessel in good condition and fit for the purpose and use intended, and provided it was not used during the "laid-up period" (in this case, defined by the insured himself as extending from November to April) for any purpose other than dismantling, fitting-out or customary overhauling. In other words, the period of active use of the vessel, so far as the insurers were concerned, was to be confined to the period from May to October (inclusive), and they were not to be liable for damage or loss sustained which was attributable to a failure on the part of the insured to maintain the vessel in a condition of seaworthiness and fitness for the purpose and use intended. It seems to me that the words "purpose and use intended" must be linked up with Question 22 on the Proposal Form, where the intended user is stated by the proposer as use for private pleasure.

Mr Whelehan SC argued that Special Warranties Nos. (i) and (ii) should be regarded as mutually exclusive, since it would be quite illogical to require that the vessel should be "seaworthy or otherwise fit for the purpose and use intended, tight, staunch, strong, sound and in good condition" at a time when it was being laid-up for necessary repairs and overhaul. I think there is a good deal of force in this argument, although it seems to involve giving the clause a meaning which is hard to reconcile with the ordinary meaning of the words used. However, the words "or otherwise fit for the purpose and use intended" seem to imply that the cover may continue during a period when the vessel is no longer seaworthy for the time being, and to this extent support the argument advanced by the defendant, who says that the two warranties can be read together and are not mutually exclusive.

Instead of attempting to resolve this difficulty, I propose at this stage to consider the implication of the second warranty given. The plaintiff's counsel contends that use of the vessel during the laid-up period for "dismantling, fitting-out or customary overhauling" is a wide enough expression to include the incidental use of the gallery and its equipment for preparation of occasional meals while the work is in progress, and that this interpretation is supported by the evidence of custom and practice among boat-owners which was tendered and which the defendant did not seek to controvert.

It seems to me, however, that the use of the cooking facilities on board the vessel, and the gas supply linked to the cooker during the laid-up period, involved for the insurance company an added risk of a not insignificant character, over and above the risks normally inherent in the use of the vessel merely for dismantling, fitting-out or customary overhauling and that they are entitled to say that it went outside the category of risks for which cover was provided. For this reason, and having regard to the very stringent provisions of s. 33 (3) of the Marine Insurance Act 1906, I have come to the conclusion that the defendant is entitled to succeed on this particular line of defence and I therefore find it necessary to dismiss the plaintiff's claim ....

The Supreme Court

FINLAY C.J. (WALSH AND HEDERMAN J.J. CONCURRING): This is an appeal by the plaintiff against the dismiss by ... O'Hanlon J, of his claim against the defendants for indemnity on foot of a policy of insurance issued by the defendants to the plaintiff....

The policy of insurance
The policy of insurance consists, firstly of a formal policy and then of two separate attached conditions, one described as 'Special Conditions Clause'

and the other described as 'Institute Yacht Clause'.

I feel obliged to comment that insofar as this combined document consists of what might be described as the ordinary policy of insurance it is wholly, completely and absolutely inapplicable to the type of risk which either the insured or the insurer is concerned. To take as a small and simple example, it is solemnly set out in this policy that the risks which are being insured are "the adventures and perils which the said company is contented to bear and does take upon itself in this voyage, they are of the seas, men of war, fire, enemies, pirates, rovers, thieves, jettisons, letters of mart and countermart, surprises, taking at sea, arrests, restraints, and attainments of all kings, princes and people of whatever nation, condition or quality soever, etc." It may well be that such terms in this policy of insurance are an attempt to bring it, by virtue of s. 2 (2) of the Marine Insurance Act 1906, within the provisions of that Act, many of which are very largely advantageous to the insurer. It is extremely undesirable from the point of view of fair dealing and clarity with regard to legal rights that a person seeking to insure a pleasure craft on inland water-ways should be presented with a document of insurance which purports strictly to bind him, which he is meant to understand and which is so wholly inappropriate, in part at least, to the purpose of the transaction being effected.

During the discussion upon this appeal, some doubt was expressed as to whether this could be a policy within the provisions of the Marine Transport Act 1906, but it is clear that upon the pleadings the plaintiff accepted it to be such and sought to rely in certain particulars upon the provisions of that Act and that it would not be now open to this Court, in my view, to consider that issue. I am assuming, therefore, without deciding, that the provisions of the Act of 1906 do apply to this particular policy of insurance.

For the purposes of the issues arising in this case, the following are the material provisions of the policy. By virtue of clause 16 of the Institute Yacht Clauses, the liability of the insurers for loss of or damage to the vessel is confined by the provision that "such loss or damage has not resulted from want of due diligence by the owners of the vessel or any of them, or by the managers or by the assured." By the special conditions clause, it is first provided that it is agreed that the information contained in the proposal made by the insured should be the basis of the contract and be held as incorporate in it and, secondly, two special warranties are provided in the following terms:

"The insured hereby warrants that at the commencement of the period of indemnity and at all times during the period of indemnity the insured vessel is and shall be:

1. Seaworthy or otherwise fit for the purpose and use intended, tight, staunch, strong, sound and in good condition.

2. During the laid-up period, laid-up in a place of safety, dismantled, not fitted-out or available for immediate use and not used for any purpose whatsoever other than dismantling, fitting-out or customary overhauling.

Relevant statutory provisions
S. 18 (1) of the Marine Insurance Act 1906 provides as follows:

Subject to the provisions of this section, the assured must disclose to the insurer, before the contract is concluded, every material circumstance which is known to the assured, and the assured is deemed to know every circumstance which, in the ordinary course of business, ought to be known by him. If the assured fails to make such disclosure, the insurer may avoid the contract.

By subs. (3) (b) of the same section it is provided that in the absence of enquiry the following circumstances need not be disclosed, namely, any circumstance which is known to or presumed to be known to the insurer; the insurer is presumed to know matters of common notoriety or knowledge and matters which an insurer, in the ordinary course of his business as such, ought to know.

S. 33 of the Act of 1906, having defined a warranty as meaning a promissory warranty, provides at subs. (3) that "a warranty, as above defined, is a condition which must be exactly complied with, whether it be material to the risk of not".

The issues

The defendants in the High Court resisted the plaintiff's claim on four main grounds. First, they asserted that the information contained in the proposal form did not reveal what they alleged was a material circumstance, namely, that whilst overhauling and maintaining the vessel during the laid-up period that the galley would be in use. Secondly, they asserted that, as far as the loss of or damage to the vessel was concerned, the plaintiff had acted without due diligence in disconnecting the geyser, even though the gas was disconnected without warning Mr Timon specifically of that fact. Thirdly, they asserted that there was a breach of Special Warranty Number I, in that the vessel was neither seaworthy at the time of the incident, by reason of the disconnection of the gas, nor fit for the purpose and use intended, namely, the overhaul and maintenance at that time. Lastly, they contended that the use of the galley was a breach of the Special Warranty Number II, and that it was a use other than one of those specified in that warranty.

Whilst those were the defendants' defences in the High Court, and whilst each of them was dealt with by the learned trial judge in his judgment, it is of considerable importance in my view that, factually, the defendant entirely concentrated on the allegation of lack of due diligence, the inadequacy of the declarations concerning the laying-up and on an allegation consistently made in cross-examination of the plaintiff and his witnesses that, apart from the question of seaworthiness it was well know to everybody concerned that one of the uses which a pleasure boat would or could be put to, while being laid-up, was the use of the galley during periods of maintenance and that the removal of the geyser without warning left it unfit for that use. The factual base for this last contention was completely inconsistent with the submission also made in the High Court, and made very strongly on this appeal, that the use of the galley during periods of maintenance and overhaul was not part of customary overhaul.

The decision in the High Court

In the course of his judgment in the High Court, O'Hanlon J. made the following findings:

1. He found that it was a matter of common notoriety or knowledge that, in the course of the maintenance and overhaul during the laid-up period of pleasure boats of this description, the galley would frequently and usually be used. The defendants cross-appealed against that finding, but did not seriously pursue that cross-appeal and indeed it would have been impossible for them to do so, because not only did the evidence support such a finding by the learned trial judge, but inevitably led to it.

2. He found that the plaintiff had not been guilty of any want of due diligence, occasioning the loss of or damage to the vessel. Again, this finding was appealed against by the defendants by way of cross-appeal, but that appeal was not pursued and, in my view, could not be pursued, having regard to the fact that it is clear that the learned trial judge applied the right test and proper legal interpretation of what is due diligence within the meaning of the policy, and that there was evidence to support his finding.

3. An issue had arisen in the court below as to whether the Special Warranty Number I was applicable during the period of the laying-up of the vessel. It was contended on behalf of the plaintiff that the two Special Warranties were, in effect, mutually exclusive, Number I being applicable to a time when the vessel was in commission and Number II being applicable to a time when the vessel was laid-up. It was contended on behalf of the defendants that both applied all the time. The learned trial judge did not resolve this issue, stating his view in the following manner:

> "Instead of attempting to resolve this difficulty I propose at this stage to con-
> sider the implications of the second warranty given. The plaintiff's counsel
> contends that the use of the vessel during the laid-up period for 'dismantling,
> fitting-out, or customary overhauling" is a wide enough expression to include
> the incidental use of the galley and its equipment for preparation of occa-
> sional meals while the work is in progress, and that this interpretation is
> supported by the evidence of a custom and practice among boat-owners
> which was tendered and which the defendant did not seek to controvert.
>
> It seems to me, however, that the use of the cooking facilities on board
> the vessel, and the gas supply linked to the cooker, during the laid-up period
> involved for the insurance company an added risk of a not insignificant
> character, over and above the risks normally inherent in the use of the
> vessel, merely for dismantling, fitting-out or customary overhauling and that
> they are entitled to say that it went outside the category of risks for which
> cover was provided. For this reason, and having regard to the very stringent
> provisions of s. 33 (3) of the Marine Insurance Act 1906, I have come to the
> conclusion that the defendant is entitled to succeed on this particular line of
> defence and I therefore find it necessary to dismiss the plaintiff's claim for
> the various forms of relief referred to in the plenary summons and statement
> of claim.

The law

I am satisfied that the learned trial judge in the conclusion which I have just quoted was in error. It would appear that his view with regard to the position of the plaintiff and the defendants under the Special Warranty Number II was coloured by and arose from a consideration of an additional or increased risk to the insurers. If there were a breach of Special Warranty Number II, then it is quite clear, having regard to the terms of s. 33 (3) of the Marine Insurance Act 1906 that the presence or absence of an additional or increased risk becomes wholly immaterial. Furthermore, the learned trial judge refers to the very stringent provisions of s.33. There can be no doubt that insofar as s.33 requires an exact compliance with warranties under the Act, that is something wholly different from and to be separated from the principles applicable to the interpretation of a warranty. What seems to me first necessary, before considering whether there has been an exact compliance with this special warranty, is to consider on the evidence in the case as well as on the terms of the policy itself as to what the true meaning of the Special Warranty Number II is.

The principle applicable to this interpretation is, I am satisfied, similar to the principle which would be applicable to the interpretation of a contract proffered by one person to another. District Justice E. Hoffman in *The Christie*,[69] dealing with an express warranty in a marine insurance policy, stated:

> "As far as the vagueness claim is concerned, plaintiffs are quite correct in stating that if the warranty was vague it should be construed against the insurer" (at p. 106).

In this case the ph[r]ase contained in Special Warranty Number II, "customary overhauling" is not expanded or amplified by any further definition in the policy, nor is it a phrase which has any special legal meaning. It must, in my view, therefore, be interpreted against the insurer in the light of evidence as to what is customary in this context. In the course of his judgment the learned trial judge dealing admittedly with the provisions of s. 18, but on the same topic, stated as follows:

> "A good deal of evidence was tendered for the purpose of establishing that owners of boats of the type damaged in the explosions, commonly lay them up for the Winter, either on the hard or afloat, and spend much of their spare time getting the boats ready for the new season; that it is common practice in such circumstances for the galley to be used while works of overhaul and refurbishing are in progress, and that this was well-known to the boat-owning fraternity and to their insurers — a 'matter of common notoriety', to use the words of the Act. I am prepared to accept that there is and always has been a common practice of the type referred to".

This finding was, as I have already indicated, not only well founded on the evidence but inevitable from it, and indeed in examining the only witness called on behalf of the defendants in the High Court, Mr Jones, counsel on behalf of the defendants, at Q. 490, summarised what the effect of the plaintiff's evidence so far had been, in the following question:

> "We have had evidence which I think is incontrovertible that it is within the contemplation of people overhauling boats during the laying-up period that

---

[69] [1975] 2 Lloyd's Rep. 100.

the cooker will be used. Is the boat fit for such use if the geyser has been disconnected in the circumstances described?"

I cannot see any conceivable distinction between what has been described by the learned trial judge as a common practice which is and always has been, in this context, and a custom; I, therefore, conclude that, on the true construction of Special Warranty Number II, having regard to the findings of the learned trial judge the use of the galley was part of the customary overhaul and ancillary to it and not a failure exactly to comply with this special warranty. The ground, therefore, on which the learned trial judge found against the plaintiff, must, in my view, fail.

It becomes necessary for me, however, having regard to that decision, to consider the matter not decided in the High Court, namely, as to whether Special Warranty Number I was applicable to this boat while it was laid-up afloat.

The terms of this warranty must, of course, be construed in accordance with the *ejusdem generis* rule. It is quite clear that a boat while laid-up for the purpose of maintenance and overhaul, must from time to time and in particular instances require to be rendered wholly unfit for navigation. For example, a boat laid-up in the hard may easily, during a significant part of the laid-up period, have major planks below the water line removed for the purpose of restoring and re-fitting better timbers. Such a boat could never be described as seaworthy; it could never be described as tight, staunch, strong, sound and in good condition. Applying, therefore, the *ejusdem generis* rule to the terms of Special Warranty Number I, I am satisfied that the proper interpretation would be that it is applicable only to periods when the boat is in commission rather than laid-up. A consideration of the terms of Special Warranty II, however, make this even clearer. One of the matters promised or warranted in that warranty is that the boat will not during the laid-up period be fitted out or available for immediate use. If both these warranties apply during the laid-up period, then the obligation of the insured, or boat-owner, would be, on the one hand, to have the boat fit for the purpose and use intended, and on the other hand to have the boat not fitted out or available for immediate use. Counsel on behalf of the defendants suggested that the only way in which these two warranties, applicable at the same time, could be reconciled is to give to the word "use" in each of them quite a separate and different meaning. Having regard to the fact that these warranties must be construed against the insurers who proffered them, I am satisfied that such an interpretation is not warranted.

I am, therefore, satisfied that the terms of Special Warranty I do not apply during the laid-up period and that no question of a breach of them, therefore, arises in this action.

I would, therefore, allow this appeal....

GRIFFIN J: In this appeal, Mr Butler SC, on behalf of the appellants confined his argument to the net issues of whether there was a breach on the part of the plaintiff of either or both of the Special Warranties (I) and (II) incorporated in the policy of insurance issued by the respondents to the plaintiff.

Before dealing with these issues there are two matters on which I should like to make some general comments. First as to the Marine Insurance Act 1906 (the Act). Towards the end of the last day on which the appeal was at hearing, the question was raised as to whether the Act had any application to this policy of insurance. In his pleadings the plaintiff relied on provisions of the Act, the entire hearing in the High Court proceeded on the basis that the Act applied, both sides relied on certain provisions of the Act to advance their respective arguments, and the greater proportion of the appeal proceeded on the basis of the application of those provisions in the Act. In my opinion, in these circumstances insofar as this case is concerned it would not be open to this Court to consider that issue and the appeal should be determined on the assumption that the Act does apply.

Secondly, although the policy of insurance has included in it several provisions which might seem to be inappropriate to an insurance in respect of a small cruiser in inland waters, policies of insurance of this kind are in standard form and in general use in marine insurance. It is highly likely that they have been drawn up with the accumulated insurance experience of very many years, if not of centuries, and although some provisions of such policies might with advantage be brought-up-to-date, and the wording revised, I would be reluctant to criticise them on that score. In any event, the proposal form and the policy form the basis of the contract between the parties.

Special Warranties

S. 33 (1) of the Act provides:

> "A warranty ... means a promissory warranty, that is to say, a warranty by which the assured undertakes that some particular thing shall or shall not be done, or that some condition shall be fulfilled, or whereby he affirms or negatives the existence of a particular state of facts."

It is provided by subs. (3):

> "A warranty, as above defined, is a condition which must be exactly complied with, whether it be material to the risk or not...."

In respect of such warranties, the true legal position was concisely and clearly stated by McNair J. in *Overseas Commodities Ltd* v. *Style*[70]:

> "It has long been well-established law that an express warranty requires a strict and literal performance: see now the Marine Insurance Act 1906, s. 33 (3). As is stated in *Arnould on Marine Insurance*, 14th ed., s. 632, 'Every policy, in fact, in which an express warranty is inserted is a conditional contract, to be binding if the warranty be literally complied with, but not otherwise'" (at p. 558).

The special warranties incorporated in the policy of insurance in this case, insofar as they are relevant to the case, are in the following terms:

---

[70] [1958] 1 Lloyd's Rep. 546.

Special Warranties

The insured hereby warrants that at the commencement of the period of indemnity and at all times during the period of indemnity the insured vessel is and shall be:

I. Seaworthy or otherwise fit for the purpose and use intended, tight, staunch, strong, sound and in good condition.

II. During the laid-up period, laid-up in a place of safety, dismantled, not fitted-out or available for immediate use and not used for any purpose whatsoever other than dismantling, fitting-out or customary overhauling.

Counsel for the appellants submit that there has been a breach of *both* I and II. In respect of Special Warranty I they allege that the vessel was not at the material time seaworthy and was unfit for use because of the defective gas installation then in the vessel. In short, they allege that the warranty as to seaworthiness continued to apply at all times even when the vessel was laid-up and was not in commission, and that they were therefore entitled to repudiate the policy. The plaintiff, on the other hand, submitted that the two [S]pecial Warranties were mutually exclusive and that the Special Warranty I applied only when the boat was in commission. Having regard to the conclusion to which I have come to in relation to Special Warranty II. I do not consider it necessary to decide whether there was any breach of Special Warranty I on the part of the plaintiff. If, however, it was necessary to decide that question, I would find it difficult to agree with the proposition that a vessel which is laid-up and undergoing (say) major repairs to its hull was required to be kept seaworthy at all times.

In respect of Special Warranty II, in my opinion, on the facts of this case, there was a breach of that warranty on the part of the plaintiff. The warranty required that the vessel should not be "used for any purpose whatever other than dismantling, fitting-out or customary overhaul". I do not consider that there was any ambiguity in relation to the use of "customary overhaul" in the policy, or that these words needed to be defined. Indeed, in the course of the hearing in the High Court, it was not alleged that there was any such ambiguity. The plaintiff's case was that the use of the galley and cooking facilities in the course of fitting-out or overhauling the boat was a use which was a customary user of a boat by the owner as being incidental or ancillary to the work being carried out on the vessel.

It was the custom of the plaintiff and his friend Mr Timon to cook meals for themselves in either the plaintiff's boat or Mr Timon's boat when they were working on one or other of their boats. On this occasion, however, Mr Timon went to Lowtown alone, with the intention of working on his own boat only. He had a key to the plaintiff's boat. As his own boat was laid-up on the bank on its side, he was unable to use the cooking facilities on that boat. He had brought his food with him and it is not in question that he would have cooked his meals in the plaintiff's boat whether the weather deteriorated or not. The work being done on his own boat was external work. When the weather turned wet, he decided to go into the plaintiff's boat and then proceeded to cook his meal which included steak. As he had time while the steak was cooking he freed the outlet on the sink, which was giving trouble, and put new hoses on it. When he had finished his meal, he washed up, locked up the boat and returned to work on his own boat for several hours. He then decided to quit as it came close to 5 o'clock, and invited two other men working there on to the plaintiff's boat for a cup of tea. It was when he lighted the gas to boil the kettle for the tea that the explosion occurred.

Dealing with the use by boat-owners of the galley when the boats are laid-up, the learned trial judge said in his judgment:

> "A good deal of evidence was tendered for the purpose of establishing that owners of boats of the type damaged in the explosions (*sic*) commonly lay them up for the Winter, either on the hard or afloat, and spend much of their spare time getting the boats ready for the new season; that it is common practice in such circumstances for the galley to be used while works of overhaul and refurbishing are in progress, and that this was well-known to the boat-owning fraternity and to their insurers — a 'matter of common notoriety', to use the words of the Act. I am prepared to accept that there is and always has been a common practice of the type referred to" (at p. 673).

Undoubtedly, this practice of which evidence was given would cover the use of the cooking facilities by the owner of the boat while overhauling and refurbishing was in progress for himself, the members of his family and his friends who would be assisting him in the work while it was being done on that boat — it would be necessarily ancillary or incidental to the work being carried out on the boat. But that is in my opinion a far cry from the situation in which a friend of the plaintiff, whilst working on his own boat, could make use of the cooking facilities in the plaintiff's boat for his own purposes and for the purposes of friends or acquaintances whom *he* would invite on board. This would in my opinion not be a use for or incidental or ancillary to dismantling, fitting-out or customary overhaul, being the only users permitted under the terms of the warranty. Such a use would be analogous to the situation in tort where a servant is on a frolic of his own. Whilst it might be arguable that Mr Timon, in doing some small job whilst his meal was being cooked on the plaintiff's boat, was within the permitted use, in my view no such argument can be made in respect of the use by him of the boat several hours later, when he returned to the boat to make tea for the use of himself and his invited friends.

In my opinion, therefore, at the time when the explosion occurred the use being made of the plaintiff's boat was a use prohibited by the Special Warranty II and the defendants were entitled to repudiate liability on foot of the policy. One can have considerable sympathy with the plaintiff, who could not remember whether he had read the provisions of the Special Warranties or not, and who in any event thought that he was fully insured against all risks. This however cannot assist him where the warranties, as in this case, require a strict and literal performance. The learned judge took the view that such user was an added risk of a not insignificant character over and above the risks normally inherent in the use of the vessel for dismantling, fitting-out or customary overhauling. In my view, added risk is irrelevant having regard to the fact that these warranties must be strictly and literally complied with. I differ from the learned trial judge only in that respect.

I would dismiss the appeal.

Dillon *v.* McGovern (on behalf of certain underwriters at Lloyds)
Unreported, 16 March 1993
The High Court

GEOGHEGAN J: This is a claim for £34,422.04 damages for alleged breach of an insurance contract.

The insurance related to 79 head of cattle. There was to be an indemnity to the Plaintiff in the event of a failure to pass what was referred to as "the routine *brucellosis* test". The contract document took the form of a certificate issued by Thoroughbred Insurance Services Limited ("Thoroughbred") effectively acting as a broker or agent for certain underwriters at Lloyds. The basic printed form contract or certificate was primarily used to cover the death of a racehorse and many of the clauses would have been appropriate only to that category of insurance. Thoroughbred has been issuing these policies since about 1974. From the beginning and from time to time this standard policy document was used to cover cattle compulsorily destroyed by reason of either tuberculosis or brucellosis under the Diseases of Animals Act, 1966 or both. A form of Memorandum and Extension Clause drawn up in the Lloyds offices in London in the seventies was furnished to Thoroughbred to be added to the standard certificate when this kind of cattle cover was desired. These forms had been invariably used up to the time at least that the Plaintiff put forward the present claim.

The added Memorandum read as follows:—

> "*Memorandum No. 1*
> It is noted and agreed that cover under this certificate applies only in respect of failure to pass routine brucellosis tests as per wording attached and all reference to mortality cover is deleted.
> WARRANTED NO PREVIOUS INCIDENTS OF FAILURE TO PASS BRUCELLOSIS TESTS IN THE ASSURED'S HERD."

The reference to "as per wording attached" was a reference to the Extension Clause which in this case related to brucellosis only. The Extension Clause read as follows:—

> "In the event of the insured animal(s) being compulsorily slaughtered under the provisions of the Diseases of Animals Act 1966 and subsequent amendments following failure to pass the routine brucellosis test — this certificate is extended to provide indemnity up to but not exceeding the sum(s) insured shown on the Schedule.
> It is further noted and agreed that all carcass value and Government compensation shall become the undisputed property of underwriters."

To complete the picture I should refer to the main Schedule attached to the document and forming part of the contract. Under the main heading "the animals insured" there are five columns. In the first column under the subheading "name" and "breed" there is entered the following:—

> "Eighty head of cattle as specified on four schedules attached".

The entry in the fourth column under the sub-heading "use" is:—

"Failure to pass routine brucellosis test".

While this policy was still in force 15 of the 79 head of cattle failed the test which would clearly fall within the description "routine brucellosis test". The Department of Agriculture and Food, however, required the slaughter of the entire herd of 79. Because of the danger of infection the remainder of the animals, even though they had not failed the test, were "deemed to be reactors". As a consequence the entire herd was destroyed. The Plaintiff claims to be entitled to indemnity in respect of all the animals, whereas the Defendant, sued on behalf of Lloyds, maintains that the indemnity only covers the 15 head of cattle that failed the test. This is the sole issue in the case.

It has been forcefully argued by Mr McGovern, Counsel for the Defendant, that the words of the Extension Clause are quite clear and are open to only one meaning. If he was right in that submission, it would not be permissible to adduce parol evidence to explain or vary the Clause. This is a general principle in the law of contract but with reference to insurance contracts the principle is neatly stated and discussed in *MacGillivray and Parkington* Insurance Law sixth edition at p. 1176. The parol evidence, however, would at any rate be admissible to show the circumstances under which the parties contracted and the general context within which the contract was entered into.

In the event, I took the view that there was some ambiguity in the Clause in that, depending on the minds of the parties, the expression "following failure to pass the routine *brucellosis* test" might not necessarily have been intended to mean that all the animals slaughtered had to fail a specific test. I also considered that the expression "failure to pass" was slightly ambiguous in that it could be held to cover animals which had been tested but had neither failed nor passed the test.

Accordingly, I decided that parol evidence could be admitted to assist me in determining the true intention of the parties as well as for the purpose of placing the contract in context. I am satisfied, however that as a matter of law I am entitled to have regard to the parol evidence only for the purpose of helping me to construe the written words in the light of the intention of the parties and the general context and not for the purpose of varying the written agreement.

It is now necessary to examine that evidence. The story began in 1985 when the Plaintiff, Mr Dillon, contacted Mr Reddin of Thoroughbred whom he knew. The Plaintiff gave the following account of what he had said to Mr Reddin on that occasion.

"I asked him would he insure my whole herd against brucellosis". Mr Reddin's evidence exactly corresponds with the Plaintiff's evidence. Mr Reddin said there was a very brief conversation which he described in evidence as follows:—

"He asked me would I insure his entire herd for brucellosis".

I accept Mr Reddin's evidence that he told the Plaintiff that he would check with the underwriters. It is common case that a proposal form which was really only a schedule in which the animals were to be listed was then sent to the Plaintiff. The Plaintiff filled it up and sent it back to Mr Reddin. The policy or certificate then issued with the clauses already cited. I am quite satisfied from the evidence that the Plaintiff would, at all material times, have assumed that he was covered in the event of depopulation of the herd as a consequence of some animals failing the brucellosis test. Clearly on the terms of the actual verbal request for cover, depopulation would have been included. I am equally satisfied that the issue was never considered by Mr Reddin because at the time that this insurance was effected he was quite unaware that animals, other than those that had specifically failed the test, could be required by the Department of Agriculture and Food to be slaughtered. The evidence establishes that "depopulation" started to be used as a weapon by the Department in its fight against brucellosis in or about 1982 or 1983. Mr Reddin impressed me as a truthful witness and I believe him when he says he was unaware of the new practice at the time of issuing this policy. Furthermore, the evidence suggests that "depopulation" was applied very sparingly before 1985 at least.

The insertion of the words "failure to pass the routine *brucellosis* test" had nothing whatever to do with avoiding liability for "depopulation" since that possibility was not considered at all by Mr Reddin. Presumably that wording was used to exclude liability for animals slaughtered under the Diseases of Animals Act, 1966 by reason of disease other than brucellosis. It was the same wording which had been used since 1974.

How then should this Court construe the policy in the context of the dispute, the subject matter of this action? I have come to the conclusion that if the wording was at all open to being construed by an ordinary farmer, such as the Plaintiff, as embracing cover for depopulation by reason of some of the herd failing a brucellosis test, then the relevant Lloyds underwriters are liable for the full indemnity claimed. Having regard to the elements of ambiguity in the wording to which I have already drawn attention, combined with the parol evidence, both as to the discussions leading up to the issue of the policy and as to the respective states of mind of each of the parties at that time, I am quite satisfied that the Plaintiff is entitled to recover on the basis of indemnity for all 79 animals. I think that the conclusion which I have reached would be correct independently of the so called "contra proferentem" rule. But the application of that rule greatly strengthens me in the view which I have taken. Counsel for the Plaintiff, Mr Gordon, has referred me to *In re Sweeney and Kennedy's Arbitration*[71] and in particular to the following passages in the judgment of Mr Justice Kingsmill-Moore at p. 98:—

> "But even if I am wrong in my conclusion that the interpretation is reasonably free from doubt, the case must be decided against the underwriters if the words are ambiguous. The wording of the proposal form and the policy was chosen by the underwriters who knew, or must be deemed to have known, what matters were material to the risk and what information they desired to obtain. They were at liberty to adopt any phraseology which they

---

[71] 1950 I.R. 85. See p. 185 of this book.

desired. They could have provided clearly and expressly that no driver should be employed who was under 21 years of age or had less than 12 months experience and they could have done this by means of a special condition or by an addition to the final proviso under the heading "description of drivers" in the policy. Indeed they could have secured their object (if it was their object) with perfect clarity in half a dozen ways. If, then, they choose to adopt ambiguous words it seems to me good sense, as well as established law, that these words should be interpreted in the sense which is adverse to the person who chose and introduced them: *Anderson* v. *Fitzgerald*[72] per Lord St Leonards, at p. 507; *Fowkes* v. *Manchester and London Life Assurance and Loan Association*[73] per Cockburn C.J. at p. 925 and per Blackburn J. at p. 929; *Fitton* v. *Accidental Death Insurance Company*[74] per Willes J. at p. 135".

That passage is highly relevant to this case. I am quite certain that if Thoroughbred or its principals had been at all aware of the "depopulation" possibility a simple clause would have been added to the policy making it quite clear that the cover was confined to the actual animals which failed the specific test and that a verbal communication to this effect would have been made to the Plaintiff. A farmer, such as the Plaintiff, dealing with Thoroughbred would have been entitled to assume that Thoroughbred and its principals undertaking this kind of insurance were aware of the methods by which the provisions of the Diseases of Animals Act, 1966 and the Regulations made thereunder were implemented in relation to the eradication of brucellosis. Any such farmer could reasonably expect that, if there was an exclusion of liability for depopulation following on a failure of some animals to pass a specific test, this would have been expressly stated in the policy. I accept, of course, that even though the policy covered all 79 animals a cover which embraced depopulation significantly extended the risk and I also accept that if the underwriters had been aware that slaughter under a "depopulation" direction by the Department as an anti-brucellosis measure was included in the request for cover, either no such cover would have been given or the premium would have been substantially higher.

Nevertheless, the Plaintiff was entitled to interpret the policy in the way he did and the Defendant must be held bound for the reasons which I have indicated by that interpretation. *Sweeney's* case is a particular application of a wider principle explained in *MacGillivray and Parkington* on Insurance Law 6th edition at par. 1173 as follows:—

"Ambiguity and the *contra proferentem* rule. If there is any ambiguity in the language used in a policy, it is to be construed more strongly against the party who prepared it, which means in the majority of cases against the Company. This rule of construction, that verba chartarum fortius accipiuntur contra proferentem, is a principle applicable to all commercial transactions where only one party has prepared the form of contract. A party who proffers

---

[72] 4 H.L. 484.
[73] 3 B. & S. 917.
[74] 17 C.B. (N.S.) 122.

an instrument cannot be permitted to use ambiguous words in the hope that the other side will understand them in a particular sense, and that the Court which has to construe them will give them a different sense. The result of using ambiguous expressions is generally a decision against those who deal in such ambiguities."

As I have already indicated, the question of whether a particular form of wording is ambiguous or not depends, not merely on the actual reading of the wording, but also on the context and surrounding circumstances in which the wording was formulated.

Although I have not found it necessary to base my Judgment on it, there is considerable force in the argument of Mr Gordon, Counsel for the Plaintiff, that the 64 animals deemed to be reactors must be regarded for that very reason as having failed to pass the routine test within the meaning of the Extension Clause and indeed the evidence establishes that they were never regarded as having passed the test. "Reactor" is defined in the relevant regulations which were the *Brucellosis in Cattle (General Provisions) Order, 1980.*[75] The definition reads as follows:—

"Reactor" means an animal which by reason of the result of a test or otherwise a veterinary inspector believes to be, or suspects of being, affected with brucellosis or capable of affecting other animals with brucellosis".

It was never intended even by the underwriters that the clause in the policy was to be given too literal an interpretation because, on a literal interpretation, not even the 15 animals that failed the specific test would be covered in that none of those animals were strictly speaking "compulsorily slaughtered". The incentive method of combining a movement permit with the payment of compensation if certain conditions were fulfilled was adopted. But liability for the 15 animals has not been in dispute. The notices and movements permits which were served listed and applied to all 79 animals, irrespective of whether they had failed the specific test or not, because by virtue of the words "or otherwise" in the definition of "reactor" all the animals were deemed to be reactors.

Finally, there is one other matter to which I should refer. It may well be that in the light of the decision of Mr Justice Lardner in *Lucey and Madigan* v. *The Minister for Agriculture and Food & Others*[76] and the slightly earlier unreported Judgment of Mr Justice Murphy in *Howard* v. *The Minister of Agriculture*[77] that there was no power at all compulsorily to require the slaughter of any of the 79 animals but, in my view, the parties must be taken to have contracted on the basis of the law as then understood. I therefore give Judgment to the Plaintiff.

---

[75] S.I. No. 286 of 1980.
[76] Unreported. High Court 19/12/90.
[77] [1990] 2 I.R. 260.

CHAPTER 7

Non-disclosure of Material Fact

The duty of an insured to disclose facts material to a proposal for insurance arises from the very nature of the contract of insurance and forms one of the essential cornerstones of Insurance Law. Insurance contracts, differing from contracts in general, are contracts "uberrimae fidei", or contracts of utmost good faith. An insured must not only refrain from making false representation of material facts, but is also obliged to disclose all material facts known to the insured, but not to the insurer. This duty arises both at the inception of the policy of insurance and at each of its subsequent renewals. The origin and justification of the duty are succinctly explained in the extract from Baron Foster's judgment in the case of *Abbott* v. *Howard* (1832).

If any material facts are not disclosed to an insurer, that insurer is entitled to repudiate the policy, declaring it void from inception and returning all premiums paid. In so doing an insurer avoids all obligations otherwise arising under the policy. An insurer's knowledge of material facts in general only arises as a result of investigations carried out at the time of a claim under the policy and therefore because of the potential for abuse the Irish courts have been quick to involve themselves in examining the justification behind any insurer's decision to repudiate thus.

Because a repudiation for non-disclosure denies the very existence of the policy, cases are litigated — as opposed to going to arbitration, as with most insurance contract disputes — and a fruitful and varied body of case law has evolved.

While there have been many cases over the years, the present application of the law has its foundation in the judgment of Mr Justice Kenny in the decision of the Supreme Court in *Chariot Inns Limited* v. *Assicurazioni Generali S.p.a. and Coyle Hamilton Hamilton Phillips Limited* (1981). All decisions of the courts since it have regarded it as a correct declaration of the law. Having examined the law regarding non-disclosure in general, Mr Justice Kenny stated that the test as to what facts are to be regarded as material was to be an objective test as set out in sect. 18 (2) of the Marine Insurance Act, 1906; namely, those facts "which would influence the judgment of a prudent insurer in fixing the premium, or determining whether he will take the risk". The onus is very much on the insurer so to prove, and while it is open to it to call "independent" prudent insurers to support its decision, the final arbiter of an insurer's prudence is the court. This was emphasised in *Aro Road and Land Vehicle Limited* v. *The Insurance Corporation of Ireland Limited* (1986) where the deference shown by Ms Justice Carroll to the views of independent insurers was strongly criticised and her decision overturned on appeal by the Supreme Court.

The duty of disclosure by an insured is not absolute and the Irish courts have been quick to circumscribe it — the exact extent and scope of the duty depending largely on the identity of the parties involved, the nature of the policy in question and the precise manner in which the policy came into being. This is particularly evident in the judgment of Mr Justice Henchy in the *Aro Road and Land Vehicles* case, where insurers were happy to provide cover over the phone and without the benefit of a proposal form. In such circumstances they had to bear the consequences of material facts not being disclosed to them. Equally, in the very recent decision of the Supreme Court in *Kelleher* v. *Irish Life Assurance Company Limited* (1993) it was held that the nature of the policy, how it was marketed and the manner in which the proposal documents were presented to the insured meant that insurers had effectively waived their entitlement to be advised of facts which would otherwise most certainly have been regarded as material. In so doing, the Supreme Court overturned the decision of Mr Justice Costello in the High Court.

In *Keating* v. *New Ireland Assurance Company Plc* (1989)[1] the Supreme Court further emphasised that the onus was very much on the insurer to prove that the material facts alleged to exist were indeed known of by the insured at the time of the alleged failure to disclose those facts.

Similarly, in *Kreglinger and Fernau Limited and Others* v. *Irish National Insurance Co. Limited* (1956) it was held that an insurer could not rely exclusively on the insured's duty to disclose in circumstances where, had proper enquiry been made by the insurer the material facts would have come to light, the insured not deliberately concealing those facts. Closely related to this is the principle that if the facts alleged to be material were known to the insurer or the servants of the insurer at the time when they ought to have been disclosed, then the insurer cannot rely on the insured's failure, however culpable, as the insurer has not in effect been in any way prejudiced by that failure. In *Latham* v. *Hibernian Insurance*

---

[1] This judgment appears in Chapter 8 at p. 312.

Company Limited and Peter J. Sheridan and Company Limited (No. 1) (1991) the insured alleged that the Hibernian could not rely on his failure to disclose material facts because a clerk in the company was aware of them. The argument failed on the facts and in principle. That case is also interesting in that it deals with a failure by the insured to disclose facts arising subsequent to inception and prior to renewal of the policy.

The two recent High Court cases *of Harney v. The Century Insurance Company Limited* (1983) and *Curran v. Norwich Union Life Insurance Society* (1987) are particularly illuminating in that while both cases involved facts not entirely dissimilar, in *Harney* the insurers were unsuccessful while in *Curran* the insurers did successfully discharge the onus of proof. The distinction between the two being the evidence given by each insurer as to the effect the disclosure of the facts would have had on them. In *Curran* the evidence was that cover would have been postponed or suspended until the insured's medical position had been clarified. The court held that being precluded from exercising such an option was not sufficient justification to support repudiation of a claim.

In passing, it is interesting to note the more liberal and equitable approach adopted by the Supreme Court in all cases before it, as opposed to the more "legal and strict" stance adopted by many of the High Court judges. With only one exception insurers have failed to convince the Supreme Court of their reasonableness in repudiating contracts of insurance and in that case, *Chariot Inns*, the insurance broker arranging cover was held liable in negligence for the insured's loss.

Abbott v. Howard[*]
(1832) Hayes 381
Court of Exchequer

FOSTER B: ... In no contracts does it appear to me, that the parties deal on so unequal terms, as in contracts of insurance. One party has all the information, and the other is perfectly ignorant. It is with reference to this view, that the principle has been clearly established, that that inequality of knowledge ought to be rectified as much as possible, before the contract is entered into. It may be asked, — Must a party, before effecting an insurance, give a minute detail of every trifling incident of his whole life? The answer is, — Those incidents and occurrences which are trifling, he need not communicate; but he is bound to give information of every *material* circumstance, and none else. The deciding upon their materiality, is the province of the Jury: and, by that doctrine, the interests of the party insured will be a little endangered....

---

[*] Extract.

Chariot Inns Ltd *v.* Assicurazioni Generali S.p.a. and Coyle Hamilton Hamilton Phillips Limited
[1981] I.R. 199
The High Court

KEANE J: These proceedings arise out of a fire which extensively damaged the premises known as the Chariot Inn in Ranelagh, Dublin on the 14th May 1978. At the time of the fire, the Ranelagh premises, which were the property of the plaintiffs, were insured by the first defendants (whom I shall call "the insurers") and the insurance had been effected on behalf of the plaintiffs by the second defendants (whom I shall call "the brokers"). After the fire, the plaintiffs were informed by the insurers that they were repudiating liability in respect of the fire because of the alleged failure of the plaintiffs to disclose a material fact to the insurers at or before the time that the insurance was effected. The fact which was alleged to be material and which, it was claimed, had not been disclosed to the insurers was that the plaintiffs had been paid a sum of £8,000 by another insurance company in respect of furniture owned by the plaintiffs which had been damaged in a fire at the premises known as No. 82 Lower Leeson Street, Dublin. The plaintiffs claimed that Mr Harte, the representative of the brokers who arranged for the insurance of the Ranelagh premises, had been fully aware of the Leeson Street claim and had advised the plaintiffs that there was no necessity to disclose it to the insurers. Mr Harte died suddenly between the effecting of the insurance and the fire at the Ranelagh premises.

The insurers maintained their position so far as repudiation was concerned, and the brokers denied any liability in the matter. Proceedings were issued on behalf of the plaintiffs claiming, as against the insurers, a declaration that the relevant policy or policies in respect of the Ranelagh premises was or were valid and subsisting and, as against the brokers, damages for breach of contract, negligence and breach of duty. In their defence, the insurers relied on the alleged non-disclosure and pleaded that the fire at the Ranelagh premises had been started deliberately by the plaintiffs, their servants or agents; this plea was withdrawn by the insurers during the course of the trial. The brokers, in their defence, denied that they were guilty of the alleged negligence, breach of contract or breach of duty and pleaded that, in so far as the plaintiffs had sustained damage as a result of the alleged breach of contract, negligence or breach of duty, it was caused or contributed to by the negligence of the plaintiffs.

The Ranelagh premises were acquired[2] by the plaintiff in either, December 1975, or January 1976. The principal shareholders in the plaintiff company were Mr Desmond Wootton and his wife. Prior to that acquisition, the Ranelagh premises had been run as licensed premises in the conventional sense. Mr Wootton had been concerned previously in the entertainment business in premises called the Revolution Club at Rutland Place, Dublin. His intention in relation to the Ranelagh premises was to carry on a form of

---

[2] See [1976] I.R. at p. 240.

cabaret entertainment there in addition to the business of the licensed premises.

Not long before the plaintiffs acquired the Ranelagh premises, Mr Wootton became interested in the premises at No. 82 Lower Leeson Street which were owned by a company called Consolidated Investment Holdings Ltd. Mr Wootton decided to acquire an interest in the Leeson Street premises with a view to operating them as a hotel, with a discotheque in the back of the premises. The finance for the acquisition was provided jointly by Mr Wootton and a Mr Mockler. It was decided to effect the acquisition by means of a transfer of the shares of Consolidated Investment. In view of Mr Wootton's known involvement in the entertainment business and of Mr Mockler's social and business connection with him, it was decided that the shares should be purchased in the maiden names of their respective wives. That was because Mr Wootton and Mr Mockler were apprehensive of objections to any necessary applications under the licensing and planning codes being made by persons in the neighbourhood if he, or Mr Mockler, were known to be associated with the project.

When the Leeson Street premises were acquired in 1975, Mr Wootton's insurance affairs were being handled by the brokers. Mr Wootton's dealings with the brokers were principally conducted through Mr Harte, who arranged for the insurance of the Leeson Street premises with the Sun Alliance and London Insurance Group. The insurance policy which was issued by Sun Alliance was for a period from 15th May, 1975, to the 15th May, 1976. The "property insured" is described in the schedule to that policy as "... building four stories and basement in height — brick, stone or concrete built and roofed with slates or tiles — two storeyed extension at rear constructed of concrete and corrugated asbestos — all situate 82 Lower Leeson Street, Dublin, and at present unoccupied ... £82.00." The first premium was stated to be £246 and the renewal premium was stated to be the same.

When the Ranelagh premises were acquired, Mr Wootton decided to carry out certain alterations and renovations to them in order to render them more suitable for the cabaret business which he proposed to carry on there. That necessitated the demolition of a large room at the rear of the Ranelagh premises; the furnishings from that room were removed to the Leeson Street premises for storage there. It appears that Mr Harte became aware of the storage of the furniture in the Leeson Street premises and, as that property had been expressly insured as "unoccupied", he advised Mr Wootton that an endorsement should be added to the Sun Alliance policy so as to include the furniture. That was done by means of an endorsement (dated the 24th November, 1975) on the existing policy containing the legend "adding furnishings £15,000". Towards the end of 1975, Mr Wootton decided to transfer his insurance business to another firm of brokers, i.e., Corcoran Insurances Ltd.

On the 19th April, 1976, a fire took place at the Leeson Street premises and caused extensive damage to the upper storeys; as a result of that fire some of the furniture from the Ranelagh premises (which was being stored in the Leeson Street premises) was destroyed. A claim was made under the policy with Sun Alliance and that company appointed Messrs Thornton (a firm of loss adjusters) to deal with the matter on their behalf. The claim of Consolidated Investment in respect of the Leeson Street fire was ultimately settled by Sun Alliance for the sum of £47,500 and, on the 15th June, 1977, that sum was paid to Consolidated Investment and a receipt therefor was given to Sun Alliance. The claim in respect of the furniture was settled for the sum of £8,000. Since it seemed clear that the fire at the Leeson Street premises had been started deliberately, a malicious-injury claim was lodged with Dublin Corporation and, by a document also dated the 15th June, 1977, Consolidated Investment agreed to assign to Sun Alliance any award made against Dublin Corporation and authorised Sun Alliance to take any necessary proceedings in its own name for that purpose. In the event, an award of £55,000 was ultimately made against the Corporation by the Circuit Court.

At the date of the acquisition of the Ranelagh premises by the plaintiffs, those premises were already insured by the General Accident Insurance Company. That policy was due for renewal on the 1st December, 1976, and Mr Corcoran, who had been dealing with Mr Wootton's insurances since the end of 1975, advised Mr Wootton that he should have an new, and more extensive form of policy so as to cover other risks in addition to damage by fire. Mr Wootton accepted that advice and, through Mr Corcoran's agency, a new policy was effected with General Accident — the period of cover being from the 1st September, 1976, to the 1st January, 1978.

The plaintiffs were notified that the premium for the General Accident policy, relating to the Ranelagh premises, would be increased by 50% on the next renewal date. Thereupon, Mr Wootton sought alternative quotations and, to that end, was in contact with at least two firms of brokers, namely Connolly Wickham & Co. and the brokers. He again dealt with Mr Harte so far as the brokers were concerned and the latter obtained quotations for him from three insurance companies, of which the lowest was that of the insurers. On the 22nd February, 1978, Mr Wootton met Mr Harte at the Ranelagh premises and, on behalf of the plaintiffs, signed two proposal forms. Both forms emanated from the insurers. One was in respect of "liabilities" and the other was in respect of "material damage." In the case of the "liabilities" proposal form, there are references (under the heading "Claims experience over last five years") to three claims; two of them relate to public liability and the other relates to a theft of money and national insurance stamps. In the case of the "material damage" proposal form, there appears the following heading:— "Give claims experience for loss over the last five years (i.e. date, nature of loss, amount paid or outstanding. Brief details of how loss occurred). If none in any class, say so." Beneath those words, there is the word "none" in handwriting.

The completed proposal form was duly transmitted to the insurers and on the 24th February, 1977, the brokers issued a cover note. They wrote again on the 9th March, 1978, to Mr Wootton (the letter being signed by Mr Harte) confirming certain alterations in the cover so far as the actual amounts insured were concerned.

After the fire at the Ranelagh premises on 14th May, 1978, the plaintiffs presented a claim to the insurers. On the 27th June, the insurers' solicitors wrote to the plaintiffs as follows:—

> "We act on behalf of Assicurazioni Generali S.P.A. whose London office have been in touch with us regarding the recent fire in the above premises. We

have been instructed to write to you formally to advise you by reason of the non-disclosure of material facts in the proposal form as submitted, on the basis of which a policy of insurance was issued, our clients are regarding this policy as void ab initio and consequently they are repudiating all liability arising out of the recent fire in the premises."

The plaintiffs' solicitors wrote on 3rd July to the insurers' solicitors asking for particulars of the material facts which it was alleged had not been disclosed. On the 4th July the insurers' solicitors replied as follows:—

"The material facts not disclosed in the proposal form signed by Mr Wootton on behalf of your client are set out in the fourth paragraph of your letter. It would appear, as you have admitted, that your clients received £8,000 for damage to their goods as a result of a fire in the premises 82 Lower Leeson Street on the 19th April, 1976. Notwithstanding the fact that these monies were paid to Consolidated Investment Holdings Limited (which was controlled by its director Mr Wootton who was also controlling director of your client company) nevertheless the goods in respect of which insurance money was paid were goods belonging to your clients and this was not disclosed to our clients. We note the contention in the fifth paragraph of your letter that the facts were notified to the representative of the insurance brokers, when the proposal form was being completed. Unfortunately, as your client is aware, this representative is now deceased. It certainly was not disclosed to the underwriters and in any event we would point out that the brokers are your clients' agents."

I shall consider first the claim against the insurers. The "material damage" proposal form contained a declaration, which was signed by Mr Wootton, in the following terms:— "I/we warrant that all the statements made by me/us or on my/our behalf on this form are true and complete and I/we agree that this proposal shall be the basis of the contract between me/us and the company. I/we agree to accept a policy in the company's usual form for this class of insurance."

The law is thus stated in MacGillivray & Parkington on Insurance Law (6th ed. at para. 829):—

"If a warranty is not fulfilled, the insurers' liability ceases, whether or not the fact warranted affected the risk or in any way influenced the insurer when he took it." It would follow that, if the answer given to the question as to the previous claims experience was wrong, the insurers would have been entitled to repudiate the policy, irrespective of whether the insurers would have been affected in taking the risk had a correct answer been given.

The claim in respect of the loss of furniture in the Leeson Street fire represented a relatively small proportion of the total Leeson Street claim but, if the answer given is to be regarded as wrong, that would not appear to be material. On the assumption that the answer given was incorrect, it would follow that, even if the furniture of the plaintiffs which was damaged in that fire consisted of only one chair, the insurers would none the less have been entitled to avoid the policy. Such a result would be so palpably unjust that one would naturally scrutinise the answer with some care in order to determine whether it was wrong. I am satisfied that the answer given to the question was strictly accurate. The question manifestly related to the claims experience of the proposer, i.e. the plaintiffs. The plaintiffs had not made any claim in respect of the fire at the Leeson Street premises; the insurance of those premises was effected by Consolidated Investment, the claim was presented by that company and the amount in respect of the furniture was paid to that company, as the receipt dated the 15th June 1977, makes clear. Doubtless, in law, Consolidated Investment held the sum of £8,000 (the amount recovered in respect of the furniture) in trust for the plaintiffs; but it remains the fact that the plaintiffs were not insured under the Leeson Street policy and had made no claim under it.

But the mere fact that the answer to this question was technically correct does not conclude the question of the insurers' liability. This was a contract of insurance and, accordingly, the duty of *uberrimae fides* rested on both parties. It is clear that that duty requires the disclosure by the insured of all material facts which are known to him. It is also clear that this duty is a common-law duty which arises from the general common-law principles of insurance; it is not merely a contractual duty arising from the terms of the particular contract:— see *Joel* v. *Law Union & Crown Insurance Co.*[3] at p.892 of the report. Accordingly, if the fact that the sum of £8,000 was paid to Consolidated Investment in respect of the furniture was a material fact, then its non-disclosure entitled the insurers to avoid the contract. Furthermore, if the Leeson Street fire and the claim and payment in respect thereof were material facts in relation to the proposal for the insurance of the Ranelagh premises, then their non-disclosure also entitled the insurers to avoid that contract. It was not seriously contended by either of the plaintiffs or the brokers in this context that the fact that Consolidated Investment and the plaintiff company were technically different legal entities was of any significance, having regard to the direct and active involvement of Mr Wootton in both companies.

It is also clear, and was accepted by all the parties, that the onus of proving the non-disclosure of a material fact known to the plaintiffs clearly rested on the insurers. At the conclusion of the evidence, counsel for the brokers and counsel for the plaintiffs submitted that the insurers had failed to discharge that onus of proof, since it necessarily required the insurers to establish that the facts allegedly not disclosed to the insurers by the plaintiffs were not actually known to the insurers. It was submitted that, as the evidence on behalf of the insurers was confined to that of independent underwriters as to the materiality of the facts alleged not to have been disclosed, the insurers had failed to establish that they were unaware of the facts in question. It was submitted that, as far as the evidence went, it was possible that Mr Harte had either communicated these facts to the insurers verbally or that he had sent them in a covering letter or memorandum which could have accompanied the proposal form when it was being sent to the insurers. Mr Liston, on behalf of the insurers, said that he was taken by surprise by this submission, and he applied for liberty to adduce evidence as to the state of

---

[3] [1908] 2 K.B. 863.

knowledge of the insurers. Paragraph 6 of the defence of the insurers expressly alleges that the fact in issue was known to the plaintiffs but not known to the insurers, although being material to be known to them. Since the onus of proving the non-disclosure of a material fact known to the plaintiffs but not known to the insurers rested on the insurers, and since the reply delivered by the plaintiffs joined issue with the insurers on their defence, it seemed clear on the pleadings that the burden of establishing lack of knowledge of the facts alleged to be material rested on the insurers and that they had not discharged that onus. However, I was reluctant to decide the case on this basis when I had been informed by counsel that evidence was available to demonstrate that it was not a basis which was founded on fact, and when counsel further informed me that the submission on behalf of the brokers (between whom and the insurers there were no pleadings) had taken him by surprise. Accordingly, I acceded to Mr Liston's application.

The evidence as to the insurers' state of knowledge was given by Mr Stephenson who, at the relevant time, was the chairman and managing director of International Underwriters. The firm was the agent for the insurers in Ireland at the time when the insurance was placed with them in respect of the Ranelagh premises. Mr Stephenson said that he dealt personally with the proposal and that no one else dealt with it until after the risk had been accepted by the insurers. He said that he first became aware of the Leeson Street fire on the Monday after the Ranelagh fire and as a result of a conversation with Mr Brooks, the loss adjuster. Mr Stephenson said that he had never met Mr Harte in his life. While it was suggested on behalf of the plaintiffs and the brokers that this did not constitute sufficient evidence for me to hold that the insurers had discharged the onus of proof, it seems probable to me, had Mr Harte known of the Leeson Street fire and communicated his knowledge of it to International Underwriters prior to the acceptance by the insurers of the risk, it would have come to the knowledge of Mr Stephenson. While it is possible that whoever contacted Mr Stephenson's office with the completed proposal form may have simultaneously conveyed the information as to the Leeson Street fire, and while it is further possible that the person in Mr Stephenson's office to whom that information was conveyed did not trouble to convey it to his principal, I do not think that either of those possibilities is particularly likely. It was further urged that, as a duty of *uberrimae fidei* rested not merely on the plaintiffs but also on the insurers, a strict duty of proof in relation to their state of knowledge rested on the insurers and that this was not discharged simply by calling Mr Stephenson as a witness. While it is certainly true that the law requires *uberrimae fidei* not merely of the insured but also of the insurer, I do not think that it follows from that principle that any greater onus of proof in regard to their state of knowledge is placed on the insurers than normally exists in a civil case. In my view, their actual state of knowledge must be determined on the probabilities. As a matter of probability, I am satisfied that the insurers were not aware of the Leeson Street fire at the time when the risk was accepted.

The next question that arises is the materiality of the facts which were not disclosed to the insurers. As I have already indicated, the relevant undisclosed facts were the damage caused to the Leeson Street premises and the furniture therein by fire, and the payment made by Sun Alliance in respect of that damage.

The most widely accepted test of materiality in all forms of insurance on property and goods appears to be set out in s. 18, sub-s. 2, of the Marine Insurance Act, 1906, which is in the following terms:—

> "Every circumstance is material which would influence the judgment of a prudent insurer in fixing the premium, or determining whether he will take the risk."

That test has been frequently stated to be applicable to non-marine insurance as well: see *Joel* v. *Law Union & Crown Insurance Co.*[4] and *March Cabaret* v. *London Assurance.*[5] Another test has sometimes been proposed, i.e., the test of whether a reasonable man in the position of the assured and with knowledge of the facts in dispute ought to have realised that they were material to the risk. But this test has been confirmed normally in its application to cases of life insurance and, possibly, burglary insurance: see Mac-Gillivray & Parkington on Insurance Law (6th ed. — paras. 749, 750). It was not suggested by any of the parties as the appropriate test in the present case and, accordingly, I propose to apply the test set out in s. 18 sub-s. 2, of the Act of 1906.

Counsel for the brokers submitted that s. 18, sub-s. 2, of the Act of 1906 should be read as though the words "in a highly competitive market" occurred after the words "prudent insurer". He said that, in the particular circumstances of the Irish insurance market to-day, that phrase was an appropriate insertion. I do not think that the addition of that qualification is justifiable. I think that the principle, as defined in the Act of 1906, accepts by implication that insurers are in the business of accepting risks whether the market be highly competitive or not, and that circumstances arise from time to time which are of such a nature that the prudent insurer, whether he be well-established or new to the market, will weigh them before accepting a risk or determining the premium applicable.

It is also clear that if the fact which was not disclosed would, if disclosed, have done no more than cause the insurers to make enquiries, perhaps resulting in delay in issuing the insurance, it is not material if the result of the enquiries would have had no effect on a prudent insurer: see *Mutual Life Insurance Co. of New York* v. *Ontario Metal Products Co.*[6]

The materiality of particular facts is a question of fact which must be determined ultimately by the Court, but it is clear that evidence may be adduced from experts in the insurance business as to insurance practice (*Yorke* v. *Yorkshire Insurance Company*[7]); such evidence was given in the present case.

It also seems clear that the test for determining materiality is an objective

---

[4] [1908] 2 K.B. 863.
[5] [1975] 1 Lloyd's Rep. 169.
[6] [1925] A.C. 344.
[7] [1918] 1 K.B. 662.

one. The fact that the particular insurer who seeks to avoid the contract would not have been affected by its disclosure in determining whether to accept the risk, or in fixing the premium, is not relevant. The law was thus stated by Samuels J. in *Mayne Nickless Ltd.* v. *Pegler*[8] as follows:—

> "Accordingly, I do not think that it is generally open to examine what the insurer would in fact have done had he had the information not disclosed. The question is whether that information would have been relevant to the exercise of the insurer's option to accept or reject the insurance proposed. It seems to me that the test of materiality is this: a fact is material if it would have reasonably affected the mind of a prudent insurer in determining whether he will accept the insurance, and if so, at what premium and on what conditions."

That passage was expressly approved by Lord Fraser of Tullybelton in giving the opinion of the Judicial Committee of the Privy Council in *Marene* v. *Greater Pacific Insurance*[9]: see p. 642 of the report. In that case, the passage was criticised in argument on the ground that it was said to be inconsistent with the statement of the law by the same tribunal in *Mutual Life Insurance Co. of New York* v. *Ontario Metal Products Co.*[10] at pp. 351–2 of the report. Lord Fraser accepted that the test stated in the Ontario Case is expressed in somewhat different words from those used in the *Mayne Nickless Case,*[11] and he suggested that the difference may be due to the fact that the *Ontario Case*[12] was concerned with a policy which was governed by the Ontario Insurance Act.

Mr Butler, in the present case, has criticised this passage in Lord Fraser's opinion on the ground that it is not supported by the wording of the Act. That may be so; but I think that, when one looks at the actual words used by Lord Salvesen when delivering the opinion of the Judicial Committee in the *Ontario Case,*[13] it appears clear that there is no difference of any real significance. He says at pp. 351–2 of the report:—

> "... the appellants' counsel ... suggested that the test was whether, if the fact concealed had been disclosed, the insurers would have acted differently, either by declining the risk at the proposed premium or at least by delaying consideration of its acceptance until they had consulted Dr Fierheller. If the former proposition were established *in the sense that a reasonable insurer would have so acted*, materiality would, their Lordships think, be established, but not in the latter if the difference of action would have been delay and delay alone. In their view, it is a question of fact in each case whether, *if the matters concealed or misrepresented had been truly disclosed, they would, on a fair consideration of the evidence, have influenced a reasonable insurer to decline the risk or to have stipulated for a higher premium.*"

---

[8] [1974] 1 N.S.W.L.R. 228.
[9] [1976] 2 Lloyd's Rep. 631.
[10] [1925] A.C. 344.
[11] [1974] 1 N.S.W.L.R. 228.
[12] [1925] A.C. 344.
[13] *Ibid.*

I think that the words in that passage which I have italicised make it clear that, in that case also, the test was taken to be an objective one. Any other view would appear to be illogical since, looked at from the point of view of the insured, on whom the duty of disclosure is imposed, it can scarcely be supposed that the duty could vary from case to case depending on the attitude of the particular insurer as to what was or was not material.

The language used in the *Mayne Nickless Case*[14] does go somewhat further in favour of the insurers than the language employed in the *Ontario Case*,[15] since the former makes it clear that the test is whether the reasonable insurer would have been affected by the information, whereas the latter might suggest that the test is whether the reasonable insurer would *in fact* have declined the risk or imposed special terms. However, having regard to the peculiar nature of the contract of insurance and the importance of the doctrine of uberrimae fidei in the context of such contracts, I think that the test formulated in the *Mayne Nickless Case*,[16] although perhaps more comprehensive than that framed in the *Ontario Case*,[17] is preferable, I am fortified in this conclusion by the endorsement of the *Mayne Nickless* test by Lord Fraser, who makes it clear that he considers it the appropriate test irrespective of whether the *Ontario Case*[18] was eventually governed by the terms of the special Act. This appears to have been the view taken in other cases; see per MacKinnon L.J. at p.60 of the report of *Zürich General Accident & Liability Insurance Co. v. Morrison.*[19]

Accordingly, I am not concerned with the question as to whether the insurers would have been affected had the facts in issue been disclosed. Mr Stephenson admitted quite frankly in cross-examination that he would not have advised his principals to repudiate in the present case were it not for the suspicions he entertained that the Ranelagh fire might have been deliberately started by the plaintiffs. While it does not necessarily follow that Mr Stephenson, in entering into the contract of insurance, would not have been affected by the disclosure of the Leeson Street fire, I think it more probable that he would not have been so affected; but, for the reasons stated, this is not relevant in determining the liability of the insurers.

It is also clear that there are two broad categories of facts which may be material: those which affect the physical hazard and those which affect the moral hazard. The physical hazard arises where the facts in issue would lead to the inference that the subject matter of the insurance was exceptionally liable to be affected by the peril insured against. This, manifestly, does not arise in the present case since the fire which was not disclosed occurred at different premises. The moral hazard arises where the facts in issue would lead to the inference that the particular proposer is a person, or one of a class of persons, whose proposal for insurance ought to be subjected to special

---

[14] [1974] 1 N.S.W.L.R. 228.
[15] [1925] A.C. 344.
[16] [1974] 1 N.S.W.L.R. 228.
[17] [1925] A.C. 344.
[18] *Ibid.*
[19] [1942] 2 K.B. 53.

consideration before it can be decided whether it should be accepted at all, or accepted at the normal rate. That, in substance, is the definition of moral hazard which appears in Halsbury's Law of England (4th ed. — vol. 25, para. 369) and it would appear from the evidence of the underwriters in the present case that it also accords with the practice of insurers. A further aspect of the moral hazard is the proposer's previous experience as regards the particular risk, and it would appear from the passage in Halsbury that this may even extend to his relations with insurers generally.

Three underwriters of wide and varied experience gave evidence. Mr Browne, who is a Lloyd's underwriter, thought that the Leeson Street fire was material to the risk and should have been disclosed. A similar view was taken by Mr Callaghan, who had been a fire underwriter for a number of years with a leading Irish insurance company; he also agreed, however, that in any event he would have been most reluctant to insure a risk of this nature, i.e. a risk in the entertainment business. Mr O'Carroll, the managing director of the American Insurance Co. Ltd. (which, in contrast, specialises in this form of insurance), said that, if he had been informed (as an underwriter) of the Leeson Street fire, he would have made enquiries as to the circumstances of the fire and the claim but that, if the results of such enquiries did not disclose any further features rendering the risk unacceptable, the mere fact of the fire having occurred and the claim having been made would not have been a factor which would have affected his decision. However, he agreed that, if the Leeson Street fire had been preceded by a number of illegal entries to the property, he might have considered requiring some form of additional security, such as having a resident caretaker in the Ranelagh premises.

Mr Liston submitted, on behalf of the insurers, that the failure to disclose the Leeson Street fire would have justified, by itself, the repudiation. But he further submitted that there were, in any event, a number of features of the Leeson Street fire and the claim made in respect of it which would have affected the mind of a prudent insurer when considering whether the risk should be accepted or the terms that should be imposed. These circumstances can be summarised as follows:—

1. The fact that the fire was non-accidental, that the premises were unoccupied and that no adequate security precautions had been taken — such as the presence of a caretaker.
2. The failure of Mr Wootton to prosecute a claim for the balance of the loss sustained by him as a result of the fire.
3. The unusually long time taken by Sun Alliance to settle the claim.
4. The disputes between Mr Wootton and Sun Alliance in relation to the claim.
5. The failure of Mr Wootton to continue insuring with Sun Alliance.

I do not think that the general principles which are applicable to all policies of insurance (which I have already mentioned) would justify the proposition that the failure to disclose any previous fire in respect of which a claim had been made would be sufficient to justify the insurers in repudiating the policy. Thus, it could hardly be argued with any plausibility that the mind of a prudent insurer who was considering insuring a multi-million pound office development would be affected in any sense by the knowledge that the entrepreneur who was proposing to insure it had successfully recovered £20 some decades previously because of a small fire which damaged an article of furniture in his house. That is an extreme example; but it makes it clear, as do the authorities to which reference has already been made, that in each case one has to consider the individual circumstances before determining whether the particular fire or fires which were not disclosed, and the circumstances which surrounded them, would have affected the mind of a prudent insurer.

Accordingly, it becomes necessary to consider the individual matters which are relied by Mr Liston in relation to the Leeson Street fire. The evidence established that at the date of that fire those premises had been unoccupied for some time, and that there had been a number of incidents of illegal entry accompanied by some degree of damage to the premises. Mr Wootton said in evidence that he had endeavoured to make the premises more secure following these incidents, that he had also reported them to the Gardaí. It was also clear that the fire was started deliberately. As I have already noted, the claim of Consolidated Investment was settled by Sun Alliance, and that company then proceeded (in its own name) to recover the sum of £55,500 from Dublin Corporation in a malicious-injury application. After taking into account the purchase price of the premises and the bank advances, the amount in question undoubtedly meant that Consolidated Investment had sustained a loss, and Mr Wootton was pressed in cross examination to explain why he did not sue Dublin Corporation for the full amount of his loss. He said that when he disposed of the site he was not at any loss and that, in any event, the settlement of the claim had been so delayed and contentious that he did not wish to be troubled any further by it.

So far as the delay in settling the Leeson Street claim and the disputes attendant on it were concerned, the relevant evidence was given by Mr Wootton and by a Mr Corcoran (who, it will be recalled, was dealing with Mr Wootton's insurances at the date of the Leeson Street fire and for some time thereafter) and by Mr Lyons, a building surveyor, who was employed in December, 1976, to prepare a claim in respect of the Leeson Street fire. No evidence was given on behalf of Sun Alliance or by Mr Brooks, the loss adjuster, of Messrs Thorntons who dealt with the matter on behalf of Sun Alliance. Mr Corcoran gave evidence that no allegation of fraud or negligence on Mr Wootton's part was made to him during the period when he was dealing with the claim. However, he did say that he found Mr Brooks difficult and unreasonable in his attitude towards the claim.

In so far as the factors relied on by Mr Liston would have affected the mind of a prudent insurer, they could only have done so in relation to the possible moral hazard. The question of moral hazard could only arise so far as a prudent insurer was concerned if the circumstances were such as to raise a serious question as to whether a proposal for insurance with which Mr Wootton was associated should be accepted at all or, if accepted, whether it should be accepted only at a special rate because of the moral hazard involved.

In my view, a prudent insurer who had been informed of the Leeson Street fire would have made enquiries in the first instance with the brokers who had dealt with the Leeson Street claim. It is possible that he might have proceeded to accept the risk without making such enquiries but, in the light of all the evidence, I think it more probable that he would have made enquiries. As I have indicated, his enquiry would have been confined to the possible existence of a moral hazard; there was no question of the physical nature of the risk being affected by the circumstances of the Leeson Street fire. The first matter that would have concerned him would have been the possibility that the Leeson Street fire and its associated claim were fraudulent. In my view, it is probable that his enquiries with Mr Corcoran would have satisfied him that there was no reason to suppose that the Leeson Street fire or the subsequent claim constituted any form of fraud on the insurers of the Leeson Street premises. I accept fully Mr Corcoran's evidence that no suggestion was made to him at any stage that the Leeson Street claim was in any way fraudulent. Nor do I think that a prudent insurer would have been affected in his judgment by Mr Wootton's failure to pursue the malicious-injury claim so far as the balance of his loss was concerned. I think that a prudent insurer would have taken the view that, had there been any suspicion of fraud, it would have been intimated at some stage by Sun Alliance to Mr Corcoran. Not merely had Sun Alliance settled the Leeson Street claim (presumably after making whatever investigation they thought appropriate) but the claim had been the subject of a malicious-injury application in respect of the sum of £55,500, which must have led to investigation by Dublin Corporation of the circumstances of the fire; again, there is nothing to suggest that the investigation indicated any fraud on Mr Wootton's part.

The only sinister motive that Mr Wootton could have had in not pursuing his claim for the balance of the loss sustained by him would have been the avoidance of an investigation which might have involved him in criminal liability; but since the presentation of the claim to Sun Alliance and the making of the malicious-injury claim to the Corporation prompted what I have no reason to assume were other than full-scale investigations by those parties, it is difficult to see what Mr Wootton had to gain in this context by not pursuing the claim further. There was a quite reasonable explanation for his not pursuing the claim for the balance, *viz.*, the fact that his losses had been recouped substantially by the sale of the site and his disinclination to involve himself in further long and contentious negotiations in relation to the Leeson Street fire.

It might be that a prudent insurer would have extended his enquiries to the insurance company itself, although I think it more probable that he would have been satisfied to accept Mr Corcoran's view that there was nothing suspicious or untoward about the Leeson Street fire or claim, so far as the plaintiffs were concerned. If I am mistaken in that opinion, however, and the prudent insurer had approached Sun Alliance for their view, the nature of their reaction must remain, at best, a matter of surmise from the insurers' point of view. In the absence of any evidence from Sun Alliance or from the person who appears to have dealt with the matter on their behalf (Mr Brooks), I am not prepared to assume that Sun Alliance would have indicated to a subsequent insurer that there was anything in the circumstances of the Leeson Street fire or claim which should weigh with him in accepting a further proposal from Mr Wootton.

The onus of proving that the fact not disclosed was material rests on the insurers and, so far as any possible fraud in relation to the Leeson Street fire is concerned, I am satisfied that they have not discharged that onus. I should emphasise that I am not treating the insurers as being in the position of a person who has made an allegation of fraud in a civil action and as having, therefore, to assume that serious burden of proof. In the context of the Leeson Street fire, the insurers need do no more than satisfy the Court that a prudent insurer, in deciding whether to accept the risk in relation to the Ranelagh premises or in deciding what terms or premium should be fixed in relation to that insurance, would have been affected by the Leeson Street fire and the consequent claim. But even to that limited extent, I am satisfied that they have failed to discharge the onus on them — at least so far as any question of fraud is concerned.

So far as negligence is concerned, it was urged that the fact that the Leeson Street premises had been invaded frequently by trespassers who succeeded in setting the premises on fire indicated a failure by Mr Wootton to take reasonable precautions in relation to the security of his property, which failure might have made an insurer cautious about accepting a new proposal for him. In considering this suggestion, I think one must have regard to the nature of the business being carried on in the respective premises. That in the Ranelagh premises consisted of licensed premises with a restaurant in which entertainment was provided on certain nights of each week. The Leeson Street premises were unused and had been unused for some time; it was ultimately proposed to run them as a hotel and discotheque when the necessary permissions under the planning and licensing codes had been obtained. One can appreciate that the mind of a prudent insurer would be affected by the fact that one or more fires had occurred, if the proposer had been carrying on the same business albeit in different premises (as happened in *Marene* v. *Greater Pacific Insurance*[20]). But here there was no question of any business being carried out in the Leeson Street premises; indeed they were expressly insured as unoccupied premises. That, of itself, would suggest that the mind of a prudent insurer would not be affected to any significant extent by the Leeson Street fire as indicating that Mr Wootton might be negligent in his approach to keeping the Ranelagh premises secure against intruders. Moreover, the unoccupied premises were situated close to the centre of Dublin; and there is nothing in the policy, nor was there any evidence *aliunde*, to suggest that Sun Alliance insisted on any particular security precautions being taken in respect of the building. They must have appreciated perfectly well that vacant premises close to the centre of Dublin would be peculiarly liable to break-ins of the nature which actually occurred. The evidence in this case suggests what, in any event, one would have thought probable, i.e., that insurance companies nowadays are very conscious of the need for proper security so far as intruders are concerned. The apparent failure of Sun Alliance to impose any specific requirements in relation to security at the Leeson Street premises suggests that they probably shared Mr Wootton's view that such precautions, in the case of that particular building, were probably not worthwhile. That is not necessarily a view which would

---

[20] [1976] 2 Lloyd's Rep. 631.

have been taken by everyone, but it appears to have been adopted by Sun Alliance as well as by Mr Wootton, it seems a tenuous basis for treating Mr Wootton as a person who was so careless of his property as to justify an insurer in being unusually cautious when confronted with his proposal for the insurance of a significantly different risk.

Then it was said that, whatever may have been the attitude of Sun Alliance when the policy was actually issued, Mr Wootton's attitude should have been different once there had been a succession of break-ins; in particular, it was suggested that the absence of a caretaker in the Leeson Street premises might have affected the mind of an insurer dealing with the proposal relating to the Ranelagh premises. Some support might be found for this in the evidence of Mr O'Carroll (to which I have already referred) but he was careful to point out that everything would depend on the result of the enquiries that an insurer made into the circumstances of the break-ins and the response of the insured to them. Mr Wootton gave evidence that he had attempted to make the Leeson Street premises more secure although without success.

In the end, one must come back to the question as to whether Mr Wootton's general conduct in relation to the Leeson Street premises was such as to affect the mind of a prudent insurer. I think that there is a basic implausibility in the suggestion that an insurer would have been affected to any significant degree by Mr Wootton's conduct in this regard. I do not think one can overlook the facts that Mr Wootton had expressly insured the Leeson Street premises as a vacant building and that he had not been required to take any specific precautions in relation to it. I do not think that that could conceivably have led an insurer to doubt Mr Wootton's attitude in relation to keeping the Ranelagh premises as secure as might reasonably be required.

There is another factor to which I must have regard, though it is not conclusive. As I have said, the Ranelagh premises were already insured by General Accident when the plaintiffs acquired their interest in them. Mr Corcoran gave evidence that, when he advised Mr Wootton that it would be desirable to take out a fresh form of insurance with that company, he informed their inspector, Mr Aubrey Shaw, of the Leeson Street fire. Mr Corcoran told Mr Shaw that furniture belonging to the Ranelagh premises had been stored in the Leeson Street premises and had been damaged in the fire there, and that he thought it was a malicious fire. Mr Shaw confirmed this in evidence and said that he recorded the information and sent it to the underwriters. Mr Smart, of General Accident, gave evidence that the Leeson Street fire was not mentioned in the proposal form for the insurance; he said that no special terms were imposed in the insurance policy issued by General Accident, nor was any special premium required to be paid. Mr Smart agreed that if Mr Shaw passed the information to the underwriter, Mr Butler, and if the latter made the usual enquiries, then Mr Butler must have been satisfied that the Leeson Street fire did not require the imposition of an additional premium or the declining of the risk on the grounds of moral hazard. Mr Butler, the underwriter, did not give evidence; it may be that he did consider the Leeson Street fire to be material and, having considered it, came to the conclusion that it did not justify any special treatment of the insurance in respect of the Ranelagh premises. Accordingly, this factor cannot be treated

as conclusive in any sense, but I cannot disregard the fact that an experienced and reputable insurance company which insured the Ranelagh premises, and which had knowledge of the Leeson Street fire, did not consider that
it merited the imposition of any special terms — still less a refusal of the
insurance. That is entirely consistent with the submission that it was not
material to the risk being insured; and, while it is not inconsistent with the
case made by the insurers, it seems to me to add weight to the contention
that the Leeson Street fire and the associated claim would not have affected
the mind of a prudent insurer in considering the proposal in relation to the
Ranelagh premises.

For these reasons, I have come to the conclusion that the insurers were
not entitled to repudiate the contract of insurance on the grounds that there
had been a non-disclosure of a material fact. As the defence of arson has been
withdrawn, it follows that the plaintiffs are entitled to a declaration in the
terms of 1(a) of their statement of claim. As a result the plaintiffs have
suffered no damage by reason of the alleged breach of contract, negligence or
breach of duty of the brokers, and so the claim against the brokers must be
dismissed.

Counsel for the insurers indicated that, in the event of his clients not
succeeding in this Court, they proposed to test the matter further in the
Supreme Court. In these circumstances, I suggested to counsel that it might
be desirable if I were to indicate the conclusions at which I have arrived in
relation to the claim against the brokers, and it was agreed by all three
parties that I should do so.

Mr Wootton maintained that the late Mr Harte knew all about the Leeson
Street fire and the claim made as a result of it, and that Mr Harte told him,
in so many words, that there was no necessity to tell the insurers about it,
since it related to a different company. Mr Wootton in evidence said that,
although Mr Corcoran had taken over his insurance affairs at the time of the
Leeson Street fire, Mr Harte became aware of that fire and the claim in
respect of it within a few weeks of the fire. He said that a meeting took place
at the Leeson Street premises around that time between himself and Mr
Harte and Mr Mockler who, it will be recalled, was Mr Wootton's partner in
the Leeson Street venture. Mr Wootton said that the object of this meeting
was to ascertain from Mr Harte the nature of the cover on the Leeson Street
premises in the light of the suggestion (which he said emanated from Mr
Brooks, the loss adjuster) that the premises were insured on an indemnity
basis only and not on a reinstatement basis. Mr Wootton said he consulted
Mr Harte in relation to this because he had arranged the cover, whereas Mr
Corcoran was merely dealing with the claim. Mr Mockler also gave evidence
confirming that this meeting had taken place; he said that it had been
convened at his request because he had become concerned at the suggestion
that the Leeson Street premises might not have been insured adequately. Mr
Wootton also gave evidence that he had a further discussion with Mr Harte at
the Leeson Street premises at a much later stage, when they had a talk about
the delay in settling the claim.

Mr Wootton said that the proposal forms for the insurance of the
Ranelagh premises with the insurers were filled out at a meeting at those
premises on 22nd February, 1978. He said that his secretary, Miss Keogh,

was present throughout the meeting. He said that, as Mr Harte went through the form with him, he (Mr Wootton) supplied the answers to the various questions. If he was not in a position to give the information immediately, he said that he asked his secretary to get out the relevant documents from the filing cabinet. He said that a file was produced which dealt generally with insurance matters and that this file included details of the claims in relation to the Leeson Street fire as well as details of other claims. He said that these claims, including the Leeson Street claim, were mentioned individually and that, when they came to the Leeson Street fire, Mr Harte said that it was totally unnecessary to disclose it on the proposal form as they were dealing with a separate company and that they only had to show what was relevant to the Ranelagh premises. Mr Wootton said that on this basis he signed the proposal form for the "material damage" policy which contained the answer "None".

Mr Wootton was cross-examined searchingly and at length by counsel for the insurers and by counsel for the brokers. Much of the cross-examination was necessarily devoted to establishing the financial position of the plaintiffs at the time the fire occurred at the Ranelagh premises, and to the circumstances of that fire. Much of this cross-examination was relevant to the issue of arson and not to the negligence and breach of contract alleged against the brokers; but Mr Barr submitted that it was material to the latter issue since Mr Wootton's answers demonstrated that he was a person of reckless business habits who would not have hesitated to treat insurance companies in the same cavalier manner in which, as Mr Barr suggested, he treated various firms with whom he had business relationships. Mr Barr said that this conduct (combined with what he described as the charade by which Mr Wootton endeavoured to obtain insurance for the Ranelagh premises after the fire by concealing his association with the premises) significantly eroded Mr Wootton's credibility on the issue between the plaintiffs and the brokers.

I think it is perfectly clear that Mr Wootton adopted towards persons having business dealings with him an attitude which was cavalier and unorthodox, to put it mildly. Nor does he appear to have taken very much trouble to ensure that the plaintiff company complied with its statutory duty to keep proper books of account. But it does not necessarily follow that Mr Wootton's version of what transpired between himself and the late Mr Harte as to the fire in Leeson Street is untrue. Counsel for the brokers, in this context, was in something of a dilemma; so far as the question of non-disclosure was concerned, he felt obliged to contend strenuously that the facts alleged not to have been disclosed to the insurers were, in any event, not material. If this view were correct, then it lends plausibility to Mr Wootton's version that Mr Harte told him that it was not necessary to disclose the Leeson Street fire to the insurers. Mr Harte, it was said, was an experienced, competent and completely honest broker — all of which I entirely accept — and, it was urged, it was most unlikely that he would have advised Mr Wootton not to disclose the Leeson Street fire. But if Mr Harte took the view that the Leeson Street fire was not material, that view was also actively supported by the brokers in this Court. I do not find anything particularly implausible in these circumstances, in the suggestion that Mr Harte advised Mr Wootton that it was not necessary to disclose it.

But Mr Wootton's claim that Mr Harte knew all about the Leeson Street fire does not rest on the unsupported testimony of Mr Wootton; his version of the meeting in Leeson Street is fully borne out by Mr Mockler. Mr Wootton's secretary, Miss Keogh, also gave evidence that fully bore out his version of the meeting of the 22nd February, 1978; she also gave evidence that Mr Harte was in the habit of calling to the Ranelagh premises fairly frequently, and that he talked about the Leeson Street claim on more than one occasion with her. Of course neither Mr Mockler nor Miss Keogh can be regarded as independent witnesses, and it is possible that not merely Mr Wootton but they also told a series of lies about this matter in the witness box; but I think that the probabilities are that their version of events is correct and that Mr Harte was aware of the Leeson Street fire but advised Mr Wootton that it was not necessary to disclose it.

The brokers also relied strongly on the evidence of Mr Cowman, a member of their firm, and on the evidence of Mr Sheridan, a member of another firm of brokers (Messrs Connolly Wickham), both of whom gave evidence of having interviewed Mr Wootton on separate occasions prior to the Ranelagh fire with a view to having completed a survey form which was necessary to obtain a quotation from the American Insurance Company. That company specialised in public-house insurance and Mr Wootton hoped to obtain a quotation from them which was lower than the premium paid to the insurers. The significance attached to this evidence on behalf of the brokers was two-fold; first, in cross-examination Mr Wootton denied having met either of the persons concerned at any stage and, secondly, it was pointed out that in these forms also no reference was made to the Leeson Street fire.

However, I do not think that the fact that Mr Wootton was demonstrably wrong in his recollection that he had never met either of these persons means that he was lying when he gave his version of the conversations with Mr Harte. As to the suggestion that the fact that these proposal forms contain no reference to the Leeson Street fire renders implausible Mr Wootton's version that he disclosed that fire to Mr Harte, it cannot be without significance that, in the case of the form for which Mr Cowman was responsible, one claim was omitted which was disclosed in the form completed for the insurers, and that, in the case of the form for which Mr Sheridan was responsible, all three of the claims disclosed in the insurers' form were omitted. Mr Wootton had no conceivable reason for concealing these other claims, since he disclosed them fully to the insurers and, in these circumstances, I do not regard the omission of the Leeson Street fire from both of these forms as of any significance. For whatever reason, neither of these forms was completed fully or accurately and it is, accordingly, not surprising to find the Leeson Street fire being omitted.

In my view, there are only four possibilities in relation to what transpired between Mr Wootton and Mr Harte. The first is that Mr Wootton did not mention the Leeson Street fire to Mr Harte because he had forgotten about it. This is wholly unlikely: that fire had happened quite recently and had been the subject of a protracted and contentious negotiation with Sun Alliance. The second is that Mr Wootton remembered the fire but did not think it necessary to disclose it. I think that this is also unlikely: Mr Wootton, as a layman, would not have been particularly conscious of the distinction so far as the two companies were concerned. Mr Harte was being paid to deal with precisely this sort of matter and there is no reason to suppose that Mr Wootton, if he had remembered the fire, would not have told Mr Harte about it and left him, in the exercise of his professional judgment, to decide whether it was necessary to include it in the proposal form. The third possibility is that Mr Wootton remembered the fire, appreciated its materiality, but deliberately decided to conceal it from Mr Harte. This is possible: but it would seem to me to follow that, if Mr Wootton were indulging in a calculated deception of this nature, it could only be because he was apprehensive that the premium already quoted would be significantly increased or the insurance declined altogether if the insurers were told about the fire. If that were Mr Wootton's frame of mind, then it would seem to me to follow necessarily that he would have pursued the same policy of concealment and lack of candour with the insurers and any persons who might be in touch with him, such as the brokers. But Mr Wootton expressly said in the witness box that, after Mr Harte's death and before the Ranelagh fire, he had a discussion with a Mr Walsh, who had taken charge of the matters with which Mr Harte had been dealing. Mr Wootton said that he had a discussion on that occasion with Mr Walsh about the Leeson Street fire and said he hoped no mistake would be made in relation to any future insurance matters of the nature which he thought had been made by Mr Harte in relation to the Leeson Street insurance. Mr Walsh did not give evidence and I am compelled to the conclusion that Mr Wootton's version of that conversation is substantially correct. If that is so, his behaviour on that occasion was utterly incomprehensible. If he had deliberately concealed from Mr Harte the existence of the Leeson Street fire, it would seem extraordinary that a few weeks later he should have a lengthy and uninhibited discussion about it with another member of the brokers. That conversation seems to me to rule out the third possibility as a credible hypothesis. That leaves one with the fourth and, in my view, the most likely possibility, i.e., that Mr Wootton remembered the Leeson Street fire and mentioned it to Mr Harte but was advised by the latter that it was not necessary to mention it.

I think it is clear that Mr Harte, as an insurance broker, owed the plaintiffs a duty of care so far as the completion of this proposal form was concerned. He owed the plaintiffs a duty to ensure that the necessary information was furnished to the insurers so as to protect the plaintiffs against a possible subsequent repudiation. In my view, Mr Harte made an error of judgment in not furnishing that information to the insurers. I think that the evidence of the various brokers in this case demonstrates that, even if a broker were satisfied that the Leeson Street fire was not material to the risk being insured, it would be normal practice to record the information and transmit it to the underwriters so that they could use their own judgment about it. This was done by Mr Corcoran so far as General Accident were concerned, and I think that it was what Mr Harte should have done in relation to the insurers in this case.

It follows that, if I should prove to be wrong in my view of the liability of the insurers, in my opinion the plaintiffs have none the less established that the repudiation by the insurers was due to the negligence and breach of contract of Mr Harte in failing to ensure that the insurers were in possession of the information relating to the Leeson Street fire.

It was also contended on behalf of the brokers that, if the brokers were guilty of negligence in failing to ensure that the plaintiffs disclosed any material facts to the insurers, the plaintiffs were equally culpable since it should have been obvious to them that these facts should have been disclosed. I do not think that there is any substance in this contention. The plaintiffs had employed the brokers as their professional advisers so far as the placing of the insurance was concerned, and the plaintiffs were perfectly entitled to rely on any advice that was given to them by the brokers in relation to the completion of the proposal form. The reasonable man who goes to the trouble of obtaining professional advice normally acts in accordance with it. In my opinion, it follows that there is no ground for finding that the plaintiffs were guilty of any contributory negligence.

It has been agreed between the parties that damages should not be assessed until all questions of liability have finally been determined between the parties.

The Supreme Court

Henchy J: I have read the judgment of Mr Justice Kenny and I agreed with it.

Griffin J: I have read that judgment and agree with it.

Kenny J: A contract of insurance requires the highest standard of accuracy, good faith, candour and disclosure by the insured when making a proposal for insurance to an insurance company. It has become usual for an insurance company to whom a proposal for insurance is made to ask the proposed insured to answer a number of questions. Any misstatement in the answers given, when they relate to a material matter affecting the insurance, entitles the insurance company to avoid the policy and to repudiate liability if the event insured against happens. But the correct answering of any questions asked is not the entire obligation of the person seeking insurance: he is bound, in addition, to disclose to the insurance company every matter which is material to the risk against which he is seeking indemnity.

What is to be regarded as material to the risk against which the insurance is sought? It is not what the person seeking insurance regards as material, nor is it what the insurance company regards as material. It is a matter or circumstance which would reasonably influence the judgment of a prudent insurer in deciding whether he would take the risk, and, if so, in determining the premium which he would demand. The standard by which materiality is to be determined is objective and not subjective. In the last resort the matter has to be determined by the court: the parties to the litigation may call experts in insurance matters as witnesses to give evidence of what they would have regarded as material, but the question of materiality is not to be determined by such witnesses.

The test of materiality which is generally accepted in all forms of insurance against risks when property of any kind is involved is stated in s.18, sub-s.2, of the Marine Insurance Act, 1906:—

"Every circumstance is material which would influence the judgment of a prudent insurer in fixing the premium, or determining whether he will take the risk."

Although that test is stated in an Act which deals with marine insurance, it has been accepted as a correct guide to the law relating to insurance against damage to property or goods of all types.

The rule to determine the materiality of a fact which has not been disclosed to an insurer was expressed by MacKinnon L.J. with his customary pungency in *Zürich General Accident and Liability Insurance* v. *Morrison*[21] at p. 60 of the report:—

"Under the general law of insurance an insurer can avoid a policy if he proves that there has been misrepresentation or concealment of a material fact by the assured. What is material is that which would influence the mind of a prudent insurer in deciding whether to accept the risk or fix the premium, and if this be proved it is not necessary further to prove that the mind of the actual insurer was so affected. In other words, the assured could not rebut the claim to avoid the policy because of a material misrepresentation by a plea that the particular insurer concerned was so stupid, ignorant, or reckless, that he could not exercise the judgment of a prudent insurer and was in fact unaffected by anything the assured had represented or concealed."

The statement of Samuels J. in *Mayne Nickless Ltd.* v. *Pegler*[22] on the law relating to the materiality of facts not disclosed to insurers was approved and followed by the Judicial Committee of the Privy Council in *Marene* v. *Greater Pacific Insurance.*[23] Samuels J. said:—

"Accordingly, I do not think that it is generally open to examine what the insurer would in fact have done had he had the information not disclosed. The question is whether that information would have been relevant to the exercise of the insurer's option to accept or reject the insurance proposed. It seems to me that the test of materiality is this: a fact is material if it would have reasonably affected the mind of a prudent insurer in determining whether he will accept the insurance, and if so, at what premium and on what conditions."

... On 14th May, 1978, a serious fire occurred at the plaintiffs' Ranelagh premises and it caused extensive damage there. In June, 1978, the defendant insurers repudiated liability because of the non-disclosure of the fire at the Leeson Street premises. From the time of the Ranelagh fire, the defendant insurers suspected that Mr Wootton had set fire to the Ranelagh premises and, during the hearing of the case, they stated that they would not have raised the issue of non-disclosure if they had not suspected that this was a case of arson.

---

[21] [1942] 2 K.B. 53.
[22] [1974] 1 N.S.W.L.R. 228.
[23] [1976] 2 Lloyd's Rep. 631.

When the defendant insurers repudiated liability, the plaintiffs brought this action against them and claimed a declaration that the policy issued by the defendant insurers, and providing for indemnity against material losses, was valid. As against the defendant brokers, the plaintiffs claimed damages for breach of contract and for negligence. The defendant insurers pleaded, amongst other defences, that Mr Wootton had set fire to the Ranelagh premises; they withdrew this plea only at the end of the plaintiffs' case.

The trial judge accepted the evidence of Mr Wootton in relation to the circumstances in which the proposal form was completed, and he held that Mr Harte knew about the fire at the Leeson Street premises. Mr Harte died suddenly on 9th April, 1978, shortly before the fire occurred at the Ranelagh premises. The trial judge decided that the non-disclosure of the fire at Leeson Street, of the fact that the plaintiffs' furnishings were stored at those premises, and of the plaintiffs' receipt of £8,000 in respect of the damage to those furnishings, did not constitute a material matter which the plaintiffs were bound to disclose to the defendant insurers. Accordingly, he declared that the policy issued by the defendant insurers was valid, and he dismissed the plaintiffs' claim against the brokers.

There has been a sustained attack on Mr Wootton's credibility and we have been invited to reverse the trial judge's finding that the proposals for insurance were completed in the way Mr Wootton described. Miss Keogh, Mr Wootton's secretary, was in the room when Mr Wootton was being interviewed by Mr Harte in connection with the completion of the proposal forms and her evidence supported Mr Wootton's testimony. The trial judge had the advantage of seeing and hearing the witnesses and, in these circumstances, I am not prepared to differ from his findings as to Mr Wootton's veracity. The question as to when an appellate court should reverse a finding by the trial judge as to the credibility of a witness was fully discussed by this Court in *Northern Bank Finance* v. *Charlton.*[24]

Three experts on insurance business gave evidence. Their unanimous view was that the fire at Leeson Street and the damage to the plaintiffs' goods were matters that were material to the risk which the defendant insurers were asked to insure. Their opinions were not conclusive on this matter. The question whether any of these matters were material is essentially an inference from facts established by evidence.

The circumstances that Mr Wootton was a director of the plaintiff company and of Consolidated Investment would not, of itself, make a fire on property owned by Consolidated Investment a fact which was material to the risk undertaken by the defendant insurers when they insured the plaintiff company against fire on its premises. However, I think that it was material to the insurance effected by the plaintiffs with the defendant insurers that goods belonging to the plaintiffs were damaged by fire in premises owned by Consolidated Investment. The answer to the query about claims made by the plaintiffs for loss over the previous five years was literally correct but, though the plaintiffs had no claim against Sun Alliance (who issued the policy in re-

---

[24] [1979] I.R. 149.

spect of the Leeson Street premises), the plaintiffs were paid by Sun Alliance the sum negotiated in respect of their stored furnishings. The circumstances in which the plaintiffs' goods were stored in the Leeson Street premises and the fact that the plaintiffs ultimately got payment in respect of them were, in my view, matters which would reasonably have affected the judgment of a prudent insurer in deciding whether to take the risk or in fixing the premium, particularly as Mr Wootton was a director of, and managed and controlled, the plaintiff company and Consolidated Investment.

It was contended strenuously by counsel for the defendant brokers that the onus of establishing that the matter not disclosed was material to the risk undertaken lay on the defendant insurers and that, in order to discharge this onus, the defendant insurers had to establish that the matter not disclosed did affect (and not merely might have affected) their judgment. I accept the first part of this proposition but not the second part. It is necessary to establish that the fact which was not disclosed would have reasonably affected the judgment of a prudent insurer if it had been disclosed. The second part of counsel's proposition contains the error which MacKinnon L.J. condemned.

The plaintiffs and the defendant brokers placed strong reliance upon the renewal by General Accident of the insurance on the Ranelagh premises after that company had been informed of the fire at Leeson Street. The evidence on this matter is not very clear. Mr Corcoran said that, when the policy relating to the Ranelagh premises was being renewed with the General Accident, he "surmised" that he told that company of the fire at Leeson Street. Mr Shaw, an official of General Accident, recollected that Mr Corcoran had informed him of the fire at Leeson Street and said that he had passed on the information to a senior official. The senior official did not give evidence and Mr Shaw's evidence did not establish when this information was given to him or the details which he was given. However, even if one assumes that Mr Corcoran gave Mr Shaw all the information about the Leeson Street fire which we now have, insurance companies may apply different considerations to taking new risks and renewing policies.

In my opinion, the plaintiffs' action against the defendant insurers should have been dismissed. I think that the appeal of the defendant insurers should be allowed.

The defendant brokers were acting as insurance brokers for the plaintiffs at the time when the proposal for material damage was completed, and Mr Harte was their employee. An insurance broker owes a contractual duty to his client to possess the skill and knowledge which he holds himself out to the public as having, and to exercise this in doing the clients' business. He is also liable in tort if he fails to exercise that skill and knowledge. Mr Harte (whom the trial judge accepted to have been an experienced, competent, and completely honest broker) should have known that the fire at Leeson Street and the subsequent payment of £8,000 to the plaintiffs were material to the risk which the defendant insurers were being requested to undertake. Therefore, the brokers are liable to the plaintiffs in both contract and tort.

The question of contributory negligence on the part of the plaintiffs was raised by counsel for the brokers but, understandably, it was not pressed. Having given the necessary facts in answer to questions put by the brokers' representative, Mr Harte (who read out the questions from the proposal form to Mr Wootton, who wrote in the answers, and who was told about the fire in Leeson Street), the plaintiffs were entitled to rely on his skill and judgment; and so it could not be held that they were guilty of contributory negligence.

In my opinion, the plaintiffs are entitled to judgment against the defendant brokers for such damages as the plaintiffs have sustained by the brokers' breach of contract or negligence....

Aro Road and Land Vehicles Limited *v.* The Insurance Corporation of Ireland Limited
[1986] I.R. 403
The Supreme Court

WALSH J: I have read the judgment about to be delivered by McCarthy J., and I agree with it.

HENCHY J: Aro Road and Land Vehicles Ltd. ("the insured company") carried on business in Rathcoole, Co. Dublin. In July, 1981, it agreed to sell and deliver a quantity of vehicle cabs and engine parts to a firm called L.R. Plant, whose premises were at Maize, Co. Antrim. The insured company's secretary, Miss Broe, telephoned the road freight section of Coras Iompair Éireann ("C.I.E.") to arrange with them to transport the goods by road to the purchaser's premises. She made the arrangement over the telephone with a Mr Spelman. She told him what the goods were, she gave him the names and addresses of the consignor and consignee, and she estimated the value of the goods at £200,000. Mr Spelman quoted transport charges at £2.00 per £1,000 worth of goods.

On the 13th July, 1981, the insured company placed a firm order by telephone for the transport of the goods and it was made clear by Mr Spelman that they would be carried at owner's risk. Accordingly he suggested that they be insured, and offered to arrange the insurance. He had to hand blank insurance certificates from the Insurance Corporation of Ireland ("the insurers"), and (apparently without disclosing the identity of the insurers), read out over the telephone the extent of the insurance cover that would be provided, namely, "against the risks of fire and theft only, but including physical loss or damage directly resulting from collision or over-turning of the carrying conveyance."

Mr Mansfield, the managing director of and principal shareholder in the insured company, reluctantly agreed to take out the proffered insurance. His reluctance was understandable because C.I.E. had previously carried goods for him by road to Northern Ireland and there had been no trouble.

Mr Spelman, having arranged with the insured company for the payment of the transport charges and having agreed that the goods would be transported in one 40 ft. container and three 40 ft. tilts or flats, arranged with Miss Broe that a trailer would be sent by C I.E. next day to start collecting the goods. Meanwhile the arrangement of the insurance was passed by Mr Spelman to a Mr McAdam, who was a road freight superintendent in C.I.E. He in turn passed the particulars to a firm of insurance brokers, who arranged the insurance with the insurers. The insurance was recorded by the issue of two insurance certificates by C.I.E., one dated 15th July, 1981, for £200,000 and another dated 16th July, 1981, for £50,000. Those certificates were issued and authenticated by the signature of an official in the road freight department of C.I.E. C.I.E. apparently had a master policy with the insurers covering such transport insurance, and the certificates state that the cover was to be subject to "the conditions and terms of the original policy".

C.I.E. seem to have treated the insurance as having been effected on 15th July 1981. Apart from issuing the main certificate of insurance on that date, they also on that date issued an invoice and statement for £1,180 (including £400 in respect of insurance) and on the same date one of their representatives called to the premises of the insured company and collected a cheque for £1,180 to cover the insurance premium of £400 and £780 freight charges. While a further £100 was paid by the insured company on 31st August, 1981, in respect of additional cover, C.I.E. began to collect the goods on or about 15th July, 1981, for the purpose of transporting them to their destination in County Antrim.

From the foregoing account of the transactions that took place before C.I.E. began to transport the goods, the following facts appear to emerge:—

1. The insured company reluctantly took out insurance on the goods and only at the invitation of C.I.E.

2. Before the goods were transported the only information as to the terms of the insurance that was given to the insured company was as to the extent of the cover.

3. Before the goods were transported the relevant certificates were completed by C.I.E. as agents for the insurers.

4. Before the goods were transported the relevant certificates were not issued by C.I.E. to the insured company, nor was even the identity of insurers made known to the insured company.

5. C.I.E. had been furnished with blank certificates of insurance by the insurers and apparently were empowered to effect them by counter-signature.

6. C.I.E., with that power to act as agents for the insurers, did not deem it necessary to require any proposal form from the insured company or to make any inquiries save as to the names and address of the consignor and consignee and the nature and value of the goods.

7. C.I.E., as agents for the insurers, made it virtually impossible for the insured company to give the insurers the type of information they now say they were deprived of, for on the 15th July, 1981, as soon as they got the premium agreed by the insurers, they not only completed the main insurance certificate but demanded and were paid the premium payable in respect of that certificate.

The contract of insurance in this case must be held to have been concluded (subject to a later addendum) on the 15th July, 1981. It is well established that the duty of disclosure (where such duty applies) ceases to exist as soon as the contract is concluded: see *Whitwell* v. *Autocar Fire and Accident*

Assurance Co. Ltd.[25] and *Looker* v. *Law Union Insurance.*[26]

The essential question, then, is whether the non-disclosure now relied on could have been made, or was expected to be made, before 15th July, 1981.

C.I.E. proceeded to deliver by road the four loads of goods as arranged. Three of these loads safely reached their destination, but on 20th July, 1981, the container was hijacked by a man with a pistol. It was set on fire and its contents destroyed. The insured company brought proceedings in the High Court claiming indemnity under the policy for the loss. The claim was contested on a variety of grounds, but at the end of the hearing the sole issue was whether the insurers were entitled to repudiate liability on the ground that, before the policy was effected, Mr Mansfield, the managing director of and main shareholder in the insured company, had not disclosed that in 1962 he had been convicted of ten counts of receiving stolen motor parts and sentenced to twenty-one months imprisonment. It was established that the convictions and sentence took place and that they were not disclosed to the insurers, but it was not shown that Mr Mansfield had anything to do with the malicious destruction near Newry of the container of goods. This defence was entirely a technical one under the law of insurance. It succeeded in the High Court. The judge, having heard the expert evidence and having applied the test for the duty of disclosure laid down by this Court in *Chariot Inns* v. *Assicurazioni Generali*[27] held that the insurers were entitled to repudiate the policy on the ground of Mr Mansfield's failure to disclose the convictions and imprisonment that had befallen him nineteen years earlier.

I accept without question that it is a general principle of the law of insurance that a person seeking insurance, whether acting personally or through a limited company, is bound to disclose every circumstance within his knowledge which would have influenced the judgment of a reasonable and prudent insurer in fixing the premium or in deciding whether to take on the risk. Carroll J., while personally of opinion that Mr Mansfield's non-disclosure of his convictions and imprisonment was not material, deferred to the expert opinion given in the High Court (which she accepted and considered to transcend her personal opinion) that a reasonable and prudent underwriter would regard that matter as material and would have regarded its non-disclosure as a good reason for refusing to underwrite the risk. Accordingly, she held that the insurers were entitled to avoid the policies in question and to repudiate liability. On the assumption that full disclosure of all known material facts was obligatory, I consider that the judge's conclusion could not be interfered with by this Court: see *Northern Bank Finance* v. *Charlton.*[28]

It emerged, however, in the course of the hearing of this appeal, that a particular aspect of the case was not adverted to, either in the pleadings or in the argument in the High Court. This was whether the circumstances of the case showed it to be an exception to the usual requirement of full disclosure.

---

[25] (1927) 27 LI.L. Rep 418.
[26] [1928] 1. K.B. 554.
[27] [1981] I.R. 199. See p. 233 of this book.
[28] [1979] I.R. 149.

Normally, a departure in an appeal from the case as pleaded, or as argued in the court of trial, or as circumscribed by the notice of appeal, is not countenanced. However, in view of the trial judge's expression of her personal opinion as to the effect of the evidence, and having regard to the technical nature of the defence and the general importance of this point in the law of insurance, I consider that this point should be entertained.

Generally speaking, contracts of insurance are contracts *uberrimae fidei* which means that utmost good faith must be shown by the person seeking the insurance. Not alone must that person answer to the best of his knowledge any question put to him in a proposal form, but, even when there is no proposal form, he is bound to divulge all matters within his knowledge which a reasonable and prudent insurer would consider material in deciding whether to underwrite the risk or to underwrite it on special terms.

That is the general rule. Like most general legal rules, however, it is subject to exceptions. For instance, the contract itself may expressly or by necessary implication exclude the requirement of full disclosure. It is for the parties to make their own bargain — subject to any relevant statutory requirements — and if the insurer shows himself to be prepared to underwrite the risk without requiring full disclosure, he cannot later avoid the contract and repudiate liability on the ground of non-disclosure.

An example of a contract of insurance which excludes full disclosure is where the circumstances are such as to preclude the possibility of full disclosure; or where the requirement of full disclosure would be so difficult or so impractical, or so unreasonable, that the insurer must be held by his conduct to have ruled it out as a requirement. This is exemplified by many forms of what I may call "over the counter insurance". Because this case is concerned only with fire and theft cover, I am addressing myself only to property insurance. Many concerns, such as airlines, shipping companies and travel agents — acting as agents for an insurance company and usually under the umbrella of a master policy — are prepared to insure travellers or consignors of goods in respect of luggage or of goods consigned, in circumstances in which full disclosure is neither asked for nor could reasonably be given effect to. The time factor, if nothing else, would rule out the requirement of full disclosure in many instances; an air traveller who buys insurance of his luggage in an airport just before boarding an aeroplane could not be expected to have time to make disclosure of all material circumstances. Insurance sold in that way obviously implies a willingness on the part of the insurer to provide the cover asked for without requiring disclosure of *all* material circumstances. The question in this case is whether this insurance, which the judge has held was entered into by Mr Mansfield's company in good faith and without any intention to defraud, was attended by circumstances which show that the insurers are precluded from claiming that full disclosure was a prerequisite of a valid contract of insurance.

Consider the relevant circumstances, Mr Mansfield, through his company, was sold this insurance. he did not look for it. It was suggested by C.I.E. He was reluctant to take it out; he considered it a waste of money. C.I.E. as agents for the insurers arranged the rates and filled in the relevant certificates of insurance. Once that was done, C.I.E. were ready to transport the goods. They sought no further information from Mr Mansfield and apparently deemed none necessary. Before collecting and transporting the goods, they did not furnish the certificates of insurance to Mr Mansfield or his company. They did not even inform Mr Mansfield or his company of the identity of the insurers. It is conceded by counsel for the insurers that if Mr Mansfield was to make full disclosure he would have to make such inquiries as would bring the identity of the insurers to his knowledge — or alternatively to pass the relevant information to C.I.E. as their agents. C.I.E. as well as being the insurer's agents were to be the carriers of the goods insured. Everything points to the conclusion that when, as carriers of the goods, they got the information necessary for their purposes as carriers, and then arranged insurance of the goods during transit, the insurance was for all practical purposes concluded, so that no further information could have thereafter been asked for.

The circumstances of this case seems to me to show that C.I.E., acting as agents for the insurers, accepted this insurance without expecting or requiring disclosure of *all* relevant circumstances. The informal, almost perfunctory, way in which C.I.E. effected this insurance, their readiness to collect the premium and proceed to carry the goods to their destination as soon as they had ascertained the premium, showed a failure or unwillingness to give the insured company an opportunity to make full disclosure before the contract of insurance was concluded. The relevant circumstances indicate an indifference on the part of C.I.E. as agents for the insurers as to matters such as the personal circumstances of the managing director of the insured company.

It may well be the law that even in a case such as this certain types of information may not be knowingly withheld by the insured, but this case calls only for an answer to the question whether in the circumstances of the case an innocent non-disclosure of an incident in the past life of the managing director of the insured company entitled the insurers to avoid the policy. In my opinion it did not. Insurers who allow agents such as shippers, carriers, airlines, travel agents and the like to insure on their behalf goods being carried, and to sell that insurance to virtually all and sundry who ask for it, with minimal formality or inquiry, and with no indication that full disclosure is to be made of any matter which the insurers may *ex post facto* deem to be material, cannot be held to contract subject to a condition that the insured must furnish *all* material information.

I would allow the plaintiff's appeal and remit the case to the High Court for the assessment of damages.

GRIFFIN J: I agree with the judgment of Henchy. J.

HEDERMAN J: I agree with the judgment about to be delivered by McCarthy J.

MCCARTHY J: The documentary evidence of the insurance effected is contained in two certificates which, save for date, insured value and an irrelevant detail, all in manuscript, are identical in form. They certify that the defendant "has insured the goods specified hereunder, under open policy, on behalf of Coras Iompair Éireann and/or as agents" against risks, including the event which happened, "subject otherwise to the conditions and terms of the original policy". The most obvious comment is that the certificate makes no reference to the plaintiff in this action. "The certificate represents and takes the place of the original policy and will, for the purpose of collecting any claims, be accepted as showing that the holder is entitled to the benefit of such policy to the extent set forth herein." Unlike what I understand to be the ordinary course of the insurance business, there was no proposal form; such forms ordinarily provide that the proposal form shall be the basis of the contract. Here the insurance was arranged by Frank Spelman of C.I.E. who signed the quotation of the 15th July and provided the certificates duly completed from forms pre-signed on behalf of the Insurance Corporation of Ireland Ltd. Frank McAdam, road freight superintendent, arranged the insurance through the brokers, Coyle Hamilton Hamilton Phillips Ltd. Exactly how this was done is not clear. What is clear beyond doubt is that no proposal form was completed, no questions relevant to the risk, save as to value, were ever asked. James Mansfield, managing director and principal shareholder of the plaintiff company, the insured, had, in 1962, been convicted on ten counts of receiving stolen motor parts and sentenced to twenty-one months imprisonment. Not merely was the fact of these convictions not disclosed to the insurers; not merely did it not occur to Mr Mansfield, a reluctant insured, to disclose them; they never occurred to him at all; they were a part of his past which he understandably preferred to forget. Although a great number of different matters were canvassed in the course of the trial, at the conclusion the sole issue was the right claimed by the insurers to repudiate liability on the ground of non-disclosure of these convictions, which, it is said, was a non-disclosure that a reasonable and prudent underwriter would regard as material and, therefore, on ground of moral hazard, a valid reason for refusing the risk. I think not.

Consideration of this appeal is not helped by the fact that the master policy, the open policy, was not produced in evidence. There was no evidence to suggest that between the 15th /16th and the 20th July (the day of the hijack) there was any communication passing to the insurers concerning this particular risk. Carroll J. considered that the convictions could not be material, particularly to the type of insurance where the risk only attached while the goods were in the custody of C.I.E. Nonetheless, accepting that Mr Smart was expressing the view of a reasonable and prudent underwriter, she felt that the defendants had discharged the onus on them to prove a material non-disclosure; she felt obliged, so to speak, to suppress her own view of materiality in favour of that of Mr Smart, once she assessed him to be a reasonable and prudent underwriter. Notwithstanding that she still held to her view that the convictions were not material, Carroll J. deferred to the view of Mr Smart; in my judgment, she was incorrect in so doing, being herself the sole and final arbiter.

In my view if the judgment of an insurer is such as to require disclosure of what he thinks is relevant but which a reasonable insured, if he thought of it at all, would not think relevant, then, in the absence of a question directed towards the disclosure of such a fact, the insurer, albeit prudent, cannot properly be held to be acting reasonably. A contract of insurance is a contract of the utmost good faith on both sides; the insured is bound to disclose every matter which might reasonably be thought to be material to the risk against which he is seeking indemnity; that test of reasonableness is an objective one not to be determined by the opinion of underwriter, broker or insurance agent, but by, and only by, the tribunal determining the issue. Whilst accepted standards of conduct and practice are of significance in determining issues of alleged professional negligence, they are not to be elevated into being an absolute shield against allegations of malpractice — see *O'Donovan v. Cork County Council*[29] and *Roche* v. *Peilow*.[30] In disputes concerning professional competence, a profession is not to be permitted to be the final arbiter of standards of competence. In the instant case, the insurance profession is not to be permitted to dictate a binding definition of what is reasonable. The learned trial judge depended part of her judgment upon the decision of this Court in *Chariot Inns* v. *Assicurazioni Generali*.[31] In his judgment, with which Henchy and Griffin J.J. agreed, Kenny J. stated at p.225:—

> "A contract of insurance requires the highest standard of accuracy, good faith, candour and disclosure by the insured when making a proposal for insurance to an insurance company. It has become usual for an insurance company to whom a proposal for insurance is made to ask the proposed insured to answer a number of questions. Any misstatement in the answers given, when they relate to a material matter affecting the insurance, entitles the insurance company to avoid the policy and to repudiate liability if the event insured against happens. But the correct answering of any questions asked is not the entire obligation of the person seeking insurance: he is bound, in addition, to disclose to the insurance company every matter which is material to the risk against which he is seeking indemnity.
>
> What is to be regarded as material to the risk against which the insurance is sought? It is not what the person seeking insurance regards as material, nor is it what the insurance company regards as material. It is a matter or circumstance which would reasonably influence the judgment of a prudent insurer in deciding whether he would take the risk, and, if so, in determining the premium which he would demand. The standard by which materiality is to be determined is objective and not subjective. In the last resort the matter has to be determined by the court: the parties to the litigation may call experts in insurance matters as witnesses to give evidence of what they would have regarded as material, but the question of materiality is not to be determined by such witnesses."

These observations were made in a case in which there was a proposal form, there were questions asked by the insurer and, as this Court held, there was a non-disclosure of a matter material to the risk. In the High Court (in *Chariot Inns*) Keane J., at p. 209, said:—

> "The most widely accepted test of materiality in all forms of insurance on property and goods appears to be that set out in s. 18 sub-s. 2. of the Marine Insurance Act, 1906, which is in the following terms:—

---

[29] [1967] I.R. 173.
[30] [1985] I.R. 232.
[31] [1981] I.R. 199. See p. 233 of this book.

'Every circumstance is material which would influence the judgment of a prudent insurer in fixing the premium, or determining whether he will take the risk.'

That test has frequently stated to be applicable to non-marine insurance as well: see *Joel* v. *Law Union & Crown Insurance Co. and March Cabaret* v. *London Assurance.*[32] Another test has sometimes been proposed, i.e. the test of whether a reasonable man in the position of the assured and with knowledge of the facts in dispute ought to have realised that they were material to the risk. But this test has been confined normally in its application to cases of life see MacGillivray & Parkington on Insurance Law (6th ed. — paras. 749, 750). It was not suggested by any of the parties as the appropriate test in the present case and, accordingly, I propose to apply the test set out in s. 18, sub-s. 2 of the Act of 1906."

Kenny J. did not expressly advert to this proposition but it reflects the argument advanced by the plaintiff here touching on what the insured might consider relevant or material. Keane J., at p. 207, referred to the judgment of Fletcher Moulton L.J. in *Joel* v. *Law Union & Crown Insurance* Co.[33] There it was said:—

"Over and above the two documents signed by the applicant, and in my opinion unaffected by them, there remained the common law obligation of disclosure of all knowledge possessed by the applicant material to the risk about to be undertaken by the company, such materiality being a matter to be judged of by the jury and not by the Court."

The same Lord Justice, at p.885, had some critical comments to make on the practices on the part of insurance offices of requiring that the accuracy of the answers to the proposal form should be the basis of the contract. I point to this so as to emphasise that *Joel* v. *Law Union & Crown Insurance Co.*[34] was a case concerned with a proposal form and insurance effected on foot of it as was *Chariot Inns.*[35] This is not such a case, but the test remains one of the utmost good faith. Yet, how does one depart from such a standard if reasonably and genuinely one does not consider some fact material; how much the less does one depart from such a standard when the failure to disclose is entirely due to a failure of recollection? Where there is no spur to the memory, where there is no proposal form with its presumably relevant questions, how can a failure of recollection lessen the quality of good faith? Good faith is not raised in its standard by being described as the utmost good faith; good faith requires candour and disclosure, not, I think, accuracy in itself, but a genuine effort to achieve the same using all reasonably available sources, a factor well illustrated by Fletcher Moulton L.J. at page 885 of *Joel*. If the duty is one that requires disclosure by the insured of all material facts which are known

---

[32] [1908] 2 K.B. 863 and [1975] 1 Lloyd's Rep. 169.
[33] [1908] 2 K.B. 863 at p. 892.
[34] *Ibid.*
[35] [1981] IR 199. See p. 233 of this book.

to him, then it may well require an impossible level of performance. Is it reasonable of an underwriter to say:— "I expect disclosure of what I think is relevant or what I may think is relevant but which a reasonable proposer may not think of at all or, if he does, may not think is relevant?". The classic authority is the judgment of Lord Mansfield in *Carter* v. *Boehm*[36] where, in terms free from exaggeration, he stated at p. 1911:—

> "The *Reason* of the rule which obliges Parties to disclose, is to prevent Fraud and to encourage good Faith. It is adapted to such facts as vary the Nature of the Contract; which One privately knows, and The Other is ignorant of, and has no Reason to suspect.
>
> The Question therefore must always be 'Whether there was, under the Circumstances at the time the Policy was underwritten, a *fair Representation*; or a *Concealment*; fraudulent, if designed: Or though not *designed*, *varying materially the Object* of the Policy and *changing the Risque* understood to be run.'"

If the determination of what is material were to lie with the insurer alone I do not know how the average citizen is to know what goes on in the insurer's mind, unless the insurer asks him by way of the questions in a proposal form or otherwise. I do not accept that he must seek out the proposed insurer and question him as to his reasonableness, his prudence, and what he considers material. The proposal form will ordinarily contain a wide ranging series of questions followed by an omnibus question as to any other matters that are material. In the instant case, if Mr Mansfield had ever had the opportunity of completing a proposal form, which, due to the convenient arrangement made between the insurers and C.I.E., he did not, there is no reason to think that he would have recounted petty convictions of about 20 years before the time. For the reasons I have sought to illustrate, in my view, the learned trial judge failed correctly to apply the very stringent test; in my judgment, the insurers failed to discharge the onus of proof that lay on them.

There is a second ground upon which, also, in my view the plaintiff is entitled to succeed. Without detracting from what I have said in respect of the general law of insurance, in my judgment, that law is materially affected by over-the-counter insurance such as found in cases of the present kind, in other forms of transit and in personal travel, including holiday insurance. If no questions are asked of the insured, then, in the absence of fraud, the insurer is not entitled to repudiate on grounds of non-disclosure. Fraud might arise in such an instance as where an intending traveller has been told of imminent risk of death and then takes out life insurance in a slot machine at an airport. Otherwise, the insured need but answer correctly the question asked; these questions must be limited in kind and number; if the insurer were to have the opportunity of denying or loading the insurance one purpose of the transaction would be defeated. Expedition is the hallmark of this form of insurance. Mr Whelehan suggested that the whole basis of insurance could be seriously damaged if there was any weakening in the rigidity and, I must

---

[36] (1766) 3 Burr. 1905.

add, the severity, of the principle he sought to support. The force of such an argument as a proposition of law is matched by the improbability of the event.

Mr Gleeson sought leave of the Court to argue as an alternative proposition that *Chariot Inns*[37] was wrongly decided in being an elaboration in a particular direction; that the reasonably prudent test is inherently unreasonable, biased and productive of unfairness, producing unjust results and, consequently, is not part of the common law. The issue of arguing this point was postponed until the main grounds of the appeal were determined; having regard to the outcome of the appeal, it is not necessary to elaborate further on the matter.

Hilda Kelleher *v.* Irish Life Assurance Company Limited
Unreported, 8 February 1993
The Supreme Court

FINLAY C.J. (NEM. DISS.): This is an appeal by the Plaintiff against the decision and order of the High Court made by Costello J. on the 16th December 1988 dismissing the Plaintiff's claim against the defendant insurance company for the payment of a sum alleged to be due arising out of the death of her husband which occurred on the 30th day of November 1985.

The claim was made pursuant to a policy of insurance issued on the 10th October 1985 at the proposal of the Plaintiff, the life assured being that of her husband. The sum assured was a sum of £80,000. The terms of the policy at the outset state as follows:

> "This policy is granted by the Irish Life Assurance Company Limited (hereinafter called the Company) to and accepted by the proposer named in the Schedule on the basis of the proposal made in writing and signed by the proposer and on no other basis."

It was agreed by counsel on behalf of both the Plaintiff and the Defendant, both on the hearing in the High Court and on the hearing of this appeal, that the proposal referred to in that policy consisted of two separate documents which were respectively known as the general application form and the special application form.

The general application form was signed by both the Plaintiff and her husband, and the special application form was signed by the Plaintiff's husband alone. The form in which these two documents were finally prepared and presented to the proposer and the life assured for completion resulted from what is described as a special promotional offer on life assurance and disability benefit.

This offer had been negotiated by a firm of insurance brokers, Sedgwick Dineen, who acted on behalf of the Irish Medical Organisation and who, on

---

[37] [1981] I.R. 199. See p. 233 of this book.

behalf of that organisation which, of course, has a very extensive membership, negotiated this "special promotional offer" to be available to every member of the organisation who wished to avail of it. The first document executed in time and executed by both the Plaintiff and her husband was, as originally printed, an application form for life assurance which, obviously, was in general use by the Defendant Company. On the first page thereof it contains information concerning the life to be assured, his age, occupation, the name of the proposer, the residence of the payer of the premium and details of the assurances proposed, including the amount of the premium and the periods of its payment. The second page on the printed form contained what might be described as usual questions concerning the health and activities and history of the life assured, which might be matters material to the risk. In summary, these questions were on the following topics:

1. Whether the life was suffering from any physical defect, ailment or disease, or had a tendency to any such?
2. Had the life suffered at any time from any illness, injury, requiring medical or psychiatric attention?
3. Had the life undergone any special investigations or laboratory tests, or had a surgical operation?
4. Was the life taking prescribed drugs, medicines, etc.?
5. Average weekly consumption of alcohol, average tobacco consumption per day.
6. Name and address of current medical attendant, or if changed in the last year, of previous one.
7. Had the life any intention of flying, other than a fare-paying passenger on a recognised public airline, of residing or travelling abroad except for holidays, or engaging in any hazardous sport or other activities?
8. Has any proposal on the life made to the Defendant or any other life office been accepted on special terms, declined or postponed?
9. Is the life currently proposing for assurance with the Defendant or any other life office ?
10. Has the life any existing ordinary branch assurances with the Company?

Through the entire of that page there was, before this document was presented to the Plaintiff and her husband, drawn a line of cancellation, the purpose of which was to indicate that in the special promotion which had been negotiated there was no obligation on either the proposer or on the life assured to answer these questions. After that page constituting a blank though printed as being the series of questions leading to a series of statements, the following declaration was made:

"I/We, the life to be assured and the Proposer, declare that the above statements (including any statements written down at my/our dictation) are true and complete. I/We understand that failure to disclose a material fact, being a fact which may influence the assessment and acceptance of the proposal by the Company, may constitute grounds for rejection of a claim. I/We understand that in the event of doubt as to whether a fact is material it should be disclosed)."

The "special proposal" form is headed "Application/Proposal Form for ... Pension Plan" and contains on the first page the name and address, marital status and date of birth, of the life assured. The next column, which is to provide for the method of pension and amount, is cancelled. The next column which is printed to provide for the life cover involved is a blank. Income protection benefits are then recited, providing for an income protection benefit of £10,000 per annum. A column provides for the method of payment of the premium as yearly, and for the cessor of premiums at the age of sixty-five. A question is then asked as to whether the life assured is engaged on its own account or as a partner personally acting in some trade, profession or occupation, and to that the answer was given: "Self-employed". A further question at the bottom of the page was as to whether the applicant is the holder of an office or employment, the answer was: "No".

On the next page of the document are a series of typed provisions which clearly are the special conditions provided by the "special promotional offer". The first of those is numbered 8, and is a query as to whether the Applicant contributes to any other arrangement by the Revenue Commissioners under sections of the Income Tax Act 1967. No. 9 reads as follows:

> "I hereby declare that the answers set forth above are true to the best of my knowledge and belief. I understand that no annuity under the fund shall be capable of being surrendered, assigned or commuted except as provided by sections 235 and 235A of the Income Tax Act 1967"

There was also an acknowledgement of an understanding that the contributions to the Fund will be aggregated for certain income tax purposes. That is signed by the life assured, Dr Kelleher. There then is contained, without a number, a heading: "Special Promotional Offer on Life Assurance and Disability Benefit", and it reads as follows:

> "For any member who is under sixty years old and who satisfactorily completed the declaration of health below, we can offer life cover of £80,000 free of medical evidence and annual disability benefit cover of £10,000 per annum. For those who availed of our previous offer they can top up to this amount. This offer is valid for a limited period of time."

Then there is a provision for the Applicant to indicate whether he wished to avail of the "medical free offer" of £80,000 life cover and £10,000 p.a. disability benefit cover or whether he wanted to top up an existing benefit. Then there is the declaration of health referred to in this clause, and it reads as follows:

> "I declare that I am actively at work or capable of being actively at work on today's date, that I have not been absent from work through illness or injury for more than two weeks in the three months prior to today's date, and that I have not undergone, taken or sought medical treatment during the six months prior to today's date."

This was duly signed by the Plaintiff's husband.

In the policy of insurance a page entitled "Provisions, privileges and conditions" contains at clause 6 the following:

> *"Proposal*
> If any question contained in the proposal has not been fully, correctly, and truly answered, or if there is any misrepresentation or non-disclosure concerning the health, habits or occupation of the Life Assured or if any answer to any question in the proposal is misleading, the Company shall be entitled to avoid the policy, and thereupon all premiums paid and all rights under the policy shall be forfeited to the Company."

The claim of the Plaintiff was originally defended by the Defendants on two grounds. The first of those was an assertion that the cause of death of the deceased was one of the causes of death excepted under the terms of the policy. The Defendants failed to establish that fact in evidence before the High Court, and the learned trial judge found in favour of the Plaintiff on that issue. Against that finding and judgment no cross-appeal or notice to vary has been brought before this Court.

The other ground on which the Defendants sought to defend the Plaintiff's claim was on an assertion that it was an express or, in the alternative, an implied condition of the contract of insurance between the Defendant and the Plaintiff that the failure of the Plaintiff or of the late Daniel Kelleher to disclose a material fact, being a fact which might influence the assessment and acceptance of the proposal by the Defendant, would constitute grounds for the rejection of the claim. It was established at the hearing in the High Court that the late Daniel Kelleher had received treatment for cancer of the prostate in the year 1981, and on subsequent occasions received treatment for consequential damage which had occurred by reason of radiation treatment which was given to him at that time, although the cancer had not recurred, and it was submitted that these facts were facts which might be material to the risk and accordingly should have been disclosed. Although it was pleaded in the defence, the Defendants failed to establish that any of the treatment which the Plaintiff had undergone was within six months before the date of the signing by him of the special proposal form. The learned trial judge in the course of his judgment held that the special promotional offer was obviating the necessity for producing medical evidence but that it did not obviate the obligation to make full disclosure, and that that was in fact underlined on the other document which was sent to persons availing of the special scheme. The ratio of his decision is to be found in a paragraph contained at page 9 of the judgment which is as follows:

> "In these circumstances it seems to me that there was no waiver by the Defendants of the obligation which was on the Plaintiff and on the person whose life was insured. There was no variation of the common law duty. There was a contractual duty to disclose which was stated in clear terms. In my view, the breach of that contractual duty entitles the Defendants to repudiate liability."

No challenge was made on the hearing of this appeal to the general proposition of the implied obligation on persons proposing insurance to disclose, first stated by Lord Mansfield in *Carter* v. *Boehm*,[38] and subsequently confirmed and repeated in many decisions both in England and Ireland.

The sole issue raised by the Appellant on the hearing of this appeal is a submission that upon the true construction of the two forms of proposal and, in particular, upon the true construction of the special form of proposal that the policy which is based on the two forms of proposal must be read as excluding a requirement of full disclosure with regard to the medical history of the life assured from the years 1981 to 1985 and that in addition the terms of those documents exclude any implied obligation arising under the doctrine laid down in the case of *Carter* v. *Boehm*.[39]

This doctrine was recently dealt with by this Court in the case of *Aro Road and Land Vehicles Limited* v. *ICI*.[40] In that case, Henchy J. in the course of his judgment at page 408 stated as follows:

> "Generally speaking contracts of insurance are contracts *uberrimae fidei*, which means that utmost good faith must be shown by the person seeking the insurance. Not alone must that person answer to the best of his knowledge any question put to him in a proposal form, but, even when there is no proposal form, he is bound to divulge all matters within his knowledge which a reasonable and prudent insurer would consider material in deciding whether to underwrite the risk or to underwrite it on special terms.
>
> That is the general rule. Like most general legal rules, however, it is subject to exceptions. For instance, the contract itself may expressly or by necessary implication exclude the requirement of full disclosure. It is for the parties to make their own bargain — subject to any relevant statutory requirements — and if the insurer shows himself to be prepared to underwrite the risk without requiring full disclosure, he cannot later avoid the contract and repudiate liability on the ground of non-disclosure."

The Appellant in this case says it comes precisely within the exception referred to in that portion of the judgment as being an instance where the contract itself formed on the two proposals, by necessary implication, excludes the requirement of full disclosure.

Special emphasis is placed upon the unambiguous statement contained under the heading "Special Promotional Offer on Life Assurance and Disability Benefit" in the special proposal form, whereby the insurance company, in effect, guarantees that "for any member who is under sixty years old and who *satisfactorily completed the declaration of health below* we can offer life cover of £80,000 *free of medical evidence* and annual disability benefit cover of £10,000 per annum." (Emphasis added). This, it is submitted, is the clearest possible assertion that completion of "the declaration of health below" is the sufficient entry for a person who is also a member of the organisation, namely the IMO, and who is under sixty years of age. The "declaration of health below", there referred to, I have set out in this judgment and it is one expressly confined to the work experience and the negating of excessive

---

[38] (1766) 3 Burr. 1905.
[39] *Ibid.*
[40] [1986] I.R. 403. See p. 255 of this book.

absence through illness for a period of three months prior to the date of the signing of the form and the absence of taking or seeking medical treatment during six months prior to the signing of the form. Such an unequivocal statement, it is submitted, not only clearly excludes the ordinary doctrine of *uberrimae fidei* or the implied obligation to make full disclosure with regard to the risk, but also must be read as confining clause 6 of the provisions, privileges and conditions in the policy of assurance to misrepresentation or non-disclosure confined to the precise questions and periods raised in the declaration of health. This topic is dealt with as a matter of general principle in the Eighth Edition of MacGillivray and Parkington on Insurance Law, published in 1988. There, having set out the possibility that the form of questions asked in a proposal form may make the Applicant's duty to disclose more strict than the general duty arising under the doctrine laid down in *Carter* v. *Boehm*,[41] at paragraph 646 it is stated as follows:

> "It is more likely, however, that the questions asked will limit the duty of disclosure, in that, if questions are asked on particular subjects and the answers to them are warranted, it may be inferred that the insurer has waived his right to information, either on the same matters but outside the scope of the questions, or on matters kindred to the subject matter of the questions. Thus if the insurer asks "How many accidents have you had in the last three years?", it may well be implied that he does not want to know of accidents before that time, though these would still be material. If it were asked whether any of the proposer's parents, brothers or sisters had died of consumption or been afflicted with insanity, it might well be inferred that the insurer had waived similar information concerning more remote relatives, so that he could not avoid the policy for non-disclosure of an aunt's death of consumption or an uncle's insanity. Whether or not such waiver is present depends on a true construction of the proposal form, the test being would a reasonable man reading the proposal form be justified in thinking that the insurer had restricted his right to receive all material information, and consented to the omission of the particular information in issue?"

This identical paragraph, which was contained in an earlier edition of the text-book involved, is cited with full approval by Woolf J. (as he then was) in *Hair* v. *The Prudential Assurance Company Limited*,[42] at page 673 of his judgment. In applying that principle to the facts of that particular case, Woolf J. laid particular emphasis on the last sentence of the paragraph.

I too would accept this as an accurate statement of the principle of limitation of the obligation for disclosure arising from the particular form of questions. I would also be satisfied that the true and acid test must be as to whether a reasonable man reading the proposal form would conclude that the information over and above it which is in issue was not required.

Applying that test to the form of the special proposal form in this case, I have no doubt that a reasonable man reading that would assume that, provided he could truthfully answer the two questions, namely, his absence

[41] (1766) 3 Burr. 1905.
[42] [1983] 2 Ll. L.R. 667.

from work due to illness being confined to not more than two weeks in the
previous three months, and the second question, as to his not having undergone, taken or sought medical treatment within six months, he would be
entitled, having fulfilled the other necessary qualifications of being a member
of the IMO under the age of sixty years, to the insurance.

In essence, the grounds on which the Defendants now seek to avoid payment on this policy consist precisely of a non-disclosure by the life assured,
Dr Kelleher, of his having sought and obtained medical treatment in the year
1981 and in succeeding years, but outside of the time of six months provided
for in the declaration of health contained in the special proposal form.

Whilst it is not necessary to go outside the forms of the proposal themselves, it is not without importance that what was described as the "special
promotional offer" being offered by the assurance company after negotiation
through the brokers to all the members of the Irish Medical Organisation
constitutes a very sound and probable commercial manner in which to attract
a very substantial quantity of new business by one single project. That fact
constitutes a probable reason why the Defendant should significantly limit
the disclosure required from proposers for that insurance.

I would, therefore, allow this appeal, vary the order made in the High
Court and enter judgment for the Plaintiff for the sum of £80,000, and would
hear submissions from counsel with regard to the question of the claim for
interest pursuant to section 22 of the Courts' Act 1981.

Kreglinger and Fernau Limited and Others *v.*
Irish National Insurance Company[*]
[1956] I.R. 116
The High Court

DAVITT P: ... While the duty to make full disclosure of all matters material to
the risk rests upon the insured, and it does not fall to the insurer to relieve
him of that duty by making inquiries, the converse is to this extent true, that
the insured does not have to conduct the insurer's business for him. Where
the contract, the performance of which the insurer is asked to cover, contains
a clear intimation that a matter, which is specifically referred to but not fully
set out, is of importance, and full information is to be had for the asking, it
would seem quite unreasonable and unjust to allow the insurer to repudiate
liability on the grounds that he did not know and was not told the details of
something which he was in fact told about. What Mr O'Callaghan was told by
the terms of the contract was, in my opinion, clearly sufficient to put him
upon inquiry. His attention was called in a very definite and specific way to
the undertaking which Swifts had given: and if he wished to know the price
which they were paying, or any other detail concerning the matter, he should
have asked for it. This view is, I think, supported by such cases as *Foley and*

---

[*] Extract.

Another v. *Tabor;*[43] *Asfar and Co.* v. *Blundell;*[44] *Joel* v. *Law Union and Crown Insurance Co.;*[45] *Mann Macneal and Steeves* v. *Capital and Counties Insurance Co.;*[46] *The Bedouin.*[47] I take the view that the defendants have not discharged the onus of showing that there was non-disclosure of the terms of Swifts' undertaking; and that from whatever viewpoint such alleged non-disclosure is considered a defence based thereon cannot at present succeed. The defence pleaded in paragraph 15 and based on sub-paragraphs *(d)*, *(e)*, *(f)*, *(g)* and *(h)* has not, in my opinion, so far been established.

Sub-paragraph *(i)* pleads non-disclosure of the fact that the price paid the vendors under the contract was substantially less than the prices being paid by the British Ministry of Food; and that, accordingly, the contract could not be carried out by the vendors with any reasonable expectation of profit. What I have said with regard to sub-paragraphs *(d)* to *(h)* can be applied equally to sub-paragraph *(i)* so far as the first part of this plea is concerned. As regards the second part, there is no evidence that the contract could not be carried out by the vendors with any reasonable expectation of profit; or if that were so that the plaintiffs were aware of it.

Sub-paragraph *(j)* pleads the non-disclosure of the alleged fact that the risk which the defendants were being asked to insure was not a first-class risk, but a risk of an unusual and very onerous character, and differed materially from what the defendants might reasonably have supposed and did suppose it to be. Apart from the circumstance that none of the contracts were fulfilled, which, so far as the evidence touches the matter at all appears to have been due to causes quite apart from the facts dealt with in the pleadings. I have no admissible evidence that the risk was not a first-class risk, or that the plaintiffs knew it to be otherwise than a first-class risk, or that it was a risk of an unusual and very onerous nature, or that it was otherwise than what the defendants supposed it to be. This plea must rest solely upon Mr Perceval's evidence that the matters which he was unaware of and did not disclose represented an entirely different picture from that which he had presented to the defendants: and that they were, in his opinion, material because their disclosure would have made it more difficult to negotiate the bonds. Some of these matters I have held to be immaterial, as to others I have held that the onus of proving non-disclosure has not been discharged. I do not think that the defendants could reasonably have supposed the risk to be other than it actually was. This plea has not, in my opinion, been established.

The pleas contained in sub-paragraphs *(k)* and *(l)* have already been dealt with inferentially; and this remark applies to pleas raised in paragraphs 16 and 17. What has been said with regard to paragraphs 15, 16 and 17 suffices to dispose also of paragraphs 33, 34, 35, 51, 52 and 53, which raise similar defences in respect of Contracts nos. 3 and 4.

Paragraph 59 in a "blanket" plea summarises the defences raised as to

---

[43] 2 F. & F. 663.
[44] [1896] 1 Q.B. 123
[45] [1908] 2 K.B. 863 at pp. 882, 897.
[46] [1921] 2 K.B. 300.
[47] [1894] P. 1.

alleged misrepresentation and non-disclosure, and calls for no comment in addition to what has already been said with regard to these defences. I would like, however, to add this much. In the cross-examination of Mr Perceval and in argument, the view was strongly pressed that in the course of the negotiations for the bond in respect of Contract no. 2, the proposition was put before the defendants as one to be accepted or rejected on the spot, or at most within twenty-four hours, and in such an atmosphere of speed and urgency that there could be little if any time for any inquiry by the defendants. Mr Perceval, rather strangely, in my opinion, accepted this as a picture of what happened. To my mind, the picture is far removed from reality. Negotiations were opened upon a provisional basis on the 3rd February and resumed upon the same basis on the 9th or 10th. On the 24th February, the defendants were given a copy of the contract. The cover note was issued on the 4th March and the performance bond on the 16th March. The defendants appear to me to have had ample time in which to make enquiries if they had thought fit to do so; and the suggested atmosphere of speed and urgency seems to have been absent.

I was pressed in argument also to hold that Mr Perceval's evidence was conclusive as to the materiality of the facts which he did not disclose. Taking on one hand the facts as they were and on the other the picture presented, not merely by Mr Perceval, but also by the contents and provisions of the contracts themselves and what should have been clear to the defendants if the contracts had been properly read and appreciated. I can see no material difference between one picture and the other so far as concerns the risks to be undertaken by the defendants. I do not consider that Mr Perceval's opinion as to materiality is admissible in evidence; but assuming that it is admissible, then I am not bound to accept it, and I do not, in fact, accept it. It appears to me to be based upon an incomplete appreciation of the facts and, in particular, upon an insufficient perusal and understanding of the terms of the contracts themselves. In my opinion, as the case stands at present, the defendants have not made good any defence based upon alleged misrepresentation or non-disclosure....

Dermot Latham *v.* Hibernian Insurance Company Limited and Peter J. Sheridan and Company Limited (No. 1)
Unreported, 22 March 1991
The High Court

BLAYNEY J: The Plaintiff claims against the first named Defendant (to which I shall refer as the Hibernian) indemnity, under a policy of insurance, for damage and loss sustained by him in a fire which occurred on the 23rd day of May 1985. The policy under which he claims was obtained through the agency of the second named Defendant of which the principal is Mr Peter J. Sheridan.

The Hibernian admits that it issued the policy under which the Plaintiff claims but says that it is entitled to avoid the policy for non-disclosure of material facts when the policy came up for renewal. The Plaintiff denies that there was non-disclosure and contends that, even if there was the Hibernian had knowledge of the material facts from other sources.

The Plaintiff claims that Mr Sheridan was negligent in not advising him of the necessity of disclosing the relevant facts to the Hibernian and he claims damages for breach of contract and negligence against Mr Sheridan's Company, the second named Defendant.

This Judgment is concerned solely with the issue of liability. It was agreed by the parties that the question of damages should be left over until this issue had been decided.

The basic facts in the case might be summarised as follows. In the month of May 1983 the Plaintiff and Oliver Byrne obtained a lease for 35 years of No. 22 Bridge Street, Ringsend, and they opened on the ground floor of the premises a shop selling groceries, confectionery and cigarettes. The shop was open seven days a week and 24 hours a day.

Insurance cover was obtained from the Hibernian, initially in the names of the Plaintiff and Oliver Byrne, for the 12 months from the 31st August 1993 to the 31st August 1984. A proposal form was signed on the 9th September 1983 by the Plaintiff. The form had been brought to the Plaintiff by Mr Sheridan and the questions in the form had been read out by Mr Sheridan to the Plaintiff and the answers inserted in the form by Mr Sheridan. The policy was duly issued some months later. It covered fire, burglary, loss of profits, public liability, loss of money, etc. Before the policy was renewed in August 1984, the Plaintiff bought out the landlord's interest in the premises in his own name, the lease merged, Oliver Byrne giving up his interest, and the Plaintiff became the sole owner of the premises. When the policy was renewed in August 1984 it was renewed in his sole name.

A fire occurred in the premises on the 23rd May 1985 causing substantial damage to the building and its contents and the Plaintiff made a claim to the Hibernian under the policy. On the 1st October 1985 the Hibernian repudiated liability on the ground that the policy was void for non-disclosure of material facts of which the Plaintiff was aware prior to the date of renewal.

The material facts were that the Plaintiff had on the 22nd day of November 1983 been arrested and charged with receiving stolen goods; that he had committed the offence of receiving stolen goods within a day or two prior to his arrest, and that while in custody immediately after his arrest he had admitted to the investigating Guards that he had committed the offence. The Plaintiff was subsequently sent for trial in the Circuit Court and in December 1984 pleaded guilty to the offence. In April 1985 he was given leave to change his plea to one of not guilty but in the course of his trial which took place in December 1985, having initially pleaded not guilty, he subsequently again pleaded guilty and was sentenced to three years' imprisonment.

Oliver Byrne had been arrested and charged with the same offence at the same time as the Plaintiff. And it came out in evidence that even though Oliver Byrne is not a party to the insurance policy, he has a private arrangement with the Plaintiff under which he will receive 50 per cent of any claim which is recovered from the Hibernian.

These are the basic facts in the case in respect of which there is no dispute. I will refer to other facts which are in dispute when I come to deal with the issues in the case.

The first issue is whether the Hibernian is entitled to repudiate for non-disclosure. Here, two separate questions have to be considered: firstly, whether the facts were such that they ought to have been disclosed, and secondly, if they were, whether the Hibernian is precluded from relying on non-disclosure because they had knowledge of the material facts from another source.

As regards the first question I have no doubt. I find as a fact that the Plaintiff was arrested and charged with the offence of receiving stolen goods, the goods in question being cigarettes to the value of £17,000; I find that he did commit the offence of receiving the goods in question and that, while in custody, he made a statement admitting the offence. I further find that he pleaded guilty to the offence and was sentenced to three years' imprisonment. On behalf of the Plaintiff Mr Fitzgerald submitted that the fact that the Plaintiff had pleaded guilty did not necessarily mean that he had committed the offence. He said that he could have had other reasons for pleading guilty. In my opinion there is no substance in that submission. A man who pleads guilty, whatever his reason may be, admits that he committed the offence. Furthermore, other evidence in the case makes it quite clear that the Plaintiff did commit the offence. In his statement to Detective Garda Muldoon, the Plaintiff describes how he and Oliver Byrne bought the cigarettes and took delivery of them and he said in the course of the statement:—

"At the time I received the cigarettes, I felt they were stolen."

and the notes written down by Detective Garda Muldoon of a conversation with the Plaintiff, which were signed by the Plaintiff, the Plaintiff said:—

"The cigarettes that the Detectives took from my home tonight are the cigarettes which I brought home last night. I already had some legitimate stock which they also took."

The reference to legitimate stock is a clear indication that the Plaintiff was aware that the other cigarettes that the Detectives had taken away were not legitimate, that is to say, that they were stolen.

Apart from this, in the course of his cross-examination the Plaintiff admitted that he had committed the offence. When asked:

"Is it not true to say that you committed the offence?"

He replied:

"Yes".

He went on to say:

"I am not denying that. I did my time for it and I am very embarrassed about it. I am still embarrassed about it; it was a stupid thing to have done at the time and I regret very much doing it ."

As to whether a fact is material to be disclosed to the Insurance Company, the test is that laid down in Section 18 (2) of the Marine Insurance Act 1906 which Kenny J. in *Chariot Inns Limited* v. *Assicurazioni Generali SPA and*

Coyle Hamilton Hamilton Philips Limited[48] said is a correct guide to the law in insurance against damage to property or goods of all types.

> "Every circumstance is material which would influence the judgment of a prudent insurer in fixing the premium or determining whether he will take the risk."

In the course of his Judgment Kenny J. said at page 174:

> "This standard by which materiality is to be determined is objective, not subjective. The matter has, in the last resort, to be determined by the court: the parties to the litigation may call experts in insurance matters as witnesses to give evidence of what they would have regarded as material but the question of materiality is not to be determined by such witnesses."

Two experienced underwriters gave evidence before me, Mr Denis Bergin the Assistant General Manager of the Eagle Star Insurance Company and a Mr Barry, the Property Manager of the Irish National Insurance Company. Both stated that if an applicant for insurance had committed the offence of which the Plaintiff had been convicted, and had admitted committing such offence, they would not be prepared to do business with him. It is clear from this that they regarded the commission of such an offence, and an admission that it had been committed, as very material. Even in the absence of such evidence I would have had little doubt that the fact that a person had committed such an offence, and had admitted it, would necessarily influence the mind of a prudent insurer and the evidence clearly supports this view. It is also supported by a decision of the Court of Appeal in England, *Reynolds and Anderson* v. *Phoenix Assurance Company Limited and others*.[49] In that case it was held that the material circumstances was not the fact that a party had been charged with an offence, but that he had committed the offence. What had to be disclosed was the underlying fact that a crime had been committed.

On the first question, accordingly I am clearly of the opinion that the fact that the Plaintiff had committed the offence, and had admitted doing so, were material facts which ought to have been disclosed by the Plaintiff when applying for the renewal of the insurance.

The second question is whether the Hibernian had knowledge of the relevant facts from some other source. In considering the first question I referred principally to the fact that the Plaintiff had committed the offence and had admitted doing so. There was no evidence, however, that the Hibernian had knowledge of this from any source. The only evidence referred to the possibility of their having known that the Plaintiff had been arrested and charged with the offence. Two witnesses purported to give evidence of this. The first was Oliver Byrne who said that when Mr Bernard Galligan, an inspector of the Hibernian, had visited the shop early in January 1984, he had told him about himself and the Plaintiff being arrested and charged. Mr Galligan denied this. At the end of the case, before Counsel made their submissions, I

---

[48] [1981] I.R. 199.
[49] [1978] 2 Ll. L.R. 440.

indicated that I accepted Mr Galligan's evidence and rejected Mr Byrne's evidence so the Plaintiff is confined to relying on the other evidence which was given by his daughter Danielle. Her evidence was to the effect that at a rehearsal of a Tops of the Town Show in the Bank of Ireland Buildings in O'Connell Street on an evening in November 1983, shortly after news of the Plaintiff's and Oliver Byrne's arrest and charge had appeared in the *Evening Herald* and *Evening Press*, Mr Gerry Ring, who was a clerk in the Phibsboro Branch of the Hibernian, had commiserated with her on her father having been arrested. Mr Ring was a clerk in the commercial section in Phibsboro, being the section in which the Plaintiff's insurance was being dealt with. The evidence was that Liam Barry, who was Danielle Latham's boyfriend at the time, had told some friends of Danielle's about what was in the paper and that Mr Ring was amongst those who had been told. Mr Ring denied that he had ever been told about the Plaintiff being arrested and charged and his evidence was to the effect that on the night when he was supposed to have heard of it he was at home with his parents as he left the following day with them to spend three weeks in South Africa.

I am not satisfied that Danielle Latham was a truthful witness. She appeared to be under very considerable stress while giving her evidence and it seemed to me that the only reason for her being under stress was that she was being asked to give untruthful evidence in support of her father's case. Mr Ring, on the other hand, seemed to me to be a truthful witness.

Evidence in support of Danielle Latham's version was given by Liam Barry and Paul Furey but it seems to me that they could have been mistaken as to whether Gerry Ring was in their company on the night in question when Liam Barry told them about the Plaintiff's arrest. So on the facts I am not satisfied that Gerry Ring did hear in November 1983 of the fact that the Plaintiff had been arrested and charged. Even if he did, it seems to me that his knowledge would not be the knowledge of the Hibernian. In my opinion this is clear from the following passage in MacGillivray and Parkington on Insurance Law (7th Edition) paragraph 674:—

> "It is obvious that the insurers cannot complain of having been misled by the assured's concealment when from some other source they had received knowledge of the facts which they say were not communicated. This would seem to apply even to fraudulent concealment by the assured, since the concealment could not have influenced the insurer's judgment. This principle applies where knowledge is received by an agent of the company, but is subject to the general limitation that the agent must have received it in the course of his duty and employment."

It is clear in the present case that if Gerry Ring received knowledge of the fact that the Plaintiff had been arrested and charged, he did not receive such knowledge in the ordinary course of his duty and employment but in the course of socialising with his friends. Knowledge received by him in such circumstances could not be imputed to his employers.

It is not necessary in the circumstances to consider another issue which was raised in the course of the argument, namely, whether the mere charge and arrest of the Plaintiff was a material fact which ought to have been disclosed. It was part of the Plaintiff's submission that it was not. Since it is not necessary to consider the issue I make no finding in respect of it.

I am satisfied in the circumstances that the Plaintiff's claim against the Hibernian fails. The Company was entitled to avoid the policy on the grounds of non-disclosure as it did not have knowledge from any other source of the facts which ought to have been disclosed to it.

There remains the claim against Mr Sheridan's Company. This gave rise to one important issue of fact which again I decided before Counsel made their submissions. Mr Sheridan's evidence was to the effect that he was not aware until after the fire had occurred that the Plaintiff had been arrested and charged with receiving stolen goods. I rejected his evidence on that issue preferring the evidence of Mrs Elizabeth Byrne, a sister-in-law of Oliver Byrne, who worked in the shop in Ringsend and who gave evidence to the effect that on the evening that news of the Plaintiff's arrest and charge had been published in the evening papers Mr Sheridan had come in to the shop and had said to her:—

"My God, what is this? If the boys go down, will you be carrying on?"

She gave evidence of other conversations also in which she told Mr Sheridan that the Plaintiff and Oliver Byrne were in Court and he asked

"What way are things going to go?"

Finally she said that on one occasion when Mr Sheridan gave her a lift into town in March 1985 he had again asked would she be carrying on the shop if anything happened to them, meaning the Plaintiff and Oliver Byrne.

The question which has to be considered is whether Mr Sheridan, knowing that the Plaintiff had been arrested and charged with an offence, was under a duty as his broker to inform the Hibernian of the position, or to inform the Plaintiff that this was something which he would have to disclose to the Hibernian when seeking a renewal of his policy in August 1984.

Mr Bernard Galligan, now the Manager of the Hibernian Office in London, and Mr Tommy O'Brien, who was the Head of the Commercial Section in Phibsboro in 1983, both said that if Mr Sheridan knew of the arrest and charge he should have informed the Hibernian and he also would have a duty to advise the Plaintiff that it should be disclosed. Even if there had not been positive evidence to this effect from people who are experts in the insurance field, I think I would have had to come to the same conclusion, since Mr Sheridan, as the Plaintiff's insurance broker, owed the Plaintiff a duty to exercise reasonable care in the handling of the Plaintiff's affairs. And one of his duties in exercising such care would have been to advise the Plaintiff as to the necessity of disclosing to the Hibernian that he had been arrested and charged with the offence of receiving stolen goods. His failure to do this was in my opinion a breach of duty to the Plaintiff.

Mr Sheridan's duty to the Plaintiff was both a contractual duty and a common law duty in negligence. In so far as it was a contractual duty, the mere breach of contract gives the Plaintiff a cause of action. In so far as it was a duty at common law in negligence, for liability to exist, it would be necessary also for the Plaintiff to prove that he has suffered damage. And it seems to me that he has done this. While the evidence establishes that if it had been disclosed to the Hibernian, as it ought to have been, that the Plaintiff had been arrested and charged, they would not have renewed his insurance policy, and furthermore that the probability was that he could not have obtained insurance from any other Irish insurance company either, at the same time, if the Plaintiff had been informed by Mr Sheridan that he had to make disclosure, and if as a result he had then discovered that he could neither renew his insurance policy with the Hibernian, nor obtain insurance anywhere else, he would at that stage have been able to decide whether he would or would not continue in business and run the risk of carrying on without insurance. As a result of Mr Sheridan's breach of duty, he was deprived of this opportunity. Accordingly, it seems to me that the Plaintiff has suffered damage and so he has established liability against Mr Sheridan's Company both in contract and in tort.

For the reasons I have given the Plaintiff's action against the Hibernian Insurance Company will be dismissed and his claim against Mr Sheridan's Company will be adjourned to some date in the future so that damages can be assessed.*

William Harney *v.* The Century Insurance Company Limited
Unreported, 22 February 1983
The High Court

MCWILLIAM J: The Plaintiff's claim is for the payment of disability benefits under the provisions of a health insurance policy issued on foot of a proposal submitted by the Plaintiff on 23rd May, 1979. At the end of the proposal form is the following statement. "The Office must be notified of any changes in the health and circumstances of the life to be insured prior to the assumption of risk."

The proposal was acknowledged on a form dated 8/6/79, requiring the Plaintiff to attend for a medical examination by the Defendant's doctor and stating that a report form had been sent to the Plaintiff's doctor for completion. In June, 1979 the Plaintiff attended the doctor appointed on behalf of the Defendant and informed him that he had no complaints except head colds for which he was then taking quinine tablets, that he had had general medical examinations for adopting a child and for motor racing and that the results of both had been clear. He stated that he had had these examinations five and six years previously approximately.

The Plaintiff's proposal was accepted by the Defendant by a letter dated 24th July, 1979. This letter was described as an acceptance letter but was, in fact, an offer by the Defendant setting out terms on which a policy would be issued and enclosing an acceptance slip to be completed by the Plaintiff. The letter contained the following provision:—

---

* The damages were assessed in a further judgment of Blayney J. and this judgment appears at page 510 of this book.

"Risk will be assumed only when you have fulfilled the requirements set out on the attached slip provided there has been no change in the information given in connection with this proposal. Therefore please complete and return the slip without delay, but if there has been any change in the health or other circumstances which could affect the risk we must be informed of it and written confirmation must be obtained or otherwise the contract may be void. The right is reserved to withdraw this offer at any time provided risk has not already been assumed."

As frequently happens in modern copying, the left-hand edge of the acceptance slip has not got on to the photostat before me, but the document appears to state that with it was enclosed with the policy number 9521350. The acceptance slip was intended to be signed and dated by the Plaintiff under a paragraph which probably reads:—

"I accept the terms set out in your letter dated 24.07.79. I enclose a signed direct debit mandate/other remittance." The copy furnished to me does not show that it had been completed by the Plaintiff.

Whenever the policy was furnished to the Plaintiff, the first recital stated that the Plaintiff had delivered the proposal as the basis of the policy and the second recital is as follows:

"This policy is not in force until the first premium has been paid to the Company or, if the premiums are expressed in the Schedule to be payable by monthly payments, until the first such payment has been made."

In the Schedule the "Effective Date" is expressed to be 17.08.79. On the same page the "Date Risk Assumed" is stated to be 31.08.79. The date of the policy is expressed as follows:— "Date as Date Risk Assumed in the Schedule within."

I have no note of any evidence as to the date of payment of the first premium by the Plaintiff although I have a note that he paid a cheque to his broker, but it is stated in the amended defence to have been paid on 31st August, 1979, and I think I can safely assume that it was paid after what has been described as the effective date. What relevance the effective date had to the policy is not clear to me other than that it was the date from which premiums were to be paid and calculated, but it is not suggested that anything turns on this. I feel, however, that the terms of the policy should have been stated in simple language rather than by reference to terms used without definition.

On 9th August, 1979, the Plaintiff attended his doctor complaining of a head cold and some pain in his chest. The doctor found that he had an infection of the throat which he considered to be a common minor illness and he put the Plaintiff on antibiotics for five days. The Plaintiff returned to his doctor on the 16th August complaining that he still had a cough and the doctor diagnosed an infection of the air passages in the lungs, a form of bronchitis, which he stated is a very common complication of a head cold and he put the Plaintiff on different antibiotics for a further five days. He stated in cross-examination that bronchitis could be serious if chronic but that he had no reason to consider that this was chronic and still considered that the

Plaintiff had only a minor illness which was merely of nuisance value to the Plaintiff at work. At no time during August was the Plaintiff off work and the doctor did not make any such recommendation. Both the visits to the doctor took place before the effective date and about a fortnight before the Date Risk Assumed. On 5th September the senior doctor in the practice, who had been on holiday during August, thought the Plaintiff's symptoms were only minor although annoying to him at work.

In the middle of September, 1979, the Plaintiff's condition began to get worse and he was taken off antibiotics which the doctor thought might be the cause of the trouble. The doctor advised the Plaintiff to go ahead with a holiday to America which had been arranged for the end of October. The Plaintiff did go for his holiday but on his return, he became very much worse and did not recover until September 1980. It was accepted by the Plaintiff's doctors that what happened in August was the beginning of the illness which incapacitated the Plaintiff.

Evidence was given on behalf of the Defendant by an independent insurance representative and by a representative of the Defendant who both stated that they consider it material to the risk that the Plaintiff had a cold which had not cleared up and had visited his doctor twice notwithstanding that no significance had been attached to the original information disclosed to the Defendant's doctor that the Plaintiff had a cold. I was somewhat unhappy about that part of the second witness's evidence which seemed to suggest that, because the Plaintiff's cold was a viral infection, he would have thought of cancer because he had heard that cancer is a viral illness, although no medical evidence was called to establish any connection and no suggestion of any connection was put to the Plaintiff's doctors. No medical evidence at all was called on behalf of the Defendant.

Both these witnesses stated that an insurance company would postpone or suspend a risk if it was made aware that the proposer was attending a doctor for a cold and that antibiotics had been prescribed without success. One of them also said that, if a company was made aware that a person was suffering from a cold the company would postpone the risk until it had cleared up. He agreed that he could refuse, load or accept the risk but said he would postpone to see if the infection cleared up.

On behalf of the Plaintiff it is argued that the continuation of the Plaintiff's cold was not material to the risk, particularly as there was a deferred period of thirteen weeks before any liability for illness could arise. It was urged that the test of materiality is whether knowledge of the continuation of a cold and the visits to the doctor would at that time have caused a prudent insurer to refuse the insurance and that the onus of proving materiality is on an insurer. I was referred to the cases of *Chariot Inns Ltd.* v. *Assicurazioni Generali S.p.a. & Others*[50] and *Mutual Life Insurance Co. of New York* v. *Ontario Metal Products Ltd.*[51]

It has not been disputed that the onus is on the Defendant to establish

---

[50] [1981] I.R. 199 and [1981] I.L.R.M. 173. See p. 233 of this book.
[51] [1925] A.C. 344.

materiality but it is urged that the evidence of the two insurance representatives does establish that the information which was withheld was material and would have been so considered by a prudent insurer. Although the amended defence suggests that this aspect was considered no argument was advanced on the basis that there was a contractual duty to disclose the Plaintiff's condition in August arising by reason of the statement at the foot of the proposal form and the recital in the policy that the proposal was delivered as the basis of the policy.

The submission and evidence on both sides related solely to the question of the materiality of the non-disclosure of the visits by the Plaintiff to his doctor in August and I propose to confine myself to a consideration of this.

The following passage from the judgment of Kenny J., at page 226 of the *Chariot Inns*[52] case sets out how I must approach my consideration of this question. He said

> "What is to be regarded as material to the risk against which the insurance is sought? It is not what the person seeking the insurance regards as material nor is it what the insurance company regards as material. It is a matter of circumstance which would reasonably influence the judgment of a prudent insurer in deciding whether he would take the risk, and, if so, in determining the premium which he would demand. The standard by which materiality is to be determined is objective and not subjective. In the last resort the matter has to be determined by the Court: the parties to the litigation may call experts in insurance matters as witnesses to give evidence of what they would have regarded as material, but the question of materiality is not to be determined by such witnesses."

In the case of the *Mutual Life Insurance Co. of New York*,[53] which concerned a policy of life insurance, Lord Salvesen giving the judgment of the Privy Council, said at page 351 "the appellant's counsel suggested that the test was whether, if the fact concealed had been disclosed, the insurers would have acted differently either by declining the risk at the proposed premium or at least by delaying consideration of its acceptance until they had consulted Dr Fierheller. If the former proposition were established in the sense that a reasonable insurer would have so acted, materiality would, their Lordships think, be established but not in the latter case if the difference of action would have been delay and delay alone."

To this I would add that the options open to an insurer are to accept the contract, refuse the contract or make a new offer at an increased premium. There cannot be any course of accepting the premium and waiting until it was seen how the proposer's health progressed so that, if the infection cleared up the proposer would be held covered in future with his premium based for future reference as of the effective date but that if some complication developed, the proposer's premium would be returned to him and the policy cancelled.

Having regard to the decisions to which I have been referred I am of

---

[52] [1981] I.R. 199 and [1981] I.L.R.M. 173.
[53] [1925] A.C. 344.

opinion that the evidence has not established the probability that the non-disclosure of the visits by the Plaintiff to his doctor in August were material to the risk. On this assessment the Plaintiff is entitled to succeed in his Action.

Olive Curran *v.* Norwich Union Life Insurance Society
Unreported, 30 October 1987
The High Court

BARR J: In February, 1985 William Curran, the late husband of the plaintiff, entered into a contract with the defendant Society which was primarily an investment scheme but which also provided life cover in the sum of £12,330.00 payable should the insured die during the currency of the contract and while the market value of units purchased on his behalf from monthly instalments of £70.00 payable by him to the defendant was less than the sum insured.

The contract was based upon a written declaration dated 16th February, 1985 and duly signed by the deceased which, inter alia, is in the following terms:—

> "... to the best of my knowledge and belief I am presently in good health and I am not in receipt of medical treatment."

No medical examinations or investigations were envisaged by the defendant as being necessary in the ordinary course in connection with such contracts.

It will be observed that, unlike the detailed medical and allied information sought in most proposal forms for life insurance, a person making the declaration in question is asked only to confirm to the best of his knowledge and belief that at the time of making it he is in good health and not undergoing any medical treatment. The reasons given by Mr Goss, the defendant's principal underwriter in Ireland, why such declarations are so limited in nature by comparison with the norm are twofold. First, the life insurance element in such contracts very rarely gives rise to claims because it is usually of comparatively short duration and is of minor practical significance to the underwriter. Secondly, such contracts are available only to persons who already hold life policies with the defendant and, therefore, proposal forms containing detailed health information would have been already submitted by them. For these reasons the defendant's underwriters take the view that in this particular type of transaction they need enquire only into the state of health of the proposer at the date of his application for cover.

I am satisfied that although the contract in question is primarily a scheme for saving and investment, it contains in it a significant element of life insurance and that the declaration made by the applicant, which I have quoted, relates to the life cover which forms part of the parcel on offer. Accordingly, as with all forms of insurance contract the standard required of the declarant as to the disclosure of all information relevant to the insurance required is uberrima fides.

The medical/surgical background to the declaration made by Mr Curran is as follows:—

In March, 1984 he suffered a severe head injury in a traffic accident which necessitated intermittent lengthy hospitalisation for about 6 months. He was discharged from Lourdes Rehabilitation Hospital at Dún Laoghaire in September, 1984 and I am satisfied from the plaintiff's evidence that her husband had good reason to regard himself as having made a full recovery at that time subject only to regaining strength and mobility. He was not warned of the risk of epilepsy in the future, nor was he advised to remain under any form of medical supervision or treatment. His rehabilitation proceeded uneventfully and by the following February he appeared to have been restored to his full pre-accident state of good health. Accordingly, having regard to the wording of the declaration, he would have had no obligation to disclose the head injury sustained by him in 1984 but for an event which took place shortly before the declaration was signed by him and submitted to the defendant. During the night of 13th/14th February, 1985, two days before the declaration was made, Mr Curran while in bed asleep had a severe attack of shivering which was witnessed by his wife. He was unaware of having had the attack and seemed to be in good health and none the worse of it on the following morning. However, the plaintiff was disturbed by what she had seen and, contrary to her husband's wishes, she contacted the family doctor, Dr Patrick Mangan, who also gave evidence. He related the attack to the deceased's head injury and concluded that it was likely to have been a minor epileptic manifestation which might never occur again but which in his opinion required daily medication for at least one year as a precautionary measure. He visited the deceased on 14th February and believes that he explained to him his diagnosis and the necessity for taking the prescribed medication. In the event, unknown to his wife and doctor until after his death, the deceased did not take the tablets which had been prescribed for him.

On 16th February, 1985 Mr Curran signed the declaration and submitted it to the defendant thus indicating to them that to the best of his knowledge and belief he was then in good health and was not receiving any medication. His application was duly accepted and the required policy document was issued. On 28th June, 1985 the insured was found dead in his garage/workshop where he had been working alone for some hours. The plaintiff, who is executrix of the estate of the deceased, claimed from the defendant the death benefit of £12,330.00 payable on foot of the policy. The insurer repudiated liability on the ground that the deceased's declaration of good health on which the contract was based was untrue to his knowledge at the time when it was made.

The standard of care required for a proposer for insurance as to the disclosure of facts material to the insurance sought by him has been laid down by the Supreme Court in *Chariot Inns* v. *Assicurazioni Generali*[54] — see in particular the opening paragraphs of the Judgment of the Court delivered by Kenny, J. at pp 225/6 which are as follows:—

> "A contract of insurance requires the highest standard of accuracy, good faith, candour and disclosure by the insured when making a proposal for

---

[54] [1981] I.R. 199 and [1981] I.L.R.M. 173. See p. 233 of this book.

insurance to an insurance company. It has become usual for an insurance company to whom a proposal for insurance is made to ask the proposed insured to answer a number of questions. Any misstatement in the answers given, when they relate to a material matter affecting the insurance, entitles the insurance company to avoid the policy and to repudiate liability if the event insured against happens. But the correct answering of any questions asked is not the entire obligation of the person seeking insurance: he is bound, in addition, to disclose to the insurance company every matter which is material to the risk against which he is seeking indemnity.

What is to be regarded as material to the risk against which the insurance is sought? It is not what the person seeking insurance regards as material, nor is it what the insurance company regards as material. It is a matter or circumstance which would reasonably influence the judgment of a prudent insurer in deciding whether he would take the risk and, if so, in determining the premium which he would demand. The standard by which materiality is to be determined is objective and not subjective. In the last resort the matter has to be determined by the Court: the parties to the litigation may call experts in insurance matters as witnesses to give evidence of what they would have regarded as material, but the question of materiality is not to be determined by such witnesses".

In the light of the foregoing it is clear that Mr Curran had a duty to disclose to the insurers the fact that a few days previously he may have suffered a minor epileptic seizure for which his doctor deemed it wise to prescribe continuing medication and that he might be at risk of a further similar attack in the future. These were material facts which I am satisfied a prudent insurer would be likely to investigate further and to take into account in its assessment of the risks proposed. I accept the evidence of Mr Goss in that regard. It was immaterial to the deceased's duty of disclosure in the circumstances of the case that he himself may have bona fides believed, notwithstanding his doctor's diagnosis, that the episode on the night of the 13th/14th February was not epileptic in nature and had no connection with his prior head injury. The inescapable fact remains that he had good reason, based on professional medical advice, to believe that he may have had such an attack and that itself was a material fact which should have been disclosed to the insurers regardless of what his personal opinion as to what his state of health may have been. Likewise, he had a duty to disclose that continuing medication had been prescribed for him by Dr Mangan. Accordingly, in the premises I am obliged to hold that the defendant was entitled to repudiate the contract on the ground that the declaration of health made by the deceased was misleading in material particulars pertinent to the insurer's assessment of the risk proposed.

I wish to make clear however that I accept unreservedly the evidence of the plaintiff regarding the probity and integrity of her late husband. There is no evidence to suggest that in making the declaration he consciously and deliberately set out to deceive the defendant. It seems highly unlikely that he adopted that course.

Accordingly, I allow the defendant's appeal and discharge the Order of the Circuit Court. No order as to costs.

CHAPTER 8

Warranties

A warranty is essentially a term in the contract of insurance whereby the insured vouches that certain statements of fact made by him are entirely accurate or that he will perform a specific obligation in a given manner. In the event of a breach of such a warranty the insurer is entitled to repudiate all liability under the contract from the date of breach, irrespective of the materiality of that breach to the contract or to a loss arising. Because of the obvious significance of determining whether or not a given statement is a warranty, much early judicial discussion concentrated on distinguishing warranties from mere representations, which would have to be material before their breach would justify repudiation. This is particularly evident in the early case of *Quin* v. *National Assurance Company* (1837) and shortly thereafter in *Anderson* v. *Fitzgerald* (1853). In the latter case the House of Lords held that the onus was very much on the insurer to prove that it was indeed a warranty that had been breached and that the insurers had used clear and unambiguous language in incorporating it into the contract of insurance. Even then it was to be construed very much against the insurer. This is echoed in the earlier case of *Scanlan* v. *Sceals* (1841) and in almost all cases involving warranties since then. In *Rose* v. *Star Insurance Company* (1850), it was further emphasised that the warranty under consideration had to be further interpreted in a manner in keeping with common sense, and emphasising the non-legal character of the persons effecting such policies of insurance.

Virtually all the Irish cases to date have dealt with breaches of warranties of fact by the insured at the inception of the policy and made by the insured when proposing for insurance. It has long been a practice of insurance companies to incorporate answers in proposals forms into the contract of insurance and to have the insured warrant the veracity of the answer given. This is done by means of a "basis of contract" clause whereby the answers given are said to form the basis of the contract and that the correctness of an answer given will be a condition precedent to liability under the policy. This practice is evident in the early cases and more recently in *Farrell* v. *South East*

Lancashire Insurance Company Limited (1932) and *Irish National Assurance Company Limited* v. *O'Callaghan* (1934). Both cases involved policies in which the answers to questions in the proposal forms were warranted to be true and the insurers were successful in both. Similarly in *Griffen* v. *Royal Liver Friendly Society* (1941) insurers were also successful.

The most graphic example of how such a basis of contract can be utilised by insurers is to be seen in *Keenan* v. *Shield Insurance Company Limited* (1987). A trivial incorrect answer which had been warranted to be true, though in no way material to the policy of insurance or the loss claimed, was held to entitle the insurer to repudiate liability under the policy.

The very strict approach of the courts in interpreting the scope and extent of what are alleged to be warranted answers in a proposal form is also evident in the judgment of Mr Justice Keane in *Chariot Inns Limited* v. *Generali Assicurazioni Spa and Coyle Hamilton, Hamilton Philips Limited* (1981).[1]

The Supreme Court, however, in *Keating* v. *New Ireland Assurance Company plc* (1989) was extremely critical of the use by insurers of such warranties and basis of contract clauses. While it was accepted that parties to an insurance contract were free to contract as they pleased, the Court emphasised that if such a clause were to be given effect it would be necessary for insurers relying on it to have used exceptionally clear language and to have explained carefully to the insured exactly what was being warranted and the legal implications of such a warranty. In addition, any such warranty was to be read restrictively and against the insurer. New Ireland were not able to satisfy these requirements and their attempt to avoid paying out under the policy failed.

Few cases involving promissory or continuing warranties have come before the Irish courts. Such warranties exist throughout the term of the policy and exist to ensure primarily that there is no increase in the risk or the insurer's potential liability under the policy. The courts are wary of construing warranties as so continuing. In *In Re Sweeney and Kennedy's Arbitration*[2] it was held that a reply in a proposal form duly warranted to be true only related to facts existing at the time the answer was given and not to facts existing during the term of the policy. The High Court held that if the insurers had so intended they should have used clear and unambiguous language. This was something entirely within the insurer's own control and any

---

[1] This case appears in Chapter 7 at p. 233.
[2] This case appears in Chapter 6 at p. 185.

such failure by them to use such clear and unambiguous language would be fatal.

Quin *v.* National Assurance Company[*]
(1839) Jo. & Car. 316
Exchequer Chamber

JOY C.B: This case comes before the court, on a bill of exceptions, to the charge of my Lord Chief Justice Bushe. It was an action on a policy of insurance tried at Monaghan, at the Summer assizes, 1836, the defence was, that there was a misdescription of the premises, and the question left to the jury, was, whether the description given was false, if so, was that description material? Upon this, there arise two questions, first, whether, the description is to be considered as a mere representation, and not material? or, second, whether it amounts to a warranty, for if it is a warranty, it must be true in fact, whether the difference is material or not. There is no doubt there was a misdescription here, but then it is said on the part of the plaintiff, that it is merely a representation and of a fact not material; let us then first consider whether there was not a misrepresentation, and in a material point too, let us see what was the description, and compare it with the actual state of the premises; the description is this, "The building of a dwelling house, then "occupied by a care-taker, brick and stone built, and slated", the evidence was that it was an unfinished house, in which a carpenter carried on his trade, for ten months, with another carpenter occasionally assisting him, and using the drawing-room as a workshop. There was much argument at the bar on the meaning of the word dwelling-house; Mr Andrews contending that because a gentleman had lived in it, though in room to which he could only get access by a ladder, that constituted it a dwelling-house, and Mr Napier insisting that the question whether dwelling-house or not, was a strict question of law; we are not, however, to consider it as a question of law, but the question is what a person ordinarily using these words would mean; what one would understand by these words, as used by another, it must be taken in its popular sense, and if the house here had remained in its confined state in the occupation of a care-taker merely, that would not in my opinion increase the risk, I should not take it to be a misdescription; but it appears that this building was occupied by a working carpenter, who kept the drawing-room for his workshop, brought in another carpenter occasionally to assist him in his trade, and for ten months carried on his trade there, having no other workshop or place of residence, therefore this is not at all like the case of a gentleman residing, and calling in a carpenter to do an occasional job; all the work he did for ten months, was done in the drawing-room, does not the fact of two carpenters working among shavings, chips, &c., increase the risk? He is described as a caretaker, is that true? Certainly not. It appeared that twenty-five pounds worth of timber was put into the house, into the kitchen; together

---

[*] Extract.

with straw, turf and potatoes. We all know his wife would have to go there every day for potatoes, and for turf, and the carpenters for timber: the windows of the room were all built up, the room was dark, and how they could go into a dark room for these several articles, we may all conjecture. It is not, therefore, at all surprising that the fire broke out there. With respect to the materiality of this, the test is whether the company would have required a larger premium if the description had been according to the fact. The issues that the parties agreed should go to the jury were, first, whether the premises were duly described, or so as to cause the insurance to be effected at a lower premium than proposed by the table, referred to in the eighth proposal. Second, whether the premises were duly described, and were not described otherwise than as they really were, so as to cause the insurance to be effected at a lower premium than they ought to have been. Third, whether from the description and representation of the plaintiff, the premises were insured at a lower rate of premium than they ought to have been. In the two last of these there is no mention of, or allusion to the proposals contained in the table. These issues relate not to what might have taken place with other companies, but what would have been the case with the defendant's company had they known the actual circumstances of the premises; this is important in relation to Todhunter's evidence, who had been for eleven years officer of the company, and whose evidence goes entirely to show what effect the knowledge of the actual circumstances of the premises would have had on the defendants, but then it is said that the judge should have left the question to the jury, whether the misdescription was material or not. Was it not the leaving it to the jury, as the judge did, to say whether they believed his evidence, substantially leaving it to them to say whether the misdescription was material, and so it must have appeared to the plaintiff's counsel, at the trial, for there is no exception taken to the charge of the learned judge on this head. We must therefore take it that it was so left, and that it was material. The exception is to the admissibility of Todhunter's evidence, *not* the effect of it, now the question was not what the insurance companies in general would do, but what this insurance company would do in such case, and how would that be proved, save by the evidence of a person, who knew what they had theretofore done in like cases; Todhunter states from his experience, that if the facts had been known, it would have increased the premium. The remark of Gibbs, C.J., in *Durrell* v. *Bedderly*,[3] is relied upon by the plaintiff's counsel, as decisive upon the point that this evidence was inadmissible but I never could assent to this authority; such evidence had been admitted in two cases which came before Lord Mansfield, *Carter* v. *Boehm*,[4] and *Syers* v. *Bridge*.[5] As to its weight, in *Carter* v. *Boehm*,[6] Lord Mansfield thought it had very little, as the opinion of the witness was not founded on any precedent or usage, but the very reason which Lord Mansfield there gives, bears strongly in favour of the admission of, and credit to be given to Todhunter's evidence here; for *his*

---

[3] Holt, N.P.C. 283.
[4] 3 Burrow, 1905.
[5] Dougl. 527.
[6] 3 Burrow, 1905.

opinion is founded entirely *"on precedent and usage"*, on his own knowledge of what had been always done in like cases by the defendants; in *Syers* v. *Bridge*,[7] the opinion was still more objectionable, for the witnesses could say nothing of any usage, and knew of no instance; what was the purpose for which the witnesses were called in *Durrell* v. *Bedderly?*[8] To prove that if the rumours, stated had been communicated *to them*, they would not have engaged in the risk, not what underwriters in general would have done. Gibbs C.J. says rightly, that was matter of fancy, and in which the diversity might be endless; and he does not say underwriters generally, but the underwriters who were called for the purpose above mentioned.

Having observed upon this mere *nisi prius* decision of Justice Gibbs, I shall now just advert to the authorities on the other side, for the admissibility of such evidence. In *Bertham* v. *Loughman*,[9] the opinions of underwriters as matter of judgment, whether particular facts, if disclosed to an underwriter, would make a difference as to the amount of the premium, were admitted by Holroyd, that was a *nisi prius* opinion, and I set it off against the other already adverted to, but I now come to a case decided before the full court, in *Richard's* v. *Murdoch*,[10] it was held that the opinion of underwriters, as to the materiality of a fact not communicated, was properly received in evidence, Lord Tenderden, in giving judgment makes some observations upon this kind of evidence, in the reasons of which I entirely concur; I therefore think Todhunter's evidence was admissible; but independently of this view of the case, I am clearly of opinion that this was a *warranty*, not a representation, and the materiality of the misdescription is then out of the question. In *Newcastle Fire Insurance Compy.* v. *Macmorran & Co.*,[11] Lord Eldon lays down the law accordingly,

> "It is a first principle of the law of insurance on all occasions, that where a representation is material, it must be complied with; if immaterial, that immateriality may be enquired into and shewn, but if there is a warranty, it is part of the contract that the matter is such as it represented to be: therefore the materiality or immateriality signifies nothing, whether the misdescription arose from mistake, fraud or any other cause, it makes no difference. The only question is as to the mere fact, for in warranty it must be actually true."

His remarks as to printed proposals (on which such stress has been laid in the present case), are to the point;

> "In the appellants case it is stated that the printed proposals formed part of the contract, and that besides being referred to, a copy is always delivered to the party insuring, and that it is there set out that if any person or persons, shall insure, &c, &c., and cause same to be described &c., &c., so as the same shall be insured at a lower rate of premium than that proposed in the table,

---

[7] Dougl. 527.
[8] Holt, N.P.C. 283.
[9] 2 Stark N.P.C. 259.
[10] 10, B. & C. 540.
[11] 3 Dow. P.C. 255.

such insurance shall be of no force; as to their setting it out in their printed
proposals, in the case of a warranty, it is unnecessary to consider that; for if
there is a warranty, the person warranting undertakes that the matter is
such as he represents it; and unless it be so, whether it arise from fraud,
mistake, negligence of agent or otherwise, then the contract is not entered
into, there is in reality no contract".

To what then do the proposals apply? The proposals apply to a case of
mere representation, and not to a case of warranty, in a case of warranty they
have no effect. And if it was a warranty, Todhunter's evidence was not
necessary for the defendant, and they were the only party entitled to *quarrel*
with the judge's charge for not ruling it to be a warranty; it did not lie in the
plaintiff's mouth to complain. A warranty according to Mr Justice Parke, in
his treatise on insurance is that which makes a part of the written policy; a
representation is not part of the written contract, but collateral to and independent of it, so Lord Mansfield in *Pawson* v. *Watson*,[12]

> "There is no distinction better known to those who are conversant with the
> law of insurance, than that which exists between a warranty or condition,
> which makes part of a written policy, and a representation of the state of the
> case, (and adds) where it is part of the written policy, it must be performed
> strictly".

Instructions given for effecting the policy, are not part of the written policy,
but mere representation, and Lord Mansfield said, in answer to an inquiry
from the underwriters, that to make written instructions binding as a warranty, they must be inserted in the policy....

Anderson *v.* Fitzgerald[*]
(1853) 4 H.L. Cas. 484
The House of Lords

CRANWORTH L.C: ... Thus, if a person effecting a policy of insurance says — "I
warrant such and such a thing, which is here stated, and that is a part of the
contract", then whether they are material or not is quite unimportant. The
party must adhere to his warranty, whether material or immaterial; but if the
party makes no warranty at all, but simply makes a certain statement, if that
statement be made *bona fide*, unless it is material, it does not signify whether
it is false or not false. Indeed, whether made *bona fide* or not, if it is not
material, the untruth is quite unimportant. If the man, on entering into the
policy, had said that he arrived at Dublin three days previously, whereas he
had only arrived that morning, it would be quite immaterial. If there be no
fraud in the representation of that sort, it is perfectly clear that it forms no
part of the contract. Even if it be material in such a case, if there be no fraud
in it, and it forms no part of the contract, it cannot vitiate the right of the

---

[12] Coup 785.
[*] Extract.

party to recover. There are several cases which are collected together in *1 Douglas*, in which this principle is well illustrated. But, my Lords, it appears to me that the principle has no application to a case where it is part of the contract, as it is here, that if a particular statement be untrue, then the contract shall be at an end. That distinction appears to me to have been overlooked by the learned Judges, and that oversight has been the ground of which I must consider to be the erroneous conclusion at which they arrived. My Lords, it is within this narrow compass the case lies. We have had the assistance of eleven of the learned Judges of this country. They all took the same view of this case, and were of the opinion that the learned Judges in Ireland committed an error in supposing that this doctrine of representation, as distinguished from a warranty, was applicable to the present case, in which the representation is itself embodied in the contract. They thought the conclusion at which the learned Judges in Ireland arrived was erroneous. My Lords, in that view of the case I entirely concur. Therefore, I shall think it is my duty to move your Lordships that judgment be given for the plaintiff in error.

Scanlan *v.* Sceals and The Caledonian Insurance Company*
(1843) 6 Ir. L.R. 367
Court of Exchequer of Pleas

PENNEFATHER B: I concur in opinion with the Chief Baron, that these exceptions should be overruled, and I do so very much on the grounds upon which he has put the case. It is quite true that matter of warranty must be literally complied with; but I think it is not going too far to say, that parties contracting upon such strict terms, should very clearly demonstrate their intention and meaning; and that if a policy is to be avoided by a literal deviation from what is stated, although that deviation be not substantial — although it be not material — and although no injury has been thereby sustained, such a contract ought to be clearly and unequivocally expressed.

It was formerly the rule that matter of warranty should appear on the face of the policy, and that it should be contained in the instrument itself, but a relaxation of that rule has taken place; and it is now, as I apprehend, clearly settled, that conditions although not contained in the policy or actually on the back of the instrument, may be so referred to by it as to be incorporated with, and made to form part of it. But to give them that effect, the intention so to incorporate them must be clearly and unequivocally expressed. In the case of the policy of the Atlas Insurance Company, which came before the Court of Common Pleas in England, in *Everett* v. *Desborough*,[13] referred to by the Chief Baron, the conditions indorsed on the policy contained amongst other things these words in No. 9:—

"The names and residences of two gentlemen to be referred to respecting the

---

* Extract.
[13] 5 Bing. 503.

present and general state of health of the life to be assured — *one to be the usual medical attendant of the party*".

That clause is followed by these words:—

> "A declaration as to all the above points will be considered as the basis of the contract between the assured and the Company. If the above declaration shall not be in all respects *true*, then the policy will become void, and the premiums that may have been paid will be forfeited."

That clause was in the conditions indorsed on the policy; and in the declaration as well as in the policy itself, is contained a proviso

> "that the policy and the assurance thereby effected, should at all times and under all circumstances, be subject to such conditions and stipulations as were contained in the printed proposals indorsed thereon, in the same manner as if the same were wholly and actually repeated and adapted to the present case".

So that not only were the conditions and the declaration made in compliance therewith, free from ambiguity (for they use the word "true", and that alone), but the policy itself refers to the entire of the declaration, not taking out or selecting particular parts of it, but alluding to the whole as if the same were inserted therein in words and figures.

The parties contracting therefore knew, and must have known what they were contracting about. There was no ambiguity there; it was perfectly clear that the Company stipulated that the declaration should be strictly observed in all its parts; that it should be, as it were, inserted in the policy; and the person whose life was insured agreed to these terms; and consequently, if he imposed any thing on himself he was aware of it, and did so voluntarily and with his eyes open.

But is that the present case? In the first place, is the declaration itself unequivocal? [I]s it so free from ambiguity that a party must be quite aware that if he deviates from the statements made, although in a matter which may be immaterial, his policy is to be thereby avoided and lost? The conclusion of the declaration is in these terms:

> "I, Edmond Fitzmaurice," &c., "do hereby agree, that what is above set forth and stated by me, is the strict truth, and shall be the basis of the contract of this insurance between the Caledonian Insurance Company and me; and if it shall hereafter appear that any of the matters set forth, have not been truly and fairly stated, or if any material fact connected with the health or habits of the life proposed for insurance shall be withheld from the knowledge of the Directors", &c., "then the insurance to be null and void."

Now the fair and reasonable construction of that declaration seems to be this:— "I stipulate that this declaration shall be the basis of my contract to this extent, that if any thing be untruly and unfairly stated — if any material matter have been misrepresented, then the policy is to be void."

The declaration in this case then differs, in my mind, essentially from that in the case of the Atlas Insurance Company, in *Everett* v. *Desborough*.[14]

In order to ascertain the true nature of the contract in this case, we must look to the declaration and the policy. In construing these different instruments, we must compare them one with the other, and endeavour to find out exactly the meaning of the contracting parties, keeping in mind the proposition I set out with, viz.:— that where any thing is to be made a matter of warranty, or in other words, where the Company mean to rely on the mere truth of a fact, whether material or not, they should take care to have their intention clearly and specifically expressed.

The declaration then being so framed, the Company having it in their power to take out of it and select such parts as they thought fit to make a matter of warranty — (for it is not disputed that they might make the most immaterial thing matter of warranty), we find they enter into the policy in these words:—

["Form of life assurance declaration, always to be referred to as the *bona fide* basis of agreement between the Company and the assured. Submitted, 21st of June 1838. Disposed, 26th of June 1838. Policy, No. 1169.

Name, residence, and profession or occupation of the person effecting the assurance with the Company — 'Edmond Fitzmaurice, writing clerk, Dominick-Street, Cork'

Name, residence, and profession or occupation of the person on whose life the assurance is to be made — 'Edmond Fitzmaurice (same).'

Place and date of birth — 'Ballylongford, county Kerry; February 1789.'

Age next birth-day — 'Fifty years.'

If been abroad beyond Europe, how long, and where? — 'No.'

Term for which the assurance is to be made with the Company — 'For life.'

Sum to be assured — '£1,500.'

State if the life had the measles and small pox, or cow pock? — 'Yes, all of them.'

State if the assured at any time has been afflicted with gout, insanity, asthma, habitual cough, dropsy, liver complaint, fits, hernia, rheumatism, disease of the heart, erysipelas, delirium tremens, or been subject to chest disease, consumption, or spitting of blood? — 'No.'

Or if at any time been subject to, or afflicted with any other disorder or ailment tending to impair the constitution or shorten life, or has he suffered any severe accidents in his lifetime — 'No.'

Is the life proposed for insurance of active, and *strictly temperate* habits? — 'Yes.'

Has he always been so? — 'Yes.'

Is he warranted now in a state of perfect good health? 'Yes.'

Is the proposer aware, or has he heard of any circumstance not specially included among the preceding inquiries, which would probably affect the acceptance of the proposed insurance, by the Directors, or the amount of premium to be paid in respect thereof? —'No.'

Reference to the usual medical attendant, on the life, or their family, as

---

[14] 5 Bing. 503.

to the present, past, and general state of health and habits of the life to be assured? — 'Never had a medical attendant until Dr Ludgate dressed his leg when it was scalled, his certificate accompanies this.'

Similar reference to a private friend? — 'Mr Michael Barry, sent herewith.'*

I, 'Edward [sic] Fitzmaurice', the party proposing the preceding assurance, do hereby declare and agree that what is above set forth, and stated by me is the strict truth, and shall be the basis of the contract of this insurance between The Caledonian Insurance Company and me. And if it shall hereafter appear, that any of the matters set forth have not been truly and fairly stated, or any material fact connected with the health or habits, occupation, or my interest in, and of the life proposed for insurance, should be withheld from the knowledge of the Directors, or if my said interest in the policy shall cease, then all monies which shall have been paid in consequence thereof shall be forfeited, and the insurance itself shall be absolutely null and void. And I do hereby declare my accession to the articles of agreement of the Caledonian Insurance Company, recorded in the books of council and session on the 20th day of December 1833, in Scotland; by which it is declared that no member or partner shall incur or be liable to any personal responsibility for the claims of the insured or others, on the said Company; nor the real or personal estate of any partner or member, as an individual, be affectable by the same in any way whatever; and I hereby agree that in the event of any difference arising between the Company and myself, when claim comes to be made, that the same shall be submitted to arbitration, according to the terms of the Company's conditions.

Dated at Cork, and signed by me upon the 20th day of June 1838.

Edmond Fitzmaurice."]

... We may perceive by this, that in the first place the declaration is received as the basis of the contract, and that if it be materially untrue, it shall vitiate the policy; but it then goes on to state what are the material parts of that declaration, and among other things describes the age, the health, and the habits of the insured.

The declaration had been made more than a month before, and had remained with them for that time, and they then take out such parts of it as they consider should be inserted in the policy; not referring, as in the case of the Atlas Company, generally to all the printed conditions, but so that the person contracting would see only so much as had been extracted from the declaration on the face of the policy. It then goes on at the conclusion —

"Provided nevertheless, that in case any untrue or fraudulent allegation be contained in the said declaration, deposited in the office as aforesaid, or that any information respecting the past health or habits of the party assured, or other circumstance important for the Directors to know, shall have been

---

* This document, which was entitled "Private Friend's Report", contained the answers to a series of questions submitted by the Directors of the Company to Mr Barry, regarding the health and habits of Fitzmaurice, substantially similar to the questions proposed in the declaration.

withheld from them", &c, "then, and in every such case the policy shall be null and void", &c.

Now, coupling that with the words which I have already referred to in the declaration, it appears to me to convey to the understanding of all parties, that the meaning to be attached to them was,

> "that such parts of this declaration as have been previously inserted in the policy shall be deemed matter of warranty, and that the other parts of the declaration shall be considered important only to the extent of their being material".

To that extent it appears to me, that there is a reference to the declaration in the policy, and beyond that there is none.

In other words, I think the declaration is not incorporated with the policy by any words of reference, beyond the matters therein particularly set forth, and that the other matters stated in the declaration, but omitted in the policy, are, by the agreement of the parties, to be considered of consequence, and to be taken into account only so far forth as they are material. That appears to me to be the true construction to be put upon this instrument, as otherwise it would be holding out a trap for the unwary, and inducing those who had not considered fully all the legal principles that may be brought to bear to defeat their claim, to enter into a contract in which the Company would have the certainty of receiving the premiums, and the party insured the certainty of receiving nothing in return....

Henry Rose *v.* Star Insurance Company
[1850] 2 Ir. Jur. 206
Court of Exchequer of Pleas

PENNEFATHER, B: This action is brought by Mr Henry Rose against Thomas Vanner and others, representing the Star Insurance Company, for a sum secured on an insurance effected in 1844 on the life of Mr Marony. The declaration states the policy in the usual manner, There were several special pleas on the part of the defendant, of which three — the 3rd, 7th and 8th — are relied on. Of these the 7th is put out of the way, by showing that no such statement as that averred in the 7th plea was made by the plaintiff. The 3rd plea avers that a declaration was made by the plaintiff and that this declaration was not true in all its parts. Here we must consider the exact words of the policy; and that clause particularly, as to the construction of which we have heard so much argument. The policy contains an allegation that Mr Marony was not afflicted with gout, cough, &c., or fits since infancy; and had not any other ailments, diseases, or habits having a tendency to shorten life. It was said that in 1841 he was afflicted with a disorder which endangered his life, and that he was bound to inform the company of it. The words "tendency to shorten life", must be connected with "ailments", as well as with "habits", as otherwise it would be impossible to effect any insurance whatsoever. The clause mentions gout, cough, and other disorders, all of a *continuing* character. The word "infancy" applies to fits and disorders of that description, because infants are peculiarly liable to these ailments. As to the others they have all a *continuing tendency* to shorten life, and are therefore mentioned particularly to avoid disputes afterwards. The company say, We will not insure any persons who have had these diseases, or any diseases having the same continuing character, and thus exclude from the category of excepted diseases, all those which have no continuing tendency to shorten life. If the true construction is, that the disease should have a continuing tendency to shorten life — if that is the construction which can be collected from the other diseases enumerated, then this ailment in the throat is not a disease within the meaning of this policy, as having a tendency to shorten life — if this is the true construction, then there is no averment, within the meaning of this policy, made by the plaintiff which was untrue. This disposes of the third plea, and leaves only the eighth. The private friends reported that Marony was a temperate person, and the judge was called on to direct a verdict for the defendant if the jury believed that Marony was not a temperate person, even if they did not believe his intemperance was such as had a tendency to shorten life. We must now consider whether the plaintiff was bound by the statement of the private friends, that Marony was a person of temperate habits. The plaintiff himself replies very cautiously, and does not answer directly; but it is said that he authorised others, and was bound by the answers of the persons he had named. He was only bound by their replies so far as he agreed the questions should be submitted to them — namely, as to the state of his health — and so far as they went beyond this, they gave their answers not under the authority of the plaintiff, and so far may be considered as strangers. It is further said that the plaintiff is to be bound, and must be considered as having given authority, because he signed a printed paper in the same form as that signed by the private friends. The printed paper he signed he filled cautiously; and it is said, that because that paper had the form with the other he must be bound by that other. He can't be bound by a paper he never saw, nor gave any authority to sign. It is said he is bound by the general words in the printed paper signed by him — "That if, in the declaration, or in any paper furnished by me, there be contained any fraudulent matter, the policy should be void". And it is contended, that by reason of these general words, and the paper having been furnished before the completion of the contract, the policy was void. It would be monstrous, considering that this is the paper of the company, to give it a construction adverse to common sense. If this be so, what security would there be for any person insuring? The paper should have been furnished by him, or by his authority. The motion should be refused, and with costs.

RICHARDS B: Unless in the case of personation, it is most unjust to allow a company to disturb insurances after having taken the money of the party. The parties ensuring, are frequently country gentlemen, ladies, and other persons, knowing nothing about the law. The papers are generally filled in the office of the company, and signed merely as a matter of form.

LEFROY B: On all points my brother Pennefather has said so much, and so well, it would be a waste of time to say anything more. The documents seem to be so framed that one part should do away with the effect of the other, and calculated to turn what might be representation into warranty with all its consequences.

John B. Farrell *v.* South East Lancashire Insurance Co. Ltd.
[1933] I.R. 36
The Supreme Court

KENNEDY C.J: This is an appeal on the part of the plaintiff from a judgment of Mr Justice Hanna dismissing the action. The claim arose out of the destruction by fire of an omnibus motor vehicle the property of the plaintiff. The vehicle was, at the time of its destruction, on the road, carrying a number of passengers, of whom two were fatally injured and eleven others claimed to have sustained personal injuries. Subsequently nine actions were instituted in the High Court and four actions in the Circuit Court, by persons alleging that they had sustained personal injuries which they alleged were caused by the negligence of the plaintiff and his agents in the management and control of the omnibus. All the actions were defended by the present plaintiff, and all were dismissed with costs. An appeal was taken to this Court by one of the plaintiffs but it did not proceed to a hearing.

The present action was brought against the defendant Insurance Company by the plaintiff to enforce his claim to be entitled to be indemnified by the Company in respect of the amount of the loss he has sustained by the destruction of the omnibus and also to be indemnified on respect of the costs and expenses incurred by him in the defence of the several actions. His claim was made under a policy of insurance dated the 19th of December, 1928, made by the defendant Company.

Mr Justice Hanna, at the conclusion of the evidence given on behalf of the plaintiff, dismissed the action and gave judgment for the Company with costs. His judgment was based upon the inaccuracy of one of the statements contained in the plaintiff's proposal for insurance, the truth of which statement the Judge held to be the basis of the contract and a condition precedent to the liability of the Company.

The facts as they appear in the Judge's Report may be shortly stated:—

The plaintiff, who was engaged in engineering work, saw a Dennis motor vehicle advertised for sale in December, 1928. He bought it for £140: paid carriage upon it:— £12 6s. 8d., and customs duty:— £52 13s. 4d., bringing the total original cost to the sum of £205. It was a Dennis 20 horse power car of the year 1926. He brought it home, overhauled it, painted it and presented it to the licensing authority as a twenty-seater vehicle. He was required to alter it to a sixteen-seater and to make other alterations which he did, and on the 20th of December he was granted a licence for the vehicle to carry sixteen passengers. He says it cost him about £50 in addition to the original cost to put it on the road.

He had never had an omnibus before. On the recommendation of a friend he went to Messrs Coyles' described as "Insurance Brokers" on the 17th of December, 1928, with a view to obtaining a policy of insurance for the vehicle. In Messrs Coyles' office he interviewed a clerk or assistant employed in the office named William Dunne, and having told him of his business, Dunne procured in the office a printed form of proposal issued by the defendant Company, and discussed with him the amount, nature and extent of the indemnity which he desired to have covered by the proposed insurance. Dunne then took from the plaintiff the particulars required to be filled into the proposal form which had blank spaces to receive such particulars. The plaintiff stated in his evidence that he told Dunne of his purchase, where he had purchased the vehicle and the price he had paid for it, as well as the duty and the freight, and he alleged that he told Dunne that he wished to insure it for £600. Dunne entered particulars on the form in a space reserved for that purpose. The plaintiff enquired as to whether the premium might be paid by instalments as to which Dunne said he would have to put it before his chief and promised to inform him later and in the meantime the plaintiff paid £25 on foot of the premium. Later in the day the plaintiff informed Dunne by telephone that he wished to increase the amount for which he was insuring the omnibus from £600 to £800. He stated in his evidence that he believed that he was entitled to insure it for the sum of £800, believing that it would cost about that sum to replace it.

The proposal form which consisted of a single page, headed at the top "Commercial Motor Proposal Form", contained the following particulars written into the tabulated form as follows:—

Make and type of body . . .	Dennis
H.P.	20
Year of make	1926
Date of purchase	12/12/'28
Actual cash price paid . . .	~~£700.~~ £800
Present Value	~~700.~~ £800
Seating capacity	Twenty-seater
Carrying capacity (including weight of vehicle) .	2 tons 3 cwt.
Number of trailers	—
Registration letter and number . .	S.M. 3560.

In the lower part of the page other particulars were set out, including the name address and occupation of the plaintiff as proposer, the purpose for which the vehicle was to be used, namely, "bus work" whether other insurance desired, where usually garaged and whether previously proposed for insurance, none of which are material to the present case.

At the foot of the page under all these tabulated entries, was the following, in print:—

"I/We warrant the truth of the foregoing and declare that I/We have not concealed any circumstances affecting the risks to be insured against"

under which, in the space for the signature, was the signature of the plaintiff, "J.B. Farrell" and the date, "17th day of December, 1928", which were the only parts of the document in the handwriting of the plaintiff.

The policy of insurance issued by the Company was dated the 19th of December, 1928. On the front page there was, first, a Schedule setting out particulars of the description of the vehicle taken from the proposal form, but, curiously enough, omitting the statement of price paid for which there was no heading in the tabulated schedule, but inserting under the head, "Value of vehicle and accessories" — £800. This was followed by a schedule containing particulars of the policy, the premium, the Company's liability under several headings in respect of any one accident, and at foot, introductory to the operative part of the actual contract which followed on the next page, there was set out prominently an introductory recital as follows:—

> "Whereas the above described Assured has proposed to the effect an insurance with the South East Lancashire Insurance Company, Limited (hereinafter called 'The Company'), and has signed and delivered to the said Company a proposal which the Assured has agreed shall be the basis of the contract for which the insurance hereby intended to be made; and the Assured has paid to the Company the sum set forth in Schedule B. as the premium or consideration for the proposed insurance for the period stated in Schedule A.

On the second page of the policy particulars of the indemnity which the Company bound itself to give to the assured were set out under an agreement in these terms:—

> "Now it is hereby agreed as follows: During the currency of this Policy that is to say at any time before the expiration of the above-mentioned period and during any subsequent period in respect of which the Assured shall pay and the Company shall be willing to accept a Renewal Premium the Company shall be willing to accept a Renewal Premium the Company shall upon and subject to the conditions set out below or endorsed hereon and provided the Assured duly observes such conditions and performs his obligations thereunder such conditions being so far as the nature of them respectively will permit precedent to the right of the Assured to recover hereunder indemnify the Assured against ..."

A number of conditions were set out on the third page of the Policy of which the following condition is relevant to this case:—

> "The due observance and fulfilment of the terms, conditions and endorsements of this Policy by the Insured in so far as they relate to anything to be done or complied with by him, and the truth of the statements and answers in the said Proposal shall be Conditions precedent to any liability of the Company to make any payment under this Policy, and if the insured shall make any claim knowing the same to be false or fraudulent this Policy shall become void and all claims hereunder shall be forfeited".

At the trial the only witnesses examined for the plaintiff were, the plaintiff himself, his solicitor who defended the several actions on his behalf, and a mechanical engineer who gave evidence as to having examined the omnibus on several occasions on behalf of the defendant Company, and who stated that in his opinion the omnibus was worth £200 before the fire and that it would not be repaired now for less than £300. As I have said, no evidence was called on behalf of the Company. William Dunne was not called for either party. The learned Judge did not, however, accept as accurate all the evidence of the plaintiff, having heard him examined and cross-examined before him, but, at the same time stated that he did not believe that the plaintiff intended to defraud by the inaccurate statement as to the price inserted in the proposal. Notwithstanding that the plaintiff denied that there was any discussion as to fixing the amount at £700, the figure so appears under an erasure in the proposal. The Judge held that there must have be some discussion as regards that figure, and he expressly found that Dunne as a result of some such discussion inserted the amount "£700" in the document in the first instance, that is to say, during the interview at which the proposal was signed by the plaintiff. No evidence was given as to the relationship between Messrs Coyle and the defendant Company, nor as to the relationship between Dunne and Coyle beyond the fact appearing from the plaintiff's evidence that Dunne was in Coyle's office as an employee of some kind —produced the proposal form in blank and, when the mode of paying the premium was discussed after the particulars had been filled in, said he would have to put it before "his Chief".

The learned Judge found as a fact that, in filling this form, Dunne was acting not on behalf of the Insurance Company nor of Coyle, but as an agent or friend of Mr Farrell, the plaintiff, and that anything he did was done as agent of the plaintiff.

In these circumstances the Judge held that it was irrelevant whether the untruthful statement inserted in the proposal was an important statement or not inasmuch as the policy contained a proviso that the truth of the statements in the proposal should be the basis of the contract, and he held it to be irrelevant whether the statement made was fraudulently or unintentionally untruthful inasmuch as the truth of the answers was made a condition precedent to the liability of the Company. He accordingly dismissed the action, with costs.

We have heard Mr Gavin Duffy make a learned argument in a gallant attempt to get outside the very obvious difficulties of the case. I will indicate his principal points without attempting to do full justice to them. In the first place he contended that the page containing the proposal was divided into two parts. I cannot agree with this submission. The entire form is contained within a single surrounding line or frame, headed at the top "Commercial Motor Proposal Form" and signed at the foot immediately after the warrant of the "truth of the foregoing". In my opinion, the warranty covers all the statements within the frame of the form including the statements as to price paid and present value, though for my own part, I find it difficult to suppose that a warranty of truth of the present value of a motor vehicle which has been on the road for several years, can be other than a warranty as to the honest belief of the person affirming it that such is the value, or his estimate of the value, of the vehicle at that time, at least in the absence of evidence as to any generally recognised or accepted standards of depreciation in value from original price, depending (say) upon mileage travelled or upon mere age. The warranty as to the price, however, is a wholly different matter. It is a warranty of a fact as to which there can be only one truthful statement, and whether the figure inserted in the space provided in the form for "*actual cash price paid"* was £600, or £700 or £800, it was definitely untrue to the knowledge of the plaintiff, who, indeed, stated that he informed Dunne of the price actually paid in fact, and said that Dunne nevertheless inserted the figures which appeared in the form and which were vouched by the plaintiff's signing the warranty of truth.

Next, assuming, as the Judge found, that the figure of £700 was inserted before the plaintiff put his signature to the document and was altered subsequently as a result of the instructions — perhaps of a misunderstanding of the instructions — which the plaintiff afterwards gave to Dunne by telephone, Mr Gavin Duffy argued that Dunne should not be regarded as the agent of the plaintiff to make the untruthful statement as to the price and value of the vehicle, and he discussed the well-known authorities in this connection.

There was a complete lack of even the slightest evidence to prove or support an inference of fact that either Coyle or his employee Dunne was in any sense an agent of the Company save perhaps, by inference, to the extent of receiving from proposing insurers signed proposal forms for transmission to the Company. There was no evidence that he had authority from the Company even to negotiate with intending insurers for contracts of insurance. On the other hand, there was evidence to support the Judge's finding of fact that Dunne filled in the blanks for particulars in the proposal form, acting in a friendly way on behalf of the plaintiff, in the character of a mere amanuensis writing in to the best of his ability the particulars from the information given him by the plaintiff, making, however, one grave error. But the plaintiff chose to entrust him with the doing of the task, and, adopting it as his own, signed it, vouching the truth of the matters stated. Is there any doctrine or principle of law which compels the Court in face of that state of facts to hold that as a matter of law Dunne was the agent of the Company, and as such agent was possessed for the Company of the truth as to the cash price of the vehicle and that he made the erroneous entry as agent of the Company. I know of none. Even the much distinguished *Bawden* v. *The London, Edinburgh and Glasgow Assurance Co.*[15] would not support such a contention. The opinion of Palles C.B. in *Taylor* v. *Yorkshire Insurance Co.*[16] will be accepted as stating the law on this matter as regards agents of insurance companies in this country, and I respectfully adopt it, noting at the same time that it is not clear whether that opinion was a decision of the Court or not, because the question of an insurance agent's position when filling a proposal form, while Boyd J. merely concurred without stating to which of the other judgments his concurrence was to be attributed.

The Company relied upon:— (1). The express warranty in the proposal of truth of the statements made therein: (2) The recital in the policy that the plaintiff agreed that the proposal should be on the basis of the contract for insurance: (3) The condition endorsed on the policy that the truth of the statements and answers in the proposal should be a condition precedent to

---

[15] [1892] 2 Q.B. 534.
[16] [1913] 2 I.R.I. at pp. 16,17. See p. 489 of this book.

any liability of the Company to make any payment under the policy: (4) The
express agreement in the policy that the endorsed conditions were to be so far
as the nature of them would permit respectively precedent to the right of the
assured to recover thereunder.

Against this formidable array of defensive provisions which the Company
had to hand in the contractual documents, the plaintiff advanced a number of
contentions.

The word "warrant" was said to be a doubtful term not conveying any
certain meaning to the plaintiff. The Judge's report, however, does not show
that the plaintiff made any such case when giving evidence. There is no
suggestion of any doubt or misunderstanding by him of this provision in the
proposal signed by him.

It will be observed that this was not a warranty as to the continuance in
the future of a certain course of conduct but a warranty by which he engaged
himself as to the truth of certain statements of fact then made and (amongst
others) as to his having paid a cash price of £800 for the car. See the distinction drawn by Scrutton L.J., *In re Morgan and Provincial Insurance Co.*[17]
The fact which he undertook to be true was made the basis of the contract in
the policy. The question of materiality of the fact warranted does not enter
into the issue in these circumstances, the truth of the fact, whether material
or immaterial , having been agreed to be the basis of the contract. The argument that evidence of the materiality of the fact to the insurance should have
been adduced by the Company is, in my opinion, wholly untenable in the
existing state of the law in this country. Compare *Newsholme Brothers* v.
Road Transport and General Insurance Co., Ltd.;[18] *In re Morgan and Provincial Insurance Co., Ltd.;*[19] *Dawsons, Ltd,* v. *Bonnia*[20] (in which case the proposal form contained no warranty of the truth of the statements made ; while
the policy contained a condition that *material* mis-statement should render
the policy void); *Mutual Life Insurance Co. of New York* v. *Ontario Metal
Products Co.*[21] (in which case the Court had to deal with special legislation of
the Province raising the materiality of mis-statements).

Looked at from the point of view of description of the risk insured, it is
patent that the insurance risk of a 1926 omnibus sold in 1928 for £140 is a
different insurance risk from that of a similar vehicle sold for £800.

This is undoubtedly a very hard case. But the fact is that the plaintiff, no
doubt innocently, warranted the truth of the statements inserted in the
proposal by Dunne for him, including the untrue statement (made without
fraud, probably by mistake), that the cash price paid for the vehicle was £800
and the contract of insurance was made expressly on the basis of the truth of
that and other statements. The statement was not true and the contract fails.
The appeal must be dismissed with costs....

---

[17] [1932] 2 K.B. 70 at 79 *seq.*
[18] [1929] 2 K.B. 356
[19] [1932] 2 K.B. 70 at 79 *seq.*
[20] [1922] 2 A.C. 413.
[21] [1925] A.C. 344.

FITZGIBBON J: I agree.

MURNAGHAN J: I also agree.

Cornelius O'Callaghan v. Irish National Assurance Co. Ltd.
(1934) 68 I.L.T.R. 248
The High Court

SULLIVAN. P: In this case the Irish National Assurance Company, Ltd., have appealed from a decree for £135 given by Circuit Judge Kenny at Cork in favour of the plaintiff, Cornelius O'Callaghan, in an action in which the plaintiff claimed £165 alleged to be due on foot of five insurance policies effected by him on the life of his father, Timothy O'Callaghan, who died on the 18th April, 1932. The defendant Company resisted the said claim on the grounds (*inter alia*) that the policies in question were void, inasmuch as they had been taken out and granted on the basis that the answers on the proposal forms were true; that the truth of those answers had been warranted by the plaintiff, and that some of those answers, notably those relating to the age of the life assured were untrue. It was proved at the trial before the Circuit Judge, and it was not contested, that the age of the life assured was misstated on the proposal forms forming the basis of the policies.

The Circuit Judge, however, came to the conclusion that he was at liberty to disregard the untrue statements on the proposal forms provided he reduced the amount of the plaintiff's claim to that sum for which the defendant Company would have insured the life of Timothy O'Callaghan if his age had been correctly stated. I am of the opinion, however, that the learned Judge's decision was erroneous.

... The [proposal] forms were either filled in and signed by the plaintiff or signed by him after they had been filled in by the Company's agent. All the proposal forms contained declarations that the answers given were true and correct in every particular. It was not contended for the plaintiff that, in the case of the forms filled in by the agent, the statements were taken from statements contained in policies which the plaintiff had taken out with other companies, and that the onus lay on the defendant Company of proving that the plaintiff knew that the ages stated were incorrect.

In my opinion, however, that contention is unsustainable. The plaintiff was bound by his signature of the declaration warranting the truth of the statements contained in the proposal forms, and some of those statements were untrue. The policies issued to him by the Company on the basis of the answers in those proposal forms were void.

It has been stated in argument that Insurance Companies often made payments in respect of policy moneys where there were incorrect answers to the questions on the proposal forms; but it is necessary to point out that, at least in cases such as this, where the proposal forms contain declarations warranting the truth of the statements therein, which is signed by the proposer for insurance, there is no legal obligation on the Company to make any such payments.

HANNA J: I concur. In cases such as this where the proposal form contains a declaration, signed by the proposer for insurance, that the answers to the questions contained in the proposal form are true, the truth of those answers is the basis of the contract with the Company, and if the answers are untrue the policy is avoided. I am satisfied, on the evidence, that the plaintiff knew this side of insurance business thoroughly, as he had himself been an agent for an insurance company. I am satisfied also that the plaintiff supplied the ages which appeared on the proposal forms. Now it has been taken as common case here that those ages are untruly stated. The Circuit Judge, nevertheless, appeared to have thought that he would disregard the untruth of the answers relative to the ages stated on the proposal forms, and that he could adjust the proposals and the policies to the correct ages in order to calculate what was due, on the assumption that the correct ages had been stated on the proposal forms. I am of opinion, however, that the Circuit Judge had no power to do this and that he should have dismissed the action on the ground I have already stated, namely, that the policies were avoided by the untrue statements.

Ellen Griffen *v.* Royal Liver Friendly Society
(1942) 76 I.L.T.R. 82
The High Court

MURNAGHAN J: ... This was a difficult case. This was an action founded on contract, in which the Plaintiff sued for money alleged to be due under a policy of assurance. The policy was effected early in 1939, the premium being 6d. per week. Shortly afterwards, in August, 1939, the insured died, at which time the Plaintiff had paid only a small amount of premiums. She now sued for the full amount of the policy, namely £48 8s. 6d. The question raised by the Company was, whether the contract was enforceable, having regard to the fact that there were embodied in the contract statements which were contained in the proposal form, for which, it was stated, the Plaintiff was responsible, and which were in fact incorrect.

The Plaintiff's husband was quite a young man, about thirty years of age, at the date of the proposal. He had been working for some months before the insurance was effected. Mr Johnston, one of the Company's officials, had seen him from time to time when he had called to collect premiums on another policy taken out by the deceased.

The Plaintiff did not initiate the policy at all. The deceased had a similar policy for £56 7s. 0d., and the Company's agent suggested to the Plaintiff that she should take a further insurance policy in order to bring the amount up to £100. Before that policy was taken out, Mr Johnston had seen the deceased man frequently, and he made a declaration, required by the Company, recommending Mr Griffin as a good life. But ... it now transpired that Mr Lane, an eminent Dublin surgeon, had had this man under his care at intervals during the preceding eight years, and that he had had several operations, including the excision of a kidney in 1931. In fact, the deceased was suffering from a deep-rooted disease of a tubercular nature, from which he subsequently died.

It was only fair to the Plaintiff to point out that several people had seen her husband at regular intervals, and had regarded him as a normal, healthy man. There was no suggestion that the Plaintiff effected the policy with full knowledge that he was stricken down by disease.

The question of law was, whether the answers on the proposal form, embodied in the contract, contained misstatements of fact which would vitiate the contract. It was asked in this form — was the proposed in good health? That was not a very searching question, and did not go as far as many companies required in the case of life assurance. The second question was as to the nature of the last illness, and the answer given was: "None". That answer was clearly incorrect. The Plaintiff did not justify her answers at all. She said that she did not give the answers; that the form handed to her was blank, and she signed it in order to show that she was the wife of the proposed. The officials of the Company, however, said that the answers, down to the answer to the second question, were put in before the Plaintiff signed the form, and that the purport of the questions was put to her. They did not say that the exact words of the questions were put to her, but that was not material. The Plaintiff, in her evidence, said that when the Company's doctor examined her husband in connection with the policy, her husband was stripped, and that a remark was passed by the doctor, concerning a scar caused by an operation for appendicitis, that he did the right thing in having the appendix removed. The doctor, Dr O'Sullivan, said that Mr Griffin did not strip at all. He asked him to open his chest, examined him for pulmonary tuberculoses. Mr Griffin passed the medical examination as required by the Insurance Company. ... [I believe] that the doctor's account of this examination was more accurate than the Plaintiff's.

The second point against that Plaintiff was that she said that she signed a paper without reading it. But she signed a declaration, which was as follows:—

1. I declare and warrant that the above answers are true, and I agree that the above answers and this declaration shall be the basis of the contract between me and the Society for effecting the Assurance hereby proposed, and that any Policy issued thereon shall become absolutely void, and all, premiums paid shall be forfeited to the Society, in the event of any answer being untrue or if any material fact has been withheld. And I also agree that such Assurance shall be subject in all respects to the Rules (present and future) of the Society.
2. I declare that the Policy is to be taken out by me and that the premiums thereon are to be paid by me.

She said that she just put her name to the paper. That might have occurred, and people might sign forms without reading them, but when a number of witnesses told ... [me] that the form was filled in before, and only the person signing it said the contrary, and without having read the proposal form, ... [I cannot] accept that answer.... [I think] that the substantial parts of the form were filled in before signature. It would have been better if the agents had not asked the Plaintiff to sign the form before all of it was filled in. The agent was ill advised to fill in the answers to certain questions after the form had been signed. If the point were material, ... [I] would have held that Mrs Griffin did not answer other questions filled up after she had signed the form.

The officers of the Society said that they put the question about her husband working, and that Mrs Griffin told them where he was working. She herself admitted she mentioned where he was working. ... [I am] satisfied that there was on the form when she signed it, the answer to the questions, which, as he had said, was an incorrect answer.

It was said on behalf of the Plaintiff that the agents were the agents of the Company to put in the answers to the questions. That point might possibly be made if the form actually put in as a summary of the information the Plaintiff gave to the agents of the Company, it did not seem to ... [me] to be material. There was, of course, the criticism that the agents were too ready to fill in the desired answers to the questions in order to procure the issue of the policy.

There had been very great difficulty about this class of insurance, and the British Legislature had made special provisions dealing with it, as had also Oireachtas Éireann, but subsequently, to the material times in this action. Section 20 (4) of the Industrial Insurance Act, 1923, the British statute, a précis of which appeared on the back of the policy, was as follows:—

"If a proposal form for an industrial assurance policy is filled in wholly or partly by a person employed by the society or company, the society or company shall not, except where a fraudulent statement in some material particular has been made by the proposer, be entitled to question the validity of the policy founded on the proposal on the ground of any misstatement contained in the proposal form:

Provided that —

a) if the proposal form contains a misstatement as to the age of the person whose life is proposed to be assured, the society or company may so adjust the terms of the policy, or of any policy, which may be issued in substitution or in lieu thereof, as to make them correspond with the terms which would have been applicable if the correct age of the person had been originally inserted in the proposal;

b) where but for this sub-section the validity of a policy could have been questioned on the ground of any misstatement in the proposal form relating to the state of health of the person upon whose life the assurance is to be taken out at the date of the proposal, nothing in this sub-section shall prevent such a question being raised, if raised within two years from the date of the issue of the policy founded on the proposal.

The section was referred to on the back of the policy , and in the body of the contract as governing the contract. Although not part of the law in Éire at the time, it was ... made by agreement part of the contract entered into between the parties. That incorporation meant that when the form was filled in by the Company's agents, the ordinary law was gone, that misstatements innocently made could be relied on to avoid the contract. That was a considerable incursion on the general law, but, owing to the Legislature's knowledge of that class of insurance, it was found to be a desirable amendment. ... [I find] that Mrs Griffin had no fraudulent intention at all, but these provisions contained the second proviso ... [I have] mentioned above regarding a misstatement concerning the health of the person to be assured. ... [I have] examined the clause very closely, and Mr Sainsbury had given his comment on it, and ... [I think] that Mr Sainsbury was right — that if an innocent mistake was made where the form was filled in by the officials of the Company, that point could be raised within two years of the date of the issue of the policy. That having been done in this case ... [I] must hold that, even though there was no fraud, there was an innocent misstatement of a material fact, and that that misstatement was sufficient to avoid the policy, as the objection had been made within two years of the issue.

As regarded the point of estoppel raised by Mr Crivon, ... [I do] not see that he could hold that because the doctor — whose position had not been developed beyond this, that he was asked to report on the life — did not find out tuberculosis of the kidney, although he might have had the opportunity of doing so, that he had actual or constructive knowledge of the condition of the assured.

This appeal ... must be dismissed, and the Order of the learned Circuit Judge affirmed.

Patrick Keenan v. Shield Insurance Company Limited
[1987] I.R. 113
The High Court*

BLAYNEY J: This is a claim by the plaintiff to set aside an arbitration award made on the 31st October, 1984. The parties have agreed that the claim raises a single issue and this has been referred to this court for its decision. The issue is as follows:—

"Having regard to the findings of fact set out by the arbitrator in his award herein and as enumerated (1), (2), (3), on p. 3 of the said award, did the arbitrator err in law in reaching his conclusion as set out in para. (4) on p. 3 of the said award?"

The facts giving rise to the arbitration are as follows:—

"1. By a proposal form dated the 22nd September, 1975, signed by the insured, the insured applied to the insurers for insurance cover in respect of the private residence of the insured at Painstown, Donadea, Naas in the County of Kildare and the contents thereof and pursuant to such proposal an insurance policy was issued by the insurers being an "all-in" policy number 80048578 in which the sum insured was given as £14,000 in respect of the buildings therein described and £2,000 in respect of contents of same; the period of insurance being given as 24th September, 1975, to 24th September, 1976; and in addition to the insured the interest of Kildare County Council was noted on the said policy.
2. A fire took place at the said premises on or about the 8th October, 1975,

in respect of which the insured claims to be entitled to be indemnified by
the insurers for destruction of the said premises and the contents
thereof.

3. The insurers have disputed their liability to pay to the insured the sums
claimed by the insured or any sum whatever, on the following grounds:—

   a) It is claimed that there was a misrepresentation of fact and a non-
   disclosure of relevant information by the insured to the insurers
   when making the proposal for said insurance cover, of such nature as
   to entitle the insurers to repudiate liability under the policy and the
   insurers have repudiated liability accordingly."

Other grounds were also set out in the reference, but in light of the terms
of the award they are not relevant.

The arbitrator's award recites the first two paragraphs which I have just
cited from the reference and then sets out as follows the grounds on which the
defendant disputed its liability to indemnify the plaintiff:—

"a) That by virtue of the incorrect reply to question no. 8 on the proposal
form and also by virtue of the declaration at the end of the proposal form
signed by the insured as to the veracity of the answers to the questions
and the acknowledgement that the answers would form the basis of the
contract between the insured and the company there had been a failure
of a condition precedent to the contract of insurance between the insured
and the company and

b) that the answer given to question 8 on the proposal form amounted to a
misrepresentation or concealment of a material fact by the insured."

After some further recitals the arbitrator then made his award in the
following terms :—

"Now I the said James A. Nugent having heard and duly considered the submission of the said parties made through their counsel and the evidence
adduced on their behalf do hereby make and publish this my award of and
concerning the matters so referred to me as aforesaid in the manner following that is to say:—

1) I find that the declaration signed by the insured on the proposal form
whereby he declared that the particulars and answers given by him in
the proposal form were true and complete in every respect and that no
material fact had been suppressed or withheld and further declared that
where any such statement and particulars were in the writing of any
person other than the insured such person should be deemed to have
been the agent of the insured for the purposes of filling in the proposal
form and whereby he agreed that the said declaration and the answers
given on the said proposal form should be the basis of the contract
between the insured and the company constituted a condition precedent
of the contract between the insured and the company that the answers
on the proposal form should be true and complete in every respect.

2) I find that the answer to question no. 8 on the proposal form was not true
nor complete.

3) I find that although the answer to question 8 on the proposal form was

> not true and complete that its inaccuracy and incompleteness did not amount to a misrepresentation or concealment of a material fact by the insured.
>
> 4) I therefore award and adjudge that the insured is not entitled to recover any sum in respect of his claim against the company under the said policy and that the company is under no liability to the insured under the said policy.

Mr Gilligan's principal submission on behalf of the plaintiff was that, in view of the finding in para. (3) of the award that the inaccuracy and incompleteness of the answer to question no. 8 did not amount to a misrepresentation or concealment of a material fact by the plaintiff, the arbitrator was wrong in law in making an award in favour of the defendant. His argument might be summarised as follows. The declaration made by the plaintiff at the foot of the proposal form commenced as follows:— "I hereby declare that the above particulars are true and complete in every respect and that no material fact has been suppressed or withheld...." This amounted to a declaration that the plaintiff, in answering the questions, had not withheld or suppressed any material fact. It was only answers which withheld or suppressed a material fact which would be a breach of the declaration. The answer to question no. 8 did not suppress or withhold any material fact. That the plaintiff had within the previous year been paid £53 in respect of a claim for fire damage to a pump was not material to the insurance being sought, and so the plaintiff had correctly answered "no" to question no. 8 which had asked whether he had "ever sustained loss or damage by any of the risks or liabilities" he wished to insure against.

The basis on which this argument reposes is the construction that Mr Gilligan gives to the sentence I quoted from the declaration, but it seems to me that this construction cannot be supported. In my opinion the sentence in question contains two separate statements:— Firstly, that the "particulars and answers are true and complete in every respect" and, secondly, "that no material fact has been suppressed or withheld." The first statement relates to the obligation of the plaintiff to give the correct answers, since these are made the basis of the contract, and the second relates to his obligation at common law, arising from the nature of a contract of insurance, to make full disclosure of all material facts. Mr Gilligan's contention was that the two parts of the sentence should be read together with the result that the second part would be imported into and qualify the first. But in my opinion the language does not lend itself to such a construction. If Mr Gilligan's contention were to be accepted it would involve treating the second part of the sentence as if it read "and that *in the answers to the questions* no material fact has been suppressed or withheld." I can see no justification for adding in this qualification, and accordingly, I must reject this submission.

Mr Gilligan referred me to a passage in the judgment of Kenny J. in *Chariots Inns* v. *Assicurazioni Generali*[22] in support of his contention that it is only inaccurate replies which relate to material matter affecting the

---

[22] [1981] I.R. 199. See p. 233 of this book.

insurance which entitle an insurance company to repudiate a policy. At first sight one of the statements in the passage does appear to have this effect but on further consideration it seems clear that Kenny J. was not dealing with what is in issue here, namely, answers which by agreement were being made the basis of a contract of insurance. In the absence of such an agreement it is only a misstatement of a material fact which would entitle an insurance company to repudiate. The passage in question is to be found at pp. 225–226 of the report:—

> "A contract of insurance requires the highest standard of accuracy, good faith, candour and disclosure by the insured when making a proposal for insurance to an insurance company. It has become usual for an insurance company to whom a proposal for insurance is made to ask the proposed insured to answer a number of questions. Any misstatement in the answers given, when they relate to a material matter affecting the insurance, entitles the insurance company to avoid the policy and to repudiate liability if the event insured against happens. But the correct answering of any questions asked is not the entire obligation of the person seeking insurance: he is bound, in addition, to disclose to the insurance company every matter which is material to the risk against which he is seeking indemnity."

While Kenny J. refers to misstatements in answers to questions, it seems clear that he is doing so in the broad context of the common law obligation to make full and complete disclosure and he is not referring to the situation which exists in the present case, namely, one where the insured has warranted that the answers to the questions are complete and accurate. As will appear later from this judgment, in such a situation the materiality of the subject matter of the question is irrelevant.

Mr Gilligan further submitted that the inaccuracy in the reply to question no. 8 was trivial, and that because of this the defendant would have to show that it was prejudiced before it would entitled to repudiate. In support of this contention he referred me to MacGillivrary & Parkington on Insurance Law (7th edition) para. 586 where the learned authors say:—

> "If a misstatement is trivial, the court may well form the opinion that it could not have affected the mind of a reasonable underwriter at all, or induced him to enter into the contract, as where the premises were described as roofed with slate whereas a small part of them was roofed with felt, but the misdescription was immaterial."

This paragraph occurs in the chapter dealing with fraud and misrepresentation and is in the section of that chapter which is entitled "Characteristics of Actionable Misrepresentations". It is concerned with the nature of a misstatement which on its own would entitle an insurance company to repudiate. It is not concerned with inaccuracies in replies to questions which, as here, have been warranted by the insured to be true and complete in every respect. The relevance of inaccuracies in that context is dealt with by the learned authors in paragraph 725:—

> "It has always been the law since Lord Mansfield's day that there must be a strict and exact compliance with the obligation or statement which is

warranted, so that, as he himself said in *Pawson* v. *Watson*,[23] 'Nothing tanta-mount will do or answer the purpose". It is, therefore, not open to the assured to say that the obligation has been substantially complied with, or that the answer he made to a question was more or less accurate. This rule is presumably related to the general doctrine that a warranty is independent of any question of materiality, since an assured who gave an answer which was false only in a trifling detail, and contended that it was accurate, might in a sense be contending that the difference was not material or important to the insurers' calculations".

It is this principle which applies in the present case and not the principle set out in para. 586 on which Mr Gilligan sought to rely. So even if I were to conclude that the inaccuracy in the reply to question no. 8 was trivial, that would be no obstacle to the defendant repudiating the policy in view of the accuracy of the answers in the proposal form having been warranted by the plaintiff.

Mr Gilligan also referred me to para. 724 of the same work, but this equally is of no assistance to his case, and in fact the opening sentence of the paragraph is wholly against his submission that it is only inaccurate replies in regard to matters which are material that enables an insurance company to repudiate for breach of warranty. That paragraph is as follows:—

> "It is convenient to bear in mind two exceptions to the general rule that materiality is of no account in warranty law. First, when the intention of the parties to give a particular term the status of a warranty is in doubt, the fact that it is material to the risk is, as we have seen, a good indication that a warranty was intended. Secondly, the effect of the breach of warranty may be cut down by a proviso which states that the policy can only be avoided for untrue statements or concealment of material facts. In that case, the mater-iality of the false answer is made a relevant issue. There is also a possible third exception, inasmuch as a court may be more ready to construe a war-ranty in the assured's favour, in order to find that he had complied with it, if the matter warranted was trivial and not fundamental to the risk."

The facts of the present case do not bring it within any of these exceptions with the result that the general rule applies, namely, that the materialy of the answers to the questions in the proposal form is of no account.

Mr Gilligan further submitted that it was unusual for an arbitrator to set out his reasons for his award and he inferred from that the arbitrator must have been troubled about what conclusion he should come to. It is correct that the award may be fuller in form than is usual, but I can see no justification for the inference which Mr Gilligan draws from this. There would appear to be an obvious explanation for the form of the award. The defendant was making two separate contentions — firstly, that it was entitled to repudiate liability because the accuracy of the answers to the questions was a condition precedent to its liability under the policy, and secondly, that it was entitled to repudiate because the reply was a material misrepresentation and so a breach of the plaintiff's obligation at common law. The arbitrator had to deal

---

[23] (1778) 2 Cowp. 785, 787.

with both of these contentions, and as he was finding in favour of the first and against the second it was understandable that he should settle his award in a form in which this could clearly be understood.

I reserved my judgment because of the insistence with which Mr Gilligan pressed his submissions, and because of the undoubted hardship to his client, as he pointed out with great force, in failing in his claim because of what appears to be a relatively unimportant inaccuracy in an answer to a question in the proposal form, but having now considered them fully, with considerable regret I have to rule against them. I am satisfied that the arbitrator did not err in law in the conclusion he reached in para. (4) of his award. That conclusion followed necessarily from his findings in para. (1) and (2) that it was a condition precedent of the contract between the plaintiff and the defendant that the answers on the proposal form should be true and complete in every respect and that the answer to question no. 8 was not true or complete. His finding at para. (3) was in no way inconsistent with his conclusion as it merely ruled against the second and separate ground on which the defendant claimed to be entitled to repudiate liability.

I find accordingly that the arbitrator did not err in law in reaching his conclusion as set out in para. (4) of his award.

Elizabeth Ann Keating *v.* New Ireland Assurance Company, plc.
[1990] 2 I.R. 383
The Supreme Court

FINLAY C.J: I agree with the judgments about to be delivered by Walsh and McCarthy J.J.

HAMILTON P: I agree with the judgment about to be delivered by McCarthy J.

WALSH J: I have had the opportunity of reading the judgment which is about to be delivered by Mr Justice McCarthy and I agree with it. There are however a few general matters I would like to deal with.

A contract of insurance is one of *uberrimae fidei* and it requires a full disclosure of all the facts and circumstances affecting the risk and is vitiated by their non-disclosure whether that be innocent or fraudulent.

In the present case the defendant sought to establish that the deceased, James Joseph Keating, made false statements as to his state of health. The contract of insurance which was effected was based upon a proposal and the answers to the questions therein and upon the answers given in, and as the result of, a medical examination required by the defendant.

This contract of insurance was a policy covering two lives, namely, that of the plaintiff and that of her late husband and the money was payable upon the death of either of them but not otherwise. In other words it was a whole life policy payable only in the event of death and the premiums were payable until such an event. Therefore the longer either of the parties lived the longer was the period over which the premiums would have had to be paid. The proposal was made out in the handwriting of the district manager and it was apparently his decision for a reason which has never been explained, that a medical examination should take place and that six of the questions were not required to be answered. They were questions of particular importance referring to the fact of whether the late Mr Keating ever had a major illness or had medical investigation or treatment or advice of any kind in the previous five years, or had any reason to believe that he had a health defect or disability at the time of the making of the proposal, or whether he had ever abused drugs or had been addicted to alcohol or whether he smoked cigarettes. Mr Smith, the district manager who wrote out the proposal form on the 16th May, 1985, was never called to give evidence. The declaration signed by the late Mr Keating was to the effect that he and his wife had read the statement and answers in the proposal and that "we declare that they are true and complete". It was agreed that the written statements of the proposers and answers to be made to the company's medical examiner in connection with the proposal together with the declaration already made should form the basis of the contract between them and the company.

It was not established in the High Court, and from the evidence given there is no inference which must necessarily be drawn, that the deceased or his wife made any false statements as to the state of health of the late Mr Keating or that they told anything other than what they believed to be the truth. The proof that the late Mr Keating or his wife knew facts not stated falls upon the defendant. The basis for the insurance policy was based upon a representation that every material circumstance raised by the questions would be truthfully answered. The declaration in this particular proposal form, in my view, must be construed as one to the effect that the statements are true to the best of the proposer's knowledge and belief and that any untrue statement or any concealment of facts should forfeit the rights. If there had been a misrepresentation then the insurance would be void even if the statement of a material fact contained in the declaration was not true though not to the knowledge of the assured. In the present case the defendant claimed that false answers were given, therefore there was a fraudulent misrepresentation. That has not been established in the evidence and it is totally different from saying that there had been an innocent misrepresentation. The evidence does not disclose that there was any misrepresentation or that there was any statement of fact material to the contract known to the deceased or his wife which was not disclosed. There was no evidence by which it could be held that he was aware of the fact that he had angina pectoris or that such condition was ever revealed to him by his medical advisers. He had disclosed that he had a medical examination for an ailment which on the face of it appeared to be a digestive problem and he made all this information, including the names of the doctors who had treated him, available to the insurance company's doctor. It seems to be quite clear that the medical examiner on behalf of the insurance company did not follow up all the names given to him to the point of ascertaining from them precisely what, if any, condition they had discovered.

The second defence upon which the defendant rested was the claim that the declaration by the insured in a proposal form amounted to a warranty.

Insurers may stipulate for any warranty they please and if an assured undertakes that warranty, although it may be something not within his or her knowledge, he or she must abide the consequences. But when insurers intend that there is to be a warranty of that sort they must make it perfectly plain that such is their intention and they must use unequivocal language, such as persons with ordinary intelligence may without any difficulty understand. No such language is to be found in the proposal form in the present case. What has been sought to be established in the present case is that there was a warranty which amounted to a pure and absolute condition that the proposer was a good life irrespective of his knowledge of the subject. Therefore it would follow that because it subsequently transpired that the proposer had, although unknown to himself, such an impairment of his health as not to be a good life the contract would be void upon that fact being established. In a case where there is such a warranty or condition then nothing need be told but it must in subsequent litigation, if that question is raised, be proved that the life in fact was a good one. Even in such circumstances the life may be a good one even though it may be suffering from some particular infirmity. The question would be whether it was in a reasonably good state of health and was such that it could be insured on ordinary common terms.

A life insurance contract is in essence a wagering contract. In a life policy obviously it is not a wager that the assured would never die. It is appropriate to recall the words of Lord Mansfield in *Ross* v. *Bradshaw*[24] that:—

> "Such a warranty could never mean that a man has not in him the seeds of some disorder. We are all born with the seeds of mortality in us. A man, subject to the gout, is a life capable of being insured, if he has no sickness at the time to make it an unequal contract."

If the present case had been one of warranty or pure condition then the insured would have taken it upon themselves to prove in the case of death that at the time the insurance was effected the parties were in such a good state of health as not to suffer from anything which was dangerous to life at the time of the insurance. If it was proved that he simply had some ailment which was troublesome or inconvenient but not a danger to his life then there would have been no breach of the warranty. In the present case the condition of angina was a danger to life but the policy was not written on the basis of a warranty. Therefore the insurers took the risk upon themselves and cannot avoid the policy unless they can prove that there was a misrepresentation fraudulent or innocent in some material circumstance. In my view, that has not been established from the evidence and the policy therefore cannot be avoided.

HEDERMAN J: I also agree with the judgments of Walsh and McCarthy J.J.

McCARTHY J: The insurer appeals against a judgment and order of the High Court (Egan J.) that the plaintiff do recover from the insurer the sum of £35,000.00 together with interest on foot of a claim made by the plaintiff

---

[24] (1761) 1 Wm. Bl. 312.

pursuant to a policy of insurance dated the 14th June, 1985, on the life of her husband who died on the 14th December, 1985. The insurer repudiated the claim on two grounds:—

1) The non-disclosure by the insured, now deceased, of a material fact, to wit, that he was suffering from angina.

2) That the policy being conditional upon full and true disclosure having been made in the proposal for insurance that, irrespective of non disclosure, the existence of the condition of angina at the time of the proposal and of the issue of the contract of insurance invalidated the policy.

The facts

The late James J. Keating was a building contractor living with his wife and family at Daingean, County Offaly. At some time in March, 1985, he went to see his general practitioner, Dr Kidney, in respect of a stomach complaint. Dr Kidney referred him to Dr Taaffe at Tullamore Hospital, and he sent Mr Keating to Dr Gearty, a cardiologist, in Baggot Street Hospital, Dublin, where he was seen on April 11th, 1985, and later admitted for investigation on April 25th to 27th. As early as the 12th April, 1985, Dr Gearty had told Dr Taaffe that angina was likely although the complaint was of recurring epigastric discomfort. On admission to hospital Mr Keating had extensive cardiac investigations including a stress E.C.G. and an angiogram. He was prescribed two drugs which were specific for angina, the prescription being conveyed to Dr Kidney by letter of the 7th May. Whilst it was Dr Gearty's "usual practice... to explain the investigations in prospect" ... Dr Gearty was unable to state that he had, in fact, so informed James Keating who signed a consent form for the purpose of the angiogram.

Dr Kidney who, on the 23rd March, 1985, referred Mr Keating to Dr Taaffe, did not see him again until the 16th July and, up till that date, had not informed Mr Keating of what had been conveyed to Dr Taaffe by Dr Gearty by letter of the 7th May, 1985.

On the 16th May, Mr Keating and the plaintiff, his wife, had made cross proposals to the insurer for a whole life insurance on both their lives, this being done by a form in which the details were inserted by a representative of the insurer, J. Smyth, who arranged a medical examination as a result of which neither proposer was asked to answer a question on the form — "Have you had medical investigation, treatment or advice of any kind in the last 5 years?" A medical examination of both proposers was duly arranged and carried out on the 28th May, 1985, by Dr K. Duffy of Daingean, who, in fact, was the family general practitioner although Mr Keating attended another general practitioner — Dr Kidney. Dr Duffy recorded on the appropriate from provided by the insurer the several answers given by Mr Keating, the record being Dr Duffy's summary of information given to him. In answer to the question — "For what ailments and injuries, since childhood, have you had medical or surgical advice?", it was stated "epigastric discomfort — 1985 — two days — Dr Geraghty (sic) Baggot Street Hospital — Nil abnormal discovered" and, after a denial that there was any affection of the heart, blood or circulatory system, in answer to a question about the stomach, intestines, or abdominal organs, — "No — apart from epigastric discomfort". Dr Duffy, in his report which classified the proposer as a first class life, remarked "knowing him for 10–12 years I would say he is nervous of medical examination and this probably accounts for his slight elevation of B.P. He was checked by Dr Geraghty (sic) in Baggot Street Hospital this year and obviously had clear cardiac assessment."

The prescription for drugs given by Dr Gibney, junior assistant to Dr Gearty, was transcribed by Dr Kidney on to his own headed note paper shortly after the stay in Baggot Street Hospital. Mr Keating did not know the nature of the tablets nor their purpose; his wife was not aware of her husband having a heart condition of any kind. Dr Gearty ... thought "he should have known that the whole area of interest was the heart and that we were dealing with x-ray pictures of the heart and we were treating him with tablets for the heart...."

The learned trial judge found as a fact that the deceased did not know that he was suffering from any heart condition, angina or otherwise. Ground No. 4 of the grounds upon which the appeal is founded contended that on the evidence it was not open to the learned judge to find as a fact that at the time of execution of the policy on the 14th June, 1985, the deceased did not know he was suffering from angina.

In the course of the hearing of this appeal the issue raised by this ground was compared to the question as to whether, in the event of the trial being before a judge and jury, the question of the deceased's knowledge would have to be left to a jury. Counsel for the defendant correctly conceded that such would be the case. That being so, in accordance with the jurisprudence of this Court over many years and identified most recently in *Dunne* v. *National Maternity Hospital*[25] there being evidence to support the finding made, this Court cannot interfere with the finding of primary fact.

Non-disclosure of a material fact

The materiality of the condition of angina is not in doubt; the deceased died from the underlying condition. The insurer contends, however, that there is further evidence of such non-disclosure in that:—

1. The deceased had been seen by Dr Taaffe at Tullamore Hospital.
2. He had undergone certain tests — the stress E.C.G. and the angiogram.
3. He had been prescribed medication.
4. He had been instructed to come back for a check-up in six months.
5. He had angina.

The deceased did tell Dr Duffy of his visit to Baggot Street Hospital under the care of Dr Gearty and Dr Duffy concluded that there had been a clear cardiac assessment. There is no positive evidence that the deceased had been given any drugs consequent on Dr Gearty's direction much less that he, the

---

[25] [1989] I.R. 91.

deceased knew the nature and/or purpose of such drugs. The answers recorded by Dr Duffy must be read in the light of the insurer's decision to have a medical examination which obviated the need to answer the questions I have quoted earlier in this judgment.

The insurer might well contend that the deceased *ought* to have known that there was some problem arising with his heart; the onus, however, of proving that he *did* know lies upon the insurer; it is not sufficient to prove that he *ought* to have known. The fact that the three doctors concerned *did* know does not impute knowledge to the deceased, to whom the medical examiner for the insurer (Dr Duffy), was enjoined by the examination form to give no information as to the result of the examination.

The insurers were not informed of these material facts; was it a non-disclosure? One cannot disclosure what one does not know, albeit that this puts a premium on ignorance. It may well be that wilful ignorance would raise significant other issues; such is not the case here. If the proposer for life insurance has answered all the questions asked to the best of his ability and truthfully, his next-of-kin are not to be damnified because of his ignorance or obtuseness which may be sometimes due to a mental block on matters affecting one's health.

Support for this view is to be found in my judgment, with which Walsh and Hederman J.J. agreed, in *Aro Road and Land Vehicles Ltd.* v. *Insurance Corporation of Ireland Ltd.*[26] In that case, as in this, reliance was placed on the observations of Kenny J., in *Chariot Inns Ltd* v. *Assicurazioni Generali Spa.*[27] *Chariot Inns*[28] was, like this, a proposal form case; the decision turned upon the determination of what is material; such is not the issue here. The *Aro Road and Land Vehicles Ltd.*[29] case was decided upon a preliminary point as to materiality and, accordingly, the expressed challenge to the reasonably prudent test as outlined in *Chariot Inns*[30] did not arise.

The legal basis

Section 2 of the policy reads:—

"1. Legal Basis
    a) The Policy is conditional upon full and true disclosure having been made in the proposal and medical statement, if any, of all material facts of which the Company ought to have been informed for the purposes of the contract of assurance.
    b) The allocation of Units to the Policy shall not constitute the Company or any other person a trustee of such units on behalf of the owner of the Policy."

Accepting, as he does for the purpose of this part of the argument, that

---

[26] [1986] I.R. 403. See p. 255 of this book.
[27] [1981] I.R. 199. See p. 233 of this book.
[28] *Ibid.*
[29] [1986] I.R. 403. See p. 255 of this book.
[30] [1981] I.R. 199. See p. 233 of this book.

neither the deceased nor the plaintiff were aware of the heart condition, counsel for the insurer contends that on the true construction of the policy, combined with the proposal form, there was an absolute warranty by the deceased as to the state of his health; that his health was not as warranted and, accordingly, the insurer was entitled to repudiate liability under the policy. In short, he says, the deceased warranted the answer to be correct — it was not correct. It is argued that it is immaterial that the insured believed his health to be satisfactory save as to the stomach upset, if the fact was that he had a heart condition. He points to the declaration contained in the proposal form:—

> "We, the proposer/s and the life/lives proposed, have read the statements and answers written in this proposal and we declare that they are true and complete.
>
> I/We, the proposer/s, agree that they, together with the written statements and answers, if any, made or to be made by the life/lives proposed to the Company's medical examiner in connection with the proposal and together also with this declaration, shall form the basis of the proposed contract between me/us and the Company.
>
> I/We, the proposer/s, hereby apply for a policy subject to such privileges, terms and conditions as are contained in the policy ordinarily used by the Company for a contract of the kind proposed.
>
> I, the life proposed and I, the second life proposed, hereby respectively consent to the Company seeking information from any Doctor who at any time has attended me and from any insurance office to which at any time a proposal of insurance of any kind on my life has been made and I authorise the giving of such information.

Such declarations and provisions are known as "basis of the contract" clauses. The contention is that their effect in law is that all answers in the proposal form are incorporated into the contract as warranties and that, if any one of them is inaccurate, the insurer may repudiate the contract for breach of warranty without regard to the materiality of the particular answer to the risk; *Thomson* v. *Weems*.[31] The corollary is that the fact that the insured may have answered the questions in good faith and to the best of his knowledge and belief is irrelevant if the answers are in fact inaccurate. It is not difficult to think of instances where a serious symptomless condition exists affecting the life expectancy of a proposer for insurance and is unknown and unknowable; yet if he were to die and it be discovered that such condition had existed at the time of the creation of the contract of insurance, the contract, it is said, it vitiated. In support of this argument , counsel for the insurer relied upon a wealth of authority as cited in MacGillivray and Parkington on Insurance Law (8th Edition) at paragraphs 732 and 737 and cited some of the authority (namely, *Duckett* v. *Williams;*[32] *MacDonald* v. *Law Union Fire and Life Insurance Co.;*[33] *Thomson* v. *Weems*[34] and *Reid* v.

---

[31] (1884) 9 App. Cas.671 at p. 689.
[32] (1834) 2 Cr. & M. 348.
[33] (1874) L.R. 9 Q.B. 238.

Employers' Accident Assurance Co.[35]). In *Duckett* v. *Williams*[36] an insurance company in proposing a re-insurance of its risk on a life policy stated in the proposal that it agreed that if any untrue answers were contained in the proposal or if the facts require to be set forth therein were not truly stated the insurance would become void. It was held that "untrue" did not mean untrue to the knowledge of the party but simply "inaccurate" without reference to his knowledge. But in *Joel* v. *Law Union and Crown Insurance Co.*,[37] Fletcher Moulton L.J. appeared to question this when he said:—

> "To make the accuracy of these answers a condition of the contract is a con-tractual act, and, if there is the slightest doubt that the insurers have failed to make clear to the man on whom they have exercised their right of requir-ing full information that he is consenting thus to contract, we ought to refuse to regard the correctness of the answers given as being a condition of the validity of the policy. In other words, the insurers must prove by clear and express language the animus contrahendi on the part of the applicant; it will not be inferred from the fact that questions were answered, and that the party interrogated that his questions were true."

It was in the course of that judgment that Fletcher Moulton L.J., said:—

> "Unfortunately the desire to make themselves (insurance companies) doubly secure has made them depart widely from this position by requiring the assured to agree that the accuracy, as well as the bona fides, of his answers to various questions put to him by them or on their behalf shall be a condi-tion of the validity of the policy ... I wish I could adequately warn the public against such practices on the part of the insurance offices."

In *Zürich General Insurance Company* v. *Morrison*[38] Lord Greene M.R. at p.58 described such clauses as being traps for the insured. In *Anderson* v. *Fitzgerald*[39] Lord St Leonards (the dual Lord Chancellor) was of the opinion that to give effect to such a clause would render the policy not worth the paper upon which it was written and liable to produce a result whereby:—

> "No prudent man (would) effect a policy of insurance with any company without having an attorney at his elbow to tell him what the true construc-tion of the document is.
> A policy ought to be so framed that he who runs can read. It ought to be framed with such deliberate care that no form of expression by which, on the one hand, the party assured can be cut, or by which, on the other, the com-pany can be cheated shall be found upon the fact of it. Nothing ought to be wanting in it, the absence of which may lead to such results".

Whilst acknowledging that parties are free, subject to legislative

---

[34] (1884) 9 App. Cas. 671 at p. 689.
[35] [1898] S.C. 1031.
[36] (1834) 2 Cr. & M. 348.
[37] [1908] 2 K.B. 863.
[38] [1942] 2 K.B. 53.
[39] (1853) 4 H.L.C 484. See p. 290 of this book.

interference, to make such lawful contracts as they may wish, in my view there are certain clear principles that must be applied in construing a contract of insurance of the kind with which the court is presently concerned. Some of these may be stated as follows:—

1. Parties of full age and competence are, subject to any statutory impediment, entitled to contract as they wish.
2. Whilst acknowledging the right of parties to express the pre-contract representations as being the basis of the contract, same must be read in the light of the actual terms of the contract subsequently executed. The contract, so to speak, takes over from the proposal.
3. If insurers desire to found the contract upon any particular warranty, it must be expressed in clear terms without any ambiguity.
4. If there is any ambiguity, it must be read against the persons who prepared it (see *Anderson* v. *Fitzgerald*[40] and *Thomson* v. *Weems.*[41])
5. Like any commercial contract, such a policy must be given a reasonable interpretation.

"The Policy is conditional upon full and true disclosure" means that it is a condition of the policy that there has been full and true disclosure. Disclosure can, plainly, be only of matters within the knowledge of the person making the disclosure. What are to be disclosed are "all material facts of which the company ought to have been informed for the purposes of the contract of assurance". This must be construed as related to the questions asked in the proposal form and in the answers to the examining doctor. As the learned trial judge said in his observation of enviable brevity when dealing with this matter — "How can it be said that a person ought to disclose some fact which he does not know about?" How is the proposer for life insurance to comply with the requirement of full and true disclosure in answer to questions in a proposal form and from the medical examiner of all material facts of which the company ought to have been informed, if he does not know of some fact of which the company might well say it ought to have been informed? To read s. 2 of the policy (The legal basis) as conveying a warranty that the proposer is accepting a contract on the basis that he had disclosed something of whose existence he was wholly ignorant is demonstrably an irrational interpretation. It is neither irrational nor inappropriate in seeking to find a reasonable interpretation of a commercial contract to pose the question as to how the casual onlooker or, indeed, the officious bystander, would react if told of the construction favoured by one party or another. I would think such an individual would react in more forceful terms than those used by Fletcher Moulton L.J., as I have quoted. An alternative test of reasonable interpretation may be to extend Lord St Leonards' observation thus. If the proposal form were to contain a statement by the proposer that the statements and answers written in the proposal together with the written statements and answers made to the company's medical examiner shall form

---

[40] (1853) 4 H.L.C. 484 at 503, 507, 514. See p. 290 in this book.
[41] (1884) 9 App. Cas. 671 at 682, 687.

the basis of the proposed contract "even if they are untrue and incomplete for reasons of which I am wholly unaware", would there be any takers for such a policy?

In my judgment, upon a reasonable interpretation of what is called the legal basis of the policy, the insurer has failed to establish either material non-disclosure or a breach of warranty as alleged. I would dismiss the appeal and affirm the order of the High Court.

CHAPTER 9

Fraud

Fraud at its simplest is the use of deception for unlawful gain or unjust advantage. In the various cases involving fraud, the Irish courts have not seen fit to provide any hard and fast definition of what amounts to fraud, and essentially it appears that the court will decide in each individual case whether or not it believes fraud to be present. More so than any other area of insurance law, the facts of a given case take precedence over the law and it is clear from the cases that the primary matters in issue have related almost exclusively to the facts in question and the ability of the party alleging fraud — invariably the insurer — to establish same successfully on the strength of the facts available. The law plays a very minor and supporting role. In the insurance context, fraud arises principally in two areas.

Firstly, at the inception of the policy where material facts have been deliberately withheld or a true state of affairs misrepresented. This has given rise to very few reported cases. Seldom have there been circumstances where the insurer could not simply rely on the defence of innocent non-disclosure or misrepresentation to defeat a claim successfully, rather than raise the seemingly more complicated issue of fraud. Those cases that do exist have arisen in the claims context and are all of very recent origin. Historically Irish insurers have relied on indirect and unrelated defences to avoid paying what they believed to be a fraudulent claim. With many of these defences no longer available, insurers now faced by what they believe to be a fraudulent claim are forced to confront head-on the issue of fraud.

Secondly, fraud arises in the claims context. It so arises in two distinct, but not exclusive, areas. Firstly, in circumstances where the insured is responsible for the insured peril occurring; and secondly, in relation to the claim as submitted.

Mr Justice Lynch stated clearly that in *P.J. Carrigan Limited and P.J. Carrigan* v. *Norwich Union Fire Society Limited (No. 2)* (1987) the onus of proof of fraud rested with the party alleging its existence, and that the onus of proof was on the balance of probabilities. He was satisfied on the facts that the insured was indeed responsible for the burning of his own home and he held in favour of Norwich Union. The case of *Euro Foods Ireland Limited* v. *Meath County Council* (1985) illustrates the type of facts which influence a court's decision in determining fraud, and while not strictly an insurance case, it is worthy of inclusion for that reason. While each case involving fraud is decided very much on its own facts, the type of facts advanced by insurers successfully to infer fraud are surprisingly few. In very general terms, the sort of factors include financial problems of the insured, lack of a plausible alibi, attempts to maximise the return for the loss by the removal of items either into or out of the risk premises in advance of the loss, increases in the sum insured, and so on.

In the much more recent cases of *Michael Fagan* v. *General Accident Fire and Life Assurance Corporation Plc* (1993) and *Superwood Holdings Plc and others* v. *Sun Alliance Insurance Group and others* (1991) the origin of the event giving rise to the claim was not in issue. The allegation of fraud in both related solely to the claim as submitted by the insured. In the *Fagan* case, Mr Justice Murphy was satisfied that not only did some of the items included in the claim not stand up to scrutiny but that, in addition, many areas of the claim were so grossly exaggerated as to amount to fraud. Making reference to the additional contractual protection which most insurers afforded themselves in modern policies, and the fact that the duty of utmost good faith existed throughout the insurance relationship, up to and including the making and submission of a claim, and not just playing a role on the inception of the policy, he confirmed that in circumstances where part only of the insured's claim was found to be fraudulent, the entire claim was forfeited by that fraud.

Mr Justice O'Hanlon's two judgments in the *Superwood* case are illustrative of the very close relationship between an insured's obligations in relation to the making of a claim in general and the duty owed by the insured to co-operate fully and assist insurers in relation to the investigation of a claim. In his first judgment he held that the insured had been in breach of their contractual obligations so to assist and co-operate with insurers, while in his second judgment he confirmed that those same facts were such as to constitute fraud within the meaning of the policy. At the time of writing, both the *Fagan* and *Superwood* cases are on appeal to the Supreme Court.

In *Una Gray* v. *Hibernian Insurance Company Limited* (1993) Mr Justice Barron had to consider the common law duty of the courts to refuse to enforce an agreement when it was alleged to be contrary to public policy, it being advanced that the insured himself was responsible for the insured peril occurring. The Hibernian sought to avoid an agreement to pay sums under a policy when it was subsequently held in entirely separate civil proceedings that the insured was responsible for the destruction of his own public house.

On the facts before him where the insured had previously been acquitted of the arson in a criminal prosecution while alive and where the Hibernian had entered into an agreement to pay in full knowledge of the allegations being made against the insured, he was not prepared to hold that to enforce the agreement would be contrary to public policy. While he was not prepared to state precisely what he believed the correct standard of proof to be in such cases, where public policy was invoked, he did state that he was of the view in light of the seriousness of the plea that it was greater than mere balance of probabilities. He was satisfied on the facts that whatever the onus was, it had not been discharged by the Hibernian.

P.J. Carrigan Limited and P.J. Carrigan & Norwich Union Fire Society Limited *v.* Scottish Union and National Insurance Company Limited (No. 2)[*]
Unreported, 11 December 1987
The High Court

LYNCH J: ... I now come to the main defence to this action, namely, that the whole claim is fraudulent because the Plaintiffs or their associates set fire to the house for the purpose of getting the insurance money. The onus of proof of this issue rests on the Defendants. The standard of proof is the balance of probabilities.

At the outset I should say that I am quite satisfied that there were no intruders into the Glebe on the night of the 21st/22nd of May 1981. The second Plaintiff stated positively to Detective Garda Dermot Neill shortly after the fire that there were no intruders and he repeated this in evidence before me. No signs of any break in or attempted burglary were discovered by any of the investigators of this fire. I am satisfied therefore that if the fire was started deliberately it was started by the second Plaintiff and/or persons acting in consort with him.

Two fire experts who were called as witnesses on behalf of the Defendants have given evidence that in their opinion the fire was not accidental but was started deliberately. These two witnesses are first of all Detective Garda Seamus Quinn who was on the scene and examined the house on the day of the fire the 22nd of May 1981 and the following two days the 23rd and 24th of May 1981. The second such expert witness was Dr Diarmuid A. Mac Daeid who examined the scene on the 8th and 27th of June 1981. I have no doubt but that their opinion evidence raises a prima facie case that the fire was started deliberately.

The second Plaintiff has denied on oath that he set fire to the Glebe. The plaintiffs also called an expert who has given evidence that in his opinion the fire was not started deliberately. This witness was Mr John Connolly and he

---

[*] The first part of this judgment appears in Chapter 5 at p. 127.

investigated the scene on the 10th, 12th, 15th, 18th and 22nd of November 1987, that is to say some 6½ years after the fire and also went back about three times during the course of the trial to check various matters. I have to decide whether I accept the second Plaintiff's sworn testimony that he did not set fire to the Glebe and the opinion of Mr Connolly that the Glebe was not deliberately set on fire as outweighing the opinion evidence of the two experts Detective Garda Quinn and Dr Mac Daeid and other circumstantial evidence relied upon by the Defendants.

I have to say at the outset that I found the second Plaintiff an extremely evasive witness under cross-examination. In addition he was clearly prepared to lie on oath when he thought it necessary to do so even though, as it turns out, his most obvious lie was a completely unnecessary one.

In the course of the Plaintiffs' case reference was made to a photocopy cheque which appears at page 107 of the Book of Discovered Documents. This cheque was referred to by the second Plaintiff as evidence of payment of some of the premiums by his brother Owen Carrigan so as to substantiate the Plaintiffs' case that the Company was owned by Owen Carrigan and Kathleen Carrigan. Samples of the second Plaintiff's signature and of his brother's signature were subsequently proved to my satisfaction. From these samples it was quite clear that the cheque for £115.60 although it was one of Owen Carrigan's personal cheques having his name printed thereon was in fact signed by the second Plaintiff and not by Owen Carrigan. It was also clear of course that there was nothing wrong in the second Plaintiff signing on behalf of Owen Carrigan because he appeared to have authority to do so and the cheque went through without any trouble arising in respect of it. However, the second Plaintiff insisted under cross-examination that he had not signed this cheque and that his brother Owen Carrigan had signed it himself. This was clearly untrue but the second Plaintiff went further and explained the similarity of the signature on this cheque to his own signature by swearing that his own signature, his brother Owen Carrigan's signatures and his mother's signature were so alike that they could be confused with each other.

Examples of the Plaintiff's signature and of Owen Carrigan's signature which were produced in evidence in the form of originals and photocopies clearly refute this evidence. There are samples of the second Plaintiff's signature on the contract for the purchase of the Glebe dated the 11th May 1978, on the undated proposal form for the insurance, on two claim forms in respect of the fire, on an affidavit of discovery in the proceedings, on a specimen signatures form for the Lombard and Ulster. There are samples of Owen Carrigan's signature on the Lombard and Ulster signature specification form, on the joint and several guarantee to the Lombard and Ulster, on two proposals to the first named Defendants for other insurances and twice on the Company register documents. A comparison of these samples of the two signatures demonstrates beyond yea or nay that there is no similarity whatever between them.

Apart from the foregoing disregard of the solemnity and obligations of an oath, the second Plaintiff was shown to be a person willing to go to extraordinary lengths to evade liability for his proper share of the cost of maintenance of his wife and two children and to evade his wife's rights under the provisions of the Family Home Protection Act 1976 in respect of the Glebe. I have already dealt with the circumstances of that evasion in the earlier part of my judgment.

There are a number of circumstantial facts which suggest that the fire was deliberately started by the second Plaintiff and/or other persons acting in consort with him. The policy of insurance was index linked so that the amounts were revised at each renewal on the 31st of July. As at March 1981 the Glebe was insured for £71,584 and its contents for £26,568. These figures would in the ordinary course of the index linked policy have been adjusted on the 31st of July 1981. However, the second Plaintiff arranged for an increase in these figures in the month of March 1981 some four months or so only before they would be revised anyway, to the figures already mentioned at the outset of this judgment, namely £110,000 in respect of the Glebe and £35,000 in respect of its contents. The fire occurred some two months later.

The Glebe was on offer for sale through Mr William Carey, Auctioneer of Enfield, Co. Meath, from about November 1980 to February 1981. During that time there was a reserve price on the Glebe of £75,000 but no offer whatever was received in respect of the property. Mr Carey had advised that this reserve price was unrealistically high. The Glebe was withdrawn from sale by Mr Carey or otherwise concurrently with the increase in the insurance thereon from £71,584 to £110,000.

In addition to having the Glebe entrusted to him for sale Mr Carey also had a grandfather clock in his showrooms in Enfield the property of the second Plaintiff which was for sale. This grandfather clock had been in the showrooms for some months but there had been no offer made in respect of it at all although some enquiries had been made but when it was found not to be actually in working order no offer was forthcoming. On the evening of Thursday the 21st of May 1981 the day before the fire this grandfather clock was collected by the second Plaintiff from Mr Carey's premises and brought out to the Glebe where it was destroyed in the fire the following morning.

The inference which I am invited to draw by the Defendants is that the second Plaintiff had hoped to raise money by the sale of the Glebe and this clock but having failed to get an offer for either he decided to get the money through the insurance policy instead.

The Defendants further rely as suspicious circumstances on the contradictory statements made by the second Plaintiff to members of the Gardaí when contrasted with his evidence in Court. For example, he told Detective Garda Neil Leinster that five gallons of paraffin which he had bought the day before had been stored in a shed but there was no signs of it found by the Gardaí. His explanation in Court was that he put it into a hot water wash in a shed. He had also given different accounts of his movements on the day before the fire to those given by him in evidence in Court.

Having carefully weighed up all the evidence adduced by the parties on this issue I have come to the conclusion as a matter of high probability that the fire was started deliberately by the second Plaintiff and accordingly the claim is fraudulent and I dismiss the Plaintiffs' action.

Euro Foods (Ireland) Limited *v.* Meath County Council
Unreported, 31 October 1985
The High Court

KEANE J: The Applicant Company, of which Mr Vincent Tynan is the principal shareholder, bought a hotel called the Mill House at Dunleek [sic] as a going concern in August 1982 for the sum of £185,000. The hotel was extensively damaged by a fire which was deliberately started on the 29th September 1984. An application for compensation in respect of the damage thus caused was resisted by the respondents on the ground that Mr Tynan was responsible for the fire himself. The application was dismissed by the learned Circuit Court Judge and from that decision this appeal is now brought.

The evidence established that, during the early part of 1984, the acquisition of this premises had proved a financial disaster for Mr Tynan. The hotel business as such had been discontinued, most of the staff had been let go and the only activity being carried on was the bar trade and occasional functions. The applicants were indebted to Allied Irish Finance Limited in the sum of approximately £240,000. Some time prior to the fire, Mr Tynan had decided to sell the premises and had instructed a firm of auctioneers accordingly. The auction was due to take place on October 3rd, i.e. a few days after the fire actually occurred.

Mr Tynan was also the owner of a licensed premises in Dublin called "The Judge and Jury". The business in this premises was also in poor shape in the summer of 1984, to the extent that the E.S.B. had cut off the electricity supply for non-payment and the premises were being serviced by a generator.

At the time of the fire, Mr and Mrs Tynan were the owners of a bungalow in the vicinity of the Mill House Hotel. Up to the night of the fire, however, Mrs Tynan had been sleeping in the hotel premises. On that night, Mr Tynan drove her and her brother to Dublin where they had a meal in the Gresham Hotel. They later attended a party being given at another hotel to celebrate the engagement of their son. They both said in evidence that they returned at about 2 a.m. to find that the hotel had been seriously damaged by fire. Both said that it had been their intention to spend that night in the hotel and not in the bungalow.

The barman in the hotel, one Michael Robinson, also went to Dublin on the night of the fire. Mr and Mrs Tynan both said in evidence that when they came back to the hotel in the early hours of the morning to find it damaged by fire, he was present at the scene. There was no other member of the staff residing in the hotel at the time. When the fire brigade arrived to fight the fire, they found the front door locked and there were no signs of a break-in. Mr and Mrs Tynan both said in evidence, however, that there was a window at the rear of the premises which was possible to open. It was obvious that the fire had been started at more than one point and that an accelerant of some sort, probably petrol, had been used.

Mr Tynan said that the reason the barman had gone to Dublin that night was to help out in "The Judge and Jury." He said that it was intended that he should then come on to the engagement party. In the event, however, he had not gone to the engagement party. The barman did not give evidence in the

Circuit Court or in this hearing. Mr Tynan denied that he (Mr Tynan) had anything to do with the burning of the hotel.

The hotel bedroom which Mr and Mrs Tynan said they proposed to occupy survived the fire unscathed. Sergeant O'Leary of the Gardaí, who carried out the investigation of the fire, said that there were no articles of clothing or toiletries of any sort in the bedroom or the adjoining bathroom. Mrs Tynan agreed in evidence that she had removed all her personal belongings from the hotel some time beforehand, but said that this was because she had made it clear to her husband that she did not want to go on living in the hotel and that she intended to move into the bungalow the next day. In a statement made to Sergeant O'Leary shortly after the fire, Mrs Tynan said that she had intended to move into the bungalow after the auction on October 4th.

Sergeant O'Leary also found a number of items of furniture from the hotel, including chairs and curtains, in the bungalow. Mr and Mrs Tynan said in evidence that these had been removed from the hotel as it was not intended that they should be included in the contents to be auctioned on October 4th.

Two dogs belonging to Mr and Mrs Tynan survived the fire, because they were kennelled for the evening in an outhouse. Sergeant O'Leary said in evidence that the appearance of the outhouse suggested to him that it had not been used for the kennelling of the dogs for any significant period of time. Mr and Mrs Tynan both said in evidence, however, that the dogs had been kennelled in the outhouse for some weeks prior to the fire, as they had been causing damage in the hotel itself.

Section 12 (3) of the Malicious Injuries Act, 1981 provides that:—

> "Compensation shall not be payable under this Act ... where it is proved to the satisfaction of the court that the person who suffered the damage or loss to which the application relates connived at, assisted in or actively facilitated the causing of the damage or was, at the time the damage was caused or the loss was suffered, associated with, combined with or in league with the person by whom the damage or loss was caused."

It was, of course, the law before this enactment that an applicant could not take advantage of his own wrong to claim compensation under the malicious injuries code. The intention of this section, which is closely modelled on s. 4(3) of the Northern Ireland Criminal Injuries Act 1956, appears to be to extend that principle to a case where the applicant is a member of an organisation (such as a group of terrorists) which is responsible for the damage.

In Artificial Coal Company and Hamon v. *Minister for Finance*[1] Kennedy C.J. said:—

> "It is, of course, fundamental that, if the applicant appears to be himself the perpetrator of the damage, he cannot take advantage of his own wrong to claim compensation; but it follows, in my opinion, from established principle: *Hire Purchase Furnishing Co. Ltd* v. *Richens;*[2] *Williams* v. *East India*

---

[1] [1928] I.R. 238 at p. 244.
[2] 20 Q.B.D. 387 at p. 389.

Company,[3] that he begins with a presumption of innocence in his favour, and that the burden of proof to the contrary is on the respondents, should they seek to question his innocence, if the facts as proved by him are consistent with such innocence."

There is nothing in the language of Section 12 (3) to suggest that the legislature intended to alter the position as to the burden of proof. It is clear that the onus is on the respondents to satisfy the Court that the case falls within the exception provided by Section 12 (3) (a). However, although establishing that the case falls within this statutory exception may involve an allegation of criminal conduct, I think it is clear that the issue is to be determined on the balance of probabilities. That this is the onus on the applicant in malicious injury proceedings is clear from the decision of Pringle J., in *Cavendish Woodhouse (Holdings) Limited* v. *Dublin Corporation*[4] and it seems to me that the same considerations should apply to a case being made by the respondents under Section 12 (3) (a). *Thurtell* v. *Beaumont*[5] which appeared to suggest that the degree of proof in such circumstances was the same as in a criminal case, was expressly disapproved of by Kennedy C.J. in *Artificial Coal Company and Hamon* v. *Minister for Finance.*[6]

It may be that where the evidence supporting a malicious injury by another party and the causing of the damage by the applicant himself is equally balanced, the presumption of innocence might determine the issue in favour of the applicant: see *Harvey* v. *Ocean Accident and Guarantee Corporation.*[7] Or on the other hand, it may be that where the respondents have failed to prove affirmatively on the balance of probabilities the complicity of the applicant but grave suspicions remains, the applicant may not be entitled to succeed and there are certainly passages in the judgment of Kennedy C.J. in *Artificial Coal Company and Hamon* v. *Minister for Finance*[8] which would support that proposition. Whichever test is applied, however, in the present case, it is clear that the applicant cannot succeed.

As I have already indicated, there was virtually no evidence of any attempt to break into the premises. No person, other than the applicants, had any conceivable interest in destroying them by fire. They had been insured in the sum of £135,000 and, although the applicants had failed to pay the necessary premium to renew the policy shortly before the fire, the finance company, whose indebtedness was secured by a mortgage of the premises, had made the necessary payment by way of salvage. After deduction of certain fees and commissions, they had been paid the sum of £112,000 on foot of the policy so that the applicants' indebtedness to them was pro tanto reduced. So far as the malicious injury was concerned, the damage was agreed in the sum of £165,662.4 [sic] and, while the insurers by subrogation

---

[3] 3 East, 192.
[4] [1974] I.R. 171.
[5] 1 Bing. 339.
[6] [1928] I.R. 238.
[7] [1905] 2 I.R. 126. See p. 148 of this book.
[8] [1928] I.R. 238.

would be entitled to the sum of £135,000 this would still leave a balance available to the applicants. Bearing in mind the state of the business in both the hotel and "The Judge and Jury" and the financial indebtedness of the applicants, it was obvious that there was much to be gained from a destruction of the premises by fire. Moreover, no adequate explanation was given as to why the hotel bedroom and bathroom had been completely denuded of all clothing, night attire, cosmetics and toiletries, although it was the claimed intention of Mr and Mrs Tynan to spend the night there. The removal of substantial quantities of furnishings to the bungalow must also weigh heavily against the applicants and the possibility, even though it may be no more than a possibility, that the dogs were kennelled outside for the first time on this occasion cannot be disregarded. In addition, the movements of the barman, Michael Robinson, on the night of the fire and his curious disappearance from the scene shortly afterwards serve only to confirm that the evidence in this case points consistently in one direction and one direction only. While it might well be insufficient to discharge the criminal burden of proving the guilt of a person beyond reasonable doubt, I am satisfied that the probabilities are that the applicants connived at or actively facilitated the causing of the damage or, applying the alternative test to which I have referred, that grave suspicion remains that they did so. It follows that, in my view, compensation is not payable in this case having regard to Section 12 (3) (a) of the Malicious Injuries Act, 1981.

The Order of the learned Circuit Court Judge will accordingly be affirmed.

Michael Fagan *v.* General Accident Fire and Life Assurance Corporation plc
Unreported, 19 February 1993
The High Court

MURPHY J: In substance this is a claim by the above named Defendants, General Accident Fire and Life Assurance Corporation plc (to whom I shall refer as "the Company") for a declaration that they are entitled to repudiate a policy of insurance issued by them on the contents of the Plaintiff's house at Donaghmore, Kilkerley, Co. Louth.

There was no dispute between Counsel on behalf of the parties as to the nature of the duty of an insured in putting forward a claim on foot of a policy of insurance. Obviously the Insured must refrain from making any statement which is fraudulent in any material respect and in that context "a claim is false not only if it is deliberately invented but also if it is made recklessly, not caring whether it is true or false but only seeking to succeed in the claim" see *Lek* v. *Mathews.*[9] In addition, the duty to exercise the utmost good faith (upon which attention is more frequently focused at the stage when the assurance company is considering whether or not to accept the risk offered) continues

---

[9] (1927) 29 Lloyd's L.R. 141 at 145.

throughout the relationship up to and including the making of a claim on foot of a policy. Mr Justice Hirst dealt with that aspect of the matter in *Black King Shipping Corporation* v. *Massie*[10] in the following terms:—

> "Moreover, in the leading and now authoritative textbook, the law relating to fire insurance, by Baker Wellford and Otter-Barry 4th edition 1948 the paragraph under the heading "fraudulent claims" on page 289 starts:—
>
>> Since it is the duty of the Assured to observe the utmost good faith in his dealings with the insurers throughout, the claim which he puts forward must be honestly made....
>
> However, in contrast to the precontract situation, the precise ambit of the duty in the claims context has not been developed by the authorities; indeed no case has been cited to me where it has been considered outside the fraud context in relation to claims. It must be right, I think, by comparison with the Style and Liberain cases to go so far as to hold that the duty in the claims sphere extends to culpable misrepresentation or non-disclosure".

The consequence of making a fraudulent claim is summarised in MacGillivary 8th edition at paragraph 1926 in the following terms:—

> "The law is, that a person who has made such a fraudulent claim could not be permitted to recover at all. The contract of insurance is one of perfect good faith on both sides, and it is most important that such good faith should be maintained. It is common practice to insert in fire policies conditions that they should be void in the event of a fraudulent claim; and there was such a condition in the present case. Such a condition is only in accordance with legal principle and sound policy. It would be dangerous to permit parties to practice such frauds, and then, not withstanding their falsehood and fraud, to recover the real value of the goods consumed. And if there is a wilful falsehood and fraud in claim, the insured forfeits all claim whatever upon the policy".

The author having quoted the foregoing passage from *Britton* v. *Royal Insurance Company*[11] went on to say as follows:—

> "The clause is most frequently invoked where the Assured includes a claim for goods which he either never had or disposed of before the fire. It may also be invoked where the Assured makes a deliberate over-valuation of the stock...."

Attention was also directed to the decision of the Supreme Court in *Banco Ambrosiano* v. *Ansbacher*.[12] Counsel on behalf of the Company referred to that Judgment as authority for the proposition that the onus of proof in a case of fraud is no more and no less than the ordinary burden of proof in a civil action. Counsel on behalf of Mr Fagan drew attention to the remarks of Mr Justice Henchy in the same Judgment to the effect that the inference of fraud

---

[10] [1985] 1 Lloyd's Rep. 437 at 512.
[11] (1866) 4 F & F 905.
[12] [1987] I.L.R. M. 669

must not be drawn lightly or without due regard to all the relevant circumstances (page 702). Counsel on behalf of the Company referred to the observations of the Official Referee in *Albian Mills* v. *Hill*.[13] The Official Referee said in relation to a claim under a policy of insurance as follows:—

> "What was the motive for making this claim in this way? Whether there was a motive or not is immaterial. It was made by the man who was trusted by the Plaintiffs, and one cannot suppose that he did not know perfectly well what he was doing. I believe there was ample motive having regard to Mr Harry Simmons [sic] position. I have come to the conclusion that the plea of fraud has been made out and therefore I have not gone into the question as to whether there was fraud in the prices charged".

The difficulty for the parties in presenting and arguing the instant case is that many of the material facts have their origin in events going back more than thirty years and concern the history of numerous household articles which were of comparatively small commercial value. I must attempt to put some shape or structure on what is understandably a diffuse history.

The Plaintiff, Michael Fagan, was born in 1935 in Northern Ireland, where he qualified as a Marine Engineer. In 1957 he emigrated to New Zealand and two years later he married there his first wife, Mary Agnes. They had six children.

Originally Mr Fagan was earning about £150 Sterling per week but he did take up a variety of different occupations and indeed resided in different parts of New Zealand before he and his wife and children returned to Ireland in 1978.

Mr and Mrs Fagan came back to Ireland for a three month holiday in 1965. In 1978 Mrs Fagan had returned to Ireland for domestic reasons before the rest of the family. When the family did come back they brought with them or arranged to have sent over all of the furniture and belongings which the family had accumulated over the years.

In 1979 Mr Fagan purchased the house known as "Mountain View", Donaghmore, Kilkerley near Dundalk, Co. Louth with the assistance of mortgage finance provided by the Irish Permanent Building Society. In 1982 further finance was obtained to make some additions to the house. Since his return to Ireland Mr Fagan has been the effective proprietor of companies which carry on a light engineering business in the Dundalk area. Clearly it is a business of some substance. It employs eight people. Unfortunately in May 1984 the first Mrs Fagan died. In addition to the personal tragedy for Mr Fagan and his children, it is clear that the death of Mrs Fagan deprived them of the valuable assistance which she could have given in relation to the acquisition and cost of the household goods. The house itself was insured by Mr Fagan from 1979 onwards. The Building Society would have insisted on that. However, the contents of the house were first insured in May 1987 in circumstances which were explored in some detail. Also in 1987 Mr Fagan met Sylvia McStay who was a well-qualified and highly motivated Social Worker in Northern Ireland. Again, later that year, the 24th November 1987,

---

[13] (1922) 12. Lloyd's L.R. at p. 98.

Mr Fagan entered into two agreements for the sale of his house and the adjoining premises for sums totalling £80,000.00. It was a provision of both agreements that the closing date should be postponed to the 30th September 1988. On the 3rd September 1988 Michael Fagan and Sylvia McStay were married and when they left for a three week honeymoon it was expected that the sale of the premises would be completed immediately upon their return. Mr Fagan had negotiated the purchase of a new house at Warrenpoint which they intended to make their new home. In fact when Mr Fagan and his wife returned from their honeymoon it emerged that there were difficulties in completing the sale — problems relating to planning permission — which gave rise to litigation which culminated with an Order for Specific Performance made by Judge Patrick Smith in the Circuit Court on the 10th of March 1989. That Order provided that the damages payable to the purchaser were to be assessed at a later date. In fact Mr Fagan was subsequently ordered to pay a sum of £12,000.00 in damages, together with the cost of the proceedings.

The first of the very many surprising features of this case is that Mr and Mrs Fagan decided to celebrate what would have appeared to have been an adverse legal decision by spending the weekend commencing Friday the 10th March 1989 at a hotel in Dublin. At that stage Mr Fagan's eldest daughter Eileen had married and was living nearby. Two other daughters were sharing a flat in Dundalk but usually returned home for the weekends. However, it was arranged that they would remain in Dundalk and that the two younger brothers, Gerard and Liam, would stay with their eldest sister. Accordingly the house was empty for the weekend and Mr Fagan arranged with a neighbour, who is a member of the Garda Síochána, to keep an eye on it. Unfortunately a fire broke out in the house sometime after midnight on Saturday the 11th of March which caused extensive damage to the house and to the contents thereof. In addition to the damage it seems clear that goods of a wide variety and in very large numbers were removed from the house by miscreants at the time of the fire.

At this stage I think it may be helpful to return to the negotiations which took place in relation to the issue of the insurance policy on the contents of the house.

In April or May 1987 Mr Fagan applied to the Irish Permanent Building Society in Dundalk as agents of the General Accident Fire and Life Assurance Corporation for insurance cover on the contents of the premises "Mountain View". The General Accident were already carrying the cover on the buildings but it does not appear that Mr Fagan had any insurance protection on the contents prior to May 1987. In making the application Mr Fagan was assisted by his daughter Eileen Fagan (subsequently Clinton). It is clear that Eileen was a close confidant and ally of her father. When her mother died in 1984 Eileen was a student in Dublin but returned to Dundalk to help her father not only with the rearing of the family but also with the running of his business. She appears to have been a devoted daughter and sister as well as a very competent administrative assistant.

The original application for insurance cover on the contents of the house was filled out by Eileen Fagan under the direction of her father. In part of the application form which provides for setting out an inventory of contents the form provides that articles of not more than five years old should be valued on a replacement basis but articles older than five years should be taken at a current price less an allowance for wear and tear. The amount originally filed into that part of the application form was £113,931.00 and it appeared from notes appended thereto that the contents of the "back lounge" amounted to £5,686.00 which should have been added thereto, giving a total of £119,617.00. In addition the original proposal form included "all risks" items amounting to £17,455.00 giving a grand total for contents of £137,072.00. It was the evidence of both Mr Fagan and his daughter that an official of the Irish Permanent Building Society advised as to the premium which would be payable on the basis of the figures aforesaid and it was decided that the quotation was excessive. On the same day, that is to say, the 1st of May 1987, a fresh form was completed showing the value of the contents of the house at £74,012.00 as against the original value of £137,072.00. It was the evidence of Mr Fagan that this reduction was achieved by dropping "inessential" items but it is quite clear from the original or draft application and the amendments thereto that no items were dropped but merely the value of most items reduced by about 50%. It must be said, as Counsel on behalf of Mr Fagan emphasised, that the original application form did not form the basis of the contract of insurance between the Company and the Insured: there is no question of the Company having been misled by that application. The merit of that form (of which the Company and its advisers had no knowledge prior to the hearing of the case) and indeed of the application form itself is the assistance they gave in relation to the value of the contents of the premises. However, the point on which the Counsel on behalf of the Insured places the greatest emphasis is the fact that the total sum in respect of which cover was sought, as opposed to the stated value of the contents, was the sum of £40,00.00 under the heading of General Cover and an additional £6,585.00 in respect of the items covered for "all risks", thus the total amount of the claim is £46,585.00 irrespective of whether the figure stated in the original draft or the amended proposal was the correct one. However, in this context it may be proper to advert to the fact that the covernote issued by the Irish Permanent Building Society omitted two articles of jewellery which had been specified in all of the proposal forms, presumably on the basis that those two items exceeded £500.00 in cost and that no valuations had been submitted in respect thereof as required by the terms of the proposal.

A claim was made immediately after the fire on the 13th of March 1989 and the Company instructed Messrs Scully Tyrrell and Company, Loss Adjusters, to investigate the claim. Because of the then current litigation Mr Fagan received advice from his solicitors, Messrs Terence C. Grant & Co. [sic] in relation to the matter but more specifically he instructed Mr O'Connor of Messrs Balcombes, Loss Assessors, to advise him in relation to the insurance claim. Both parties dealt expeditiously with the matter.

On Tuesday the 14th of March 1989 a meeting took place between Mr Tyrrell, his assistant Mr Shanley and Mr Fagan at the premises. By the 21st of March 1989 a list of the contents believed to have been stolen was handed into the Garda Síochána at Dundalk by Mr Fagan. On the 30th of March 1989 a meeting took place at Mr Tyrrell's office at which the Plaintiff and Mr O'Connor attended. On the 3rd of April 1989 Mr O'Connor forwarded to Mr

Tyrrell a list (the April list) which was described as "the contents claim". Mr O'Connor contended in that letter that the loss was total and that the policy holder would be entitled to receive the full amount insured, including the full amount insured on the "all risks" items.

Two further meetings took place at Mountain View; the first on the 11th April 1989 and the second on the 19th April 1989. Subsequent to those meetings Messrs Balcombes submitted a further list (the May list) on the 8th of May 1988 of the contents in the house and the value placed on them. As the May list contained fewer items than the April list Scully Tyrrell inferred that certain items had been abandoned but this was not correct. The purpose of the May list, as explained by Mr O'Connor, was to give such additional information as had been obtained, particularly in relation to the more valuable items.

By letter dated the 7th June 1989 the Solicitors on behalf of the Company notified Mr Fagan that they were repudiating liability on foot of the policy issued by them in so far as it related to the contents of the house.

Subsequently Mr Fagan sought to have the dispute referred to arbitration and this was rejected by the Company. However, it was not until the 10th October 1989 that the Solicitors on behalf of the Company set out in detail the grounds for repudiating liability. In that letter the case made by the Company is set out in general terms in the first paragraph thereof as follows:—

> "The claim submitted by Michael Fagan (the Insured) on his behalf is grossly exaggerated and the values set out in the claim, in respect of the individual items, are in many cases grossly inflated. The explanations given by the Insured in respect of the existence and the value of many items have been wholly unsatisfactory and in many cases totally contradictory. The Insured has changed his explanation in relation to the various items on a number of occasions. In addition claims have been submitted for items which have subsequently been withdrawn and are now admitted not to have been damaged or to have already been claimed under a different heading".

The letter then goes on to specify what are alleged to be major breaches of condition six of the policy. I would paraphrase those allegations as follows:—

1. At the meeting on the 14th of March 1989 the Insured informed Mr Tyrrell that a number of particular items, including three radios, a wallet containing cash, a jewellery box, a mink coat, a television set and cardboard cartons containing household goods and wedding presents had been stolen. Mr Fagan gave no indication on the 14th of March that a very large number of goods, having a value in excess of £34,000.00 was in fact missing.
2. That the lists submitted claimed for items of jewellery which had never been specified in the proposal forms.
3. That a price of £1,200 for a JVC stereo player was nearly twice the market price of such equipment.
4. That a sum of £550 attributed to a brass chandelier with matching wall lights was more than three times the replacement cost of those items.
5. That on the 11th of April 1989 the Insured gave to Mr Tyrrell two small rugs which he identified as being Indian tapestry rugs (item 6

(j)) and to be valued for £200 (or £300) when the maximum value of those rugs was £20. Subsequently the Insured explained that in fact neither of the small rugs related to item 6 (i) or 6 (j) and that those items had been destroyed in the fire.

6. The Insured claimed (item 9 (f)) for four wardrobe mirrors at £80.00 each amounting to £320. He contended that these mirrors had been screwed on to the inside of certain wardrobes. It was subsequently established that there were no screw marks in any of the wardrobe doors. It was subsequently contended that the mirrors were fixed to the wardrobe doors with "double adhesive" though no trace of such adhesive was ever found.

7. A Bontempi electric organ and stand (item 98) was claimed at £250 whereas it had been bought for £89 Sterling.

8. Eight sheepskin rugs were claimed at £50 each making a total of £400 (item 10 (c)) where the replacement value of these rugs was £232.

9. A wall clock (item 11 (a)) was claimed at £1,000 where its replacement value was less than £200.

10. The contents of the freezer was claimed at £700 when in a point of fact the freezer was empty and was not in use at the time of the fire.

11. A dining-room table and six chairs (item 13 (f)) was claimed at £1,200 where the replacement value of these items was £380.

12. A clock (item 13 (n)) was claimed at £500 when its maximum value was £100.

13. The carpeting of the house (item 13 (o)) was claimed at £5,500 when the replacement cost was less £3,000.

14. The claim for ladies clothing was exaggerated.

15. Items were deleted without explanation.

The greater part of the evidence and argument before the Court was directed to the issues raised in that letter.

Mr Tyrrell gave evidence of the four meetings which he had with Mr Fagan. It was his evidence that these meetings took place in a reasonable atmosphere and that Mr Fagan co-operated fully at the meetings. He expressed the general view that it would be most unusual to find that a house like Mountain View would have contents to the value of anything like £100,000.00. Figures of that magnitude would not ordinarily arise unless the householder collected paintings or valuable furniture. It was Mr Tyrrell's evidence that the photographs which were put in evidence indicated furniture of a moderate or ordinary quality and not such as one would associate with valuable contents. It is also the evidence of Mr Tyrrell that at his meeting with Mr Fagan on site on the 14th of March 1989, Mr Fagan attached relatively little importance to the "missing items". Mr Fagan did, according to Mr Tyrrell, advert specifically to a television set and two or three radios as well as certain cardboard cases that were missing but said nothing to suggest that the loss under this heading could be anything like £30,000.00. At the meeting on the 11th of April the parties discussed the contents of the April list and in that connection Mr Tyrrell sought receipts, statements, paid cheques, bank accounts or, specifically in relation to goods which had been imported and on which duty had been paid, customs declarations or receipts.

No such documentation was ever produced in relation to any of the many items comprised in the list. Instead the May list did contain a considerable body of information purporting to set out the history of many of the items; where [they] were purchased and the price paid for them or their replacement value.

These lists comprised more than twenty pages, each describing a variety of "items" identified by letter. There were over six hundred such items but for the purposes of appreciating the magnitude of the task involved, both for those by whom the lists were prepared and those to whom they were submitted, it must be recognised that some of these "items" contained numerous individual sub-lots. For example item 3 (p) referred to fifty blouses of assorted colours valued at £25 each and totalling £1,250.00. The total of the constituent items must amount to several thousand. From the point of view of the Insured the problem with regard to the preparation of the lists was magnified by the fact that his first wife, by whom many of the items had been purchased had, as I have noted, died some years earlier. But that was not all. After the remarriage of the Insured in September 1988 his present wife did bring to the house (notwithstanding the plans which they had at the time to move to Warrenpoint) some of her furniture and goods as well as a great deal of clothing. Again Mr and Mrs Fagan received a number of wedding presents some of which had not even been unpacked at the time the fire took place. It was clear that no one person would have had the knowledge to compile a detailed inventory of the house at the time of the fire less still to place a value on its contents. In addition to problems of personal recollection the Insured explained to Mr Tyrrell that he was further hampered by the fact that the filing cabinet which had been damaged or looted in the course of the fire contained the greater part of his personal and financial records which might otherwise have assisted in substantiating the claim.

The problem for the Company was to obtain independent verification of the existence and value of items included on the lists. Without such verification the Company would be virtually — or in the case of the missing goods wholly — dependent on the co-operation, competence and integrity of the Insured.

At the meeting on the 11th of April 1989 Mr Tyrrell queried a number of items and the nature of his queries and the responses given by Mr Fagan were a matter of controversy. In this and in other respects, therefore, it is necessary to assess the credibility of the material witnesses.

Mr Tyrrell impressed me as a man of complete integrity and competence who gave his evidence fairly and carefully. If necessary I would have little difficulty in relying on his credibility. As it happened the more controversial evidence given by Mr Tyrrell was verified to an extraordinary extent by documentation produced in evidence and made available to the company for the first time in the course of the hearing and subsequent to the evidence given by Mr Tyrrell. In my view his credibility was established beyond question.

Mr Fagan is a mature and experienced businessman. He was a quiet-spoken and courteous witness. Whilst no doubt the case imposed enormous pressures on him and evidence was given (which I fully accept) that he had had a serious accident during the year and even in the course of the hearing was only recovering from a viral infection, he seemed to give his evidence with composure and to be unruffled by his lengthy cross-examination and the difficult questions asked of him. One very burdensome feature of his cross-examination was the constant cross-referencing from one list to another and the task of reconciling real or apparent inconsistencies and contradictions. Whilst Mr Fagan did not seem to me to be distressed — although he did drink a glass of water from time to time — it did appear that many of his answers seemed to be inconsistent with known facts. As Mr Fagan appeared to give his evidence with a combination of innocence and sincerity, I was reluctant to draw the conclusion that he was not telling the truth. However, towards the conclusion of his evidence under cross-examination, he gave an account of his affairs arising out of his dealings with the Irish Permanent Building Society which his Counsel subsequently on his behalf necessarily admitted was wholly untrue.

In the context of a significant expenditure on luxury items the Insured was cross-examined about the extent of his liability to the IPBS in 1987. He did admit that he was indebted to the Building Society and explained that there was an arrangement that his indebtedness would be cleared off by the completion of the sale of "Mountain View" in September 1988. It was then put to him that he was in arrears with current payments in 1987 before he entered into the contract for the sale of his house. This he disputed. He denied that proceedings were brought by the Building Society to recover possession of his premises and he seemed to me to be genuinely amazed by the series of letters from the 14th October 1986 to the completion of the sale in 1988 drawing attention to his failure to meet his mortgage repayments. It seemed incredible that Mr Fagan could have overlooked such letters. What was even more surprising was that he thought that these letters might be explained on the basis that they related to a different Michael Fagan. It was only with difficulty that he was convinced that they all related to him and his account with the IPBS. He then offered the explanation that due to pressure of business he had put some of his domestic matters in the hands of an Accountant who was looking after his affairs. That explanation seemed inconsistent with the fact that such payments as were made appeared to have been made by cheques enclosed with letters written in manuscript either by Mr Fagan or his daughter. When Mr Fagan insisted that such arrears as existed did not indicate that he had any financial problems, his attention was drawn to the fact that a cheque for £258.59p drawn in favour of the IPBS on the 25th of March 1988 was returned marked "refer to drawer". Mr Fagan thought that this might have been due to the fact that he changed his account from the Allied Irish Bank on which the cheque was drawn. That explanation seemed inconsistent with the fact that he asked the Building Society to represent the cheque. This unhappy chapter concluded with the reference to a letter from the Building Society to Mr Fagan dated the 16th of September 1988 in which the Building Society indicated that the Abbey National Building Society sought information with regard to his account but that they were unwilling to give such information without his authority. They did however express their view in their letter to Mr Fagan that his account had been unsatisfactory from May 1986 "as a result of business problems encountered by him". When the letter requesting information from the Abbey National to the Irish Permanent Building Society was produced in evidence it appeared that the Mr Fagan in question was identified as "Michael William Fagan". Mr Fagan denied that "William" formed part of his name or that he had any dealings with the Abbey National. When Counsel on behalf of the Company drew the attention of Mr Fagan to the fact that the proposal form was headed "Michael William Fagan", I warned the witness of the seriousness of his position and adjourned the matter giving his Counsel permission to advise him in relation to his situation. In explaining that Mr Fagan's evidence as to his name and his dealings with the Abbey National was untrue, Counsel drew attention to his client's health, the pressure of the case and the length of his cross-examination. Even making allowance for these factors, one must conclude that Mr Fagan is an unreliable witness to put it at its mildest.

Mrs Eileen Clinton was another important witness whose evidence was challenged. In the course of her evidence it emerged first, that a number of documents had escaped destruction in the fire and secondly, that a number of preliminary lists of damaged or stolen goods had been prepared by a variety of people and thirdly, that very important notes had been appended by Mr Fagan and by Mr O'Connor to the copies which they had had of the April list. This additional documentation or information complicated still further the task of reconciling the evidence of any given witness with what appeared to be contemporary records. Let it be said that the immediate burden of this increased body of information fell on Counsel for the Company. The notes that were made by Mr Fagan and by Mr O'Connor in 1989 had been in their possession and were available for review, discussion and revision up to the hearing of the trial. Counsel for the Company received this documentation during the course of the cross-examination carried out by him. This is not a matter for complaint as the Company did not obtain or seek discovery — for the reason that it had been understood that all material documents had been destroyed. However, it is a point to be borne in mind considering the pressure which was undoubtedly felt by the witnesses concerned in explaining or reconciling their own documentation.

In addition to the annotated lists and the preliminary lists, Mrs Clinton produced a document consisting of twenty-three foolscap pages in her own writing, entitled "Please Note" and dated the 15th April 1989. In essence this was a list of the contents of the house which had been damaged or stolen and the prices attributed to those items. The first page of the document summarised the items under different headings and in certain respects the document would appear to be an attempt to reconcile the claim of the Insured with the figures set out in the actual or revised proposal for the contents insurance. However, in assessing the credibility of Mrs Clinton as a witness, the most important fact concerns the date or dates on this document. The first page was, as I say, dated the 15th April 1989 and a number of subsequent pages were dated the 15th March 1989. Thereafter the dates move on up to and including the 13th of April 1989. Understandably Mrs Clinton was cross-examined carefully, and in my view fairly, as to the purpose of this document and the manner in which it was compiled. Clearly it was material to establish whether this document pre-dated the April list or whether it formed the basis of the May list. It seemed to me that the answering of the witness in this regard was very unsatisfactory indeed. Certainly I found it difficult to understand whether it was her contention that the pages were dated before or after the items were described or their values inserted and whether the list of items on any given page was completed before the next page was started. In particular I was unconvinced by the explanation given by Mrs Clinton as to how she came to erase the date originally put on the front of the document and substitute therefor the 15th April 1989. These matters were explored at some length but the one matter which most assuredly was not suggested by Mrs Clinton was the explanation given by her Counsel the following day, namely, that all of the dates had been written in from memory not in 1989 but some two or three weeks before the trial, that is to say, more than two and a half years after the event, and for that reason errors might have occurred.

The evidence of Mrs Clinton in that regard must be considered in conjunction with what she said about another document also in her handwriting, entitled "replies made to questions asked by Mr Joe Tyrrell at final meeting and inspection of contents of house".

That document is dated the 29th October 1992 and Mrs Clinton says it represented the transcription by her of a manuscript letter written by her father to queries raised by Mr Tyrrell. It was the evidence of Mrs Clinton that she did not direct her mind to the contents of this document. That seemed improbable in any event but in the context that she was preparing or reviewing other notes at the same time is quite unbelievable. Not only is there nothing wrong with the witnesses reviewing the evidence in anticipation of the trial, I would have thought it was entirely proper that they should do so. What is far more unlikely is that a person who was to be an important witness in the case could transcribe a letter or document which was crucial to the case some weeks before the trial without directing her mind to the contents thereof. Regretfully, I must conclude that Mrs Clinton was not a reliable witness either.

The other member of the family to give evidence was the present Mrs Fagan. Whilst she gave her evidence with confidence and apparent sincerity such documentation as does exist did cast doubt upon her veracity. One of the primary issues with which she was concerned was the value of a fur coat lost at the time of the fire and in respect of which a claim was made. There is no doubt that Mrs Clinton owned a mink fur coat. There was a photograph of her with her brother put in evidence showing her wearing a 5/8 length mink coat. Evidence was given by an expert, based on that photograph and the description of the coat, which put its value in the order of £2,500.00. It was the evidence of Mrs Fagan that she had bought the coat in Corfu or had it made for her there at a cost of £2,600.00 Sterling delivered in Belfast. The April list shows the cost or value of this cost at £2,000.00 and the May list gives it at £1,600 Sterling. Mrs Fagan herself produced a carbon copy of the contract for the purchase of this cost which showed the cost price at £2,600.00. However, when Counsel for the Company drew attention to the fact, it was indeed clear that this document had been interfered with by the insertion of the figure 2 so as to give a total cost of £2,600.00 and a balance of £2,500.00, having given credit for a deposit of £100.00. It was the unequivocal evidence of Mrs Fagan (and in this she was supported by a friend who has been present at the transaction) that she had indeed paid the full sum of £2,600.00 for the coat, however the document came to be in its present form.

Another controversy arose from the style and sizes of the women's clothing which remained after the fire. There was evidence from an expert witness, Miss Norma Tucker, that the clothing was of two sizes, that is to say, size 12 and size 14 and also that there were two styles of clothing, one old fashioned and the other modern or trendy. Presumably the implication was that the older style (which coincided with the larger size) represented clothing which had been worn by the late Mrs Fagan, where the more modern style related to the clothing of the present Mrs Fagan. This possible inference was utterly repudiated by Mrs Fagan who maintained that all of the clothing was her property and that she acquired the full range of styles and that she wore different sizes, depending upon such styles. The controversy in this regard focused to a large extent on what was described as "a sequinned-top" dress which was shown in photograph number 4 of the folder relating to ladies garments. This was a garment which Ms. Tucker described as being "extremely dated". This was a view which Mrs Fagan hotly disputed and she said in evidence (and all of the lists furnished confirmed) that this garment had been bought in September 1988. However, Mrs Fagan went on to give the place of purchase as Fungerola, Spain and on the face of it this appeared to be in conflict with the May claim where the place of purchase is given as "Hillsborough Boutique" and the price £120 Sterling. This was explained by Mrs Fagan on the basis that indeed the shop in Fungerola was owned by two girls from Northern Ireland who traded under the name "Hillsborough Boutique" and that the garment had been purchased for altering as she and her husband were short of local currency. When the photograph which had been put in evidence was enlarged it showed that the label on this dress contained a statement "Hand Embroidered — Made in China".

On the other matter that cast doubt upon Mrs Fagan's explanation was the fact that the list prepared by her and incorporated in the May list contains a column headed "shop/place" and under that heading a shop and a town is given in respect of every individual item contained in the list prepared by her so that anybody reading the list would infer that "Hillsborough" identified the place where the particular garment was bought and certainly it is astonishing that the list did not contain any reference to Spain in that context.

It does seem to me that objectively the evidence given by Mrs Fagan in these respects seems improbable. On the other hand it seems difficult to find any reason why she would lie particularly in relation to the place in which the sequinned garment was purchased. The material evidence was that it was purchased by or for her as recently as 1988. The location of the purchase and even its price was not material in this context. With regard to the alteration of the contract relating to the fur coat, it is hard to believe that anyone would attempt to deceive an insurance company by the production of such an amateurish forgery. Perhaps the more probable explanation is, as Counsel on behalf of Mr Fagan contends, that the document was altered by the vendors or their agent.

I turn now to consider particular areas of controversy and more particularly those areas in which the Company contends that the Insured made deliberate material misrepresentations in respect of particular items.

1. Carpeting:

This item was described in the April list (item 13 (0)) as "house fully carpeted wall to wall and underlay £5,500". It was Mr Tyrrell's view that much of the carpeting was of inferior quality so that this figure was exaggerated. On the 11th April he removed part of the carpeting, with the permission of Mr Fagan, and his view as to the value of the carpeting was confirmed by expert evidence. Let it be said that the valuation was revised down to £3,560 in the May list which (together with the letter accompanying that list) explained that the error had been caused by a mistake as to the quality of the carpeting used in part of the house. It does seem, however, that the explanation aforesaid is far from complete or adequate.

It is the evidence of Mr Fagan that the entire house was carpeted by County Carpets Ltd, as a single contract carried out in the year 1986 for the sum of £3,566. This Mr Fagan purported to confirm with an invoice or estimate provided by that company dated the 24th of April 1989. Apart from that document Mr Fagan had no record relating to the purchase of the carpeting. He did, however, have a detailed recollection with regard to the matter. He recalled the work being carried out and remembered the circumstances in which it was completed. He drew a cheque for the payment of the contract but at the request of the suppliers, cashed the cheque and discharged the bill in cash. It was a substantial transaction by any standards but particularly for Mr Fagan who, in 1986, was being pressed by his Building Society to meet his mortgage repayments. I find it astonishing that he did not recall in April 1989 that the carpets had cost £3,500 and not £5,500. However it is even more remarkable that when he sought insurance for the contents of the house in May 1987, that is to say, in the year following its purchase, he valued the floor covering at a sum in excess of £8,500.

In these circumstances it seems to me to have been demonstrated clearly the claim made in April was manifestly excessive and the explanation given for the correction inadequate.

2. Curtains:

This item was described at page 11 (b) in the April list in the following terms "curtain drapes and curtain rails and netting full house £2,000". Mr Tyrrell contended that much of the curtains in the house were of poor quality and queried this item. Again he removed a sample of these curtains with the permission of Mr Fagan. It was Mr Tyrrell's evidence that Mr Fagan explained that the curtains had been made up by his daughter Eileen prior to his wedding in September 1988. The evidence of Mr Tyrrell in that respect was confirmed in detail by the contemporaneous note made by Mr O'Connor on his copy of the April list at the meeting of the 11th of April 1989. His note in that regard was repeated in the May list. This explanation raised the question why would Mr and Mrs Fagan have replaced the curtains on the Dundalk premises seeing that it was their plan to vacate those premises at the end of the month. It was the evidence of Mrs Clinton that in fact the claim for £2,000 was made up on the basis that her father intended to remove from the Dundalk house only the good curtains in the front lounge and that she made up the remainder of the curtains required for the Warrenpoint house. The evidence of Mrs Clinton in this respect was supported by the evidence of Mrs Fagan who explained that she had spent nearly £800 on purchasing material for the new curtains.

Having regard to the terms in which the claim was made and the absence of any reference to the house in Warrenpoint, I find it very hard to accept that the claim for £2,000 was intended to relate to anything other than curtains in the Dundalk house and I am driven to the conclusion that the Insured has endeavoured to justify what was a grossly excessive valuation on the basis of an account which is untrue.

3. The Clocks:

The items which caused the greatest controversy and which were explored in the greatest depth were two clocks, that is to say items 11 (a) and 13 (n). The first of these items was described in the April list in the following terms:—

> "Wall clock ex New Zealand (pendulum chiming New Zealand inlaid wood[)] £1,000".

The second of these items was described as:—

> "Mantle Clock (Paua shell) presentation gold frame £500".

There is no doubt that on the 11th of April 1989 Mr Tyrrell took away with him two clocks shown in photographs 37 and 40 respectively of the first album of photographs. The clock in photo 37 was undoubtedly the wall clock and the first question which arises in this context is whether the clock in photograph 40 was the "mantle clock".

As the clock shown in photograph 40 is not in fact a mantle clock why should Mr Tyrrell suggest that it is the clock in question? The answer is that Mr Fagan so informed him. That was the evidence which Mr Tyrrell gave with confidence and on which he was challenged. However, it subsequently appeared that not only was Mr Tyrrell's evidence corroborated by the notes taken by Mr O'Connor but that Mr Fagan's own note made at or shortly after the meeting of the 11th April 1989 in relation to the mantle clock reads as follows "queried? and took the clock to be valued: small paua clock 1978".

What Mr Fagan says is, that notwithstanding that evidence, the clock shown in photograph 40 is not the mantle clock. If Mr Fagan was correct in that evidence the question would then arise as to what became of the real mantle clock which had been valued for the purposes of the claim at £500. Mr Fagan now says it was stolen but if it was stolen why was it never included in the list given to the Garda Síochána of the missing or stolen property?

Further evidence was given as to the location at the time of the fire of the mantle clock alleged to have been stolen. The evidence of Mrs Clinton was that it had been packed in anticipation of the move to Warrenpoint and then unpacked because it was required in the kitchen. The circumstances in which it was needed in the kitchen were confusing. Apparently the original kitchen clock became defective so that Mrs Clinton replaced it with a Seiko clock which had been given to her stepmother as a wedding present. That clock would not work either and it was in those circumstances that Mrs Clinton unpacked the mantle clock or at any rate transferred it to the kitchen. What makes this complicated story unreal is the fact that the evidence of Mrs

Fagan places these events in September 1988 when none of the family was living in the house and only Mrs Clinton was coming in to look after it from time to time. Moreover if the clock shown in photograph 40 was not the mantle clock no claim was made for it at all. Mr Fagan explained this on the basis that the clock in the photograph was of little value and that is why no claim had been made for it. Seeing that claims were made for items of as little value as £2 it is difficult to accept that explanation. In all of the circumstances it seems to me that I am forced to accept that Mr Fagan was correct when he originally identified the mantle clock (item 13 (n)) as the clock given to Mr Tyrrell and shown subsequently as photograph No. 40. On that basis it would be common case that the claim as to its value was grossly inflated.

The pendulum clock was taken away by Mr Tyrrell and it was his view that it was a relatively cheap mass-produced article. This opinion was confirmed by an Irish expert in fine arts, Mr Douglas Bennett and an expert who came from New Zealand to give evidence, Mr Wilkinson. There is no doubt but that the mechanism in the clock was a cheap battery operated system made in Taiwan. There was a dispute between the witnesses called on behalf of the Company and those who gave evidence on behalf of the Insured as to when and how this clock was constructed.

The experts called on behalf of the Company expressed the opinion that it had to be constructed after 1963. It was Mr Wilkinson's view, based on a very considerable knowledge of the trade, that the production of these articles did not begin until that time. Mr Bennett said that battery operated clocks of this type were not made before 1965. On the latter point his evidence was in direct conflict with that given by Commander Tuite, an expert Horologist, who gave compelling evidence to the effect that battery operated clocks were well known prior to that date.

As to the date of manufacture: Mr Tyrrell swore that he was told by Mr Fagan at their meeting on the 11th of April 1989 that he had bought the clock in New Zealand in 1978 for 2,000 New Zealand dollars. Mr Tyrrell was challenged on this evidence and it was put to him that in fact the clock had been bought by Mr Fagan in Wanganui in 1959 as a present for his wife on their first wedding anniversary. This is one of a number of points under which Mr Tyrrell's evidence was wholly vindicated by contemporaneous documents produced by the Defence. The May list submitted by Messrs Balcombes and in the handwriting of Mr O'Connor gives the following particulars in relation to that clock, namely:—

> "Wall Clock — Paua shell finish — 1978. Wanganui, North Island. Purchased NZ$2,000".

Moreover it would seem that the foregoing description was based on the notes made by Mr O'Connor at his meeting with Mr Tyrrell and Mr Fagan on the 11th of April 1989. Those notes confirm precisely the evidence given by Mr Tyrrell in regard to the date and price of this article as furnished by Mr Fagan.

There is no doubt whatever but that Mr Fagan informed those present in April 1989 that he purchased this particular clock in 1978 for 2,000 New Zealand dollars. If he purchased it in 1959 he would have bought it for pounds which was then the unit in New Zealand. Moreover if he had spent £2,000 (or even £1,000) in 1959 it would have been a very substantial sum of money by any standards but particularly by reference to his weekly salary of £150.

Whilst Mr Fagan's recollection as to the street in which the clock was bought was vindicated at least to the extent that there is a Queen's Street in Wanganui — a fact which Mr Wilkinson emphatically denied — I regret to say that I do not believe the account which Mr Fagan has given as to the date when he bought this article or the price which he paid for it.

However, the more important fact is that the quality of the article itself. Mr Fagan believed it was made out of a variety of special local hard woods and that it was hand crafted. He was supported in this by Commander Tuite who said that the clock was not mass-produced and in particular he, Commander Tuite, pointed to the decoration on the front of the clock which he believed was gold leaf applied by hand. He did not attach particular value to the gold leaf so much as to the hand work involved in its application.

Mr Bennett was emphatic that the clock was cheap, mass produced and made of soft wood. In one respect at least there may have been a misunderstanding as to what the parties meant by "mass-produced". It seems to me that Mr Bennett was rejecting the concept that the woodwork or the moulding had been hand carved. Indeed he explained that, in his belief, the moulding would have been cut out in sets or batches of a dozen at a time and in fact that evidence coincides precisely with that given by Commander Tuite.

As to the real conflict between the experts it seems to me that I must prefer the view of Mr Bennett who had the opportunity of inspecting the article in question and formed his opinion at a stage when he must have assumed that if his view was to be challenged by any other expert that the article itself would be available and any error made by him would be exposed. It seems to me inconceivable that an acknowledged expert in fine arts could fail to tell the difference between a hard wood and a soft wood when the particular object was in his hands.

I am again forced to the conclusion that the figure given in the April and May lists in respect of this clock were to the knowledge of Mr Fagan grossly in excess of the cost or value of the article.

4. *The Persian Rugs:*

Items 6 (i) and 6 (j) are described as "floor rugs Indian/Singaporian" and "Indian tapestry rugs" respectively. It is certain that two rugs were produced at the meeting of the 11th of April 1989, identified by Mr Fagan as being some of the rugs involved in one or other of these claims and were taken away by Mr Tyrrell to be valued. All parties would agree that the rugs so identified were valued for only a fraction of the amount claimed in the April list. It was subsequently said on behalf of Mr Fagan that an error had been made and that the rugs handed over were unrelated to this claim and indeed no claim had been made in respect of them.

So what were the rugs in respect of which claims amount to £1,000 were made? It was my understanding of Mr Fagan's evidence that the rugs in question were purchased by the late Mrs Fagan in Singapore when she was returning alone to Ireland in 1978 for a sum equivalent to approximately

IR£1,000. These rugs were delivered directly to New Zealand and, as the family were returning to Ireland, were not opened in New Zealand but transported to Ireland instead, where they remained in their packing until the night of the fire.

If this was the final version or correct account as to what took place I would be surprised that these valuable rugs were unused and virtually untouched for more than 10 years. This would be particularly so in the context of a family moving to a new house which they had to furnish and carpet fully. It is astonishing that these expensive rugs were never used in that context.

But this was not the final version of the story. It would seem from the notes made by Mr Fagan on the April list that at least one of the rugs was bought in Hong Kong in 1965, presumably for a sum of £400 or its local equivalent and it was the three Indian tapestry rugs which were bought for £600. This would suggest that the rug described as Singaporian was bought in Hong Kong and the ones described as Indian tapestry were bought in Singapore.

It seems to me that the available evidence, no matter how it is interpreted, makes it clear that the claim for £1,000 is grossly excessive and must have been known by Mr Fagan to be such.

5. *The Additional Jewellery:*

A number of items of jewellery are set out at page 23 of the April list. Mr Fagan was cross-examined as to why the more valuable of the items in that list (Items (e) and (f)) were not specified at item H in either of the proposal forms. The fact that the more valuable items of jewellery were not included in that section of the proposal form certainly calls for explanation. The first explanation given by Mr Fagan was that the items were omitted on the grounds of expense. Clearly that explanation was unsatisfactory as the draft proposal for insurance comprised articles to a value in excess of £100,000 and the issue of expense does not appear to have arisen until Mr Fagan and his daughter discussed the draft proposal with an official of the IPBS. Mr Fagan then explained it was the wish of his first wife that the jewellery in question be divided between her three daughters so that the insurance was really a matter for them rather than him. But if this was so why was the jewellery not distributed amongst the beneficiaries between 1984 and 1989? Mr Fagan explained that it was decided the jewellery should not be distributed as long as his daughters were living with him. As two of his daughters were living — at least part of the time — in a flat in Dundalk and his eldest daughter was married with her own household, it is difficult to accept that explanation. An additional or alternative explanation was that he was anxious to wait until the girls were in a position to appreciate the value of the jewellery. As the evidence was that all of the girls did possess jewellery of their own this explanation too lacks conviction.

In relation to this item, therefore, it seems to me that a real doubt was cast upon either the existence or the value of the jewellery in question. It should have been within the competence of the Insured to resolve this doubt. So far from doing so his numerous and somewhat conflicting explanations tend to confirm the misgivings of the Company.

6. J.V.C. Stereo:

This stereo system was claimed at £1,200, where the expert evidence given by Mr Lawless put the current price of the equivalent model of the same machine at IR£500. The figure for the equipment in the invoice prepared by Toners was supported by inquiries which Mr O'Connor had made from Power City, who are a very large suppliers of electrical equipment.

The only valid basis for disagreement between the parties as I see it, would be a misunderstanding as to the quality of the particular equipment in question. In this regard it is significant that the invoice from Toners does not give a model number but refers to "4 x 70 watt speakers" where the claim refers to 2 x 30 watt speakers. Again it would seem that Mr O'Connor did not identify the particular model in the inquiries he made from Power City.

There should have been no difficulty in identifying the equipment beyond any question of debate. This stereo did survive the fire and more particularly the notes prepared by Mrs Clinton for the purpose of the proposal form in May 1987 identified the equipment and each component part thereof by its model number. Whatever misunderstandings may have arisen at the time when the claim was prepared, it is extraordinary that Mr Fagan and his advisers did not, subsequent to the receipt of the letter of the 8th October 1989, investigate this matter in such a way as to put the issue beyond doubt, if that was possible.

As matters stand I am convinced that the particular equipment was not worth more than £700 and that Mr Fagan did not pay more than that for it. Accordingly this claim too is grossly exaggerated.

7. Brass Chandelier and Matching Wall Lights:

The claim in respect of this item (5 (1)) is £550. The Company contends that the true value thereof is £134. The company was able to value this item with precision because there was a sticker on the back thereof identifying it as "BHS lot number 1323". Whilst the evidence in this regard is somewhat confused it may be possible to explain, as Mrs Clinton sought to do, the discrepancy between the two prices on the basis that the claim related to a larger number of light fittings than might appear from the description contained in the lists.

8. The Wardrobe Mirrors:

This was a small but very controversial claim relating to four wardrobe mirrors (item 9 (f)) amounting to a total of £320. The expert evidence would suggest very strongly that there were never any mirrors attached by any means to the inside doors of the wardrobe but particularly the wardrobe in the master bedroom. On the other hand Mrs Fagan gave positive evidence of having herself used such mirrors and a carpenter was called to give evidence that he had in fact installed them by attaching them to the inside doors with a particular form of adhesive.

The issue with regard to these mirrors did not arise in the first place as to their existence or their value. I am satisfied that the point was taken by Mr Tyrrell that they were fixtures and as such formed part of the house and not the contents. In their discussion in April 1989 Mr Fagan explained that the mirrors had been screwed to the wardrobes and that he intended to unscrew them and transfer them to his new house in Warrenpoint. It was only when Mr Tyrrell's assistant adverted to the fact that there were no screw holes on the wardrobe doors that Mr Fagan said that the mirrors had been affixed by a double adhesive. If that had been the case it seems unlikely that Mr Fagan would have been entitled as a matter of law or could as a matter of fact have moved these mirrors (if they existed) to his new house. It seems to me that the only way in which the evidence given in relation to these mirrors can be reconciled is to conclude that the mirrors had been removed somehow from the wardrobe before the fire occurred. Certainly I accept, on the basis of the forensic evidence and what appears from the photographs of the wardrobes, that there was no mirror on the inside door of the wardrobe in the master bedroom when the fire occurred. In relation to the conflict of evidence between Mr Tyrrell and Mr Fagan as to the existence of the mirror after the fire and the attention of Mr Tyrrell being drawn behind a radiator in the bathroom, I prefer the account given by Mr Tyrrell.

9. The Bontempi Electric Organ:

The insured made a claim (item 98) in respect of this article for £250. The evidence of Mr Tyrrell was that he saw the packaging for the organ in the house after the fire and that it showed a price tag of Sterling £89.95 which he brought to the attention of Mr Fagan but which Mr Fagan said did not relate to the particular item. Inquiries made by Mr Tyrrell from the shop which appeared to supply the goods put its price at £79.95 Sterling. Mr O'Connor himself made some inquiries about this article and this produced the figure of £250. Mr O'Connor was indignant that his attention was not drawn to the label on this package or indeed to the price tag on the brass chandelier but there is no question of this information being kept from the Insured or his advisers. In any event one would expect that the Insured would have made more specific inquiries if not before the 8th of October at least after that date to resolve this problem and at least explain how the error occurred. I am satisfied that the figure of £250 was a grossly excessive valuation and certainly not the cost paid for this article.

10. The Sheepskin Rugs

This item (10 (c)) was described as "eight sheepskin rugs £50 each £400". Apart from the fact that there was a difference between the experts on behalf of the respective parties as to the unit cost of a sheepskin rug in 1978 — the year in which they are alleged to have bought — it transpired that some of these rugs were doubles and others were what is known in the trade as "Quatros". Certainly the more substantial rugs would have been very much more expensive. Whilst it is surprising that no reference was made in either list to "doubles" or "quatros" I would accept that there may have been a misunderstanding about this item.

11. Freezer Contents:

This item (13(b)) was claimed at a sum of £700. It is not clear whether this item was withdrawn by the Insured from his claim or whether it was his contention that the claim should have related to the freezer itself. If the latter was the case it seems to be common case that the freezer was not in the house proper at the time of the fire but was in a basement or garage awaiting repairs. The fact is that the sum of £700 is precisely the figure set out in the insurance schedule issued by the Company in respect of the period from the 4th of May 1987 to the 19th of June 1987 under the description "deep freeze or refrigerator contents £700". Undoubtedly Mrs Clinton recognised that she did have regard to the proposal documents in preparing the claims lists but it seems to me that in this and other respects that figures were taken from the proposal documentation without any regard whatsoever for the actual cost or value of the goods in question.

12. The Dining-Room Table and Chairs (item 13 (f)):

There is no doubt that this item existed before the fire and was virtually destroyed by it. The table and a dresser of similar material is shown in photographs which were produced in the course of the evidence given on behalf of the Insured.

With the benefit of the information supplied by the Insured and the opportunity of inspecting the damaged goods, Mr Tyrrell made his own enquiries and established to his satisfaction that the value of the table and the six chairs was approximately £380, less than one third of the figure put on these goods by the Insured. How could this discrepancy arise? These goods were bought by the Insured to be installed in the house which he had purchased in 1978. The table was manufactured in Ireland and the suppliers were identified. The Company called an official from the named supplier who supported in general the figure for which the Company contended. He denied that the table had been supplied by his Company to the Insured in 1983 as he contended. Mr Carey made available in Court his records in support of his evidence. It was then put to the witness by Counsel on behalf of the Insured that the table might have been purchased in 1982. Fortunately Mr Carey had records in Court in respect of that year also and again denied that the table or dresser was supplied in that year either. It was only when Mrs Clinton was giving evidence some days later that she gave evidence with confidence that the table had been purchased in or before 1981 as she recalled doing her homework on the table for her Intermediate Examination in that year. In relation to this item it seems to me that not only is this claim grossly inflated but that successive and unconvincing efforts were made to justify the date of the purchase and the amount paid.

13. The Ladies Clothing:

Whilst I suspect there may have been a degree of exaggeration in relation to this item and I was surprised that Mrs Fagan prepared lists as to the goods which were destroyed or missing without herself inspecting what remained after the fire, I do not believe that the claim put forward by the Insured in this regard was either fraudulent or mala fide.

14. The Quantity of Goods Stolen:

Even allowing for the state of shock in which the Plaintiff must have been at the time, it is extraordinary that he did not at his first meeting with Mr Tyrrell advert to the fact that 16 packing cases of goods were missing from the house.

The Company had contended originally and proved in the course of the hearing that the Insured had ascribed values or prices to a small but significant number of goods which were grossly excessive. Counsel for the Insured emphasised the problems with which the Insured was faced in compiling the various lists discussed in evidence. It was not surprising — Counsel argued — that errors, even substantial errors, should arise with regard to the value or cost of a relatively small number of the goods in the circumstances. If such errors occurred or if, in the absence of specific information or appropriate documentation, the Insured had claimed for figures which were excessive in the sense that they represented an extremely optimistic view of the value of the items in question, that would not, in my view, justify the Company in repudiating liability on foot of the policy.

This was not a case in which an Insured sought to correct or explain errors or to revise claims proved to be insupportable. So far from it the Insured and his family sought to justify as correct facts and figures which, in my view, were untrue. The tragedy of the case is that no financial purpose appears to have been served by inflating the claim and the attempt to justify figures which could not be sustained created unnecessary and embarrassing problems for all of the witnesses.

In the circumstances it seems to me to have been established on the evidence as a whole that the Insured, in breach of both his general and contractual obligations to the Company, claimed a loss under the policy based on figures which were deliberately over-stated in the original claims and persisted in on the hearing of the action. In those circumstances it seems to me that the Company is entitled to repudiate liability on foot of the policy issued by it and to have such declaration as may be necessary to give effect to that decision.

I have reached this conclusion with regret because it is beyond dispute that the Insured had a valid policy of insurance which covered a loss up to approximately £46,000.

It is common case that he did suffer loss which fell within the terms of that policy and by any reckoning it would seem that his loss must have been a substantial one. Moreover, I suspect that the unsatisfactory evidence may be explained in part by the way in which the Insured and his family divided between them the responsibility of presenting the claim and in part by the anxiety of every member of the family loyally to support the evidence of the others. Nevertheless it seems to me for the reasons which I have given that the Plaintiff's claim herein must be dismissed.

(This case is on appeal to the Supreme Court.)

Superwood Holdings plc and Others *v.*
Sun Alliance and London Insurance plc t/a Sun Alliance
Insurance Group and Others (No. 1)[*]
Unreported, 13, 14 and 15 August 1991
The High Court

O'HANLON J: Throughout the foregoing Sections of the present judgment I have made findings of fact in relation to the various topics under review, which I do not find it necessary to recapitulate at this stage. I propose now to summarise my overall views in regard to the claim.

I find that the destruction of the storage building at the Superwood complex in Bray gave rise to a valid claim for compensation under the Fire Policy in respect of the cost of reinstatement on the building and for the value of the goods destroyed in the fire.

I find that it also gave rise to a valid claim under the Consequential Loss Policy for loss of gross profit on turnover, and Increased Cost of Working, attributable to the disruption in the business of the Company brought about by the loss of the storage building and the stores of raw waste plastic and granulated material contained therein.

Superwood claim that but for the fire there was every likelihood that in the financial year 1987/88 they would have achieved the sales and profits projected in their Prospectus, involving sales of plastic products on the home market in the region of £1m and in the export market of a sum in excess of £600,000 (sterling).

The actual sales achieved in the period referred to fell far below these figures, and the Group showed a loss instead of the substantial profits which were forecast.

The claim made in the present proceedings is that the entire differential between the sales projected and the sales achieved, and the entire differential between the profits projected and the loss which as actually incurred, are attributable to the loss of the double-haybarn structure used for storage and sorting purposes, coupled with the shortage of working capital flowing from the Defendants' failure to make any payments on account under the Consequential Loss Policy pending final settlement of the claim.

The task which faced Thorntons, Scully [Tyrrell], (loss adjusters appointed by Sun Alliance) and Stokes Kennedy Crowley in turn, was to assess the extent to which the fire damage had contributed to that overall loss, and the same task falls on the Court when the claim for damages is made in the present proceedings.

Superwood continued at all stages, down to the present, to press their claim that all their losses were brought about by the consequences of the fire and the failure of the Insurers to pay the substantial sums claimed under the Consequential Loss Policy.

In pursuing this claim I am satisfied that they did their utmost to prevent the Loss Adjusters, and later Mr Noel Cooke of SKC, from uncovering the

[*] Extract.

multiple weaknesses and deficiencies in the Group operation to which I have
already referred, and which made the projections unrealistic and unattain-
able even had the fire never occurred.

I find that there was a deliberate policy of non-cooperation adopted,
commencing in the early weeks after the fire and that everything possible
was done to prevent Mr Begg, and later Mr [Tyrrell] and Mr Sleator, from
learning the truth about the Company and its operations.

Mr [Tyrrell] and Mr Sleator wanted to know what back-up documentation
was available to support the projections, and were told that there was none,
save the computer print-outs, which they were allowed to look at, but copies
were refused. At that time Superwood were in possession of a very enlighten-
ing report from Mr Williams, Sales Manager in the UK, and a massive collection of reports compiled by Mr Morris on a weekly basis with reference to the
same market — these would obviously have been of great help to Mr [Tyrrell]
and Mr Sleator in their inquiries had they been made available. I have
already commented on the non-production of Mr Doran's tables relating to the
home market, or at least, of Mr Doran himself as the compiler of those tables.

The Plaintiffs also claim that very large sums had to be expended from
the date of the fire up to the months of March or April 1988, on the purchase
of granulated material by way of substitute for the material they could not
themselves process in the aftermath of the fire, and that the excess of cost
over and above the cost of providing their own granulated material should be
recoverable as Increased Cost of Working under the Consequential Loss
Policy.

I find that the Plaintiffs did suffer a significant disruption in their manufacturing operations by reason of the fire, and did incur substantial costs, on
a temporary basis, in the purchase of granulated materials to minimise the
loss of turnover which otherwise would have been incurred.

I find, however, that the effort to attribute the down-turn which took place
in sales and profits for the financial year 1987/88 to the fire and its consequences is wholly without foundation.

I find that there were many reasons for the poor performance of the
Superwood Group in the manufacture and sale of plastic products during the
year in question. The Group planned a huge expansion of its operation, particularly in the export market, but also on the home market at a time when,
in my opinion, it was totally unprepared to carry it into effect.

The manufacturing and office premises in Bray, and the facilities available there for storage and sorting out of waste materials, were barely adequate for the much smaller operation which up to that time had been carried
on by Superwood — and in the case of storage of materials were totally inadequate from the environmental point of view.

I am satisfied that the huge increase which was planned in the volumes of
raw waste materials to be purchased and taken in for processing would have
been quite unmanageable had the fire never occurred — both in relation to
the dumping of materials on the open ground, and also in taxing the capacity
of the storage building destroyed in the fire.

I think this finding is borne out by the descriptions of the conditions which
obtained in Johnston's warehouse during the year in question: by the descriptions of the conditions on the ground in Superwood as given by different

witnesses, and by the state of affairs in the reconstructed storage building as seen by Mr Slack on the occasion of a visit there in 1990.

I make a similar finding, in relation to the production capacity of the Company. The evidence has led me to conclude that during the 1987/88 financial year the hoped-for production of 3,500 tonnes of moulded product, or thereabouts, could never have been achieved, given the staggered installation of the machines which were to produce it; the problems involved in sourcing and providing suitable material in sufficient quantities: the problems which were liable to arise — and did arise — in the granulation process; the problems which were liable to arise — and did arise — in the moulding process; problems with the machines themselves; with the training of operatives to run them; with the demands made on the operatives by running the machines round the clock, seven days a week, with operatives standing in front of their machines for 12 hours at a stretch. I have regard to the fact that the production figures required to achieve the Company's targets far exceeded the production figures achieved previously, and that the figures for the first five months of the financial year up to the time of the fire gave no encouragement to the hope that the target figures would be achieved. I accept Mr Slack's evidence on this aspect of the case.

I make a similar finding in relation to the management and organisation of Superwood at the time when it came to the market — it appears to me that it was in no way geared to the huge expansion of the Company's business that was being demanded of it if the projections were to be realised. There was a virtual break-down in accounting and even basic book-keeping systems, with no effective financial control or stock control. Mr Davies trusted implicitly in the ability of the co-founders of the Company, Mr Bunyan and Mr Binnegan, to know exactly what was happening the stocks and finances and all other aspects of the business from week to week, but I think it has been demonstrated during the case that his confidence was ill-founded. One example may help to demonstrate this weakness in the Company structure. Mr Bunyan was asked at a very early stage in the case about the possible loss through wastage when the raw waste plastic was being put through the various processes until the finished product was ready for the market. His initial reaction was to say that while excess PVC, if its presence went unnoticed, might spoil a whole batch (which should not happen if the workers were doing their job properly), the question of waste did not really arise in the manufacturing process. He said that one aimed at producing 105% of what was required, to allow for the fact that off-cuts were made in the final fabrication process, but such off-cuts then went back into the granulation stage with raw waste materials and did not represent tonnage lost in the final analysis.

At a later stage he was prepared to accept that a wastage loss of 5%/6% might be regarded as normal. As the Company had no records of the tonnages involved in respect of goods sold and could only make a rough calculation by working backwards through tonnages produced and deducting an estimated figure for loss through wastage, no accurate figures could be produced until after the hearing of the proceedings commenced. Then a laborious exercise was carried out, both by Superwood and by Scully [Tyrrell], involving an examination of all the sales invoices and an assessment of the weights involved in each consignment. Both parties, acting independently, came up with comparable figures for tonnages sold during the 1987/88 financial year. The exercise produced the remarkable result, however, that it left approximately 250 tonnes of product unaccounted for. If wastage, then it meant that the figure for wastage soared to 23% or thereabouts — at which stage Mr Bunyan, disclaiming the universal knowledge that Mr Davies attributed to him, said that he would be the last person to be told if such were the case.

I am left with a strong impression that affairs were conducted in a similarly haphazard manner in relation to sales and costings and that the accounting systems and financial controls of the Company were inadequate to keep the management informed as to where they were going. It has at all stages been claimed that a gross profit in the region of 90% is attainable on the cost of the raw materials to the Company, but this has turned into a net loss at all stages since the year 1987/88. Although the destroyed building has long since been replaced by one which is much superior to its predecessor, and the storing and sorting problem should thereby have been eliminated, the Plaintiffs claim that their ongoing losses have been attributable to the fact that they were starved of working capital by reason of the Insurers' failure to honour their obligations under the Consequential Loss Policy. At the same time very large sums by way of alternative finance were raised by Superwood by way of bank loans, and £1m was raised on the Stock Market for the acquisition of Braithwaite Plastics.

I believe that Superwood completely underestimated the working capital they would require if they were to have any prospect of success in breaking into the English market on a large scale; purchasing and equipping new factory premises in the UK; recruiting and employing a sizeable sales force for the new UK market, and expanding the home market sales force to achieve a 150% increase in sales in a single year; organising a sales drive for the Superflow machine process on the international market, and producing the machines to meet the expected demand from overseas; carrying through a take-over of Braithwaite which had been planned for a long time before it occurred.

The claim in these proceedings has risen inexorably towards the £8m. mark — the entire loss being attributed to the loss of a haybarn type structure and its contents of raw waste plastic and granulated materials. It can only be based on the old principle that, "For want of the nail the shoe was lost, For want of the shoe the horse was lost..."

Even if the management and organisation were in place, if all four machines had been installed and in operation at the commencement of the financial year, and if sales representatives of suitable calibre had been appointed in good time for the UK, I would still remain unconvinced that the 1,000% increase of sales projected for the UK for the year 1987/88 could ever have been achieved.

The evidence I have heard, and particularly the reports coming from Mr Williams and Mr Morris, the Condon Report and the correspondence with potential purchasers in the UK, all combine to suggest very clearly that much more preparatory work was needed on the ground before a large-scale sales drive in the UK could be attempted. There was a lot of sales resistance to the Superwood product and a lot of indications that research and design work to iron out defects and deficiencies in the product and make it more attractive to the market were needed and would take time to achieve — thinking perhaps in terms of years rather than months.

In the short-term, I believe that sales could only be built up by selling goods at give-away prices on this market and it should not have been necessary to adopt this course if patient preparatory work had been undertaken beforehand.

To conclude this part of my judgment, I find that the inability of Superwood to trade profitably during the financial year 1987/88 was brought about by a multiplicity of causes — one of the contributory causes being the unfortunate destruction of the storage building at Bray with the contents therein on the 26th October, 1987.

All access to the books and records of Superwood were refused to Thorntons and Scully [Tyrrell]. Three ledgers of the Group were, after a long delay, produced for inspection by Mr Cooke, but not by Mr Begg, on the basis that Mr Cooke who was totally unfamiliar with the case, could be expected to glean whatever information was required by looking at them in the course of an afternoon meeting in the offices of Kinnear Owens Murray.

I regard the claim made by Mr Bunyan to withhold access to books and records of Superwood and to information concerning its affairs, from the Loss Adjusters, on the professed ground of having to protect the confidentiality of matters concerning a public company, as quite unwarranted and I think it is regrettable that he was encouraged in the adoption of this posture by Mr Davies, in reliance on a single letter or communication from a shareholder enquiring about rumours which were going around about Superwood's insurance claim. I think that Mr Davies' statement that he felt "comfortable" in furnishing information to Mr Cooke implies a reflection on the reliability and trustworthiness of Thorntons and Scully [Tyrrell] and Co. which is totally without justification and which is effectively rebutted by what Mr Ballesty had to say about the professional standing of the two firms concerned.

I find that Superwood did their utmost to prevent the Loss Adjusters from uncovering the weaknesses inherent in the Group management, organisation and accounting systems; from obtaining a true picture of the sales potential for Superwood products on the Irish and UK markets; from learning the truth about the production capacity of the manufacturing process: from ascertaining information they needed concerning the sources of supply of raw materials and the prices paid for such materials; from learning the truth about the measures taken by Superwood to off-set the damage caused to their production process by the loss of the storage building and its contents.

Ultimately, when this policy had been pursued by Superwood for over a year, they were asked to allow Mr Cooke of Stokes Kennedy Crowley carry out an over-all assessment of the claim, and Mr Bunyan's response was that he would not consider letting in Mr Cooke's team to Superwood without first getting an admission of liability on foot of the Policy and a substantial payment on account. According to Mr Ballesty, Mr Cooke then enquired what payment on account was envisaged and he, Mr Ballesty suggested £1m.

In my opinion, Superwood were totally unjustified in not allowing such access to their books and records as was reasonably required by the Loss Adjusters and later by Mr Cooke, for the purpose of assessing the amount which could be legitimately be claimed on foot of the Consequential Loss

Policy, and were not entitled to lay down the pre-conditions suggested by Mr Bunyan.

I have to record that I found Mr Bunyan unreliable as a witness. Again and again when the statements made by him in relation to the claim were tested by Scully [Tyrrell] by going back and examining such documentation as was made available to them, they found that they would not stand up.

In the course of the present proceedings Mr Bunyan kept asserting that the earlier proceedings brought against the Defendants in the early part of 1988 were brought for the purpose of getting the insurance policy, whereas it has emerged that the policy was actually delivered before even the Plenary Summons was served and the proceedings were continued thereafter by delivery of a Statement of Claim which did not include a claim for delivery of the policy. In the case of the proceedings started against Lloyds, even the Plenary Summons did not contain a claim for delivery of the policy.

I have also referred to the correspondence with his bankers when he was accused of having given them figures which later proved to be quite incorrect. Mr Bunyan admitted in evidence that this had happened and gave an explanation which I found far from satisfactory.

In relation to two important matters having a direct bearing on the insurance claim I believe that not merely obstruction, but actual deception, was practised on those who were inquiring into the claim on behalf of the Insurers.

I am not satisfied with the explanation given regarding the deletion from the production records of the columns giving particulars of downtime, and the reasons for downtime, when these production records were sought by the Loss Adjusters.

Mr Ballesty suggested in evidence that it was attributable to the use of an unusually small copying machine, the conventional office machine being out order at the time. His evidence on this matter I found unconvincing. He took no part in the copying process himself, and arrived late in the day to collect the material. He gave a graphic description of Mr Lyons, the Production Manager being in a state of exhaustion after a hard day copying material on a machine which was unsuitable for the purpose, but Mr Lyons, when he came to give evidence, said he had nothing to do with the work of copying; [he] had merely turned up at the end and helped to gather some of the papers together; and had no recollection of any difficulties preventing the copying being carried out in a way which would give a true copy of the documents required.

I would have expected that whoever was charged with the copying of the documents would have realised that the columns dealing with downtime and the reasons therefor would, in all likelihood, have been of considerable interest to whoever wanted to see the production records of the company, and would have ensured that full and complete copies were made available whenever it became possible to do so (on the assumption that it could not be done on the date in question).

As the matter was obviously of some importance, I would also have expected to hear from some witness who could speak with first-hand knowledge, (which neither Mr Ballesty nor Mr Lyons could do), about any difficulties which might have prevented full copies being taken on the date in question....

In an ordinary case I would be prepared to give the benefit of the doubt to the people responsible for the failure to furnish this important information, but in the present case, with its history of the withholding of information until it could be withheld no longer, I am driven to the conclusion that in all probability the deletion of these particulars from the copy documents furnished was achieved deliberately.

The second matter to which reference must be made concerns the whole question of the use made of Johnston's warehouse and the withholding of information about it until it emerged as a result of painstaking work on the part of Scully [Tyrrell] and Co., over a year after Superwood commenced using this facility.

When Mr Ballesty furnished his lengthy Interim Claim Data in March, 1988, it included a number of items which were clearly not legitimate claims under the Policy, but it made no mention of a perfectly legitimate claim — the rental charges for warehousing payable to Johnston Haulage in respect of the months of January and February, 1988. Their freight invoices were included in the Interim Claim Data, but not rental invoices and the explanation was quite simple — Mr Ballesty, the Loss Assessor for Superwood was told nothing about the renting of this warehouse space until Mr [Tyrrell] elicited this information almost a year later. In meantime the space rented had risen from 2000 square feet to 9000 square feet, and remained at that level for some months before gradually tapering off again towards the end of the year.

At some stage in May or June, according to Mr Ballesty's evidence, Mr Finnegan made a casual remark to him in the Superwood office about Johnstons having some problem about insurance, and Mr Ballesty responded by telling him that if that were so he should get a letter about it, so that it would be available later if required. Mr Finnegan said nothing to suggest that such a letter was already in his possession and Mr Ballesty was surprised to be provided with a letter at a later stage, dated 24th March, 1988, from Johnston Haulage to Superwood, expressing regret about their inability to store material owing to space constraints and inadequate insurance cover.

I have no doubt whatever that this was furnished by Mr Johnston as a result of a request emanating from Superwood, as an obligement to help prop up the claim made by Superwood that alternative storage could not be obtained due, in part, to insurance difficulties affecting warehousemen who might otherwise have dealt with them.

The contents of the letter bear no relation to the reality of the situation, which was, that on the date borne by the letter, Superwood were already firmly installed in Mr Johnston's warehouse and continued to rent it for months afterwards with ever-increasing demands on the floor space available.

Mr Ballesty was unable to say, with certainty, that he had ever delivered the letter to Scully [Tyrrell], but was sure that he had conveyed the information contained therein, and he was driven to the conclusion that the letter was back-dated, although at a later stage in his evidence he endeavoured to retreat from this position.

I am not impressed by the throwaway lines in Mr [Bunyan's]] letters of the 3rd and 30th August to Mr Allen about some use having been made of storage in Johnston Haulage, or the passing references when Mr Sleator attended meetings on the 8th and 29th July, 1988. At all stages the impression was conveyed that any facilities provided by Johnstons were of a temporary and limited nature, and were brought to an end because of insurance difficulties, none of which was correct. It merely enabled Superwood to say at a later stage that, of course, they had mentioned the matter, which being designed at the same time to forestall further inquiry.

If there were an innocent explanation in relation to the letter of the 24th March, 1988, I would have expected Mr Finnegan to be called to deal with the matter.

I think it inconceivable that the renting of up to 9000 square feet of storage space could have continued for months on end unknown to Mr Bunyan, as suggested by him in evidence. The whole critical situation for Superwood according to Mr Bunyan was brought on by lack of their storage building, and he was in constant contact with Mr Finnegan about the affairs of the Group. They worked within a matter of yards of each other at Bray; they were identified by Mr Davies as the people in charge of what was effectively a two-man firm, and between them they owned over 70% of the issued share capital of the Company. I am quite sure that they were constantly discussing with each other the problems of Superwood, and what could be done to alleviate them, and the biggest problem of all at that time — according to Mr Bunyan — was the problem of alternative storage.

Mr [Tyrrell] and Mr Sleator were constantly pressing for information as to how Superwood had managed to handle, store and process the hundreds of tons of raw waste material which it had dealt with subsequent to the fire, but they were never given a satisfactory answer. Their enquiries, however, put Mr Bunyan clearly on notice that they wanted to know all about the handling of the raw materials which were being dealt with and what alternative storage arrangements, if any, were being utilised by Superwood.

I am once again driven to the conclusion that all information about the usage of Johnston's Warehousing was deliberately withheld from the Loss Adjusters for as long as possible, in the hope that a settlement of the claim would be negotiated without full information about the alternative arrangements availed of by Superwood ever being divulged.

I conclude my findings of fact in the case by re-affirming that in my opinion, Thornton & Partners, Scully [Tyrrell] and Co., and Mr Noel Cooke representing Stokes Kennedy Crowley at all times carried out their respective functions in relation to the examinations of the claim in a highly professional and impressive manner, and they and everyone representing the Insurers showed amazing patience, reasonableness, and at the same time, tenacity, in the manner in which they dealt with the insured and everyone representing the Insured.

Mr Ballesty, who had had previous dealings with the Insurers and their representatives, was — on the whole — generous in his recognition of the high standing which they enjoyed, and said ... about the leading Insurer —

"They are a highly reputable company. I have no problems with the Sun as a Company ... I am glad you gave me the opportunity to record it.... I have no problems with the Sun Alliance. My view of the Sun is, they are an excellent company."

It is fair to say that nothing I have heard in this lengthy case has detracted in any way, in my judgment, from the tribute paid to them by Mr Ballesty.

Conclusions of Law

It will be at once apparent from the findings of fact already recited that, in my opinion, there are clear and serious breaches by Superwood of their obligations under Condition 4 of the Consequential Loss Policy, the relevant part of which reads as follows:—

> "4. On the happening of any damage in consequence of which a claim is or may be made under this policy the insured shall ... at his own expense ... produce and furnish to the insurers such books of account and other business books, vouchers, invoices, balance sheets and other documents, proofs, information, explanation and other evidence as may reasonably be required by the insurers for the purpose of investigating or verifying the claim.... No claim under this policy shall be payable unless the terms of this condition shall have been complied with and in the event of non-compliance therewith in any respect, any payment on account of the claim already made shall be repaid to the insurers forthwith.

I am satisfied that by reason of these breaches, the Plaintiffs have disqualified themselves from claiming any payment whatever under the policy and that their claim must be dismissed.

The Defendants also rely on the provisions of Condition 5 of the policy, which reads as follows:—

> "If the claim be in any respect fraudulent or if any fraudulent means or devices be used by the insured or anyone acting on his behalf to obtain any benefit under this policy or if any damage be occasioned by the wilful act or with the connivance of the insured, all benefits under this policy shall be forfeited."

As I have already decided that the Defendants must succeed in reliance on the provisions of Condition 4 of the Policy, it may not be necessary for me to decide the issue of law involved in the Defendants' further reliance on Condition 5 of the Policy, and I propose to adjourn my decision on this issue until the opening day of the Michaelmas Term when I can be informed by the parties whether they also require this issue of law to be dealt with in my judgment.

(This case is on appeal to the Supreme Court.)

Superwood Holdings plc and Others *v.*
Sun Alliance and London Insurance plc t/a Sun Alliance
Insurance Group and Others (No. 2)
Unreported, 12 November 1991
The High Court

O'HANLON J.: In the judgment already delivered by me in this case on the 13th, 14th and 15th August, 1991, I decided the action in favour of the Defendants on the basis of the findings that the Plaintiffs had been shown to be in breach of the terms of insurance policies on which they sought to rely, by reason of breaches of Condition 4 in the policies requiring them to furnish all information which might reasonably be required by the insurers for the purpose of investigating or verifying the claim.

I left over for further consideration my decision in relation to the other issue of law raised by the Defendants in their defence to the claim, which was based on Condition 5 of the policies. This Condition provides, inter alia, that all benefit under the policies was to be forfeited "if the claim be in any respect fraudulent or if any fraudulent means or devices be used by the insured or anyone acting on his behalf to obtain any benefit under this policy...."

I indicated that as I had already decided in the Defendants' favour by reason of the provisions of Condition 4 of the policies, it might not be necessary for me to deal further with the plea under Condition 5 but as one of the parties requires me to deal with this issue also, I now propose to do so.

In my judgment, the findings of fact which I have already made lead on inexorably to a finding of fraud against the Plaintiffs. A claim for compensation under the relevant policies was put forward which was, in my opinion, far in excess of the real loss sustained by the Plaintiffs for which they were entitled to claim under their Consequential Loss policies. In support of this claim the Plaintiffs did everything in their power to prevent the Defendants from carrying out a proper investigation of the loss. They deliberately concealed from the Defendants information which was in their possession or procurement which was relevant to the claim which was repeatedly sought by the Defendants' representatives, notably in relation to the trading history of the Plaintiffs; the research carried out with regard to the potential market for their products in Ireland and the United Kingdom; the production capacity of the Plaintiffs; their books of account and other trading records; the arrangements made for alternative storage while the premises destroyed by fire were being rebuilt. They also deliberately misrepresented the true position in relation to a number of these matters.

As the firms of Kinnear and Co./ Grant Thornton, Auditors and Accountants, and Balcombe and Co., Loss Assessors, were actively engaged in the presentation of the claim on behalf of the Plaintiffs, I think I should make it clear that, in my opinion, neither firm was implicated in the findings of deliberate withholding of information and fraud which I have made against the Plaintiffs.

I find that numerous breaches of Condition 5 of the policies were committed by the Plaintiffs in putting forward a claim which was fraudulent in many respects, as outlined already in the findings of fact which I have made in relation to the claim, and the action must be dismissed on this ground also, in addition to the ground already referred to in the judgment delivered on the 13th, 14th and 15th August, 1991.

(This case is on appeal to the Supreme Court.)

Una Gray *v.* Hibernian Insurance Company Limited
Unreported, 27 May 1993
The High Court

BARRON J: The Bolton Horse public house was destroyed by fire on the 30th November, 1982. The premises were owned by the Plaintiff's husband ("the deceased") and were insured with the Defendant Company. Following the fire the deceased made a claim against the Defendant under his policy. At the same time he commenced proceedings to recover damages for malicious injury. These proceedings came on for hearing on the 25th June, 1984. On that date the deceased was arrested and charged with being implicated in the fire. The malicious injury proceedings were accordingly adjourned.

The deceased was charged with arson. His trial took place on the 19th June, 1985. The nature of the evidence against him was that of two persons ("the accomplices") who maintained that they had been instructed by the decesased to set fire to the premises. The deceased himself gave evidence on his own behalf. In the event the jury acquitted him of the charge.

On the 8th July, 1985 the deceased called upon the Defendant to admit liability under the policy. The Defendant refused to admit liability until such time as the malicious injury application was concluded. It claimed to be so entitled pursuant to a term of the policy.

On the 25th February, 1986 the deceased commenced proceedings to enforce the policy. These proceedings were referred to arbitration by an Order of this Court on the 13th June, 1986. The arbitration was held on the 24th July, 1987 and the arbitrator held against the Defendant, and found that the deceased was not obliged to proceed with the malicious injury application in the absence of the determination by the Defendant as to whether or not to accept liability under the policy.

On the 11th November, 1987 the Defendant accepted liability under the policy and on the 15th March, 1988 made a payment of £100,000 on account. The parties could not agree upon the amount to be paid on foot of the policy, nor could they agree upon the appointment of an arbitrator.

Accordingly further proceedings were commenced on the 28th March, 1988 to obtain an Order for the appointment of an arbitrator. This arbitrator was appointed by the Court on the 20th June, 1988 and proceedings took place before him, including a preliminary hearing which took place on the 12th June, 1989.

Meanwhile, the Plaintiff's husband had died on the 17th September, 1988. Prior to his death some correspondence had taken place between the Solicitors for the parties as to evidence to be given in relation to quantum at the application. Following the deceased's death the Solicitors for the Defendant wrote on the 27th September, 1988 indicating that they were being prejudiced by the lengthy delay in bringing forward the malicious injury application for hearing. By a further letter dated the 27th February, 1989 they indicated that their client was no longer prepared to continue with the arbitration as to quantum and regarded themselves as no longer bound under the terms of the arbitration agreement.

On the 7th July, 1988 they commenced proceedings to stay the arbitration until the Plaintiff had disposed of the malicious injury application. These proceedings were compromised on the 12th February, 1991 in the following terms:—

> "This action is hereby settled and all further proceedings herein stayed upon the terms following:
>
> (1) The Defendant will pursue a malicious injury application against Dublin Corporation in accordance with the request already made herein pursuant to Condition 6 of the policy of insurance and with the benefit of the indemnity as to costs already given, with all reasonable expedition up to the conclusion of the same in the Circuit Court.
> (2) Upon the delivery of judgment by the Circuit Court on the said application, the Defendant shall be at liberty to proceed with the arbitration of her claim under the said policy.
> (3) The Plaintiff undertakes unconditionally that it will not withdraw its agreement to indemnify the Defendant in respect of her claim under the said policy.
> (4) Each party will bear his own costs of this action."

The malicious injury application came on for hearing on the 7th May, 1991. At that hearing evidence was given by the accomplices on behalf of Dublin Corporation. The Circuit Court Judge found that the accomplices were probably telling the truth and dismissed the application. On the following day the Defendant repudiated liability under the policy and on the day following such repudiation the present proceedings were commenced.

The Defendant submits that the Plaintiff is disentitled to succeed because the loss upon which she relies was caused by the deliberate act of her husband. Two bases are put forward for this submission. First, as a matter of public policy that a man may not recover for loss sustained by his own deliberate act. Secondly, that it is the rule of insurance law that an insured cannot recover when he has deliberately caused the event upon which policy specifies that indemnity should be payable. The Defendant relies upon the decision of the Circuit Court Judge in dismissing the malicious injury application. The Plaintiff contends that that decision does not create any estoppel as between the Plaintiff and the Defendant in these proceedings, and that the onus of establishing the wrongdoing on the part of the deceased lies upon the Defendant.

The two propositions for which the Defendant contends are fully dealt with by the House of Lords in England in *Beresford* v. *Royal Insurance Company Limited*.[14] In that case there was a policy of life assurance. It provided that if the life assured should die by his own hand whether sane or

---

[14] [1938] 2 All E.R. 602.

insane within one year from the commencement of the insurance the policy should be void as against any person claiming the amount thereby assured or any part thereof. In June, 1934 he became insolvent. He had no means of repaying his creditors save with the insurance monies. Just before the policy expired he shot himself. It was held in those circumstances that it would be contrary to public policy to allow the personal representative of the assured to recover under the policy. In the judgment of Lord Atkin he considered that there were two questions to be answered:

(1) What was the contract made by the parties?
(2) How was that contract affected by public policy?"

In dealing with the first of those questions he said at page 604:

> "On ordinary principles of insurance law, an assured cannot by his own deliberate act cause the event upon which the insurance money is payable. The insurers have not agreed to pay on that happening. The fire assured cannot recover if he intentionally burns down his house, nor the marine if he scuttles his ship, nor the life assured if he deliberately ends his own life. This is not the result of public policy, but of the correct construction of the contract."

Then on page 605 he said:

> " ... I entertain no doubt that, on the true construction of this contract, the insurance company have agreed with the assured to pay his executors or assignees on his death the sum assured, if he dies by his own hand whether sane or insane, after the expiration of one year from the commencement of the assurance ... the meaning is clear, and one may assume from what one knows of tariff conditions that it is a usual clause. There is no doubt, therefore, that, on the proper construction of this contract, the insurance company promised (its insured) that, if he, in full possession of his senses, intentionally killed himself, they would pay his executors or assignees the sum assured."

Dealing with the second question, he said at page 607:—

> "I think that the principle is that a man is not to be allowed to have recourse to a court of justice to claim a benefit from his crime, whether under a contract or under a gift. No doubt the rule pays regard to the fact that to hold otherwise would in some cases offer an inducement to crime, or remove a restraint to crime, and that its effect is to act as a deterrent to crime, but, apart from these considerations, the absolute rule is that the courts will not recognise the benefit accruing to a criminal on his crime."

In the event, the claim failed.

The reason for the first rule is that an insurer must be presumed as a matter of construction of the contract when it is silent as to suicide not to have intended to be on cover on such circumstances. Where, on the proper construction of the contract, he did so intend, then he cannot rely upon the criminal act as a pure matter of contract to repudiate liability. In my view, that is how the acceptance of liability by the Defendant should be viewed. It agreed knowing the full allegations being made against the deceased that it would honour the policy.

The settlement entered into in February, 1991 is to the same effect although stronger. The use of the words "the Plaintiff undertakes unconditionally" can only mean that the Defendant would not repudiate the policy upon any ground, and certainly not upon the ground of the deceased's involvement in the fire. Evidence has been given on behalf of the Defendant by the Solicitor acting for the Defendant in the proceedings which were compromised that the purport of that compromise was to ensure that the malicious injury application continued and that the Defendant was reaffirming its agreement to accept liability under the policy. She further gave evidence to the effect that she did not believe that use of the word ["]unconditionally["] was intended to bar the Defendant from all time from honouring the policy. Evidence was given as to the negotiations which took place prior to that settlement. The negotiations took place between the Counsel for each party. Mr Fennelly, Counsel for the Plaintiff, gave evidence that he told Mr Kelly, Counsel for the insurance company, that he wanted to ensure that the insurance company could not withdraw acceptance of liability. An attendance made by the Defendant's Solicitor at the time puts the matter slightly more strongly in that Counsel was indicating to her that Counsel for the Plaintiff wanted such an assurance.

I do not think that what occurred prior to this settlement is of any great significance. I am satisfied from the terms of the settlement itself that the insurance company with full knowledge of the allegations which were being made against the deceased had already agreed willingly to accept liability under the policy. I am satisfied therefore that as a matter of construction the Defendant agreed to pay on foot of the policy.

The issue of public policy was considered in *R* v. *National Insurance Commissioner, Ex-parte Connor*[15] an application by a widow for a widow's allowances pursuant to the Social Security Acts was refused upon the basis that she had become a widow through her own intentional criminal act. She had been convicted of manslaughter of her husband and the Court accepted that the verdict of the jury must have been based upon a belief that she had deliberately caused the act which caused his death. In judgment of Lord Lane C.J. at page 773 he quotes a passage from the charge by the trial Judge to the jury in which the trial Judge put the evidence of the wife to the jury. In that passage he ended by saying:—

> "The only issue is whether what happened was done deliberately in order to hurt, or whether it happened accidentally, and from the start to the finish, from the very first moment she opened her mouth to the police, she has maintained it was an accident."

In that case the court decided that as a matter of public policy that the widow was not entitled to the allowance she claimed.

---

[15] [1981] 1 All E.R. 769.

The two submissions made on behalf of the Defendant assumed an onus of proof upon the balance of probabilities. In my view, this is not so. The defence of illegality in relation to insurance law is a question of contract. Here, if the Defendant had not admitted liability, it would have had to prove the deceased's involvement in the malicious damage as a matter of probability. Once that defence fails, the Defendant is asking the Court to deny to the Plaintiff upon grounds of public policy the benefit of the cause of action which she has established. To succeed on this defence it must therefore establish that the deceased committed a crime. The issue arises in civil proceedings, but the defence is permitted only because to refuse it would be to allow an unconscionable result. In my view, that requires a heavier standard of proof than the balance of probabilities.

There are only two pieces of evidence which have been adduced upon this issue:

(1) the acquittal of the deceased upon the charge of arson; and

(2) the finding by the Circuit Court that the evidence of the accomplices was probably correct.

The admissibility of the latter finding has been challenged on the ground that it does not found an estoppel against the Plaintiff. I do not accept that submission. The issue being raised is not strictly an issue in personam. It is in reality an issue in rem.

There is a considerable difference in interpretation between a verdict of guilty and a verdict of not guilty. The meaning of the former is clear. The jury is satisfied beyond reasonable doubt that the accused has committed the crime with which he is charged. In the present case, no such certainty can be inferred from the verdict that the deceased was not guilty. The jury may have had a reasonable doubt, they may have believed the deceased totally, or they might have taken a view somewhere between the two. It is not appropriate in my view, as the Defendant submits, to ignore this verdict upon the basis that it is not of any value where the onus of proof is not beyond reasonable doubt, but on the balance of probabilities. That submission is based as I have already indicated upon a false premise as to the onus of proof upon the present issue.

The deceased was acquitted by a jury in a criminal trial. In the course of that trial he gave evidence on his own behalf and evidence was given against him by the accomplices. Before the Circuit Court the accomplices gave the same evidence. At this date the deceased was dead and was unable to give evidence on his own behalf. In those circumstances, can the Court be satisfied even on the balance of probabilities that if the deceased had given evidence before the Circuit Court that the Circuit Court decision would have been the same. Obviously, it cannot.

The position accordingly is as follows. The accused was acquitted at his own trial when he was there to defend himself. The evidence of the accomplices was accepted on the probabilities when he was not there to defend himself. In my view, public policy could not require the Court on such evidence to deny to his estate the benefits to which it is entitled by contract.

To do so would neither be fair nor seen to be fair. Whatever the onus of proof upon the Defendant upon this issue, it could not be so low as to be satisfied by the evidence adduced. It is accordingly unnecessary to indicate the proper standard of proof nor the evidence by which it should be established.

The issue set down for determination will be answered accordingly.

CHAPTER 10

Road Traffic Insurance

The statutory scheme of compulsory insurance for motor vehicles was originally implemented in Ireland by the Road Traffic Act, 1933. The current statutory frame work is found in the Road Traffic Act, 1961 which repealed and to a large extent re-enacted the provisions of the earlier legislation. Thus, cases relating to the provisions of the 1933 Act can still be of importance when interpreting the 1961 legislation and the subsequent amendments.

The provisions discussed in this chapter are those which have most often been the subject of judicial consideration.

Section 56 re-enacts section 56 of the 1933 Act. In essence it provides that a mechanically propelled vehicle may be used only when insured. Section 56 of the 1933 Act was considered by the High Court in *Attorney General* v. *Downes* (1959). In this case a servant of the owner was charged under the section with driving without insurance.

In *Greaney* v. *Scully* (1981) a case was stated by a Circuit Judge to the Supreme Court. Here, the defendant had been convicted under section 56 of driving his father's lorry without insurance. He appealed the conviction to the Circuit Court. The Circuit Judge took the view that the restriction of cover allowed by the Road Traffic (Compulsory Insurance) Regulations, 1962, exceeded the powers delegated to the Minister by the Act, with the result that the defendant's driving should have been covered by the policy. The Supreme Court, however, did not agree with the Circuit Judge's interpretation.

The 1933 legislation created the concept of an "approved policy of insurance" which was one that did not contain "prohibited conditions". Conditions were prohibited if they had the affect of reducing the scope of third party protection under the policy. Article 4 of the Road Traffic (Third Party Risks) Regulations, 1933, defined a "prohibited condition" as one coming within any of the classes listed in its First Schedule.

One such "prohibited condition" was considered in *McCarthy* v. *Murphy* (1938). In this case an insurance company sought to resist paying out on foot of a judgment obtained against its policyholder. The company unsuccessfully argued that cover did not operate because of the policyholder's failure to record the appropriate details in the register which the policy required the policyholder to keep. The High Court, however, held that this obligation on the policyholder was a prohibited condition and the company could not therefore rely on the policyholder's failure to keep such a record as a reason for not paying the claim.

In *O'Donnell* v. *The Yorkshire Insurance Company Limited* (1949), the plaintiff policyholder applied unsuccessfully to his insurance company for reimbursement of his own legal costs incurred in defending a claim in circumstances where the insurer had repudiated liability. Two points of interest emerge from the judgment:—

- The High Court accepted that whilst the determination of an insurer's liability by reference to an arbitration clause was a prohibited condition as between the insurer and a third party, such a clause was not necessarily a prohibited condition as between the policyholder and the insurer.

- In situations where a policy was not issued to the policyholder, any cover note issued by the insurer formed the basis of the contract with the insured.

In *Higgins* v. *Feeney* (1952) the plaintiff who had been injured in a collision with a motorcycle obtained judgment against the defendant. At the time of the occurrence the defendant was carrying a pillion passenger. One of the policy conditions provided that cover did not include "use while carrying any passenger unless a side-car is attached to the motor-cycle". The plaintiff unsuccessfully argued that this was a prohibited condition insofar as the insurer's liability was made to depend on the "construction, equipment, maintenance or state of repair of the vehicle".

Section 78 of the 1933 Act was re-enacted as section 76 of the 1961 Act. It permits an individual in certain circumstances to serve notice directly on the insurers of a claim or award against its policyholder. Having served such notice, the individual is entitled to proceed against the insurer for certain reliefs.

Judge Sheehy in *McGee* v. *London Assurance Company* (1943) discussed the intention behind s. 78 and put it into its general context.

Brady v. *Brady* (1937) involved an unsuccessful application under section 78 (1) (c) for liberty to execute judgment directly against the defendant's insurer.

The insurance policy in this case did not cover drivers who, to the knowledge of the insured, were not entitled to hold a driving licence. The policyholder in this case had been aware that his son — whose driving had caused the accident — was too young to hold the licence that had been issued to him.

Hayes v. *Legal Insurance Company Limited* (1940) is an example of the application of section 78 (1) (d) which enables the court to grant liberty to an individual to proceed against an insurer where it is "just and equitable" to do so. In this case, the owner had been killed in a traffic accident in which the plaintiff was injured. Representation to the driver's estate had not been raised and, in the absence of an application under section 78, the plaintiff could not have proceeded with his claim.

In *Kelleher* v. *Christopherson* (1956) the plaintiff brought an application under section 78 to recover an award of damages and costs. The insurance company had repudiated liability on the grounds that at the time of the traffic accident, the motor policyholder had been carrying swill in the course of a business or trade for which he was not insured. The Circuit Judge, however, had no difficulty in finding for the plaintiff.

The Supreme Court in *Whelan* v. *Dixon* (1957) held that in an application under section 78 it was for the claimant to establish that the defendant's motor car was being driven in accordance with the limitations as to use contained in the policy.

In *O'Leary* v. *Irish National Insurance Company* (1958)[1] the third party could not proceed against the insurer, as a valid policy did not exist, the insured not having an insurable interest in the motor vehicle involved in the accident.

Stanbridge v. *Healy* (1983) concerned an application under section 76 of the 1961 Act. Here, the insurance company successfully argued that a roadway in the grounds of a country house where an accident had happened was not a public place under section 3 of the Road Traffic Act and there was therefore no obligation on the defendant policyholder to be insured at that place under section 56. Thus, the plaintiff was held not to be entitled to proceed under section 76.

A similar view was expressed in *D.P.P.* v. *Molloy* (1993) which involved a traffic offence committed in Grafton Street.

Bus Éireann v. *Insurance Corporation of Ireland* (1994) arose out of a road traffic accident in which the defendants' policyholder was fatally injured. Unfortunately, his policy of insurance did not indemnify him in respect of his driving at the time of the accident.

The plaintiff contended, unsuccessfully, that section 76 created a new cause of action against the deceased's insurer and that its case therefore was not governed by the limitation period which operated in respect of claims brought against the estate of a deceased person.

The judge also accepted the defendants' contention that the extent

---

[1] See Chapter 5, pp. 115–22.

of its liability was limited to the amount of cover which section 76 specified as being compulsory in respect of injury to property.

The Attorney General (At the Prosecution of Superintendent Hayes) *v.* Downes
(1959) 93 I.L.T.R. 121
The High Court

DAVITT P: In this case the question submitted by the District Justice involves the interpretation of section 56 of the Road Traffic Act, 1933. That section, by sub-section (1), prohibits as unlawful the driving in a public place of a mechanically propelled vehicle unless, generally speaking, it is covered by insurance in accordance with the provisions of sub-paragraphs (a) (b) and (c) of the sub-section. Sub-section (2) need not concern us. Sub-section (3) makes it an offence for both owner and driver if the vehicle is driven in contravention of the section. Sub-section (4) we are not concerned with. Sub-sections (5) and (6) provide special defences for owner and driver.

On the facts as stated it is clear that Patrick Redican on the occasion in question drove a car when it was not covered by insurance. The District Justice, however, held that he had established the special defence provided by sub-section (6), as he was satisfied that Redican was driving it in obedience to the express orders of the owner, and dismissed the charge against him. He also dismissed the charge against the owner because he was of opinion that the dismissal of the charge against the driver was an adjudication to the effect that the driver had not driven in contravention of the section.

The net point is whether he was correct in this opinion.

The key word is "contravention". The section contains one, and only one, prohibition: the prohibition in sub-section (1) against driving an uninsured vehicle. The only way in which the section can be contravened is by such driving contrary to sub-section (1). It is quite clear that Redican did contravene the prohibition contained in that sub-section, even though, by reason of the special defence provided by sub-section (6) he committed no offence in doing so.

In my opinion the District Justice was wrong in the view he took and the question submitted should be answered accordingly.

HAUGH J: I agree.

MURNAGHAN J: I agree.

Greaney *v.* Scully
[1981] I.L.R.M. 340
The Supreme Court

HENCHY J: The defendant was convicted in the District Court of an offence contrary to s. 56 of the Road Traffic Act, 1961. Put colloquially, this offence was that of driving a lorry on the public road when he was not covered by insurance. S. 56 (I)(a) of the 1961 Act required that, in the circumstances, he should have had

> an approved policy of insurance whereby the user or some other person who would be liable for injury caused by the negligent use of the vehicle at that time by the user, is insured against all sums without limit (save as is hereinafter provided) which the user or his personal representative or such other person or his personal representative shall become liable to pay to any person (exclusive of the excepted persons) by way of damages or costs on account of injury to person or property caused by the negligent use of the vehicle at that time by the user.

Unfortunately, the defendant's use of the vehicle fell outside the requirements of that provision. There was in fact a policy of insurance in force in respect of the vehicle, but the person insured under it was the defendant's father, and he was the only person whose driving was covered by the policy. Consequently, if the defendant, by negligent driving on the occasion in question, had caused injury to another road user, there would have been no insurance to meet the damages that would become payable to the injured person. The defendant, therefore, as user of the vehicle, on the face of things, committed an offence contrary to s. 56, as amended by Part VI of the Road Traffic Act, 1968.

So much is common case. It was not, I think, contended on behalf of the defendant that he was not, at least prima facie, in breach of the requirements of s. 56. Accordingly, the District Justice had no option but to convict him of the offence charged. He was fined £100, disqualified from holding a driving licence for twelve months, and an order was made that particulars of the conviction and disqualification be endorsed on his driving licence.

The defendant appealed to the Circuit Court against that order. The appeal came before Judge Sheridan, sitting at Waterford. On the hearing of the appeal, the defendant's contravention of s. 56, to the extent I have indicated, was clearly established, but the point was taken (apparently by the Circuit Court judge himself) that the policy of insurance in question was an approved policy of insurance for the purpose of s. 56, notwithstanding the fact that it provided no insurance cover for any negligent driving by the defendant. Insofar as I understand the basis for this point, it would seem to be that, while the policy was issued in compliance with the Road Traffic (Compulsory Insurance) Regulations, 1962 (i.e. SI No. 14 of 1962, which I shall call 'the Regulations'), the restriction of cover allowed by the Regulations exceeded the powers delegated to the Minister to make such Regulations. Accordingly, in the opinion of the Circuit judge the limitation of cover to the defendant's father was permitted by Regulations which he (the judge) considered to be *ultra vires*, so that the defendant's driving should be held to have been covered by the policy. He would therefore have allowed the appeal and dismissed the complaint; but before doing so, he stated this case, at the request of the complainant, so that the opinion of this Court might be got as to whether the Regulations are *ultra vires* to the extent that they provide for a policy which limits cover by specifying by name the persons to be covered.

... [W]as the defendant covered by an approved policy of insurance (notwithstanding the fact that he was excluded from its cover) because his exclusion resulted from a limitation or restriction of the cover caused by Regulations which in this respect were *ultra vires*? I must confess that that statement of the point at issue may not be complete or precise, for although I have carefully read the provisional judgment which the judge annexed to the case stated, I am not sure that I understand the reasons why he was minded to hold that the Regulations are *ultra vires* and that the conviction cannot stand.

In the course of his provisional judgment, the judge said that

> the courts, it seems to me, must endeavour to safeguard the position of third parties irrespective of any contractual arrangements made between the insurers or (sic) the insured or any liability over which may exist in favour of an insurer against the user of a vehicle the subject of an approved Policy of Insurance or a Certificate of Insurance.

With respect, I cannot agree. I do not think the scheme of compulsory insurance contained in Part VI of the Road Traffic Act, 1961, imposes any such duty on the courts. It is the user of the vehicle who must ensure that the vehicle is adequately insured. If it is not, then so far as the criminal law is concerned, the user commits an offence contrary to s. 56; and so far as the civil law is concerned, a person negligently injured is left to pursue a claim for damage against the user, or against somebody who is liable in law for the user's conduct; or if such a claim would be worthless, to seek such compensation as may be recoverable from the Motor Insurers' Bureau. The object of the statutory scheme is, of course, to compel users of all mechanically propelled vehicles (save those who are covered by an approved guarantee or who are exempted persons under s. 60) to have an approved policy of insurance, so that the injured third parties will recover full compensation. But if it is found by a court that a policy of insurance relied on is not an approved policy of insurance (as defined by s. 62), I fear I cannot agree with the judge's opinion that the court 'must endeavour to safeguard the position of third parties irrespective of any contractual arrangements made'. If a court were to hold an insurance policy to be an approved policy of insurance when in fact it is not, the court would be illegally and unjustly perverting its functions. In a prosecution such as the present, where the user is charged with a breach of s. 56 by using the vehicle in a public place without having an approved policy of insurance, the sole issue is whether the prosecution have proved beyond reasonable doubt that the policy relied on by the defendant is an approved policy of insurance, having regard to the relevant statutory provisions and to duly made Regulations. As I have pointed out, it clearly does not comply with the statutory requirements. The only point remaining, therefore is: is there some *ultra vires* feature of the Regulations that prevents the policy from being an approved policy of insurance?

The suggestion apparently is that the Regulations are *ultra vires* in that they expressly allow (see Art. 5 and the First Schedule) an approved policy of insurance to contain a condition limiting the persons to be covered by specifying by name the persons to be covered. In my view, such a permitted condition has no relevance to the circumstances of this case. A scrutiny of the policy shows that it does not specify by name the persons to be covered. It simply provides that the insured (i.e. the defendant's father) is the only person who comes under the category of "Persons Or Classes of Persons Whose Liability is Covered". The defendant is an excepted person by the nature and scope of the policy (which covers liability and driving of the insured only) and not because he has been excluded by name. But even if he had been excluded by name from cover, I fail to see how the Regulations could be said to be *ultra vires* by permitting such an exclusion. A permission or a prohibition allowed or required by the Regulations to be inserted in an approved policy could be held to be *ultra vires* only if, in allowing or requiring such an insertion, the Minister in question (as the designated author of the Regulations) exceeded the powers which may reasonably be said to have been expressly or impliedly delegated to him by the Act. In different places (see, for example, s. 56 (I)(a) and s. 62 (I)(b)) the Act envisages that certain persons may be excepted persons. It stands to reason that the scheme of [C]ompulsory Insurance designed by Part VI of the Act would be unworkable unless certain persons or classes of person (such as disqualified drivers) could be excepted from the cover provided by the policy. But when the Regulations provide that any limitation or restriction on the persons or classes of persons or the physical or mental condition of persons whose driving of a vehicle is covered by the policy shall be a prohibited condition unless it is effected, *inter alia,* by specifying by name the persons to be covered, the Minister as maker of the Regulations is ensuring that an approved policy will provide a very wide range of cover and is therefore in keeping with the spirit and purpose of Part VI. Nothing in the argument propounded on behalf of the defendant has persuaded me that any part of the Regulations relied on is outside the powers delegated to the Minister.

On the assumption that the Circuit Court judge has jurisdiction to state a case on whether the Regulations were made *ultra vires,* I would reply to the questions posed in the case stated by ruling that (a) the Circuit Court judge would be wrong in law if he dismissed the complaint and (b) the relied-on parts of the Regulations are not *ultra vires* and do not detract from the fact that the defendant was in breach of s. 56 of the 1961 Act.

McCarthy v. Murphy
[1938] I.R. 737
The High Court

O'BYRNE J. (MAGUIRE P. CONCURRING): In this case the plaintiff, on the 4th day of March, 1936, recovered judgment against the defendants in the Circuit Court at Wexford for the sum of £250 and costs (which have since been taxed at the sum of £45 7s. 1d.) in respect of damage sustained by him through the negligence of the defendants' servant in the driving and management of a motor car. The car was the property of Messrs M. Murphy & Sons, Motor Garage Proprietors, of which firm the defendant, Mary Murphy, seems to be sole proprietor, and was driven by the defendant, Patrick Murphy, as servant and agent of the said firm.

On the 27th day of November, 1936, the plaintiff, pursuant to sect. 78 of the Road Traffic Act, 1933, obtained liberty from the said Court to execute the said judgment against the Union Assurance Society, Limited, being the vehicle insurers of the said firm, and this appeal is brought by the insurance company against the said order.

The policy of insurance in this case was entered into between the said insurance company and Messrs M. Murphy & Sons.... The policy is what is generally referred to as a "Garage Policy" and it covers "any motor vehicle, the property of the insured or in his custody or control, not exceeding 30 horse power...." The motor car involved in the said accident comes within the fore-going description, and was held to be the property of the insured, or in their custody or control, and, on the material date, was driven from the premises of the insured.

By memorandum attached to and forming part of the said policy, it is provided that:—

> "It is a condition precedent to any liability of the company under this policy that:—
>
> "1. Before each and every departure of a motor vehicle from the insured's premises there shall be recorded in a special register kept by the insured for the purposes of this policy the date and time of departure of such vehicle and its make, horse power, and registered number (or chassis number, if the vehicle itself is not registered)."

Particulars of the said car were not inserted in the register kept by the insured in accordance with said memorandum and, accordingly, it is con-tended on behalf of the insurance company that the car was not covered on the material journey. It will be noted that under clause 1 of the memorandum the necessary particulars should have been recorded in the register before the commencement of the journey. Clauses 2 and 3 of the memorandum deal with cases in which the particulars are to be recorded in the register after the completion of the journey. It was contended on behalf of the insurance company that clause 1 of the memorandum was severable from the remaining clauses and that the policy should be construed accordingly. It seems to me that, if the policy stood alone, there would be considerable force behind this contention; but, in view of the conclusion at which I have arrived, I am of opinion that the question does not arise and I express no opinion upon it.

On the 18th February, 1935, the insurance company issued to the insured a certificate of insurance, in pursuance of sect. 68 of the Road Traffic Act, 1933, certifying that an approved policy of insurance had been issued to the insured and purporting to state the prescribed particulars of the policy. The description of the vehicles, the driving of which is covered, is stated in the same way as in the policy. The memorandum, to which I have referred, is not set out in the certificate. There is, however, the following proviso, which was obviously intended to take the place of the memorandum, viz.:—

> "Provided that the make, H.P., index mark and registration number (or chassis number, if the vehicle itself is not registered) and dates and times of journeys made shall be recorded in the special register kept by the insured for the purposes of the policy."

This proviso is intended to be comprehensive. It does not draw any distinction between different classes of journeys, and I am of opinion that it would be a compliance with the terms of the proviso to enter the necessary particulars in the register at any time, whether before or after any particular journey, irrespective of where such journey commenced.

I turn now to sect. 69, sub-sect. 1 *(b)*, of the said Act, which provides that where an insurer has issued a certificate of insurance under sect. 68, then, if such insurer has issued to the insured such policy as is described in such certificate but the actual terms of such policy are less favourable to persons claiming under or by virtue of such policy against such insurer, either directly or through the insured, than the particulars of such policy as stated in such certificate, such policy shall as between such insurer and any other person except the insured, be deemed to be in terms conforming in all respects with the said particulars stated in the said certificate. It seems to me obvious that the terms of the policy, in the foregoing respect, are less favourable to persons claiming under the policy against the insurer than the particulars of the policy as stated in the certificate, and accordingly I am of opinion that for the purpose of this appeal I must treat the policy in this respect as being conformable with the particulars stated in the certificate.

Sect. 62 of the Act deals with and defines what constitutes an "approved policy of insurance" within the meaning of the Act. Sub-sect. 1 of that section, so far as it is material, provides that:—

"A policy of insurance shall be an approved policy of insurance within the meaning of this Act if, but only if, it complies with all the following conditions, that is to say:—
'(c) the liability of the insurer under the policy is not subject to any condition, restriction or limitation, which is prescribed as a condition, restriction or limitation (as the case may be) which shall not be inserted in an approved policy of insurance.'"

Sect. 6 provides that the Minister may by order make regulations prescribing any matter or thing which is referred to in the Act as prescribed or to be prescribed.

In exercise of the powers conferred upon him by the said Act and of certain other powers therein mentioned, the Minister for Local Government and Public Health made regulations, known as the Road Traffic (Third Party Risks) Regulations, 1933, on the 10th day of November, 1933. It was suggested by Mr FitzGibbon, in the course of his argument, that the power of the Minister to make some of these regulations might be open to question. The matter was left there and no argument was addressed to us upon the matter. In the absence of any such argument, I propose to deal with the case upon the assumption that the regulations were within the power of the Minister and were properly made.

Article 4 of the regulations provides as follows:—

"(1) In this article the expression 'prohibited condition' means and includes every condition, restriction, or limitation on the liability of the coverer under a covering instrument which comes within any of the classes mentioned in the First Schedule to these regulations or any other condition, restriction, or limitation which has substantially the same effect as a condition, restriction or limitation which is so specified.

(2) There shall not be inserted in a covering instrument any condition, restriction or limitation on the liability of the coverer which affects the right of any person except the holder of the covering instrument or an excepted person to recover by virtue [of] the covering instrument an amount under sect. 78 of the Act, or which could have the effect of reducing the amount which such a person could so recover, if such condition, restriction, or limitation is a prohibited condition."

The prohibited conditions are set out in the First Schedule to the regulations. One of the conditions, so prescribed, is "any condition under which the existence or the amount of the liability of the coverer depends on any specified thing being done or omitted to be done after any negligent driving which is covered by the covering instrument."

I have already pointed out that, in my opinion, the proviso, as contained in the certificate of insurance, would be fully and properly complied with by entering the necessary particulars in the register at any time, even after the negligent driving, and accordingly it seems to me that that proviso is a condition under which the existence of the liability of the coverer depends on some specified thing being done or omitted to be done after a negligent driving which is covered by the policy. If I am right in this, then the proviso is clearly a prohibited condition within the meaning of the Act and the regulations made under it.

I turn again to the policy of insurance. Several conditions are endorsed upon the policy. At the commencement of these conditions, appears the following:—

"Any condition of this policy and/or of any endorsement thereon, in so far as it is a prohibited condition within the meaning of Part V of the Road Traffic Act, 1933, shall not be a condition affecting the right of any person to recover an amount under and by virtue of the provisions of sect. 78 of the said Act."

It was contended by Mr FitzGibbon that this condition is operative only as between the parties to the policy, and that it does not affect the rights of third parties, even those relying upon sect. 78 of the Act. In my opinion, this argument is entirely unsustainable. In the first instance, and apart from the provisions of sect. 78, of course the policy and every clause and term thereof is binding only as between the parties thereto. The rights of the parties to the policy are contractual rights and must be determined by the terms of the contract. The rights of the plaintiff, as against the insurer, are statutory rights; but the terms of the contract must be looked at for the purpose of determining whether the provisions of the statute have been fulfilled, so as to validate a claim under the section. The question at issue in this case turns upon whether there was, or, alternatively, whether the Court is bound to hold that there was, an approved policy covering the particular risk. That the policy was intended to be an approved policy is beyond all question and the object of the condition, to which I have referred, seems to me to be quite clear.

It was obviously feared that some clause of the policy should be held to be a prohibited condition within the meaning of the Act, which would have the effect (amongst others) of defeating the claims of persons claiming under sect.

78, and the clear object of the condition was to ensure that the claims of such persons should not be defeated in this way. The condition is expressly intended to affect the rights of such third parties and, in my opinion, it should be so construed.

For the reasons which I have already stated, I am of opinion that the policy must be construed as if the memorandum to which I have referred were omitted therefrom, and the proviso contained in the certificate of insurance substituted therefor. I am further of the opinion that this proviso constitutes a "prohibited condition" within the meaning of the Act and that, under the express terms of the policy (as contained in the condition to which I have referred), it is not to affect the right of any person claiming under sect. 78, and that, for the purpose of such a claim, the policy should be construed as if the offending proviso were omitted therefrom.

For these reasons I am of opinion that the policy is an approved policy, that the particular risk was covered, that the decision of the Circuit Court Judge was right and that this appeal should be dismissed with costs.

Charles O'Donnell *v.* The Yorkshire Insurance Company Limited
[1949] I.R. 187
The High Court

Headnote:

... Pending the issue of a third party policy of insurance in respect of plaintiff's motor car defendants issued to plaintiff a certificate of insurance in the prescribed form and a cover note which stated that the risk was held covered in the terms of defendants' usual form of third party policy of insurance.... Plaintiff was involved in a motor accident in respect of which defendants repudiated liability. A third party injured in the accident obtained judgment for damages and costs against plaintiff and, by leave of the Court under s. 78 of the Road Traffic Act 1933, issued execution against defendants for the damages and costs. Plaintiff sought to recover from defendants the costs incurred by him in defending the action and sought to show that under s. 62, sub-s. 1 (b) of the Act defendants, as insurers, were liable to him for the costs on the grounds that because of the issue of the certificate of insurance an approved policy of insurance was deemed to have been issued and that defendants would, by virtue of s. 62, sub-s. 1 (b) of the Act, have thereby bound themselves to insure the plaintiff against all sums which he became liable to pay by way of costs....

DIXON J: The plaintiff's case in this Court was based on the certificate of insurance dated 13th March, 1946, coupled with the suggested effect of certain provisions of the Road Traffic Act of 1933. In particular the contention was that the statement in the certificate that an approved policy of insurance had been issued to the plaintiff imported the statutory definition of such policy in s. 62 of the Act and imposed on the defendants a statutory and contractual obligation, as defined in that section, of indemnifying the plaintiff against all sums without limit which the plaintiff should become liable to pay to any person (with certain immaterial exceptions) whether by way of damages or costs on account of injury to person or property occasioned by the negligent driving during the period of cover of the insured vehicle. Part V of the Act, however, in which this section occurs is substantially, if not wholly, concerned with the position of third parties as regards the insured on the one hand and the insurer on the other, and it does not seem to me to follow from the provision referred to that the defendants must, as regards the plaintiff, be treated as having issued to him an approved policy of insurance. The contrary seems to me to follow from the provision, in s. 69, sub-s. 1 (a) of the Act, that whenever a vehicle insurer has issued a certificate of insurance certifying that an approved policy of insurance has been issued to the insured, then, if and so long as no such policy has been issued to the insured, such vehicle insurer shall as between himself and any other person except the insured, be deemed to have issued to the insured an approved policy. The exception here of the insured himself can only mean that it is left open to the defendants to dispute or negative the existence of an approved policy as between themselves and the plaintiff or, in other words, they are not estopped by the form of the certificate as regards the insured. Another ground of excluding any question of estoppel as to the form of the policy is the endorsement on the certificate itself, which I shall have to refer to later and which may be called "the cover note." This, in my view, prescribes the actual form of the contract and is inconsistent with the defendants' having represented themselves to the plaintiff as bound by any statutory contract or obligation. Again, the plaintiff did not prove the issue of any policy to him (apart from the certificate and cover note) while the defendants proved that such a policy was not issued until after the occurrence of the event giving rise to the claim and, in such circumstances, s. 69, sub-s. 1 (a) excludes the plaintiff from the category of persons in whose favour an approved policy is deemed to have been issued. It would have been easy, if so intended, for the statute to provide that such a policy should be deemed to have been issued in favour of all persons, including the insured, when a certificate of insurance is issued.

Even, however, if I were to hold that the extent of the indemnity were to be determined by the definition in s. 62. I am clearly of opinion that this would not be sufficiently extensive to include the present claim which is, substantially, for the costs incurred in defending the claim of the third party upon the omission or refusal of the defendants to do so. The "costs" referred to in that definition are, in my view, limited to those incurred by the third party, i.e. the party injured in his person or property by the negligent driving. It is only as damages for breach of contract that the costs in question here could be claimed on the basis of the existence of a statutory contract of indemnity.

The cover note already referred to constitutes, in my view, the contract operative between the parties at the material time. The relevant portion of it provides as follows:

"The risk is hereby held covered in the terms of the Company's usual form of Third Party Only Policy applicable thereto for the period shown on such certificate...." The period shown on the certificate was one month and this indorsement was evidently intended to provide for the interval until a formal policy should be issued. The defendants have given in evidence their usual form of "Third Party Only" policy and have also proved that the policy subsequently issued was in the same form with the insertion of the relevant details and an endorsement not here material. So far as the relevant provisions are concerned, it is, therefore, indifferent whether I treat the matter as governed by the terms of the usual form or by the terms of the actual policy. In the former case, I am satisfied that the cover note is apt to import all the provisions in the usual form, so far as not illegal, and not merely the portion descriptive of the risk.

Taking either form, the liability against which indemnity is undertaken is headed "Liability to Third Parties." It then describes the liability in terms almost word for word the same as those used in s. 62 of the Act, and already quoted, with the addition of the statement: "and the Company will pay all costs and expenses incurred with its written consent." As in the case of s. 62, I think the reference to "costs" in the first part of this description relates only to the costs of the injured third party: while the inclusion of the present claim in the second part of the description is precluded by the admitted absence of any written consent to the incurring of the costs.

These considerations are sufficient to dispose of the claim so far as it is based on any express or implied undertaking to indemnify the plaintiff against any liability incurred by him to his solicitor. The amount is, however, claimed, alternatively, as damages for breach of the alleged contract of insurance in that, it is alleged, the defendants wrongfully failed and refused to indemnify the plaintiff in the proceedings brought by the third party. This arises by reason of the defendants having repudiated liability in respect of the particular occurrence, the subject matter of the third party claim, and the plaintiff having, thereupon, defended the action brought by the third party by his own solicitor and counsel. In the event, the third party obtained judgment for an amount agreed to by the present plaintiff, with costs, and, as a result of an application by the third party, under s. 78 of the Act of 1933, the present defendants were ordered to pay and did pay that amount and those costs. In the result, therefore, even though under compulsion, the defendants have indemnified the plaintiff against his liability for the damages and costs of the third party; and I cannot see that there was any breach by the defendants of any undertaking by them of indemnity in this respect. Even if there were, I do not think the incurring of the costs in question would be damages flowing from such breach. They would rather be the result of a wrongful refusal by the defendants to defend the proceedings brought by the third party. To find such a wrongful refusal would require, first, the existence of a contract by the defendants to undertake such defence. The form of policy reserves to the defendants the powers to take over and conduct in the name of the insured the defence or settlement of any claim; but this is not an undertaking by the defendants to do so in any case or to indemnify the plaintiff for any expense incurred by him (other than to the injured third party) where they do not do so. Equally, the statutory liability, if any, to indemnify the plaintiff is not more extensive than that in the policy and the same considerations would apply to the alternative claim so far as based on the statute. Again, I do not think I could imply any understanding or obligation not to repudiate liability either from the statute or from the terms of the policy; if I could, the damages claimed might reasonably be said to flow from a wrongful repudiation of liability, but the question would still be undecided whether there had been such a wrongful repudiation. The success of the application under s. 78 of the Act is not necessarily conclusive, as between the insurers and the insured, on this question.

It is true that, in the result, the expenses incurred by the plaintiff may have had the effect of reducing the damages recovered and thereby decreasing the ultimate liability of the defendants to the third party as a result of the successful application under s. 78 of the Act; but these expenses were necessarily also incurred partly, if not wholly, with the object of limiting the plaintiff's own potential liability in the absence of a successful application under s. 78 or in the event of the defendants being ultimately found to have a right of recoupment, for anything paid by them, against the plaintiff. Further, even assuming a benefit incidentally resulting to the defendants from the incurring of these costs, it does not follow that the benefit necessarily excluded the amount incurred or that the plaintiff would have any right to recoupment, by way of salvage or otherwise, even if the amount were claimed on that footing.

Taking the view that I do that there was no breach by the defendants of any contract of indemnity by them, and that the damages claimed were not the result of the breach of any such contract, it is unnecessary to decide the matters that were argued in connection with the portion of the defence founded on the arbitration clause in the policy. In deference, however, to the arguments, and as having some bearing on the question (now, on the view taken, theoretical) whether there was a wrongful repudiation of liability, I shall state my views on these matters shortly.

The defendants base this portion of their defence on condition 5 of the policy, which provides for the reference to arbitration of "all differences arising out of this policy": for the making of an award being a condition precedent to any right of action against the Company; and for the case of the Company disclaiming liability to the insured for any claim under the policy. In the latter event, it is provided that if such claim shall not, within twelve calendar months from the date of such disclaimer, have been referred to arbitration then the claim shall for all purposes be deemed to have been abandoned and shall not thereafter be recoverable under the policy.

While these provisions may constitute a "prohibited condition" within the meaning of s. 62, sub-s. 1 (c) of the Act, as interpreted by the Road Traffic (Third Party Risks) Regulations, 1933, I think it is clear from Part V. of the Act as a whole, and in particular from s.62, s. 69, sub-s 1 (a) and (b), and s. 78, and from the absence of any obligation on the insurers to issue a policy only in the form of an approved policy of insurance, that such a condition is not prohibited and may be valid as between the insurers and the insured. As a matter of law, considered independently of the Road Traffic Act, I think the present condition is not illegal: *Scott* v. *Avery;*[2] *General Omnibus Co. Ltd.* v. *London General Insurance Co. Ltd.*[3] I think, further, that the question whether the defendants were entitled to repudiate liability, as between

---

[2] 5 H.L.C. 811.
[3] [1936] I.R. 596.

themselves and the plaintiff, in respect of the particular event giving rise to a claim was a difference arising under the policy and subject to the arbitration clause (see *Heyman* v. *Darwins, Ltd.*[4]); that the time limit for submitting such difference to arbitration commenced at the date of the original disclaimer of liability; that no fresh period commenced when the costs were actually incurred or claimed (see *General Omnibus Co. Ltd.* v. *London General Insurance Co, Ltd.*[5]), and that, the period having elapsed before action brought, the particular claim was barred by the provisions of the arbitration clause.

It is a matter on which comment was justifiably made that, until the defence was served, the defendants never directed the attention of the plaintiff to the provisions relating to arbitration but, on the contrary, in the correspondence by their solicitors referred to defending proceedings and orally by their officials referred to the questions being ventilated in the Courts. This would not disentitle them from relying on the arbitration clause and the plaintiff had it in his power to acquaint himself with the terms of the policy actually issued to him or with the terms of the defendants "usual form of Third Party Only Policy", but one cannot help feeling that it would have been fairer for the defendants to have called his attention, specifically and within time, to the arbitration clause, with the existence and contents of which insurers are usually much more familiar than the insured.

For the reasons given, this appeal must be dismissed.

Higgins *v.* Feeney
[1953] I.R. 45
The High Court

DAVITT P: This is a matter which does not seem to have come up for consideration before in any Court in this country, or at all, so far as reported cases go. It depends entirely upon the condition in the policy which limits the use of the vehicle. It is expressly stated in the policy that it does not cover use while carrying a passenger unless a side-car is attached. The question is whether or not that is a prohibited condition. The answer depends upon the construction of clause 3 of the first schedule of Statutory Rule and Order, No. 130 of 1933, which reads:—

> "Any condition under which the existence or the amount of the liability of the coverer depends on the construction, equipment, maintenance, or state of repair of the vehicle the driving of which is covered by the covering instrument, or the speed at which such vehicle is driven, or the keeping or carrying of anything on such vehicle."

Clause 4 of the Regulations themselves provides that any condition to the same effect, whatever the actual wording, was to be a prohibited condition. I have accordingly to say whether the condition limiting the use of the motor

---

[4] [1942] 1 All E.R. 337.
[5] [1936] I.R. 596.

cycle to use without a passenger unless a side-car is attached is a condition under which liability depends upon the construction or equipment of the vehicle.

It is a question which does not permit of a prolonged argument and is mainly a matter of first impression. In my opinion, the condition in question is not a prohibited condition. Clause 3 refers to "construction, equipment, maintenance, or state of repair". I do not think any of these matters are involved in the condition. It is conceded that if there were no reference to the side-car the condition would be good. What is prohibited is the carrying of passengers except under certain circumstances. The onus is on the insurers to show that this does not come within s. 78 of the Road Traffic Act, 1933. Even applying all the principles which Mr Murnaghan [for the plaintiff] asks me to apply, I take the view that this condition is not a prohibited condition.

The Supreme Court

MAGUIRE C.J: This is an appeal from the refusal of the President of the High Court of an application for an order pursuant to s. 78, sub-s. 1 (c), of the Road Traffic Act, 1933, giving the plaintiff liberty to execute against the Norwich Union Fire Insurance Society Limited, a judgment for £5,000 and costs recovered by him on the 11th July, 1951.

The question for decision arises upon the meaning to be attached to a clause in the policy of insurance taken out by the plaintiff and whether that clause contains a prohibited condition within the meaning of the Road Traffic Act. The Schedule to the policy provides that the policy does not cover use while carrying any passenger unless a side-car is attached to the motor cycle.

The plaintiff contends that this condition contravenes clause 3 of the first schedule of Statutory Rule and Order No. 130 of 1933....

It is submitted that that condition is one by which liability is made to depend (a) on the construction of the vehicle, or (b) on its equipment, or (c) on the keeping or carrying of something.

The condition which is objected to prohibits the carrying of passengers on a motor cycle unless a side-car is attached. I cannot accept the contention that the condition relates either to the construction of the motor cycle or that it relates to the keeping or carrying of something on the motor cycle. The argument which has been most pressed and which gave me most trouble was that the condition related to the equipment of the motor cycle. Having considered the question with as much care as possible, I am in agreement with the President of the High Court that the condition does not relate to the equipment of the motor cycle.

I am therefore of opinion that this appeal should be dismissed.

MURNAGHAN J.: This motion raises a matter of some importance as many riders of motor cycles carry pillion passengers without a side-car. The policy of the Road Traffic Act, 1933, was to protect the public. An approved policy of insurance under that Act was one which did not contravene regulations made by the Minister. The question in this case is whether this policy contains a condition which does contravene those regulations. The policy in question contains a description of the vehicle. In that description it names the machine, giving its index mark and registration number, its cubic capacity, its year of manufacture, and the insured's estimate of the value including side-car, accessories and spare parts. There is a column for the seating capacity of side-car (if any) which in the policy is left blank.

In the beginning of the policy it is provided that the Company would indemnify the insured against loss and/or damage to any motor cycle described in the schedule and/or its accessories or spare parts, including spare tyres in, on, or about the motor cycle by certain means therein set out. In the liability clause it is provided that the Company will indemnify the insured against liability to third parties on account of injury occasioned by, through, or in connection with any motor cycle described in the schedule thereto. That refers to any motor cycle, which would include a side-car if there were one. The policy then contains certain limitations as to use, one of which is that the policy does not cover use while carrying any passenger unless a side-car is attached to the motor cycle.

My reading of these provisions is that the owner of the cycle was covered whether he had a side-car attached to his motor cycle or not. Reading it in that way, he is told by the Society that he is not covered by the policy unless a side-car is attached. It seems to me that on that reading of the condition a side-car must be carried in order that the policy may be effective and it seems clear, therefore, that a side-car is equipment which is for the carrying of passengers and, therefore, the condition is a prohibited condition which cannot be relied upon by the Society.

O'BYRNE J: I have arrived at the same conclusion as the Chief Justice. If one considers this policy, it is clear that it is intended to cover either a motor cycle alone or both a motor cycle and side-car: because, when it comes to the schedule, there is a space for the seating capacity of a side-car, if any. That seems to me to contemplate that you may have a motor cycle without a side-car, and reading it in that way no help is to be gained from the definition at the beginning of the policy. I take the view that where there is a side-car which is covered by the policy the expression, "motor cycle," is sufficiently wide to cover the entire vehicle. In this case what was insured was a definite entity with a registration mark and number and that was a motor cycle without a side-car, and it seems to me that it does not cover passengers unless a side-car is attached to the motor cycle. That merely is a condition against carrying passengers. The prohibited condition ... is contained in clause 3 of the schedule to the Road Traffic (Third Party Risks) Regulations....

It is fairly obvious that in a loose and general kind of way one might refer to a motor cycle as being equipped with a side-car. That, however, does not carry the appellant sufficiently far. The term, "equipment", must be read in its context. The vehicle covered is a motor cycle without a side-car. I am of opinion that equipment in that sense does not include a side-car. A side-car is not equipment any more than a trailer is equipment. I also agree with the Chief Justice's second point.

KINGSMILL MOORE J. CONCURRED WITH THE CHIEF JUSTICE AND O'BYRNE J.

McGee *v.* London Assurance Company
(1943) 77 I.L.T.R. 133
The Circuit Court

SHEEHY J: I have considered carefully Section 78, under which these proceedings are brought, and I have no doubt as to its meaning. It appears to have two objects. On the one hand it is to protect a person injured — a third party — through the negligence of an insured driver in the event of such insured person proving to be without assets. That is the principal purpose of the section. It provides, where a person has a claim for damages for negligence against an insured person, that if he gives notice of such action to the Insurance Company, then the Insurance Company is rendered liable jointly with the insured person. On the other hand, it is a protection for the company. It is quite clear that notice of proceedings against the insured person must be given to the Insurance Company. Otherwise a "convenient" accident could take place. A claim for a large sum could be allowed to go by default against the insured person and then the injured person could seek to recover from the Insurance Company. To avoid this danger of collusion notice must be given to the Insurance Company, before proceedings are brought against the insured person, in order to recover on foot of any judgment given in such a case from the Insurance Company. Accordingly, I allow this appeal and dismiss the case with costs here and in the Court below.

Brady *v.* Brady
[1938] I.R. 103
The High Court

O'BYRNE J: This is an application under sect. 78, sub-sect. 1 (c), of the Road Traffic Act, 1933 ... for liberty to issue execution against a vehicle insurer.

The question for me to determine is whether or not there was a valid policy of insurance in existence in this case, which insured the defendant in the action brought in this Court in respect of the accident giving rise to that action.

The defendant was insured against loss arising from accident and I have before me a copy of the policy. The accident occurred on the 28th of October, 1934, and the policy covered that date. It is admitted by the parties that this was an "approved policy" under the provisions of the Road Traffic Act.

This policy contains certain permitted exceptions: that contained in clause 1 (c) of the general exceptions is material in this case

["The Company shall not be liable in respect of (1) any accident ... or liability caused ... or incurred while any motor vehicle in respect of which insurance is granted under this policy is ... *(c)* being driven with the general consent of the insured by any person who to the insured's knowledge does not hold a licence to drive such vehicle unless such person has held and is not disqualified by order of a Court of law or by reason of age or disease or physical disability from obtaining such a licence."]

At the time of the accident the vehicle was being driven by Thomas Brady, Junior, a son of Thomas Brady, the person insured. A driving licence had been issued to Thomas Brady, Junior, but at the time of such issue he was under the required age, and his father, the insured, was admittedly aware of this. Brady Junior was born on the 16th day of August, 1918, and so was two months over the age of sixteen at the time of the accident. He then held a piece of paper in the form of a driving licence, issued under the Motor Car Act, 1903,[6] but having regard to the fact that he was under age, and so disqualified from holding a licence, I have to consider whether or not he ought to be deemed to have held a licence for the purposes of the general exception in the insurance policy.

I turn first to the Motor Car Act, 1903, under which the licence was issued. Sect. 3 deals with the issue of licences, and sect. 4 with the suspension of licences and with disqualifications. Sub-sect. 5 of sect. 3 provides that any person under the age of seventeen years shall be disqualified for obtaining a licence except in respect of a motor bicycle. Sub-sect. 5 of sect. 4 provides that if any person disqualified from obtaining a licence under the Act — and that is the case here, Brady Junior being under the age of seventeen — applies for or obtains a licence while so disqualified, that person shall be guilty of an offence under the Act, and any licence so obtained shall be of no effect. I am not concerned with the provisions creating an offence, in so far as they merely create an offence, but I am concerned with the concluding words of the sub-section as to the licence being of no effect. It is clear that the licence was obtained in contravention of this Act, and I am of opinion that, having regard to the provisions of sect. 4, sub-sect. 5, the licence so obtained was of no effect.

We next come to the Road Traffic Act, 1933 ... which came into operation during the period in respect of which the said licence purports to have been issued. Sect. 45 provides that every licence granted under sect. 3 of the Motor Car Act, 1903, and bearing date as of a day prior to the commencement of Part III of the Act of 1933 and in force at the date of such commencement shall be deemed to be a licence granted under Part III of the Act of 1933 and have the like force and effect as if granted under the Act of 1933. It is doubtful whether or not that section has any application here. It seems to me that it deals only with cases where a licence was properly granted under the Act of 1903 and not where it was granted in contravention of the provisions of that Act. Assuming, however, that this section does apply, it gives to the licence the same force and effect as if it had been granted under the Act of 1933. One is then driven to sect. 26 of the Act of 1933 which provides that a licence granted to a person over the age of sixteen but under the age of seventeen shall operate and be expressed to operate to license such person to drive a motor cycle. Hence in this case, as the driver was at the time of the accident under the age of seventeen, the only vehicle which he could be licensed to drive was a motor cycle. The vehicle involved in this accident was a motor car. Accordingly I am of opinion that, under the provisions of the Act of 1933 the driver was not entitled to hold a licence to drive a motor car and

---

[6] 3 Ed. 7, c. 36.

the "licence" issued to him was of no force or effect for this purpose. I am, therefore, bound to deal with the case as if Thomas Brady, Junior, held no driving licence and only one result can then follow. The exception in the insurance policy frees the company from liability where the vehicle in question is driven by a person who, to the knowledge of the insured, holds no driving licence. This is a valid exception. The vehicle in this case was driven by the boy with the consent of his father, the defendant in the action, and it is clear that the father knew that the son, by reason of his age, was not entitled to hold a licence.

The insurers are accordingly, in my opinion, relieved from liability by the express terms of their policy, and the present application must be dismissed.

Hayes *v.* Legal Insurance Co., Ltd.
[1941] Ir. Jur. Rep. 49
The High Court

Headnote:
Consequent upon a collision of two vehicles the driver of one of the vehicles died, and, more than four months later, representation to his estate not having been taken out, the owner of the other vehicle, which was damaged, applied for liberty to institute and prosecute proceedings in negligence against the "vehicle insurer" of the first vehicle.

Ex Parte motion.
The facts as set forth in the affidavits of the intended plaintiff, his solicitor, and a lorry driver, Denis Greene, were as follows: A collision occurred on August 13, 1940, at Maudlins, near Naas, Co. Kildare, between a lorry driven by Greene, the property of the intended plaintiff, and a motor-car driven by Lieutenant Matthews, Curragh Camp, Co. Kildare, as a result of which the latter died. Lieut. Matthews, it was alleged, was driving on the wrong side of the road, and damage to an extent of over £300 was occasioned to the plaintiff's lorry. The police report of the accident was exhibited, as was also the certificate of the Kildare County Council as to the registration in his own name of Lieutenant Matthew's car, and it appeared that the intended defendants were "vehicle insurers" in respect of the deceased and the car he was driving at the time of the collision. The head office of the insurers was Liverpool, England, and they had an address in Dublin, namely, the office of Messrs Coyle & Co. (Brokers), Ltd. A search in the Probate Office revealed that representation to Lieutenant Matthews had not been taken out.

MR W.G. FALLON, FOR THE INTENDED PLAINTIFF: Representation not having been taken out, there is no way of constituting an action or naming a defendant. Such a case as the present is covered by the words of s. 78 (1) (d) "that it is for any other reason just and equitable that such application should be granted."

MARTIN MAGUIRE J: I will make the order sought in this case. I think it is just and equitable that the application should be granted. The plenary summons and this order may be served on the intended defendants per Messrs Coyle & Co. (Brokers), Ltd.

Kelleher *v.* Christopherson
(1957) 91 I.L.T.R. 191
The Circuit Court

NEYLON J: The plaintiff on 25th day of November, 1954, at Midleton Circuit Court recovered judgment for the sum of £305 against Mr Timothy McCarthy for loss and damage sustained by the plaintiff through the negligence of Mr McCarthy in the driving of his motor car.... He was also awarded taxed costs and expenses which amounted to £135 11s. 8d. Mr McCarthy's car was insured, third party, by the Equitable Motor Policies ... being represented by the defendant, their named representative in this case. When the plaintiff sought damages and costs he was unable to recover them from Mr McCarthy. This Civil Bill is now brought by the plaintiff pursuant to the provisions of section 78 of the Road Traffic Act, 1933, for liberty to execute judgment against the defendants as the insurers of Mr McCarthy.

A number of grounds of defence were set out in the defence filed by the insurance company, but the only ground relied upon at the hearing was that set out in paragraph 3 of the defence, namely, that the policy of insurance did not cover the use being made by Mr McCarthy of the car on the occasion when the accident occurred.

Shortly stated, the facts are that Mr McCarthy, who is employed as a labourer at Haulbowline, insured the motor car ... with the Equitable Motor Policies, and the use of the car covered by the policy was for social, domestic and pleasure purposes, and the use by the insured personally in his business. His business is described as a builder's labourer. Mr McCarthy used the car to bring him to work every day. In his spare time he carries on pig farming in a small way. It is contested whether this is a business or a hobby. I have come to the conclusion that the pig farming carried on by Mr McCarthy is in the nature of a business and not a hobby or an amusement. For the purpose of feeding the pigs, Mr McCarthy got swill about three times per week at the canteen at his place of employment. The swill he carried home in containers in his motor car, the back seat having been removed to make way for them. When the accident occurred he was returning home from work and was carrying some swill in the containers in the car.

In respect of this accident the insurance company has repudiated liability under the policy on the grounds that in carrying the swill Mr McCarthy was not using the car for the business covered by the policy. The question argued before me was, what was the effect on the policy of the fact that Mr McCarthy was carrying swill in his car at the time of the accident. It was accepted that when Mr McCarthy used the car for the purpose of getting to and from his place of work merely, he was covered by the insurance policy. At the hearing in support of their repudiation of the policy the insurance company relied upon a number of authorities, but the chief case upon which reliance was placed and which, it was argued covered the present case entirely was the case of *Jones* v. *Welsh Insurance Corporation*.[7] In that case the wording of the clause regarding user in the policy was similar to that of the policy now under consideration. The insured was a motor mechanic and the business for which his car was insured was that of a motor mechanic. He was also engaged in sheep farming. On the date on which the accident occurred he asked his brother to take his car and bring two sheep and two lambs to their father's house were he had made arrangements regarding the grazing for the animals. While the sheep were being conveyed the accident occurred. The Court held that the sheep farming was a business carried on by the insured and that as the car was at the time of the accident being used for the purpose of that business the insurance company was not liable under the policy in respect of the accident.

It appears to me, however, that this cited case differs materially from the present case. The insured in the cited case was not driving the car at the time of the accident. The car was being used for the purpose of a business clearly not covered by the policy. As I have already pointed out in the present case, it was admitted that when the insured drove his car to and from his work he was covered by insurance. Thus, if Mr McCarthy had not swill in his car on the date when the accident occurred, his driving would have been covered. I have come to the conclusion that his carrying of swill made no difference to the insurance cover in this case. I cannot accept the proposition that by carrying swill he thereby converted a journey which was covered by insurance into one which was not so covered. It appears to me that when a person is using his car for a purpose which is apparently covered by his policy of insurance, there is a very heavy onus on the insurance company to discharge before it can establish that such a user has ceased to be insured by reason of some action of the insured. As in this case, it is a fact that the insured was returning home from work and thus is covered by insurance. To deprive him of this benefit it must be proved that he has done something which alters the nature of the journey or user of the car.

In my opinion the insurance company has fallen short of discharging that onus. I am compelled to hold that on the evidence in this case, firstly, that on the date when the accident occurred, the car was being used by Mr McCarthy to bring him to and from his work and, secondly, that the user was covered by insurance, and that the mere carrying of swill did not alter the nature of the use of the car.

The plaintiff, therefore, is entitled to succeed in his claim.

The plaintiff in reply to the case made by the insurance company relied upon certain provisions of the Road Traffic Act (Third Party Risks) Regulations, 1933. In the circumstances it is not necessary for me to deal with the case made by them under the regulations.

---

[7] [1937] 4 All E.R. 149.

Whelan *v.* Dixon
(1963) I.L.T.R. 195
The High Court

MURNAGHAN J: The case before me is governed by the unreported decision of Davitt P., in *O'Reilly* v. *Hennessy* [sic].[8] By that decision, I am bound to hold that the onus of proof lies on the plaintiff to establish that the defendant's motor car was, at the time of the accident the subject matter of the action, being driven within the limitations as to use contained in the policy of insurance effected by the defendant with the insurance company in respect thereof. That onus not having been discharged by the plaintiff here, I must refuse the plaintiff's application with costs.

The Supreme Court

MAGUIRE C.J: I have had an opportunity of reading the judgment about to be read by Mr Justice Lavery and I agree with it.

LAVERY J: The plaintiff has recovered judgment for £1,846 10s. 0d. damages and costs in an action for personal injuries caused by the negligence of the defendant's agent or servant in the driving of a motor car in Dame Street, Dublin on 1st July, 1954.

This judgment remains wholly unsatisfied and the plaintiff applied to the High Court on notice of motion for leave to execute the judgment against the Hibernian Fire and General Insurance Co. Ltd. (which I shall hereafter refer to as the "Company") under the provisions of section 78 of the Road Traffic Act, 1933.

It is established that at the material time there was in force a policy of insurance, issued by the Company to the defendant, and covering the vehicle involved in the accident, but with certain limitations as to use. The policy indemnified the defendant only when the vehicle was being used for the purposes of the defendant's business (stated in the policy to be that of "a greengrocer and no other for the purposes of the insurance" or for social, domestic and pleasure purposes, or necessitated by the overhaul upkeep and/or repair of the vehicle. I shall have to refer later in more detail to the terms of the policy.

The Company have repudiated liability on the ground that at the time of the accident the car was being used for a purpose other than those covered, and that, accordingly, they are not liable to indemnify the defendant, nor liable to the plaintiff under the provisions of section 78 Road Traffic Act, 1933.

The motion came before Murnaghan J. grounded on affidavits which, so far as the applicant was concerned, did no more than establish that the plaintiff had been knocked down and injured by the vehicle driven by the defendant's agent or servant, and that the defendant held a policy with the

---

[8] Unreported. High Court, 17 June 1949.

Company indemnifying him in the terms of the policy in respect of loss caused by the vehicle.

The Garda report of the accident was exhibited and certain further particulars can be found therein but it is difficult to see how such a report could be admissible in evidence to prove them.

At the time of the accident the car was being driven by one Richard Crowe and one Owen Connolly was a passenger in the car.

Neither the driver Richard Crowe nor Owen Connolly had made affidavits and they were not available to give evidence when the motion came for hearing, but the Company exhibited Statutory Declarations made by them which, if admissible to prove the facts stated therein, and deemed to be sufficient to do so, would show that the car was being used for a business purpose of Crowe and Connolly and not of the defendant and, therefore, not within the limitations as to use of the policy.

At an adjourned hearing the Company sought to put in evidence an affidavit from Owen Connolly. This affidavit would, if accepted, and not displaced by other evidence, also go to show that the car was being used outside the limitations as to use covered.

It is not clear whether this affidavit is before this Court or not. The learned Judge did not consider it as he was prepared to decide and did decide the matter on a ground which did not require him to do so. Counsel read the affidavit to this Court.

The learned Judge refused the application holding that the burden of proof of establishing that the car was being used within the limitations of use at the time of the accident rested on the claimant and that it was not sufficient merely to show that the car the driving of which had caused the damage was one covered for certain risks by the Company.

In doing so, the learned Judge said he was following a decision of Davitt P. in a case of *O'Reilly* v. *Henderson*.[9]

This Court has been supplied with the Registrar's Certificate of the case (Record No. 1948 No. 203P.) from which it appears that an issue directed by order of the 22nd April, 1949, to be tried between Seamus O'Reilly and The Insurance Company of Ireland was tried by Davitt J. (as he then was) on the 17th June, 1949. The Certificate records:—

> "The Judge decided that the onus of proof was on the plaintiff to establish that the motor car the property of the defendant Thomas Henderson was at the time of the accident the subject matter of the action, being driven within the limitations as to the use contained in the policy of insurance effected by the said Thomas Henderson with the said Company in respect of the said motor car and that the plaintiff had failed to discharge that onus and the Judge found that the said motor car was not being so used."

The claim was accordingly rejected.

Murnaghan J. was therefore correct in his statement of the decision which he held governed the case before him.

---

[9] Unreported. High Court, 17/6/49.

It is to be noted, however, that Davitt J. decided the matter on the hearing of an issue, directed by the order made on the hearing of a motion for leave to execute and after a trial on oral evidence. In an earlier case *Pattison and Co. Ltd.* v. *Martin*[10] Dixon J. having decided a similar application under section 78 against the claimant on a point as to notice said:—

> "The Court, may if necessary, adjourn the matter for hearing oral evidence and I would not preclude the respondents from having an opportunity of going into oral evidence if I thought it was necessary."

It was not necessary having regard to the view he took.
The learned Judge Dixon J. later said:—

> "It is suggested that the applicants must show that the defendant was insured against liability in the particular circumstances of this accident, but I am of opinion that the accident was of the type of those against which the owner or driver was insured by section 2 of the policy and I think it is sufficient, in order to make a *prima facie* case, for the applicants to show that the injury was caused during use for business generally, and that then the onus is shifted to the insurers to show exceptions in the particular instance ... I am simply holding that it is for the insurers to show that the vehicle was being used in a manner for which the insured was not covered."

Having regard to his decision on the point of notice these observations were clearly *obiter* but nevertheless they show a difference of judicial opinion and must be considered. From the decision of Murnaghan J. the plaintiff has appealed to this Court.

It is contended that the learned Judge and Davitt P. were in error in holding that the burden of proof was on the claimant and that the terms of the policy expressing the limitation as to use as a general exception from the indemnity granted by the policy made it the obligation of the Company to establish by evidence that the exception applied.

The submission appears to me to be that it is sufficient for a claimant to prove his judgment that the defendant had a policy covering the vehicle in certain circumstances and thereupon the burden of proof of showing that the user was outside the covered risks is shifted to the insurers, the Company.

I hope I have stated the submission accurately. In effect it is the view expressed by Dixon J. in *Pattison and Co. Ltd.* v. *Martin.*[11]

If this matter were *res integra* it would give me little trouble but the Court has been referred to certain decisions in England which it is submitted establish the proposition for which the plaintiff contends.

This is, I think, the first case under the provisions of section 78 of the Road Traffic Act 1933, to have come under review in this Court.

It must be remembered that decisions on claims by an insured person against insurers depend entirely on the terms of the contract which the policy represents and may not be applicable in applications under section 78 where

---

[10] (1947) 81, I.L.T.R. 155.
[11] *Ibid.*

the claimant is an outsider to the contract seeking to enforce the statutory right conferred by the section. It is clear of course that this right is governed by the terms of the contract but it may be that this burden of proof falling on him may not be the same as that which falls on an insured person claiming against his insurers.

I propose to consider the matter, first of all as a matter of construction of the contract between the defendant and the Company.

The structure and form of Insurance Policies has become settled after a long period of growth. Insurers are naturally loth to depart from this form which has stood the test of many years and the provisions of which have acquired definite meanings.

Nevertheless, any one who approached the consideration of a policy without any prior experience might think it a very curious document indeed.

Such a person might think it would be simple to say:— We will indemnify you against loss or damage caused when you are using the car No. XY for the purposes of your business or for your personal purposes.

But the submission made to this court is that the Company have *prima facie* contracted to indemnify the insured, (and therefore the claimant under section 78) against all loss or damage caused by the use of the vehicle, and have excepted liability to indemnify only against loss or damage caused in particular circumstances such as use for particular purposes or use by particular persons, e.g. unlicensed drivers or persons other than the insured himself and many other circumstances, and that the proof that any such exception applies in the particular case lies on the Insurers.

I shall attempt to set forth the material provisions of the Policy in as summary a manner as possible.

In consideration of the premium paid the

> *"Policy Witnesseth:*— That subject to the Terms, Exceptions and Conditions contained herein or endorsed or otherwise expressed hereon....
> *Section 11 — (Liability to Third Parties)*
> The Company will indemnify the Insured against all sums which the Insured ... shall become liable to pay to any person (other than the excepted persons as hereafter defined) by way of damages or costs on account of injury to person or property occasioned by the use of any vehicle described in the Schedule hereto.
>   Excepted persons are not here material.
>   *General Exceptions of the Policy* — The Company shall not be liable in respect of ... (b) Any loss, damage, liability and/or injury arising out of any event occurring.... (ii)While any vehicle described in the Schedule hereto is being used otherwise than within the Limitations as to use contained in such Schedule."

I have already set out the "Limitations as to Use".

It appears to me that the governing words of the contract which I have quoted demonstrate that universal cover is not given with exceptions which the grantor of the indemnity must establish but that only such cover is given in the light of these governing words and an examination of the contract as a whole appears.

If I am right in this then in a claim for indemnity by the insured against the insurers it would be for him to establish that at the time of the incident giving rise to the claim the vehicle was being used within the limitations as to use in the policy.

What is the position of the claimant under Section 78 Road Traffic Act, 1933.

I have, I fear, taken a long time to reach the section — but here it is so far as I consider it material:—

> Section 78 (1) "Where a person (in this section referred to as the claimant) ... has in any Court of Justice (in proceedings of which the vehicle insurer ... hereinafter mentioned had notice) recovered judgment against such owner or driver (i.e., The owner or driver of a mechanically propelled vehicle) for a *sum* (whether liquidated or unliquidated) *against the liability for which such owner or driver is insured by an approved Policy of insurance* ... the claimant may serve on ... the vehicle insurer by whom such policy ... was issued ... a notice in writing of the judgment for such *sum* and upon the service of such notice such of the following provisions as are applicable shall have effect, that is to say:— ... (c) Where the claimant has so recovered for such sum ... and has not recovered from such owner or driver or such vehicle insurer ... the whole amount of such judgment, the claimant may apply to the Court in which he recovered such judgment for leave to execute such judgment against such vehicle insurer ... and thereupon such Court may, if it thinks proper, grant such an application either in respect of the whole amount of such judgment or in respect of any specified part of such amount.
>
> (3) This section only applies to claims against the liability for which an insurance ... is required by this part of this Act to be effected...."

In the present case the claim is in respect of a loss against the liability for which an insurance is required to be effected.

No question arises as to notice of the proceedings in which the judgment was obtained. The Company had the notice required.

The judgment must be for a sum against the liability for which the owner or driver is insured — (see the words ... italicised.)

In my opinion, the claimant must establish this. The right given by the Act prescribes it as a necessary condition.

If I am right in this, it is unnecessary to consider the cases to which we were referred in argument as to whether the onus of proof lies in claims by insured against Insurers.

But at the risk of going outside my province I would say — and it may be *"obiter"* — that in such cases the position would be the same. Too much may be made of the burden of proof. Where an issue has been tried and all the available evidence has been put before the tribunal, the tribunal decides upon such evidence and if its decision is called in question in a higher Court the first issue will be whether there was evidence to support the decision....

... Cases may arise where insurers in answer to a claim under section 78 rely on a breach of condition but this is not such a case.

The question here is what is the risk covered. A simple if extreme example would be where a policy insured against fire risk. If the property is destroyed surely it would be for the insured to establish that it was destroyed by fire and not by flood, tempest or other cause.

In my opinion the decision on the point of law of the of the learned Judge following Davitt P. was correct....

KINGSMILL MOORE, O'DALY AND MAGUIRE JJ. CONCURRING.

Stanbridge *v.* Healy and Ensign Motor Policies at Lloyds (Notice Party)
[1985] I.L.R.M. 290
The High Court

HAMILTON J: On 9 September 1973 the plaintiff in these proceedings, Miss Claire Stanbridge suffered personal injuries as a result of an accident which she alleged was caused by the negligence of the defendant, Declan Healy, in the driving of a motor vehicle owned by him. As appears from the statement of claim issued on her behalf, and as established in the evidence, the accident occurred on: "the roadway in the grounds of Corduffstown House, Naas in the county of Kildare".

On 28 April 1982, the proceedings instituted on her behalf were compromised and judgment was entered in her favour against the defendant, Declan Healy, in the sum of £9,000 and costs.

The plaintiff has failed to recover the said sum or any portion thereof and on 28 March 1983 caused to be issued a notice of motion seeking liberty to execute in respect of the said judgment and costs against Messrs Ensign Motor Policies.

This motion was issued pursuant to the provisions of s.76 of the Road Traffic Act 1961, the relevant provisions of which are as follows:

> "76. (1) Where a person (in this section referred to as the claimant) claims to be entitled to recover from the owner of a mechanically propelled vehicle or from a person (other than the owner) using a mechanically propelled vehicle (in this section referred to as the user) or has in any court of justice (in proceedings of which the vehicle insurer or vehicle guarantor hereinafter mentioned had prior notification) recovered judgment against the owner or user for a sum (whether liquidated or unliquidated) against the liability for which the owner or user is insured by an approved policy of insurance or the payment of which by the owner or user is guaranteed by an approved guarantee, the claimant may serve by registered post, on the vehicle insurer by whom the policy was issued, or on the vehicle insurer or the vehicle guarantor by whom the guarantee was issued, a notice in writing of the claim or judgment for the sum, and upon service of the notice such of the following provisions as are applicable shall, subject to subsection (2) of this section, have effect.
>
> (c) where the claimant has so recovered judgment for the sum, or after service of the notice so recovers judgment for the sum or any part thereof, and has not recovered from the owner or user or such insurer or guarantor the whole amount of the judgment, the claimant may apply to the court in which he recovered the judgment for leave to execute the judgment against the insurer or guarantor, and thereupon the court may, if it thinks proper, grant the application either in respect of the whole amount of the judgment or in respect of any specified part of that amount."

S. 76 (3) of the Road Traffic Act 1961, provides that:

"Subsections (1) and (2) of this section apply only to claims against the liability for which an approved policy of insurance or an approved guarantee is required by this Act to be effected."

S. 56 of the Road Traffic Act 1961, sets forth the circumstances in which an approved policy of insurance or an approved guarantee is required to be effected by the Road Traffic Act 1961.

S. 56 (1) of the Act provides that:

"A person (in this subsection referred to as the user) shall not use in a public place a mechanically propelled vehicle unless either a vehicle, a vehicle guarantor or an exempted person would be liable for injury by the negligent use of the vehicle by him at that time or there is in force at the time either—

(a) an approved policy of insurance whereby the user or some other person who would be liable for injury caused by the negligent use of the vehicle at that time by the user, is insured against all sums without limit (save as is hereinafter otherwise provided) which the user or his personal representative or such other person or his personal representative shall become liable to pay to any person (exclusive of the excepted persons) by way of damages or costs on account of injury to person or property caused by the negligent use of the vehicle at that time by the user, or

(b) an approved guarantee whereby there is guaranteed the payment by the user, or some other person who would be liable for injury caused by the negligent use of the vehicle at that time by the user; of all sums without limit (save as is hereinafter otherwise provided) which the user or his personal representative or such other person or his personal representative shall become liable to pay to any person (exclusive of the excepted persons) by way of damages or costs on account of injury to person or property caused by the negligent use of the vehicle at that time by the user."

What is required by the said section to be insured against is any liability arising from the user of a mechanically propelled vehicle in a public place.

"A public place" is defined in s.3 of the Road Traffic Act, 1961, as being:

"any street, road or other place to which the public have access with vehicles whether as of right or by permission and whether subject to or free of charge."

The Notice Party, Messrs Ensign Motor Policies at Lloyds, opposed the application made on behalf of the plaintiff on the grounds that:

(a) The accident, the subject matter of the proceedings in which the plaintiff had recovered judgment did not take place in "a public place":

(b) That there was no obligation on the defendant to have at that time an approved policy of insurance or an approved guarantee: and

(c) The provisions of s. 76 of the Road Traffic Act 1961, did not apply and that as a consequence thereof the plaintiff was not entitled to an order giving her liberty to recover the amount of the said judgment against them.

The only issue which I have to determine in this case is whether or not the injuries sustained by the plaintiff were occasioned by the user of a mechanically propelled vehicle by the defendant in a public place.

I heard evidence from Mr Charles Edward Mayberry, Patrick Lynch and the plaintiff with regard to the ownership of Corduffstown House and the lands immediately adjacent thereto, including the roadway on which the accident happened and the user thereof.

It appears from the evidence of Mr Patrick Lynch, who is the Treasurer of St Corban's Conference of the Society of St Vincent de Paul, the Corduffstown House and the lands are owned in trust for the Society of St Vincent de Paul, that the house is run as a holiday home by the Council of Dublin and that it is administered by the Conference of St Corban.

The house is let during the holiday period to different Conferences of the St Vincent de Paul in the Archdiocese of Dublin.

A permanent staff is employed there but during the particular periods that it is allocated to particular conferences, these conferences bring down voluntary helpers who help to look after the people who are enjoying Corduffstown House for a holiday period.

It appears further from his evidence that the Conference does not encourage relatives to visit the senior citizens enjoying their holiday but if they come they are made welcome but encouragement is given to members of the society as stated by Mr Lynch to visit the old folk while they are in residence.

It appears to be quite clear from Mr Lynch's evidence that the people normally using Corduffstown House and entitled to be present there consisted of the senior citizens who were having a holiday there, the paid staff looking after them and members of the Vincent de Paul who would volunteer to help in their care and amusement or merely come to visit them and relatives of the senior citizens who would be made welcome there but not actively encouraged to come.

It further appears that any other people wandering in off the highway would be challenged and unless they had reason to be there would be told to go.

An access to Corduffstown House from the public carriageway was through a gateway beside which there was a gate lodge.

It does not appear to matter to me whether the gate was left open at all times or not. It is quite clear to me from the evidence that the public at large did not have access to Corduffstown House, its lands or the roadway which led from the gates up to Corduffstown House.

In the Scottish case of *Harrison* v. *Hill*,[12] the Lord Justice General, Lord Clyde, who was considering whether in the case before him, a road leading from a public highway down to a farmhouse was a road within the meaning of the Road Traffic Act, 1930 had occasion to interpret the definition: "That road means any highway or any other road to which the public has access and includes bridges over which a road passes" stated (at 16):

"It is plain from the terms of the definition that the class of road intended is wider than the class of public roads to which the public has access by virtue

---

[12] [1932] J.C. 13.

of a positive right belonging to the public and flowing either from the statute or from prescriptive user. A road may therefore be within the definition:

(1) Although it belongs to the class of private roads and,

(2) Although all that can be said with regard to its availability to the public is that the public has access to it.

I think that, when the statute speaks of "the public" in this connection, what is meant is the public generally, and not the special class of members of the public who have occasions for business or social purposes to go to the farmhouse or any part of the farm itself: were it otherwise, the definition might just as well have included all private roads as well as all public highways."

The important part of that statement is his reference to his interpretation of the meaning of the words "the public" which he interprets as meaning the public generally and not the special class of members of the public who have occasion for business or social purposes to go to the farm-house or any part of the farm itself.

It is quite clear from the evidence of Mr Lynch that the public generally do not have any access to the lands of Corduffstown House either as of right or by permission.

I am further satisfied that the meaning to be attributed to the words "the public" in the definition of a "public place" contained in s. 3 of the Road Traffic Act, 1961, is the public generally and not any particular class. That being so I have no alternative but to hold that the place where the accident occurred was not a public place within the meaning of the Road Traffic Act, 1961, and that the plaintiff is not entitled to succeed in her application for leave to execute against Messrs Ensign Motor Policies at Lloyds in respect of the judgment obtained by her against the defendant.

In reaching this decision I am fortified by the decision of Maguire P., in the case of *Judge* v. *Leonard*,[13] and by the fact that the statement of Lord Clyde referred to herein was considered and adopted in *Bugge* v. *Taylor*[14] and in *Buchanan* v. *Motor Insurers' Bureau*.[15]

The plaintiff's application is refused.

The Director of Public Prosecutions *v.* Molloy
Unreported, 3 March 1993
The High Court

MURPHY J: The case stated by District Justice Michael Pattwell on the 16th of December 1992 raises the question whether he was correct in law in determining that Grafton Street in the City of Dublin was on the 7th day of June 1991 or at any material time on that date a "public place" within the meaning of Section 3 of the Road Traffic Act 1961.

---

[13] [1941] Ir. Jur. Rep. 39.
[14] [1941] 1 K.B. 198.
[15] [1955] 1 All E.R. 607.

The question arises in this way. The Defendant, Peter Molloy, was prosecuted on three charges under the Road Traffic Acts or various regulations made thereunder. It is an ingredient of each of the charges that it occurred in a "public place". The particular place where the incidents were alleged to have occurred was Grafton Street in the City of Dublin and the time was 10.35 p.m. In the hearing of the charges before the learned District Justice, Garda Michael Whelan gave evidence that he observed the Defendant riding a motorcycle along Grafton Street, coming from the direction of St Stephen's Green in the direction of Nassau Street and that he stopped the bicycle outside Brown Thomas Department Store. Whilst no accident occurred, the Garda gave evidence that the street was crowded with pedestrians and that the Defendant had swerved in and out of them. The Garda expressed the opinion that the Defendant had driven the motorcycle in a careless fashion. Apparently it was the Garda who gave evidence that Grafton Street is closed to traffic generally and is open to traffic only on weekday mornings between the hours of 6 a.m. and 11 a.m. to enable shops to be supplied and so forth. It follows that at the time of the incident the road was closed to traffic generally. In fact the "pedestrianisation" of streets in Dublin is regulated by Statutory Instrument 109 of 1982, part IV which, so far as material, provides as follows:—

> "16 (1) A person shall not with a vehicle enter a street or portion of a street to which this rule applies, or park a vehicle in such a street or portion of a street during the period indicated by means of an information plate
> (2) This rule applies to a street or portion of a street at each entry of which sign traffic number 216 authorised by the Regulations of 1962 (as amended by the Road Traffic (Signs) (Amendment) (No. 3) Regulations, 1971[16] is erected."

The Road Traffic Act 1961, Section 2 defines a public place in the following terms:—

> "'Public Place' means any street, road or other place to which the public have access *with vehicles* whether as of right or by permission and whether subject to or free of charge."

As a person may not lawfully enter Grafton Street with a vehicle between the hours of 11 a.m. and 6 a.m. the following day, can it be said that that street is a public place during that period for the purposes of the Road Traffic Act, 1961?

In *Montgomery* v. *Loney*,[17] the Court of Appeal in Northern Ireland held that the forecourt of a filling station situate a few yards back from the edge of a public road was a "public place" within the meaning and for the purposes of Section 39 (1) of the Road Traffic Act (Northern Ireland) 1955. As there are significant differences between the way in which a public place is defined in the Northern Ireland legislation and in the 1961 Act, the decision has no

---

[16] S.I. No. 256 of 1971.
[17] [1958/59] N.I.L.R. 171.

direct application to the present matter but I would respectfully agree with the views expressed by Lord MacDermott L.C.J. at page 176 to the following effect:—

> "There can be little doubt that the main object which Parliament had in mind in enacting these provisions was the protection of members of the community from the dangers of road traffic and, in particular, from those caused by motor vehicles. That has to be borne in mind in construing 'public' and 'access', for these words have no fixed and inflexible meaning and their true signification must depend on their context and the purpose for which they are used."

The decision of Hamilton J. in *Stanbridge* v. *Healy*[18] is material to the extent that it is addressed to the proper interpretation of the words "public place" as defined in Section 3 of the Road Traffic Act, 1961. Unfortunately, however, the decision is limited to deciding that the words "the public" means that the public generally and not the special class of members of the public who had occasion for business or social purposes to traverse a private roadway leading to a farmhouse. The only authority on point which Counsel had been able to locate was the note of the Judgment of the Queen's Bench Divisional Court in *Sandy* v. *Martin*.[19] In that case the High Court in England held that a car park provided for the convenience of patrons of a public house was a public place. But even more important was their decision that:—

> "An otherwise private place was public if and so long as the public had access at the invitation of the land owner, but there was no evidence that the licensee's invitation continued an hour after closing time...."

Whilst a distinction can be drawn between property privately owned to which members of the public may be given access from time to time and publicly owned property to which access by the public may be restricted or prohibited from time to time, it does seem to me that an essential ingredient in the definition of a public place for the purposes of the Road Traffic Act, 1961 is that the public should have access thereto with vehicles so that if and so long as such access is prohibited by law, that the place in question cannot comply with the statutory definition.

In the circumstances I am of opinion that the learned District Justice was correct in law in his determination that, at the time of the offences complained of, Grafton Street was not a public place within the definition of same as appears in the Road Traffic Act, 1961.[*]

---

[18] [1985] I.L.R.M. 290.
[19] [1974] C.L.R. 258.
[*] This case is under appeal.

Bus Éireann/Irish Bus *v.*
The Insurance Corporation of Ireland Plc
Unreported, 10 May 1994
The High Court

MORRIS J: This matter [comes] before the Court pursuant to an Order of the 6th April, 1992, which directs that primary issues should be tried prior to the hearing of the action and the issues are as follows:—

1. Whether the action herein is statute-barred pursuant to the provisions of Section 9 of the Civil Liability Act, 1961.
2. If, which is denied, the defendant is liable to the Plaintiff whether or not pursuant to the provisions of Section 76 (3) of the Road Traffic Act, 1961 or Section 56 (2) (a) thereof of the said Act, the Plaintiff is entitled to seek recovery of any damages in excess of a total sum of £1,000 before any apportionment thereof.

The circumstances in which this issue arises can be summarised as follows:—

On the 19th December, 1987 a road accident occurred involving a vehicle driven by the late Mr Harry Lawless and a bus owned by Bus Éireann. In this accident the late Mr Lawless received fatal injuries. In the proceedings which followed, arising from that accident, it was determined by the High Court, on appeal from the Circuit Court, that the entire responsibility for the accident rested on the late Mr Lawless and that Irish Bus were free from blame.

It is common case that the insurance cover which the late Mr Lawless had, covering his use of his vehicle, did not indemnify him or his representatives in respect of the driving on this occasion and, accordingly, by Notice of Motion dated the 13th July, 1989, Dublin Bus sought and were granted an Order pursuant to Sections 76 (1) (d) of the Road Traffic Act, 1961 as amended, granting it liberty to issue and serve proceedings on the Insurance Corporation of Ireland in lieu of the late Mr Lawless and on foot of that Order a Plenary Summons was issued on the 31st May, 1990, seeking to recover from the Insurance Corporation of Ireland the loss and damage suffered by Bus Éireann in the accident which comprised £17,000 vehicle damage. In the Defence delivered, the Insurance Corporation of Ireland Plc raises the two issues which now fall to be determined.

Dealing with the first of these issues:—
This issue relates to the limitation period to be applied where a claim is made against an insurance company pursuant to Section 76 of the Road Traffic Act, 1961.

It is common case that the relevant limitation period for proceedings which might have been instituted against the late Mr Lawless's estate is that provided by Section 9 of the Civil Liability Act, 1961 and this provides that the "relevant period" is "within two years from the date of his death" and it is also common case that the present action, having been commenced on the 31st May, 1990, is outside of that period and that if the proceedings were instituted against the late Mr Lawless's estate they would be statute-barred. However, it is submitted that this is not a claim against the estate of a deceased person but that it is a claim based upon a cause of action expressly provided for in the Road Traffic Act, 1961 at Section 76 and that the limitation period contained in the Civil Liability Act, 1961, at Section 9 has no application.

Section 76 of the Road Traffic Act, 1961, provides, in summary, and insofar as is relevant to the present case, that where a person claims to be entitled to recover from the owner of a mechanically propelled vehicle damages and where there was in place a policy of insurance covering the use of the vehicle at the relevant time, he may, by adopting the procedures provided for in the section get leave of the Court to institute proceedings against the insurer "in lieu of the owner or user" of the vehicle and to recover in this action from the insurer any sum he would have been entitled to recover from the owner or user.

I do not accept Counsel's submission that Section 76 creates a new cause of action in respect of which a separate limitation period would be applicable. To my mind, it is clear that all that the section does is to enable an injured party to substitute for a deceased defendant the insurance company holding cover at the relevant time. In reaching this conclusion, I consider it relevant that the entire structure and wording of the section seems to me to do no more than attach to the insurance company whatever responsibility the deceased owner had. Insofar as this case is concerned, the relevant part of Section 76 is 76 (1) (d) which provides "where the claimant has not so recovered judgment for the sum, the claimant may apply to any Court of competent jurisdiction in which he might institute proceedings for the recovery of the sum from the owner or user for leave to institute and prosecute these proceedings against the insurer or guarantor (as the case may be) in lieu of the owner or user...." It is in my view clear that it is the same action but that there is an entitlement conferred upon the Plaintiff to pursue the claim against the insurance company. I consider that all that is given to the Plaintiff is the right to institute and prosecute the proceedings against the insurer or guarantor "in lieu" of the owner.

Accordingly, I am of the view that the limitation period provided by Section 9 of the Civil Liability Act, 1961 is the relevant limitation period, and there being no issue on this aspect of the case, I answer the first preliminary issue that the Plaintiff's action herein is statute-barred pursuant to the provisions of Section 9 of the Civil Liability Act, 1961.

As to the second issue:—
This issue arises in the following circumstances. The Bus Éireann bus was damaged to the extent of approximately £17,000. It is the submission of the Insurance Corporation of Ireland Plc that since Part IV of the Road Traffic Act, 1961, and in particular Section 56 thereof, provides that insurance cover is compulsory for a mechanically propelled vehicle to the extent only of £1,000 in respect of injury to property, that the provisions of Section 76 (3) limit any claim for damage to property to that amount.

From time to time the figure of £1,000 has been increased and now stands at £40,000. However, it is common case that at the relevant time the £1,000 figure applied.

On behalf of Bus Éireann it is submitted that Section 56 (1) of the Road Traffic Act, 1961 limits the obligation of a user of a mechanically propelled vehicle to the requirement of having insurance cover to the extent of £1,000. However, it is submitted, if a claimant suffers property damage in a sum in excess of £1,000 and if in fact the driver had cover in excess of that amount, then nothing in the Act prohibits the claimant from pursuing his claim against the insurance company in lieu of the driver to the full extent of his damage. It is common case that in the circumstances of this case the insurance cover which the late Mr Lawless had exceeded £1,000.

I do not accept this submission. Section 76 is made up of two enabling sub-sections which enable claimants to pursue an insurance company in respect of damages caused by a deceased owner or user of a mechanically propelled vehicle.

Subsection (3) of Section 76 is in my view clear. It provides "subsections (1) and (2) of this section apply only to claims against the liability for which an approved policy of insurance or an approved guarantee is required by the Act to be effected". In my view it is equally clear that Section 76 of the Road Traffic Act, 1961 requires that an approved policy of insurance is required to be effected "against all sums without limit save as is hereinafter otherwise provided" and subsection (2) (a) expressly limits that "insofar as it relates to injury to property be limited to the sum of £1,000 in respect of injury caused by any one act of negligence or any one [series] of acts of negligence collectively constituting one event".

I am satisfied that the Act requires an approved policy of insurance or guarantee only to the extent of £1,000 and that the entitlement to recover under Section 76 of the Road Traffic Act, 1961 is limited to that amount.

Accordingly, I answer the second issue that the Plaintiff would not be entitled in this action (even if it were not statute-barred) to seek to recover any damages in excess of a total sum of £1,000 before any apportionment thereof.

CHAPTER 11

Arbitration

Arbitration is a method of resolving disputes which exists as an alternative to the judicial process. The essence of an arbitration clause is the parties' agreement to refer any dispute coming within its scope for adjudication before a referee, or arbitrator, of their own choosing. Among its perceived advantages as compared to the judicial system are speed, privacy and confidentiality.

Arbitration clauses have long been standard features in a contract of insurance. As such they have been the subject of considerable judicial attention.

It should be borne in mind, however, that when arbitration cases come to court, it is usually because one or other of the parties is unhappy with the original decision concerning the arbitration clause and refuses to accept it. In a sense, therefore, the judges only become involved with the arbitration process at second hand.

Two broad themes may be discerned from the sixteen cases included in this chapter. The first series of six older cases considers the question as to whether an insurance company may rely on an arbitration clause in a policy which it alleges does not exist, by virtue usually — although not exclusively — of fraud on the part of the policyholder.

In *Dooley* v. *the London Assurance Company* (1879) the Court of Exchequer would not stay proceedings brought against the defendant company in favour of arbitration in circumstances where the company sought to raise the question of fraud in any such arbitration. The court, however, was aware of the advantages in general of the arbitration process.

In stark contrast is *Gaw* v. *British Law Fire Insurance* (1908) where the Court of Appeal held that the issue of fraud was a difference arising out of the policy.

Gaw was neither cited by counsel nor referred to by O'Brien L.C. in refusing to stay proceedings in *Wilson* v. *National Livestock Insurance Company* (1914) where the defendant company refused to give an undertaking not to raise the question of the plaintiff's alleged fraud.

To similar effect as *Wilson* was *Ballasty* v. *Army Navy and General*

Assurance Association Limited (1916). Although both *Gaw* and *Wilson* were cited by Counsel neither case was mentioned in the two High Court judgments.

Ballasty was expressly followed in *Furey* v. *Eagle Star and British Dominions Insurance Company* (1922).

The matter was very fully considered by Budd J. in his exhaustive judgment in the definitive case of *Coen* v. *Employers Liability Assurance Corporation Limited* (1962). Having reviewed all the leading Irish and English cases, the judge concluded that the defendant company could not rely upon grounds of repudiation of liability, which went to the validity of the existence of the contract, and at the same time rely on the arbitration clause in that contract.

The second series of six modern cases concerns the courts' attitude to and interpretation of the Arbitration Acts, 1954–80 which provide the current statutory framework for the arbitration process in this country.

The following preliminary points are worth noting:

1.   There is strong evidence of a judicial and statutory bias in favour of the arbitration process:

        a)   The judges attach considerable importance to the finality of the arbitrator's decision and lean against any unnecessary interference with those decisions.

        b)   This is mirrored by the legislation itself which does not confer an automatic right of appeal to the courts from the arbitrator's decision. A party may successfully challenge the decision only if that party can find grounds in the award which bring it within the scope of sections 35–40 of the 1954 Act.

        c)   Section 5 of the 1980 Act is even more explicit as it entitles a party to an arbitration agreement to an order staying any court proceedings instituted by the other party to that agreement.

2.   It is settled law that where the parties refer a specific question of law to an arbitrator for a decision, they cannot subsequently seek to overturn the decision simply because they believe that the arbitrator erred in that decision.

In *Walsh* v. *Shield Insurance* (1976) Hamilton J. granted the insured's application under section 45 of the 1954 Act to extend the time in which arbitration may be commenced, notwithstanding the "inexcusable delay" on the part of the insured, which, in the light of the decision, appears, in fact, to have been excused!

In *Church & General Insurance* v. *Connolly and McLoughlin* (1981) the plaintiff company was unsuccessful in its attempt to have an arbitration award remitted to the arbitrator under section 36 of the 1954 Act or to have it set aside pursuant to section 38 of the same Act. The application was grounded on a central allegation of "misconduct" in the sense that the arbitrator had allowed an error of law to appear on the face of the award.

It is also worth noting that Costello J., relying on section 27 of the 1954 Act, made it clear at the outset that the application was not in any sense to be construed as an appeal from the award.

Keenan v. *Shield Insurance* (1988) provided the Supreme Court with its first opportunity to consider the extent and scope of the arbitrator's power, under section 35 of the 1954 Act, to state a question of law for the decision of the court.

The case is of particular significance because of the statements of general principle concerning the importance of the arbitration process in the modern world. (This trend is also evident in the subsequent Supreme Court case of *McStay* (infra)).

The unanimous verdict of the five-member court was given by the late Mr Justice McCarthy who delivered a strong, pro-arbitration judgment in which he stated his disapproval of Costello J.'s approach in *Church & General*, citing it as an example of the type of "fine combing exercise which the Court should not perform when it is sought to review an award". In McCarthy J.'s opinion, judges should only interfere with an award where there was so fundamental an error of law on its face that they could not allow it to remain unchallenged.

The court also held that the arbitrator's powers under section 35 were "spent" once he had made his award.

In *Winterthur Swiss Insurance Company* v. *ICI* (1989) O'Hanlon J. examined the operation of sections 39(2) and (3) of the 1954 Act which provide as follows:—

"(2) where —

a) an agreement between any parties provides that disputes which may arise in the future between them shall be referred to arbitration, and
b) a dispute which so arises involves the question of any party having been guilty of fraud,

the Court shall, so far as may be necessary to enable the question to be determined by the Court, have power to order that the agreement shall cease to have effect and power to give leave to revoke the authority of any Arbitrator or Umpire appointed by or by virtue of the Agreement.

(3) In any case where by virtue of this Section the Court has power to order that any Arbitration Agreement shall cease to have effect or to give leave to revoke the authority of any Arbitrator or Umpire, the

Court may refuse to stay any action brought in breach of the Agreement."

The attitude adopted by the court in this case can be viewed as providing the equivalent, modern answer to the problems posed in the series of "older" cases already considered.

There are strong echoes of those cases in O'Hanlon J.'s finding that

"... it is difficult to envisage that parties who bind themselves contractually to go to arbitration in the event of disputes arising in their business dealings with each other had in contemplation a situation where one party would allege fraud against the other."

A majority decision was given by the Supreme Court in *McStay* v. *Assicurazioni Generali* (1990). This was another case involving section 35 of the 1954 Act. The net point at issue concerned the entitlement of the arbitrator to award interest in respect of the period prior to the making of an award.

In a strong judgment the Chief Justice reiterated the doctrine espoused in the *Keenan* case. In doing so, he based his judgment not on the arbitration clause in the insurance policy but rather on the reference to arbitration subsequently agreed between the parties. He held the former to have been superseded by the latter. In the light of the Chief Justice's findings, the importance of such references cannot be overstated.

The Chief Justice concluded that one of the matters referred to the arbitrator for his decision was this question of law concerning interest and, as such, the court could not interfere with that decision.

O'Flaherty J., dissenting, believed that the matter should be remitted to the arbitrator. In so doing, he adopted a new test which involved the court in a consideration of the consequences for each of the parties of a failure to remit the case.

However, it is submitted that such an approach will serve only to undermine the finality of an arbitrator's award, which O'Flaherty J. regarded as being important. This approach would seem to come very close to the judicial "fine combing" so clearly disapproved of in *Keenan*.

It remains to be seen, therefore, which, if any, of these approaches, the Supreme Court, as currently constituted, will adopt. It appears, for the moment, that the matter has not yet been finally resolved.

The Other Cases

In *Lowry* v. *Ocean Accident and Guarantee Corporation Limited* (1898) the Queen's bench division (Boyd J. dissenting) interpreted the wording of the arbitration clause in a life policy in a manner contrary to that urged upon the court by the company. O'Brien J. referred to insurance companies trying "every form of ingenuity to evade the submissions of cases against them to the Courts of Law".

Lowden v. *Accident Insurance Company* (1904) arose out of an employers' liability policy. It provides an example of the situation whereby at common law in Ireland, there was no jurisdiction in an arbitrator to award costs to the successful party. Section 29 of the 1954 Act now provides that costs are at the discretion of the arbitrator.

In *Hutchinson* v. *Law Union & Rock Insurance Company* (1935) proceedings were stayed in favour of arbitration, as urged by the defendant insurance company.

An interesting example of an insurance company successfully restricting the scope of an arbitration agreement which it had drafted is provided in the Circuit Court case of *Hogan* v. *Poland* (1939).

In *McConn* v. *The Commercial Insurance Company of Ireland* (1949) the pro-policyholder approach of the Circuit Court Judge was reversed on appeal in the High Court. The point at issue was a claim for the policyholder's costs of an arbitration which had been resolved in his favour. The Circuit Court adopted the test of Viscount Simon in *Heyman* v. *Darwin's Limited*,[1] a case that was also examined by Budd J. in *Coen* (supra).

Dooley *v.* The London Assurance
(1872) 6 I.L.T.R. 31
Court of Exchequer

PIGOT C.B: I am not prepared to accede to this application, and I regret that I cannot do so. I think that the defendants have, by their own conduct, deprived themselves of the right to stay these proceedings, which, otherwise, some members of the Court would have been disposed to stay. It appears to me that this contract is one which ought to be effectuated within all legitimate limitations;[2] but the provision which we have to administer is one which requires to be carefully scanned and considered, with reference to the conduct of the party who seeks to avail himself of it. It may be made the engine of delay, and I think it very important with a view to speed, that parties who are entitled under a contract, to which a condition of the present character is attached, and who are desirous of taking advantage of that condition, should intimate that desire to the opposite party at the earliest possible moment, in the ordinary course of business. In this case it appears that the fire took place on the seventeenth of September. Within three days after, the corporation were apprised of the calamity. Within less than twenty-one days they were furnished with particulars of the alleged loss and damage, and within the like

---

[1] [1942] A.C. 356.

[2] See *Mansfield* v. *Doolin*, I.R. 4, C.L. 37, 51.

period an examination was made by a person employed by the corporation, with a view to ascertain, as far as possible, the extent of that loss and damage. It was quite nugatory to apprise the corporation of the loss for any purpose but that of settling the amount claimed by the plaintiff under his policy, and, when they got the account they were called upon then to accede or not to plaintiff's demand. They had the means under their contract of requiring proof of the extent and nature of the loss, although they were not bound to avail themselves of that means. The policy itself gave them the opportunity, and it might be embraced in a proper case. But they made no demand of that kind. The matter so stands, and the parties are left at arm's length; the defendants being an English company, represented by a Dublin agent. The contract and the demand being before them, nothing is done until November. They know the position represented by the plaintiff: it was that of a house burned, and the insured contents burned as he represented. An investigation is made, but that investigation is not followed up. That as the result of the investigation, Doyle came to the conclusion, that twenty five pounds would compensate the plaintiff's loss, or would be enough under the circumstances, i[s] as clear as light. On the nineteenth of December, without any further investigation having been made, the defendants say that, having been carefully advised as to extent of the loss or damage, they are assured that it would be fully compensated by that sum. They had no means but that of Doyle's investigation whereby to arrive at this conclusion, so that they had then the facts before them on which this previous letter was written. Yet, it was on the nineteenth of December that they first intimated their intention to seek a reference touching the loss sustained by the plaintiff. Several communications passed between the plaintiff's attorney and their agent, with a view to the enforcing of plaintiff's demand. Delays were the result of his application. It is not to be overlooked that, from the middle of September to early December, they were not in a position or condition to say that they would avail themselves of a reference. Why did they not do so then? In none of their letters does the agent, though a settlement is demanded, make the slightest allusion to the provision of the contract to refer the dispute to arbitration. On the twenty-second of November, they are asked to name a solicitor. On the twenty-third, a reply is given by the agent, that he has put himself in communication with the head-office. If the defendants were willing then to arbitrate, that ought to have been communicated to their representatives here. Then there is the illness of their secretary. And on the twenty-seventh of November, their solicitors write to have the process forwarded to them. That was an invitation on the part of the defendants to have the process transmitted, which they then expected to be issued. There was then no suggestion of a reference, but on the fifteenth of December (the plaintiff's attorney having then issued the process, which he was all but invited to issue by the letter of the twenty-seventh of November), the defendants first suggest arbitration. That the issuing of the writ was the bringing of the action is perfectly clear to my mind. It is not the service, but the issuing of it which would save the statue of limitations. The defendants knew that it was to have been issued, but, even at the very latest period when they ought to have done so, they did not express their willingness to arbitrate. If they had done so, the writ might not have been issued. It must be taken that, on the nineteenth of

December, they knew that it had been issued. But, it is only then that we have the first intimation of any desire of the defendants to accept the privilege now sought. I am not prepared to accept the statement of the accountant (who does not say that he was aware of the proceedings of the corporation), that they were willing, at the time of the bringing of the action, to refer the matter in dispute, although I do not impeach his veracity. How does that gentleman know when this action was brought? I do not know what he may understand by the bringing of the action — the issuing of the writ or the service. If he means that it was on the thirteenth of December that this willingness existed, I see no grounds for that statement, and there is no indication of willingness, and no statement with reference to the arbitration prior to the nineteenth. Another circumstance indirectly points to the same inference, that his willingness did not arise until after the fifteenth. It was after that date that their solicitor writes, in answer to a letter of that date, that he had taken his client's instructions, and that it was after mature consideration they offered the twenty-five pounds; and it would seem that it was then that they first determined on arbitration. Why have I observed so much upon this? Because it is perfectly plain, upon the terms of the Act of Parliament, that the legislature contemplated promptitude on the part of those who sought to avail themselves of this provision. Because the time at which the liberty to use this enactment, and to withdraw the cause from the adjudication of a Court of law, is given, was when the action had been brought. It is perfectly reasonable that, before parties are tempted to commence a suit, and to incur even the small expense of issuing a writ, those who desire to stay the suit afterwards should prove that, at that time, they were willing to take advantage of the provision, of which they subsequently seek to avail themselves. I am disposed to hold that this application is not brought within the Act of Parliament. We ought to be slow to yield to such an application, unless proper promptitude has been exhibited. It is of the greatest moment to persons having demands, large or small, against such companies, that their demands should be promptly adjusted and that after considerable delay and when obliged to commence an action, plaintiffs should not be met by a proposal of this character to have the matter transferred to another tribunal. As to imposing terms, it must be borne in mind that, up to the time of the motion, no intimation was given that the defendants would not seek to rely on the question of fraud by reason of an extortionate demand. The alternative given on the nineteenth of December was not to take the twenty five pounds and arbitrate as to the remainder of the claim, but that, if this sum were not accepted, the corporation would defend; and in defending they would have been entitled to rest on the clause which nullified the policy, in the event of there having been an attempt at intentional extortion. This might, however, be provided for by terms, and by imposing the costs of the motion. But, on other grounds, the defendants have so conducted their proceedings with reference to the plaintiff's application, they have so played and parried with the plaintiff, that we ought not, I think, to send the case to another tribunal. One reason why the legislature might require an early application is, that, under this section, there is no power in the Court to refer the case at all to arbitration, but the power given to us is to stay the action, that is to impose a penalty on the plaintiff. Nor do we, by the exercise of our jurisdiction, in effect refer the matter to arbitration at once, but the parties are to be thrown at large to seek and to appoint an arbitrator. How do we know when that would be done? In a case before me, upwards of three weeks elapsed before the arbitration was agreed on.[3] Some substantial period would elapse before the tribunal was constituted, and, meantime, would slip away the opportunity of having the case tried. That is one reason why, upon the frame of the section itself, there ought to be an early act done, on the part of the person seeking the benefit of this particular clause of the contract, showing his willingness to avail himself of it. Yet I have arrived at this decision reluctantly, because, if this case were relieved from all questions of fraud, and that the only question were, what loss did the plaintiff sustain, what was the value of the goods destroyed, the course proposed would be the speedy and sensible course and one that might lead to complete justice.[4] It would be less expensive in this, that furniture brokers, acting as arbitrators, would not need the evidence of witnesses as to the value of the goods, but would act upon their own experience. I do not see that they would possess any advantage in determining, yea or nay, whether the things were in the house, but that too could be determined by the exercise of mere common sense.

FITZGERALD B: The only power vested in the Court of staying the action, in carrying out the arbitration clause of the policy, is that given by section fourteen of the Common Law Procedure Amendment Act (1856). The statute has directed us not to exercise that power, unless we are satisfied that no reason exists why the matter cannot, or ought not to be referred to arbitration. I offer no opinion upon the construction of the arbitration clause, as I am not at present prepared to do so. But I am not satisfied that no reason exists why this case ought not to be referred. As to why it ought not to be referred, it does appear to me, from what has taken place, that there would seem to have been a disposition to raise a question of fraud, by suggesting that the account given is substantially an untrue representation of the contents of the house, at the time of the fire. I do not think it was the intention of the legislature that such questions should be referred to arbitration under this section.

HUGHES B: We must not disregard how this matter is presented by both parties. Upon the abstract point, I am clearly of opinion that we are not precluded from exercising our jurisdiction of staying this action peremptorily and

---

[3] Cf. *O'Callaghan* v. *O'Callaghan*, 12 I.C.L.R. (n.s.) App. 46.
[4] In *Elliot* v. *Royal Exchange Assurance Co.,* L.R. 2, Ex. 244, Martin, B., observes —

> "This is a policy of Insurance, and it is well known to everyone that , on such a contract, there is constantly a dispute as to the value of the articles for which compensation is claimed. It is equally well known that this is a question which a jury cannot try and that, if the matter is allowed to go into Court, the parties after incurring all that expense may have to go into arbitration. Therefore, assuming the parties to be aware of this, it is the part of wise men to agree that the question of value shall be so determined at the outset."

And see *Mansfield* v. *Doolin,* Ir R. 4, C.L. 26; *Kitchen* v. *Turnbull,* 20 W.R. 253.

leaving the parties to proceed to arbitration. It is fairly admitted by Mr Purcell, that this motion was brought before the Court at the earliest moment. The defendants were not served till the twenty-third of December. The Christmas recess intervened, and then the motion was brought forward, without any delay as respects the conduct of the case. But then, it is said, that the defendants were not willing to refer the matters in dispute to arbitration at the time of bringing the action. I think that, giving a reasonable construction to the terms of the section, the period at which such willingness should be shown to have existed must be taken to be, that at which the defendants became aware of the action being brought. The process issued on the thirteenth of December. The defendants, a London corporation, reside in England, and are represented by agents in Dublin. But, at the moment that they became aware of the issuing of the writ, they write the letter of the nineteenth signifying their willingness; and their accountant testifies to the existence of that willingness. But then it said that there is a possible question of fraud. If that question is surrendered, there would be no question but as to the contents of the house, and the value of those contents at the time of the fire. It appears to me that the parties might, without any difficulty or delay, agree in appointing a proper and competent furniture broker, to arbitrate upon those questions within a week (a consent to that effect being made a rule of Court), providing that otherwise the action should proceed. In two hours a broker would come to a conclusion on these questions. On the other hand, the case might stand still till next Easter term, if it were made a special jury case and fixed near the end of the list.

Gaw *v.* British Law Fire Insurance Co.
[1908] 1 I.R. 245
Chancery Division

Ross J: The plaintiff is a cycle dealer and repairer carrying on business in Belfast.

By a policy of insurance dated 11th of April, 1905, the defendant company insured the plaintiff against loss by fire in the sum of £400 on stock and utensils in trade. There are other conditions embodied in the policy, to which I shall afterwards refer.

On the 19th August, 1905, portion of the stock was destroyed, and the remaining portion injured by fire. A claim was furnished, setting out in detail the particulars of the loss. In the correspondence that ensued it was admitted that substantial damage had been caused by fire; but a difference arose between the plaintiff and the defendant company as to the amount of the damage.

Under the conditions of the policy an arbitration was necessary as a condition precedent to any suit or action. The arbitrators on each side met on 18th October, 1905. In the correspondence there was nothing to lead the plaintiff to believe that there was anything in dispute save the amount of the damage. In the condition embodied in the policy there is a clause to the effect that if the claim should be in any respect fraudulent, or any fraudulent devices be used by the insured or any one acting on his behalf to obtain any benefit under this policy, all benefit thereunder should be forfeited.

This clause was relied on before the arbitrators. It was contended that a fraudulent claim had been put forward in respect of part of the goods insured. The arbitrators promptly decided that this had occurred. They therefore awarded the plaintiff nothing, on the ground that a forfeiture of the policy had taken place in consequence of the fraudulent claim.

It is no part of my duty at this stage to say whether this contention was well founded or not; and I express no opinion on it whatever. One thing I must say, and it is this, that it is contrary to justice to allow a man to go into arbitration believing that the only question is one of amount, and then to spring upon him the charge of fraud without previous notice.

It has been contended on behalf of the plaintiff that the question of a fraudulent device in a claim is not a difference arising out of the policy, and was therefore outside the scope of the reference altogether. It is not necessary for me to express any opinion on this contention, having regard to the view I take of the case. What I have to decide is whether the plaintiff was bound to go into the question of fraud raised before the private tribunal and to be bound by their decision, and whether he was debarred from having his case heard by the ordinary Courts of the country. Now, as regards the amount of his loss, I think he had no cause of action, until the arbitrators have ascertained the amount of it by their award. But as regards the question of forfeiture by reason of fraud, how does the matter stand?

While the decision of *Scott* v *Avery*[5] is accepted by all Courts, the language of Lord Campbell in his judgment goes much further than was necessary, and has given rise to a good deal of misconception and confusion. It is calculated to create an impression that where an agreement to refer all differences exists, accompanied by words indicating that an award is a condition precedent to legal proceedings, a party can be forced before the private tribunal, no matter what the nature of the differences may be. The matter is cleared up by the judgment of Lord Esher in *Edwards* v. *Aberayron Mutual Ship Insurance Society*[6]:"The true limitation of *Scott* v. *Avery*",[7] he says, "seems to me to be ... that if parties to contract agree to a stipulation in it, which imposes, as a conditional precedent to the maintenance of a suit or action for the breach of it, the settling by arbitration, the amount of damage, or the time of paying it, or any matters of that kind, which do not go to the root of the action, i.e., which do not prevent any action at all from being maintained, such stipulation prevents any action being maintained until the particular facts have been settled by arbitration, but a stipulation in a contract, which in terms would submit every dispute arising on the contract to arbitration, and so prevent the suffering or complaining party from maintaining any suit or action at all in respect of any breach of the contract, does not prevent an action from being maintained.... The rule is founded on public policy. It in no way prevents parties from referring disputes which have arisen to arbitration; but it does prevent them from establishing, as it were, before they dispute, a

---

[5] 5 H.L. Cas. 811.
[6] 1 Q.B.D. 563, at p. 596.
[7] 5 H.L. Cas. 811.

private tribunal which may act in contravention of the most elementary principles of the administration of justice."

This decision has been mentioned with approval by many Courts both in this country and in England. It establishes this, that it is still the law that parties cannot by contract oust the jurisdiction of the Courts in all cases.

In the words of Mr Justice Coleridge in *Scott* v *Avery*[8]: "The Courts will not enforce or sanction an agreement which deprives the subject of that resource to their jurisdiction, which has been considered a right inalienable even by the concurrent will of the parties."

The right to meet a charge of fraud before the King's public tribunals is a right that no man can part with against his will. This award purports to deprive the plaintiff of that right and cannot be allowed to stand. The proper course for the arbitrators to have adopted, was to find the amount of the loss in fact, and leave the plaintiff to enforce his award in a Court of Law. In answer to his claim it is open to the defendants to prove the fraud they allege. The only valid order I can make in this suit is to set aside and cancel the award, leaving the plaintiff to take such further steps as he may be advised. The defendant company must pay the costs of the action.

The Court of Appeal

HOLMES L.J DELIVERED THE JUDGMENT OF THE COURT: This action originated in an insurance against fire effected by the plaintiff with the defendant Company, by a policy which contained a condition that all "differences arising out of the policy shall be referred to the decision of two arbitrators, one to be appointed in writing by each of the parties in difference ... and the obtaining the award of such arbitrators ... shall be a condition precedent to any liability or right of action against the Company in respect of any claim for any loss or damage, or in respect of any other matter in difference." A fire took place after the insurance; and a claim was made by the plaintiff in respect of the loss alleged to be sustained thereby for more than the full sum insured. There followed some correspondence between the representatives of the respective parties, in which an offer was made on behalf of the plaintiff to accept the sum of £317 in settlement of his demand. His advisers seem to have been under the impression that the defendants had offered £100; but I am satisfied that in this they were mistaken. They were informed in the clearest language in two letters that the agents of the Company had not and could not make an offer on behalf of their principals, and that therefore there was no reason why the arbitration previously suggested by the plaintiff should not proceed. A draft submission to arbitration was afterwards submitted by the solicitors for the plaintiff to the defendants, which may or may not have confined the matter referred to the question of amount; but this was not accepted by the agents of the defendants, who returned it with a statement that the conditions of the policy were in themselves sufficient submission to arbitration, and no other was therefore required beyond the appointment of arbitrators in

[8] 5 H.L. Cas. 811.

writing. Accordingly the plaintiff appointed Mr Kennedy, a cycle agent, as arbitrator; and the defendants nominated a solicitor named McCutcheon as the other arbitrator. These gentlemen made their award in due course, wherein after reciting the circumstances that led to their appointment and that there was a difference as to the plaintiff's claim, and after further reciting that the reference came on for hearing before them in the presence of the claimant with his counsel and solicitor, and in presence of the solicitor and assessor of the Insurance Company, and after hearing the evidence and arguments adduced by and on behalf of the respective parties and on examination of the documents submitted to them, they find and award that the claim of James Gaw is fraudulent in a material respect, and that fraudulent devices have been used by him, or some person acting on his behalf, for the purpose of obtaining a benefit under the policy, and they accordingly find that James Gaw has forfeited all benefit under the policy, and is not entitled to recover any sum in respect of his claim.

This finding is based on a condition in the policy that if the claim of the insured be in any respect fraudulent, or any fraudulent devices are used by the insured, or anyone acting on his behalf, to obtain a benefit under the policy, all benefit thereunder shall be forfeited. In these circumstances this action was brought for the purpose of having the award declared void.... The only evidence given before Mr Justice Ross, or in this Court, were the policy of insurance, the award, and the correspondence that passed between the parties; and we have therefore no proof of what happened at the arbitration. The plaintiff's counsel account for this by saying that the object of the action is to raise the purely legal question that the arbitrators had no jurisdiction to find that the insured had forfeited all benefit under the policy for the reasons given by them. Mr Justice Ross dealt with — and I think properly dealt with — the case from this point of view; but in thus approaching it, we are not at liberty to assume that there was any disregard of the principles of natural justice, or other impropriety, on the part of the arbitrators in coming to the conclusion embodied in their award. When the learned Judge says that it is contrary to natural justice to allow a man to go into an arbitration believing that the only question is one of amount, and then to spring upon him the charge of fraud without previous notice, he lays down a proposition in which I would agree, provided the man was not given full opportunity of meeting the charge and defending his conduct. But I have no reason to hold that this is what happened in the present case. I am satisfied from the correspondence that the matter referred was whether the defendant company was under any liability to the plaintiff, and if so to what amount. I have no means of knowing that the plaintiff entered on the arbitration in the belief that the only question was one of amount. We have neither his own testimony nor that of any witness on his behalf; and I cannot without evidence ascertain what a man believed at any particular date. Furthermore I cannot assume that he and his advisers were not invited, and given full opportunity, to explain the acts that the award finds to have been fraudulent devices. He may have tried to do so and have failed; or he may have declined, as his counsel have done, to give any evidence relating thereto on the ground that these matters which the arbitrators had no jurisdiction to inquire into.

I have quoted and commented on the foregoing passage in the judgment of

Ross, J., to prevent my own views from being misunderstood; but it is right to say that it formed no part of his "ratio decidendi", which he states with characteristic clearness. He ruled in favour of the plaintiff, quite irrespective of whether the question of fraud was or was not a difference arising out of the policy, upon the ground that the plaintiff could not by any condition or stipulation be debarred from having his case heard by the ordinary Courts of the country. He held, as I understand his judgment, that the plaintiff had no cause of action until the arbitrators had ascertained the amount of his loss, but that their jurisdiction was confined to declaring such amount, and did not extend, where there was some loss, to awarding that the company was relieved from liability, either by reason of the fraud of the insured, or on any other ground. It would, I think, be difficult to exaggerate the importance of the position thus laid down. We are all familiar with the rule of law, that a term in a contract that any matter of difference arising thereon shall be referred to arbitration cannot be used as a defence to, or a ground for staying, an action brought by either party for the purpose of having the matter in difference adjudicated upon by one of the public Courts of the country. We also know that some modifications of, or exceptions to, this rule were laid down by the House of Lords in *Scott* v. *Avery*.[9] It will not be denied that that decision legalises a stipulation in a contract that any difference as to the amount of liability thereunder is to be referred to arbitration, and that no action can be maintained until the amount is so settled, and then only for such sum as shall be awarded. Speaking for myself, however, I have always been of opinion that *Scott* v. *Avery*[10] went farther than this, and is an authority that a contract may legally provide that where a difference arises thereunder relating to other matters than amount, no liability is to arise, and no action is to be maintained until the matter of difference has been made the subject of arbitration and award. This has been not only my opinion, but is, I think, the view generally taken by lawyers during the last forty years. As Martin, B., says in *Tredwen* v. *Holman*,[11] "The case of *Scott* v. *Avery*[12] decided that the insurer and the underwriter may contract that no right of action (to be enforced in a Court of law) shall accrue until an arbitrator has decided, not merely as to the amount to be recovered but upon any dispute that may arise upon the policy"; and I may also quote Amphlett, B., one of the majority of the Exchequer Chamber, in the *Aberayron Case*[13] — "It must be taken to have been the intention of the parties to give exclusive jurisdiction to the directors to settle all claims between the society and its members, and the question whether an agreement to that effect is void as being against the policy of the law, is, in my judgment, concluded by the decision of the House of Lords in *Scott* v. *Avery*.[14] It is true that in the present case the directors are to decide not the mere amount of the claims, but also any dispute that might arise

---

[9] 5 H.L. Cas. 811.
[10] *Ibid.*
[11] 1 H. & C. 72.
[12] 5 H.L. Cas. 811.
[13] 1 Q.B.D. 563.
[14] 5 H.L. Cas. 811.

respecting insurances, but so they were in *Scott* v. *Avery*,[15] and both the learned Lords who decided the case held such extension of the powers of the directors to be immaterial."

I might refer to many similar dicta of distinguished Judges, but I prefer to see what is relied on in support of the contrary view, and I find that the only authority mentioned by Mr Justice Ross is the judgment of Brett, J., in *Edwards* v. *Aberayron Mutual Ship Insurance Society*.[16] That case is curious and complicated. For my present purpose it is enough to say that the defendants were a limited Company for the mutual insurance of ships belonging to members; and the Articles of Association provided that the directors should have full power to determine all disputes arising between the Society and members concerning insurances or claims upon the Society, and the decision of the Directors should be final and conclusive, and no member should be allowed to bring any action or suit against the Society except as provided therein. The plaintiff insured, with the Society, a vessel which was wrecked, and he sent in his claim for the loss; whereupon the Directors, having heard from the master of the ship his account of the wreck, resolved that it was not lost by perils of the sea, and that the owner had no claim upon the Society. This was done behind the back of the plaintiff, who had no notice or knowledge of the meeting; and he brought an action against the defendants to recover the amount of his insurance, which came before the Court of Queen's Bench on a case stated. Not only were the foregoing facts admitted, but it was also admitted that the vessel had become a total loss by perils of the seas. There were other points argued, but the main contention turned on the Article of Association which I have quoted; and Blackburn, Mellor, and Lush, J.J., held, on the authority of *Scott* v. *Avery*,[17] the action did not lie.

The case was then brought into the Exchequer Chambers, where Archibald, J., and Pollock, B., came to the same conclusion as the Queen's Bench. Amphlett, B., took the view of *Scott* v. *Avery*,[18] which I have already quoted, and thought that the action could not be maintained unless it could be shown that the conduct of the Directors in the so-called arbitration had made it inequitable to bind the plaintiff by their finding, or to compel him to submit his claim again to their determination. This he held on an examination of the facts; and he therefore decided in favour of the plaintiff. But Lord Esher, then Brett, J., distinctly, and Kelly, C.B., with more doubt, took the narrow view of *Scott* v. *Avery*,[19] on which Mr Justice Ross has acted. It must, however, be remembered that in doing so they not only differed from the majority of the Exchequer Chamber, but from the three Judges of the King's Bench. The *Aberayron Case*[20] has, as far as I am aware, been only referred to in one subsequent, English case, *Trainor* v. *The Fire Insurance Company*,[21] in which

---

[15] 5 H.L. Cas. 811.
[16] 1 Q.B.D. 563.
[17] 5 H.L. Cas. 811.
[18] *Ibid.*
[19] *Ibid.*
[20] 1 Q.B.D. 563.
[21] 65 L.T. (N.S.) 825.

Lord Esher's view of the effect of *Scott* v. *Avery*[22] was dissented from; and in *Scott* v. *The Mercantile Accident and Guarantee Insurance Company, Limited*,[23] Lord Esher himself gave a judgment absolutely inconsistent with his dicta in the *Aberayron Case*.[24] In the *Caledonian Insurance Company* v. *Gilmour*[25] Lord Watson regarded the principle of *Scott* v. *Avery*[26] to have been embodied in the emphatic words of Lord Campbell: "'I think that the contract between the shipowners and the underwriters is as clear as the English language could make it; that no action should be brought against the insurers until the arbitrators had disposed of any dispute that might arise between them. It is declared to be a condition precedent to the bringing of any action. There is no doubt that such was the intention of the parties; and upon a deliberate view of the policy, I am of opinion that it embraced not only the assessment of damage, the contemplation of quantum, but also any dispute that might arise between the underwriters and the insured respecting the liability of the insurers as well as the amount to be paid.' He then deals with the question whether such a contract is tainted with illegality, which he answers in the negative; and the main ground of judgment is expressed by him in these terms:— 'Now, in this contract it is stipulated in the most express terms that until the arbitrators have determined, no action shall lie in any Court whatever. That is not ousting the Courts of their jurisdiction, because they have no jurisdiction whatsoever, and no cause of action accrues until the arbitrators have determined.'" I hold that every word of this passage is applicable to condition 6 of the policy in this case; that the effect of that condition is that an award of arbitrators is a condition precedent to any liability or right of action against the Company in respect of any claim for any loss or damage, or in respect of any other matter in difference, and that there is no illegality in such a stipulation.

This disposes of the ground on which judgment was given in the Divisional Court; but Mr Brown relies on two other matters on which Mr Justice Ross did not express any definite opinion. The first of these is that the question of fraud or fraudulent devises was not a matter in difference between the parties previous to the arbitration. It is true that there had been no reference to fraudulent devices in the correspondence; and probably they were not present to the mind of the advisers of either party. The matter in difference, however, was the liability of the defendant Company; and I am of opinion that they were at liberty to rely on any defence to the claim arising from the terms of the policy. Although no evidence was given at the trial of what were the alleged fraudulent devices, documents were produced without objection in the Divisional Court, and have also been seen by us, which show the nature of the fraud. The plaintiff obtained from a cycle company with which he dealt duplicates of twenty invoices of goods purchased by him shortly before the fire; and these documents were laid before the arbitrator in

---

[22] 5 H.L. Cas. 811.
[23] 66 L.T. (N.S.) 811.
[24] 1 Q.B.D. 563.
[25] [1893] A.C. 85.
[26] 5 H.L. Cas. 811.

proof of the value of the stock on the plaintiff's premises. All these duplicates are said to have been altered by the plaintiff or some one acting in his interest by adding additional goods to a considerable amount. If this was the case, the alterations were skilfully made and were evidently intended to deceive; and the moment the honesty of these invoices was challenged by the defendants' representatives, this became a matter in difference on which the arbitrators had jurisdiction to decide. Of course the plaintiff was entitled to rebut the charge if he could do so; but a letter from the arbitrators read by his counsel shows that they made their award with great reluctance, and I have no doubt they gave him ample opportunity to show that the allegation of fraud could not be supported.

I have some difficulty in following the other argument urged by Mr Brown; but, as I understand him, it turns upon the final provision of the second condition, which is to the effect that in the event of the use of any fraudulent devices all benefit under the policy should be forfeited. Mr Brown contends that this puts an end both to the policy and all differences arising thereunder. I do not think so. It is made a term of the contract that certain conduct on the part of the insured will deprive him of any benefit thereunder; and whether he has been guilty of such conduct or not is a matter of difference arising out of the policy. Therefore, I hold that the appeal ought to be allowed and the action dismissed.

Wilson *v.* The National Live Stock Insurance Co., Ltd.
(1914) 48 I.L.T.R. 77
The Court of Appeal

O'BRIEN, L.C: This is an appeal from an order of Mr Justice Boyd refusing to stay an action which has been brought by the plaintiff against the National Live Stock Insurance Co., Ltd., to recover the value of a horse which was insured with the company under circumstances which he says brings it within the contract of insurance. It has been admitted that an order under s. 14 of the Common Law Procedure (Ir.) Act, 1856, is a discretionary order. The appeal then is from a discretionary order, and although this Court will interfere with orders made under the discretionary jurisdiction, if there is a violation of some principle of law, it is slow to interfere with an order made under this section. The learned Judge was not satisfied that the defendants in this case would not raise the question of fraud, and he was justified in that because they would not adopt the ordinary course of having it taken down on the order that the plea of fraud would not be raised. The defendants were within their right as to that, and so was the Court in taking the fact into consideration when making its order.... It has been argued that the condition in the policy is in the nature of a condition precedent. On the construction of this clause it is a very arguable question indeed whether it is a condition precedent or not. I do not express any opinion one way or another, but I think in the exercise of its discretion the Court was rightly of opinion that that was a question more properly triable in the action than in a summary proceeding like this.

HOLMES L.J: This action has been brought to recover the sum of £1,000 alleged to be due under a policy of insurance made by the defendants whereby they indemnified the plaintiff in this sum against the death of a mare named "Saratoga" from natural causes, fire or accident. The policy was executed on May 13, 1913, and the mare died on Aug. 14 following. The plaintiff resides in Westmeath, and the defendant company has its registered office in London; but as the writ of summons by order of the King's Bench Division has been served in England, and as such order has not been discharged, it is to be presumed that the policy is an Irish contract. The present appeal is taken from the refusal of an application made by the defendants under s. 14 of the Common Law Procedure (Ir.) Act, 1856, for a stay of the proceedings on the ground that the parties had agreed by the policy and documents incorporated therewith that the matters in dispute in this action should be referred to arbitration, and that the obtaining of an award at such arbitration should be a condition precedent to the liability of the defendants to pay or satisfy any claim under the policy. Section 14 of the Act of 1856 enacts that where the parties to a document agree that any existing or future differences between them shall be referred to arbitration, and one of them shall, nevertheless, commence an action at law, or suit in equity against the other in respect of the matters so agreed to be referred, it shall be lawful for the Court in which the action is pending or a judge thereof upon being satisfied that no sufficient reason exists why such matters cannot be or ought not to be referred to arbitration according to the agreement to make a rule or order staying all proceedings in such action or suit. An order under this section may be described as a discretionary order; but counsel for the defendants argue that the contract in this case shows clearly that no cause of action can arise until an arbitration takes place, and an award has been obtained; and that therefore the discretion of the Court, ought to be exercised in their clients' favour. This really means that in the circumstances the action is frivolous and vexatious, and ought to be so dealt with. I cannot agree with this proposition. So far from the case being clear I think there arises a question of importance that has never been decided. I have said that we must assume that the contract between the plaintiff and the defendants is an Irish contract; but by its terms the arbitration must be an arbitration in England governed by the English law dealing with arbitrations and awards which differs substantially from the law in this country relating thereto. The plaintiff desires to argue that he is not bound by the portion of this contract; or, at the least, it does not amount to a condition precedent, and in my opinion this is a fit subject for argument and for the decision of the highest tribunal if either party so requires. Therefore, I agree with Boyd, J., in holding that the action ought not to be stayed. The defendants can raise the question in controversy by their defence; and I wish it to be understood that I have formed no opinion thereon.

CHERRY L.J: I concur, and have nothing to add.

Ballasty *v.* Army, Navy and General
Assurance Association Ltd.
(1916) 50 I.L.T.R. 114
The High Court

MADDEN J: This is an application on behalf of the defendants for an order that all further proceedings in this action be stayed and the matter in dispute referred to arbitration, the plaintiff and the defendants having by the terms and conditions of the policy of insurance sued upon agreed to refer to arbitration the matter in respect of which this action is commenced. The policy contains an arbitration clause in very wide terms, including all disputes in regard to claims of any kind under this policy. The law is settled since the decision in *Scott* v. *Avory* [sic],[27] that a clause of this kind only imposes a condition precedent, compliance with which is antecedent to a right of action arising: therefore if the present claim were under the policy the defendants would be entitled to carry their motion; but a claim that the policy and contract are not enforceable is a different thing. The ground of the decision in *Jureidini's Case*[28] is stated in the head-note, as follows:—

> "A claim was made for indemnity for the loss of goods by fire under a policy, the conditions of which provided — (1) that if the claim were fraudulent or if the loss were occasioned by the wilful act or with the connivance of the insured all benefit under the policy should be forfeited; and (2) that if any difference arose as to the amount of any loss such difference should, independently of all other questions, be referred to arbitration; and that it should be a condition precedent to any right of action upon the policy that the award of the arbitrator or umpire of the amount of the loss, if disputed, should be first obtained. The insurance company repudiated the claim on the ground of fraud and arson. *Held,* that the repudiation of the claim on a ground going to the root of the contract precluded the company from pleading the arbitration clause as a bar to an action to enforce the claim."

One condition was that in case of fraud or crime the policy should be forfeited. The question was whether the claim was founded on a crime, and the decision was that as the question sought to be referred to arbitration went to the continued existence of the policy, it could not be referred. The condition here is [7]:

> "Any material misrepresentation or concealment or omission to state any circumstance or to give any information material to be known for estimating the risk or the rate of premium or in respect of any claim by or on behalf of the insured shall render this policy absolutely void, and all premiums thereon shall be forfeited to the Association."

This is, in substance, the same condition as in *Jureidini's Case*.[29] The case

---

[27] 5 H.L. Cas. 811.
[28] [1915] A.C. 499.
[29] *Ibid.*

arose out of a motor car collision. The case of the company is that an admission of liability was concealed, so as to come within Condition 7. If this is true it renders the policy void. Two letters which have been read render their attitude clear. This is an application to refer to arbitration a question going to the root of the contract. Mr Battersby [for the insurance company] endeavoured to distinguish the present case from *Jureidini's Case*,[30] but they are indistinguishable. There are other difficulties in the case, but I only say that the intention appears to have been to have a contract governed by English law; difficulties would arise in carrying this out. We base our decision on the question in dispute being one that goes to the root of the contract.

PIM J: I concur. We do not decide this case on the ground of the inconvenience of applying the English Act or on the existence of allegations of fraud. Possibly in some cases a question of fraud might be referred to arbitration. Where one party says that the contract is gone and the premium forfeited, he cannot insist on going to arbitration under a contract which he says does not exist.

Furey *v.* Eagle Star and British Dominions Insurance Co. Ltd.
(1922) 56 I.L.T.R. 23
The High Court

Headnote:
F. Insured a motor charabanc with the defendant company. The policy contained the usual clause as to wilful misstatements, and a clause that any dispute ... "as to the extent and meaning" of the policy should be referred to arbitration....

PIM J: Mr Denning [for the insurance company] says that this case cannot be distinguished from *Jureidini's Case*[31] except by the introduction of the words "extent and meaning" in the arbitration clause. Probably those words were introduced because of *Jureidini's Case*,[32] so that, if not repudiated, the extent of the policy might be tried by arbitration, the question, for instance, whether it covered arson, which was the question in that case. But those words have nothing to say to a thing which goes to the root of the policy — namely, fraud, which makes the question whether or not the whole policy has gone. As I said in *Ballasty's Case*,[33] where one party says that the contract is gone, he cannot then insist on going to arbitration under a contract which he says does not exist. I must hold that the words "extent and meaning " of the policy do not cover this case, and the motion must therefore be refused with costs.

---

[30] [1915] A.C. 499.
[31] *Ibid.*
[32] *Ibid.*
[33] (1916) 50 I.L.T.R. 114. See p. 420 of this book.

SAMUELS J: I concur, being of the opinion that, notwithstanding Mr Denning's able argument, this case is indistinguishable from *Jureidini's*[34] and *Ballasty's Cases.*[35]

James Coen v. The Employers Liability Assurance Corporation Limited[*]
[1962] I.R. 314
The High Court

Headnote:
The plaintiff entered into a contract of insurance with the defendants in relation to the plaintiff's liability in damages arising from injuries caused by the driving of a motor car, the property of the plaintiff. A passenger in the plaintiff's said motor car recovered judgment for damages for personal injuries suffered by him as a result of an accident in which the plaintiff's car was involved. The defendants disclaimed liability to indemnify the plaintiff in respect of the damages awarded to the passenger on the grounds (1) that injury to passengers was not covered by the policy of insurance; (2) that the insured had not an insurable interest in that he was not the owner of the vehicle at material times. The contract of insurance entered into between the parties contained a condition that all disputes arising under the policy should be referred to arbitration, and that if the insurers should disclaim liability to indemnify the insured in respect of any claim under the policy and such claim should not be referred to arbitration within twelve months from the date of such disclaimer, then the claim should, for all purposes, be deemed to have been abandoned and should not thereafter be recoverable under the contract. The plaintiff did not refer the matters in dispute or the disclaimer to arbitration, but instituted proceedings in the High Court seeking a declaration that the defendants were liable to indemnify him under the contract of insurance in respect of his liability to the injured passenger....

BUDD J: A great many issues and defences were raised by the pleadings in this case but at an early stage of the case Mr Wood for the defendants took the very practical course of stating what the particular matters relied on by the defendants were as constituting both their grounds of repudiation of liability and defence. These were, first, that the cover note, as he described it, number 2, being that bearing the date the 21st June, 1956, did not cover passenger liability. This point was, of course, elaborated in argument during the trial and developed into a contest as to what was the form of the contract under which the plaintiff was insured. The second ground relied upon was that the plaintiff had no insurable interest in the car, i.e., that he was not the owner. Thirdly, the defendants contended that assuming that a contract did

---

[34] [1915] A.C. 499.
[35] (1916) 50 I.L.T.R. 114. See p. 420 of this book.
[*] Extract.

exist between the plaintiff and defendants' Company, the plaintiff had abandoned his claim by not having referred it to arbitration within the twelve months of the defendant Company's disclaimer of liability on the 12th September, 1957.

The last ground relied on by Mr Wood was a reference to the plea contained in para. 15 of the defence wherein the defendants relied upon the arbitration clause contained in the policy dated the 31st August, 1956, which was in the same terms as that already quoted, as being contained in the two specimen policies produced. At a very late stage in the proceedings this plea was later amended by leave on the terms, *inter alia*, of the plaintiff being entitled to make any necessary amendments in his reply and an amended reply was duly filed. The matters arising on the third issue as to the application and effect of an arbitration clause in the contract as regards the first two issues between the parties I shall also deal with later.

I have first to consider the validity of the ground of repudiation of liability based upon the defendants' contentions as to the nature and effect of the second document, referred to by the defendants as a cover note, issued by the defendants, so far as the matter of liability to passengers is concerned. The defendants contended that this document stood by itself and was the document constituting the contract between the parties on the date when the accident occurred. They said that the only cover that it provided was that on the document as it stands, and that, having regard to the wording of the certificate at the end of the document, the only risks covered were those required to be covered by the provisions of the Road Traffic Act, 1933, in an "approved" policy and that indemnity in respect of liability to passengers for personal injuries was not covered by such a policy. They said, further, that there was nothing to link the first certificate or the endorsement on its back with the second document and that the words, "Cover note", contained in the second document were merely descriptive of what it was; or, to put it in another way, that the words "Cover note", meant the document itself. They further submitted that the plaintiff by his pleadings only sought to rely on this second document and was tied to it by his pleading. This last contention I reject as the statement of claim seems clearly to rely upon the cover note endorsed on the back of the first certificate and the first certificate, as well as what is contained in the second document, as constituting the contract between the plaintiff and the defendants on the date of the accident. I have, then, to determine what the real contract of insurance between the parties was on the true construction of either or both documents.

The plaintiff had applied through his sister and the brokers for the insurance of his car, including third party cover. In response he had, prior to the date of the accident, received the first document, dated the 9th June, 1956, obviously issued by the defendant Company with the intention that it should be given to him. It contained on the back the endorsement I have stated. The document was therefore two things: it was a certificate of insurance of a type required to comply with the provisions of the Road Traffic Act, 1933, and it was by virtue of the endorsement on the back, usually called a cover note, a contract of insurance between the plaintiff and the defendant Company relating to the insurance of the use and driving of the motor car mentioned in the certificate with the index mark and registration number IZ

7238, which I shall assume for the present was the plaintiff's property for the purpose of the matter which I am now considering. The risk was held covered, according to the terms of the endorsement, in the terms of the Corporation's usual third party fire and theft policy which I have already referred to as the "standard" form of policy. It is the fact that that form of policy covers liability to third parties and does not except indemnity in respect of liability to passengers. The endorsement contained no exception as to indemnity in respect of passenger liability. It is therefore clear that had the accident occurred during the currency of the first certificate with this endorsement the plaintiff would have been covered in respect of Michael Kavanagh's claim by virtue of the contract of insurance contained in the endorsement and the relevant portions of the certificate as to the person insured, period of cover and identification of the vehicle.

There is no evidence that in the interval between the issue of the two documents the defendant Company decided to alter the contract they had entered into or that any agreement had been come to between the parties involving any alteration as to the risk covered or the nature of their contractual relationship. It remains in that state of affairs to analyse and construe the true meaning of the second document viewed in the light of the existing circumstances.

The second document, dated the 21st June, 1956, current at the date of the accident, is in my view a certificate of insurance and is so described in its heading. It complies with the provisions of the Road Traffic Act, 1933. It is not on its heading described as a cover note and is not, taking the document as a whole, properly describable as a cover note. It is, I think, properly describable as a certificate of insurance referring to a cover note. But it contains at its foot a certificate saying that an approved policy has been issued to the plaintiff covering all liabilities required to be covered by the said Act. I need scarcely say that a policy which gives greater cover than that which is required by the Act fulfils the requirements of the Act as to the cover which an approved policy should contain. A certificate such as this is not in itself or on the face of it a contract of insurance. It is a certificate that a contract of insurance exists between the plaintiff and defendant Company and it seems to me that by its issue by the defendant company to the plaintiff the defendant Company must be taken, in the circumstances that existed and having regard to their pre-existing relationship, as representing to the plaintiff that at least some contract of insurance existed between them during the period covered by the certificate. What contract of insurance, then, is referred to? Opposite to the words, "No. of the Policy of Insurance", we have the words, "Cover Note". Normally, where a policy of insurance in the full form we are accustomed to see has been issued, the number of that policy is, of course, inserted where the words, "Cover note", appear. The purpose of this is to identify the policy in respect of which the certificate of insurance is issued. Therefore the place where these words appear is the appropriate place in which to state and identify the document containing the contract of insurance between the body issuing the certificate and the person receiving it and named in it. That is, in fact, the document by means of which the insured person obtains cover. What is the true inference to be drawn, on construing the document, on finding these words inserted in this particular place in the certificate? Undoubtedly they must mean that some cover is in existence and *prima facie* that it was contained in the cover note. I would agree that in certain circumstances — such as where an owner of a motor car had applied for insurance for his motor car and received in return from an insurance company a certificate of insurance, without more — the document might be construed as containing the contract between the parties, and the addition of the words, "Cover note", if no other cover existed, might well aid in such a construction. But that is not the position here. Having regard to the fact that there existed already between these parties a cover note containing a contract of insurance for a stated period in the shape of the cover note endorsed on the back of the first certificate, I can only construe this second certificate, containing these words where they are placed, as referring to the cover or contract of insurance which the plaintiff already had, and the only cover or contract of insurance that existed was that contained in the cover note endorsed on the back of the first certificate together with the relevant parts of that certificate. The certificates should, then, in my view, be properly construed as indicating that the type of cover which the insured had during the currency of the second certificate was that contained in the said endorsement and the relevant part of both certificates. In my view, therefore, when the defendant Company issued the second certificate to the plaintiff in the circumstances existing they thereby impliedly represented to, and agreed with, the plaintiff, as the person intended to receive and receiving the certificate, that he was held covered by the Company on the terms of the cover note contained in the first certificate and the relevant parts of both certificates and that the cover was extended to the 8th July, 1956. That, then, was, in my view, the contract existing between the parties on the date of the accident and it involved the result that the usual terms of the Company's "standard" policy were incorporated into the contract. It follows that the plaintiff was therefore covered against the risk of injury to passengers on the date when the accident occurred and that the defendant Company is liable to indemnify the plaintiff in respect of Michael Kavanagh's claim in so far as the documents I am construing are concerned and unless there be some other circumstance which relieves them of liability.

The second matter relied upon by the defendant Company is that the plaintiff was not the owner of the motor car at the time when the accident giving rise to the claim against him occurred and when the contract of insurance was effected and, as a result, had no insurable interest in the car. The legal result of that state of affairs is, the defendants say, that no valid contract of insurance ever came into existence and hence they cannot be liable to indemnify the plaintiff. In this connection the defendants relied upon my own decision in *O'Leary* v. *Irish National Insurance Co. Ltd.*[36] I said in that case that if a person purports to take out a policy of insurance in respect of a certain car, of which he is not in fact the owner, no valid contract of insurance ever comes into existence for want of subject-matter and lack of insurable interest. The circumstances here, it seems to me, indicate that it

---

[36] [1958] Ir. Jur. Rep. 1. See p. 115 of this book.

was understood that the plaintiff was the owner of the motor car. Naturally, I accept the defendants' contention as to the proposition of law involved and it will be applied to relieve the defendants of liability if the fact is that the plaintiff was not the owner of the motor car in question.

A good deal of evidence was directed to the matter of the sale of this car to the plaintiff by his brother-in-law and a great deal of criticism was made of the evidence adduced on behalf of the plaintiff to prove the sale. Some suggestion was made that the car was not sold to the plaintiff, but merely insured in his name so as to get a cheaper rate of insurance. That suggestion did not seem to me to have been substantiated. The onus is, of course, on the plaintiff to establish that he was the owner of the car when he insured it, but it is all a question of fact dependent upon what evidence I accept as true and what I believe to be the true state of affairs. Although there were some curious features of the transaction, I believe that the plaintiff's brother-in-law was the owner of this car and sold it to the plaintiff for the sum of £90. The contract of sale was, I am satisfied, made on the 8th June, 1956, before Mrs Smith got in contact with the brokers. That this was the date is corroborated by the letter of the 8th June, 1956, from the brokers to Mrs Smith which is consistent with other evidence given that there had been a previous contract between Mrs Smith and the brokers about arranging the insurance on behalf of the plaintiff. Since I reject the suggestion that the car remained the property of Mr Smith or Mrs Smith or was insured in the plaintiff's name for some ulterior motive, the fact that the plaintiff, as I believe, got this car insured in his own name supports the view I take, as to the sale to him having taken place. I further accept the evidence that the plaintiff obtained the key of the car and took it over and drove it on several occasions before the accident occurred; but, in any event, the property in the motor car passed to the plaintiff and he became the owner thereof on the 8th June when the contract was made in accordance with the provisions of the Sale of Goods Act, 1893. In my view, therefore, the contract of insurance was not invalidated for want of insurable interest.

The third ground of repudiation relied on by Mr Wood was that assuming that a contract existed between the parties the plaintiff must be held to have abandoned his claim, not having referred it to the arbitration within twelve months of the defendant Company's disclaimer of liability. This point had reference to para. 18 of the pleadings, as they then stood, which involved one particular matter: but as amendments of the pleadings were allowed several points now arise for decision with relation to the applicability and construction of an arbitration clause. The defendants in their original defence pleaded that if they did insure the plaintiff, the cover was provided under, and by virtue of, the policy of insurance of the 31st August, 1956, and that such cover was subject to certain express conditions which were those contained in the arbitration clause of that policy. This clause is in the same terms as those contained in the Company's "standard" and "approved" policies.... The plaintiff contended during the hearing that the defendants had tied themselves by their pleading to the arbitration clause contained in that particular policy and that if I should hold that the cover given was not by that policy, but rather by the contract dependent upon the endorsement on the first certificate and the relevant words of the two certificates, the plea was not relevant and did not constitute a defence. Accordingly, the defendants asked for, and obtained, liberty to amend their pleading by deleting the portion of para. 15 of their defence, referring to the policy of the 31st August, 1956, so that the paragraph, as amended, raised the plea that if the defendants had insured the plaintiff the cover provided was subject to the express conditions set out in the paragraph, which are in fact the same as those contained in the arbitration clause contained in the Company's "standard" form of policy above recited. As my findings so far made would make the conditions of the "standard" form of policy part of the contract between the plaintiff and defendants it was then open to the defendants to rely on the terms of the arbitration clause contained in the "standard" form of policy. They accordingly contended that according to its terms all differences arising under the policy must be referred to arbitration, that the making of an award was a condition precedent to any right of action and that as the Company had disclaimed liability in respect of a claim under the policy and such claim had not been referred to arbitration within twelve calendar months from the date of disclaimer, the claim must be deemed to have been abandoned and not recoverable under the policy. The defendants say that they repudiated liability by their letter of the 12th September, 1957, and that since the difference thus arising was not referred to arbitration within twelve months of that date this action is not maintainable. The repudiation relied upon was that the policy did not indemnify the insured in respect of persons being carried in the motor car referred to in the policy. The defendants, at the very conclusion of the case, also relied on the further repudiation contained in the letter dated the 18th March, 1958, based on the allegation that the plaintiff was not the owner of the motor car on the date of the accident and likewise say that as that second difference was not referred to arbitration within twelve months the plaintiff's claim is not sustainable. Liability was in fact technically disclaimed in both letters under the terms of the policy of 31st August 1956, but no point as to this was made at the hearing and both parties treated the repudiations of liability as being applicable to whatever contract of insurance existed between the parties.

The defendants were, of course, only given liberty to amend on terms as to costs to be decided later and that the plaintiff should be entitled to amend his reply to meet the new case made. The plaintiff duly amended his reply. Paragraph 4 of the amended reply is in these terms:— "The matters in issue in this action do not constitute difference arising out of the policy of insurance within the meaning of condition No. 5 of the defendants' usual form of third party, fire and theft policy on the relevant date (referred to in this action as the 'standard policy') and accordingly the defendants are not entitled to rely on the said condition".

In this case I accept the contention of the plaintiff that the first ground of repudiation of liability relied upon by the defendants — that the second certificate (called by Mr Wood the cover note) did not cover passenger liability — raised an issue in this case as to what was the contract of insurance between the parties, or, to put it in another way, raised an issue as to whether the plaintiff was covered by the terms of a "standard" policy or of an "approved" policy and I have determined that he was covered under the terms of a "standard" policy. Under that type of policy no question arises as to whether it

covers liability to passengers. It is conceded that it does. There cannot be said
to be any difference between the parties arising out of the terms of the
"standard" policy within the meaning of the arbitration clause, which refers
to "differences arising out of this policy", on the question of liability to passengers and therefore there arises nothing on this score which the defendant
Company could claim should be referred to arbitration. The real point in
issue, then, by reason of the plea in para. 4 of the amended reply is as to
whether, under the correct construction of the arbitration clause in a "standard" policy, a question as to whether the plaintiff was insured under that
form of policy or some other form of policy can be said to be a difference arising out of the policy and therefore one to which the arbitration clause applies.
As regards the second point, namely, that of insurable interest, the same
issue arises as to whether or not that question falls within the arbitration
clause.

The plaintiff, however, relied on other matters in paras. 5 and 6 of the
amended reply, which read as follows:—

> "5. The defendants, having denied the existence of any contract of insurance
> between the parties, and, in particular, the existence of the contract of insur-
> ance relied on by the plaintiff in this action, are not entitled to rely upon the
> arbitration clause contained in the said condition.
>
> 6. The plaintiff, while not admitting that the defendants are entitled to
> claim in this action that the contract of insurance relied upon by the plaintiff
> is void or ineffective, says that the defendants cannot at the same time rely
> upon the alleged lack of insurable interest in the plaintiff or the alleged
> absence of subject-matter for the said insurance, and upon the said arbitra-
> tion clause."

The pleas in these two paragraphs should logically be dealt with before
the plea contained in para. 4. Further, the case law relevant on these two
issues has some considerable bearing on the matters relied on in para. 4 of
the amended reply and I feel that I should deal with it before coming to any
final conclusion on the matter of construction of the arbitration clause.

These two pleas raise questions of approbation and reprobation that have
given rise to great difficulty in many cases. First, Mr Connolly [for the
Plaintiff] relies on two Irish decisions, *Ballasty* v. *Army, Navy and General
Assurance Association, Ltd.*[37] and *Furey* v. *Eagle, Star and British Dominions
Insurance Co., Ltd.*[38] In the former case the policy contained a clause that any
material misrepresentation or concealment should render the policy void. The
company alleged that an admission of liability was concealed and that that
contention, if correct, would render the policy void. There was also an
arbitration clause and the company moved to stay the proceedings and that
the matter in dispute be referred to arbitration. The arbitration clause was, if
anything in wider terms than that contained in the "standard" policy here.

... The Court refused to stay the proceedings. Mr Justice Madden said in
the course of his judgment:— "We base our decision on the question in

---

[37] (1916) 50 I.L.T.R. 114. See p. 420 of this book.
[38] (1922) 56 I.L.T.R. 23. See p. 421 of this book.

dispute being one that goes to the root of the contract." Pim J., concurring, said:— "Where one party says that the contract is gone and the premium forfeited, he cannot insist on going to arbitration under a contract which he says does not exist."

The latter case was also a motion to stay proceedings. The policy there in question contained a clause that if any wilful misstatement was made in the proposal form the policy should become void. It also contained an arbitration clause....

The company repudiated the claim on the ground of non-disclosure of material facts. Counsel argued that the addition of the words, "extent and meaning", in the arbitration clause, which were not contained in the arbitration clause in *Ballasty's Case*[39] covered the question as to whether the plaintiff was guilty of wilful misstatement and that they covered an inquiry as to whether the policy was gone or not. The Court, consisting of Pim J. and Samuels J., refused a stay. Mr Justice Pim, *inter alia*, held that the addition of the words had nothing to say to a thing which goes to the root of the policy, namely, fraud, which makes the question whether or not the whole policy was gone. He added that, as he had said in *Ballasty's Case*,[40] "where one party says that the contract is gone, he cannot then insist on going to arbitration under a contract which he says does not exist." Mr Justice Samuels, who concurred, also said that he was of opinion that the case was not distinguishable from *Ballasty's Case*.[41] It is right to add, however, that both learned Judges also relied on *Jureidini* v. *National British and Irish Insurance Co., Ltd.*[42] which has been held in later English cases to have been of limited application.

Mr Connolly also relied on the terms of the order of the Supreme Court as stated in the concluding portion of the judgment of Kennedy C.J. in *Kennedy* v. *London Express Newspapers*,[43] where the Supreme Court did stay proceedings on a policy to allow the dispute between the parties to be determined by arbitration, as indicting by implication that the Court would not have stayed the proceedings if any question going to the root of the contract had been raised. The Chief Justice stipulated that the company were to be bound not to raise in such arbitration proceedings any question of fraud or other matter going to the root of the existence or validity of the contract which for the purpose of the arbitration was to be taken as admitted. It is, again, right to add that the Chief Justice also in that case pointed out that the scope of the decision in *Jureidini's Case*[44] had been extended without justification. He pointed out that the arbitration clause in that case only applied in terms to the amount of loss or damage, while the issue in the action was fraud and arson which would forfeit all benefit under the policy.

The matter has also been dealt with in many decisions in the Courts in

---

[39] (1916) 50 I.L.T.R. 114. See p. 420 of this book.
[40] *Ibid.*
[41] *Ibid.*
[42] [1915] A.C. 499.
[43] [1931] I.R. 532.
[44] [1915] A.C. 499.

England and I feel that I should deal with the contentions based on them also. In *Toller* v. *Law Accident Insurance Society*,[45] the Court of Appeal reversed an order refusing to stay proceedings on an application by the defendants alleging that the case fell within an arbitration clause. The question at issue was whether or not the contract of insurance covering the plaintiff's driving on a certain date was in existence or not. If it was, the contract would have been subject to an arbitration clause covering all differences arising out of the policy. During the course of his judgment, Greene L.J. (as he then was) referred with approval to the following statement of law by Romer L.J. in *Stevens & Sons* v. *Timber and General Mutual Accident Insurance Association Ltd.*[46] as follows:—

> "A person who repudiates the contract *in toto* obviously cannot be allowed at the same time that he is repudiating it to avail himself of a clause contained in it. Where, therefore, a defendant who has so repudiated his contract applies to the Court to refer to arbitration the question of the legality of such repudiation, his application must necessarily fail. For if the repudiation was justified the arbitration clause has gone. An arbitrator, therefore, who purported to award in favour of the defendant's repudiation would at the same time be making an award against the existence of his own jurisdiction."

He then went on himself to say:—

> "Now, the class of cases where the defendant insurance company is denying the existence of a contract is totally different from the class of case where the defendant, while admitting the existence of the contract, is relying on some clause in it to escape liability. It is very important in my view that language should be accurately used and there is great danger in the use of such words as 'repudiation'; repudiation of a contract may mean that, having admittedly made a contract, you decide to break it and break it in such a way that you intend not to proceed with it. Another use of the word 'repudiation' is where you say: 'There never was a contract at all between us.' If it turns out that there was a contract, the act of one party denying the existence of it is to repudiate it; but supposing it turns out he was right and there never was a contract, then 'repudiation' is used in a different sense from that in which it would be used when an existing contract is broken by a refusal to perform."

Later in his judgment the learned Lord Justice points out that if the plaintiff succeeds the plaintiff will be entitled to receive a policy which will contain the usual arbitration clause. He says it may be when the plaintiff claims that it must be treated on the footing that that clause is enforceable against him and it may be that the defendants will not be liable. He adds:— "I do not know." These remarks, however, seem to have reference to claims which the plaintiff might have in respect of certain accidents he was involved in and cannot, I think, have had any reference to the matter of the plaintiff's

---

[45] [1936] 2 All E.R. 952.
[46] 102 L.J.K.B. 337.

right to have the question as to whether he was covered by insurance on the vital date determined by the Court. Lord Justice Scott ends his judgment by saying that in his view "the right of the plaintiff to have his action tried in the Courts in a case where the whole contract is denied or repudiated is quite clear."

The whole subject of the meaning of repudiation and the result of a total repudiation of a contract of insurance was later dealt with in great detail by the House of Lords in *Heyman* v. *Darwins, Ltd.*[47] That case involved a dispute as to whether an arbitration clause in a contract applied in the circumstances of the case. The House of Lords held that it did and that the action should be stayed. The decision of the House turned upon the view of their Lordships as to the nature of the alleged repudiation of the contract and its effect and the terms of the arbitration clause. The nature of various types of repudiation and their effect on arbitration clauses were also considered. There are, however, some general statements of law which seem to me relevant to what I have to decide in this case. At p. 362, Viscount Simon says:—

> "If the respondents were denying that the contract had ever bound them at all, such an attitude would disentitle them from relying on the arbitration clause which it contains, but that is not the position they take up."

At p. 366, he said:—

> "An arbitration clause is a written submission, agreed to by the parties to the contract, and like other written submissions to arbitration, must be construed according to its language and in the light of the circumstances in which it is made. If the dispute is whether the contract which contains the clause has ever been entered into at all, that issue cannot go to arbitration under the clause, for the party who denies that he has ever entered into the contract is thereby denying that he has ever joined in the submission. Similarly, if one party to the alleged contract is contending that it is void *ab initio* (because, for example, the making of such a contract is illegal), the arbitration clause cannot operate, for on this view the clause itself also is void."

Lord Macmillan, at p. 370, said:—

> "If it appears that the dispute is whether there has ever been a binding contract between the parties, such a dispute cannot be covered by an arbitration clause in the challenged contract. If there has never been a contract at all, there has never been as part of it an agreement to arbitrate. The greater includes the less. Further, a claim to set aside a contract on such grounds as fraud, duress or essential error cannot be the subject-matter of a reference under an arbitration clause in the contract sought to be set aside."

Lord Macmillan stated that Lord Russell agreed with his opinion on all points. Lord Wright, at p. 378, said:—

---

[47] [1942] A.C. 356.

"Repudiation of a contract is sometimes used as meaning that the defendant denies that there ever was a contract in the sense of an actual consensus *ad idem*. If that is the case, a submission of disputes under the contract never comes into operative existence any more than the contract to which it was to be ancillary."

It is right to say, however, that both Lord Wright and Lord Porter later both appear to take the view that, where the contention is that the appearance of consent was vitiated by illegality, fraud, duress or mistake, it depends upon the terms of the submission as to whether a claim to set aside the contract on such grounds could properly be the subject-matter of a reference to arbitration. For example, at p. 384, Lord Wright says:—

"Nor are the appellants helped by the rule that, generally speaking, a dispute whether the contract ever existed, as contrasted with the question whether it has been ended, is not within the usual form of submission of differences arising out of the contract or the like; because, if there was never a contract at all, there could never be disputes arising out of it. *Ex nihilo nil fit*. It is all a question of the scope of the submission. Hence, if the question is whether the alleged contract was void for illegality, or, being voidable, was avoided because induced by fraud or misrepresentation, or on the ground of mistake, it depends on the terms of the submission whether the dispute falls within the arbitrator's jurisdiction."

Further, at p. 392, Lord Porter says:—

"Meanwhile, I think it essential to remember that the question whether a given dispute comes within the provisions of an arbitration clause or not primarily depends on the terms of the clause itself. If two parties purport to enter into a contract and a dispute arises whether they have done so or not, or whether the alleged contract is binding on them, I see no reason why they should not submit that dispute to arbitration. Equally I see no reason why, if at the time when they purport to make the contract they foresee the possibility of such a dispute arising, they should not provide in the contract itself for the submission to arbitration of a dispute whether the contract ever bound them or continues to do so. They might, for instance, stipulate that, if a dispute should arise whether there had been such fraud, misrepresentation or concealment in the negotiations between them as to make an apparent contract voidable, that dispute should be submitted to arbitration. It may require very clear language to effect this result, and it may be true to say that such a contract is really collateral to the agreement supposed to have been made, but I do not see why it should not be done."

The question as to what principles of law are to be derived from the judgments is the next matter to determine. Deriving them to the best of my ability it seems to me that the majority of the House took the view that if the dispute be as to whether a party entered into a contract at all or whether there was a binding contract, the issue cannot go to arbitration. That also seems to me to have been the view of the Court of Appeal in *Toller* v. *Law*

Accident Insurance Society.[48] Thus it would appear that if one party to the contract alleges that it is void *ab initio* on such grounds as fraud, duress or illegality, the arbitration clause cannot operate. According to the views of Lord Wright and Lord Porter the question as to whether any particular case should be submitted to arbitration under the arbitration clause where the dispute is as to a contract being void for illegality, fraud, misrepresentation or mistake would depend on the terms of the submission. Indeed, Lord Porter's view would appear to be that a dispute as to whether the parties had ever made a binding contract might, if the words of the clause were sufficiently wide, fall within the terms of an arbitration clause.

Assuming for the purpose of dealing with the matters raised in the paragraphs of the amended reply that I have referred to that there were disclaimers by the defendants of liability under the contract which I have held to exist, which would include the conditions of a "standard" policy, I have to consider the applicability of the statements of law I have quoted to the facts of the present case.

The contentions of the plaintiff contained in paras. 5 and 6 of the reply seem to me to be supported by the two Irish decisions relied on. The *Ballasty Case*,[49] in particular, is strongly in favour of the plaintiff in that the company in that case repudiated liability under a condition of the policy in respect of something done by the insured after the policy had come into existence. They did not say that there never had been a contract of insurance between the parties. In *Furey's Case*[50] also it is to be noted that an actual clause in the policy itself was relied on, the breach of which it was alleged rendered the policy void, yet the decision was that a party who says that the contract is gone cannot then insist on going to arbitration under a contract which he says does not exist. It seems to me that these cases go further than the facts of the present case in that in the first case it was held that the arbitration clause did not apply, even though the insurance company did not allege that a valid contract had not been entered into but relied on terms of the policy, and in the second case the insurance company relied on an actual clause of the policy for its repudiation thereof. They seem to be authorities for the proposition that a defendant insurance company will not be permitted to approbate and reprobate in circumstances more favourable to the defendants in these cases than those existing in this case. There is also, it seems to me, to some degree contained in the judgment of Kennedy C.J., which I have referred to, an indication that matters of dispute going to the root of the existence or validity of a contract of insurance are not matters falling within the ambit of an arbitration clause. As a Court of first instance I feel that I should follow these two Irish decisions which are of very long standing, even though it may be suggested that they go further than is warranted by later English decisions of weighty authority. The application of them would seem to entitle the plaintiff to succeed on the contentions contained in paras. 5 and 6 of the amended

---

[48] [1936] 2 All E.R. 952.
[49] (1916) 50 I.L.T.R. 114. See p. 420 of this book.
[50] (1922) 56 I.L.T.R. 23. See p. 421 of this book.

reply as regards both issues relating to the nature of the contract and insurable interest.

I feel, however, that before finally deciding the matter I should also examine the validity of the defendants' defence based on the arbitration clause and of the contentions of the plaintiff contained in paras. 5 and 6 of his reply in the light of the English decisions I have referred to. The point to be decided is as to whether or not what I believe to be the general principles to be derived from these decisions support the plaintiff's contentions. The defendants in their first letter of disclaimer say that the policy, which is that of the 31st August, 1956 (No. 26507), does not indemnify the insured in respect of any person being carried in the vehicle referred to in the policy, which is the plaintiff's Hillman car. That is a reliance upon a contract which I have held did not exist between them and that, it seems to me, impliedly involves a repudiation of the contract that I have held did exist which would cover passenger liability. The pleadings — and the first issue stated by the defendants at the trial to arise on them — likewise amount to a denial of the existence of the type of contract which the plaintiff says existed between the parties. The pleadings, indeed, go further and deny the existence of any cover for insurance at all and thus deny the existence of any contract. The defendants further by their contentions at the trial took the attitude of denying the existence of the contract which I have held to have existed. While it might be said that a dispute as to which type of contract exists between the parties is not quite the same thing as saying that no contract exists, I think that where that dispute involves in fact the repudiation of the existence of that type of contract which one of the parties relies on, as it does here, the same principle applies and the repudiating party cannot be allowed to approbate and reprobate. He cannot thus be allowed to say:— "I deny the existence of the contract which you say exists between us, but I also rely on a term of that contract which contains a provision which bars you from bringing proceedings on foot of any claim not arbitrated upon within twelve months of the date of disclaimer." It seems to me, therefore, that as regards the repudiation of the contract the case falls also within the English decisions referred to and that the plaintiff is under them also correct in his contention contained in para. 5 of the amended reply, that the defendant Company cannot in the circumstances rely upon the arbitration clause. The defendants' defence based on the arbitration clause as regards this particular dispute, therefore, fails in accordance with those English decisions.

As regards the second ground of disclaimer, based on the lack of insurable interest, the same reasoning would *prima facie* seem to apply since the disclaimer amounted to saying that the contract was void *ab initio* and also amounted to a repudiation of the contract. On this point I felt some hesitation by reason of certain views expressed by Lord Sumner in his judgment in *Macaura* v. *Northern Assurance Co.*[51] This case was not adverted to at the hearing and I had not the benefit of hearing argument upon it.

In that case the appellant sold timber to a company in consideration of

---

[51] [1925] A.C. 619.

receiving shares in the company. He was in fact the sole shareholder and a substantial creditor also. He subsequently insured the timber against fire by policies effected in his own name with several insurance companies. Most of the timber having been destroyed by fire, he sued the insurance companies to recover the loss. The actions were stayed and the matter was referred to arbitration. The arbitrator held that the claimant had no insurable interest. The House of Lords also held that he had no insurable interest. It also held that the appellant having allowed the matter of insurable interest to be raised before the arbitrator without objection, it was not open to him to question the authority of the arbitrator to decide the point. While these appear to have been the main grounds of the decision, the question as to whether a dispute as to insurable interest fell within the particular arbitration clauses in the policies was also dealt with in the opinions of the House. It is, I think, to be inferred from Lord Buckmaster's opinion that such a dispute did in his view fall within the arbitration clause. Lord Atkinson concurred, but gave no separate judgment. Lord Wrenbury did not deal separately with the point, but concurred with Lord Sumner's judgment.

Lord Sumner said, at p. 631:—

"There remains the contention that the respondents were incompetent to raise the absence of insurable interest upon the arbitration. This seems to me to be a pure misapprehension. It is said that the defendants could not have got the order, which stayed the action and referred the matter in dispute to arbitration, if they had stated that they meant to rely on this point or rather, if they had not actually intimated that they would not. The argument rests on the contention that to put the plaintiff to proof of an insurable interest is the same thing as pleading the Gaming Act, and saying that the policy is null and void and that there is no contract for arbitration or anything else, but in truth the defendants have said no such thing. The letters written before the order was made did not, either affirmatively or negatively, show anything of the kind. The plaintiff had averred an insurable interest in his pleading. The defendants, who moved for a stay before putting in a defence, simply denied liability, and the issue so raised was the matter in dispute. The case of *Jureidini*[52] is not in point. There persons, who had repudiated the whole contract of insurance, afterwards relied on a limited arbitration clause contained in it, which required the amount payable to be determined by arbitration, and said that, until he had obtained such an award, the plaintiff could not complete his case. It was held that the defendants could not both repudiate the contract *in toto* and require the performance of a part of it, which only became performable when liability was admitted or established. The present case is the converse. Here an arbitration and award are conditions precedent to any action to enforce the policy. The defendants do not repudiate the policy or dispute its validity as a contract; on the contrary, they rely on it and say that, according to its terms, express and implied, they are relieved from liability: see *Stebbing's Case*;[53]

[52] [1915] A.C. 499.
[53] [1917] 2 K.B. 433.

Woodall v. *Pearl Assurance Co.*[54] It is a fallacy to say that they assert the policy to be null and void. They do not plead or mention the Gaming Act, and have no need to rely on it. The contract made in the policy was that, if the plaintiff could prove, among other things, that he had, at the time of the loss, such an insurable interest in the timber as the law recognises, the insurers would pay, and not otherwise. No gaming contract was ever made, nor any agreement to pay, interest or no interest. It is we who would make the contract a gaming contract, if we were to accept the appellant's contention. The respondents say, and truly say, that a fire insurance policy is not an aleatory contract, but is a contract of indemnity, under which the assured must aver and prove interest at the time of the loss. This is a part of the law of insurance, quite independently of the Gaming Act, though the consequence of failure to prove interest is the same — namely, that the policy is unenforceable by an uninterested assured. It was open to the defendants to raise this case at any time. Under the policy arbitration was the only legal proceeding open, and the order was made as a matter of course."

These observations would indicate that the matter of insurable interest was a matter properly to be dealt with by the arbitrator having regard to the nature of the particular arbitration clauses contained in the policies under consideration.

Any observations of Lord Sumner are without doubt entitled to great respect, but from the point of view of deciding whether they should be applied in this case I have some considerable difficulty. To begin with, what he said was not the main reason for the decision of the House. The case also has, from the point of view of what I have to decide, the unsatisfactory feature that, as I read the report, counsel was not permitted to argue the very point here in issue. Counsel submitted (at p. 622) that in as much as the want of insurable interest is a question going to the root of the contract, the arbitrator had no jurisdiction to entertain it. Lord Buckmaster L.C. said the point was not open to the appellant. Counsel appears to have accepted that ruling in that he did not attempt to argue the point further. The House did not therefore have the benefit of having before it such argument as there might be *contra*.

It seems to me, however, that in the first place the case is distinguishable on the facts in that the respondents in that case relied on the contract and did not dispute its validity. In this case the defendant Company repudiated liability under the contract which the plaintiff relies on, and has established as existing, and have argued that it was void *ab initio*. They raised the matter of the ownership of the car in their letter of the 18th March, 1958, in such fashion that the only reasonable inference is that they were relying on the ground of lack of insurable interest as a further ground of repudiation of liability. They maintained an attitude of repudiating liability in the pleadings by denying ownership of the car and pleading that the plaintiff had no cover for insurance. They also took up the attitude at the trial that the contract was void *ab initio* as is shown by their reliance on the case of *O'Leary* v. *Irish*

---

[54] [1919] 1 K.B. 593.

National Insurance Company Ltd.[55]

Their attitude being that they repudiated the contract on this ground seems to bring the case within what I conceive to be the principles to be derived from the judgments of the majority of the House of Lords in *Heyman's Case*.[56] Even if the case was not distinguishable on the facts and one were to accept that Lord Sumner's view was that the allegation of a lack of insurable interest was not a matter disentitling a party raising such a point from relying on an arbitration clause, I cannot reconcile that with what I conceive to be the views of the majority of the House of Lords in *Heyman's Case*[57] to the effect that if a party to an alleged contract says it is void *ab initio*, or if it appears that the dispute is whether there has ever been a binding contract, that issue cannot go to arbitration, and I prefer to follow the views expressed in *Heyman's Case*.[58]

I take the view that the case falls, as regards the second ground of repudiation, within the view of the majority of the House in *Heyman's Case*[59] and that as to that particular dispute also, the defendant Company, having taken up the attitude which it did, is not entitled to rely on the arbitration clause contained in the "standard" policy as regards this dispute.

My final conclusions therefore are that, applying the Irish cases referred to and the views of the majority of the House of Lords in *Heyman's Case*,[60] the defendant Company cannot rely upon either of the grounds of repudiation of liability relied on going to the validity of the existence of the contract and at the same time rely on the terms of the arbitration clause in the same contract. The defendants' defence based on the right to rely upon the arbitration clause therefore fails as to both disputes. It follows that the plaintiff is entitled to succeed in respect of the pleas raised in both paras. 5 and 6 of the amended reply. Having regard to the other findings I have already made in these proceedings the plaintiff is therefore entitled to succeed in this action.

Without departing in any way from the view I have just expressed I would not feel it right to conclude my judgment without reference to the argument that was addressed to me on the scope of the particular arbitration clause in the "standard" policy, especially having regard to the view of two of the Law Lords in *Heyman's Case*[61] that the question as to whether a particular dispute should be referred to arbitration depends upon the wording of the arbitration clause in question. As I have formed a view as to the correct construction of this clause in reference to the matters in issue I feel that I should express it.

The contention of the defendant Company is that the wording of the arbitration clause in the "standard" policy is wide enough to cover the disputes which have arisen. It is contended in para. 4 of the amended reply that it is not.

---

[55] [1958] Ir. Jur. Rep. 1. See p. 115 of this book.
[56] [1942] A.C. 356.
[57] *Ibid.*
[58] *Ibid.*
[59] *Ibid.*
[60] *Ibid.*
[61] *Ibid.*

The plaintiff's contention, based on this plea, is that the matters arising for decision under the first two issues in this case are not, within the meaning of clause 5 of the conditions of the "standard" policy, "differences arising out of the policy". He says that the first issue was in reality as to what was the contract between the parties; was the insured covered under the terms of a "standard" policy covering liability to passengers or an "approved" policy which did not cover liability to passengers, and that that is not a difference arising out of any policy. Likewise, as regards the second issue of insurable interest, dependent upon the ownership of the motor car, he says that that again is not a difference arising out of the policy but a question as to whether any contract exists between the parties at all for want of insurable interest. The plaintiff says that the condition must be construed as a whole and that accordingly the last paragraph of the condition, barring an insured's claim if arbitration shall not take place within twelve months of a disclaimer, must be construed as referring to such claims as can properly be described as "differences arising out of the policy", because it is only such differences that the condition stipulates must be referred to arbitration. The plaintiff says that the differences arising on the first two issues in the case are not such differences and that the clause therefore has no application and that the last paragraph of the condition cannot be relied upon as a bar to these proceedings.

The defendants' contention in answer to this plea in the reply is that the arbitration clause is wide enough to cover the first two issues which I have dealt with, and should be widely construed so as to cover all difference arising between the parties. Mr McKenna relied upon certain portions of the judgment of Holmes L.J. in *Gaw* v. *British Law Life Insurance Co.*[62] in support of these contentions. That case involved a policy of insurance against fire. The policy contained a condition that if a claim should be fraudulent, all benefits thereunder should be forfeited. It also contained an arbitration clause, providing that all differences arising out of the policy should be referred to arbitration and that the obtaining of an award should be a condition precedent to any liability or right of action against the insurers in respect of any claim for loss or damage or in respect of any other matter in difference. The insured property was damaged by fire. A claim was sent in and arbitrators duly appointed. The award found that the claim was fraudulent and all benefit under the policy was forfeited. Mr Justice Ross held that the right of the plaintiff to have the question of fraud decided by the Court was not ousted by the conditions of the policy. His decision was reversed by the Court of Appeal, which held that the making of an award was in the circumstances of the case a condition precedent to the maintenance of an action, that the plaintiff was barred by the award against him and could not sue on the policy. Mr McKenna says that the particular passage in the judgment of Holmes L.J. on which he relies is applicable to the facts of this case and shows that the wording of the arbitration clause in the Company's "standard" policy is sufficiently wide to bring the matters raised in the first and second issues in this case within its scope. Before referring to that passage, however, and to enable one

---

[62] [1908] 1 I.R. 245. See p. 411 of this book.

to appreciate its import, it is necessary to understand and appreciate the point and matters that were in issue before Lord Justice Holmes. As I read his judgment he was in the main dealing with the extent of the decision in *Scott* v. *Avery*.[63] He had pointed out the grounds of the decision of Ross J. in these words, at p. 255:—

> "He ruled in favour of the plaintiff, quite irrespective of whether the question of fraud was or was not a difference arising out of the policy, upon the ground that the plaintiff could not by any condition or stipulation be debarred from having his case heard by the ordinary Courts of the country. He held, as I understand his judgment, that the plaintiff had no cause of action until the arbitrators had ascertained the amount of his loss, but that their jurisdiction was confined to declaring such amount, and did not extend, where there was some loss, to awarding that the company was relieved from liability, either by reason of the fraud of the insured, or on any other ground. It would, I think, be difficult to exaggerate the importance of the proposition thus laid down."

He proceeded:—

> "We are all familiar with the rule of law, that a term in a contract that any matter of difference arising thereon shall be referred to arbitration cannot be used as a defence to, or a ground for staying, an action brought by either party for the purpose of having the matter in difference adjudicated upon by one of the public Courts of the country. We also know that some modification of, or exceptions to, this rule were laid down by the House of Lords in *Scott* v. *Avery*.[64] It will not be denied that that decision legalises a stipulation in a contract that any difference as to the amount of liability thereunder is to be referred to arbitration, and that no action can be maintained until the amount is so settled, and then only such sum as shall be awarded. Speaking for myself, however, I have always been of opinion that *Scott* v. *Avery*[65] went farther than this, and is an authority that a contract may legally provide that where a difference arises thereunder relating to other matters than amount, no liability is to arise, and no action is to be maintained until the matter of difference has been made the subject of arbitration and award."

Having quoted certain passages from other judgments in support of that view and what had been relied upon to the contrary, he indicated, by what he said at p. 257, his view that Ross J. had taken the narrower view of *Scott* v. *Avery*.[66] Finally, with regard to the correct view to be taken of *Scott* v. *Avery*[67] he refers, at p. 257, with apparent approval to what Lord Watson regarded as the true principle of *Scott* v. *Avery*[68] in these words:—

---

[63] 5 H.L. Cas. 811.
[64] *Ibid.*
[65] *Ibid.*
[66] *Ibid.*
[67] *Ibid.*
[68] *Ibid.*

"In *The Caledonian Insurance Company* v. *Gilmour*[69] Lord Watson regarded
the principle of *Scott* v. *Avery*[70] to have been embodied in the emphatic words
of Lord Campbell: 'I think that the contract between the shipowners and the
underwriters is as clear as the English language could make it: that no
action should be brought against the insurers until the arbitrators had
disposed of any dispute that might arise between them. It is declared to be a
condition precedent to the bringing of any action. There is no doubt that such
was the intention of the parties; and, upon a deliberate view of the policy, I
am of opinion that it embraced not only the assessment of damage, the
contemplation of quantum, but also any dispute that might arise between
the underwriters and the insured respecting the liability of the insurers as
well as the amount to be paid.' He then deals with the question whether such
a contract is tainted with illegality, which he answers in the negative; and
the main ground of judgment is expressed by him in these terms:— 'Now, in
this contract it is stipulated in the most express terms that "until the
arbitrators have determined, no action shall lie in any Court whatever". That
is not ousting the Courts of their jurisdiction, because they have no jurisdiction whatsoever, and no cause of action accrues until the arbitrators have
determined.'"

Lord Justice Holmes then used the words relied on by Mr McKenna:—

"I hold that every word of this passage is applicable to condition 6 of the
policy in this case; that the effect of that condition is that an award of arbitrators is a condition precedent to any liability or right of action against the
Company in respect of any claim for any loss or damage, or in respect of any
other matter in difference, and that there is no illegality in such a stipulation."

From the passages I have cited, and reading the case as a whole, the point
which Holmes L.J. was dealing with seems to me clearly to have been
whether the narrower or wider view of the decision in *Scott* v. *Avery*[71] should
prevail and as I understand his judgment, his view was that the wider view
should prevail, namely, that a clause making a submission to arbitration a
condition precedent to suing was a good and valid condition even where the
clause provided not only for the arbitrator deciding the amount of damage,
but also the question of the liability of the insurers. The words which Mr
McKenna has relied upon were an acceptance of what had been stated in the
passages which Holmes L.J. had quoted and should, in my view, be construed
in that light. In short, he was addressing his mind to the wording and effect
of the condition in the policy and found that in the particular circumstances
of the case it made the award of the arbitrators a condition precedent to
liability and that there was no illegality in such a stipulation. It is true that
he did refer to any matter in difference, but these words must be read in the
light of the facts of the case in which differences had arisen out of the terms

---

[69] [1893] A.C. 85.
[70] 5 H.L. Cas. 811.
[71] *Ibid.*

of the policy. The particular policy in question, it must be remembered, contained a clause to the effect that if a claim were fraudulent, all benefit under the policy should be forfeited, and therefore the question whether a claim was fraudulent or not was a matter of difference arising out of the policy and properly a matter for the arbitrator to decide. I think that the words in the judgment relied on should be read in the light of the facts of the case and should properly be taken as intended to apply to the facts of the case before the Court and were thus meant to refer to difference arising out of the policy. I do not believe that Holmes L.J. was laying down any general proposition that any difference arising between an insured and an insurer must necessarily fall within an arbitration clause of the kind under review here or that the words he used were intended to cover such cases as where one party denied that any contract, or a particular contract, of insurance existed between the parties. If there be any doubt upon the matter, what I have said is, I think, reinforced by the second last sentence in the judgment, referring to counsel's contention as to the meaning of the final provision in the second condition relating to the loss of benefit through the use of fraudulent devices. As to it, Holmes, L.J. says:—

> "It is made a term of the contract that certain conduct on the part of the insured will deprive him of any benefit thereunder: and whether he has been guilty of such conduct or not is a matter of difference arising out of the policy."

I accept, of course, as binding on me the view of Holmes L.J. that the wider view as to what was decided in *Scott* v. *Avery*[72] is to prevail, but the decision — and what was said by Holmes L. J. — should not, in my view, be extended to something that was not in issue in the case and to which the learned Lord Justice was not addressing his mind, namely, whether a dispute as to whether a certain type of insurance existed between the parties or, indeed, the existence of any contract of insurance at all, both matters going to the root of the contract, could be held to fall within the terms of a particular arbitration clause. I take the view, therefore, that the decision in *Gaw* v. *British Life Insurance Co.*[73] is not applicable to the matters in issue in this case; but I have still to determine on this aspect of the case the issues raised in para. 4 of the reply as to whether the first two issues in the action are differences within the meaning of the arbitration clause in a "standard" policy and as to whether the defendants are entitled with regard to these issues to rely on the condition that a claim shall be barred if not arbitrated on within twelve months of disclaimer in the particular circumstances of this case.

The clause is not the first instance so worded as to cover expressly the first matter in issue. Nor does it, in my view, cover such a matter by implication. The Company rely on the latter portion of the clause which in effect provides that if the Company shall disclaim liability in respect of any claim "hereunder" and such claim shall not have, within twelve months of disclaimer, been referred to arbitration "under the provisions herein contained",

---

the claim is to be deemed abandoned. The clause must be construed as a whole. The latter portion of the clause must, by reason of the reference to claims "hereunder" which have not been referred to arbitration, be taken as referring to such claims as it is provided in the clause should be referred to arbitration. The claims that it is intended should be arbitrated on are shown by the opening words of the clause to be all differences arising "out of this policy". A dispute as to whether the plaintiff was insured under that policy or not does not arise out of the policy. Therefore I take the view that on its true construction the arbitration clause does not apply to such a dispute with the result that the provision that claims not arbitrated upon within twelve months of disclaimer shall be deemed to have been abandoned does not operate to bar the plaintiff's action and the defendants' defence based on this contention fails, in so far as it relates to the dispute relating to the nature of the contract entered into. There remains to be decided the question as to whether or not the second disclaimer relied on by the defendant Company can be said to come within "the wording" of the arbitration clause....

The defendants' letter of the 18th March, 1958, can, I think, only be construed in the circumstances of the case as involving a further repudiation of the contract in the sense of denying its existence, since the only intelligible reason for stating in the particular circumstances that it had come to light that Mr Coen was not even the owner of the car was put forward as a further ground on which the defendant Company was not liable and that ground was one which would also avoid the contract *ab initio*. The pleadings, of course, also contain a denial of the ownership of the car and Mr Wood's second point was that there was no insurable interest because of this. The defendants again at the trial took the attitude that the lack of insurable interest rendered the contract void *ab initio,* as is shown by their reliance on the case of *O'Leary* v. *Irish National Insurance Company Ltd.*[74]

It seems to me that the same reasoning that applies to the construction of the arbitration clause as regards the first question in dispute likewise applies to the second matter in dispute. The clause, as I have pointed out, refers to all differences "arising out of this policy". A dispute as to whether or not the policy is void *ab initio* for want of insurable interest does not arise out of any term of the policy; it is a matter going to the existence of the contract. I take the view, therefore, that the arbitration clause cannot properly be construed as applying to this second matter in dispute and that the defendants' contention that the plaintiff's action is barred by his failure to refer this second disclaimer to arbitration within twelve months also fails.

Having regard to my findings on the issues in this action, the plaintiff is entitled to succeed....

---

[74] [1958] Ir. Jur. Rep. 1. See p. 115 of this book.

Desmond Walsh *v.* Shield Assurance Co. Ltd.
[1976–7] I.L.R.M. 218
The High Court

HAMILTON J: This is an application brought by the applicant pursuant to the provisions of s.45 of the Arbitration Act 1954 in which he claims relief set forth in detail in the notice of motion issued by him on 2 July 1976.

The facts are set forth in the affidavits of the applicant sworn herein on 30 June 1976 and 7 October 1976, and of Michael P. O'Rourke, the secretary to the respondent company, sworn on 15 July 1976 and the exhibits therein referred to.

From these it appears that:

1. The applicant was the holder of a policy of insurance, described as a "shopkeeper all-in bonus policy" with the respondents.

2. The period of cover was from 22 July 1970 to 22 July 1971.

3. The said policy covered all aspects of employers' liability.

4. On 5 October 1970 the applicant's employee, one Paul Jones, suffered injury in the course of his employment by the applicant.

5. The respondent was duly notified of the accident and by letter dated 13 October 1970 addressed to Messrs Maher & Richardson Ltd, insurance brokers, repudiated liability on foot of the said policy on the grounds set forth in the said letter. In addition they draw the attention of the said brokers to the terms of condition 15 of the policy which provided that:

> "All differences arising out of this policy shall be referred to an arbitrator to be appointed by the parties in accordance with the statutory provision in that behalf for the time being in force.
>
> Where any differences is by this condition to be referred to arbitration the making of an award shall be a condition precedent to any right of action against the company.
>
> Claims not referred to arbitration within twelve calendar months from the date of disclaimer of liability shall be deemed to have been abandoned."

6. By letter dated 25 July 1971 the applicant was notified by the injured party's solicitor of his intention to hold the applicant liable for damages for the injuries, loss and damage which he had suffered as result of the said accident.

7. A copy of this letter was forwarded to the respondents but returned by them on 13 July 1971 on the grounds that they had no further interest in the claim being made upon the applicant.

8. There was correspondence between the applicant's solicitor and the respondents during the period 21 February 1972 to 30 January 1973 during the course of which the respondents reiterated their position which was in effect:

> (1) That they repudiated liability on foot of the policy.
>
> (2) That the time fixed by the policy for reference to arbitration of the dispute had expired.
>
> (3) That it would be necessary for the applicant to apply to the Court to extend the time, and

(4) That they would oppose such application.

9. By letter dated 17 January 1973 the applicant's solicitor stated, inter alia, that:

"We reiterate that it is our intention to, and we hereby, on our client's behalf, refer the matter to arbitration and nominate Mr Liam Hamilton SC as arbitrator."

10. By letter dated 23 January 1973 the respondent stated:

"We are in receipt of your letter of the 17th instant. We believe that we made our position in this matter clear in our letter to you of 8 December 1972. To remove any further doubt however, we wish to confirm that we are not prepared to indemnify your client in respect of any liability he may have incurred to the plaintiff.

We formally advised your client's insurance brokers to this effect on 13 October 1970. We have reminded you that under condition 15 of the policy of insurance held by your client 'claims not referred to arbitration within twelve calendar months from the date of disclaimer of liability shall be deemed to have been abandoned'. You will therefore have to apply to the court to see whether permission will be given to your client to commence arbitration proceedings when he is in breach of the terms of his contract on this point. We cannot be responsible for costs which your client may incur through being in breach of the conditions of his contract.

Our solicitors Messrs George D. Fottrell & Company will look after your interests.

Yours faithfully,
P.J. Kennedy
Claims Manager."

11. The correspondence terminated with the letter dated 30 January 1973 from the applicant's solicitor to the respondents in which they state that:

"We have returned papers to counsel in this case to draft the necessary motion and we will be in communication with you again relative thereto."

12. The notice of motion was issued on 2 July 1976.
13. S.45 of the Arbitration Act 1954 provides that:

"Where
(a) the terms of an agreement to refer future disputes to arbitration provide that any claim to which the agreement applies shall be barred unless notice to appoint an arbitrator is given or an arbitrator is appointed or some other step to commence arbitration proceedings is taken within a time fixed by the agreement and
(b) a dispute arises to which the agreement applies, the court, if it is of opinion that in the circumstances of the case undue hardship would otherwise be caused, and notwithstanding that the time so fixed has expired, may on such terms, if any, as the justice of the case may require, but without prejudice to s.42 of this Act, extend the time for such period as he thinks fit."

14. S.42 of the Arbitration Act 1954 provides that:

"The statutes of limitation shall apply to an arbitration under an arbitration agreement as they apply to action in court."

15. S.3(1) of the Act provides that:

"For the purpose of this Act ... an arbitration shall be deemed to be commenced when one party to the arbitration agreement serves on the other party or parties a written notice requiring him or them to appoint or concur in appointing an arbitrator...."

16. The applicant's letter dated 17 January 1973 can be interpreted without any difficulty as a request to the respondents to concur in the appointment of the person therein named as an arbitrator and by virtue of the terms of s. 3(1) of the Arbitration Act the arbitration is deemed to have been commenced on that date.

17. The applicant's problem however is that the agreement provides that:

"Claims not referred to arbitration within twelve calendar months from the date of disclaimer of liability shall be deemed to have been abandoned."

18. The applicant's claim to be indemnified was not referred to arbitration within twelve months from the date of disclaimer of liability which was made on 13 October 1970.

19. There has been inexcusable delay on the part of the applicant in (1) commencing arbitration proceedings and (2) bringing an application to this Court in accordance with the provisions of s.45 of the Arbitration Act 1954.

20. However I am quite satisfied that the respondent has not been in any way prejudiced by such delay. The respondent has repudiated liability on foot of the policy on the grounds set forth in their letter dated 13 October 1970 and if these grounds are valid, the delay has not in any way affected them or prevented them from being in a position to make the case before the arbitrator.

21. I am satisfied that undue hardship would be caused to the applicant if I were not to extend the time for referring the matter to arbitration and I will make an order:

(1) deeming that the arbitration proceedings commenced on 17th January 1973 and
(2) extending the time for commencing the said arbitration proceedings to 30 January 1973.

The applicant is to be responsible for the costs of this motion and is not to be awarded the costs of the arbitration if he is successful therein.

In the Matter of the Arbitration Act, 1954
Church and General Insurance Co.
v. Connolly and McLoughlin[*]
Unreported, 7 May 1981
The High Court

COSTELLO J: The plaintiffs agreed to insure the Defendants against loss resulting from fire damage to premises in Bandon, Co. Cork, used by the Bandon Youth Centre Committee as a youth centre. A disastrous fire occurred at the premises some years ago and a dispute arose between the parties as to what sum (if any) was payable to the Defendants under the policy. The dispute was referred to arbitration and the arbitrator made an interim award in which he determined the basis on which the Defendants were entitled to recover, leaving the amount of compensation to be fixed at a later date. The plaintiffs contend (a) that there is an error of law on the face of the award, (b) that the arbitrator was guilty of "misconduct" in that his award has the effect of enforcing an illegal contract, and (c) that the award is inconsistent. They seek to have the award set aside or remitted to the arbitrator.

The facts necessary to determine the issues which I have to decide can be gleaned from the submission to arbitration which the parties signed. The insured were permitted to use the premises for the purposes of a youth centre. They claimed that they were tenants of the owner of the premises but they admitted that the exact nature of their interest in the premises was not known. The premises and contents were destroyed and damaged by a fire which occurred on the 22nd October 1975 and the Defendants claimed to be indemnified to the amount of the full value of the premises and contents. The Plaintiffs repudiated liability under the policy on the ground that the Defendants had no insurable interest in the premises; alternatively they contended that their liability was confined to indemnifying the Defendants against damage or loss in respect of the actual interest (if any) which they had in the premises. On the other hand the Defendants contended that they were entitled to full indemnity in respect of the damage and loss caused to the owners in fee of the premises (a company called Irish Taverns Limited) in addition to such damage and loss as were caused to the limited interest which the Defendants themselves enjoyed.

The Plaintiffs submit that in these proceedings I am entitled to look at the terms of the Policy. It was issued on the 8th April, 1975. The name and address of the insured was given as "The Committee for the time being, Bandon Youth Centre, Bandon, Co. Cork", the premises were described as the "Youth Centre at Kilbrogan Hill, Bandon", the total sum insured was £160,000. The Plaintiffs agreed, subject to the terms, exceptions limits, conditions and warranties contained in the policy that

> "If the property described in the Schedule hereof or any part of such property be destroyed or damaged by (1) fire ... the company will pay to the

---

[*] Extract. A further extract from the judgment appears in Chapter 5 at p. 101.

insured the value of the property at the time of the happening of its destruction or the amount of such damage or at its option reinstate or replace such property or any part thereof provided that the liability of the Company shall in no case exceed in respect of each item the sum expressed in the said schedule to be insured thereon or in the whole the total sum insured hereby....

The Plaintiffs draw attention to the fact that the only name appearing on the policy is that of the Committee for the time being of the Bandon Youth Centre and that, in particular nowhere is it expressly stated what the Defendants' insurable interest in the premises is or that any interest in the premises other than that of the insured is to be covered by the policy.

To resolve the dispute between the parties four questions were referred to the arbitrator but it was agreed that the fourth question relating to the amount of compensation (if any) payable to the insured should be deferred and that the arbitrator should make an interim award on the first three questions.

Question (1) was —

"Whether or not the Insured are entitled to claim indemnity from the Insurer in respect of the fire which occurred on the 22nd October 1975, and if so whether such indemnity should be measured on the basis of the interest of the Insured only or should include indemnity in respect of loss and damage caused to the owners in fee of the said premises (Irish Taverns Ltd)."

The arbitrator answered this question as follows —

"I award and determine that the Insured are entitled to claim indemnity from the Company in respect of the fire which occurred on October 22nd 1975, and that such indemnity should include indemnity in respect of loss and damage caused to the owners in fee of the premises."

Question (2) was —

"Whether or not the Insurer is entitled to repudiate on the grounds that the Insured had no insurable interest in the premises at the material time."

The arbitrator answered this question as follows —

"I award and determine that the Company is not entitled to repudiate on the grounds that the Insured had no insurable interest in the premises at the material time."

Question (3) was —

"What was the extent of the Insured's insurable interest in the premises on the 22nd October 1975."

The arbitrator answered this question as follows —

"I award and determine that the extent of the insurable interest of the Insured in the premises on October 22nd 1975 was their right to occupy the premises as tenants at will of the owners in fee with the responsibility for payment of rates and care and maintenance of the premises whilst in their occupation".

It will be seen that the arbitrator has made certain findings of fact on matters which had been in dispute. He has found that the insured had an insurable interest in the premises and that that interest was their right to occupy the premises as tenants at will of the fee simple owners, with responsibility, inter alia, to care and maintain the premises. These findings of fact are not now contested. The gravamen of the Plaintiffs' first complaint relates to the arbitrator's determination that notwithstanding the Defendants' limited interest and the fact that the interest of the fee simple owner in the property is not referred to in the policy the insured were entitled to an indemnity which should include loss and damage caused to the fee simple owner of the premises.

There is one point I should stress at the outset of this judgment before examining the Court's power to remit or set aside an arbitrator's award. Section 27 of the Arbitration Act, 1954 provides that unless a contrary intention is expressed in an arbitration agreement (and none was expressed in the parties' agreement in this case) the arbitration agreement is deemed to contain a provision that the award to be made by the arbitrator shall be final and binding on the parties. It is perfectly clear therefore that this is not an appeal from the arbitrator's award. The Plaintiffs must carry out its terms unless they can show that the Court has jurisdiction to set it aside or remit it, and that it should exercise its discretion in the Plaintiffs' favour.

The Court is given a general discretion to remit a case to an arbitrator under section 36 of the 1954 Act and a power to set aside an award under section 38 when the arbitrator had "misconducted" himself. The Plaintiffs rely on both sections and firstly ask the court to set aside the award under section 36 alleging that there was "misconduct" on the arbitrator's part. They accept that although the power to remit is given in very general terms it is a discretionary power which must be exercised according to well established principles. They submit as a general principle that if misconduct is established a power to remit under the section arises, and claim that the "misconduct" under section 36 was that the arbitrator permitted an error of law to appear on the face of the award. They say that this "misconduct" also entitles them to have the award set aside under section 38. In addition they claim that by his award the arbitrator has enforced an illegal contract, that this also amounted to "misconduct" entitling them to an order under section 38.

As to the first submission there is no doubt that at common law the Court can either remit or set aside an award if there is an error of law on its face. In support of the view that such an error amounts to "misconduct" under the corresponding English statute I have been referred to a passage in Volume 2 paragraph 126 of Halsbury's Laws of England, Third (Simonds) Edition which states that "misconduct" occurs if on its face an arbitrator's award is erroneous in a matter of law and the Court has a statutory power to remit. But I note that this passage is not repeated in Volume 2 of the Fourth (Hailsham) Edition of the "Laws of England", nor does the proposition find support in Russell on "Arbitration", nor from the cases in the footnote to paragraph 126 to which I was referred. I do not consider that when such an error occurs it should be regarded as "misconduct". In my view the Court's jurisdiction to set the award aside in such circumstances is given by the common law. Although the Plaintiffs' claim was not pleaded in this way I should nonetheless consider it and decide whether or not the alleged error was made....

Keenan v. Shield Insurance Company Limited*
[1988] I.R. 89
The Supreme Court

McCARTHY J. (FINLAY C.J., WALSH, GRIFFIN, HEDERMAN J.J. ALL CONCURRING): The plaintiff Patrick Keenan (the insured) appeals from an order of the High Court (Blayney J.) dismissing a special summons in which, as amended, the insured sought an order setting aside the award of an arbitrator and substituting an order to the effect that the insured is entitled to succeed in his claim as against the defendant (the company). At the start of the hearing this Court raised the question of the jurisdiction of the High Court to entertain the claim. No such question was raised at the hearing in the High Court because, as counsel informed the Court, the company had been advised that the objection could not be successfully maintained having regard to the decision of Costello J. In *Church and General Insurance Co.* v. *Connolly and McLoughlin.*[75]

The Facts

1. "By a proposal form dated the 22nd September, 1975, signed by the insured, the insured applied to the insurers for insurance cover in respect of the private residence of the insured at Painstown, Donadea, Naas in the County of Kildare and the contents thereof and pursuant to such proposal an insurance policy was issued by the insurers being an "all-in" policy number 80048578 in which the sum insured was given as £14,000 in respect of the buildings therein described and £2,000 in respect of the contents of same; the period of insurance being given as 24th September, 1975, to 24th September, 1976; and in addition to the insured the interest of Kildare County Council was noted on the said policy.

2. A fire took place at the said premises on or about the 8th October, 1975, in respect of which the insured claims to be entitled to be indemnified by the insurers for destruction of the said premises and the contents thereof.

3. The insurers have disputed their liability to pay to the insured the sums claimed by the insured or any sum whatever, on the following grounds:—
   (a) It is claimed that there was a misrepresentation of fact and non disclosure of relevant information by the insured to the insurers when making the proposal for said insurance cover, of such nature as to

---

* See also the High Court judgment in Chapter 8 at p. 307.
[75] Unreported, High Court, 7th May 1981. See p. 446 of this book.

entitle the insurers to repudiate liability under the policy and the insurers have repudiated liability accordingly."[76]

The proposal form, *inter alia*, contained the following:—

"8. Have you ever sustained loss or damage by any of the risks or liabilities you now wish to insure against? If so give particulars ... No
   I hereby declare that the above particulars and answers are true and complete in every respect and that no material fact has been suppressed or withheld and I further declare that if such statements and particulars in the writing of any person other than myself, such person shall be deemed to have been my agent for the purpose of filling the same and I agree that this declaration and the answers above given shall be the basis of the Contract between me and the Company."

After some delay, the dispute was, pursuant to the contract, referred to the arbitration of James A. Nugent, senior counsel, no intention contrary to s. 27 of the Arbitration Act, 1954, being expressed. Mr Nugent duly entered upon the arbitration and on the 31st October, 1984, published his award in which he found:—

1. That the declaration (*supra*) constituted a condition precedent of the contract between the insured and the company that the answers on the proposal form should be true and complete in every respect.
2. That the answer to question No. 8 on the proposal form was not true nor complete.
3. That although the answer to question 8 on the proposal form was not true and complete that its inadequacy and incompleteness did not amount to a misrepresentation or concealment of a material fact by the insured.
4. That the insured was not entitled to recover any sum in respect of his claim against the company under the said policy and that the company is under no liability to the insured under the said policy."

The Preliminary Point

Although the issue was not taken in the High Court this Court must reserve its right, in an appropriate case, to raise a question fundamental to the jurisdiction of the High Court, whence the appeal to this Court comes. Accordingly, the matter has been fully argued as a preliminary issue and this judgment is confined to that issue. It is necessary to examine the procedure of the Arbitration Acts, 1954 and 1980.

Arbitration

Until 1954 the submission to and enforcement of arbitration was governed by common law rules; the Arbitration Act, 1889[77] did not apply to Ireland, the

---

[76] Cited from the reference to Arbitration dated 31st January, 1984.
[77] 52 & 53 Vict., c. 49.

only relevant statutory provisions which related to enforcement being the statute [an Act for determining differences by Arbitration, 1698][78] and the Common Law Procedure Amendment Act (Ireland), 1856[79] with the procedural amendments made necessary by the Supreme Court of Judicature Act (Ireland), 1877.[80] The Act of 1954 was "to make further and better provision in respect of arbitrations". It took as its model the English Acts of 1889 and of 1950 and was intended to provide a comprehensive scheme whereby matters commercial, such as in construction, insurance, financial services, shipping and kindred and other industries might be resolved without recourse to the courts and, in many instances, by those best equipped for that purpose by training and experience in the particular field. There was no purported exclusion of the supervisory or enforcement role of the courts as a "back-up" to the arbitration procedure which, itself, allowed for reference to the courts in different ways when appropriate. The underlying intent, however, was to provide a private and appropriate forum, largely for business disputes, reminiscent of the motives that led the Dublin business community to found the Dublin Chamber of Commerce (see L.M. Cullen "Princes and Pirates", Dublin Chamber of Commerce (1983)). This statutory intent is particularly to be inferred from s. 12 repealed in 1980 and re-enacted in altered form by s. 4 of the Arbitration Act, 1980. The power to stay proceedings where there is an arbitration agreement was, under s. 12 of the Act of 1954, to be exercised when the court was satisfied that there was not sufficient reason why the matter should not be referred in accordance with the agreement, but s. 5 of the Act of 1980 which precludes the court from making an order staying the proceedings:— "unless it is satisfied that the arbitration agreement is null and void, inoperative or incapable of being performed or that there is not in fact any dispute between the parties with regard to the matter agreed to be referred," — plainly emphasises the extra-curial nature of arbitration procedure.

The Act of 1980 is entitled "an Act to enable effect to be given to the Convention on the Recognition and Enforcement of Foreign Arbitral Awards done at New York on the 10th day of June, 1958, and to certain provisions of the Convention on the Settlement of Investment Disputes between States and Nationals of other States opened for signature in Washington on the 18th day of March, 1965, and otherwise to amend the Arbitration Act, 1954."

It was in that context that s. 5, with its marked shifting of emphasis, was enacted.

Sections 23 to 28 of the Act of 1954 make provisions as to awards including (ss. 25, 26 and 27) provision that unless a contrary intention is expressed therein, every arbitration agreement, shall where such a provision is applicable to the reference, be deemed to contain a provision that:—

- (s.25) the arbitrator or umpire may, if he thinks fit, make an interim award;
- (s. 26) the arbitrator or umpire shall have the same power as the Court to

---

[78] 10 Will. 3, c. 14 (Ir.).
[79] 19 & 22 Vict., c. 102.
[80] 40 & 41 Vict., c. 57.

order specific performance of any contract other than a contract relating to land or any interest in land; and,

(s. 27) the award to be made by the arbitrator or umpire shall be final and binding on the parties and the persons claiming under them respectively.

Under the heading of *"Special Cases, Remission and Setting aside of Awards* etc." the Act provides:—

"35. — (1) An arbitrator or umpire may, and shall if so directed by the Court, state —
    (a) any question of law arising in the course of the reference, or
    (b) any award or any part of an award, in the form of a special case for the decision of the Court.

(2) A special case with respect to an interim award or with respect to a question of law arising in the course of a reference may be stated, or may be ordered by the Court to be stated, notwithstanding that proceedings under the reference are still pending.

36. — (1) In all cases of reference to arbitration, the Court may from time to time remit the matters referred or any of them to the reconsideration of the arbitrator or umpire.

(2) Where an award is remitted, the arbitrator or umpire shall, unless the order otherwise directs, make his award within three months after the date of the order.

37. — Where an arbitrator or umpire has misconducted himself or the proceedings, the Court may remove him."

The Plaintiff's Submission

The thrust of Mr Gilligan's argument was that:—

(1) If a question of law is submitted to arbitration, and the arbitrator decides that question, there is no form of judicial review available even though it may be argued that the decision was wrong.

(2) If, however, a submission to arbitration leads to an expressed decision of law which is wrong on its face, then there is an available form of judicial review, in this instance, by way of the special summons procedure.

It is the second part of the submission that is material for the purpose of this judgment. He relied upon the judgment of Costello J. In *Church and General Insurance Co.* v. *Connolly and McLoughlin*[81] and a series of English authorities.

As a "fall-back" to his argument, which would not have been appropriate in the circumstances that prevailed in the High Court, Mr Gilligan relied upon ss. 35 and 36 of the Act of 1954.

In my view the operation of s. 35 ends once the arbitrator had made his award, without any qualification. No request was made for the stating of any question of law or any part of the award in the form of a special case. It is now too late to do so. Section 36 is substantially the same form as s. 22 of the

---

[81] Unreported, High Court, 7th May 1981. See p. 446 of this book.

English Arbitration Act, 1950;[82] s. 10 of the Arbitration Act, 1889, and s. 8 of the Common Law Procedure Act, 1854, corresponding to the Irish Act of 1856.

Section 36 would appear to be the procedure appropriate, for example, to a case of a patent mistake in monetary calculation, in the giving or not giving of a particular credit, in an award that is on its face ambiguous or uncertain, in a case where the arbitrator, himself, seeks to rectify some error and, perhaps, where fresh evidence has become available subject to the standard rules of an appellate court in such cases. No case cited to the Court in the course of argument concerns the application of the like section in England and no Irish case has been cited on the point. In my view neither s. 35 nor s. 36 affords any relief to the plaintiff; I express no opinion on the question as to whether or not either section may be so used by this Court, which is not the Court referred to in the sections, when such an application is made as of first instance on the hearing of an appeal.

Church and General Insurance Company v. *Connolly and McLoughlin*.[83] In that case the plaintiff did apply under s. 36 alleging that the arbitrator permitted an error of law to appear on the fact of the award and that this constituted a misconduct under s. 38, an argument rejected by Costello J., who expressed the view (p. 7 of his judgment) "that there is no doubt that at common law the court can either remit or set aside an award if there is an error of law on its face", and, later, "in my view the court's jurisdiction to set the award aside in such circumstances is given by the common law." The precedents cited establish that, before the passing of the Act of 1954, the jurisdiction to set aside an award because of an error of law that appeared on the [face] of the award had been established as part of the common law. In addition I would point to *Ex parte Strabane R.D.C.*[84] and *The Honourable the Irish Society* v. *Ministry for Finance*.[85] This jurisdiction was abolished in England by the Arbitration Act, 1979.[86] This feature of the common law was described in Russell on Arbitration 19th Ed. (1979) at p. 437 as a somewhat anomalous extension of the rule that an award which, on its face, fails to comply with the requirements for a valid award, will be remitted or set aside.

The concept that a long established common law principle necessarily requires legislation to effect a change in it has little appeal for me since the common law, itself, by definition, reflects the changing demands of society, adapting itself to meet perceived needs. Where, however, the legislature has intervened in a particular branch of the law, and has not expressly negatived an existing common law jurisdiction, such a jurisdiction must have survived, albeit that it must be administered so as to accommodate the legislation.

Arbitration is a significant feature of modern commercial life; there is an International Institute of Arbitration and the field of international arbitration is an ever expanding one. It ill becomes the courts to show any readiness to interfere in such a process; if policy considerations are appro-

---

[82] 14 Geo. 6, c. 27.
[83] Unreported, High Court, 7th May 1981. See p. 446 of this book.
[84] [1910] 1 I.R. 135.
[85] [1958] N.I. 170.
[86] 23 Eliz. 2, c. 42.

priate as I believe they are in a matter of this kind, then every such consideration points to the desirability of making an arbitration award final in every sense of the term. *Church and General Insurance Company* v. *Connolly and McLoughlin*[87] itself is an example of the type of fine-combing exercise which courts should not perform when it is sought to review an arbitration award. There may be instances in which an award which shows on its face an error of law so fundamental that the courts cannot stand aside and allow it to remain unchallenged. This is far from such a case. Indeed, the judgment of Blayney J. in the instant case[88] demonstrates this to the full. Even without such judgment, it is clear that it is, at best from the plaintiff's point of view, merely an arguable case. It is far from satisfying any test of obvious error and, in my view, should not have been entertained in the High Court.

I would dismiss the appeal.

Administratia Asigurarilor de Stat, Winterthur Swiss Insurance Company and Others *v.* The Insurance Corporation of Ireland plc
[1990] I.L.R.M. 159
The High Court

O'HANLON J: In these proceedings a total of fourteen plaintiffs whose names appear in the full title in the pleadings claim relief under a large number of different headings against the defendants, the Insurance Corporation of Ireland plc, a limited liability company in respect of which Mr William McCann was appointed administrator on 25 March 1985, pursuant to the provisions of the Insurance (No. 2) Act 1983.

The defendants have at all material times carried on business as an insurance company and the plaintiffs are insurance or reinsurance companies who, between the years 1980 and 1984, agreed to reinsure certain classes of business which had been written by the defendants.

The plaintiffs now claim to be entitled to repudiate liability under the reinsurance contracts made between the plaintiffs and the defendants in respect of the said period, and these proceedings are brought primarily for the purpose of establishing whether they are entitled to do so, and if so, what forms of relief are available to the plaintiffs whether by way of declaratory orders, payment of damages or other monetary compensation, or otherwise.

The reinsurance contracts between the plaintiffs and the defendants contained an arbitration clause, part of which reads as follows:

> It is hereby mutually agreed between the parties that if and whenever any dispute, difference or question arises between the company and the reinsurer with reference to the construction, validity or performance of this agreement, it shall, as a condition precedent to any right of action

---

[87] Unreported, High Court, 7th May 1981. See p. 446 of this book.
[88] [1987] I.R. 113.

hereunder, be referred to two arbitrators, one arbitrator to be appointed by each party and an umpire shall be appointed by the arbitrators before they enter upon the reference.

Some correspondence had taken place between the solicitors representing the plaintiffs and the defendants prior to the formal repudiation of liability under the contracts by the plaintiffs. By letter of 4 December 1987, the plaintiffs' solicitors wrote to the defendants' solicitors, stating (*inter alia*):

A number of matters cause us grave concern. What we have seen, in the absence of any satisfactory explanations, convinces us that these treaties are tainted by fraud. Given the seriousness of our conclusion, we believe it is only right that you and your clients should have a chance of commenting upon findings.

Details of the matters relied upon were then given. The allegations were denied in a letter of reply from the defendants' solicitors, dated 31 December 1987. A further letter then followed from the plaintiffs' solicitors, dated 15 January 1988 reiterating the suggestion previously made that the transactions referred to were of a fraudulent nature, and this was followed by a further letter of 20 January 1988, from the plaintiffs' solicitors to the defendants' solicitors, giving formal notice of repudiation of liability under the contracts by the plaintiffs. The letter contains the following passage:

Without limitation to any other facts, the matters or things which may hereafter come or be drawn to their notice, the grounds on which our clients rely in avoiding their writings are
— non-disclosure and misrepresentation of information both at inception and during the currency of the treaties, and
— the breach of the duty of utmost good faith and fair dealing owed to them by the ICI.

The defendants did not accept that the plaintiffs or any of them were entitled to repudiate liability under the said contracts, and on 3 February 1988, the defendants served a notice of arbitration on Winterthur Swiss Insurance Co., the 13th-named plaintiff in these proceedings, and nominated the arbitrator appointed by the defendants. They further called upon the said plaintiffs to appoint their arbitrator within one calendar month in accordance with the provisions of the arbitration article contained in the reinsurance contract. By letter of 2 March 1988, the solicitors for the said plaintiffs gave notice that the said plaintiffs had appointed Mr David Donaldson QC as arbitrator "without prejudice to their right to seek a stay of this arbitration".

The present proceedings were commenced by plenary summons dated the 30 May 1988. Brussels Reinsurance Co. were added as a plaintiff in addition to other reinsurers who had repudiated liability prior to the service of notice of arbitration on 3 February 1988. Subsequently, on 14 June 1988, notice of discontinuance was served on behalf of the tenth-named plaintiff, National Underwriters (Reinsurance) Ltd, and the action is now proceeding in the names of the remaining 13 plaintiffs.

By notice of motion dated 7 June 1988, notice was given on behalf of ... Winterthur ... of intention to apply for an order pursuant to s. 39 of the

Arbitration Act 1954, that the alleged arbitration agreement between ... [it] ... and the defendants should cease to have effect and that the said plaintiff should be entitled to revoke the authority of the arbitrators allegedly appointed by or by virtue of the said agreement.

On 8 July 1988, notice of arbitration was served on behalf of the defendants on the remaining plaintiffs other than Winterthur Swiss Insurance Co. who were continuing with the proceedings and by notice of motion dated 13 July 1988, the said plaintiffs gave notice of their intention to apply for similar relief to that already referred to in the notice of motion served on behalf of the 13th-named plaintiff on the 7th June 1988.

By notice of motion dated 11 July 1988, the defendants gave notice of their intention to apply to the court to stay the proceedings herein, and the issues raised by the said respective notices of motion now fall for determination by this court.

The arbitration agreement between the parties is to be found in Article 16 of the contract made between the defendants and each of the plaintiffs, which said contract is entitled "general miscellaneous quota share reinsurance agreement". The full text of Article 16 reads as follows:

"Article 16.

Arbitration
It is hereby mutually agreed between the parties that if and whenever any dispute, difference or question arises between the company and the reinsurer with reference to the construction, validity or performance of this agreement, it shall as a condition precedent to any right of action hereunder be referred to two arbitrators one arbitrator to be appointed by each party and an umpire who shall be appointed by the arbitrators before they enter upon the reference.

The award of the arbitrators or in the event of their disagreement the award of the umpire shall be final and binding upon all parties without appeal.

The costs of and incidental to the reference and award shall be in the discretion of the arbitrators or umpire as the case may be and they shall determine the amount and direct to and by whom and in what manner the costs of any part thereof shall be paid and they shall have power to tax the costs in such manner as they think fit and to award costs to be paid as between solicitor and client.

In the event of either party refusing or neglecting to appoint an arbitrator within one calendar month after the other party requests it to do so or if the arbitrators fail to appoint an umpire within one calendar month after they have accepted their appointments, such arbitrator or umpire as the case may be shall upon the application of either party be appointed by the chairman for the time being of the fire offices' committee, London, and the arbitrators and the umpire shall thereupon proceed to the reference as above stipulated.

This agreement shall be interpreted rather as an honourable engagement than as a legal obligation and the award shall be made with a view to effecting the general purpose of this agreement rather than in accordance with the literal interpretation of its wording. The arbitrators and the umpire may abstain from judicial formality and from following strictly the rules of law.

Arbitration shall take place in Dublin unless the disputants agree otherwise. Except as hereinbefore provided the terms of the statutes for the time being in force in Eire relating to arbitrations shall apply to the arbitration hereunder.

This submission shall be construed as a separate and independent contract between the parties hereto."

The relevant statutory provisions are contained in s.5 of the Arbitration Act 1980, (replacing the earlier provisions found in s.12 of the Arbitration Act 1954), and in ss. 39 (2) and (3) of the Arbitration Act 1954.

S. 5 of the Act of 1980 now curtails the discretion of the court to refuse to stay proceedings brought in apparent breach of an agreement to refer disputes to arbitration, to a much greater extent than did s. 12 of the Act of 1954. It reads as follows:

"5.(1) If any party to an arbitration agreement, or any person claiming through or under him, commences any proceedings in any court against any other party to such agreement or any person claiming through or under him, in respect of any matter agreed to be referred to arbitration, any party to the proceedings may at any time after an appearance has been entered, and before delivering any pleadings or taking any other steps in the proceedings, apply to the court to stay the proceedings, and the court, unless it is satisfied that the arbitration agreement is null and void, inoperative or incapable of being performed or that there is not in fact any dispute between the parties with regard to the matter agreed to be referred, shall make an order staying the proceedings.

(2) Nothing in this section shall be construed as limiting or otherwise affecting the power conferred on the High Court pursuant to s. 39 (3) of the Principal Act to refuse to stay any action brought in breach of an arbitration agreement."

The text of s.39(2) and (3)of the Act of 1954 reads as follows:

"(2) Where —

(a) an agreement between any parties provides that disputes which may arise in the future between them shall be referred to arbitration, and
(b) a dispute which so arises involves the question whether any party has been guilty of fraud,

the court shall, so far as may be necessary to enable the question to be determined by the court have power to order that the agreement shall cease to have effect and power to give leave to revoke the authority of any arbitrator or umpire appointed by or by virtue of the agreement.

(3) In any case where by virtue of this section the court has power to order that any arbitration agreement shall cease to have effect or to give leave to revoke the authority of any arbitrator or umpire, the court may refuse to stay any action brought in breach of the agreement."

These are the provisions relied on by the plaintiffs in resisting the defendants' present application to stay their proceedings, and in seeking an order that the arbitration agreement shall cease to have effect and that the plaintiffs should be entitled to revoke the authority of the arbitrators appointed by virtue of the said agreement.

The plaintiffs say that the dispute which has arisen between themselves and the defendants involves a question whether the defendants have been guilty of fraud and that it is an appropriate case for the court to exercise the discretion which remains vested in it under the above-mentioned provisions of s.39 (2) and (3) of the Act of 1954.

The defendants respond by saying that the allegations of fraud now made are in the nature of an afterthought; form only an insignificant part of the causes of action upon which the plaintiffs seek to rely; have not been substantiated to the extent that should be required before the court would exercise its powers under s.39(2) and (3); and that, in any event, the general policy of the courts has been to leave the parties to their agreed procedure by way of arbitration unless the party against whom fraud is alleged desires to have that matter investigated in open court.

It is worthy of note that whereas the opening letters from the plaintiffs' solicitors, dated respectively 4 December 1987, and 15 January 1988, specifically referred to a suggestion that fraud had been disclosed on the part of the defendants, the letter of 20 January 1988, containing the formal repudiation of liability under the contracts referred to "non-disclosure", "misrepresentation" and "breach of the duty of utmost good faith and fair dealing" but did not expressly allege fraud.

However, the general indorsement of claim on the plenary summons which followed, claimed (*inter alia*), a declaration that the reinsurance contracts were void; recision of the said contracts, and damages for fraudulent or alternatively negligent misrepresentation.

The draft statement of claim (later filed on 29 June 1988), exhibited in the affidavit of Christopher Elwen, swore herein 10 June 1988, which is a very lengthy document, recites, in paragraph 5, a number of representations allegedly made by the defendants to the plaintiffs for the purpose of inducing them to enter into, and to renew, or not to cancel their participation in the general miscellaneous treaty of reinsurance. It is further pleaded that these representations did so induce them, and were untrue, and were in some instances made fraudulently.

Particulars of the terms, representations and breaches thereof are then given in sections A to P of the draft statement of claim. Fraud is alleged against the defendants in respect of representations made about the estimated premium income (section A); in alleged "premium stripping" on the part of the defendants in effecting joint reinsurance protection, (retrocession cover) for themselves and the plaintiffs, whereby the defendants effected such retrocession cover not for the benefit of the plaintiffs but for the benefit of and/or to generate the payment of commission to the defendants, their servants or agents (section K); in ceding "treaty business" to the general miscellaneous treaty and charging commission at a higher rate in their own favour than was permissible under the terms of the treaty (section L); and, (although the term "fraud" or "fraudulently" is not expressly used), in compiling statistics of premiums received and claims made under the general miscellaneous treaty for the information of the plaintiffs, knowing the same were inaccurate and incomplete or having no reasonable grounds for believing them to be accurate or complete (section B).

In a series of schedules which is incorporated in the draft statement of claim, examples are given of the matters alleged under the various headings dealt with in sections A to P. The entire pleading comprises over 80 pages.

The allegations of fraud are dealt with in the following manner in the affidavit of Christopher Elwen, of the firm of Holman, Fenwick and Willan, the plaintiffs' English solicitors, sworn herein 10 June 1988, and filed on behalf of the 13th-named plaintiff, Winterthur, in support of their application under s. 39 (2) of the Arbitration Act 1954.

He refers to the letter of 4 December 1987, written by his firm to the defendants' London solicitors, in which the allegation of fraud appears to have been made for the first time, and in which examples were give of the fraud alleged. He then refers to the letter of 31 December 1987, received from the defendants' English solicitors, in which the said allegations were refuted. There followed another long letter from his firm to the defendants' solicitors in which the allegations previously made were reiterated and expanded.

He states that the affidavit is made from facts within his own knowledge or gleaned from documents in his possession; from instructions received from the plaintiffs and from information supplied by one, Roy Ward, who has been retained by the plaintiffs for the purpose of gathering evidence in relation to the dispute so that the plaintiffs' solicitors may consider same and advise thereon. He states that Mr Ward was given access to some of the documents in the defendants' possession, acting on behalf of the plaintiffs. He does not, however, exhibit any report hitherto made by Mr Ward.

He states in paragraph 15 of the affidavit, that he believes the facts stated in the draft statement of claim to be true, and he gives details of the allegations of fraud made under the various headings already referred to and of the plaintiffs' grounds for believing that these allegations were well-founded.

A replying affidavit, sworn by Andrew Michael Higgs of the firm of Davies, Arnold and Cooper, the defendants' English solicitors, on 8 July 1988, has been filed herein. Mr Higgs deals with the history of the dispute which arose between the defendants and certain of the reinsurers under the general miscellaneous treaty and makes the point that only a small fraction of the total number of reinsurers who participated with the defendants in the general miscellaneous treaty business during the period from 1980 to 1984 had supported the allegations of fraud now put forward on behalf of the plaintiffs, and that the plaintiffs account for only 10–20% approximately of such reinsurers. He does not, however, attempt to reply in detail to the various allegations made in Mr Elwen's affidavit and these allegations appear to be left hanging in the air insofar as the evidence on affidavit presently before the court is concerned.

It is now necessary to consider the legal principles upon which the court should act when exercising the discretion vested in it by the provisions of s.39(2) and (3) of the Arbitration Act 1954.

The general approach in the past has been to allow the arbitration process to proceed and to stay legal proceedings where the parties have bound themselves by agreements to follow this course, but this has not been an inflexible rule as the courts have been given a greater or lesser degree of scope for refusing to stay legal proceedings by statutes enacted from time to time.

In the case of *Wallis* v. *Hirsch*,[89] the application to stay the proceedings involved a consideration of s.11 of the Common Law Procedure Act 1854. Cockburn C.J. said:

> "I think we should be extremely reluctant to interfere to prevent the full benefit of the enactment in question where the parties have in writing agreed expressly that the differences between them shall be submitted to arbitration. But at the same time, as the Act of Parliament has given us a discretion to enforce the reference or not as we may deem it expedient, it is incumbent on us to look at all the circumstances in order to see whether or not the party objecting to the reference has made out a case to warrant us in limiting the operation of the agreement to refer. In this case I think the objection is well-founded. It cannot be supposed that the parties contemplated to refer a case of fraud. The affidavits suggest that the plaintiffs *bona fide* believe that a gross fraud has been attempted to be practised upon them ... I must say I do not think that is at all a fit question for reference to two brokers."

Another member of the court, Williams J., said:

> "I am of the same opinion. The plaintiffs have by their affirmation pledged themselves that this action is founded on fraud. I doubt whether the terms of this contract, large as they were ever intended to meet such a case as that. And, if it be a matter for the exercise of our discretion, I am clearly of opinion that the tribunal proposed is not the proper one to entertain it."

In *Russell* v. *Russell*,[90] the court took the view that in exercising its discretion under the same Act, it should generally refuse to stay legal proceedings where a party against whom fraud was alleged sought to have his reputation vindicated in open court, but that the converse would apply where the party opposing the stay on legal proceedings was the party alleging the fraud.

The following passage appears in the judgment of Jessel M.R. (at p.474):

> "I can perfectly understand the court saying 'I will not refer your character against your will to a private arbitrator'. It seems to me in that case it is almost a matter of course to refuse the reference, but I by no means think the same consideration follows when publicity is desired by the party charging the fraud ... I must say that I am by no means satisfied that the mere desire of the person charging the fraud is sufficient reason for the court refusing to send the case to arbitration....

> If the mere making of a charge of fraud would entitle the person making it to call upon the court in the exercise of its discretion, to refuse to refer to arbitration, there would be a very easy way of getting rid of all these clauses of arbitration.... There must be sufficient *prima facie* evidence of fraud, not conclusive or final evidence, because it is not the trial of the action, but sufficient *prima facie* evidence."

---

[89] (1856) 1C.B. (n.s.) 316.
[90] (1880) 14 Ch.D. 471.

In *Camilla Cotton Oil Co.* v. *Granedex*,[91] the House of Lords had to consider the application of s. 24(3) of the English Arbitration Act, 1950, which largely corresponds with the provisions of s. 39 of our Act of 1954. Lord Wilberforce said (at p.16):

> "Under s. 24(3) of the Arbitration Act 1950, it is necessary that the dispute involves the question whether any party has been guilty of fraud. To satisfy this, a concrete and specific issue of fraud must be raised. Moreover the fraud relied on must be fraud by the party opposing the stay — see *Russell* v. *Russell*,[92] so that any alleged fraud by the appellants is irrelevant.... I do not therefore regard this as a reason against the stay."

The rule was restated in less sweeping fashion by Woolf L.J. in *Cunningham-Reid* v. *Buchanan-Jardine*.[93] He considered that the House of Lords in the *Camilla Cotton*[94] case intended to give effect to the view which had been expressed by Jessel M.R. in *Russell* v. *Russell*,[95] which he summarised as follows:

> "First of all, before a court will refuse a stay where fraud is alleged, there must be sufficient prima facie evidence of fraud. Second, if the application is made in a case where there is sufficient prima facie evidence of fraud and the application is opposed by the party charged with the fraud, then almost as a matter of course the court will in fact refuse a stay so that the matter can proceed to trial. However, third, in the case where the party charging the fraud wishes the action not to be stayed but to proceed in the court, the court has a discretion to either refuse or grant a stay. Whether or not it does grant or refuse a stay will depend on all the circumstances of the case."

I think that the general approach adopted by Woolf L.J. represents the correct approach in giving effect to the provisions of s.39(2) and (3) of the Arbitration Act 1954. The provisions of the section do not fetter in any way the manner in which the court should exercise its discretion and I do not see any reason for reading into the section any qualifications which are not already inherent in the words used by the draftsman. Accordingly, it is a matter of staying or refusing to stay the legal proceedings, having regard to all the salient features of this particular case.

As to the suggestion made in some of the English cases that the party opposing a stay on legal proceedings must establish a *prima facie* case of fraud against his opponent, I prefer the approach adopted by the Irish Queen's Bench Division in the case of *Workman* v. *Belfast Harbour Commissioners*[96] where Kenny J. expressed himself as follows (at p. 244):

> "Therefore, without offering any opinion whatever as to the merits of the

---

[91] [1976] 2 Lloyd's Rep. 10.
[92] (1880) 14 Ch.D. 471.
[93] [1988] 2 All E.R. 438.
[94] [1976] 2 Lloyd's Rep. 10.
[95] (1880) 14 Ch.D. 471.
[96] [1899] I.R. 234.

plaintiff's claims, I am convinced that they are made with perfect *bona fides*, and with a deliberate intention of prosecuting them, and that on the documents before us there is no foundation for the contention that they are either sham or frivolous, or that they are put forward with the object of placing an obstacle in the way of a compulsory reference under s.14 of the Common Law Procedure Act 1856."

He went on to say that on the affidavits in that case he thought, in any event, that a sufficient case was made, not of personal fraud, but of constructive and equitable fraud, and that afforded sufficient grounds, within the scope of the common Law Procedure (Ireland) Act 1856, for refusing to stay the proceedings. He relied also on the fact that the case raised serious and difficult questions of law for determination, which made it appropriate that it should be retained in court and not referred to arbitration.

In the present case I am satisfied that the allegations of fraud are made *bona fide* and are not introduced for the purpose of placing an obstacle in the way of an application to stay the proceedings. I express no opinion on the merits of the case. There is a well-recognised principle that counsel should not sign pleadings containing allegations of fraud against any party unless they are satisfied that their client has substantial grounds for making and relying on such allegations, and I think the court is entitled to anticipate that this rule of practice will be observed by counsel.

Were it necessary for me to make a finding that a *prima facie* case had been made out against the defendants — and I prefer to reserve my decision on this point — I would consider that the plaintiffs have gone far enough to satisfy this requirement, having regard to the contents of the affidavits and the exhibits referred to therein, and to the response hitherto received from the defendants to the allegations made.

I consider that the case is one of great seriousness and complexity and involves the resolution of difficult questions of law. I cannot recollect having seen a statement of claim of such length and containing such a wealth of detail, in any previous proceedings, and the magnitude of the claim may be assessed by reference to the estimate of net losses on the general miscellaneous treaty business, given in the affidavit of Mr Elwen, as "between US $200 and US $300 million".

The arbitrators already nominated are a prominent and experienced member of the Inner Bar in Ireland and an English Queen's Counsel, each of whom would be well-equipped to grapple with such legal and technical problems as might arise during the course of arbitration proceedings. An umpire has not yet been nominated, as envisaged by the arbitration agreement, and there is no obligation to choose a person drawn from the legal profession, although it seems more than likely that the arbitrators would do so, if the occasion arose. If they fail to agree on an umpire, the appointment is to be made by the chairman of the fire offices' committee, London.

For a number of reasons, however, I have come to the conclusion that the proper course to take in this case is to retain the proceedings before the court and to refuse the defendants' present application for a stay to enable the matters in dispute to be resolved at arbitration.

I am influenced in reaching this decision by the magnitude and complexity of the claim and the difficult questions of law which are sure to arise for decision in the course of the case. It appears to me that a hearing before the High Court, with a right of appeal on questions of law to the Supreme Court, offers a much better procedure than a hearing before two arbitrators drawn from different jurisdictions and an umpire whose qualifications or sphere of operation are at present unknown.

Most of the previous decisions in cases where applications were made to stay proceedings and allow disputes to proceed to arbitration have related to fairly small-scale commercial transactions — break-up of partnerships and so forth — where a hearing by an arbitrator presented no obvious difficulty. Even in the *Camilla Cotton*[97] case, where the amount involved was very large, it arose merely out of default on the part of one of the contracting parties to make deliveries of large consignments of peanuts to the purchasers.

For a claim of the magnitude and complexity of the present claim, proceedings by way of arbitration can present many problems, which would not arise if the matter were being processed by way of ordinary litigation before the court. Resort must be had to the court in any event for orders of discovery, interrogatories, and for many other forms of relief incidental to the proceedings. Questions of law may be referred by case stated from an arbitrator or umpire to the court, and must be if so directed by the court. The control which can be exercised by the arbitrators or umpire over the course of the proceedings is not as satisfactory as that which can be exercised by the court, using the comprehensive code of procedure provided by the Rules of the Superior Courts. An example of the manner in which the hearing of arbitration proceedings can be held up indefinitely by lack of co-operation on the part of one of the parties to a dispute was seen in the case of *Mahony and others* v. *Lysaght*.[98]

The claim in the present case has already been long delayed, in part by circumstances outside the control of the parties, and I consider that it would proceed much more expeditiously were it to be allowed to continue from its present stage where the plenary summons and statement of claim have been delivered, rather than calling a halt to the proceedings at this stage and allowing the matter to start again following upon the appointment of an umpire in addition to the two arbitrators already appointed.

I accept what was urged by Mr McCracken in the course of his submissions on behalf of the defendants, that the plaintiffs represent only a small contingent of the total of 84 reinsurers who were involved in the contract during the relevant period, and that their stake in the reinsurance liability is also not very large in proportion to the entire amounts covered. Nevertheless, the amounts involved for which the plaintiffs may or may not be liable in their capacity as reinsurers (depending on the outcome of their claim) are still enormous, and are measurable in millions rather than in thousands of pounds.

---

[97] [1976] 2 Lloyd's Rep. 10.
[98] [1988] I.R. 29.

I do not consider that the fact that the defendants appear to be in the process of negotiating successfully on a commercial basis with the remainder of the reinsurers, nor the fact that the primary causes of action relied on by the plaintiffs are based on misrepresentation rather than fraud are sufficient reason to stay the proceedings.

I agree with a comment made in a number of the decided cases, that it is difficult to envisage that parties who bound themselves contractually to go to arbitration in the event of disputes arising in their business dealings with each other, had in contemplation a situation where one party would allege fraud against the other. This may apply with even greater force in the present case where the article dealing with arbitration states that the agreement is to be interpreted rather as an honourable engagement than as a legal obligation, and that the arbitrators and the umpire may abstain from judicial formality and from following strictly the rules of law. I believe that we are here dealing with a situation which was not within the contemplation of the parties when entering into an agreement in those terms, and that this is a further reason why proceedings by way of litigation in court may be more appropriate.

For these reasons I have come to the conclusion that I should not accede to the defendants' application to stay the proceedings and that in lieu thereof I should grant the relief sought by the plaintiffs by granting an order that, in so far as may be necessary to enable the question whether the defendants have been guilty of fraud as alleged against them by the plaintiffs to be determined by the court, the arbitration agreement between them shall cease to have effect, and by granting leave to revoke the authority of any arbitrator or umpire appointed by or by virtue of the agreement.

For the reasons already stated, it appears to me that it would be very wasteful of time and resources to divide up the causes of action outlined in the statement of claim and require all issues of fraud to be tried by the court while reserving for the consideration of the arbitrators and umpire all other claims put forward on behalf of the plaintiffs as entitling them to repudiate liability under the reinsurance contracts.

It is submitted on behalf of the defendants that the defendants are entitled, as of right, to a stay on the proceedings, in so far as relief is claimed on grounds other than the allegations of fraud, irrespective of any decision that may be made by the court in exercise of the jurisdiction conferred on it by s.39(2) of the Act of 1954.

I do not construe the provisions of s.39(3) in this manner. It provides that in any case where the court has power by virtue of s.39 to order that any arbitration agreement shall cease to have effect or to give leave to revoke the authority of any arbitrator or umpire, the court may refuse to stay any action brought in breach of the agreement. I interpret that provision as meaning that the court is given a discretion in such circumstances to refuse to stay any action brought in breach of the arbitration agreement where a dispute has arisen between the parties involving the question whether any party has been guilty of fraud, and that the words "any action" are sufficiently wide to encompass proceedings where other issues are raised in addition to the issue of fraud.

I therefore propose to refuse the defendants' application to stay the proceedings, or any part thereof, which have been brought by the plaintiffs against the defendants.

McStay (Receiver of Hotel Holyrood Ltd)
v. Assicurazioni Generali S.p.a. and Maguire
[1991] I.L.R.M. 237
The Supreme Court

FINLAY C.J. (HEDERMAN J. CONCURRING): This is an appeal brought by the Plaintiff against the Order of the High Court made by Carroll J. on 23 June 1989 dismissing the Plaintiff's claim.

The claim of the plaintiff

The plaintiff's claim as pleaded and apparently to some extent, at least, as pursued in the High Court was for:

1. An order directing the second-named defendant to state a question of law referred to in his award on an arbitration in the form of a special case for the decision of the High Court and, in the alternative

2. An order remitting the portion of the award made by the second-named defendant which *inter alia* determined that he had no jurisdiction or power in law to award interest to the plaintiff for any period between the date of the event giving rise to the plaintiff's claim and the date of the award for his reconsideration.

It would appear that the first relief sought was either not fully pursued or expressly abandoned in the High Court, and the claim for it was dismissed by the learned High Court judge and no appeal has been brought against the dismissal.

With regard to the appeal against the dismissal of the claim for an order remitting portion of the arbitrator's award for his reconsideration, it arises out of the following facts. The plaintiff is the receiver over the assets of Hotel Holyrood Ltd (the company) by virtue of two appointments dated 9 July 1986 and 13 February 1987. By two separate policies of insurance taken out by the company with the first-named defendant (the insurance company) both of which were dated 9 October 1984, the company insured its premises, contents and business of a hotel in Harcourt Street in Dublin, in the one instance against loss or damage by fire and certain other perils ... and in the other instance in respect of consequential loss.

Whilst those policies were in force the hotel premises were, on 25 February 1985, damaged by fire. Subsequently, portion of them had to be removed to comply with Dublin Corporation's requirements for safety, and certain payments on account of the responsibility of the insurance company were made in respect of that operation in May of 1985. Disputes then arose between the company and the insurance company as to the amount payable under each of the two policies.

The company instituted proceedings in the High Court claiming the amounts which they alleged were due on foot of the said policies and in those proceedings the insurance company applied to the High Court pursuant to the provisions of s.5 of the Arbitration Act 1980 for an order staying the proceedings by reason of the existence of an enforceable agreement to refer the dispute between the parties to arbitration. An order staying those proceedings was made by the High Court, apparently without opposition on the part of the plaintiff, and an agreement was then entered into between the plaintiff and the insurance company, dated 20 June 1988, referring the matters in dispute to the arbitration of the second-named defendant. Clause 2 of the matters agreed in that reference read as follows:

> The said arbitrator shall have power to direct what pleadings are to be delivered by the parties hereto, and such other steps of an interlocutory nature as may reasonably be necessary or convenient for the conduct of the said arbitration and in his award to give directions and make declarations as to the rights of the parties as to the time and manner of payments, including (if he shall think fit) the amount of interest (if any) to be payable on such amount and the period in respect of which interest (if any) may be payable and to determine and direct by which party and in what amounts the costs of the arbitration and of the award may be borne.

Prior to the actual execution of that agreement to refer the disputes to arbitration the solicitors for the insurance company had raised with the plaintiff particulars of the claims being made, and in reply to those a claim was made for interest at 11% from various dates in respect of both the building loss and the consequential loss. Of even date with the execution of the reference to arbitration the insurance company entered points of defence to the claim of the plaintiff and at paragraph 11 thereof stated as follows:

> The claimant is not entitled to interest upon any payment found recoverable under either policy;
> (a) There is no jurisdiction under either policy for an award of interest in respect of any period prior to the determination by an arbitrator.
> (b) No amount has at any time to date been ascertained as due and recoverable under either policy, such as would attract an entitlement to interest.
> (c) The claimant alone has been responsible for any delay in bringing about an ascertainment of the amounts payable under either policy by virtue of his failure to comply with the conditions thereof and to make and vouch claims thereunder as aforesaid.

The arbitration was heard by the arbitrator on a number of dates between 27 September 1988 and 24 October 1988, and he issued his award on 16 November 1988. At paragraph 1(d) of that award he determined as follows:

> I award and determine that I am not entitled as arbitrator to adjudicate on the claim of the claimant for interest on the sum referred to at paragraph 1(b) hereof, save and expect as hereinafter provided for in respect of the period as and from the date of this award until payment, accepting as I do the submission on behalf of the respondent that I as arbitrator do not have in law any jurisdiction or power to award interest on any sums payable by the respondent, save and except such interest as I may in my discretion award as and from the date of this my award. The respondent herein requested that I as arbitrator should state a special case for the decision of the High Court under s. 35 of the Act of 1954 in the event that I should

decide that I had in law jurisdiction to award interest for any period, between the date of the event giving rise to the claim, and the date of this my award. In the event, it is unnecessary for me to state this part of my award in the form of a special case for the decision of the High Court.

It was agreed by the parties in the High Court and again on appeal in this Court that at no stage during the hearing of the arbitration was any application made on behalf of the plaintiff for the stating of a special case to the High Court under any conditions or in any event pursuant to s. 35 of the Act of 1954.

The plaintiff's claim

The plaintiff claims that the provisions of s. 22 of the Courts Act 1981, enabling the judge concerned in any proceedings where a court orders the payment by any person of a sum of money also to order the payment by the person of interest at the rate per annum standing specified for the time being in s.26 of the Debtors (Ireland) Act 1840, was by virtue of the principles of common law an authority and jurisdiction vested in the arbitrator to whom a dispute which was maintainable in the courts had been referred, in the absence of an agreement to the contrary. In the alternative, it was the claim of the plaintiff and appellant that the terms of clause 2 of the reference to arbitration, which I have already quoted in this judgment, amounted to an agreement by the parties that the plaintiff was entitled to interest on the sums due to him in respect of the insured liability from the appropriate date at an appropriate rate of interest and that the only matter left to the decision of the arbitrator was as to the appropriate period and rate.

Submissions on behalf of the defendants

Counsel on behalf of the insurance company submitted that upon the true construction of the reference to arbitration the question of law as to whether the arbitrator had jurisdiction to award interest prior to the date of the award was expressly and unambiguously submitted to the determination of the arbitrator. It was further contended that once that had been done and a question of law was expressly submitted for the determination of the arbitrator that the arbitrator's decision was final, subject to his right to state a special case to the High Court for guidance on the issue of law and subject to the rights of either of the parties prior to the making of a final award, to request the High Court to direct the stating of such a case. It is contended that this principle is fundamental to the finality of arbitration and is well supported by judicial authority.

The judgment of the High Court

The *ratio decidendi* of Carroll J. in dismissing the claim of the plaintiff is essentially contained in the following paragraph from her judgment[99]:

Therefore I agree with the first-named defendant's submission. The

---

[99] [1989] I.R. 248, 251.

arbitrator was given power to decide a specific question of law, namely, the plaintiff's entitlement to interest. He decided that question by deciding that he did not have power to award interest. The plaintiff could have asked for a special case to be stated for the High Court on the point. Having failed to do so he is bound by the arbitrator's decision on the point and it does not matter whether that decision was erroneous at law or not. Having decided that, it is not necessary for me to decide whether the decision was in fact erroneous.

The decision

Counsel on behalf of the appellant conceded that if the proper interpretation of the reference to arbitration was that it submitted to the decision of the arbitrator the specific question of law as the learned High Court judge decided as to whether or not he did have power to award interest prior to the date of the award, then he could not contend that the court could now intervene with regard to the arbitration or remit the matter to the arbitrator, even if he could establish that the decision made by the arbitrator was erroneous in point of law.

I do not rest my decision on this concession, but I am satisfied that it was a proper and inevitable one.

A fundamental ingredient of the concept of arbitration, as contained in the common law, is the finality of the decision of the arbitrator, subject, of course, to certain qualifications and precautions. Broadly speaking, however, as one might expect, the law appears to acknowledge that where two parties agree to refer a particular question which is in dispute between them to the decision of a particular individual by way of arbitration, they are taken to have abandoned their right to litigate that precise question.

To that broad principle qualifications and exceptions have developed, both in the common law and in statutory provisions, which protect a party against injustice.

Without attempting exhaustively to list them, they include the following.

1. The power of an arbitrator to state any question of law arising in the course of the reference or any award or any part of an award in the form of a special case for the decision of the High Court.

2. The power of the court, upon application, to direct an arbitrator to state such a case.

Both these provisions are contained in s. 35 of the Arbitration Act 1954, but are, indeed, necessarily steps which can be taken only prior to the making of a final award, as has been decided by this Court in *Keenan* v. *Shield Insurance Company Ltd*[100] at p. 95 of the judgment of McCarthy J.

3. An arbitrator who has misconducted himself or the proceedings may be removed by the Court (s.37 of the 1954 Act).

4. Where an arbitrator has misconducted himself or the proceedings or an arbitration or award has been improperly secured, the court may set the award aside (s.38).

---

[100] [1988] I.R. 89. See p. 307 and p. 449 of this book.

5. The appointment of an arbitrator who may be partial is capable of being revoked by the court (s.39)

6. I am satisfied that at common law where an arbitrator decides a question of law in the course of an arbitration where a general issue in dispute is submitted to him, but where that precise question of law has not been submitted to him for his decision the court may in its discretion and in particular cases where the decision so expressed is clearly wrong on its face, intervene by way of remitting the matter or otherwise in the interests of justice. This was the situation presented to this Court in *Keenan* v. *Shield Insurance Company*[101] and in the judgment of McCarthy J. was accepted, subject to what I am satisfied were appropriate warnings as to the limited number of instances in which it is appropriate for the court, even in that situation to intervene. A decision made by an arbitrator upon the reference to him of a specific question of law which appears on its face to be erroneous is not covered by any of these qualifications.

This fact is not only recognised by the concession made by the counsel in this case, which I have already noted, but is also inherent in the submission of counsel on behalf of the insured and appellant in *Keenan* v. *Shield Insurance Company*[102] where he made a similar concession. The matter is most succinctly and , in my view, accurately dealt with by the speech of Lord Russell of Killowen in *Absalom Ltd* v. *Great Western (London) Garden Village Society*[103] when he stated at p. 607 as follows:

> My Lords, it is, I think, essential to keep the case where disputes are referred to an arbitrator in the decision of which a question of law becomes material distinct from the case in which a specific question of law has been referred to him for decision. I am not sure that the Court of Appeal has done so. The authorities make a clear distinction between these two cases, and as they appear to me, they decide that in the former case the court can interfere if and when any error of law appears on the face of the award, but that in the latter case no such interference is possible upon the ground that it so appears that the decision upon the question of law is an erroneous one.

I am therefore satisfied that the first issue which necessarily arises for determination on this appeal is as to whether the clause of the reference to arbitration which I have set out in the course of this judgment constitutes a reference of the specific question as a matter of law as to whether the arbitrator had jurisdiction to grant interest.

In my view, on a careful consideration of the terms of that reference, and they supersede the original arbitration agreements contained in the polices of insurance to which we were not even referred, it is an inescapable conclusion that one of the matters referred to the arbitrator who, of course, was a distinguished member of the Senior Bar, was this precise question of law. I would be satisfied, as was the learned trial judge, that that is the correct interpretation of the reference. Whilst my decision could not rest upon it, I

---

[101] [1988] I.R. 89. See p. 307 and p. 449 of this book.
[102] *Ibid.*
[103] [1933] AC 592.

am confirmed in that view by the fact that on the facts of this case as presented on the appeal it is clear that the parties in the arbitration made submissions on that precise issue of law to the arbitrator, and that one of them, namely, the insurance company, indicated a desire for a stating of a case by the arbitrator in the event of his inclining to a view contrary to their express contention that he had no power to award interest.

I cannot accept the contention submitted on this appeal on behalf of the plaintiff that this clause of the reference could possibly be construed as indicating an acceptance by the parties of the power of the arbitrator to award interest, and the reference to him merely of the question as to whether on the particular facts of the case he should award such interest and, if so, how much. Neither can I accept the contention which appears alternatively to have been made that the terms of the reference themselves, quite apart from any transference to the arbitrator of powers vested in a judge by s. 22 of the Act of 1981 should be construed as an express agreement that he would have such power to award interest prior to the date of the award.

Either of these two constructions appears to me to do violence to the terms of this reference.

I am, therefore, driven to the conclusion that the decision so clearly expressed by the arbitrator as being a decision on a question of law, namely, the jurisdiction vested in him under law to award interest prior to the date of the award is a decision which cannot be interfered with by way of setting aside or remitting the matter to the arbitrator by reason of the fact that it is established to be erroneous.

That being so, I accept that it was appropriate for the learned trial judge to abstain in the High Court from deciding whether in fact this decision was erroneous or not. Counsel on behalf of the insurance company in this Court have taken up the attitude not only that that was correct but also that they should not be involved on the hearing of this appeal in a dispute concerning the question as to whether the decision of the arbitrator that he had no such jurisdiction was correct in law.

Apart from his contention that the reference to arbitration constituted an agreement that the arbitrator had jurisdiction to award interest if on the facts he thought it just to do so, counsel for the appellant submitted that on the principles of common law the arbitrator had, having regard to the provisions of s. 22 of the Court Act 1981, though not directly under them, power to grant interest. He relied for this submission on the decision of the Court of Appeal in *Chandris* v. *Isbrandtsen-Moller Co. Inc.*[104] In addition he relied on the unqualified obligatory nature of the duty of the court upon the making of an application to stay, pursuant to s. 5 of the Arbitration Act 1980.

I am satisfied that having reached the conclusion which I have reached concerning the submission by the parties in their reference of the precise question of law as to the arbitrator's jurisdiction to grant interest prior to the date of the award to the decision of the arbitrator, it would not be proper for me to express any view on the issue as to whether the decision which he has

---

[104] [1951] 1KB 240.

expressly made that he has no such jurisdiction is or is not correct in law.

I fully appreciate that if, when this question comes finally to be decided, either in the High Court or in the Supreme Court, in a case when it is at issue it is found that the arbitrator has under the circumstances arising in a case such as this a jurisdiction to grant interest, that there is a possibility that as a result of the arbitrator's decision in this case the appellant would appear to have suffered an injustice.

Even the possibility of such an injustice cannot, in my view, permit me to reach a conclusion which would alter the legal consequences of the agreement to refer this precise point of law to the determination of the arbitrator. Those consequences undeniably are, as a matter of fundamental law, that the parties are bound by his decision. Such a provision is just and adequate, bearing in mind the right which the parties had at all times up to the issue of the final award by the arbitrator to seek the stating of a case by him to the High Court in order to have the point of law determined. I would, accordingly, dismiss this appeal.

O'FLAHERTY J: The essential facts of this case and the course the proceedings took in the High Court have been set out in the judgment of the Chief Justice. At the arbitration hearing it appears that submissions were made to the arbitrator at various stages relating to his jurisdiction to award interest in respect of any period prior to the award itself. Certainly both parties addressed the arbitrator on this topic in the course of their closing submissions. It was submitted on behalf of the insurance company that the arbitrator had no jurisdiction to award interest in respect of the period prior to the award itself and that neither courts nor arbitrators have a power at common law to award interest in respect of late payments of a debt, except where the contract out of which the debt so provided as part of the agreement between the debtor and creditor.

It appears that the contrary submission was put forward on behalf of the appellant, viz. that the arbitrator had an inherent jurisdiction to award interest and the basis for this submission was that since a court (or more accurately a judge) can award interest for a period prior to the actual award of damages he could not have been taken to have contracted out of his entitlement to interest which he would have got in a court. In other words, so the argument went, arbitrators act with a parallel jurisdiction to a court and have as ample a power as a court to do essential justice between the parties, certainly as far as the awarding of interest is concerned.

It is clear that the insurance company requested the arbitrator to state a special case for the decision of the High Court under s. 35 of the Arbitration Act 1954 should he decide that he had in law jurisdiction to award interest for any period. The appellant did not seek such a special case from the arbitrator because the view was taken on his behalf that the arbitrator had no power to state a case concerning a matter of his own jurisdiction. In the circumstances the arbitrator determined that he was not entitled as arbitrator to adjudicate on the claim of the appellant for interest.

In this Court, while it was argued that the arbitrator has an inherent jurisdiction to award interest, greater emphasis was placed on the entitlement to interest which, it was submitted, is contained in the arbitration agreement. On behalf of the insurance company, however, it is stated that the reference to interest is only relevant if it were to be found that the arbitrator had an inherent jurisdiction to award interest in the first place. Furthermore, it is submitted that the appellant had a chance of seeking a special case and did not avail of it and should now be precluded from getting any relief by way of the proceedings at present before the court. In this regard, reliance was placed on the decision of this Court in *Keenan* v. *Shield Insurance Company Ltd.*[105] At p. 96, McCarthy J., speaking for the court said:

> Arbitration is a significant feature of modern commercial life; there is an International Institute of Arbitration and the field of international arbitration is an ever expanding one. It ill becomes the courts to show any readiness to interfere in such a process; if policy considerations are appropriate as I believe they are in a matter of this kind, then every such consideration points to the desirability of making an arbitration award final in every sense of the term. *Church and General Insurance Company* v. *Connolly and McLoughlin*[106] itself is an example of the type of fine-combing exercise which courts should not perform when it is sought to review an arbitration award. There may be instances in which an award which shows on its face an error of law so fundamental that the courts cannot stand aside and allow it to remain unchallenged. This is far from such a case.

In the circumstances, it appears to me that there are three questions for resolution:

(1) What is the arbitrator's jurisdiction to award interest at common law and under statute?

(2) Did the instant arbitration agreement give the arbitrator an entitlement to award interest from a date prior to the date of the award?

(3) If it is found that the arbitrator had the entitlement to award interest has the appellant now any remedy in the light of his failure to avail of the special procedure provided for by the 1954 Act?

(1) Arbitrator's jurisdiction

S.34 of the Arbitration Act 1954, provides that a sum directed to be paid by an award shall, unless the award otherwise directs, carry interest as from the date of the award and at the same rate as a judgment debt. It will be observed that the entitlement to interest under this section follows automatically unless, for some reason, the arbitrator should direct otherwise.

In my judgment the arbitrator does not have jurisdiction to award interest at common law in respect of a period prior to the award. Neither do I think can such a power to award interest be implied along the lines indicated by the Court of Appeal in England in *Chandris* v. *Isbrandtsen-Moller Co. Incorporated.*[107]

I find it impossible to take the leap required from finding that prior to

---

[105] [1988] I.R. 89. See p. 307 and p. 449 of this book.
[106] Unreported. High Court, 7 May 1981. See p. 446 of this book.
[107] [1951] 1KB 240.

1981 an arbitrator had no power to award interest (aside from agreement) to a finding that such a power is to be implied in agreements because of s.22 of the Courts Act 1981. That clearly reserves the entitlement to award interest to a "judge"; not even to a "court": see judgment of Finlay P. (as he then was) in *Mellowhide Products Ltd* v. *Barry Agencies Ltd.*[108]

(2) The Arbitration agreement

I believe that paragraph 2 of the agreement empowered the arbitrator to declare that the appellant was entitled to interest on the award from a date prior to the date of the award. He was given full power to make declarations as to the rights of the parties and this was to include the amount of interest (if any) that should be payable on such amount and the period in respect of which the interest (if any) would be payable. It is inconceivable that this is simply a reiteration of what is contained in s.34 of the 1954 Act because s.34 is self-executing, i.e. the interest follows the making of the award unless the arbitrator orders otherwise. So, therefore, it appears to me that the parties clearly intended that the arbitrator should have the same power as a court to award interest and that this was done by their express agreement. Even if there were no reference to interest in the paragraph I would think that the parties, having given the arbitrator power to make declarations 'as to the rights of the parties', were conferring on him a power to award interest. In other words, if it was intended that the arbitrator should not have the power to award interest on foot of making such a declaration, such an exclusion should have been expressly stated in the agreement. This is for the very simple reason that a party who recovers many years later an award without interest is simply not getting his "rights": his just entitlement.

While the parties made this agreement, nonetheless, they appeared to lose sight of its relevance in the course of the arguments that were presented to the arbitrator. The appellant, for his part, relied on the point that the arbitrator has an inherent power to award interest which he has not but, on the other hand, the insurance company placed great reliance on the fact that their policies had no provision for the payment of interest. In this, it is clear, that both parties were under a mutual misapprehension as to the importance of the arbitration agreement in the scheme of things. While there is no doubt that courts and arbitrators seek the same end, viz. to do justice between the parties, nonetheless, it should be borne in mind that there may be many differences between proceedings in a court and how an arbitration proceeds. In *Bremer Vulkan Schiffbau und Maschinenfabrik* v. *South India Shipping Corporation,*[109] the House of Lords was concerned with whether an arbitrator could dismiss a claim for want of prosecution in the way that a court might do. In the course of his speech Lord Diplock pointed to "a whole variety of procedures used in arbitrations for the resolution of disputes between the parties." Most of them, he said, do not reflect at all closely the pattern of procedure in an action in the High Court. At p. 983 he pointed to the

---

[108] [1983] I.L.R.M. 152.
[109] [1981] A.C. 909.

fundamental difference between an action at law and arbitration.

> "The submission of the defendant to the jurisdiction of the High Court to
> determine a dispute that has arisen between him and the plaintiff is com-
> pulsory. If he wants to resist the claim he has no other choice. The plaintiff
> has a choice whether or not to bring an action in a court of law to enforce a
> disputed claim against the defendant, but if he does want to enforce it the
> only forum in which he can do so is a court of law, unless he and the defen-
> dant mutually agree to submit their dispute about the plaintiff's claim for
> determination in some other way. As plaintiff and defendant in an action the
> parties assume no contractual obligations to one another as to what each
> must do in the course of the proceedings: their respective obligations as to
> procedure are imposed on them by the rules and practice of the court. In
> contrast to this, the submission of a dispute to arbitration under a private
> arbitration agreement is purely voluntary by both claimant and respondent.
> Where the arbitration is in a clause forming part of a wider contract and
> provides for the reference to arbitration of all future disputes arising under
> or concerning the contract, neither party knows when the agreement is
> entered into whether he will be claimant or respondent in disputes to which
> the arbitration agreement will apply."

I respectfully adopt and follow this reasoning and in my judgment the
importance and central position of the arbitration agreement must always be
kept in the forefront in determining the respective rights of the parties to it.
If it has to be kept in the forefront in procedural matters then it is all the
more necessary that it should be so regarded in matters of substance.

(3) Remedy
There is no doubt that the parties were at cross purposes as to the arbitrator's powers in the way that I have attempted to describe. Nonetheless,
there was a simple matter for resolution and that was whether or not the
arbitrator had power to award interest. The procedure laid down by s. 35 of
the 1954 Act is obviously the correct procedure to invoke in those circumstances. I can sympathise with counsel for the appellant's submission that to
seek such a case stated at the beginning of the arbitration and thus to put the
making of the award off for a further length of time was not a pleasant
prospect but I find it less easy to understand why it would not have been
possible for *both* of the parties to invite the arbitrator to make a finding on
the entitlement to interest and, indeed, to set out what interest (if any) he
would have awarded and reserved to the court the determination of whether
he had power to award interest or not. Unfortunately, that course was not
pursued and, therefore, the arbitrator, having decided that he had no jurisdiction to award interest, and not having been invited by the appellant to
state a case made his award without stating a case.

I agree with everything that has been urged that it is important that there
should be finality in arbitrations; that, indeed, is often the point of having
arbitrations at all. There may be other reasons, such as lack of publicity and,
perhaps, speed of disposal of the matter in dispute and so forth. Nonetheless,
I believe that there was a fundamental misapprehension by both parties as to
the effect of the agreement in this case. While I have no doubt that the

matter should have been resolved by reliance on s. 35 of the Act of 1954, I am entitled to ask what possible injustice can the insurance company suffer (that cannot be met on terms as to costs) by not having a reference under this section. On the other hand, if the appellant is shut out from his entitlement to claim interest (I make no comment as to what, if any, interest may be awarded) then, indeed, he could suffer a grave injustice. I believe the justice of the case does call for the intervention of the court and that the matter should be remitted to the arbitrator with a direction that he is entitled to entertain an application for interest prior to the date of his award. I believe that this jurisdiction to remit is one that should be sparingly exercised but I believe it should be exercised in this case.

In the Matter of an Arbitration between the Executors of Daniel Lowry, deceased, and the Ocean Accident and Guarantee Corporation Ltd.
(1898) 32 I.L.T.R. 126
Queen's Bench

KENNY J: It appears from the affidavit made for the purpose of this application that the late Mr Lowry was insured against accident in the Ocean Accident and Guarantee Corporation for the sum of £4,000, and the policy of assurance shows that it was contemplated that the policy should become a claim against the company in either of two events — either in the event of Lowry meeting with an accident not resulting in his death, or in the event of his meeting with an accident causing death. The question in dispute between the parties is whether the death of the insured was the result or not of an accident which occurred to him some time before his death, within the meaning of the condition of the policy — i.e. whether that accident was or was not the "actual and direct cause of the assured's death." Efforts were made on the part of the Company to have the matters in dispute referred to arbitration under clause 10 of the policy

["Upon any difference arising between the Corporation and the assured as to the construction, meaning, or extent of the contract hereby made, the amount of any claim thereunder, or the fulfilment of the conditions thereof, or any question, matter, or thing concerning or arising out of this assurance, it is a condition of this policy, which the assured by acceptance thereof agrees to abide by notwithstanding any law to the contrary, that every such difference shall be referred to the arbitration and decision of a neutral person agreed upon by the Corporation and the assured, and the decision of the arbitrator shall be final and binding on both parties, and shall be conclusive of the amount, if any, payable in respect of the said claim."]

and they have now instituted the present summons under s. 15 of the Common Law Procedure Act, 1856, asking that one of the gentlemen named in the summons should be appointed arbitrator.

This clause had been framed in the most general language, and if I were to judge of the intention of the parties from the clause alone I would come to the conclusion that it was intended to meet the double event contemplated by the policy itself — namely, accidents not resulting in death, and accidents from which death resulted where no arbitrator had been appointed during the lifetime of the assured. There is, however, this peculiarity about the clause, the arbitrator is to be appointed by "the Corporation and the assured", not "the assured or his personal representative". It is obvious that in the event of the policy becoming a claim during the life of the assured this clause would be applicable; but it was contended by the Corporation that if the assured person died, then the parties to join in the arbitration would be his personal representatives and the Company. I cannot agree with this construction of the clause. Throughout the policy, wherever a reference to personal representatives was necessary, they are specifically mentioned, and this provision of the contract between the parties being an abrogation on the part of these Common Law right[s], we cannot, unless wholly satisfied that such was their intention, allow the Common Law rights of the parties, or those claiming under them to be cut down or curtailed. If, however, I was satisfied that the words "or his personal representatives" could be incorporated in clause 10, I would feel bound to grant the application.

In *In re Percival*,[110] Mathew J., a judge of the widest experience in commercial cases on an application somewhat similar to the present, held that what was in the contemplation of the parties was that there should be a personal selection of the person who should act as arbitrator, and that the exercise of personal judgment by the parties was requisite, and that, one of them being dead, that had become impossible. That is to say, that as there is no mention of personal representatives the scope of such a condition as is contained in clause 10 cannot be extended to include them. The motion must therefore be refused.

BOYD J: I am of opinion that the condition does apply, and that the matter should be decided by the tribunal agreed on by the parties to the contract. The liability of the Corporation, in the event of the death of the assured, was in contemplation of the parties to the contract when it was entered into, and is expressly provided for in the policy. It is contended that the arbitration clause does not apply, because it stipulates that the reference shall be to a neutral person agreed upon "by the Corporation and the assured", and that the assured, being dead, cannot now agree to such a person. I hold that the personal representatives of the assured represent him, not only for the purpose of receiving the money payable under the policy, but also for the selection of the arbitrator. [His Lordship having referred to *Willesford* v. *Watson*,[111] continued.] I think that the word "assured" in the 10th clause should be construed to mean the person or persons entitled to make a claim under the policy. I think the case comes within ss. 14 and 15 of the Common Law Procedure Act, 1856, and that the application should be granted.

---

[110] 2 Times L.R. 150.
[111] L.R. 14 Eq. 572, and L.R. 8 Eq. 473.

O'BRIEN J: I concur with Mr Justice Kenny. Ever since *Scott* v. *Avery*,[112] insurance companies have tried every form of ingenuity to evade the submission of cases against them to the Courts of law. Certainly clause 10 has been constructed with great skill to avoid any possibility of an appeal to the Courts. It is not possible for an insurance company by a clause like this to oust the ordinary jurisdiction of the Court. The 10th clause omits the words "or his personal representatives", and it is an argument of great weight to find the "representatives", of the assured mentioned in other parts of the policy, and their rights provided for, and to find them omitted in clause 10. This case is governed expressly by *Re Percival*.[113] Though the facts are not the same, the principle is, and I entirely agree that the language of such a clause as this implies a personal confidence on the part of the assured in the person to be selected.

Lowden v. Accident Insurance Co.
(1909) 43 I.L.T.R. 277
King's Bench Division

PALLES L.C.B. (**ANDREWS AND JOHNSON J.J.** CONCURRING): The question in this case is a nice one. It is whether the umpire had jurisdiction to award the costs of the reference, and, of course, it is well known that in order to award these costs there must be a provision in the submission either express or implied to that effect. In every submission in England since the Act of 1889,[114] unless the contrary is expressly provided for, such a provision is absolutely incorporated in the submission by reason of the schedule to the Arbitration Act, 1889. If we are to hold that the English Act of 1889 is made part of this submission, then the award is good, but upon the other hand it is well known that one of the differences between English and Irish law is that in Ireland there is no provision equivalent to that of the English Arbitration Act, and that, consequently, in Ireland to give the arbitrator power to award these costs there must be a special provision to that effect. When the case was first argued before us it occurred to me that in determining the point of the case, it might be material to know where it was that this contract was entered into, and further affidavits showing that fact were filed. On the facts disclosed I have no hesitation in saying that this contract was entered into in Ireland. There was a proposal sent forward from Ireland to England to effect this insurance, but the rate that was to be paid for the insurance was not mentioned in the proposal. The proposal was made the subject of a so-called acceptance in England, but the rate was introduced in England for the first time, and the introduction of the new term rendered it impossible to say that there was any contract existing until the policy was sent back to Ireland and delivered there by the agent of the insurance company to Lowden and

---

[112] 5 H.L. Cas. 811.
[113] 2 Times L.R. 150.
[114] The Arbitration Act, 1889.

accepted by him. I am of opinion that the contract was completed, and, therefore, entered into in Belfast. We have, therefore, to take that into consideration in construing the contract. Serjeant Dodd's contention for the plaintiff
was that, assuming this to be an Irish contract, we are obliged to construe
this document so that some effect will be given to every word in it, and that
there was no reason why an Irish contract should not incorporate in it the
provisions of an English Act of Parliament as part of the contract, and that
the Arbitration Act, 1889, and the conditions contained in the schedule are so
incorporated in this contract as to give the umpire jurisdiction to award costs.
I am clearly of opinion that at one period of our legal history little weight
would have attached to that argument, but in modern times, at least since
Russell v. *Niemann*,[115] and even earlier, the courts came to the conclusion that
where you are construing a document which is in a stereotyped and printed
form, and intended to apply to various and varying states of fact, it ought to
be construed with reference to the particular state of facts, and that,
therefore, the construction of a document, which is composed by filling up in
writing a form largely in print, and largely used for general purposes, the
construction need not be necessarily the same as if it were a special document
prepared for a special occasion. [The arbitration clause was as follows:

> "in case of any dispute or difference of any kind arising under this policy,
> such dispute or difference shall be referred to the arbitration of an impartial
> person if mutually agreed upon or to the arbitration of two arbitrators to be
> chosen by the employer and the company respectively, and all the provisions
> of the Arbitration Act, 1889, and the Arbitration Act (Scotland) 1894 (where
> applicable), and such Arbitration Acts as may be in force for the time being
> shall apply to any such arbitration."]

I have come to the conclusion that the meaning of this clause is:— "We are
English, and we are willing to effect insurances under circumstances in which
some of our contracts will be English contracts, some may be Irish and others
Scottish, and we shall incorporate into this contract the Acts relating to
arbitration in the country in which the contract is entered into." Therefore, I
have come to the conclusion that the Act of 1889 is not incorporated in this
document, and therefore, the umpire had no jurisdiction to give costs. I shall
state shortly the reasons which have led me to this conclusion. In the condition we have, first of all, a reference to the English Act, then a specific
reference to the Scottish Act. Immediately following are the words "where
applicable", which words I do not limit to the Arbitration Act of Scotland, but
in my opinion qualify as well the reference to the English Act. Therefore, the
first thing we have to do is to find if these Acts, or either, is applicable to the
facts under consideration. Now, plainly, we must find, as a matter of fact, that
the Act is applicable before we can hold, that they are included in the
contract. They are plainly not incorporated until some such decision has been
arrived at. Immediately following are the words: "and such arbitration Acts
as may be in force for the time being." These are general words which would
include all Acts relating to England, Scotland or Ireland, and would comprise

---

[115] 17 C.B.N.S. 163.

Acts in any of these countries that were in existence at the time when this printed form was first prepared, and all Acts that had been passed afterwards, and that were in force at the time when the form was actually signed by the directors and assumed the character of a policy of insurance. These three codes of laws are in many respects essentially different, and could we reasonably impute to the parties that their contract was to be of such a description, that it was to be part of the contract that all the arbitration laws relating when the form was prepared, to Ireland, England and Scotland were incorporated? I cannot come to that conclusion. I think that the plain meaning of the words is that there are certain places where the Act of 1889 is applicable, and to which the Act of 1894 is applicable, that the Acts are to apply in the places where the legislature itself has made them applicable, and that the law of the place where the contract is made is to apply to it. This, in the case of an Irish submission, does not give the right to award the costs. I do not know whether I should say that I regret the conclusion that I have come to, but I do regret it, as I think that the successful party in any litigation should be indemnified as to costs. The award is void in this particular, and a declaration must be made to that effect.

Hutchinson *v.* Law and Rock Insurance Co. Ltd.
[1940] Ir. Jur. Rep. 7
The Circuit Court

DAVITT J: I am satisfied that the second proviso contained in the policy of insurance [... "Provided also that if a difference of any kind whatever shall arise between the Company and the Insured or the Insured's representatives in respect of this Policy or any claim thereunder the said difference shall be referred to arbitration (subject to the statutory provisions from time to time in force relating to arbitration) as a condition precedent to the commencement of any action and no action shall be brought on the Policy except for the sum if any awarded to be due on such arbitration"] in this case clearly expresses the intention of the parties that all differences (including the present one) between them should be referred to arbitration, that such reference should be a condition precedent to the commencement of any action, and that any right of action upon the policy should be limited to the amount of the award."

I am of the opinion that this case, so far, at least is not affected by the reasoning in *Yeates* v. *Caruth*.[116] In that case the parties had signed a submission to two named arbitrators, one of whom refused to act, and the submission, neither by itself nor with the aid of the provisions of the Common Law Procedure Act, 1856, provided any way out of the difficulty. Even giving the agreement of the parties its full force and effect, and calling in aid the provisions of the statute in question, failed to afford any means of deciding the difference between the parties. In this case that is not so. In the first

---

[116] [1895] 2 I.R. 146.

place there has been no "submission" to arbitration in the legal sense. There has been none at common law since no arbitrator has been appointed, nor have I been referred to any enactment such as section 27 of the Arbitration Act of 1889, which would render the proviso already referred to a "submission". There is, however, a binding agreement between the parties to refer the dispute to arbitration, and as the defendants are willing to proceed upon that basis I can see no good reason why the plaintiff, setting up the policy and suing upon it, should not be bound by all its terms, including the proviso as to arbitration. In this case, giving the agreement between the parties full force and effect, there is a method of settling the difference between them. I do not know what form the submission to arbitration may take or what difficulties may arise thereunder. In the circumstances, however, I see no good reason why the matter should not go to arbitration and I shall accordingly stay these proceedings until the issues between the parties have been duly submitted to arbitration and an award made or until further order....

Hogan *v.* Poland
[1940] Ir. Jur. Rep. 4
The Circuit Court

SHANNON J: This is an action to recover a sum of £16 alleged by the plaintiff to be due to him by the defendant on foot of an award made on the 7th December 1938. In the month of May of that year the plaintiff's motor car was damaged in an accident, and he claimed to be indemnified by the defendant and others against the loss accruing to him by reason of such damage. This claim was made on foot of a policy of insurance dated the 7th July 1937 to which the defendant was one of several signatories. In this action the defendant represents and in the arbitration proceedings represented all the said signatories. The plaintiff's claim was repudiated by the insurers on the ground that he had failed to comply with condition 4 of the policy which required him to maintain the car in efficient condition. Following upon this repudiation the plaintiff's solicitor wrote to the defendant's solicitors on the 27th June 1938 that the plaintiff had incurred expense by reason of his having to hire a car owing to the delay in having his damaged car repaired, and that he would claim compensation in respect of this expense and his liability for garage fees. The policy in question exempts the insurers from liability to pay the plaintiff for loss of use of his car, and the claim contained in the letter referred to could not be sustained under the policy.

The policy contains a condition [no. 5] that "all differences arising out of" it should be referred to an arbitrator.... By an agreement in writing dated the 17th October 1938 and made between the plaintiff and the defendant, after reciting that disputes and differences had arisen and were then pending respecting the liability of the underwriters under the said policy to indemnify the insured against loss, damage and liability in consequence of an accident to his Ford Car, and after reciting that the parties had agreed to refer the said matters to arbitration pursuant to condition 5 of the policy, it was agreed that all disputes and differences which then existed between the said parties, and also all other disputes and differences which might thereafter arise between them and be laid before the arbitrator thereinafter named at any time before he should make his award, should be referred to arbitration.

In pursuance of this submission the arbitrator duly made his award in writing on the 7th December last. In this he recites the agreement of the 17th October 1938, specially referring to the parts there referred....

He then found and awarded as follows:

["1. I find as a fact that the said insured did take all reasonable steps to safeguard from loss or damage, and to maintain in efficient condition the said Ford 8 h.p. car, and I do accordingly award that the said underwriters shall pay to the said insured the said sum of forty pounds five shillings and eightpence in respect of the cost of repairing the said damage to the said car. 2. And I find as a fact that the completion of the necessary repairs to the said 8 h.p. Ford Car was unduly delayed, that said delay was due to the refusal of the underwriters to admit such liability as aforesaid and that the insured suffered loss thereby, which I assess at the sum of sixteen pounds (£16). 3. I find that the underwriters are legally liable to the insured in respect of his said loss of sixteen pounds. I do accordingly further award that the underwriters shall pay the insured, in addition to the sum hereinbefore mentioned, the sum of sixteen pounds (£16). And I do further award that the underwriters shall pay the insured their costs of and incidental to this Arbitration."].

No questions as to the £40 5s. 8d. or the sums awarded as costs and expenses arise. All these have been paid, but the defendant has refused to pay the said sum of £16 on the ground that he did not refer to the arbitrator any difference or dispute as to whether the underwriters were liable to pay the plaintiff in respect of loss occasioned by the refusal of the underwriters to admit liability to indemnify the plaintiff in respect of the damage to the car. It appears to me that if the award shows upon its face that the arbitrator had jurisdiction to deal with the matters he purports to deal with, then any decision he made thereon must be final and binding upon the defendant so long as the award is not set aside by a competent Court. If the defendant in this action can show by reference to the award and any documents therein referred to that the arbitrator has exceeded his jurisdiction, then the award is not, in regard to such excess, binding upon the defendant.

Condition 5 of the policy provides that "all differences arising out of the policy" should be referred to arbitration. The agreement of the 17th October 1938, recites that disputes and differences had arisen respecting the liability of the underwriters under the policy to indemnify the insured against loss and damage and liability in consequence of an accident to his Ford car. This recital is repeated in the award, and no exception can be taken as to its correctness. If the arbitrator said in effect that the plaintiff claimed £16.00 under the policy and awarded it, I do not think the defendant could say the award was bad upon its face.

But the arbitrator has not awarded £16 as money due under the policy. He has awarded it as damages to the plaintiff because the underwriters did not admit liability for repairs to the car within a reasonable time after the accident. I am not concerned to say whether he was right or wrong in law. I am only concerned to see whether the defendant can show from the award itself that the arbitrator should not have dealt with such a claim. It must be conceded for the purposes of this case that such a claim was made. The question is does this award show on its face that the underwriters did not submit such a claim to the decision of the arbitrator. The plaintiff says that when the agreement of the 17th October 1938 submits "all other disputes and differences" it submits what it literally says, whereas the defendant argues that the submission when looked at as a whole is a submission of all existing and future differences "arising out of the Policy".

In my view this is the correct interpretation of the submission, and a disputed claim in the nature of a claim for damages for the refusal of the underwriters to admit their liability to indemnify the plaintiff in respect of damage to his car is not a claim "arising out of" the policy but a claim for damages for breach of contract. As it is clear from the award that the £16 was not awarded as money payable under the policy, and as it is equally clear that it was awarded in settlement of a dispute which was not one which "arose out of" the policy, then I think it is clear that it was made in respect of a dispute which was not submitted to the arbitrator by the defendant.

For these reasons I think the claim fails and the action must be dismissed with costs.

McConn *v.* The Commercial Insurance Company of Ireland Limited
(1949) 83 I.L.T.R. 142
The Circuit Court

CONNOLLY J: The defendants by a policy of insurance dated 24th day of June, 1936, agreed to indemnify the plaintiff against all sums which the plaintiff should become liable to pay to any employee in respect of any personal injury by accident or disease as described in the 6th Schedule to the Workmen's Compensation Act 1934 (No 9) while engaged in the service of the plaintiff, in case the plaintiff should be liable to make compensation for such injury as therein, and in addition all costs and most expenses incurred by the plaintiff, with the consent of the defendants, in defending any claim for such compensation, but subject to the conditions stated in the said policy.

In the month of February, 1941, Joseph Melvin, an employee of the plaintiff, sustained an injury arising out of and in the course of his employment with the plaintiff. By an order of the Circuit Court, Western Circuit, County of Mayo, dated the 29th day of April, 1941 the plaintiff was ordered to pay compensation to the said Joseph Melvin at the rate of £1 4s. 0d. a week from the 10th day of February, 1941, and his costs and expenses. The said Joseph Melvin was an employee of the plaintiff who was covered by the said policy.

The defendants disputed their liability under the policy to indemnify the plaintiff as such insured as aforesaid. Thereupon, the plaintiff had to have recourse, under the terms and conditions of the policy, to arbitration to enforce his right of indemnity thereunder.

Both parties to the policy agreed to refer the dispute to the decision of a single arbitrator, and for this purpose duly signed a submission to arbitration. The dispute, or difference, so referred to arbitration was:— Whether the Company was liable under the Terms and Conditions of the said policy to indemnify the plaintiff in respect of all monies payable or to become payable by him to the said Joseph Melvin for compensation, costs and expenses under and by virtue of the provisions of the Workmen's Compensation Act, 1934, in respect of an accident alleged to have occurred to the said Joseph Melvin on the 5th day of February, 1941, while in the service of the plaintiff. This submission, which was dated the 24th day of March, 1942, did not empower the arbitrator to deal with the costs of and incidental to the arbitration nor the arbitrator's fee. It did provide that both the submission and the award thereunder might be made a rule of the High Court of Justice by either party.

The arbitrator having duly heard the evidence, both oral and documentary, submitted to him by the respective parties duly made and published his award in writing on the 31st day of May, 1942, whereby he decided and awarded that the defendants were liable under the terms and conditions of the said policy to indemnify the plaintiff in respect of all monies payable, or to become payable, by him to the said Joseph Melvin for compensation, costs and expenses under or by virtue of the provisions of the Workmen's Compensation Act, 1934, in respect of the accident alleged to have occurred to the said Joseph Melvin, while in the service of the plaintiff. The plaintiff duly paid the arbitrator's fee of £15 15s. 0d. and thereupon the arbitrator issued his said award to him. On the 27th day of July, 1943, the said submission and award were made a Rule or Order of the High Court. The plaintiff claims in this action the said sum of £15 15s 0d., paid by him to the arbitrator, and in addition his costs and expenses of the said arbitration amounting in all to £196 18s. 3d. ... as damages for breach by the defendants of the contract of indemnity contained in the said policy.

The defendants by their defence apart from mere traverses or denials contend (a) First that the claim herein is a difference, or dispute, within the meaning of the said policy, and that accordingly same should in pursuance of the relevant condition therein be referred to the decision of an arbitrator, and that as the plaintiff had not referred the said difference, or dispute, to arbitration the action is not maintainable, and (b) secondly that the said condition provided that if the defendants should disclaim liability to the plaintiff for any claim under the said policy and such claim should not, within twelve calendar months from the date of such disclaimer, have been referred to arbitration under the provisions of the said policy the said claim should, for all purposes, be deemed to have been abandoned and should not be recoverable under the policy and (c) thirdly that as the defendants had disclaimed liability for the plaintiffs claim in this action and as more than twelve calendar months had elapsed since such disclaimer without arbitration the claim is not recoverable, and this action is not maintainable. As proof of such disclaimer the defendants rely on two letters from their solicitors to the plaintiff's solicitor dated 23rd day of October, 1943, and 30th day of March, 1944, respectively.

The contention in these letters is that the plaintiff is not entitled to recover the amount of his claim as aforesaid as the arbitrator's said award did not award costs to the plaintiff. In neither of these two letters is it specifi-

cally alleged or contended that the claim herein was a difference arising out
of the policy. The relevant condition is Number 7 which is as follows:—

> "7. All differences arising out of this policy shall be referred to the decision of
> an arbitrator to be appointed in writing by the parties in difference or if they
> cannot agree upon a single arbitrator to the decision of two arbitrators one to
> be appointed in writing by each of the parties within one calendar month
> after having been required in writing so to do by either of the parties or in
> case the arbitrators do not agree of an umpire appointed in writing by the
> arbitrators before entering upon the reference. The umpire shall sit with the
> arbitrators and preside at their meetings and the making of an award shall
> be a condition precedent to any right of action against the company. If the
> company shall disclaim liability to the insured for any claim hereunder and
> such claim shall not within twelve calendar months from the date of such
> disclaimer have been referred to arbitration under the provisions herein con-
> tained then the claim shall for all purposes be deemed to have been aban-
> doned and shall not thereafter be recoverable hereunder."

It was by reason of the defendants' repudiation of their liability under the
said policy that the award of an arbitrator became a condition precedent to
any right of action against the defendants as insurers.

It was well known to both parties that in resorting to arbitration the fee of
the arbitrator should be provided for, and that in accordance with the usual
practice the successful party would take up the award and pay the arbitrator's fee. The submission to arbitration was prepared by the defendants
solicitors and submitted by them to the plaintiff's solicitor for execution by
his client. It contained no provision empowering the arbitrator to award costs
and expenses of and incidental to the arbitration. In the absence of such a
provision the arbitrator had not, in my opinion, jurisdiction to award such
costs and expenses.

The plaintiff's costs and expenses were properly and necessarily incurred
by him in prosecuting his claim under the indemnity in the said policy before
the tribunal which the defendants had prescribed for the determination of
any difference arising out of the policy and further requiring the making of an
award a condition precedent to any right of action against the defendants.

In the events which have happened the defendants must be deemed to
have wrongfully repudiated their liability to the plaintiff under the said
policy, and by reason of such repudiation to have committed a breach of
contract between them and the plaintiff. In consequence of such breach the
plaintiff contends that he was damnified and that he is entitled to recover
from the defendants by way of damages the amount of the costs and expenses
incurred by him, as aforesaid in connection with the said arbitration as well
as the amount of the arbitrator's fee. At the trial the defendants relied on
Clause No. 7 of the conditions of the said policy and contended that their
liability for such costs, expenses and arbitrator's fee was a difference arising
out of the said policy and consequently should have been referred to arbitration as provided by the said clause, and they now rely on this clause as a bar
to the plaintiff's right to recover the amount of his claim in this action. It was
contended on behalf of the plaintiff that his claim in this action is not a
difference arising out of the said policy but arose *dehors* the said policy.

Mr Casey [for the defendant] cited *Heyman* v. *Darwins Ltd.*[117] I have carefully read the judgments in it. I do not consider it necessary to analyse them beyond referring to that part of the judgment of Viscount Simon at page 360 as follows : "The answer to the question whether a dispute falls within an arbitration clause in a contract must depend on (a) What is the dispute and (b) What disputes the arbitration clause covers." I think in applying these observations to the terms of the policy in this action there can be no doubt that the dispute related to the liability of the defendants under the indemnity in the policy and that the arbitration clause covered such dispute. The words "All differences arising out of this policy" in clause No 7 of the conditions therein can, in my opinion, relate only to the specific matters comprised in the indemnity contained in the said policy. The fundamental dispute was the matter referred to arbitration by the parties. It was as a consequence of having to arbitrate on such dispute that the plaintiff suffered the loss and damage he claims in this action. The limitation of twelve calendar months contained in clause No. 7 of the conditions can only, in my opinion, be applicable to a claim arising out of the indemnity contained in the policy and not otherwise. The extended meaning which the defendants seek to attach to the said words "All differences arising out of this policy" is in my opinion contrary to the true intendment of the policy. The scope of the arbitration clause should be strictly confined to the disputes and differences which, on a reasonable interpretation of the contract, could be deemed to arise thereout, under the indemnity therein contained. The costs and expenses which the plaintiff had to incur in connection with the said arbitration are, in my opinion, consequential damages arising out of the defendants' breach of contract, in repudiating their liability to the plaintiff under the indemnity contained in the said contract, and as such are *dehors* the said policy; accordingly I am of the opinion the plaintiff is entitled to recover in this action such costs, expenses and arbitrator's fee as damages for breach of contract. I give a decree for £196 18s. 3d. with costs and expenses when taxed and ascertained.

The High Court

MAGUIRE J in the course of his judgment said that there had been no breach or repudiation of the contract by the Insurance company. The facts in the case were very simple, and were not in dispute. The amount claimed had been correctly made up.

The company's answer to the claim had been, first, that the sum claimed was irrecoverable under the contract of insurance. The case was an important one, and his lordship gladly would have stated a case for the opinion of the Supreme Court, but apparently the parties had decided that they did not want a case stated, and it fell upon his lordship to decide on the facts what was the liability, or otherwise, of the company under the contract. The contract was the policy of insurance, and the costs of the arbitration did not arise under the policy. He could not find that the contract under the policy

---

[117] [1942] A.C. 356.

had at any time been repudiated by the company, in the sense that it was not binding. There had been no attempt by the company at any time to escape their obligation or their contract. On the contrary, the insurance company had appeared right through, even in that Court, to rely on the contract and not in any way to depart from its terms.

His Lordship had to decide in that case, whether or not there had been any breach of contract, or repudiation of the contract itself, and he was unable to find any breach of contract, or repudiation of contract, there. Accordingly, he regretted that he was unable to agree with the Circuit Court Judge, and he was obliged to dismiss the action.

CHAPTER 12

The Role of the Insurance Intermediary

The insurance intermediary plays a very significant role in the Irish insurance market. It is surprising, in light of the strong presence of intermediaries, that relatively few cases involving them have come before the Irish courts. As a consequence, although the duties and obligations of intermediaries and to whom those duties and obligations are owed, are, with the benefit of foreign precedents, well established in theory, few practical Irish examples exist to illustrate the scope and extent of those obligations and duties.

In the Irish market there are different classes of intermediary, primarily the independent broker and the tied agent. The distinction between the two — and thus their responsibilities and duties — is governed by the Insurance Act, 1989. Depending on their classification, difficulties can often arise in establishing whether at given times in the life of the insurance contract — such as at the completion and submission of the proposal, at the collection of premiums, at the estimation, submission and settlement of claims, at the renewal and so on — the intermediary is acting as the agent of the insured or of the insurer, thereby determining to which of the two the primary responsibilities of the intermediary are owed. The 1989 Act is of minor assistance and deals only with a few limited situations, such as the completion of proposal forms by tied agents and the offering of advice by tied agents who are also employees of the insurer.

At common law it has been accepted generally that the independent broker is indeed the agent of the insured, unless specifically stated to the contrary. In most cases this is simply taken for granted and not given specific judicial attention. However, in the case of *Taylor* v. *The Yorkshire Insurance Company Limited* (1912) it had to be decided whether the consequences of the default of a broker at inception were to be borne by the insured or the insurer. The broker was held to be acting as agent of the insured in the submission of the proposal, and therefore the insured bore the burden of his misdeeds. In *Sanderson* v. *Cunningham* (1919) the status and authority of the broker was examined to determine where exactly the contract of insurance had been completed, thereby ascertaining in which of two jurisdictions a dispute was to be litigated. Again the broker was held to be acting on behalf of the insured.

The nature and extent of a broker's responsibilities to a client have been examined in a number of cases. In this respect the duties owed by the broker to the client are no different from those owed by any professional to those to whom services are provided. Brokers must discharge their obligations in a competent and professional manner, reaching and maintaining the standards of their fellow brokers. In very general terms, they must advise on the suitability and adequacy of the policies supplied, examine all the alternatives, explain fully the content and scope of a policy and ensure that nothing has occurred that might invalidate that policy in any way.

More often than not what will be in dispute is the simple absence of cover and, as seen in the case of *Richard Curtis t/a Agencies Transport* v. *Corcoran Insurances Limited* (1973), it is very much a dispute on the facts to determine exactly the instructions given by the insured, the broker's understanding of same and where the fault ultimately lies for the absence of cover.

In circumstances where the broker has failed utterly to secure the cover as instructed, the issue of negligence is easily decided — the only matter in dispute, as illustrated by *Amethyst Limited (in liquidation)* v. *Galway Insurance Brokers Limited and McGovern* (1991), being the assessment of the client's loss as a result of that failure.

Most disputes, however, involve allegations that brokers have not fulfilled their professional obligations, by failing to explain adequately the actual cover provided by a policy or alerting the client as to the existence of specific exclusions and conditions. Equally a broker will be considered negligent for failing to make a proper enquiry of a client as to the existence of facts which might render the policy void, or alternatively, where the broker is aware of such material facts, for failing to advise the client that those facts ought to be disclosed. In *Chariot Inns Limited* v. *Asscurrazoni Generali S.p.a. and Coyle Hamil-ton Hamilton Philips Limited* (1981)* it was held that the broker was negligent in the circumstances where he failed to advise his client of the necessity to disclose to the insurers a previous related claim, of which he was aware, that claim being held to be material fact which ought to have been so disclosed. He was held responsible for the resulting absence of cover. Similarly, in the more recent case of *Latham* v. *Hibernian Insurance Company Limited and Peter J. Sheridan & Company Limited* (1991),† the broker was again held liable for

---

* This judgment appears in Chapter 7 at p. 233.
† This judgment appears in Chapter 7 at p. 272.

the absence of cover when the insurers successfully voided the policy *ab initio* for failure to disclose a material fact, the broker being aware of the same, having learnt of the material fact from a source other then the insured. He was under a duty of enquiry to examine those facts thoroughly and advise his client as to their materiality.

The *Latham* case is also of interest as the material facts arose after the inception of the policy, but prior to renewal, the facts not being disclosed to the Hibernian on that renewal.

Also of interest in the *Latham* case is the fact that the issue was not addressed as to whether or not the insured should have realised the materiality of the facts in question himself and, as such, not placed reliance on his broker so to advise him. Equally, in the second *Latham* decision, in which the Court was determining what the insured's loss was and thereby assessing the claim against the broker, no evidence was called by the broker to illustrate that, had the material facts being disclosed, the insured could not in all probability have obtained insurance elsewhere, especially as that had been the Hibernian's evidence in the first case. The second *Latham* decision is also important as it provides an excellent illustration of how an insured's losses are to be assessed where a policy of insurance had in fact been in existence. It will also provide a good guide as to the assessment of damages in cases where an insurer is unsuccessful in refusing to handle a claim, though in such circumstances the issue of "bad faith" will also be a factor.

Taylor *v.* The Yorkshire Insurance Company Limited[*]
[1913] 2 I.R. 1
King's Bench Division

PALLES C.B: This is an action on a policy of assurance for £1,000, effected by the defendant company with the plaintiff on the 9th November, 1909, against loss by death from accident or disease of his stallion "General Symons".

The policy recites that the plaintiff had caused to be delivered to the company a proposal which the insured hath agreed shall be the basis of this policy, and be considered as incorporated herein.

The proposal thus referred to, and made the basis of the policy, is signed by the plaintiff and contains six questions, which were required to be answered by the proposer. The third is: "Are they" (the animals proposed to be insured) "or have they been insured elsewhere? Have you had a proposal for L.S." (live stock) "insurance declined? Have you been paid claims? If so, how many and by whom ?"

At the foot of the proposal there is the following declaration, "I, the

---

[*] Extract.

undersigned." (i.e., the plaintiff), "do hereby warrant and declare the truth of all the above statements; that all animals are, and have been, in good health; and that *I have not withheld any important information;* and I agree that this declaration and proposal shall be the basis of the contract between me and the Yorkshire Insurance Company, Limited."

Thus, the contract sued on contains a condition that the plaintiff has not withheld any important information; and I desire to state that my judgment is based solely on this condition and not on the 10th condition endorsed on the policy, which avoids the policy if it be *obtained through* the withholding of material facts. The consideration of this latter condition involves a question of causation which, in a case such as the present, depending as it does, upon a strict discrimination between the functions of the Judge and the jury, is materially different from that which I proceed to discuss.

In canvassing for and procuring the proposal for this insurance, in forwarding that proposal to the company's office in Dublin, in handing to the plaintiff the policy, which was sent to him from the Dublin office, and in receiving the premium, one Scollen acted as agent for the defendants.

"General Symons", the animal insured, although a most valuable horse for stud purposes, had a serious malformation of the forelegs. The fetlocks of these legs were so much turned in that, instead of walking, he could merely hobble. There is evidence that this diminished, to a substantial degree, his power of locomotion and of taking exercise; and consequently may have affected his power of digestion, and through it, his general health.

Prior to the policy sued on, the horse had been insured in various companies. In 1904 and 1905, he was insured with the Scottish Live Stock Company, and, in 1906 and 1907, in the Army and the Navy Company. These four policies were effected through the intervention of the same Mr Scollen, who in reference to them acted as agent of the respective insuring companies. In February, 1908, the Army and Navy Company declined to re-insure; and the fact that they so declined was known at the time to both the plaintiff and Scollen; but Scollen was not, at that time, nor until the month of June following, an agent for the defendants.

In 1908 and 1909, the horse was insured with the National Live Stock Company, for whom Coyle & Co. were agents. On the 17th of July, 1909, this company sent Mr McKinney, a veterinary surgeon, to examine the horse, and, after his visit, this company did not send the plaintiff the usual notice requesting him to renew the policy.

Under these circumstances, Scollen, who had been agent of the Army and Navy Company at the time that company had declined to re-insure, and had since become an agent for the defendant company, asked the plaintiff to insure the horse with the latter company, which, after some demur, the plaintiff agreed to do.

The proposal for the insurance bears date the 29th October, 1909, and is signed by the plaintiff; but the answers are in Scollen's handwriting. The plaintiff and Scollen differ as to the circumstances of the preparation of this document. The plaintiff says that Scollen filled up the answers; that he (the plaintiff) did not read them; that he told Scollen all he knew; that he was not dealing with the company direct, but with Scollen; that if he had been allowed to fill the form he would have filled it differently, and given all the information in his power. Scollen, on the other hand, swore that the plaintiff told him to fill up the form; that he read out the questions; and that the plaintiff answered them.

For the purpose of this case, I deem the difference between these two accounts immaterial; but, in the determination of this motion, I assume, as I am bound to do, that the plaintiff's account is the correct one. It is, to my mind, undoubted, and indeed, was ultimately admitted by Serjeant Moriarty, that, in filling up the answers, Scollen must be taken to have acted as the plaintiff's agent, and that the plaintiff is bound by the declaration he signed, as if he had read it, and knew the answers it contained: *Biggar* v. *Rock Life Assurance Company*.[1]

As, however, during the early part of the argument, it was suggested that this decision, which was that of a single Judge — the late Mr Justice Wright — was inconsistent with the previous decision of the Court of Appeal in *Bawden* v. *The London, Edinburgh and Glasgow Assurance Company*,[2] and must, therefore, be taken not to be law, I do not like to altogether abstain from referring to this question.

In *Bawden's Case*[3] the plaintiff was an illiterate man, and, to the knowledge of the defendant's agent, was almost unable to read or write, although he could write his name. He had but one eye. Quin, the company's agent, saw this when the plaintiff applied to him to be insured. The form of the proposal was a complicated one, and contained a note: "If not strictly applicable, particulars of any deviation must be given at back"; which may well be taken to have been a direction, not to the proposer, but to the agent. Lord Esher, M.R., rested his judgment on the imputation to the company of the knowledge acquired by their agent during the negotiations for the policy, that the proposer had but one eye. Lindley and Kay, L.JJ., however in addition to relying on this imputation of notice, held that a duty lay upon Quin, in reference to the filling up of the proposal, Lindley, L.J., stating it was his duty "to put it in shape", and Kay, L.J., that it was his duty to see that it was filled up correctly, and to have written at its back that the proposer had but one eye — a fact which rendered the form not strictly applicable. Thus, one Lord Justice expressly and certainly, and the other probably, bases the duty which it is alleged makes the company's agent an agent of the proposer to fill up the answers, on the special circumstances of that particular case. This is the view taken of it by Wills and Phillimore, JJ., *Levy* v. *Scottish Employers' Insurance Company*.[4]

Agreeing as I do with them, I hold not only that, as a general rule, no such duty devolves upon an insurance company's agent, but that the expressions relied on do not indicate an opinion that it does. On the contrary, I hold with Mr Justice Wright that although "he may have been an agent to put the answers in form," the agent of an insurance company cannot be treated as their agent to invent the answers to the questions in the proposal form; and

---

[1] [1902] 1 K.B. 516.
[2] [1892] 2 Q.B. 534.
[3] *Ibid.*
[4] 17 Times L.R. 229.

that, if he is allowed by the proposer to invent the answers, and to send them as the answers of the proposer, the agent is, to that extent, the agent, not of the insurance company, but of the proposer. In arriving at this conclusion, I have not overlooked the fact that both in *Biggar* v. *The Rock Company*[5] and *Levy's Case*[6] there was a provision in the proposal that verbal statements to the agent should not be imputed to the company; but, in relation to this question of authority, as distinct from that of imputations of notice, this is immaterial.

I have read, with pleasure and advantage, the judgment of Field, J., in delivering the unanimous opinion of the Supreme Court of the United States, in *New York Life Insurance Company* v. *Fletcher,*[7] relied on by Mr Justice Wright, which well repays perusal.

I revert now to the third question, which I have already read: "Are they, or have they been, insured elsewhere? Have you been paid claims? If so, how many, and by whom?" The answer is, "Yes; with Coyle & Co., Dublin."

Thus part only of that question is answered, viz., that part of the question which asks, "Are they insured elsewhere?" The answer omits to state (1) that the horse had been insured with the Army and Navy Company; (2) that that Company had declined to re-insure; nor did the answer disclose (3) that the National Company, the principals of Coyle & Co., Dublin, intended not to continue their insurance. I, however, leave out of consideration this third matter not disclosed, as it may be that whether the plaintiff knew of this intention of the National Company involved a matter of fact for the consideration of the jury. Be this, however, as it may, every other matter I have stated was undisputed, and, in fact, was the common case of both parties.

The defendants, by their defences, relied upon the physical condition of the horse and his having been previously declined for insurance, as constituting breaches of the condition, and, also upon the concealment of those matters being fraudulent. To the former the plaintiff replied, that when they effected the policy, the defendants knew of the condition of the horse, and that he had been previously declined for insurance, and that they had waived the compliance with the conditions. At the trial the defendants withdrew the charge of fraud.

The jury found that the fact of the insurance having been declined by another company was important, as was also the malformation of the legs; but, I am not to be taken as deciding that the mere fact of the questions in the proposal, making inquiry as to these matters, did not *per se* make the answers or the omission to answer material. The jury were told by the learned Judge that the meaning of the word "withheld" in the proposal was "not disclosed in that proposal," but they disregarded that direction by failing to agree on another of the questions left to them — whether the information in reference to these matters, which was, in fact, not disclosed by the answers, was withheld by the plaintiff.

Upon these findings of the jury, Mr Justice Dodd entered a verdict for the

---

[5] [1902] 1 K.B. 316.
[6] 17 Times L.R. 229.
[7] 117 U.S. 519.

defendants, refusing to leave to the jury questions suggested by Mr Serjeant Moriarty as to the knowledge by Scollen of the material facts omitted from the proposal.

Mr Serjeant Moriarty, for the plaintiff, now moves for a new trial; and relies on *Armstrong* v. *Turquand*,[8] as establishing that knowledge by the company, at the time of the policy, of the matters omitted from the proposal, is a good answer to a defence relying upon the breaches of the condition.

In that contention I agree with the learned Serjeant. No doubt, the questions in the two cases are not identical, the knowledge of the breach of condition in *Armstrong* v. *Turquand*[9] having been acquired after, and not, as here, at the time of the policy; but the *ratio decidendi* there (as explained in the elaborate judgment of Mr Justice Christian), that "void" in the condition should be construed as void at the election of the insurers, and that the receipt, with such knowledge, of a premium payable under the policy was an election by the insurance company to affirm the policy, seems equally applicable here....

As to the second question, I agree with the learned Judge that material information within the knowledge of the plaintiff, not disclosed in the proposal, was "withheld," within the meaning of that word in the proposal.

One of the objects of a proposal is to lay before the insuring company such facts within the knowledge of the proposer as, in the opinion of the company, are material in valuing the risk they are asked to undertake. The mode adopted by the company in attempting to obtain knowledge of these facts is, first, by asking certain specific questions and requiring a warranty that the answers given to these are true. But that alone is not sufficient. It is essential to the true valuation of the risk that, not only shall there not be any false representation, but that there shall be no concealment of any material matter. So essential is this that the very nature of the contract involves a duty in the proposer to state all material facts within his knowledge; and Sir George Jessel, in *London Assurance Company* v. *Mansel*,[10] uses the words "non-disclosure" and "concealment" as synonymous in reference to matters which it is one's duty to disclose. "Concealment, properly so called," says that very learned Judge, "means non-disclosure of a fact which it is a man's duty to disclose".

Now, in my clear opinion, the effect of the words in the proposal "I have not withheld any important information", amounts to an express condition at least as extensive as that which is implied by law in a contract of insurance, that the information given is *all* the information, material to the insurance, within the knowledge of the proposer; and that, therefore, any such information not communicated is, within the meaning of the document, "withheld," just as, within the meaning of the insurance law, it is concealed.

How does the contract provide that this information is to be communicated? To answer this we must look to the nature of the document. Its object was to communicate information for the purpose of valuing the risk.

---

[8] 9 I.C.L.R. 32
[9] *Ibid.*
[10] 11 Ch. D 363.

The risk, undoubtedly, was to be valued at the head office of the company — whether in Dublin or London does not appear — by the officials there; not in Mullingar by Scollen. Therefore, the information to be communicated should be put in such form that it should reach the head office. Again the information was to be covered by a condition by the proposer in a document which was to bear his signature; and, therefore, the only mode of communication sufficient to satisfy the intention of the parties was disclosure in the proposal itself. I am therefore of opinion that the true meaning of "I have not withheld" in the proposal is "I have not withheld from this proposal," and that everything material which was within the plaintiff's knowledge, and which was not disclosed in the answers, was withheld; that the fourth question really involved matter of law only; and that the learned Judge rightly treated the disagreement of the jury upon it as immaterial.

For these reasons, I am of opinion that the verdict and judgment should stand, and that this application should be refused with costs.

GIBSON J: ... Where a broker is employed — whether in marine insurance or otherwise — the principal may be affected by knowledge which the nature of the broker's business would naturally enable the latter to possess, but in all such cases the notice is closely connected in point of time with the particular contract: *Blackburn* v. *Vigors;*[11] *Blackburn* v. *Haslam.*[12] In these cases the notice was sought to be attributed to the insured, not to the insurers.

In none of the insurance cases relied on for the plaintiff, where the insurers were held bound by the agent's knowledge, was such knowledge acquired otherwise than in discharge of duty in relation to the particular contract. *Bawden's Case*[13] (plaintiff's main authority) turned, as the judgment of Kay, L.J., explains, and in the actual negotiation of the policy. The case is a peculiar one. An illiterate one-eyed man, in good faith, at the instance of the company's agent, made a proposal, which seemed in terms to apply to a person without defects, and possessed of two eyes. The Court held that the contract must be construed with reference to the known facts present to the minds of the parties, and also that the agent was guilty of breach of duty. The same result might have been arrived at by a different process of reasoning — estoppel, rectification, or the view that the policy was not procured by a representation known to be contrary to the fact or mistaken. Knowledge derived from personal inspection of the person or thing insured, contemporaneous with the insurance, is wholly different in character and consequence from knowledge of a collateral matter affecting the risk, acquired previously and detached from the contract. I hold, therefore, that the knowledge acquired by Scollen in February, 1908, cannot affect the defendants, and that the case (as between plaintiff and defendants) must be dealt with as if Scollen had never heard of the refusal to renew. On that assumption, how does the matter stand?

---

[11] 12 A.C. 531.
[12] 21 Q.B.D. 144
[13] [1892] 2 Q.B. 534.

Scollen was the plaintiff's agent in filling the proposal, and the plaintiff is thereby bound. Sergeant Moriarty admits the point, which is indeed decided in *Biggar's Case*.[14] Taylor was an educated man, had effected many insurances, and was aware of the materiality of the refusal of February, 1908. He attempts to put the blame of the omission to disclose such refusal on Scollen; but, if the latter was his agent, such excuse is of no avail. Scollen, thinking only of his commission, was acting entirely outside the duty he owed the company; and Taylor who ought to have known this, cannot be heard to say otherwise, or to claim, by reason of Scollen's default, exoneration from the obligation to disclose the rejection known by him to be material....

Sanderson *v.* Cunningham and Others[*]
[1919] 2 I.R. 234
The Court of Appeal

SIR JAMES CAMPBELL C: The sole and only question for decision in this case is whether, upon its facts, the contract of insurance was completed in London or in Dublin; and the answer to this question must largely depend on the nature and extent of the authority of Coyle & Co., the insurance agents or brokers, who effected the insurance on behalf of the plaintiff.

We are all of opinion, differing in this respect from the judges in the King's Bench Division, upon the affidavits and correspondence in the case, that Coyle & Co. had full authority from the plaintiff to negotiate for and effect on his behalf the contract contained in the particular policy sued on. We are also satisfied that the proposal was for a specific policy, known to Coyle & Co. as a Dreadnought Motor policy, which to their knowledge would contain the conditions usual in a policy of this description, and, in the absence of any evidence or suggestion that the conditions of the policy in question were in any respect unusual in this sense, we must hold that plaintiff, through his authorised agents, received the precise form of policy for which he had bargained. We cannot therefore, accept the view upon which the King's Bench Division acted in holding that the proposal was for a Dreadnought policy which was to contain no conditions, or that the insertion of the usual conditions of such a policy required an opportunity for the inspection of the document by the plaintiff, or his authorised agents in Dublin, before the contract could be treated as complete. If the plaintiff, or Coyle & Co., upon the receipt of the policy, had objected to it on the ground that the conditions, in whole or in part, were not usual in a policy of this particular description, it would have been open to them to repudiate it at their risk in the event of it being subsequently found that the conditions were in fact only such as were usual; but this consideration cannot affect the question as to the venue in which the contract was completed.

---

[14] [1902] 1 K.B. 316.
[*] Extract.

Further, we are of opinion that in the circumstances of this case this contention on behalf of the plaintiff wholly fails upon another ground, because it appears from the correspondence that when the original policy was executed by the defendants, and received in Dublin by Coyle & Co., as the agents for the plaintiff, it was returned by them with a request for one alteration only, namely, a correction in the description in the policy of the particular vehicles to be insured. No objection whatever was taken at that time by Coyle & Co. to the conditions, which were in print, and were presumably the usual conditions in a Dreadnought policy; but the defendants, instead of returning it with the desired alteration, executed a fresh policy, which was precisely the same as the other in every respect, save as to the amended description.

These facts seem coercive as to the knowledge of Coyle & Co. that they had received a policy which agreed in form and effect with that for which they had proposed; and if it is the fact, as alleged on the part of the plaintiff, that this fresh policy was never seen by him, I think his acts, in subsequently refunding to Coyle & Co. the premium which, as their agents, they had paid on their account to the defendants, and in bringing this present claim upon foot of the policy, are coercive to the conclusion that Coyle & Co. had the fullest authority from him to complete the transaction.

It is always possible that a presumed acceptance of an offer may introduce a new term into the contract proposed, but the argument on behalf of the plaintiff would seem to lead to this, that in every contract the person who makes the offer is entitled by law to a reasonable interval in order to enable him to determine whether the acceptance is in fact in strict compliance with the offer, and that consequently the contract can never legally be complete until he has been afforded such an opportunity — a contention which is directly in conflict with the principles which determine the completion of contract in all cases of an offer, followed by an unqualified acceptance. In this case we are of opinion that when the defendants executed the fresh policy and forwarded it from London to the authorised agents of the plaintiff, they both in fact and in law accepted the precise proposal that had been made to them, and consequently completed the contract. The contract was complete at the latest when, by forwarding the policy from London to Coyle & Co. in Dublin, they thereby communicated their acceptance of the proposal to the agents of the plaintiff, and as this was done in London we must reverse the order appealed from, and discharge the order for services of the writ outside the jurisdiction, with costs both here and below. It only remains to add that our decision in no way conflicts with any of the Irish authorities that were cited in argument, as in each of them the Insurance Company had an agent in Dublin to whom they forwarded the policy for delivery to the insured, so that the communication of the acceptance by this act of delivery and the consequent completion of the contract took place in Ireland.

RONAN L.J. AND O'CONNOR L.J. CONCURRED IN SEPARATE SHORT JUDGMENTS.

Richard Curtis, Trading as Agencies Transport *v.* Corcoran Insurance Limited
Unreported, 13 July 1973
The High Court

PRINGLE J: The Plaintiff, who has been carrying on business as a Haulage Contractor for thirty years, claims damages against the Defendants who are Insurance Brokers and Consultants. The claim is based alternatively on two grounds — first that the Defendants were guilty of a breach of contract in failing to carry out the Plaintiff's instructions to insure comprehensively a Ford Tractor unit and Trailer Registered Number RZU 65 and alternatively that they were guilty of breach of contract or negligence on failing to advise the Plaintiff fully and properly in regard to the insurance of the said vehicle. That the Plaintiff sustained loss to the extent of £5000 owing to damage to the vehicle in an accident which occurred on 2nd January 1970 and that it was not at the time of this accident comprehensively insured is not in dispute and the questions in issue are (1) were the Defendants instructed by the Plaintiff to have comprehensive insurance cover effected for this vehicle and (2) if not, was there a breach of duty by the Defendants in not advising him to have comprehensive insurance effected and (3) if so, did this breach of duty cause the loss sustained by the Plaintiff?

The Plaintiff first employed the Defendants to act as his Insurance Brokers in the month of March 1969 in connection with all his insurance business which had previously been carried out by another company. A Schedule of his various existing insurances was prepared by the Defendants and he was advised to, and did, take out certain further policies in regard to employment insurance, public liability etc., and on 9th September 1969 he was sent by Mr William O'Brien, the Defendants' manager, a report on his insurance policies which set out particulars of six policies with The Yorkshire Insurance Company and two with The Royal Insurance Company. The policies in regard to vehicles were all with The Yorkshire and they consisted of three different policies, one for three private vehicles, which were shown as being insured third party, fire, theft, open driving, one for general haulage (referred to in evidence as the Fleet or Block Policy) showing five vehicles covered third party and fire, and third for special types of vehicles comprising three vehicles, a "Conveyancer" valued at £3,000, which was covered comprehensively, and two Fork Lifts each valued at £1,000 which were covered only for hire and reward, third party and fire.

On or about Friday 17th October 1969 the Plaintiff acquired the new vehicle in question at a purchase price of £6,718 and on 20th October 1969 he entered into a hire purchase agreement with The Hire Purchase Company of Ireland in respect of this vehicle, the hire purchase price being £7819.8.0. This agreement contained an agreement by the Plaintiff, in Clause 1 (h) thereof, immediately at his own expense to insure the vehicle comprehensively against all risks including loss or damage by fire, theft and accident and to keep it insured throughout the period of hiring, which was for three years. The purpose for which the Plaintiff acquired this particular vehicle was to enable him to carry out a contract which he was at the time negotiating with Irish Shell Limited to transport their oil from Manchester via Liverpool to Dublin. This of course involved bringing the vehicle by sea forwards and backwards to England.

Before the hire-purchase agreement was entered into, the Plaintiff spoke to Mr O'Brien on the telephone on 17th October 1969 in regard to insurance cover for the vehicle. There is a conflict of evidence as to what was said in the course of this conversation. The Plaintiff says that he told Mr O'Brien about the purchase of the vehicle, the purpose for which it was required and its value, and he swore that he told Mr O'Brien that he wanted "proper" insurance cover on it and that Mr O'Brien gave him temporary cover. He also swore that he told Mr O'Brien that he wanted the cover on a Van Registered Number HZE 253 suspended from that day, as he had not work for it at that particular moment. He said he told Mr O'Brien that he wanted the cover on this van suspended indefinitely. This van was one of the vehicles which was insured third party and fire only on the "Fleet" Policy referred to in Mr O'Brien's report of 9th September 1969. Mr O'Brien's version of this conversation is that the Plaintiff told him of the purchase of the vehicle and said that he wanted it included in the Commercial Vehicle Policy, that is the Fleet Policy, and that he wanted another vehicle HZE 253 deleted from that Policy. He agreed that he was given a description of the vehicle, its registered letters and numbers and its value, £5,200 on the Tractor and £1,200 on the Trailer. He said that he had no recollection of the word "proper" being used and that he thinks it was not used, as if it had been, he would have asked for clarification. He also said that he had no recollection of the Plaintiff using the word "suspended" in regard to the cover on the Van. He was quite clear that the Plaintiff made no reference to hire-purchase and the Plaintiff in cross-examination eventually agreed that this was so.

The Plaintiff admitted that he would not say that he had a good memory and I am satisfied that on a number of matters his memory is defective and his evidence, particularly in regard to the precise words used at any of the conversations deposed to is unreliable and, when contradicted by either Mr O'Brien or Mr Corcoran, I accept their evidence rather than that of the Plaintiff. Consequently I cannot accept that the words "proper insurance" were used by the Plaintiff and I accept Mr O'Brien's evidence that what the Plaintiff asked for was that the new vehicle was to be included in the Fleet Policy in place of the Van HZE 253. The Plaintiff does not contend that the agreement in relation to comprehensive cover on which he relies was reached on 17th October, but says that it was arrived at during a later conversation with Mr Corcoran on 23rd October 1969. Apparently the Plaintiff was under the impression that Mr O'Brien was only effecting temporary cover for the vehicle, but the evidence is that he was sent two Certificates of Insurance showing that the vehicle was covered from 17th October 1969 to 27th July 1970. One of those Certificates is dated 20th October 1969 and Mr O'Brien's evidence was that they were issued on 22nd October 1969, but they may not have reached the Plaintiff before the conversation on 23rd October. They should however have indicated to the Plaintiff that the vehicle was covered for a year, but of course they did not indicate the nature of this cover.

On 23rd October the Plaintiff rang Mr Corcoran the Proprietor of the Defendants, who had been a personal friend of his for many years and he swore that he then went down to see him at his office. Mr Corcoran says that the Plaintiff never came to his office that day and that the entire conversation took place on the telephone. This is one of the matters on which I think the Plaintiff's memory is at fault, but it is not of much importance where the conversation took place. It is agreed that Mr Curtis told Mr Corcoran that Irish Shell insisted on cover being obtained on their oil in transit. The Plaintiff swore that Mr Corcoran said "Well now Dick, there is a lot of money involved in RZU 65 and I advise you to have the vehicle, as well as the goods, comprehensively covered" and that he agreed. Mr Corcoran swore that what he told the Plaintiff was that, while the vehicle was on board ship, there would be no cover for damage to the vehicle, but only third party, and that Mr Curtis said "Fair enough, get me a quotation for that also". I am satisfied that the entire of this conversation related to the taking out of a Marine Policy and the Plaintiff said in his evidence that Mr Corcoran told him that he would require a special Marine Policy to cover the goods and vehicle on board ship and that a special policy would be required for this. Furthermore in a letter which Mr Curtis wrote to the Irish Shell on 28th October 1969 he said "Our brokers are having the insurance on the vehicle and *goods in transit* compiled. They advise us to have a fully comprehensive cover which we agreed to." This letter I think bears out the conversation related only to the insurance of the goods and vehicle in transit.

The Plaintiff relies on this conversation as constituting an agreement by the Defendants to have comprehensive cover effected on the vehicle for all purposes and not limited to the period while it was on board ship. I am satisfied that the only agreement reached related to the cover of the vehicle while on board ship and the oil from door to door. It is unfortunate that Mr Corcoran did not consult Mr O'Brien or ask for the file to ascertain what cover already existed on the vehicle, but, as the conversation related solely to the question of a Marine Policy, his failure to do so is understandable. I do not accept the Plaintiff's evidence that he signed a Proposal Form that day or at all. After this conversation the matter of obtaining quotations for the Marine Policy was handed over by Mr Corcoran to Mr O'Brien and I am satisfied that telephone conversations took place between Mr O'Brien and Mr Curtis relating to the quotations obtained from the Insurance Corporation of Ireland, and by two letters both dated 20th November 1969, one relating to the cover on the oil from Manchester to Dublin and the other relating to the vehicle from Liverpool to Dublin were sent out by the Defendants to the Plaintiff confirming that the premium for the former was £125 and for the latter £100. Unfortunately the Plaintiff says he never received these letters which should have made it quite clear that the comprehensive cover on the vehicle was only while it was on board ship. I am satisfied that those letters were in fact sent and that they reached the Plaintiff's office but for some reason, probably due to his illness, were not seen by the Plaintiff himself and I accept that the first time he knew of these letters was when he received copies from the Defendants in January 1969 after the accident. These letters stated that the policy would reach the Plaintiff in a week, but I am satisfied that in fact what happened was that the policy had not reached the Plaintiff when, on December 15th, he notified the Defendants that shipments under the projected contract with Irish Shell had not started and that the marine cover was to be held up and the Insurance Company notified when shipments started.

I am not satisfied that there ever was any instruction given by the Plaintiff to the Defendants to insure the vehicle comprehensively, except for the time it was on board ship, and the Defendants were therefore in my opinion not guilty of any breach of contract in failing to carry out any instructions from the Plaintiff.

In arriving at the conclusions stated above as to the conversations of 17th and 23rd October, I was influenced by the fact that in conversations which took place after the accident the Plaintiff, when he was told that he had no comprehensive cover and therefore no claim, did not rely on any instructions given by him to the Defendants either on 23rd October or on 17th October. He simply said he thought he had comprehensive cover.

As regards the Plaintiff's alternative claim, it is pleaded that it was the duty of the Defendants to advise the Plaintiff fully and properly in regard to the insurance on the said vehicle, and to advise fully comprehensive insurance which by reason of (a) the terms of the H.P. Agreement under which the Plaintiff was purchasing the vehicle from the Hire Purchase Company of Ireland Limited and, (b) the value of the said vehicle in relation to the other vehicles owned by the Plaintiff and insured through the Defendants was the proper insurance.

The Plaintiff relies on the fact that the Defendants held themselves out to be not only Insurance Brokers but Consultants. Mr Ellis contended that under the circumstances existing, there was a legal duty on the Defendants to advise the Plaintiff that he should have this valuable vehicle comprehensively insured, or at least to point out the options which were open to him, so that he could decide whether to have it comprehensively insured or not. It was submitted that there was a particular duty in the circumstances of this case on the Defendants to advise the Plaintiff fully because of the fact that this vehicle was so much more valuable than the other vehicles insured under the existing Fleet Policy and by reason of the fact that it was the subject matter of a Hire Purchase Agreement which the Defendants ought to have known would contain a covenant to insure it comprehensively. Furthermore the Defendants were aware, as Mr Corcoran admitted in his evidence, that Mr Curtis "left a little to be desired business-wise". Mr Ellis further submitted that if the instructions given by the Plaintiff were vague or ambiguous there was at least a duty on the Defendants to enquire from him what type of insurance he required.

Mr Murphy, in reply to these submissions, contended that the instructions which were given by the Plaintiff to Mr Curtis were quite clear, that is to say that the vehicle was to be included in the Fleet Policy in the place of the Austin Van and that the Defendants were entitled to assume that the Plaintiff was aware from the report furnished to him in September that all the vehicles insured under this policy were only insured third-party and fire. In regard to the vehicle being the subject matter of a Hire-Purchase Agreement, Mr Murphy submitted that the evidence established this fact was not brought to the Defendants' notice and I accept that this was so, and, as I have pointed out, this was admitted by the Plaintiff in his evidence. Mr Murphy submitted that there is no duty cast on an Insurance Broker or Consultant to advise a client as to what particular form of cover he should have unless he is asked for advice, or unless his instructions are ambiguous and that, even if his instructions are not clear, the Broker is not liable if he bona fide acts on a reasonable interpretation of his instructions. I think that this submission of the law is correct and is borne out by the decision in the case of *James Vall and Co.* v. *Van Oppen and Co. Limited.*[15] In that case the Plaintiffs had engaged the Defendants, who were shipping agents to insure certain goods which were to be carried from Leeds to Barcelona. Their instructions were to insure "against all risks". One of the bales of goods was never delivered and the Plaintiffs failed to recover from the Insurance Company because the Policy effected by the Defendants did not cover non-delivery. The evidence established that the Policy did not cover all risks covered by an ordinary Marine Policy and Mr Justice Roche held that the Defendants were not liable. In his judgment he said

> "No doubt the Plaintiffs might have intended to instruct the agent to obtain the widest possible insurance but the question was whether he understood his instructions in another sense, and if so, whether it was reasonable for him to do so."

The learned Judge then held that a reasonably competent agent could have understood the instructions as the Defendants had done and that they were not therefore guilty of negligence. Finally Mr Murphy submitted that even if there was a breach of duty by the Defendants, it had not been established that this breach caused the damage sustained by the Plaintiff as the latter, who was according to Mr Corcoran "cost-conscious", might have decided that he would not go to the expense of having comprehensive cover and furthermore it might not have been possible to obtain comprehensive cover for the vehicle.

The duty of an Insurance Broker to his client is in my opinion the same as that of any other agent, to his principal, that is to say he is under a legal duty to exercise reasonable care and skill in the performance of the duty which he undertakes under the particular circumstances existing. The question of whether reasonable care and skill has been exercised is a question of fact and the evidence of persons engaged in the same profession is admissible as to what would, in the circumstances, have been reasonable care and skill (See *Chapman* v. *Walton*[16]). Mr Henry Barnewell, an experienced Insurance Broker, gave expert evidence on behalf of the Plaintiff. He said that in his opinion the duties of a person who held himself out as a Consultant were higher than those of an ordinary Insurance Broker and that his duty was to advise a client who was insuring a new vehicle as to the type of cover which he should seek. He said that if a client said he wanted to substitute a new vehicle worth £6,400 for a vehicle worth £200 on an existing policy, a prudent broker would at least suggest to the client that he should try for comprehensive cover. He agreed that it would be very unusual for a person involved in the transport business for a number of years not to know the difference between third-party and comprehensive cover. Mr O'Brien in his

---

[15] [1921] 37 TLR 367.
[16] [1833] 10 Bing 57.

evidence agreed that, if a client's instructions were not clear as to the type of insurance which he required, his duty would be to ask him what his requirements were, but he said that his instructions were quite clear, namely to substitute one vehicle for another in an existing Policy under which there was only third-party and fire, and as nothing was said by Mr Curtis indicating that the cover which he required was to be different from that of the other vehicles on the Policy, he assumed that no alteration in the cover under the Policy was required. I have already said that I am satisfied that Mr Curtis *did* indicate to Mr O'Brien that what he required was that the new vehicle would be included in the Fleet Policy in the place of the Van. In his evidence the Plaintiff did say in answer to a question from me as to whether there was any connection between his instructions as to the two vehicles "No connection whatsoever only that we had a Fleet Policy which was held to ten vehicles and by suspending this we had ten vehicles at that time and on the suspension of HZE, RZU came into the picture at the same time the Van was suspended". I think it is unfortunate that Mr O'Brien did not say so to Mr Curtis "You know that this means that "your new van will only be covered third-party and fire", but in my opinion it was reasonable for him to assume that when Mr Curtis asked for the new vehicle to be included in the place of the Van in the Fleet Policy, he knew that this meant that it would not be comprehensively insured. Mr O'Brien's instructions were not in my opinion ambiguous and there was no legal duty imposed on him to enquire what type of cover was required or to advise that the vehicle should be covered comprehensively. The position would probably have been different if he had been dealing with a client who was simply asking him to obtain cover on a valuable new vehicle. I consider that Mr O'Brien was not guilty of any breach of duty to the Plaintiff. In regard to Mr Corcoran as I have said I am satisfied that the conversation which he had with the Plaintiff on 23rd October was solely concerned with Marine Insurance and there was in my opinion no duty on him, either as a Broker or Consultant to advise the Plaintiff on his road traffic cover on the vehicle unless he had been asked for advice, and he too was not guilty of any breach of duty to the Plaintiff. In regard to the question as to whether, if there had been a breach of duty, the onus of proving that this breach of duty caused the damage which the Plaintiff sustained, was discharged, I would have held that on the balance of probabilities the Plaintiff (notwithstanding his cost-consciousness) would have decided to insure the vehicle comprehensively having regard to its value and his obligations under the Hire Purchase Agreement and I also think that such cover would probably have been obtainable. There is one further submission on behalf of the Plaintiff with which I have not dealt and that is that the Defendants were guilty of a breach of duty in not notifying within a reasonable time of the nature of the cover which they had obtained. I think it is very unfortunate that they did not do so, but again I think it cannot be said that the Defendants were not reasonable in assuming that they had carried out their instructions. Furthermore I agree with the decision of Mr Justice

McNair in the case of *United Mills Agencies Ltd.* v. *R.E. Harvey Bray and Co.*[17] In that case one of the grounds upon which it was sought to hold the Defendants liable for Negligence was that they failed to notify the Plaintiffs promptly of the cover obtained. In fact the Defendants in that case notified the Plaintiffs three days after the insurance had been placed, but unfortunately the goods were destroyed by fire before this notification reached the Plaintiffs and they were not covered by the Policy effected by the Defendants. Mr Justice McNair said

> "On that point, evidence was called from an independent broker — and I think substantially agreed to by Mr Davey — that it is the practice of, at any rate, these two offices of Insurance Brokers (and I have no doubt the practice of brokers as a whole) that when cover has been placed, the clients are notified as soon as possible. That seems to be good business and prudent office management, but on the evidence, I am completely unable to hold that it is part of the duty owed by the broker to the client so to notify him, in the sense that a failure so to notify him would involve him in legal liability. No case was cited in which any broker had ever been held liable or had ever paid any client money in respect of such a failure. It seems to me to put quite an intolerable and unreasonable burden on a broker to say that as a matter of law, apart from prudent practice, he is bound to forward the cover note as soon as possible. It is no doubt prudent to do so, both to allay the client's anxiety, and possibly to enable the client to check the terms of insurance. That is a very different thing from saying that it is part of his duty."

I agree with this statement of the legal position. It certainly was contrary to good practice for the Defendants not to notify the Plaintiff as to the cover effected as soon as possible, but I do not consider that their failure to do so renders them liable. I cannot but be sorry for the Plaintiff in the serious loss which he sustained and which I believe he has convinced himself was due to the default of the Defendants, but in my opinion he has no claim in law against them and this action must accordingly be dismissed.

Amethyst Limited (in liquidation) *v.* Galway Insurance Brokers Limited and Raymond P. McGovern on behalf of certain Underwriters at Lloyds
Unreported, 16 May 1991
The High Court

BARRON J.: The premises of the Plaintiff Company at Williamscourt, Limerick were destroyed by fire on the 1st of July 1985. The Company believed itself to have been insured against this risk in respect of its stock in trade, its fittings and fixtures and in respect of consequential loss. Owing to the negligence of the Defendant, its insurance brokers, the insurances were not in

---

[17] [1952] 1 T.L.R. 149.

place. The present proceedings are brought to recover damages for that negligence. The sole issue is as to the measure of damages. There is no dispute as to the amount recoverable in respect of stock in trade and fittings and fixtures. This sum amounts to £29,386. There is however a dispute as to the amount now payable in respect of the failure by the Defendant to obtain cover for the Plaintiff for consequential loss.

The Plaintiff makes its claims under two heads. First, it claims such sum as it would have recovered by way of insurance moneys if the cover had been effected: secondly, it claims loss of profits by reason of not having received these moneys. The evidence given on behalf of the Plaintiff sought to establish an anticipated growth in turnover which would have translated itself into a growth of profits. The evidence on behalf of the Defendant approached the matter on a similar basis. This evidence contested the rate of growth and suggested a much slower rate of growth. It was also submitted that the Plaintiff should have ceased trading sooner than it did and that this would have avoided such trading losses as it incurred after such date.

The Plaintiff Company was at all material times beneficially owned by Taghd Kearney. He had a number of years experience in the retail jewellery trade in Limerick. He had managed the Limerick Branch of a Galway firm for several years at its premises at No. 2, O'Connell Street, Limerick. From 1981 he had run the same branch in his own name but on a smaller scale. In November 1983 he moved to new premises in Williamscourt which were run by the Plaintiff but under the name of its owner. These premises had a large window frontage to William Street. They form part of a new shopping centre created out of premises previously used as a drapery store. Following the fire, the Plaintiff was out of business for five months and then opened on a temporary basis in premises at 109 O'Connell Street pending the reconstruction of the Williamscourt property. Premises in Williamscourt were ready for occupation in June 1987. The Plaintiff moved back into these premises at that time but as a result of bad trading results closed the business in June 1988. It was subsequently wound up by the Court and a liquidator appointed on the 24th of October 1988.

The sum for which the Plaintiff ought to have been insured for consequential loss was the sum of £50,000 per year for a period of two years. The amount payable was to be the loss of gross profit due to (a) reduction in turnover and (b) increase in cost of working, less any sum saved during the indemnity period in respect of such of the charges and expenses of the business payable out of gross profit as might cease or be reduced in consequence of the damage. The policy further contained a proviso for reduction of the amount payable in the event of underinsurance. In order to arrive at the amount which would have been covered it was necessary to consider what turnover might have been achieved and what expenses would have been incurred in arriving at that turnover. For the purpose of the policy the relevant turnover was the anticipated turnover during the two years following the fire.

The evidence adduced on behalf of both parties concentrated on the increase in turnover which might have been anticipated. Both parties used actual turnover figures before the fire to justify the figures which they gave in evidence. In addition the Plaintiff relied on the business experience of its sole beneficial shareholder to justify the rate of expansion suggested. The

Defendant on the other hand regarded increases in profits as being generally of a minimal nature. There was no real evidence given as to how the projected level of expenses was calculated. It was clear from the evidence on behalf of the Plaintiff that it was not a guess, even an educated one, because there was reference to allowance for additional sales' staff, but no real details were given in evidence. For the Defendant, expenses were increased in the first projected year at half the rate of the projected increase in turnover, but again there was no real breakdown given. Another problem in determining the likely course of the Plaintiff's business is that neither party purported to show how the break in trade in the premises in Williamscourt would have affected the Plaintiff's results on its return to those premises. Other matters which were not dealt with in evidence were the source of additional capital to finance the Plaintiff's expansion, the cost of such capital and the effect of underinsurance. It seems to me that as no evidence was given on many of these matters that I must draw only such inferences as are reasonably clear from the evidence as a whole. I propose therefore to confine myself to a resolution of the issues raised in evidence save where it seems to me that this will not give a true result.

It is clear from the evidence that the performance of the business of the Plaintiff depended upon two things: the name Kearney and the location of its premises. There are no longer records of the business being carried on before its move to Williamscourt. There is however nothing to suggest that its trading was specially dependant upon its name. It seems probable that its trading suffered from the number of other retail jewellers in O'Connell Street and its relatively poor position vis à vis such traders. Its move to Williamscourt may have shown an immediate improvement. I doubt that however because its first 13 months' trading achieved for Mr Kearney a salary of £10,000 a year plus profits of £2,000, which was hardly a return commensurate with his position in the Limerick business world. Nevertheless it is probable that he expected better and these expectations were beginning to be fulfilled when the fire occurred. Having regard to what occurred when the Plaintiff reopened temporarily in O'Connell Street after the fire, it seems probable that this increase in trade was accounted for by the location of the premises rather than by its trading name. The premises in which the Plaintiff reopened temporarily were at 109 O'Connell Street which was relatively as poor a position as the original premises in O'Connell Street had been. I think therefore that it is reasonable to suppose that if the Company had been properly capitalised on its return to Williamscourt that it would have been profitable. My reference to properly capitalised is intended to mean that it had sufficient capital or credit to expand in accordance with the plans of its management. It is hard however to see it trading in its first or even second year after its return to its premises following the two year disruption caused by the fire as if during those two years it had traded as it would have done had there been no fire.

In the two years following the fire, the claim is for both loss of insurance moneys payable on the consequential loss policy and for loss attributable to non-payment of those moneys when they should have been paid. These two claims are not mutually exclusive. The more that is technically recoverable under the second heading, the less in theory would be payable under the first heading. This has been recognised by the witnesses who dealt with these matters since they concentrate on the actual turnover to establish the loss of profits. I think that this is a reasonable approach but in effect the evidence has not segregated the two claims. The Plaintiff does seek to claim actual losses during this period, but in the absence of evidence as to how the consequential loss element would have been lessened, I am not in a position to assess the appropriate figures.

The turnover figures produced for the trading period before the fire have confused the issue. There are in fact several set of figures, not through any dishonesty, but because the Plaintiff in addition to its real business dealt also in the first six months of trading in buying and exporting gold. Some of this turnover appeared in its VAT returns although it was not subject to VAT while other of it did not. Again although the entire turnover appeared in the accounts the turnover kept by the Plaintiff did not include this aspect of the business. Because of these different figures, a correlation between turnover figures for 1984 and 1985 produced a different trend from that shown by the figures for VAT returns.

The sales' records for the period January to June 1984 showed a turnover of £27,477. The sales' records for the same period in 1985 which ended with the fire showed a turnover of £51,020; an actual increase of 85.9% over the previous year. The VAT returns for the same period in 1984 showed sales of £36,287. The VAT returns for the same period in 1985 showed sales of £50,421; an actual increase of 39%. Evidence of the likely progress of the Plaintiff was given by Hans Droog, a partner in Ernst and Young. Relying upon what he was told by Mr Kearney as to the latter's expectations he anticipated that the turnover for the remainder of 1984 would have been increased in the months of July, August and September by 100% over the previous year; in October and November by 85% and in December by 120%. He projected a further increase during 1986 at a rate of 50% of this increased turnover and thereafter for 1987 at a further 25% increase, for 1988 and 1989 15%, for 1990 20%, for 1991 15% and for 1992 12%. On the basis of these projections the projected turnover was indicated by him to be for the years ending 30th of June 1986 £194,000; for the year ending 1987 £272,000; for the year ending 1988 £331,000; for the year ending 1989 £380,000; for the year ending 1990 £444,000; for the year ending 1991 £525,000; and for the year ending 30th of June 1992 £598,000. The actual turnover for the periods of trading after the fire were: for the year ending the 30th of June 1986 £47,657; for the year ending 30th of June 1987 £82,683; and for the year ending 30th of June 1988 — taken from the VAT returns — £72,680. On behalf of the Defendants, William Twamley, a Chartered Accountant and a member of Loss Adjusters, Aston and Associates, specialising in consequential loss claims, gave evidence based on the 39% increase in the VAT returns between the figures for the first six months of 1984 and those for the same six months in 1985. He also allowed further increases for the year 1985 at 8%, for the year 1986 at 8%, for the year 1987 at 5% and for the year 1988 at 6%. He took these fig-ures as a result of enquiries which he made of increase in turnover figures for a retail concern with five outlets in the South of Ireland. However he had no details of the turnover of these outlets nor of the individual figures for each outlet.

In dealing with expenses which might have been anticipated, Mr Droog estimated that overheads for the period for the two years ending 30th of June 1987 would have been £158,000 whereas the actual overheads for those two years allowing for the fact that the Plaintiff was not trading for the first five months after the fire were £112,000. Mr Twamley on the other hand estimated projected overheads at £147,000 and actual overheads at £101,000. His projected turnover figure for the two years was £313,000.

It was agreed that the gross profit on turnover should be calculated at the rate of 49.4%. In arriving at the appropriate figure payable under the consequential loss policy it was also necessary to consider the expenses incurred which would not otherwise have been incurred. There was again a considerable difference of opinion between the two witnesses. Mr Droog had to revise his figures in the course of the evidence since they had not been calculated in accordance with the policy. Ultimately his figures for the increase in cost of working were increased bank interest £6,499, increased insurance £5,766, increased rent £10,911 and cost of temporary premises £14,000 which came to a figure of £37,176. Mr Twamley on the other hand allowed only £1,000 for insurances, nothing for bank interest and accepted the other two figures.

It was clear from the figures that the proviso for averaging contained in the policy would have had to have been applied. Taking Mr Droog's figures in their entirety the claim came to £68,226. Applying Mr Twamley's figures the amount payable under the policy would have been £45,000.

Although they reached the figure for savings by a different route both witnesses arrived at the same figure, that is £46,000 for this item. Where the difference arises is on the figure for loss of gross profit and on the figure for increased cost of working. In the course of the hearing it became apparent that Mr Twamley was correct in a number of matters in relation to the calculation of the amount payable under the consequential loss policy. Accordingly it seems to me that his figure of £26,000 for increased cost of working is more reliable than the figure of Mr Droog. However it does seem to me that he has underestimated the figure for interest and the figure for insurances. In practice he accepted that insurers would probably have allowed some sum for interest and his figure for insurance is set out as a negotiating figure. In the circumstances I propose to allow £30,000 for this item. As regards the anticipated gross profit it seems to me that Mr Twamley is wrong to have relied upon the 39% increase for the VAT returns. The figures for turnover show 85% increase over the last six months of trading. I think it reasonable that this would have continued and would have continued at something like the increase which Mr Droog with the assistance of Mr Kearney has calculated. There may be some excess in this figure and I propose to allow the figure of £300,000 instead. As a result the claim will read.

(a) Gross profit reduction on turnover 49% times £300,000		£147,000
(b) Gross profit reduction on increase in cost of working		£30,000
	Total	£177,000
Less cost saving		£46, 000
	Total	£131,000

As a result the calculation for underinsurance will have to be altered. The gross profit is now on a budgeted turnover of £430,340. Forty nine per cent [of] that comes to £210,867. The equation accordingly is 100,000 times £131,000 over £210,867 which comes to £62,124.

As I have already indicated I do not propose to allow anything in respect of the actual loss sustained during this two year period. It is necessary now to consider what losses were incurred by reason of the failure of the Plaintiff to receive its insurance moneys in time. The evidence shows that these moneys would have been received before the premises would have reopened in the beginning of December 1985. Accordingly it seems to me that none of the post-fire trading experience would have occurred anyway.

The Plaintiff's figures were criticised upon a number of bases. It was suggested that the Plaintiff's stock levels at the time of the fire belied the projections. Evidence was given that a retail jeweller turned over his stock one and a half times in a year. The stock at the time of the fire was £50,000; average mark up was 100%; so turnover for the year could be taken at £150,000. This is however in my view a rather crude method of arriving at a correct projection, though I accept that it is not unreasonable to use it as Mr Twamley did as a yardstick to confirm figures reached by a different route. However, £50,000 was put forward as having been an increase in stock. Allowing for the fact that the stock of the 31st of December 1984 was £35,500 and that the stock sold in December before mark-up represented purchases of some £10,500, £50,000 represented stock levels very nearly 10% higher than those obtaining at the beginning of the busiest month in the year. It seems to me to justify a belief that business was increasing substantially and that the following months would increase in tourist traffic. Even with the increased turnover in January/June the Plaintiff would have expected a turnover considerably less than in the previous December and yet had a larger stock. The projected rate of increase in turnover was said to be too high. I accept the 85% increase in turnover as a reasonable starting point for the second half of 1985. I also see nothing impossible about projecting a continuation of a trend with only marginal acceleration both on the basis of actual figures and the stock figures. Commonsense also indicates that if some businesses did not grow at these sort of rates but at those suggested by Mr Twamley that businessmen would be more inclined to seek employment with others and to put their money in Government bonds than to take the risks inherent in trading.

My problem is to accept that turnover on the business' return to Williamscourt would have been at the level at which it has been projected, as if there had been no fire. There is also difficulty in accepting the figure for expenses. It may be that the additional turnover in the year 1985 would have merely taken up spare capacity and that it could have been as was in fact for the first six months achieved without employment of extra staff and other additional expenses.

Once the Williamscourt premises reopened, the Plaintiff's difficulties became apparent. When it opened in O'Connell Street after being out of business for five months it was not really affected by the loss of its insurance moneys. Yet its turnover was on a par with that achieved at Williamscourt two years before. Having regard to my view that the latter location was superior, it seems to me that some of the increased turnover had stayed with the Plaintiff. It was soon lost as is reflected in the turnover figures which stagnated. As a result when the Plaintiff returned to Williamscourt it had lost the benefits of its trading success in those premises before the fire. Accordingly its trading pattern bore no relation to what it would have been. It had lost more than its goodwill; it was severely restricted by financial considerations which had also affected its O'Connell Street trading. Even if there had been no problems with payment of the insurance moneys, the disruption caused by the fire must have had an impact. There was also the matter of underinsurance. Still it seems to me that the impact of this could well have been cushioned by leaving the profits in the business.

To arrive at a realistic scenario for the period July 1987 to June 1992, it seems to me that I should concentrate more on net profits than on turnover. While the 1985 turnover might well have been accommodated by little increase in expenses, it seems to me that there would have been a much closer relationship between turnover and expenses thereafter.

The experience of December 1985 suggests that July 1987 to June 1988 would have produced a turnover somewhere between the 1984 and the 1985 projected figures. Assuming £150,000 this would have resulted in an approximate break-even position. Similarly assuming somewhere between 1985 and 1984 figures for the following year's turnover then if this is taken at £240,00, it should give a net profit of around £25,000 allowing for an increase in expenses in the manner I have indicated. Thereafter with a closer relationship between turnover and expenses, I would accept a net profit averaging £30,000 a year.

It has been suggested that the Plaintiff ought to have closed in Williamscourt once it found that it was trading at a loss. I accept that the Plaintiff could not have continued trading at a loss indefinitely in Williamscourt. However I consider it reasonable for the Plaintiff to have continued for a year in those premises. It was clear at that stage that it would have been unreasonable to have continued. Accordingly I propose to allow the loss sustained during that period. It is the Plaintiff's wish to have the liquidation annulled. If so then there is a further £31,000 of liquidation expenses to be provided for. In my view this must be allowed as part of the claim against the Defendant.

There will be judgment for the two sums which would have been received as insurance moneys, for the sum of £115,000 for loss of profits, for the trading loss from the reopening of the business in Williamscourt to the closure of the business, and for the legal and liquidator's expenses attributable to the winding-up.

Dermot Latham *v.* Hibernian Insurance Company Limited & Peter J. Sheridan & Company Limited (No. 2)
Unreported, 4 December 1991
The High Court

BLAYNEY J: In a Judgment delivered on the 22nd March of this year[18] I dismissed the Plaintiff's claim against the first named Defendant and held that the second named Defendant is liable to the Plaintiff for damages for breach of contract and negligence. I now have to assess the damages.

The detailed facts of the case are set out in my previous Judgment so all that needs to be done now is to summarise those which are relevant to the issue of damages.

The Plaintiff owned No. 22 Bridge Street, Ringsend, a three storey building on the ground floor of which was a shop. The shop was opened in the month of May 1983 and the business continued until the 25th May 1985 when the building was destroyed by fire.

The second named Defendant is a Company carrying on the business of an insurance broker. The business is managed by Mr Peter Sheridan. The Plaintiff retained Mr Sheridan to insure No. 22 Bridge Street with the Hibernian Insurance Company. Mr Sheridan duly obtained a policy from the Hibernian in August 1983 covering all the usual risks for a shop business and the policy was renewed for 12 months from the 31st August 1984.

Prior to the policy being renewed, the Plaintiff, on the 22nd November 1983 was arrested and charged with receiving stolen goods. Mr Sheridan heard of this but failed to advise the Plaintiff, when the policy was being renewed in August 1984 that this circumstance had to be disclosed to the Insurance Company. The Plaintiff himself was not aware that it ought to be disclosed. By reason of the non-disclosure the policy of insurance was repudiated by the Hibernian. In my previous Judgment I held that they were entitled to do so. The issue to be decided now is what damages the Plaintiff should be awarded to compensate him for the loss and damage sustained as the result of Mr Sheridan's negligence in failing to advise him that the fact of his having been arrested and charged ought to have been disclosed to the Hibernian when the policy was being renewed in August 1984.

The issue is an extremely difficult one. At first sight the measure of damages would appear to be what the Plaintiff would have recovered from the Hibernian under his policy of insurance with them if they had not been entitled to repudiate it. But this assumes that were it not for the negligence of Mr Sheridan the Plaintiff could have recovered under his policy with the Hibernian. But such is not the case. The evidence at the previous hearing, which I accepted, was that if the fact of the Plaintiff having been arrested and charged had been disclosed to the Hibernian, as it ought to have been, they would have refused to renew the policy, and furthermore, no insurance company in Ireland would have been prepared to accept the risk either. So the position is that if Mr Sheridan had not been negligent, but had advised the

---

[18] See Chapter 7, p. 272.

Plaintiff to make the necessary disclosure, insofar as having insurance cover from the Hibernian was concerned, the Plaintiff would have been in no better position. The Hibernian would have refused to give him cover. So it was not Mr Sheridan's negligence that was the cause of the Plaintiff not being covered by the Hibernian, it was in fact that he had been arrested and charged with receiving stolen goods.

So it seems to me that the loss attributable to Mr Sheridan's negligence has to be approached in a different way. One has to look at what the position would have been had Mr Sheridan not been negligent, that is to say, if he had advised the Plaintiff that he had to disclose to the Hibernian on the renewal of the policy that he had been arrested and charged, and was awaiting trial. If Mr Sheridan had done this, the Hibernian would have refused to renew the policy and the Plaintiff would then have had the opportunity of seeking insurance elsewhere.

The question that has to be considered then is whether he would have been able to obtain such insurance. I am satisfied on the evidence given at the original hearing that he would not have been able to obtain insurance in Ireland. Once the Plaintiff had been refused by the Hibernian, none of the other companies here would have been prepared to take him on. But there was still the possibility of seeking insurance in England from a Lloyd's syndicate or from some other insurance company there. Whether this was a possibility only, or whether it was probable that the Plaintiff could have got insurance there, was something on which very little evidence was given. The Plaintiff called a single witness and Mr Sheridan did not offer any evidence at all.

The Plaintiff's witness was Mr Peter Hanlon, an Insurance Broker from the firm of Messrs McMahon, Galvin and Keeney. He said that in February of this year he was asked to get a quotation for insurance for the Plaintiff for a shop business, disclosing that the Plaintiff had been convicted of receiving stolen goods three years previously. He said that he had got a quotation from Lloyds, but that none of the Irish companies were prepared to quote. The rates quoted by Lloyds were between 25% and 50% higher than the normal rates.

The onus of proof is on the Plaintiff to prove what damage and loss he suffered as a result of Mr Sheridan's negligence. If he is to be awarded what he should have recovered if he had been insured, which is the main basis on which his claim is put, he must prove that he could have obtained insurance in England. While the evidence offered to establish this is slight, as no evidence has been produced by Mr Sheridan to contest it, I consider it is adequate to discharge the onus of proof. I accept Mr Hanlon's evidence that he was able to get a quotation from Lloyds for the Plaintiff, disclosing his conviction for receiving stolen goods, and I consider that on the balance of probabilities the Plaintiff would have been able to get a similar quotation in August 1984.

I am satisfied also that the Plaintiff would probably have sought insurance cover in England. While he said in his evidence that he did not know what he would have done if the Hibernian had refused to renew his policy in August 1984, his partner, Mr Oliver Byrne, said that he would have tried to get insurance in England and I have little doubt that he would have adopted this course. The only alternatives would have been to carry on without insurance, something that no sensible businessman would have done, or to have sold the business, which I think the Plaintiff would have been slow to do as both he and Mr Byrne considered that it was very profitable.

In the circumstances I propose to approach the assessment of damages on the basis that the Plaintiff would have been able to obtain insurance cover with Lloyds and that such cover would have been in existence at the date of the fire in May 1985. As to the nature of the cover, I think I am entitled to assume that it would have been similar to what was provided by the Hibernian policy at the time of the fire, that is, cover for the building, the stock, fixtures and fittings, and loss of profits for one year.

This cover corresponds to three of the categories of loss in respect of which the Plaintiff is claiming, but with this qualification, that in respect of loss of profits the claim is for a continuing loss up to the present. I will deal separately with each of these items of loss later on. In addition the Plaintiff claims for the loss of the rent from six flats which were over the shop. I am not prepared to allow this claim. There was no cover for the loss of rent in the Hibernian policy which included the following memo:

> "The building is occupied by the insured as a retail sales shop and otherwise as a private dwelling."

There is no reason to believe that the Plaintiff would have sought different cover when applying to Lloyds, and accordingly nothing could have been recovered under the policy in respect of loss of rent from the flats. This being so, the Plaintiff cannot recover such loss from Mr Sheridan.

Before entering on the details of the Plaintiff's damage and loss it is necessary to refer to something which has an important bearing on the amount of the Plaintiff's claim. The Plaintiff, under the malicious injury code, obtained an award of compensation from Dublin Corporation for the damage caused by the fire. The amount of the compensation was agreed between the Corporation's assessor and the Plaintiff's assessors at the sum of £66,370.07, being £48,460 for the reinstatement of the building, and £17,890.37 for the stock, fixtures and fittings in the flats and the shop. This sum was agreed, with a statutory deduction of £100, in October 1988. Whatever figure I ultimately determine as being the amount of the Plaintiff's loss will have to be reduced by the amount which he recovered from Dublin Corporation. The Plaintiff's loss has been mitigated by the compensation he received.

I will now consider separately each of the heads of claim.

1. *The Building*
The first issue to be decided is whether the Plaintiff's loss should be calculated on the basis of an indemnity or on the basis of reinstatement. And this depends on the nature of the cover which the Plaintiff would have obtained from Lloyds. The Plaintiff's loss is limited to what he would have recovered under the policy. As I indicated earlier, I am assuming that the cover would have been similar to that contained in the Hibernian Policy. At the time of the fire, this provided for an indemnity only. So it seems to me that the correct approach is to see what the Plaintiff's loss would have been on the basis of an indemnity. But there is a difficulty in following this approach. The only evidence given was much more relevant to reinstatement. Mr Brian Whelan, Quantity Surveyor, was called on behalf of the Plaintiff,

and he produced a Bill of Quantities, the main item in which was "reinstatement". The only witness for Mr Sheridan was Mr Henry Sheppard, a Building Costs Surveyor with Dublin Corporation, who had negotiated with Mr Whelan in connection with the malicious injury claim, (the negotiations being conducted on the basis of Mr Whelan's Bill of Quantities) and agreed with him the amount of compensation to be paid in respect of the building. Mr Sheppard said that the settlement with Mr Whelan was on the basis of reinstatement; Mr Whelan said it was on the basis of indemnity. It seems to me, however, that Mr Whelan took this view because Mr Sheppard had disallowed the professional fees which would be incurred in connection with reinstatement. But there is no doubt whatsoever that the Bill of Quantities had been prepared to support a claim for reinstatement.

It was common case that a party entitled to reinstatement would recover more than a party entitled to an indemnity only. Since the Plaintiff, under his policy with Lloyds, would only have been entitled to an indemnity, I am satisfied that he would not have recovered more under that policy than was agreed between his Quantity Surveyor and Mr Sheppard. Mr Whelan in fact referred to that figure as having been agreed on the basis of an indemnity so I see no reason for allowing a higher figure. Accordingly, apart from the question of interest which I will deal with at the end of this Judgment, I consider that the Plaintiff's loss in respect of the building was fully satisfied by the amount he received from Dublin Corporation.

2. The Stock, Fittings and Fixtures
There was no dispute in respect of the stock; while £2,150 was claimed in the malicious injury proceedings, the figure of £1,170 was agreed and the Plaintiff did not seek a figure in excess of this.

Separate figures were claimed in respect of the fixtures in the flat, and those in the shop. Mr Owen O'Connor, a Loss Assessor in the firm of Messrs Balcombes, gave evidence on behalf of the Plaintiff, and Mr Sheppard gave evidence on behalf of Mr Sheridan. The basis of the Plaintiff's claim was an inventory of loss and damage prepared by Mr O'Connor in connection with the malicious injury claim. In those proceedings Mr O'Connor had accepted a reduction of 35% on his figures on the ground of betterment, but he stated in evidence that he considered the 35% very high, and he had agreed to it only because the Plaintiff was anxious to have the matter settled quickly. He said that were it not for that he would have held out for a 20% reduction.

I accept his evidence that a reduction of 35% was very high, but on the other hand he might not have succeeded in holding out for 20%. It seems to me that a reduction of 25% would be reasonable. On the basis of such a reduction the figures for the fixtures and fittings in the flat would work out as follows:

Amount claimed	£6,832
25%	£1,708
	£5,124

The appropriate amount for the fixtures and fittings in the shop is more difficult to calculate as there was disagreement as to whether some items should have been included and in addition Mr Sheppard took the view that the overall figure should be reduced by £1,550 for salvage. In the circumstances it is not possible simply to apply a reduced percentage of 25% instead of 35%. Having considered the evidence of Mr O'Connor and [Mr] Sheppard I think it would be reasonable to increase the figure of £11,758.50 allowed by the Corporation to £13,090.

The total to be allowed for the stock fixtures and fittings would then be as follows:

Stock	£1,170
Fixtures and Fittings in flat	£5,124
Fixtures and Fittings in shop	£13,790
Total	£20,084

To this must be added 3% for the Loss Assessor's fees, which amounts to £602.52, which gives a final total of £20,686.52. From this must be subtracted the amount of £17,890.37 received from the Corporation, leaving a balance of £2,796.15. The Plaintiff is entitled to recover this figure as a part of his damages.

3. *Loss of Profits*

The first matter to be considered is the period in respect of which the loss is to be allowed. On behalf of the Plaintiff it was submitted that it should be from the date of the fire right up to the present time. It was argued that Mr Sheridan ought to have been able to foresee that, in the event of a fire, the Hibernian could repudiate the policy and the Plaintiff would be left with a burnt-out building which he would not have the funds to repair until he received damages from Mr Sheridan, and accordingly until then he would be without the profits from his business and should be entitled to recover them as damages. In my opinion such damage would be too remote. I accept that Mr Sheridan could reasonably have anticipated that the Plaintiff would not have the funds to reinstate the building, but I do not agree that he could reasonably have anticipated that the Plaintiff would not be able to borrow what was required. It appears from the evidence that an attempt was made to raise the necessary fund and that it failed. There was no evidence as to why it had failed. If it had been successful, the Plaintiff, could have recovered the interest he had to pay on the loan. In *Murphy* v. *McGrath*,[19] the Plaintiff who had had to borrow money to have repairs carried out to his car which had been damaged by the negligence of the Defendant, was held to be entitled to recover the interest he had had to pay on the borrowed money. O'Higgins C.J. said in his Judgment:

> "Damages lead to necessary repairs and these repairs necessarily had to be paid for. The question is by whom — by the Plaintiff, of course. The Plaintiff had to be put to the necessary task of borrowing finance and accordingly, I see no break in the chain of causation from the original tort. This I believe to be the commonsense view and I say this without studying the authorities that if a man has to go to a bank to borrow the necessary finance to effect

---

[19] [1981] I.L.R.M. 364.

repairs to his motor car which was damaged as a result of the Defendant's negligence, then he is entitled to claim interest thereon. The claim for interest is not too remote or extreme."

In the present case, if the Plaintiff had borrowed money in order to re-instate the premises this likewise would have been caused by Mr Sheridan's negligence. But his inability to borrow the money, and so to reinstate, is not the result of his negligence, and so damage resulting from it is too remote.

It seems to me, accordingly, that the appropriate measure of damages is what the Plaintiff would have recovered if he had been insured, which is twelve months' loss of profits, as this is the extent of the loss which was covered under his policy with the Hibernian and which I have assumed would also have been covered under any policy he might have obtained from Lloyds.

The evidence as to the profits earned by the shop business prior to the fire rested principally on three accounts prepared by the Plaintiff's Accountant, Mr Pascal Bergin. The first account was for the six months ended on the 19th February 1984; the second for the twelve months ended on the 28th February 1985, and the last one for the three months' period ended on the 20th May 1985, three days before the fire. But it was only the first of these accounts that was prepared from proper records. The other two accounts were prepared earlier this year by Mr Bergin on the basis of information provided by suppliers to the business, on the basis of the Plaintiff's bank account at the time and Mr Bergin's knowledge of the overheads of the business. They were also prepared on the assumption that the Plaintiff and Mr Byrne each took £500 a week from the business.

While I have no doubt that Mr Bergin made a genuine attempt to ensure that the second and third accounts would be as accurate as possible, it seems to me that no reliance can be placed on them. The material to prepare proper accounts just was not available. Furthermore, the information he was given in regard to the drawings of the Plaintiff and Mr Byrne was inaccurate. He was told that the earnings of the business were the sole source of their drawings. This was not so. The bank account kept by the Plaintiff shows that there were substantial earnings also from a disco business carried on by himself and Mr Byrne.

In these circumstances I consider that the only reliable evidence as to the profits being made by the business is to be found in the first account covering the six months ended on the 19th February 1984. That account showed a net profit of £9,664 for the six months. According to the Defendants' Accountant, Mr John Bouchier-Hayes, 56% of the annual turnover would have been realised in the six months in question. The profit of £9,664 would accordingly have represented 56% of the profit for the year, which would give an annual profit of £17,257. On the basis of the turnover for the six months in question, and applying the Consumer Price Index between 1984 and 1986, Mr Bouchier-Hayes calculated that the profit for the year May '85 to May '86 would have been £15,000.

The Plaintiff had a very exaggerated idea of what the business was making. He said that the profit was £2,000 a week. He accepted that Mr Bergin's figure of £9,664 for the first six months was correct. Relying principally on this figure, I consider that a reasonable sum to allow for loss of profits for the 12 months following the fire is £17,500.

In addition to claiming damages, the Plaintiff claims also interest under Section 22 of the Courts Act 1981. [S]ubsection (1) of that section provides as follows:

> "(1) Where in any proceedings a court orders the payment by any person of a sum of money (which expression includes in this section damages), the judge concerned may, if he thinks fit, also order the payment by the person of interest at the rate per annum standing specified for the time being in section 26 of the Debtors (Ireland) Act, 1840, on the whole or any part of the sum in respect of the whole or any part of the period between the date when the cause of action accrued and the date of the judgment."

I am satisfied that this is a case in which I ought to order the payment of interest. Were it not for the negligence and breach of contract of Mr Sheridan, the Plaintiff would have been compensated about five years ago for the loss he sustained as a result of the fire. In these circumstances he is entitled to such interest as I have jurisdiction to award him under the section.

The interest on the amount due for loss of profits creates no problem and is easily calculated. I take as the starting point the 1st June 1986, being the date by which I consider the Plaintiff should have received the £17,500, and I allow interest at the statutory court rate of 11% up to the 23rd January 1989, when the rate of interest was reduced by Ministerial Order to 8%, and at 8% from the 24th January 1989 to the 23rd October 1991. I calculate that the interest at 11% comes to £5,050, and the interest at 8% to £3,850 giving a total of £8,900, but these figures can be checked by Counsel.

A problem arises in regard to allowing interest on the amounts in respect of the building and the stock fixtures and fittings. I would have been prepared to allow interest on these amounts for the part of the period between the date of the fire and October 1988, when they were paid to the Plaintiff by Dublin Corporation, but it seems to me that it cannot be done under the section. Interest may only be given "on the whole or any part of the sum" the payment of which is ordered by the Court. There is not going to be any order for the payment of the amounts in respect of the building or the stock fixtures and fittings, except for £2,796.15 in respect of the latter. So it is only in respect of this figure that it seems to me I have jurisdiction to award interest. However, as this issue was not argued in the course of the hearing, I will hear Counsel on it before deciding it finally.

If interest is allowable on the £2,796.15 only, I will award it from the 23rd January 1986 for three years at 11%, which comes to £922.68, and from the 24th January 1989 to the 23rd October 1991 at 8%, which comes to £615.12, giving a total of £1,537.80.

Subject to the verification of the calculations, and to my hearing Counsel further on the question of interest, the total damages will be:

Loss of Profits	£17,500.00
Interest	£ 8,900.00
Stock fixtures and fittings	£ 2,796.15
Interest	£ 1,537.80
Total	£30,733.95

From this must be deducted from the estimated amount by which the premium paid to Lloyds would have exceeded that paid to the Hibernian. On the basis of Mr Hanlon's evidence it seems to me that this would have been about £700, reducing the damages to £30,033.95.

There is one final point that needs to be attended to. The Defendants submitted that the Plaintiff, not being the sole owner of the shop business, but having an equal partner, Mr Oliver Byrne, with him, could only recover half of the actual loss. This submission was contested by the Plaintiff, but in the event of my accepting it, it was submitted that Mr Byrne could be added as a Plaintiff. In my opinion that is what ought to be done and accordingly, provided Mr Byrne agrees to this course, I will add him as a Plaintiff.

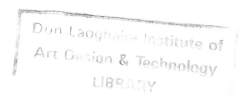

CHAPTER 13

Rights of Third Parties

Insurance contracts, as is the case with all contracts are subject to the common law doctrine of privity of contract. In essence, it states that persons not party to a contract cannot acquire enforceable rights from it. This being so, even if the particular contract was ultimately for the benefit of a specific third party, that third party cannot sue under the contract.

However, because of the social significance of insurance contracts and the apparent harshness of the doctrine, in certain cases the legislature has intervened in limited circumstances to alter the common law position and thereby confer upon third parties rights under the policy.

The most important statutory intervention is section 76 of the Road Traffic Act, 1961 (formerly section 78 of the Road Traffic Act, 1933). A third party claiming against an insured motorist can, in certain specified circumstances, proceed directly against that motorist's insurers:—

Firstly, if judgment has been obtained against the insured and it remains undischarged, provided the insurers had prior notice of the proceedings, the third party may seek leave to execute the judgment direct against the third party's insurers. Judge Sheehy in *McGee* v. *London Assurance Company* (1943) discusses the intention behind section 78 of the 1933 Road Traffic Act, and puts it into its general context. As illustrated by *Whelan* v. *Dixon* (1957),* it is still necessary for the third party to prove that the judgment obtained is for an amount in respect of which both a valid policy and valid policy cover exist. In *O'Leary* v. *Irish National Insurance Company Limited* (1958),** the third party could not proceed against the insurer as no valid policy existed, the insured having no insurable interest in the motor vehicle. Secondly, if the insured cannot be found or if the insured is outside the State, or if the court considers it is "just and

---

* This judgment appears in Chapter 10 at p. 389.
** This judgment appears in Chapter 5 at p. 115.

[518]

equitable" to do so, the third party can seek liberty to proceed directly against the insurer. In *Hayes* v. *Legal Insurance Company Limited* (1941),* the insured was dead and no representation raised to his estate. The third party was given liberty to proceed against the insurer.

An insurer's ability to refuse to deal with a third party under section 76 is slight. Insurers cannot rely on breach of policy conditions by the insured to deprive the third party of payment under the policy. The Road Traffic (Compulsory Insurance) Regulations, 1962 as amended and extended prohibit almost all conditions which might possibly reduce the rights of redress of a third party. While the insurer cannot rely on such prohibited conditions *vis-à-vis* the third party, as evidenced in *O'Donnell* v. *Yorkshire Insurance Company Limited* (1949),** they are still operative as between the insurer and the insured. Furthermore, in section 76 itself, the insurer cannot rely on any fraud, misrepresentation, or false information on the part of an insured to defeat a third party's claim. In *Stanbridge* v. *Healy* (1983)*** the insurers against whom the section 76 application was brought satisfied the court that the section did not apply to the circumstances of the accident, as the defendant was not obliged to have a valid policy of insurance to cover the accident in question as it did not occur in a "public place".

In 1987 the Supreme Court emphasised once again the doctrine of privity in all circumstances except those directly within the ambit of section 76. In *Boyce* v. *McBride* (1987) it refused to allow the insurers to remain in the existing proceedings, stating that same would be fruitless, as any ultimate liability on them would lie in contract and not negligence as in the existing action.

The only other statutory exception to the privity rule is to be found in section 62 of the Civil Liability Act, 1961. It is the only equivalent in Ireland of the English Third Party (Rights Against Insurers) Act, 1930. It is a long section which essentially states that where an insured has a policy of insurance in respect of liability for a wrong and monies are payable by an insurer to discharge that liability and — depending on the status of the insured — should the insured be wound up, dissolved or declared a bankrupt, any moneys so payable under the policy are to be paid in discharge of that liability and are not to be paid to the insured. In the case of *Dunne* v. *P.J. White Construction Limited (in liquidation) and Michael Payne* (1989), the Supreme Court held that if the section was to be of any effect, it was

---

* This judgment appears in Chapter 10 at p. 386.
** This judgment appears in Chapter 10 at p. 377.
*** This judgment appears in Chapter 10 at p. 394.

to be read as entitling a third party plaintiff to proceed directly against an insurer. In order so to proceed, it was necessary for the third party to satisfy a number of criteria. The third party must prove:—

(i) That the insured in question had effected a policy of insurance in respect of liability for a particular wrong;

(ii) That that the insured had obtained judgment for damages arising out of the particular wrong in question;

(iii) That the insured had been wound up, dissolved or made a bankrupt.

Having satisfied these criteria, the onus then shifted to the insurer to prove that there were justifiable and substantial policy reasons why indemnity should not be provided, as was being alleged by P.J. White's insurers. This aspect of the case was referred back for determination by the High Court and was ultimately compromised.

In very rare circumstances a court will be prepared to hold that monies due to be paid by an insurer to the policy-holder are to be held by that policy-holder in trust for, and for the benefit of a third party. While such cases are few, a fine example is to be found in the case, *In the Matter of Irish Board Mills Limited (in Receivership)* (1980). Mr Justice Barrington held that, though a personal accident policy on its face was for the benefit of the insured, on the evidence presented, the dependants of a deceased employee had successfully discharged the onus of proving that the sums payable were to be held in trust by the insured for their benefit. In the course of his judgment Mr Justice Barrington emphasised the extent of the onus to be discharged by third parties and suggested that there would have to be significant evidence available before such a trust would be held to exist.

Mr Justice Barrington's remarks were followed in the very recent case of *Patrick Desmond McManus* v. *Cable Management (Ireland) Limited, Radford Communications Limited and Hibernian Insurance Company plc* (1994). On the application of the Hibernian, Mr Justice Morris dismissed proceedings brought direct by the injured plaintiff against the Hibernian. The plaintiff who was suing his employer, Radford Communications Limited for injuries sustained in the course of his employment, alleged that his employer, when entering into an employers' liability policy with the Hibernian (which the Hibernian had since repudiated), had acted in the capacity as trustee for the plaintiff and that he was therefore a beneficiary under the policy, thereby entitling him to sue the Hibernian direct. Having considered the nature of both the policy and the cover provided, Mr Justice Morris held on the facts before him that no such trust in favour of the plaintiff existed.

The only other significant circumstance in which an insurer will be obliged to deal directly with a third party, and which, while not strictly to do with insurance law is worthy of mention, is where an insurer by its actions and representations induces a third party to alter their legal position. If the insurer then attempts to act differently from what was specified in their original representations, to the detriment of the third party, the courts will intervene to prevent the insurer from so doing. Such an intervention owes its origins to the doctrine of estoppel. Attempts to invoke its protection are to be seen in the cases of *Boyce* v. *McBride* (1987) and *Doran* v. *Thompson* (1978). In the first, it was submitted that insurers had impliedly promised or assured a third party that they would not rely on the invalidity of existing proceedings. In the second, it was that insurers would not rely on the Statute of Limitations. In both cases it was held on substantive grounds that the insurers were not so estopped and they could proceed as they intended. Estoppel is not an easy doctrine to invoke and, as these cases illustrate, the courts will only allow its protection in extreme cases.

Joseph Boyce v. Peter McBride
[1987] I.L.R.M. 95
The Supreme Court

HENCHY J. (FINLAY C.J. AND GRIFFIN J. CONCURRING): In July 1979 a motor car driven by one Peter McBride of Omagh, Co. Tyrone, collided on a road near Letterkenny, Co. Donegal, with a motor car driven by the plaintiff. The plaintiff's car was substantially damaged and he himself suffered somewhat severe personal injuries. As to Peter McBride, he died from injuries received in the accident.

The plaintiff instructed a Letterkenny firm of solicitors to bring the necessary proceedings in the High Court to recover damages for personal injuries suffered by him in the accident. Because the motor car driven by the late Peter McBride was owned and insured by his father Joseph McBride, one would have expected the claim to have been made against Joseph McBride, particularly as it was contended by the plaintiff that Joseph McBride's insurers should be held liable. That, however, is not what happened.

On 19 October 1981 a plenary summons was issued by the plaintiff claiming damages against Peter McBride. Why the deceased Peter McBride was chosen as defendant remains a mystery, but it was not for want of notice that he was then dead. By letters dated 8 July 1981 and 8 October 1981 the insurers of Peter McBride had intimated to the plaintiff's solicitors, by heading those letters "Peter McBride (Deceased)". It goes without question, therefore, that when the plenary summons was issued against Peter McBride the plaintiff's solicitors ought to have known that Peter McBride was then dead. Yet no explanation has been given why proceedings so plainly unsustainable were issued and carried on against a deceased defendant. The error is made all the more inexplicable by the fact that two days after the plenary summons was issued a further letter headed "Peter McBride (Deceased)" was written to the plaintiff's solicitors by the insurers.

In January 1982 a statement of claim based on the invalid plenary summons was delivered. There followed a desultory correspondence dealing mainly with arranging on behalf of the insurers a medical examination of the plaintiff. A notice for particulars was sent by the insurers' solicitors in March 1982 and it was replied to by the plaintiff's solicitors in April 1982. The correspondence between the parties petered out in November 1982 before a defence was delivered.

In January 1983 the plaintiff brought a notice of motion in which he sought liberty to join the insurers as defendants in place of Peter McBride deceased. That motion does not seem to have been moved. Another motion in roughly the same terms was brought in January 1984. This motion was grounded on an affidavit made by his solicitor in which he says that he issued the plenary summons without realising that Peter McBride was dead. No explanation was given for that statement. As I have pointed out, the correspondence showed that on at least three occasions the insurers had written letters to him headed "Peter McBride Deceased". To be fair, however, it has to be said that the plaintiff's solicitor does not complain that he was misled by the insurers.

That second motion was not proceeded with either. In April 1984 a third motion to the same effect was brought. It came on for hearing in the High Court in February 1985 when it was ordered that the insurers nominate some person to defend the action and that in default of doing so within two weeks the court would join the insurers as co-defendants. The present appeal has been brought by the insurers as that order.

The basis of the order under appeal is a finding that in the circumstances the insurers are estopped from opposing an order joining them as defendants in the existing proceedings. Of course, the natural remedy for a situation such as has risen would be to discontinue the existing proceedings and to issue fresh proceedings against the personal representative of Peter McBride deceased. Unfortunately, such new proceedings would now be statute barred and we have been told that if they were brought the insurers would plead the statute.

I fear I cannot agree with the conclusion that the insurers are estopped from objection to being joined as defendants. Before the insurers could be thus estopped it would have to be shown that by clear and unambiguous words or conduct they promised or assured the plaintiff that the invalidity of the proceedings would be relied on by them. The law on the matter is correctly and succinctly stated as follows by Griffin J in *Doran* v. *Thompson Ltd.*[1]:

> "Where one party has, by his words or conduct, made to the other a clear and unambiguous promise or assurance which was intended to affect the legal

---

[1] [1978] I.R. 223. See p. 535 of this book.

relations between them and to be acted on accordingly, and the other party has acted on it by altering his position to his detriment, it is well settled that the one who gave the promise or assurance cannot afterwards be allowed to revert to their previous legal relations as if no such promise or assurance had been made by him, and that he may be restrained in equity from acting inconsistently with such promise or assurance."

See the judgment of Kenny J. to the same effect in the same case at p.237.

While it is to be said that the insurers might very well have pointed out to the plaintiff's solicitors that the pending proceedings were invalidly constituted and that their defence to the claim would rely on that invalidity, I find nothing in the insurers' conduct to support the submission of counsel for the plaintiff that they impliedly promised and assured that they would not rely on the invalidity of the proceedings. Indeed the affidavit of the plaintiff's solicitor markedly refrains from asking making any such suggestion.

In those circumstances I must hold that the case for estoppel has not been made out.

But even if the factual basis for the estoppel claimed existed, so as to enable an order to be made allowing the plaintiff to join the insurers as defendants, such an order would be fruitless. The pending action is one founded on an allegation of negligence. It would not be legally possible for a court to find against the insurers in negligence. They were not themselves guilty of any negligence and they could not be held to be vicariously liable for the negligence of the insured or of any person whose driving was covered by the policy. The liability of the insurers (if any) arises as a matter of contract under the policy of insurance. A third party cannot claim against insurers under the policy, save where that is specially allowed by statute — as it is under s. 76 of the Road Traffic Act 1961. Since no such statutory provision applies in this case, it would be pointless to join the insurers or their nominee as defendant.

I would accordingly reverse the order allowing the insurers or their nominee to be joined as defendant, thus allowing the insurers' appeal.

Michael Dunne *v.* P.J. White Construction Co. Ltd (in Liquidation) and Michael Payne and Others
[1989] I.L.R.M. 803
The Supreme Court

FINLAY C.J. (HENCHY, GRIFFIN, HEDERMAN AND MCCARTHY J.J. CONCURRING): This is an appeal brought by the plaintiff against the dismiss by the High Court of his claim against the second-named defendants (the respondents). The plaintiffs' claim against the respondents was for a declaration:

"That the sum of £143,586 and costs which were awarded to the plaintiff herein on 16 February 1982 before a High Court judge and jury constitutes an award for a wrong and the second-named defendants are obliged under the terms of the policy of insurance entered into with the first-named defendant to pay the required monies to the plaintiff herein and to discharge the said sum for damages and costs pursuant to the provisions of the policy of insurance."

In the High Court, Murphy J., at the conclusion of the evidence for the plaintiff dismissed the claim on an application made on behalf of these defendants. He did so on the grounds that as a matter of law the onus was on the plaintiff, not only of establishing that a policy of insurance existed, issued by these defendants to the first defendant, which covered the risk of an accident such as the accident in respect of which the plaintiff had obtained his damages, but that there was also on the plaintiff the onus of proving as a negative that a right asserted or alleged by these defendants in the pleadings to rescind or repudiate the policy of insurance had not arisen. The learned trial judge held that the plaintiff had failed to discharge this latter onus and accordingly dismissed the claim.

It is against that decision that the plaintiff has appealed, and there has been no cross-appeal. The net issue before this Court, therefore, is as to whether the learned trial judge was correct in his view of the onus which the law placed on the plaintiff.

The plaintiff brings this action under the terms of s.62 of the Civil Liability Act 1961. The relevant parts of that section provide that where a person who has effected a policy of insurance in respect of liability for a wrong as a corporate body is wound up, monies payable to the insured under the policy shall be applicable only to discharging in full all valid claims against the insured in respect of which those monies are payable, and no part of those monies shall be assets of the insured or applicable to the payment of the debts, other than those claims of the insured in winding-up.

The accident in this case occurred in 1977 and proceedings were instituted in respect of it by the plaintiff against his employers the first defendants. In the course of these proceedings and before the action had been set down, while pleadings were being delivered, the first-named defendant went into liquidation. That defendant did not further defend the plaintiff's claim and he obtained his judgment for damages for negligence in default of a defence.

Whilst the matter was not raised in the pleadings in the High Court nor referred to in the arguments there, some debate took place in this Court as to whether the plaintiff had a right to bring an action by reason of s.62 against the insurers. I am quite satisfied that since the issue has not been raised, either in the pleadings or in the High Court, I must deal with this case on the basis that the plaintiff has clearly got such a right. I would express the view, however, notwithstanding the fact that a full debate has not taken place on this issue, that it seems to me that an inevitable consequence of the terms of s. 62 itself is that such a right of action is created by it.

S. 62 of the Act of 1961 is specifically designed to protect an injured plaintiff in the precise position of Mr Dunne in this action so as to ensure that monies payable on a policy of insurance to an insured who is dead, bankrupt, and, in the case of a corporate body, who is gone into liquidation, will not be eaten up by other creditors, but will go to satisfy his compensation, and with that purpose in mind the section must, it seems to me, give to the plaintiff a right to have that right enforced and protected by the courts and that means that he has got a right to sue, as he has sued in this action.

The case made on behalf of these defendants is that having sued, he is to be found in the position, as I understand their submission, that once they have merely stated or alleged in their document of pleading (as they did by amendment in this case) that they were entitled to and did rescind or repudiate the contract, that the plaintiff then has an onus to disprove that by his evidence. It is quite clear that such a legal position would be a breach, and a very wide breach, of the ordinary rule with regard to the question of the onus of proof that he who alleges must prove. Furthermore, it would be a breach, in my view, without any conceivable justification for it. But the matter seems to go further than that. It is conceded on behalf of these defendants that the insured in an ordinary case of a dispute with his insurance company has the advantage of a presumption in law that the policy is good unless and until the insurer establishes a right to rescind or repudiate it. Yet it is suggested that the injured party with the special statutory protection arising under s. 62 of the Civil Liability Act, 1961, as Mr Dunne has in this case, is deprived of that very valuable presumption. It is quite clear that as a matter of justice, such a person may, in many cases find it impossible and, in most cases, must find it immeasurably more difficult than the insured would, to negative a rescission or a right of repudiation. In my view, there would be no warrant for such an unjust application of rules of procedure or of a question of the onus of proof in an action and I would not be prepared to subscribe to it unless I saw anything, either in the general principles of law or in the terms of s. 62 which make it necessary for me to do so. I do not see anything in either of those areas.

On the contrary, I think properly to implement the protection given by the legislature in s. 62 to a person in the precise position of this plaintiff, it is necessary that the onus of proof should be the other way. I am, therefore, satisfied that the learned trial judge erred, that the appeal should be allowed, and that there must be a re-trial and that the matter should be sent back for further hearing on the issue, the onus being on the defendants.

In the Matter of Irish Board Mills Ltd (In Receivership); William McCann v. Irish Board Mills Ltd, James O'Hara, Patrick Hickey, Peter Thomas and Frances Lynch[*]
[1980] I.L.R.M. 216
The High Court

BARRINGTON J: The applicant in this case is the receiver of Irish Board Mills Ltd. The first named respondent is the said company. The second, third and fourth named respondents are the trustees named in an assignment of a personal accident insurance policy No 7427X50399 dated 16 August 1978 and wherein the respondent company is named as the insured. The last named respondent is the widow and personal representative of the late David

---

[*] Extract.

(otherwise Daniel) Lynch who died, as a result of an accident, on 7 July 1978.

Irish Board Mills Ltd was incorporated under the name Inisturk Ltd on 8 April 1974 and changed its name to Irish Board Mills Ltd on 26 June 1974.

Irish Wallboard Co. Ltd, a company incorporated on 9 February 1939, after several changes of name, changed its name to Irish Board Mills Ltd on 17 August 1973 and subsequently changed its name to Inisturk Ltd on 26 June 1974 and by agreement dated 17 December 1974 transferred its assets to the respondent company with effect from 4 May 1974.

On 29 October 1973 the company, then bearing the name Irish Board Mills Ltd, through their then brokers, Bowater Hammond Ltd, made a proposal to the Norwich Union Fire Insurance Co. Ltd for a group personal accident and sickness policy under the insurance company's optional scheme for cover for eight employees of their company. The insurance company's proposals form is headed as follows:

> "PERSONAL ACCIDENT AND SICKNESS — GROUP
> Injury to an employee can cause loss to a business through the absence from work of such person. The loss may be —
> 1. Fall in turnover consequent upon non-performance of the work normally undertaken by such person.
> 2. Increased cost of another person having to do this work.
> 3. The payment to the injured person of some part of his/her normal wage. Provision for such loss or extra expense can be made by a personal accident insurance providing compensation for injuries to employees during the course of employment only or during leisure and employment.
> Incapacity by sickness can also be covered to provide even wider protection."

The policy number filled in to the proposal form is 74210A50020. The final question in the personal form was 'to whom are the benefits under the policy to be payable?' and this was answered in the case of both types of benefits with the words 'the employer'.

A policy dated 22 March 1974 was issued on foot of that proposal for a period from 22 October 1973 to 21 October 1974. Condition 4 of that policy states that in the event of a claim under the policy any benefit should be payable to 'the insured'; the words 'person who is the subject matter of that claim or his or her personal legal representative' being struck out. This policy may well have been renewed from year to year in subsequent years but the plaintiff, as receiver, has not been able to find any such policies.

On 22 October 1975 the deceased Mr Lynch was offered and accepted the position of Marketing Co-ordinator with the defendant company under the terms of a letter dated 22 October 1975. There is no mention in that letter of any insurance scheme other than the contributory life assurance/pension scheme. Mr Lynch while he held the important position of marketing co-ordinator, and, later, marketing manager, with the company was not at any time a director of the company.....

On 18 July 1978 a policy number 7427X50399 was issued by the insurance company and was expressed to be for the period 1 July 1978 to 30 June 1979. It was in similar terms to the policy mentioned earlier except that it covered 14 officers and employees of the company including a marketing manager, in respect of whom the sum of £60,000 was to be payable if he should sustain bodily injury caused by accident which injury, solely and independently of any other cause, resulted in his death.

As previously stated Mr Lynch died on 7 July 1978 as a result of an accident and the sum of £60,000 accordingly became payable under this policy to the company. On the face of the policy itself this sum of £60,000 would appear to be payable to the company for the company's sole benefit and the receiver has, therefore, properly sought a direction from the court as to whether this sum of £60,000 is properly to be treated as assets of the company or whether, in the events which have happened, it is to be treated as being the property of the legal personal representative of the late Mr Lynch. The receiver has clearly taken great pains to lay all the relevant material before the court and the court is grateful to him for his effort in that behalf.

The court has also had the assistance of affidavits from several directors of the company who state that, even though the insurance policies referred to were expressed to be for the benefit of the company, in fact the settled policy of the company was that benefits payable in respect of an employee were to be paid to the employee or, in the case of death, for his dependants, and that the company did not intend to accept any benefit under these policies. The Norwich Union Insurance Co., I have been told, admits that the sum of £60,000 is payable and is prepared to pay it in accordance with any direction made by the court....

In approaching this case I am satisfied that the insurance policy referred to is on its face for the benefit of the company and not from the benefit of the employees. I must, therefore, approach it on the basis that on the date of Mr Lynch's death on 7 July 1978, *prima facie*, monies payable under the policy as a result of his death were the property of the company and that the onus of proof rests on anyone who seeks to prove otherwise. I am also satisfied that it is not sufficient for a person seeking to discharge this onus of proof to show that Mr Lynch would have had a "reasonable expectation" that his dependants would benefit under the policy in the event of his death. In this respect I fully accept the law as laid down by the English Court of Appeal in *Green* v. *Russell*.[2]

Mr Murphy SC (for the widow and personal representatives of the late Mr Lynch) accepts that the onus of proof is on him to establish that a trust exists in favour of his client. He submits that the trust which he seeks to establish is a trust of pure personalty and does not therefore need to be in any particular form: see *Re Kayford Ltd*.[3] He submits that there is no doubt as to the subject matter of the trust property or the objects of the trust. The only problem is to prove the intention of the company to create a trust. Mr Murphy SC claims to be able to prove this from the conduct of the directors going back over a number of years, see *Bolton (Engineering) Co. Ltd* v. *J.J. Graham & Son Ltd*,[4] and from the other matters hereinafter referred to.

A number of affidavits have been filed on behalf of directors and officers of the company who state that the understanding of the board at all times over

---

[2] [1959] 1 Q.B. 28.
[3] [1975] 1 W.L.R. 279.
[4] [1957] 1 Q.B. 159.

a number of years past has been that the insurance policy, though expressed
to be in the name of the company, was in fact taken out for the benefit of the
[dependants] of certain officers of the company and was, in effect, a perquisite
of office of these officers. The deponents referred to have not been cross-
examined. They have no personal interest in the outcome of these proceedings. They come before the court as reputable businessmen and I have no
hesitation in accepting that they have told the truth.

Looked at in the light of these considerations there are four factors which
convince me that the insurance policy, though taken out in the name of the
company and not referred to in the deceased's conditions of employment, was
in fact, at the date of the deceased's death, held by the company in trust for
the deceased and his dependants.

1. The first is the traditional practice of the company and its predecessors
in business in relation to insurance policies of a similar kind. Mr Jeffrey R.
Morgans in his affidavit says that for many years the defendant company was
a partly owned subsidiary of Bowater Corporation Ltd, a company incorporated in the United Kingdom, and that the policy of conditions of employment in the defendant company followed the general conditions laid down by
Bowater Corporation Ltd for its subsidiaries. He says that some time in 1973
Bowater Corporation Ltd sold its shares in Bowater's Irish Board Mills Ltd to
Inisturk Estates Ltd and that it was a term and condition of the said agreement for the sale of the shares that all existing contractual obligations
between employees of Bowater's Irish Board Mills Ltd would be upheld and
accepted in full by Inisturk Estates Ltd. He exhibited a copy of a memorandum dated 8 May 1968 and entitled "Bowater Staff Benefits". Among the
"benefits" listed are "personal accident insurance". This section of the memorandum contains the following sentence:

> "All staff will be insured by the company during all times when employed on
> the company's business, for a sum equivalent to four times the annual salary
> and payable in the event of death from accidental causes."

The memorandum continues:

> "Having regard to general conditions applicable to this type of insurance, the
> policy is in favour of the company who must retain certain rights over the
> allocation of any money received under a claim."

It appears to me that if the insurance policy had been taken out for the
benefit of the company it would be inappropriate to refer to it in a memorandum headed "Staff benefits". It also appears to me that the reference to
the policy being in favour of the company "who must retain certain rights
over the allocation of any money received" is inconsistent with an intention
on the part of the company to keep the insurance monics itself.

There is no doubt that there was a certain reticence on the part of the
company as to exact purpose of the insurance cover. But it is not difficult to
visualise reasons for such reticence. It appears to me that this staff policy of
the Bowater Corp. Ltd casts some light on the policy of the respondent company and helps to explain the purpose of the insurance policy in the present

case and the reason why there is so little reference to it in the records of the company.

2. In fact Mr O'Hara who was chairman of the respondent company for many years and who took an active role in the management and decision of the company says, in his affidavit, that one of the reasons why the insurance was effected in the manner outlined was to ensure that the insurance monies would not become part of the deceased's estate, in the event of death, and that they could be paid to the widow or appropriate representative of the deceased without waiting for a grant of representation to be raised. Mr O'Hara also remembers Mr Lynch being appointed marketing manager some time around 1977. At that time Mr Lynch was making frequent trips to Nigeria in the course of the company's business. Nigeria was then in an unsettled condition and on one occasion Mr Lynch unwillingly found himself on the fringe of a riot and narrowly escaped serious injury. Mr Lynch was, in the circumstances, understandably nervous about returning to Nigeria but Mr O'Hara was able to reassure him that he was covered by the company's insurance policy and make a remark to the effect that if anything happened to Mr Lynch his wife would be a rich widow. Mr Patrick Hickey, who was also a director of the company was present and confirms Mr O'Hara's recollection on this point

Mr Peter Thomas who was also a director of the company, confirms that the insurance policy was frequently referred to at board meetings and that the general intention of the board was that the policy should be held for the benefit of certain employees and not for the company. This was also the understanding of Mr Manuel Macedo who was elected a director of the company in January 1976. In these circumstances one can ask oneself the question as to what the position would have been had the late Mr Lynch been killed in Nigeria after the conversation referred to with the chairman of the board in the presence of another director. Surely no court would have allowed the company to repudiate the chairman's promise in such circumstances. Mr Lynch was not killed in Nigeria. Indeed it does not appear that the accident which resulted in his death took place in the course of his employment with the company. Nor of course is the company attempting to repudiate the chairman's promise. But nevertheless the question casts light on the purpose of the insurance policy and the nature of the relationship between the parties.

3. The receiver has discovered among the papers of the company the following document. It is headed: "Amendment to the Minutes of the Board Meeting of Irish Board Mills Limited held at Athy, County Kildare on 5 April 1977". It is signed by Mr O'Hara, the chairman of the board, and by Mr Macao a director. The text of the document reads as follows:

> "It was agreed by the Board of Irish Mills that the payment of life insurance benefits under the group's personal accident policy be paid to the dependants of the insured as beneficiaries and that the company waives all rights to claim any benefits which may arise now or in the future under this personal accident policy."

This document, if authentic, is decisive. The receiver has misgivings about it for two reasons and he has properly placed these misgivings before the court. The two reasons are that it was not found in the minute book of the company and that it does not bear any date. On the other hand Mr O'Hara and Mr Macedo have both sworn that the minute is authentic and, while they cannot state the date on which they signed it, Mr Macedo has sworn that they signed it before Mr Lynch's death. Moreover, while the document was not found in the minute book of the company it was found in the book of the company entitled "Copies of Minutes" and which contains other important records of the company. In the circumstances I have no hesitation in accepting the word of Mr O'Hara and Mr Macedo that it is an authentic amendment to the minutes.

4. Finally, on 16 August 1978 the company executed the assignment of the insurance policy above referred to to the trustees. In this assignment they recited that the policy was executed by the company as a perquisite of office of certain employees and on the understanding that all sums of money which would be paid to the company pursuant to the said policy would be received by the company as trustee for the benefit of the insured persons. The deed went on to assign the policy to trustees and contains declarations by the trustees that they hold the policy in trust for the employees referred to and an undertaking to pay all monies which become due or recoverable upon any claim pursuant to the policy to the employee who is the subject of the claim or to his legal personal representative. In my view the company in this assignment of 16 August 1978 was merely formally ratifying what was already the position.

Taking the view, which I do, that the company was not dealing in this assignment with assets of its own but merely with assets which it held on trust, I do not find it necessary to deal with Mr Murphy's alternative submission that the deeds of 16 August 1978 constitutes an independent disposition of the insurance monies for the benefit of Mr Lynch's personal representatives.

In the circumstances there will be a declaration that the sum of £60,000 payable in respect of the death of one David (otherwise Daniel) Lynch on 7 July 1978 and on foot of a personal accident and sickness insurance policy number 7427X50399 effected by the company with the Norwich Union Fire Insurance Society on 19 July 1978 and covering the period from 1 July 1978 to 30 June 1979 on foot of a proposal dated 29 October 1973 was at the date of the appointment of the plaintiff as receiver of the defendant company on 29 September 1978 held by the defendants James O'Hara, Patrick Hickey and Peter Thomas in trust for the personal representatives of the said David (otherwise Daniel) Lynch and a direction that the said sum of £60,000 together with any interest should be paid to the said personal representative accordingly.

Patrick Desmond McManus *v.* Cable Management (Ireland) Limited, Radford Communications Limited and Hibernian Insurance Company plc
Unreported, 8 July 1994
The High Court

MORRIS J: This matter comes before the Court as a Motion pursuant to Order 19 Rule 28 of the Rules of the Superior Courts seeking an Order dismissing the Plaintiff's claim against the Third-named Defendant herein on the grounds that the Pleadings disclose no reasonable cause of action and/or are frivolous or vexatious. In the alternative the same Order is sought pursuant to the inherent jurisdiction of the High Court.

The circumstances in which the application arises can be summarised as follows:—

The Plaintiff claims that he was employed by the First or in alternative the Second-named Defendants and on the 24th of April, 1991 while he was in their employment and while engaged in installing cable television at a dwellinghouse in Athlone, Co. Westmeath he was required to work at the top of a ladder and while he was doing so the ladder slipped and he suffered personal injuries which he says arose by reason of the negligence and breach of duty of either the First or Second-named Defendant for their joint negligence.

The claim that he makes against the Third-named Defendant is contained in paragraphs 6,7,8 and 9 of his Statement of Claim and it is that there was in existence an employer's liability policy of insurance at the relevant date whereby the Third-named Defendant contracted to indemnify the Second-named Defendant in respect of a claim for personal injuries, loss or damage sustained by an employee in the employment of the Second-named Defendant. He says that the Third-named Defendant has intimated to the Plaintiff its refusal to indemnify the Second-named Defendant in respect of the Plaintiff's claim herein, being a claim in respect whereof the Second-named Defendant is entitled to such indemnity and in respect of which the Plaintiff is entitled to such benefit as would accrue to him under the policy. The Plaintiff claims that the Third-named Defendant's refusal to indemnify the Second-named Defendant is unlawful and he seeks, in so far as the Third-named Defendant is concerned "an Order that the Third-named Defendant indemnifies the Second-named Defendant in respect of the Plaintiff's decree and Order for costs herein".

Counsel for the Third-named Defendant, the moving party, bases his submission on two grounds

(a) That there is no privity of contract between the Plaintiff and Third-named Defendant ("the insurance company") and accordingly he has no entitlement to maintain these proceedings.

(b) While Section 62 of the Civil Liability Act, 1961 confers on the Plaintiff in certain circumstances a right to sue the insurance company, those circumstances do not exist in this case because the Second-named Defendant, being a corporate body, is not wound up. It is accordingly submitted that *Dunne* v. *P.J. White Construction Company Limited (In Liquidation) and Others*[5] has no application.

Counsel on behalf of the Plaintiff accepts that he is not entitled to maintain the proceedings pursuant to Section 62 of the Civil Liability Act, 1961 and agrees that it has no application to the present case. He bases his claim to be entitled to maintain these proceedings solely on the basis that the Second-named Defendant, in entering into the employers liability insurance

---

[5] [1989] I.L.R.M. 803. See p. 523 of this book.

policy, acted in the capacity of a trustee for the Plaintiff and that the Plaintiff
is a beneficiary under the policy in which capacity he would be entitled to
maintain these proceedings.

Counsel for the Plaintiff has referred me to the authorities which are set
out in the Schedule to this judgment.[6] In my view most of these relate to the
issue of whether there was in the particular circumstances of the case a presumption of advancement in favour of the beneficiary under a policy of insurance and are not relevant to the circumstances of this case. There are however two exceptions. The first is *Green* v. *Russell, McCarthy (Third Party)*[7]
This case dealt with the circumstances which arose when an employer took
out a personal accident group insurance policy which after reciting "whereas
the insured is desirous of securing payment of benefits as hereinafter set
forth to any insured person", it provides that "if any insured person shall
sustain bodily injury" resulting in death the insurance company would pay a
specified sum and that "the company shall be entitled to treat the insured as
the absolute owner of this policy and shall not be bound to recognise any
equitable or other claim to or interest in the policy and the receipt of the
insured ... alone shall be an effective discharge". The policy described the
employer as "the insured" and named as the "insured persons" certain of his
employees. One of the employees named as an "insured person" died in a fire
which occurred at the employer's premises and his mother brought an action
under the Fatal Accident Acts in England in which liability was admitted and
damages were agreed and the question was whether the agreed damages paid
under the policy by the insurance company in respect of the death to the
employee's solicitors and paid, or about to be paid, by them to the employee's
mother was a benefit arising out of the death which should be taken into
account in assessing damages under the Act so as to reduce the mother's
"financial dependency" on the deceased.

It was held that the deceased employee had no right at law to the policy
monies since he was not a party to the contract of insurance and therefore
could not sue on it. It was further held that "the mere intention to provide
benefits was insufficient to create a trust and accordingly the deceased
employee did not have any equitable interest in the policy monies". This

---

[6]   SCHEDULE
                                                References
        (a) *Re Richardson* (1882), 47 L.T. 514.
        (b) *Royal Exchange Assurance* v. *Hope* [1928], 1 Ch 179.
        (c) *In Re Webb* [1941], 1 Ch 225.
        (d) *In Re Fosters Policy* [1966], 1 W.L.R. 222.
        (e) *Re Clay's Policy of Assurance* [1937], 2 All E.R. 548.
        (f) *Re Burgess Policy* (1915), 113 L.T. 443.
        (g) *Re Foster* [1938], 3 All E.R. 357.
        (h) *Williams* v. *Baltic Insurance Co.* [1924], 2 K.B. 282.
        (i) *Prudential Staff Union* v. *Hall* [1947], K.B. 685.
        (j) *Vandepitte* v. *Preferred Accident Insurance Corporation* [1933], A.C. 70.
        (k) *Green* v. *Russell* [1959], 2 Q.B. 226.
[7] [1959] 2 Q.B. 226.

authority does not, in my view, assist the Plaintiff's case.

The other authority referred to by Counsel was *Prudential Staff Union* v. *Hall*.[8] This is a case in which a Union, whose members consisted of members of the staff of an insurance company, effected a policy of insurance with Lloyds Underwriters covering the loss by any of its members who should be members during the currency of the policy arising from certain perils including burglary or housebreaking. In the policy, the Union was described as "the insured". The Underwriters contracted to pay the Union in case of a loss occurring within the policy. Certain burglaries and housebreakings occurred and the members suffered loss. In an action by the Union against the Underwriters in respect of the alleged loss, the insurance company pleaded that the Union had no cause of action and that the action should have been taken by the members who claimed to have suffered the loss. It was held that the Union had no insurable interest in the money. Nevertheless the Union was entitled to sue because the Underwriters had contracted, in the event of the loss, to pay the Union who would thereupon become trustees for the members.

Counsel for the Plaintiff sought to rely on this as authority for the proposition that the Second-named Defendants in this case became, upon entering into the contract of insurance with the Insurance Company, trustees of whatever benefits flowed from that contract in favour of the Plaintiff because it was a contract entered into for his benefit.

In my view this does not reflect the realities of the situation. Unlike the Prudential Staff Union case, the Plaintiff never stood to benefit under the contract of insurance which was in its nature an indemnity for the Second-named Defendants in the event of it being called upon to pay compensation to the Plaintiff. It is true that under the terms of the policy the definition of "the insured" is to include not only the Second-named Defendant but also "if the insured specified in the Schedule hereto so requires ... any person employed by the insured under a contract of service or apprenticeship". Leaving aside the fact that there is nothing in the papers to indicate that any request was made that the Plaintiff be deemed to be the insured, there still remains the fundamental point that the clause was intended only to provide an indemnity for the Plaintiff in the event of *his* injuring a third party. To that limited extent only might the Second-named Defendant be deemed to have entered into the policy as a trustee for the benefit of the Plaintiff but not so as to confer on the Plaintiff any rights under the policy in respect of injuries which he sustained.

The very point at issue here came before the House of Lords in England in *Bradley* v. *The Eagle Star Insurance Company Limited*.[9] In that case the Plaintiff over a period of 24 years in the employment of a cotton mill contracted a respiratory disease by the inhalation of cotton dust. The textile company was voluntarily wound up. In 1984 the Plaintiff brought proceedings against the insurers of the textile company pursuant to the Third Parties

---

[8] [1947] 1 K.B. 685.
[9] [1989] 1 All E.R. 961.

(Rights against Insurers) Act, 1930 on the basis that her injuries were caused by the negligence of her former employers which had insured against those risks with the Respondents during the relevant period. The matter came before the House of Lords on an application for discovery. It was held that an insured person's right of indemnity under a policy of insurance against the liability to third parties did not arise until the existence and amount of his liability to the third party had first been established either by action, arbitration or agreement and since the employer's liability to the Plaintiff had never been established, the Applicant's claim failed. In the course of his judgment, Lord Brandon expressed agreement with the decision of Lord Denning M.R. in *Post Office* v. *Norwich Union Fire Insurance*[10] when he said

> "I think the right to sue for these monies does not arise until the liability is established and the amount ascertained".

Lord Brandon says at p. 965

> "In my opinion the reasoning of Lord Denning and Salmon L.J. contained in the pages of their respective judgments in the Post Office case set out above on the basis of which they conclude that under a policy of insurance against liability of a third party the insured person cannot sue for an indemnity from the insurers unless and until the existence and amount of his liability to a third party has been established by action, arbitration or agreement is unassailable and correct."

Again [*In the Matter of Irish Board Mills Ltd (in Receivership; McCann* v. *Irish Board Mills Ltd. And Others*[11]] Barrington J. in considering the position of employers and officers of a company in receivership where the benefits under a policy of insurance covered accidents to employees of the company said as follows:—

> "In approaching this case I am satisfied that the insurance policy referred to is on its face for the benefit of the company and not for the benefit of the employees. I must therefore approach it on the basis that on the date of Mr Lynch's death on the 7th July 1987 [sic — died 1978] prima facie monies payable under the policy as a result of his death were the property of the company and that the onus of proof rests on anybody who seeks to prove otherwise. I am also satisfied that it is not sufficient for a person seeking to discharge this onus of proof to show that Mr Lynch would have had a "reasonable expectation" that his dependants would have benefited under the policy in the event of his death."

I am satisfied on these authorities that no case can be made out on the Plaintiff's behalf to indicate that he had any entitlement to the benefits payable under the policy and I am satisfied on the authority of *Sun Fat Chan* v. *Osseous Limited*[12] that there is vested in the High Court an inherent

---

[10] [1967] 1 All E.R. 577.
[11] [1980] I.L.R.M. 216. See p. 525 of this book.
[12] [1992] I.R. 425.

jurisdiction identified by Costello J. in *Barry* v. *Buckley*[13] in an appropriate case, to dismiss an action on the basis that, on the admitted facts, it cannot succeed.

I am of the opinion that this is such a case and accordingly I make the Order sought and I direct that the Plaintiff's proceedings against the Third-named Defendant be struck out on the grounds that they disclose no reasonable cause of action against the Third-named Defendant.

Kevin Doran *v.* Thomas Thompson and Sons Limited
[1978] I.R. 223
The Supreme Court

HENCHY J: To prevent the guillotine from falling on these proceedings, it is necessary for the plaintiff to show that the defendants are estopped by representation from pleading the Statute of Limitations, 1957. Otherwise, the claim must stand dismissed for, as the defendants have pleaded, the plaintiff's claim for damages for negligence was not commenced within three years after the cause of action arose — as the statute requires.

Where in a claim for damages such as this a defendant has engaged in words and conduct from which it was reasonable to infer, and from which it was in fact inferred, that liability would be admitted, and on foot of that representation the plaintiff has refrained from instituting proceedings within the period prescribed by the statute, the defendant will be held estopped from escaping liability by pleading the statute. The reason is that it would be dishonest or unconscionable for the defendant, having misled the plaintiff into a feeling of security on the issue of liability, and, thereby, into a justifiable belief that the statute would not be used to defeat his claim, to escape liability by pleading the statute. The representation necessary to support this kind of estoppel need not be clear and unambiguous in the sense of being susceptible of only one interpretation. It is sufficient if, despite possible ambiguity or lack of certainty, on its true construction it bears the meaning that was drawn from it. Nor is it necessary to give evidence of an express intention to deceive the plaintiff. An intention to that effect will be read into the representation if the defendant has so conducted himself that, in the opinion of the court, he ought not be heard to say that an admission of liability was not intended.

What representation did the defendants' insurers make as to the issue of liability? The answer is "None". Aside from the first letter written by the plaintiff's solicitor in October, 1973, in which a query was put as to what proposal the defendants had for compensating the plaintiff, and the insurers' neutral reply saying that the circumstances of the accident were being investigated, not a word was written or spoken during the three-year period of limitation on the question of liability. Other than those two opening letters,

---

[13] [1981] I.R. 306.

the only communications that passed were those between the solicitor and the insurers, and these consisted of five letters on each side and two telephone conversations. In none of them was any reference, direct or oblique, made to the question of liability.

The plaintiff's solicitor assumed at all stages that liability would not be in issue; but what lured him into that state of mind was the plaintiff's account of how the accident happened. There is nothing in what the insurers said or did that could be reasonably be held to have nurtured his assumption that liability would be admitted. For reasons that are not obvious he excluded the possibility that the plaintiff's explanation of the cause of the accident might prove wrong or that, even if right, the defendants might still escape liability by pleading the statute. This fallacious thinking stemmed entirely from considerations subjective to the solicitor. I find nothing in the conduct of the defendants' insurers that could reasonably be said to have been causative of the impression that the issue of liability had disappeared from the case.

In holding that there was estoppel by representation, the judge in the High Court saw three matters as supporting that inference. First, he held that it was reasonable for the solicitor to conclude from the account of the accident given by the plaintiff that liability would not be denied. It was certainly reasonable for the solicitor to *hope* or *expect* that liability would not be denied, but I do not think it was reasonable for a plaintiff's solicitor in such circumstances to risk the extinction of his client's claim by *assuming* that liability would not be contested. Because the defendants' version of how the accident happened might not tally with the plaintiff's, or for any one of a number of other reasons (such as that the ostensible negligence of the defendants might turn out to be that of a third party), the issue of liability could not have been safely written off. At any rate, the solicitor's state of mind in this respect was formed and maintained without reference to any representation by the insurers.

Secondly, it was held that it was reasonable for the solicitor to expect that an offer of settlement would be made after the defendants' surgeon had carried out a medical examination. Doubtless it was reasonable for him to cherish that expectation, but not to the extent of ignoring the period of limitation. As the three-year period drew to its close, the insurers' silence on the issue of liability cried out for a direct question to be put to them asking whether liability was being admitted or not, and if a satisfactory reply were not received, for an originating summons to be issued. The issue of the summons would have cost little; it did not even have to be served to defeat the statute; it would have been valid for 12 months; and it could have been renewed at the end of 12 months. However, such routine precautions never crossed the solicitor's mind. The self-induced *idée fixe* that he had formed diverted his attention from the palpable and imminent disaster. His preoccupation with the quantum of damages to the exclusion of the issue of liability was the cause of his inactivity, and not anything in the nature of a representation by the insurers.

Thirdly, it was held that the insurers' willingness to make available a copy of their surgeon's medical report justified the solicitor's assumption that a reasonable and realistic approach to settlement would be taken by them, and that it was probable that the report would be treated as an agreed one.

Assuming, without so holding, that to be so, I do not think it advances the plaintiff's claim that the defendants are estopped by representation from pleading the statute. The agreement to give the plaintiff's solicitor a copy of the medical report was a concession requested by him and agreed to by the insurers because the plaintiff would have no medical representative present at the medical examination. The solicitor had no reasonable grounds for assuming that the result would be an agreed medical report, or that the medical examination was but a prelude to a settlement.

Looking at the matter without the benefit of hindsight, I consider that no reasonable legal adviser who read the file of the plaintiff's solicitor at the stage when the end of the limitation period was approaching could have reasonably believed that the issue of liability had been or would be abandoned. At best he could only have hoped or expected that such would be the case, and the basis for that hope or expectation would have been the plaintiff's instructions and not anything said or done by the insurers.

The insurers had exercised their right to remain silent on the issue of liability. There was no onus on them to deny the allegation of negligence that had been made in the opening letter. It was for the plaintiff's solicitor to pursue the matter in correspondence and, in the absence of a satisfactory reply, to issue proceedings. His failure to do so was not supported by any causative representation by the insurers. As many a would-be plaintiff has learned, it is a fact of life in the world of insurance that a not unusual way for insurers to dispose of unprosecuted claims is to allow them to die of inanition. That is what happened here.

It is with regret that I differ from the conclusion reached in the full and careful judgment under review. I feel, however, that the plaintiff's case on this question was put fairly and at its highest by the solicitor himself when, at the end of his evidence in the High Court, he was asked a final question by the judge to explain why the necessity of issuing proceedings did not enter his mind. The solicitor's reply was:—

> "My attitude in this case ... was that my opinion on the circumstances of the accident as explained to me by my client was that it was a pretty clear case on liability, and I had the correspondence and the telephone conversations with the insurance company relating to the carrying out of the examination, and my object was to facilitate them as far as I could in arranging that examination and, indeed, I was anxious to get medical evidence myself, and I was quite confident that when the medical evidence was available the claim could and would be settled without the necessity of any proceedings."

There, frankly, fairly and at its full length, stands the plaintiff's case for avoiding the closure applied by the statute. It shows that the solicitor misread the situation. He erred in good faith in thinking that the question of damages was all that was in issue. He failed to apprehend that the defendants could plead the Statute of Limitations: but the error was of his own making. It was not induced by any representation made by or on behalf of the defendants. The result is the sort of unfortunate situation that persuades prudent solicitors of the necessity to be adequately insured against the consequences of their negligence. I would allow the appeal and rule that the plaintiff's claim is statute-barred.

GRIFFIN J: The facts in this case are not in dispute. On the 20th July, 1972, the plaintiff was employed by the defendants as a steel erector. On that date, whilst working for the defendants in erecting a steel structure at Carlow, he was injured when he fell to the ground from a height of approximately 20–25 feet. He consulted his solicitor during the latter half of October, 1973, which was 15 months after the accident.

On the 31st October, 1973, his solicitor wrote to the defendants and referred to the fall and the fact that his client was still totally incapacitated at that time and was attending the doctor each week. The letter concluded as follows:— "From the instructions we have received it appears that the accident was due to your failure to provide a safe system of work, and we shall be glad to hear from you as to what proposal you should have to compensate our client for the loss and damage he has sustained." The defendants passed this letter to their insurers who replied thereto on the 18th December, 1973. In their letter, having stated that they were "investigating the circumstances of the accident to which you refer", the insurers inquired whether the plaintiff had effected a full and complete recovery from his injuries and, if not, they requested the usual facilities for a medical examination of the plaintiff by their medical officer. Between that date and the 16th June, 1975, further correspondence took place between the insurers and the plaintiff's solicitor: in addition, there were three telephone conversations between the principal of the firm of solicitors and officials of the insurers. This correspondence and the telephone communications related *exclusively* to the medical examination of the plaintiff which was sought on behalf of the defendants: some difficulty had arisen in connection with the attendance of a doctor on behalf of the plaintiff at such examination. In the result, it was arranged that the defendants' doctor should examine the plaintiff without the necessity for the attendance of a doctor on behalf of the plaintiff, provided that a copy of the medical report was made available to the plaintiff's solicitor. The examination took place on the 29th July, 1975, and on the 29th September, 1975, a copy of the medical report was sent to the plaintiff's solicitor by the insurers.

Proceedings on behalf of the plaintiff were not commenced within the three years specified in s. 11 s2(b), of the Statute of Limitations, 1957. This action was instituted on the 18th February, 1976, and the defendants pleaded in their defence that the plaintiff's claim was barred by virtue of the provisions of that statute. As the plaintiff in his reply pleaded (inter alia) that the defendants were estopped by their conduct and the conduct of their agents from relying on the provisions of the statute, an issue of law as to whether they were so estopped was directed; it was tried by Mr Justice Costello.

Four witnesses gave evidence at the oral hearing, and these included the principal of the said firm of solicitors. The latter conceded that the question of liability was not discussed at all in the telephone communications between him and the insurers, that the discussions were purely confined to the arrangements for a medical examination and that there were no negotiations whatever. He stated that he had not issued legal proceedings during the period between October, 1973, and the end of July, 1975, and he stated his reason as follows:—

"I did not really consider the question of issuing proceedings because I had been arranging with the insurance company for this medical examination which was proving so difficult. There was never any discussion as to liability. It seemed to me that the case was a clear one and that the only question at issue was the extent of the man's injuries and the amount of damages and as long as I was still in discussions with the insurance company to arrange this medical examination, the question of issuing proceedings did not enter my mind."

He said that he was quite confident that when he got a copy of the doctor's report and probably submitted it to his doctor for his views on it, he would then have negotiations with the insurance company as regards the settlement of the claim. In answer to the last question (Q.101) put to him (by the trial judge), he summarised his attitude as follows:—

"My attitude in this case ... was that my opinion on the circumstances of the accident as explained to me by my client was that it was a pretty clear case on liability, and I had the correspondence and the telephone conversations with the insurance company relating to the carrying out of the examination, and my object was to facilitate them as far as I could in arranging that examination and indeed, I was anxious to get medical evidence myself, and I was quite confident that when the medical evidence was available the claim could and would be settled without the necessity of any proceedings."

Having heard all the evidence, and considered the correspondence, the trial judge held that the defendants were estopped by their conduct from pleading the statute. He was satisfied that the words and conduct of the defendants' insurers led the plaintiff's solicitor to believe that the case was a clear one, that liability would not be contested, and that it would be settled without the necessity of instituting proceedings; and that without the necessity of instituting proceedings; and that this belief was one which was reasonable for him in the circumstances to draw from that conduct.

It is with the utmost regret that I also differ from the trial judge. Where one party has, by his words or conduct, made to the other a clear and un-ambiguous promise or assurance which was intended to affect the legal relations between them and to be acted on accordingly, and the other party has acted on it by altering his position to his detriment, it is well settled that the one who gave the promise or assurance cannot afterwards be allowed to revert to their previous legal relations as if no such promise or assurance had been made by him, and that he may be restrained in equity from acting inconsistently with such promise or assurance. The representation, promise, or assurance must be clear and unambiguous to found such an estoppel: see Bowen L.J. at p. 106 of the report of *Low* v. *Bouverie*.[14] But this does not mean that the representation must be one positively incapable of more than one *possible* interpretation. Where, however, more than one construction is possible, the meaning relied upon must clearly emerge in the context and circumstances of the case, although in other contexts or other circumstances the same words might possibly have borne a different construction. In

---

[14] [1891] 3 Ch. 82.

addition, the party relying on the representation must show that the representation was *reasonably* understood by him in a sense materially inconsistent with the allegation against which the estoppel is attempted to be set up: see Cairns L.J. at p. 306 of the report of the decision of the Court of Appeal in *Woodhouse Ltd.* v. *Nigerian Produce Ltd.*[15] where he explained and analysed the celebrated passage of Bowen L.J. in *Low* v. *Bouverie.*[16]

If the defendants' insurers had made a clear and unambiguous representation (in the sense I have explained) that liability was not to be in issue, and the plaintiff's solicitor had withheld the issue of proceedings as a result, I would have held that the defendants were estopped from pleading the Statute of Limitations. In my opinion, however, on the agreed facts there was no promise, assurance, or representation made by the insurers to the plaintiff's solicitor, and none can be inferred from the correspondence, the telephone conversations, or the conduct of the insurers. Apart from stating in their first letter that they were investigating the circumstances of the accident, the insurers thereafter made no reference, express or implied, to the circumstances of the accident or the question of liability.

It is contended on behalf of the plaintiff that the insurers' failure to deny the statement in the first letter from the plaintiff's solicitor (to the effect that, from the instructions they had received, it appeared to the solicitors that the accident was due to the defendant's failure to provide a safe system of work) amounted to a representation that the insurers were not contesting liability. However, this is not the law as, in the absence of a duty to speak out, mere silence or inaction is not such conduct as amounts to a representation. A duty to speak arises whenever one party knows that the other party is acting on an erroneous assumption of some liability undertaken by the former. There is no question of any such knowledge in this case.

Whilst the plaintiff's solicitor undoubtedly believed that, on the information he had received from his own client, the case was a clear one and that it would be settled without the necessity of instituting proceedings, that belief was not induced by the insurers. Indeed, with the utmost candour and fairness, when he was giving evidence the principal of the solicitors' firm, in reply to questions 78 and 101 (already quoted), did not suggest that his belief that the case was a clear one was induced by the insurers. There was no promise, assurance, or representation on the part of the insurers within the meaning of the principles already mentioned and, accordingly, the defendants are not estopped from pleading the statute.

It is the invariable practice of some solicitors, upon first receiving instructions and opening a new file in a case in which personal injuries are received in an accident, to put in bold figures, on the outside of the file, the date prior to which a plenary summons must be issued unless the case is settled. This, or some appropriate variation of it, is a practice which might, with advantage, be universally adopted. If the action has not been settled by the date which appears on the outside of the file, prudence requires that a plenary summons

---

[15] [1971] 2 W.L.R. 272 & [1972] A.C. 741.
[16] [1891] 3 Ch. 82.

should be issued though not necessarily served. In any event the small cost of issuing the plenary summons will be recovered on any subsequent settlement. If there is no settlement, the plaintiff's rights are protected. I would allow this appeal.

KENNY J: ... The issue as to whether the defendants were estopped or in any way precluded from pleading the Statute of Limitations was tried by Mr Justice Costello on the 26th May, 1977. Oral evidence was given and, in a most careful and conscientious judgment, he held that they were. His first ground for so holding was that the defendants' insurers, by not informing the plaintiff's solicitors that they were contesting liability, led the solicitors to conclude that the insurers were not contesting it and that the case would be settled without the necessity of instituting proceedings. His second ground was that it would be inequitable to allow the defendants to go back on the position which their insurers' words and conduct had brought about. He thus based his first conclusion on the developing doctrine of promissory estoppel. I regret that I cannot agree with either of the grounds he relied on.

Both parties accepted as being correct the statement of the law on promissory estoppel at p. 563 of the 27th edition (1973) of Snell's Principles of Equity which has the authority of having been edited by Mr Justice Megarry (now the Vice-Chancellor) and Professor Baker. It reads:—

> "Where by his words or conduct one party to a transaction makes to the other an unambiguous promise or assurance which is intended to affect the legal relations between them (whether contractual or otherwise) and the other party acts upon it, altering his position to his detriment, the party making the promise or assurance will not be permitted to act inconsistently with it."

It was argued that the plaintiff's solicitors made a claim by their letter of the 31st October, 1973, that the defendants were liable to compensate their client, that the answer by the insurers was that they were investigating the circumstances of the accident and that they never informed the plaintiff's solicitors what the result of the investigations were and never denied liability, so that, it was contended, the solicitors were justified in assuming that the insurers were accepting liability.

In court pleadings what the defendant does not deny in a plaintiff's statement of claim is admitted, but this is the result of a rule of court (O.19. r 13, of the Rule of 1962) and cannot and should not be applied to correspondence. The failure to reply to a charge in correspondence may have some tenuous evidential value if there is some ground for the complaint but silence on receipt of an accusation (be it criminal or civil) can never be an acceptance of the allegation unless the person against whom the charge is made is under a duty to deny it. One of the penalties of being a judge is the receipt of letters from disappointed litigants. At present I get numerous letters from two litigants accusing me of corruption, acceptance of bribes and gross partiality. Do I admit these charges by ignoring the letters, and am I to be held to have led the writers to believe that I accept the accusations because I do not answer them?

The rule of the law on this matter was summarised by Lord Tomlin when delivering the judgment of a particularly eminent House of Lords in *Greenwood* v. *Martins Bank*.[17] At p. 57 of the report he said:— "Mere silence cannot amount to a representation, but when there is a duty to disclose deliberate silence may become significant and amount to a representation."

Then it was said that the request for the medical examination by the insurers was an admission of liability or a representation that the case had become one in which the amount of the damages was the only issue. In every case in which damages are claimed for personal injuries, the defendant or his insurer asks for a medical examination of the proposed plaintiff at the earliest possible date. This is because the defendant's surgeon or doctor may ultimately have to give evidence and in some cases, where the plaintiff is not wealthy, it may be possible to settle the case for a small sum and avoid the heavy costs of litigation. If the surgeon or doctor retained by the defendant does not examine the plaintiff at an early stage, his evidence will be compared unfavourably with the plaintiff's surgeon or doctor who will have examined him shortly after the accident and many times afterwards.

In my opinion there was no representation of any kind by the insurers or the defendants that they were admitting liability, or that the only issue in the case was the amount of damages, or that they would not rely on the Statute of Limitations. Therefore, there is no foundation for the application of the doctrine of promissory estoppel.

The other argument was that it would be inequitable to allow the defendants to rely on the Statute of Limitations. If the defendants had accepted liability and had entered into negotiations to arrive at an agreed sum, and if the plaintiff's solicitors had refrained from bringing proceedings because they relied on the admission of liability or the negotiations being conducted, it would be inequitable to allow the defendants to rely on the time-bar. But they never accepted or admitted liability and never represented that they did, nor did they carry on any negotiations for the purpose of settling the case. They did nothing which could give the plaintiff's solicitors the impression that they need not issue proceedings nor did they mislead them in any way. I cannot see how the conduct of the insurers was dishonourable in any respect and I do not think that anything they did makes it inequitable for them to plead and rely on the Statute of Limitations. If the plaintiff's solicitors thought that liability was being admitted, the defendants and the insurers did nothing to cause or contribute to that belief.

Counsel for the plaintiff relied strongly on the decision of this Court in *O'Reilly* v. *Granville*.[18] That was an application to add a party as a defendant in a motor accident case. Objection to this step was taken on the ground that, at the date of the application, the time limit of three years had expired. Complicated questions as to the effect of order 15, r. 13, were discussed but this has no relevance to the present case. In that case the defendant's insurers within the statutory period of three years wrote to the plaintiff's solicitors asking for details of the special damages, and added:— "We shall see if we

---

[17] [1933] A.C. 51.
[18] [1971] I.R. 90.

can arrange a settlement with you." Subsequently the defendant's insurers asked the plaintiff's solicitors by letter how much the plaintiff expected to be paid in settlement of his claim apart from special damages which (the letter added) "no doubt can be agreed by negotiation." It was in these circumstances that Ó Dálaigh C.J. said that a plea of the Statute of Limitations "would be not only wholly unmeritorious but, I feel it my duty to add, unconscionable and plainly dishonest." Therefore, there was conclusive proof that an admission of liability had been made by the defendant's insurers: in this case no such admission was made either expressly or by implication and so *O'Reilly* v. *Granville*[19] does not help the plaintiff.

The question whether an admission of liability without more makes it unequitable to rely on the Statute of Limitations or whether the admission of liability must have been relied on by the plaintiff's solicitors as a ground for not issuing proceedings was not discussed in argument and, in any event, does not arise. I find it difficult to reconcile the remarks of the former Chief Justice with the reasoning in *The Sauria*[20] on this point, and so I reserve this for future consideration.

In my opinion the issue ordered to be tried by the order of the 14th February, 1977, should be answered by finding that, in this case, the defendants are not estopped or precluded in any way from pleading or relying on the Statute of Limitations, 1957.

---

[19] [1971] I.R. 90.
[20] [1957] Lloyd's Rep. 396.

CHAPTER 14

Conditions Precedent to Liability

The insured is bound by the contract of insurance to fulfil certain of its terms as a necessary prerequisite to his right of recovery against the company. It is in this context that some of the terms of the policy are described as being conditions precedent to the liability of the insurer to provide an indemnity to the insured.

Although a particular form of words is not required to make a term of the contract a condition precedent, nevertheless, contracts are usually very clear in identifying those terms which are to be regarded as such. The question as to which terms constitute conditions precedent is to be determined by the intentions of the parties. Thus, the absence of a specific designation may not prevent a court deciding that the term is a condition precedent.

Traditionally, judges were reluctant to interfere with the contents of a contract freely entered into by the parties. This "laissez-faire" approach, however, fails to take account of the inequality of bargaining power which is central to the relationship between the policyholder, on the one hand, and the insurer on the other.

Gamble v. *The Accident Assurance Company* (1870) is an example of this strict "laissez-faire" approach. Here, the Court of Exchequer held that a policy provision making it a condition precedent to the insured's right of recovery that notice of an accident be delivered within seven days applied even to a case of instantaneous death!

To similar effect was *Patten* v. *The Employers Liability Assurance Corporation* (1887) where Gamble was expressly followed.

In contrast to these cases is *Weir* v. *The Northern Counties of England Insurance Company* (1879). In this case a provision in the policy requiring that an account of items damaged by a fire be delivered within fifteen days was held, on the construction of its wording, not to be a condition precedent to recovery.

In *Car and General Insurance Corporation Limited* v. *Munden* (1934) an insurer had discharged its obligation under a motor policy before establishing whether the insured had complied with a condition precedent to liability which the policy imposed upon him. In fact, the insured had been in breach of the condition and this would have entitled the insurer to repudiate liability in the usual way. The question for determination was whether, in the circumstances of the case, the insurer had a right of action in damages against the policy-holder as a result of his breach.

The High Court found that a condition precedent contained a negative undertaking on the part of the policyholder and that the company was entitled to sue in damages for the breach of this undertaking. In reaching this conclusion, the judge accepted that a party could waive compliance with a contractual condition which was exclusively for its benefit, and this had been done by the insurance company in this case.

In Re the Equitable Insurance Company Limited (1968), a case arose under the Insurance Act, 1964. The applicant policy-holder had given notice of an accident to his insurance company, then in liquidation, thirteen months after it had occurred.

The issue for the High Court, and on appeal to the Supreme Court, was whether he had given notice "as soon as practicable", as required by a condition precedent to the liability of the company. All the judges held that he had not done so. In the leading Supreme Court judgment, Budd J. rejected the argument that the phrase was to be construed from an insured's own point of view.

In *Gaelcrann Teoranta* v. *Payne* (1983) an arbitrator stated a case for the opinion of the High Court. Two issues were involved:—

(a) Whether the word "or" in a condition precedent was to be given a conjunctive or disjunctive meaning and;

(b) Whether actual prejudice on the part of the company was necessary before it could repudiate liability for breach of the condition precedent to liability.

Gannon J., after a detailed examination of the matter, adopted a disjunctive interpretation. He also found that there was not any onus on the company to show actual prejudice.

Although *Munden* was not expressly referred to or cited, the court also concluded that compliance with a condition precedent could be waived.

Gaelcrann was followed by Costello J. in *Capemel Limited* v. *Lister* (1989).

Gamble v. The Accident Assurance Company (Limited)
(1870) Ir.R. 4 C.L. 204
Court of Exchequer

PIGOT C.B: Two propositions were urged, on the part of the Plaintiff.... First, it was contended, that the sixth condition, referred to and incorporated by reference in the policy of insurance sued on, and endorsed upon it, did not, according to the terms and import of the contract, apply to the case of the instantaneous death of the assured resulting from the accident. Secondly, that, since the death was instantaneous, the provision in that condition, that, in the case of a fatal accident, notice should be given of it to the Company within seven days after it should have occurred, was discharged by the act of God, which made the death instantaneous.

As to the first of these propositions, the policy, in the body of it, contains a stipulation, that

> "the said policy, and the insurance thereby effected, were, and should be, subject to several conditions, instructions, stipulations, and notice thereupon endorsed, so far as the same should be applicable, in the same manner as if the same respectively were repeated and incorporated in the said policy."

By the sixth condition, so endorsed, it is provided as follows:—

> "In the event of any accident, *whether fatal or not*, occurring to the insured within the intent and meaning of this policy, notice thereof in writing *must be delivered* to the Company at their chief office, in London, within seven days after the occurrence of the accident; stating the nature and date of the injuries, the place where, and the manner in which, they were received, with the name, address, and occupation of the person injured; but any notice delivered, or coming through any agent of the Company, shall not be sufficient to satisfy this condition."

Then, immediately succeeding that provision, comes the following:—

> "In case the accident shall not prove fatal, *he shall*, within seven days from the accident, furnish to the Company a full written report by a medical practitioner (who shall be duly qualified and registered) on the facts of the case; and further, shall, when required by the Company, from time to time *submit himself* to be examined by their medical officer, and, if possible. either at their chief office or at the address given by the insurer as aforesaid, at their option; and shall at all times give them such further information by certificate, solemn declaration, or otherwise, as they may from time to time require, or as may be necessary or proper, in order to ascertain and prove the nature and extent of such injury."

In the course of the argument it was suggested (and I was at one time disposed to consider that there was some ground for the argument), that, connecting the sixth condition with the notice endorsed on the policy (which notice is also referred to and incorporated in it), the entire might be construed as importing, that the parties contemplated only giving of such a notice, in pursuance of the condition, as could be given by the *insurer himself*. If that were the true import of the contract taken as a whole, the provision for giving notice within seven days could not, of course, by any reasonable construction, be treated as contemplating the giving of the notice by the insured, in the case of his instantaneous death resulting from the accident. The notice endorsed on the policy is headed "Special notice *to Insurers*". The notice states:

> "In every case of accident where a claim *is intended to be made*, notice of the

accident must be delivered at the chief office, 7, Bank Buildings, corner of Old Jewry, London, within seven days, in pursuance of the sixth condition; and *insurers are informed*, that notice given to or by any local agent will not be a compliance with that condition, and in this respect time shall be considered as the essence of the contract."

It was argued that, as this notice was specially addressed to insurers, and as "insurers" were informed of what was to be done, the Company, by the notice, intended to convey, and did convey, what was to be done by "insurers", and not what was to be done by others. It was argued that the matters required by the notice (which contains in substance a repetition of requirements contained in the sixth condition), were matters to be done by the insurers, and not by others. And it was argued, that it therefore followed, that when the death of the insurer, who was also the insured, was instantaneous (an event plainly within the range of the contract and contemplated in it), since those matters could not be done by the insurer, they need not be done at all.

The fallacy of this argument is made apparent by adverting to the terms of the sixth condition, and of the notice. The notice is addressed to insurers, because it is with them that the Company deals. *They* are "informed" of what the Company requires, because they are the persons who are interested in measures being taken for the doing of that which the Company so requires. And, although a man cannot serve a notice after he has ceased to live, it is perfectly practicable for him so to arrange that what is required by the Company shall be done by a survivor. The terms of the sixth condition, and of the notice, specify two classes of requirements: first, what is to be done "in the event of *any* accident, whether fatal or not, occurring to the insured"; secondly, what is to be done "in case the accident shall not prove fatal". In the latter case, *the insurer* is required, within seven days from the accident, to furnish a full written report by a medical practitioner of the facts of the case; and the insurer is to furnish further information, and to submit himself to examination, in the manner described in the sixth condition. But the former provision, which is expressly applied to *any* accident, whether *fatal or not*, does not specify by whom the notice shall be given, but peremptorily requires that the notice shall be given within seven days. The matters of which such notice is required are not matters lying within the knowledge of the insured alone. They can be learned by any surviving member of his family, by any surviving friend, or by any person having means of inquiring into the facts. They are — the nature and date of the injuries; the place where and the manner in which they were received; and the name, address, and occupation of the person injured. The omission to state *by whom* the notice required by the first provision, and the express statement that the insured shall give the information required in the second provision, shows that the parties to the contract stipulated that the requirements of the first provision should be complied with, by whomsoever that should be done — whether by the insurer himself or by some other person. It contemplated a fatal accident, and it must have contemplated that deadly injuries might make it impossible for the insured to do what was required; and, consequently, that cases might occur in which it must be done by another.

The provision, applied to instantaneous death, was represented in the argument as a most unreasonable condition. Even if it were, it would still be binding, if its meaning were clear. If the words were capable of two constructions, we might adopt one which was reasonable, and reject one which was not. But the language of the first proviso of this sixth condition is clear and unambiguous; and we cannot free either of the parties from a contract which they have both made for themselves, because *we* may think it was very unwise in one of the parties to engage in it. But I confess I do not think this was an unreasonable provision. This Company must be considered as having framed their policies with a view to the possibility of many casualties of various kinds. In order to protect themselves against unfounded or aggravated claims, it was very important that they should, in every instance in which a casualty should occur likely to originate a claim against them, have the earliest opportunity, when the facts should be recent, and when evidence could be more easily and satisfactorily procured than it could be after the lapse of any considerable time, of inquiring into the circumstances of the casualty, the nature of the injury, and the position of the insured. After a prolonged interval, other casualties might happen, and new claims might arise; and the Company might be encumbered with a multitude of claims and inquires, beyond the power of their ordinary staff to examine sufficiently into the facts, and to report upon then fully to the Company. Upon the true, and (I think, on consideration) the clear and manifest construction of this contract, it was a condition precedent to the right of recovering on the policy, that the notice required by the first provision of the sixth condition should be given to the Company by *some* one, even in the case of the accident causing the instantaneous death of the insured.

As to the second argument urged on the part of the Plaintiff, that the condition was discharged by the act of God, in the instantaneous death of the insured, it is answered by the contract itself. If the contract was, as I conceive it was, that the required notice *should* be given by *some* one, the instantaneous death of the insured did not render it impossible to do what the condition required, since it could have been done by a survivor. The Plaintiff's counsel relied on the averment in the Summons and Plaint, that "no other person having knowledge of the existence of the said policy, or of its having been executed, or of the aforesaid contract of assurance, had, within such seven days, any knowledge or notice of such occurrence, or could give the Defendants any notice thereof." That averment only shows that the insured did not take the necessary means of enabling some one who was likely to survive him, if he should meet immediate death by a sudden accident, to give the necessary notice, by apprising some of his family or friends of the policy, and of the strict condition contained in it. The dispensation of Providence, in his instantaneous death, would not have occasioned the omission to give the necessary notice, but for his own neglect in not providing for that contingency. The case is, therefore, entirely without the range of those exceptions to the rule laid down in *Paradine* v. *Jane*,[1] and in the class of authorities of which

---

[1] Aleyn, 26.

several are cited in the note to *Walton* v. *Waterhouse*,[2] of which exceptions *Taylor* v. *Caldwell*[3] is one of the latest examples. In those cases it was held that, in the nature and import of the contract itself, there was that which involved an implied condition that the destruction of the person, or the thing, with which the contract dealt, should absolve from its performance — which was the case of *Taylor* v. *Caldwell*.[4] There, A agreed with B to give him the use of a music hall on certain specified days, for the purpose of holding concerts, with no express stipulation for the event of the destruction of the music hall by fire. It was held that both parties were excused from the performance of the contract. "In none of those contracts," says Mr Justice Blackburn in his judgment, "is the promise in words other than positive, nor is there any express stipulation that the destruction of the person or thing shall excuse the performance; but that excuse is by law implied, because, from the nature of the contract, it is apparent that the parties contracted upon the basis of the continued existence of the particular person or chattel." "In the present case" (he continues), "looking at the whole case, we find that the parties contracted on the basis of the continued existence of the music hall at the time when the concerts were to be given; that being essential to their performance." In this case of *Gamble* v. *The Accident Assurance Company*, now before us, the distinction, to which I have already adverted, between the language of the sixth condition, where it deals with all accidents which do not prove fatal, and its language where it deals with all accidents, whether fatal or not, appears to me to exempt this case from the application of the class of authorities to which *Taylor* v. *Caldwell*[5] belongs. There is nothing stipulated for in the sixth condition, which, in the case of a casualty fatal to the insured, could not have been done by a survivor, whom the insured had taken the precaution of making acquainted with the policy.

We are of opinion that the Defendants are entitled to judgment on this demurrer.

Patton *v.* The Employers' Liability Assurance Corporation (Limited)
(1887)20 L.R.I. 93
Court of Common Pleas

HARRISON J: We are of opinion that the condition, [Condition no. 3:—

> "In the event of any accident, hereby assured against, happening to the assured, he, or his representatives, shall give notice thereof in writing to the Corporation within 10 days [and 14 days in the case of the second policy] of its occurrence, stating the number of the policy, the nature and date of the

---

[2] 2 Wms. Saund. 422, a.
[3] 3 B. & S. 826.
[4] *Ibid.*
[5] *Ibid.*

injuries, the place where and the manner in which they were received, the
extent of the disablement, and the name and then present address and
occupation of the person injured; and also, within fourteen days of the
accident, forward to the head office of the Corporation a written report from
the assured's medical attendant, who shall be a duly qualified and registered
medical practitioner, of the facts of the case, and nature and extent of the
injuries received; and shall, at his or their own expense, forward to the said
office, within the space of seven days after demand, such certificate, statements, and declarations, in proof of the identity of the assured, the origin,
nature, and extent of the injuries received, the title of the claimant, and
generally all such information in support of the claim as the Directors for the
time being shall reasonably require; and unless this condition shall have
been complied with, both as to time and otherwise (time being of the essence
of the contract), no person shall be entitled to claim under this policy."]

indorsed on these policies respectively requiring the assured, or his representative, in the event of the happening of any accident assured against, to
give notice in writing to the Corporation within ten days in the case of one of
the policies, and fourteen days in the other, stating the particulars specified
in the condition, apply to the case of an accident resulting in death, as in the
present instance, and is a condition precedent, which must be performed
before any claim can be made under the policy.

The policies are substantially in the same terms, and both recite that the
assured desired to effect an assurance against accident. They then provide
that, if the assured should sustain any personal injury, caused by accident
within the meaning of the policy and conditions, and such injuries should be
the immediate cause of the death of the assured within a certain time, or if
such injury should not result in death, but in permanent total disablement,
the Corporation would pay to the assured, or his legal personal representative, the sum of £500, within one calendar month after such death and the
cause thereof (or after such personal injury and the cause thereof), shall have
been proved to the satisfaction of the directors, and such verification of the
proposal of the assured as they shall require, and such information as is
required by the conditions, shall have been furnished. The policies therefore
contemplated an injury happening which might result in death, and in such
case the information required by the conditions is to be furnished before the
person assured, or his legal personal representative, should be entitled to
receive the sum assured.

Now the condition endorsed on the policies relied on by the defendants
specifies the information which the assured, or his representative, is to give
the Corporation within the time specified, before any person should be
entitled to claim under the policy; such information is to be given, in the
event of *any accident*; and as the policy assured against the result of accidents
which should be the immediate cause of death, as in this case, the furnishing
of such information is as much required to be given in that event as in the
case of an accident causing disablement; and the condition provides, that unless this condition shall have been complied with, both as to time and otherwise (time being of the essence of the contract), no person shall be entitled to
claim under this policy. In the case of a fatal accident, resulting in death, the
assured could not himself give the required notice, but the condition does not

require that in every case the assured is to give the notice, but that it should be given by him or his representatives.

The term "representative" does not, in my opinion, here mean legal personal representative, but some person who had been appointed by the assured to act in such a case and represent him by furnishing the required notice in writing within the specified time.

In the case of *Gamble* v. *The Accident Assurance Co.*[6] cited in the argument, the Chief Baron in his judgment ... says:— "Although a man cannot serve a notice after he has ceased to live, it is perfectly practicable for him so to arrange that what is required by the Company shall be done by a survivor." And in a later portion of the judgment, in answering the argument that the conditions requiring notice was discharged by the act of God, in the instantaneous death of the insured, the Chief Baron says...: —

> "That objection is answered by the contract itself. If the contract was, as I conceive it was, that the required notice should be given by some one, the instantaneous death of the insured did not render it impossible to do what the condition required, since it could have been done by a survivor."

The averment, in the summons and plaint, that no other person having knowledge or notice of the contract, had, within the specified time, knowledge or notice of the occurrence, or could give notice thereof, only shows, says the Chief Baron,

> "that the insured did not take the necessary means of enabling someone who was likely to survive him, if he should meet immediate death by a sudden accident, to give the necessary notice by apprising some of his family or friends of the policy and of the strict condition contained in it. The dispensation of Providence in his instantaneous death would not have occasioned the omission to give the necessary notice, but for his own neglect in not providing for that contingency."

It is clear that the Corporation (the defendants in this case) would require the information specified in the written notice, or the greater portion thereof, as much in a case of fatal injury resulting in death, as in one causing permanent or partial disablement. "The nature and date of the injuries, the place where, and the manner in which they were received", are all essential matters for them to inquire into, and there is no reason why the furnishing of this information should not be as much a condition precedent to the recovery of any claim under the policy in the case of instantaneous death as of death ensuing after a time from fatal injuries. According to the plaintiff's contention, no information of the death of the assured, or of its cause or particulars connected therewith, need be furnished to the defendants within any specified time; and they might be called on long after the death, which might have occurred in any part of Europe, to pay the whole sum assured, without having any information previously furnished to enable them to make the necessary investigations to satisfy them that the claimant was entitled to

---

[6] (1870) Ir. R. 4 C.L. 204. See p. 545 of this book.

recover under the policy. Such, in my opinion, is not the meaning of this contract, and the non-fulfilment of the condition in question furnishes, in my judgment, a complete answer to the action. As regards the condition requiring a written report from the assured's medical attendant, within fourteen days after the accident, it is possible that if the assured had no medical attendant, the non-furnishing of this report might not be held to be fatal to the claim under the policy; but such an excuse for not furnishing such report should be replied and proved if the Corporation defendants relied on the absence of such report as they do here.

The defendants, in my opinion, are entitled to have the verdict and judgment entered for them, with costs.

MURPHY J: I concur. This case cannot be distinguished in principle from that of *Gamble* v. *The Accident Insurance Co.*[7] The Chief Baron says...:

> "This Company must be considered as having framed their policies with a view to the possibility of many casualties of various kinds. In order to protect themselves against unfounded or aggravated claims, it was very important that they should, in every instance in which a casualty should occur likely to originate a case against them, have the earliest opportunity, when the facts should be recent, and when evidence could be more easily and satisfactorily procured than it could be after the lapse of any considerable time, of inquiring into the circumstances of the casualty, the nature of the injury, and the position of the assured."

All that applies more forcibly here, because it is of more vital moment, as applying to the case of fatal accidents, than any others. Therefore it is right to suppose that the Company, in guarding themselves against false claims, should insert conditions with respect to the notices that should be given in order to give them ample opportunity of investigating the claim.

In *Gamble's Case*[8] the Chief Baron says: "It was a condition precedent to the right of recovering on the policy that the notice ... should be given to the Company by *some* one." I am of opinion that it is not necessary that his representative should be a person appointed by him in his lifetime. Any person who took upon himself the duty of serving the notice on behalf of those interested in the policy would, in my opinion, be capable of giving notice under the term "representative". Did not this case illustrate the importance of it? There was a very extraordinary case to inquire into, viz. whether this man was accidentally drowned in eighteen inches of water. When should the Company have received the notice that would enable them to make inquiry into the circumstances under which the assured met his death? Independently of the authority of *Gamble's Case*,[9] we have no doubt as to the decision we should come to in this case.

---

[7] (1870) Ir. R. 4 C.L. 204. See p. 545 of this book.
[8] *Ibid.*
[9] *Ibid.*

Weir *v.* The Northern Counties of England Insurance Company
(1879) L.R.I. Vol. IV
Court of Common Pleas

LAWSON J: This was an action upon a policy of insurance against fire, effected with the Defendants' Company on the 29th of November, 1878. The case was tried at Belfast Spring Assizes, 1879, before Mr Baron Dowse and a special jury, and resulted in a verdict for the Plaintiff for £262. A rule was obtained to set aside this verdict....

... Mr Boyd for the Company, contending that he was entitled to a verdict, upon the defence that Plaintiff had not delivered an account within fifteen days after the happening of the loss. This turns upon the construction of the fifth condition endorsed on the policy, which is in these words,

> ["On the happening of any loss or damage by fire to any of the property hereby insured, the insured is forthwith to give notice in writing thereof to the Company, and, within fifteen days at latest, to deliver to the Company as particular an account as may be reasonably practicable of the several articles or matters damaged or destroyed by the fire, with the estimated value of each of them respectively, having regard to their several values at the time of the fire, and in support thereof to give all such vouchers, proofs and explanations as may be reasonably required, together with, if required, a statutory declaration of the truth of the account; and, in default thereof, no claim in respect of such loss or damage shall be payable until such notice, account, proof and explanation respectively are given and produced, and such statutory declaration, if required, is made."]

Notice was given forthwith of the loss, but the Plaintiff did not deliver an account within fifteen days after the happening of the loss, though he did so before action. This raises the question, whether upon the true construction of this clause, the delivery of the account within fifteen days is a condition precedent to the right to recover; and that turns upon the meaning of this condition taken as a whole.

This particular form of condition, though now commonly adopted in fire policies, does not seem to have been the subject of judicial decision. If the condition had stopped before the words, "and in default thereof", etc., the case would have been clear upon the authorities. The early case of *Worsley* v. *Woods*[10] followed in *Mason* v. *Harvey*[11] shows that the delivery of such account and particulars is a condition precedent where the clause requires that delivery. In that case Pollock, C.B. says,

> "By the contract of the parties the delivery of the particulars of loss is made a condition precedent to the right to recover. Such a condition is in substance most reasonable; otherwise a party might lie by for four or five years after the loss, and then send in a claim when the Company perhaps had no means of investigating it."

---

[10] 6 T.R. 710.
[11] 8 Exch. 819.

The same point was decided in *Roper* v. *Lendon*,[12] where it was decided that the delivery of the particulars was essential before action, and that it should be within fifteen days after the loss.

The question then is, do the subsequent words used here take away from the force of the preceding, which, if they stood alone, would be conclusive against the Plaintiff's claim? No precise form of words is necessary to make a condition precedent, but the question must depend on the intention of the parties, to be collected from the instrument. Here the Plaintiff contends that the words "in default thereof", that is, in case the party fails to comply with the condition to give particulars within fifteen days, no claim shall be payable until such notice, account, etc., are given and produced, have the effect of only deferring the right to payment until the notice and account are given, and thus enlarging the time; and undoubtedly if that be the construction, it has the effect of rendering practically inoperative the words "within fifteen days at latest" and would enable the assured to withhold his account until a time when it might be impossible for the Company to check it. Why then are these words added, without which the clause would have had the stringent operation of a condition precedent? Is it not for the purpose of defining what shall be the consequence of failure to comply with the requirements of giving the notice and account within the time limited; and instead of saying that in default no action shall be brought or payment made, it says, that no claim shall be payable *until* such notice and account, etc., are given, thus giving an enlarged time for doing it, provided it is done before the claim is payable? This is the ordinary grammatical construction of the words, and it may well be that those words were added in order to get over in favour of the assured the stringency of the prior words, as interpreted by the cases to which I have referred. It would be very hard on an assured if, by reason of absence from the country when the fire took place, he could not send in his account until after fifteen days, that he should lose the benefit of the policy; and such a condition might deter persons from insuring in an office which imposed it. Besides, the words are those of the Company's own form, and the maxim applies, *fortius contra proferentem*. We are, therefore, of opinion that the delivery of the account within fifteen days is not a condition precedent to the right to recover. The cause shown must, therefore, be allowed with costs, and judgment given for the Plaintiff for £262.

Car and General Insurance Corporation Ltd.
v. Patrick J. Munden
[1936] I.R. 584
The High Court

MEREDITH J: As the result of a collision between the defendant's motor car and a bus belonging to the Magnet Bus Co. the defendant suffered personal injuries and also damage to his car. Against the latter risk he was insured

---

[12] 1 E. & E. 824.

with the plaintiffs, but, although he was also insured with them against certain grave personal injuries, he was not so insured against loss from the injuries actually suffered. Acting on instruction from the plaintiffs the defendant made a claim against the Magnet Bus Co., and the claim for the personal injuries was settled for the sum of £40. The correspondence and all the circumstances of the case made it clear, as in fact has now been admitted by a representative of the Magnet Bus Co., that the settlement was only in respect of the personal injuries, but, by an oversight, the receipt for the £40, which was on a printed form, expressly discharged the Bus Co. from claims in respect of damage to property as well as in respect of personal injuries, and, up to the hearing of this action by the Circuit Court Judge, the plaintiffs believed the receipt would be a bar to any claim against the Bus Co. for damage to the car. If it were such a bar the plaintiffs were in a very awkward position, for, exercising an option reserved to them under the policy, they had undertaken the repair of the car and had paid the firm of Messrs Treacy the sum of £130 for the repairs. They thus lost the protection, given to them under the conditions of the policy, of repudiating liability because of the defendant's breach of condition 2 of the policy. [Condition 2 ... provided that "no admission, offer, promise, payment or indemnity shall be made or given by or on behalf of the assured without the written consent of the Corporation which shall be entitled, if it so desires, to take over and conduct in the name of the assured the defence or settlement of any claim, or to prosecute in the name of the assured for its own benefit any claim for indemnity or damages or otherwise, and shall have full discretion in the conduct of any proceedings or in the settlement of any claim...," and condition 9 made the due observance and fulfilment of the terms and provisions of the policy a condition precedent to any liability of the Corporation to make any payment under the policy.] Accordingly they brought this action and now seek to recover the £130 from the defendant as money paid by them for the use of the defendant, or, in the alternative, they claim the £130 as damages sustained by reason of the breach by the defendant of the terms and conditions of the policy.

At the hearing before the learned Circuit Court Judge, Judge Davitt, attention seems to have focused entirely on the questions: first, whether the receipt was a breach of condition 2 of the policy, and, second, whether the receipt under all the circumstances would enable the Bus Co. successfully to defend an action for the damage to the car. The learned Circuit Court Judge, in a judgment which is altogether convincing on these points, held that the receipt made an admission which constituted a breach in condition 2, but that the settlement was only in respect of the personal injuries. The latter finding, however, he held, and I think quite rightly, did not affect the question as to the breach of the condition. That being so, he held that the plaintiffs "are under no liability to pay Mr Munden for the damage done to his car." The judgment of the learned Circuit Court Judge then continues in these words: "The car went to Mr Treacy and received repairs on their responsibility. Accordingly, I think the money paid to Mr Treacy was paid on behalf of Mr Munden, and the Car and General Insurance Co. had no liability for it. It was done at his request."

The difficulties attending these further steps do not appear to have been stressed in the argument that had been addressed to the Court. The liability of the plaintiffs to make good the damage done to the defendant's car was not an issue in the action, for the plaintiffs had already discharged that liability. The plaintiffs by discharging their liability under the contract had lost their right of relying on condition 2 as a condition precedent, for breach of which they could repudiate liability. A party can always waive a condition exclusively for his benefit, and may do by conduct: *Panoutsos* v. *Raymond Hadley Corporation of New York*;[13] and accordingly, when the plaintiffs chose to discharge their liability without waiting to see that the defendant would observe the conditions imposed on him, they have to look round for some remedy other than that of repudiating liability.

The claim to recover the £130 as money paid for the use of the defendant is altogether unsustainable. There was certainly no express request. Though the car was originally given to Messrs Treacy by the defendant, the matter was taken out of his hands by the plaintiffs, who exercised their option. It was on the plaintiff's instructions that Messrs Treacy repaired the car, and the plaintiffs, as debtors, paid Messrs Treacy's account — and the learned Circuit Court Judge himself seems so to have held. The only ground, then, on which a request can have been thought to have been implied is the subsequent fact that the defendant did something which would have entitled the plaintiffs to disclaim liability if they had left the repairs in the defendant's hands. But such an *ex post facto* matter cannot make the transaction something which it was not at the time.

The question, however, of the plaintiffs' right to claim damages for breach of the condition is a much more difficult question. In any case the claim for the £130 is unsustainable. That claim was based on the assumption that the receipt clearly put an end to any action against the Magnet Bus Co. As that assumption is quite unwarranted, the damages, if any, resulting from the breach of the condition are altogether hypothetical, but, if there has been a definite breach of contract, the plaintiffs may be able to recover nominal damages. Consequently, it is necessary to consider if the loss of the right to rely on condition 2 as a condition precedent does not still leave the plaintiffs with a right of action for damages for breach of contract.

The nature, extent and full effect of the waiver implied by reason of a party to a contract accepting liability thereunder notwithstanding the non-performance of a term which is a condition precedent to his liability raise difficult questions, which have been considered in a number of cases, many of which have been complicated by the provisions of certain statutes, such as the Sale of Goods Act or the Statute of Frauds, or by the fact that the contract is one for the sale of land. One of these questions is whether, in a particular case, the effect of the waiver is to eliminate the term from the contract, the term being treated as a condition which, being waived, "the party is in the same situation as if it had never existed," per Tindal C.J. in *Alexander* v. *Gardner*,[14] or whether the wavier is only of a right to repudiate liability, wavier of which right leaves the term of the contract standing as one for

---

[13] [1917] 2 K.B. 473.
[14] 1 Bing. N.C. 671 at p.677.

breach of which compensation in damages may be recovered, as, for example
in *Bentsen* v. *Taylor*.[15] To say that the claim for damages remains when the
condition ceases to be available as a condition precedent seems to imply
either that the term of the contract may be analysable into two distinct
factors, namely, an undertaking on the one hand, and, on the other, a provision for a certain remedy in the event of a breach, or else that the contract
may be construed by reference to matter *ex post facto*. The latter alternative
view seems to be that favoured by Pollock C.B. in *Ellen* v. *Topp*[16]: —

> "It is remarkable that, according to this rule, the construction of the instru-
> ment may be varied by matter *ex post facto*; and that which is a condition
> precedent when the deed is executed may cease to be so by the subsequent
> conduct of the covenantee in accepting less."

The comments of Lord Shaw on this view in *Wallis, Son & Wells* v. *Pratt and
Haynes*[17] do not favour its adoption. The judgment of Fletcher Moulton L.J. in
Wallis, Son & Wells v. *Pratt and Haynes*,[18] and in particular, the observation
(at p. 1013): "But in the case of a breach of a condition he has the option of
another and a higher remedy, namely, that of treating the contract as repudiated" favours the first alternative. On this view, where, in a particular case,
the right to bring an action for damages survives the waiver of the condition
as a condition precedent, it is because there is an undertaking which has been
broken, and the ordinary remedy for the breach is not affected by waiver of
the right to resort to the higher remedy, provision for which is regarded as a
distinct element. To say, however, that, in a particular case, the right to bring
an action for damages is lost once the condition precedent is waived seems to
imply either that there is no distinct undertaking, but only a provision that
liability is to be subject to a certain condition, or else that, though there is an
undertaking, the right to repudiate liability in toto on a breach of the
undertaking can only be got rid of by a discharge of the obligation in one way
or another. In each of these latter cases once the condition disappears as a
condition precedent nothing remains on which to bring an action for damages.
It is hardly necessary to point out that the different cases present their
different special difficulties, such, for example, as the discharge of an
obligation under an executed contract.

The consideration in the abstract of the different positions that may arise
is much more difficult than the consideration of the position in a given,
particular, case. In the present case the only difficulty that seems to present
itself is that of saying whether or not condition 2 contains a definite
undertaking, express or implied, on the part of the insured not to do certain
things. Looking to condition 1 and 5 it might very plausibly be said that these
conditions do not impart an undertaking on the part of the insured to give
certain notices or to maintain his motor car in efficient condition, and that
these are matters entirely for himself, but that if he chooses not to comply

---

[15] [1893] 2 Q.B. 274.
[16] 6 Exch. 424, at p. 441.
[17] [1911] A.C. 394, at p. 400.
[18] [1910] 2 K.B. 1003 at p.1013.

with the conditions the insurers are, under condition 9, exempt from liability, which exemption is the beginning and end of the matter. In the same way it may be said that the insured does not under condition 2 undertake not to do the things there mentioned, and that the condition must be read in conjunction with condition 9 and that, taking both together, one meaning alone is to be extracted, namely, that, it the insurers are to be liable, the insured is not to do any of the things mentioned.

Of course, so long as the higher remedy of repudiating liability continues to exist the question of damages for breach of a purely protective condition of this kind, considered as involving a simple undertaking, does not arise. At common law a party is in all cases left free to break his contract and pay damages for so doing. Hence, where the payment of damages does not enter into the question because of the completeness of the remedy of repudiating liability altogether, the character of the condition as involving a simple undertaking, and the remedy of payment of damages for breach, both remain in the background or may be said to be merely latent. Furthermore, a condition precedent is naturally worded more explicitly in reference to the higher remedy. But, once the right to insist on the higher remedy is waived, the latent character of the simple undertaking emerges and comes to the front. It seems doubtful, if in those cases in which the rule to which Pollock C.B. refers in *Ellen* v. *Topp*[19] applies, the construction is really varied by matter *ex post facto*, and not merely directed to a latent character of the condition which is entirely obscured so long as the remedy of repudiation remains open. But, however that may be, this much is clear from *Ellen* v. *Topp*[20] and other similar authorities, that either the construction of a condition precedent may be varied by matter *ex post facto*, so as to allow an action for damages for breach of contract to be brought, or else a stipulation which in itself gives rise to an action for damages for breach may have that fundamental character almost entirely obscured while it is clothed and parades as a condition precedent.

These considerations dispose of the main difficulty in the present case, which is simplified by the fact that the character of a condition precedent is given to condition 2 by a separate condition which appears as condition 9. This latter condition has been waived by the conduct of the plaintiffs who have discharged their liability without waiting to see if the defendant would in all respects faithfully observe condition 2. Accordingly, condition 9 may be disregarded, and the question is then whether condition 2 contains an undertaking that the defendant will not do what the condition says he is not to do, and what the learned Circuit Court Judge has rightly held he has done. On the authorities it is clear that either the condition, as I would think, immediately involves such an undertaking, though it may be only as an implicit and latent undertaking, or else that, while not originally such an undertaking, it is now available as such owing to the subsequent waiver of the condition as a condition precedent. On either view the plaintiffs are entitled to damages for the breach.

---

[19] 6 Exch. 424.
[20] *Ibid.*

The plaintiffs anticipated that they would have no difficulty in showing that, owing to the receipt given by the defendant, he had lost his right to recover anything from the Magnet Bus Co. in respect of the damage to his car, and that they had been damnified accordingly. Having failed to show the loss of defendant's right of action, they are in the position of having failed to prove damage. The award of £130 by the learned Circuit Court Judge must be varied to one for nominal damages.....

SULLIVAN P. CONCURRED.

In the Matter of the Equitable Insurance Company Limited and in the Matter of the Companies Acts 1908 to 1959 — John Butler, Applicant
[1970] I.R. 45
The High Court

KENNY J: On the 21st March, 1959, the Equitable Insurance Company Limited issued a private motor-car policy to Mr Butler in relation to motor car IR 8900. This provided under the heading "Insured driving other vehicles" that, subject to the limitations on liability for driving the car mentioned in the Schedule (IR 8900), the Equitable would indemnify Mr Butler in respect of any event while he was personally driving a car not belonging to him. The Equitable's liability to indemnify Mr Butler in respect of the car was expressed to be "subject to the terms, exceptions and conditions contained herein or endorsed or otherwise expressed hereon". Under the heading "Conditions" on one of the pages of the policy, there appeared a clause which read: "The Insured shall give notice in writing to the Head Office or any Branch Office of the Company as soon as practicable after the occurrence of any event in consequence of which the Company may become liable under this Policy with full particulars thereof..."

On the 27th May, 1963, this Court ordered that the Equitable was to be wound up. On the 24th June, 1963, when the policy issued by the Equitable was in force, Mr Butler was driving a car owned by Mr Kieran Kenny for which a policy issued by the Ocean Accident Insurance Company was in force. Mr Kenny was a passenger in the car on that day and was injured because of Mr Butler's carelessness. The accident policy of the Ocean company, I have been informed, contained a clause under which that insurance company was not liable to indemnify the driver against a claim by Mr Kenny.

The Equitable did not get any notification of Mr Butler's claim for indemnity against them until the 31st July, 1964.

Mr Kenny subsequently got judgment against Mr Butler for £3,100 damages and for costs which were subsequently taxed at £504 14s. 1d. The official liquidator repudiated all liability of the Equitable to indemnify Mr Butler who has now applied under s.3, sub-s. 3, of the Insurance Act, 1964, for an order that I should find the amount awarded by the judgment to be reasonable and for an order for payment under s.3, sub-s, 1. of that Act.

In my opinion, Mr Butler did not give the Equitable notice of the occurrence of the event, creating a liability to indemnify, as soon as practicable. Mr Butler's belief (that there was no purpose in giving notice as the Equitable was known to be insolvent) did not free him from his obligation to notify them of the accident. He committed a breach of one of the conditions of the policy and the Equitable are not liable to indemnify him against Mr Kenny's claim.

Before I can make an order for payment out of the insurance fund it must be shown that there is a sum "which is due to a person under a policy" issued by the Equitable — see s. 3, sub-s. 1, of the Act of 1964. There was a delay of 13 months in giving notice and it had not been suggested that Mr Butler was incapable of giving notice immediately after the accident. There is nothing due to Mr Butler under the policy issued by the Equitable and I refuse the application.

The Supreme Court

BUDD J: The applicant in this case, John Butler, held a motor-car policy with the Equitable Insurance Company (which I shall call "the company")....

So far as this case is concerned the relevant conditions are Conditions No. 1 and 6 which are as follows:—

> "1. The Insured shall give notice in writing to the Head Office or any Branch Office of the Company as soon as practicable after the occurrence of any event in consequence of which the Company may become liable under this Policy with full particulars thereof, or, where such event did not occur in the Insured's presence, within 48 hours after the occurrence of such event first came to his knowledge together with such particulars of such event as are in his knowledge or procurement."

> "6. The due observance and fulfilment of the terms provisions and conditions of this Policy and/or of any Endorsement thereon in so far as they relate to anything to be done or complied with by the Insured and the truth of the statements and answers in the said proposal shall be conditions precedent to any liability of the Company to make any payment under this Policy."

... The applicant appeals to this Court on the ground that the learned judge was wrong in law in holding that the proper inference from the facts was that the applicant was in breach of Condition no. 1 of the policy, and on the ground that the learned judge misdirected himself in holding that the expression "as soon as practicable" in Condition No. 1 means only as soon as possible having regard to the circumstances of the accident and the state of health and physical capacity of the insured. A further ground was that the judge was wrong in law in determining that the liability of the company under the policy was properly repudiated by the liquidator but this ground was not pursued and it is, in any event, unsustainable. The final ground was that the learned judge was wrong in law in determining that no sum was due to the applicant by the company under the policy.

The accident involving injury to Mr Kenny was obviously an event in consequence of which the company might become liable under the policy, and it was equally clear under the terms of Condition No. 1 of the policy that the applicant was under an obligation to give notice of the accident to the company "as soon as practicable" after its occurrence. Condition No. 6 made the due observance and fulfilment of the condition of the policy a condition precedent to the liability of the company to make any payment under the policy. If the applicant did not comply with Condition No. 1 the company was under no liability to him. The issue before the court below and before this court was whether the applicant gave notice to the company "as soon as practicable" after the accident. The applicant did not himself give Mr Sandys, the official liquidator of the company, notice of the accident until the 7th November, 1964. Therefore, notice of the accident was not given by the applicant for a period of over sixteen months from the happening of the accident. It is true that the official liquidator did receive notice of the accident from Mr Kenny's solicitors on the 31st July, 1964. That notice was not given in accordance with the terms of the policy which requires that the notice should be given by the insured. But even assuming (though not so deciding) that the notice of the 31st July, 1964, could be held to be effective under the terms of the policy, there would have been a delay in giving notice of over 13 months.

The first reasons given by the applicant for not giving prompt notice were that he was not aware of the intention of Mr Kenny to bring proceedings, that he thought Mr Kenny's insurers would indemnify him or that Mr Kenny would proceed against them. The obligation under the condition in question, I may observe, was not to give notice of anyone's intention to proceed nor to give notice of proceedings against him. It was to give notice of the accident as an event in consequence of which the company might become liable under the policy. Therefore, these two alleged reasons for not giving notice of the accident are irrelevant. He also says, however, that when the plenary summons was served on him he did in fact forward it to the official liquidator on the 7th November, 1964, and he had therefore given notice as soon as practicable in the circumstances of the case. The circumstances relied on were that prior to the accident he had received a letter from the company advising him to insure with some other company and that he had read in the newspapers that the company was in liquidation. He says that he believed that in such circumstances there was no possibility of the company being in a position to meet any claim which Mr Kenny might bring in respect of the accident.

The argument founded on the applicant's alleged belief amounts to this, that it was not practicable to give notice of the accident to the company before he did so because no useful purpose would be served in giving notice to a company which the applicant believed to be insolvent and unable to pay; and it was on this branch of the case that most of the argument took place.

It is contended on behalf of the applicant that the words in the condition must be looked at from his point of view and thus should be construed having regard to the end intended to be achieved by the insured, namely, the obtaining of payment by way of indemnity from the insurer. It was submitted that the words of the condition involved the insured in having to make a decision as to what was practicable in the particular circumstances of the case. It was further submitted that the relevant circumstances in the eyes of the applicant were that he believed that the company could not pay and that it was impracticable, in the sense that nothing was to be achieved thereby, to give notice to the company. In colloquial language this seems to me to mean that it was not a practical proposition to give notice which would achieve nothing, and that the word "practicable" should be construed in this sense. If so construed, it was contended that there had been no breach of the condition by reason of the failure of the applicant to give prompt notice. Driven to its logical conclusion, it would seem to me that the contention came to this: that the condition should be construed from the point of view of the insured (that is to say, from his subjective standpoint) and that it should be construed as only requiring notice to be given to the insurer when it became apparent to the insured that a practical object (namely, that of being paid) could be achieved.

I agree that, in deciding whether or not something has been done "as soon as practicable" after a particular event, regard must be paid to the context in which the words are used and the surrounding circumstances. In this case the words are used in a motor insurance policy providing for the indemnity of the insured by the insurer in certain circumstances. Furthermore, they are used in that part of the contract between the parties which places an obligation on the insured to perform certain obligations to the insurer before the insurer becomes liable to indemnify the insured in respect of the event insured against. Having regard to the nature of the policy, the prima facie object of a clause such as Condition No. 1 in this policy is to give the insurer some reasonable protection against unsustainable or fraudulent claims by giving him the opportunity to investigate the circumstances of an event which may give rise to liability, such as an accident, at the first opportunity when the facts can be ascertained most easily and the insurer can thus ascertain his position as regards liability.

Some indication of what is in the contemplation of the parties to the contract may be derived from the wording of the second part of the condition which provides that, where the event under which the company may become liable under the policy did not occur in the insured's presence, the insured must give notice of the occurrence within 48 hours after the event first came to his knowledge, and must supply such particulars of the event as are within his knowledge. There also appears on the front of the policy the following words:— "In case of accident immediate notice must be given to the Company." Stress is thus laid on the importance of the company being put in possession of the facts immediately after or within a short time of the occurrence. The only reasonable object would appear to be to enable investigations to be made. If that be so, it could not reasonably be said that the giving of information as soon as practicable was to depend upon what the applicant thought his obligation was, or that his failure to give notice might be justified by a consideration of what he thought his chances were of recovering ultimately a sum to be paid in respect of such liability as he might have incurred to the injured party by reason of the accident.

The words of Condition No. 1 of the policy must be construed according to their ordinary and grammatical meaning. The meaning to be ascribed to the word "practicable" is of first importance. I have had occasion previously to consider the meaning of the word "practicable" in the case of *O'Donovan* v.

The Attorney General.[21] In that case I pointed out that Lord Goddard L.C.J. in *Lee* v. *Nursery Furnishings Ltd*.[22] had accepted the meaning "practicable" as contained in the Oxford Dictionary as "capable of being ... carried out in action ... feasible," and I do not see any reason for thinking that the word should be given any other meaning by reason of its use in the present context. I think the same reasoning applies in this case as was applied in *O'Donovan's Case*,[23] namely, that "As to what is 'practicable' depends upon the relevant circumstances" and that "In order to discover what is practicable in the circumstances thus involves determining what difficulties there are that should properly be taken into consideration having regard to that which is enjoined to be done." In accordance with the views I have just expressed, the words in the condition "as soon as practicable" should be construed in the sense of "capable of being ... carried out in action ... feasible." In deciding whether or not the applicant has complied with Condition No. 1, account can only be taken of such difficulties as make the giving of notice not feasible or not capable of being carried out in action. Any view that the applicant may have had that there was no point in giving notice to the company, because of the applicant's belief in its inability to pay, is irrelevant. Such a view does not create any difficulty in giving notice or make it not feasible to give notice. Further, from the definition of the word "practicable" which I have accepted, it follows that the type of difficulty that one has to consider in deciding whether or not it was practicable to give notice sooner than was done is one of a practical nature such as a difficulty arising through illness or through a break-down in communications, or some other difficulty of the same nature. Having regard to the views which I have expressed, it seems to me that there were no difficulties of the kind that it would be legitimate to consider in the construction of the condition which made it impracticable for the applicant to give the necessary notice to the company immediately, or within a very short time, after the occurrence of the accident.

In fact no notice of any kind reached the company or the official liquidator until some 13 months after the accident and, in my view of the circumstances of the case, the notice then given could not be regarded by any stretch of the imagination as a compliance with the condition requiring notice to be given as soon as practicable. The same observation applies *a fortiori* to a notice given some 16 months after the occurrence of the accident. It being a condition precedent to the liability of the company that notice should be given as soon as practicable after the occurrence of an event in consequence of which the company might become liable under the policy, and such notice not having been given, there has been a breach of the conditions of the policy and the company, in my view, are not liable to indemnify the applicant. It follows that there is so sum due to the applicant under the policy and that no order can be made under s. 3 of the Insurance Act, 1964, and that the court below was right to dismiss the application. I would dismiss this appeal.

---

[21] [1961] I.R. 114, 132.
[22] (1945) 61 T.L.R. 263.
[23] [1961] I.R. 114, 132.

FITZGERALD J: ... The net point argued before Mr Justice Kenny and before this Court is whether the applicant had given notice of the accident to the company as soon as practicable so as to comply with Condition No. 1 of the policy and to establish his right to indemnity in respect of his potential liability to Kenny.

It was submitted by Mr Gannon on behalf of the applicant that the notice given on the 31st July, 1964, by Mr Kenny's solicitor was a compliance with Condition No. 1 on the basis that the delay in giving notice (from the 24th June, 1963, the date of the accident, until 13 months later) was explained and justified on two grounds. First, that the company being in liquidation and notice of cancellation of the policy having been received from the liquidator, the applicant believed that the company would not be in a position to meet his claim under the policy and, secondly, that he believed that Mr Kieran Kenny would claim against his own insurance company and not against the applicant. Mr Gannon argued that the words "as soon as practicable" in Condition No. 1 of the policy must be construed having regard to the existing circumstances. He submitted that, the insurance company being in liquidation and the liquidator having cancelled the policy, the applicant reasonably believed that the company was not in a position to pay, and consequently that it was not practicable to give notice as it could not have produced any final satisfactory result for the applicant. He further submitted that the applicant's belief that Kenny would not claim against him was a further justification for earlier notice to the company not being practicable. He submitted that the word "practicable" should be distinguished from the word "possible" and that, while it would have been possible to give notice earlier, it was not practicable for him to give notice prior to the 31st July, 1964, in the existing circumstances of the company's inability to pay or indemnify him and of his belief that Kenny would not claim against him. Mr Murphy, on behalf of the liquidator, did not contest the point that the word "practicable" should be construed differently from the word "possible", but he did contend (correctly, in my opinion) that the existing circumstances did not make it impracticable for the applicant to give notice prior to the 31st July, 1964.

The obvious purpose of Condition No. 1 is to enable the insurance company at an early date to investigate the circumstances of the accident and to decide whether the policy covers the accident, whether they will take over the contest of the action on the insured's behalf, whether they will contest the third party's claim and, if so, on what basis. Notwithstanding the fact that at the time of the accident the company was in liquidation, the liquidator was entitled to be put in the same position as the company to make the necessary investigation. The failure of the applicant to give prompt notice deprived the liquidator of the opportunity to make such an early investigation. The applicant's belief that the company or the liquidator could not meet a claim may have justified a belief that a notification by him would be of no benefit to him — although even that belief was proved subsequently to have been erroneous having regard to the provisions of the Act of 1964 which made funds available. Quite apart from that, the applicant disclosed no reason for believing that the company would be unable to pay any part of his claim as distinct from meeting it in full. Even if the word "practicable" is to be construed as meaning "not worthwhile" from his point of view, his belief that the company would have no funds at all to meet a claim was unjustified. The applicant's belief that Kenny would not claim against him seems to have sprung from an intimation from Kenny that he would claim against his own insurance company. Kenny's insurance policy was not exhibited, nor does it appear that the applicant ever inspected it. It would be surprising if that policy provided for any benefit to Kenny which would correspond with the verdict which he subsequently obtained against the applicant. In any event Kenny was entitled to change his mind and proceed against the applicant. There was no reasonable justification for the belief of the applicant that Kenny precluded himself from looking to the applicant for compensation for his injuries.

Even assuming that the applicant was justified in his belief that the insurance company had no money to meet the claim under the policy and that Kenny would not claim against him, there was no practical difficulty about the applicant giving notice to the company. He knew that his policy covered his liability; he knew the facts of the accident and he knew that Kenny was injured. He elected against notifying the company, not because of any impracticability in doing so but because he thought it was not worth his while. He chose to ignore the fact that the condition requiring notice to be given was one for the protection of the insurance company. In my opinion the applicant was clearly in breach of Condition No. 1 of the policy and the decision of Mr Justice Kenny that the company was not liable to indemnify him was correct. There being no liability of the company to indemnify the applicant, his application for an order for payment out of the insurance fund was properly refused. The appeal should be dismissed.

In the matter of the Arbitration Act 1954, and of an Arbitration between Gaelcrann Teoranta and Michael Payne and Others, Underwriters at Lloyds
[1985] I.L.R.M. 109
The High Court

GANNON J: Pursuant to the provisions of a policy of insurance, described in the policy as contractor's liability insurance, under which the above-named underwriters contracted to indemnify the above-named insured (therein and hereinafter described as "the assured") against claims in respect of employer's liability a dispute thereunder was referred to arbitration. In the course of the arbitration a question arising out of interpretation of the conditions of the policy was raised for determination and on this the arbitrator Mr Frederick Morris, SC requests the advices of the court by this case stated.

The policy which is a Lloyd's policy contains under the heading "General Conditions attaching to this Insurance" a paragraph in the following terms:

> 5. Claims procedure.
> The assured shall give to O'Leary's Insurance Ltd, 7 South Mall, Cork immediate notice in writing, with full particulars of the happening of any occurrence which could give rise to a claim under this insurance, or of the

receipt by the assured of notice of any claim and of the institution of any proceedings against the assured. The assured shall not admit liability for or
offer or agree to settle any claim without the written consent of the underwriters who shall be entitled to take over and conduct in the name of the
assured the defence of any claim and to prosecute in the assured's name or
underwriters' benefit any claim for indemnity or damages or otherwise
against any third party and shall have full discretion in the conduct of any
negotiations and proceedings and the settlement of any claim. The assured
shall give to the underwriters such information and assistance as the underwriters may reasonably require.

A sub-heading in relation to the conditions in this section of the policy states
"All conditions are precedent to liability under this insurance". Two claims
were made by one of the employees of the assured in relation to personal
injuries on two different occasions in the course of employment with the
assured. The injured employee instituted proceedings in the High Court
against the assured by the issue and service in 1977 of two plenary summonses, one alleging injury in June 1975 and the other alleging injury in
August 1975. The assured notified the underwriters of these claims and
transmitted to them the two plenary summonses on 15 November 1977 and
claimed indemnity under the policy. The underwriters disclaimed liability by
reason of the alleged breach of condition 5 of the general conditions of the
policy and claimed to be prejudiced by the failure of the assured to comply
with that condition. To determine whether or not the assured is entitled to
recover the amounts of indemnity claimed under the policy the arbitrator
wishes to be advised:

> (a) On the true interpretation of the said contract of insurance, has the
> assured, by giving notice of a claim and of the institution of proceedings
> against the assured and the institution of the proceedings against him, com-
> plied with clause 5 of the agreement or in the alternative was he obliged,
> notwithstanding the aforesaid notice, to give full particulars in writing of the
> happening of an occurrence which could give rise to the claim?
> (b) Is the claims procedure as set out in clause 5 a condition precedent to the
> liability of the underwriters particularly having regard to the heading "all
> conditions are precedent to liability under this insurance"?
> (c) In the event of there being a finding of fact that the underwriters were in
> no way prejudiced by the failure on the part of the assured to give immediate
> notice in writing with full particulars of the happening of the occurrence
> which could give rise to a claim under the insurance, are the underwriters
> entitled to nevertheless rely upon this clause to avoid liability on the policy?

The questions as submitted in the case stated are expressed in a manner
which would seem to require findings of fact by this Court.

For the underwriters Mr Hill SC, argues that the word "or" where it first
appears in condition 5 of the general conditions is used in a conjunctive and
not a disjunctive sense so as to impose on the assured the obligation of giving
immediate notice in writing of all three matters. He submitted that failure on
the part of the assured to give notice of the happening of an occurrence which
could give rise to a claim in relation to which notice of institution of proceedings is later given releases the underwriters from liability because the

conditions as to giving notice are included in those under the heading "All conditions are precedent to liability under this insurance". He contended that because the condition as to giving notice is a condition precedent to liability the question of prejudice to the underwriters by the non-compliance of the assured with such conditions is irrelevant. In presenting his argument for the assured Mr O'Driscoll SC emphasised at the outset that because the policy document was a contract drawn by the underwriters which the assured had to adopt without alteration it should be construed strictly against them. He pointed out that in condition 5 of the general conditions the word "or" is used throughout in a disjunctive sense and that it should not be given a conjunctive meaning where first used as if the word "and" had been intended at that point only but was not used where it could have been used if so intended. He argued that unless all of the conditions described as being precedent to liability can be treated as conditions precedent none should be so read, and he referred to the wording used in some of the conditions which he submitted is inconsistent with such interpretation. He contended that the requirement of giving immediate notice in writing relates only to particulars of the happening of an occurrence which could give rise to a claim but not to the receipt by the assured of notice of a claim nor to the institution of proceedings against the assured. He submitted that the purpose of the requirement of giving immediate notice is to avoid any prejudice, caused by loss of time, to investigation of facts, and, where the facts are ascertained without reference to the assured there is no prejudice and liability cannot be avoided.

Some helpful observations on the principles to be applied in the construction of statues and documents and in particular on the interpretation of the words "or" and "and" which are capable of different use according to context are to be found in the opinions expressed in the House of Lords in *Reg.* v *Federal Steam Navigation Company Ltd.*[24] The provisions of s. 1(1) of the English statute the Oil and Navigable Waters Act 1955 which creates an offence of pollution for which a ship owner or master could be liable was under consideration. The word "or" was given a conjunctive meaning, rendering both the owner and the master liable to prosecution, on the ground that the alternative interpretation with disjunctive meaning would be absurd or unintelligible. Lord Reid in the course of a dissenting opinion says[25]:

"In my judgment the question here is whether there is anything in the Act or in surrounding circumstances which it is permissible to consider, which could justify striking out the word 'or' and substituting the words 'and ... each'. It would be necessary to put in the word 'each' because otherwise 'owner and master' could suggest a joint offence — a result for which no one contends.

There is a multitude of cases where courts have considered whether it is proper to substitute one word for another, and in particular whether it is proper to substitute 'and, for 'or' or vice versa. There may be some difference

---

[24] [1974] 1 W.L.R. 505.
[25] [1974] 1 W.L.R. 508.

between commercial or informal writings, on the one hand, and deeds and statutes on the other. One is entitled to expect greater skill in drafting deeds and statutes. A great number of different words have been used in stating the criteria, and I do not think it would be useful or indeed possible to examine them all.

Cases where it has properly been held that a word can be struck out of a deed or statute and another substituted can as far as I am aware be grouped under three heads: where without each substitution the provision is unintelligible or absurd or totally unreasonable; where it is unworkable; and where it is totally irreconcilable with the plain intention shown by the rest of the deed or statute. I do not say that in all such cases it is proper to strike out a word and substitute another. What I do say is that I cannot discover or recall any case outside these three classes where such substitution would be permissible."

In stating his opinion supporting the majority Lord Salmon states ... in the same report[26] as follows:

"My Lords, I do not suppose that any two words in the English language have more often been used interchangeably than 'and' and 'or'. However unfortunate or incorrect this practice may be, many examples of it are to be found in all manner of documents and statutes. There are many reported cases which turn upon whether, in its particular context, the word 'or' is to be read conjunctively or the word 'and' disjunctively.

There is high authority for the view that the word 'or' can never mean 'and' although it is sometimes used by mistake when 'and' is intended: See Sir George Jessel M.R, in *Morgan* v. *Thomas*[27] and McKinnon, J. In *Brown & Co.* v. *T. & J. Harrison.*[28] On the other hand, there is also the high authority of Bankes and Aitken L.JJ. on appeal in *Brown & Co.* v. *T. & J. Harrison*[29] that 'or' is quite commonly and grammatically used in a conjunctive sense. In *Southerland Publishing Co. Ltd.* v. *Caxton Publishing Co. Ltd.*[30] MacKinnon, L.J., was able pungently to restate the contrary view which he had expressed eleven years previously. The Oxford Dictionary seems to support Sir George Jessel, M.R. and MacKinnon, L.J. I do not, however, attach any real importance as to whether the one school of thought or the other is right on this interesting grammatical point. In *Brown & Co.* v. *T. & J. Harrison*[31] the Court of Appeal agreed with MacKinnon J., as to the effect of the relevant statutory provision. MacKinnon J., reached his conclusion by holding that the word 'or' should be substituted for the word 'and'. The Court of Appeal reached their conclusion by holding that the word 'or', on its true construction meant 'and'. The result was the same.

There is certainly no doubt that generally it is assumed that 'or' is intended to be used disjunctively and the word 'and' conjunctively.

---

[26] [1974] 1 W.L.R. 523.
[27] 9 Q.B.D. 643, 645.
[28] (1927) 43 T.L.R. 394.
[29] 96 L.J.K.B. 1025.
[30] [1938] Ch. 174.
[31] 96 L.J.K.B. 1025.

Nevertheless, it is equally well settled that if so to construe those words leads to an unintelligible or absurd result, the courts will read the word 'or' conjunctively and 'and' disjunctively as the case may be; or, to put it another way, substitute the one word for the other. This principle has been applied time and again even in penal statutes; see for example *Reg* v. *Oakes*.[32]

A number of cases are cited by the Law Lords in their opinions in that case illustrating the application of the principle of the construction in circumstances in which the conjunctive use of the word "or" was rejected or accepted. It is implicit in these and many other judgments on the construction of statutes and documents and on the interpretation of words used therein that the court of construction will always credit the draftsman of the document with the degree of care and skill to be expected of him. In one of the cases cited in argument by Mr O'Driscoll SC in *Re Diplock, Wintle* v. *Diplock*[33] the English Court of Appeal refused to give the word "or" a conjunctive meaning as its use as a disjunctive is its primary use and was suitable and made sense in the context notwithstanding that its effect was to defeat a charitable purpose indicated in the Will. The court will not look for ambiguities or inadvertencies or doubtful alternative meanings. A particularly high degree of care and skill will be presumed and attributed to the drafting of a penal statute on the one hand whereas allowance for lack of skill or inadvertence may be made in the construction of a will drawn by a testator.

Adopting and applying the principles stated in the cited and other cases it seems to me that the word "or" where first used in condition 5 of the general conditions of the policy can be used in its *prima facie* ordinary and most common sense consistently with the rest of that condition and with all the other provisions of the policy. An examination of the scope of the policy shows that liability could arise, for example, for damage to property from faulty or insufficient workmanship, materials or design, in respect of which it might not be possible to give notice with particulars of the happening of an occurrence which might give rise to a claim. The wording of the general conditions is intended presumably to comprehend in their application a wide variety of circumstances. Consequently, the use of disjunctives more probably expresses truly the intentions and purpose of the parties. The use of the punctuation commas in the first sentence of condition 5 may contribute to the difficulties of interpretation which have arisen. Had the second comma been placed after the word "particulars" or after the word "happening" or after the word "claim" where it secondly appears in that sentence the meaning of the sentence would be less difficult to ascertain. The expression "to give notice" is almost invariably followed with the word "of" in relation to the objective matter but this is not so here with the second comma after the word "insurance". I can find nothing in the expressed purpose of the condition or in the sense to be derived from other terms or expressions to be found anywhere in the policy from which I should find an unintelligible or absurd meaning in the use of that word "or" in its primary disjunctive sense where it first occurs in the first

---

[32] [1959] 2 Q.B. 350.
[33] [1941] 1 Ch. 253.

sentence of condition 5. I accept that condition 5 could also bear an intelligible and sensible meaning if the word "or" where first used were to be given a conjunctive use, but, the mere existence of an acceptable alternative is not a sufficient reason for rejecting the prima facie disjunctive meaning and use of the word.

Having regard to the range of cover afforded by the policy and the variety of the nature and circumstances of the possible claims to which the general conditions are expressed to apply it seems to me the obligations imposed in condition 5 are expressed in the alternative in order to provide for the varied types of the alternatives which might be presented by the circumstances giving rise to and the nature of the claims. I think that the true and correct interpretation of condition 5 [as] expressed is that it imposes on the assured one or other alternative obligation with respect to notice of claims and in addition an obligation in respect of the institution of proceedings. The use of the conjunctive "and" which introduces the reference to the institution of proceedings joins this obligation, to give immediate notice in writing thereof, to whichever of the alternatives in respect of notice of claim may be applicable in the circumstances. Upon this construction of condition 5 as expressed in the policy the interpretation which I advise should be applied in relation to the obligations imposed on the insured is that:

(1) In every instance in which to the knowledge of the assured an occurrence happens which he recognises could give rise to a claim under the policy he must give to the nominated agent of the underwriters immediate notice in writing of the happening of such occurrence, or alternatively give them the like immediate notice of his receipt of the claim if such be made;

(2) In the event of a claim being made or received which arises from no identifiable occurrence as a happening, or of the happening of which the assured was unaware, he must give the nominated agent of the underwriters immediate notice in writing of his receipt of notice of such claim;

(3) In every case he must give to the nominated agent of the underwriters immediate notice in writing of the institution of proceedings.

The remaining two questions govern the entitlement of the assured to indemnity under the policy and the liability of the underwriters thereunder in the event of non-compliance with the condition as to notice of claim and they are inter-related. It was recognised in the course of argument that a distinction must be made between a condition expressed in a contract to be a condition precedent and one which is not so described in the contract. Counsel referred to In *Re Coleman's Depositories Ltd*[34] and in particular to the judgment of Fletcher Moulton, L.J. from which it would appear that upon non-compliance with the condition that is stated to be a condition precedent performance of the obligation of the contract cannot be enforced by the party in default. Nevertheless, Fletcher Moulton, L.J. says in reference to what he calls a trifling default at page 807 of the report:

The courts have not always considered that they are bound to interpret

---

[34] [1907] 2 K.B. 798.

provisions of this kind with unreasonable strictness, and although the word "immediate" is no doubt a strong epithet I think that it might be fairly construed as meaning with all reasonable speed considering the circumstances of the case.

In the event of non-compliance with a condition not described as a condition precedent the party in default may be able to establish a right to the benefit of the contract subject to an assessment in damages for the consequences of the default or may be unable to enforce the contract. It was also accepted in the course of argument that compliance with a condition expressed in either form could be waived by the party to benefit by it either expressly or impliedly from conduct. But a difficulty has been created by some observations of Lord Justice Denning M.R. in his judgment in *Lickiss* v. *Milestone Motor Policies at Lloyd's*[35] also reported as *Barrett Bros. (Taxis) Ltd* v. *Davies.*[36] In that judgment Denning, M.R. stated at page 975...:

> First, it was unnecessary for the motor cyclist to send documents to the insurers. They had all the relevant facts, and that absolved the motor cyclist from doing more. The police headquarters at Blackpool by their letter of 18 January 1964 gave to the insurers all the material information. The insurers would be entitled, if they so wished, to send their own representative to the Magistrates' Court and watch the proceedings or, indeed, to take such other steps if any, as they were entitled to take. Seeing that they had received the information from the police, it would be a futile thing to require the motor cyclist himself to give them the self-same information. The law never compels a person to do that which is useless and unnecessary.

In that case the motor cyclist was obliged under the terms of his policy to notify immediately the insurers of intended prosecution and had failed to do so. Towards the end of his judgment Lord Denning adds the following observation at page 976:

> Condition 1 was inserted in the policy so as to afford a protection to the insurers so that they should know in good time about the accident and any proceedings consequent on it. If they obtain all the material knowledge from another source so that they are not prejudiced at all by the failure of the insured himself to tell them, then they cannot rely on the condition to defeat the claim.

When a similar point was taken before McKenna, J. in *Farrell* v *Federated Employers Ltd*[37] those observations of Denning, M.R. were cited to him. In his judgment McKenna, J. says at page 363 of the report:

> Counsel for the plaintiff in his able argument contended that there could be no breach of a condition entitling the insurers to repudiate liability unless the breach had caused actual prejudice to the insurers. For this surprising

---

[35] [1966]2 All E.R. 972.
[36] [1966]1 W.L.R. 1354.
[37] [1970]1 All E.R. 360.

proposition he cited *Lickiss* v. *Milestone Motor Policies at Lloyd's*.[38] In that case the insurers relied on a failure of the insured to inform them of the receipt by the insured of a notice of intended prosecution. The insurers had received information of this matter from the police. There was also some evidence that they had waived the condition entitling them to such notice.

McKenna, J. then quotes the passage which I have quoted above from the judgment of Lord Denning M.R. in the cited case. McKenna J. then went on at page 364:

> I distinguish that case from the present. There the insurers had contemporary knowledge from another reliable source of the matter which the insured failed to notify. Here the insurers had no knowledge from any source of the issue of the writ until they received the letter of 2 March 1966. I do not regard Lord Denning, M.R.'s judgment as authority for the wider proposition that an insurer cannot rely on a breach of condition unless he has suffered actual prejudice.

An appeal from the decision of McKenna, J. came before the Court of Appeal in England over which Lord Denning, M.R. presided. That court in upholding unanimously the decision of McKenna, J. carefully avoided expressing any approval or acceptance of the proposition advanced by Lord Denning, M.R. in 1966. To the extent that any of the observations of Lord Denning as stated in the 1966 case seem to be at variance with the statements of the law as expressed by Fletcher Moulton, L.J. In *Re Coleman's Depositories Ltd*[39] I would not be prepared to adopt them.

In the policy under consideration by the arbitrator condition 5 is expressed to be a condition precedent to liability under the policy. Non-compliance with the provisions of that condition, if such there be, may be waived by the underwriters or they, the underwriters, may be found to have waived impliedly their right to rely on non-compliance. If they were found to have led the assured by their conduct to believe that their right to rely on the non-compliance was being waived by them the matter of prejudice might possibly arise for consideration. Save in the investigation of such matters of fact it seems to me there is no onus on the underwriters to show that they are prejudiced by a non-compliance with condition 5. That is to say in the absence of waiver the underwriters are entitled without the obligation of proof of prejudice to their position to rely on non-compliance with condition 5 as releasing them from liability to meet a claim under the policy.

Instead of replying to the queries submitted in the case stated in the form in which they are posed I would advise the arbitrator as follows:

1. Compliance with condition 5 is a condition precedent to liability of the underwriters.

2. Unless the non-compliance with condition 5 is trivial or has been waived expressly or impliedly by the underwriters they are not obliged to show that they are prejudiced by the non-compliance.

---

[38] [1966]2 All E.R. 972.
[39] [1907] 2 K.B. 798.

3. The assured is obliged by condition 5 to give to the nominated agent of the underwriters immediate notice in writing either of the happening of an occurrence likely to give rise to a claim or of the receipt by the assured of such a claim.

4. The assured is obliged by condition 5 to give to the nominated agent of the underwriters immediate notice in writing of the institution of proceedings in every case.

In advising the arbitrator in this manner I have left the arbitrator free to make all findings and inferences of fact. As the hearing before the arbitrator has not concluded he may require to hear further evidence on facts pertinent to the issues arising in view of the foregoing advices on the interpretation of the policy constituting the contract between the parties.

Capemel Limited, Charles Roche, Ellen Roche, William Roche, David Roche, Cathal Roche and Geroid Roche *v.* Roger H. Lister (No. 1)
[1989] I.R. 319
The High Court

COSTELLO J: The plaintiff carries on business as manufacturers of kitchen furniture and employs 18 men in its factory in Dublin.

The plaintiff entered into a policy of insurance with a firm of Lloyd's Underwriters with effect form 1st August, 1985, to 24th June, 1986. The policy included employer's liability indemnity. On 27th March 1986, one of the plaintiff's employees, John Holt, was injured in an accident. At the time of the injury to Mr Holt, Mr Charles Roche senior, who was the principal director of the plaintiff and its founder, was ill and had only recently come out of hospital. Mr Charles Roche senior was the director responsible for such things as insurance in relation to the staff and premises and during his illness the business was carried on by his two sons and his place was taken by them. Because Mr Roche had returned briefly to work, his sons assumed that he would he would notify the insurance brokers of Mr Holt's accident and I think that Mr Roche had assumed that his sons, or one of them, would do so. But whatever the reason for the failure to do what Mr Roche senior accepts he would normally do, namely, notify the brokers of the accident, this was not done.

On 15th October, 1986, Mr, Holt's solicitor wrote to the plaintiffs and this letter was sent on to the brokers and then sent on to the Lloyd's underwriters. Thus the Lloyd's underwriters had no notice of the accident to Mr. Holt until some time shortly after 15th October, 1986.

The general conditions attaching to the insurance policy, which are in a separate part of the policy headed "All conditions are Precedent to Indemnity under this Insurance", contain in paragraph 4 under the heading "Claims procedure" the following words:—

> "The Assured shall give to Underwriters immediate notice in writing, with full particulars of the happening of any occurrence which could give rise to a

claim under this insurance, or of the receipt by the Assured of notice of any claim or of the institution of any proceedings against the Assured."

In this case the issue is whether this clause entitles the defendant to repudiate liability because it did not receive immediate notice in writing with full particulars of the happening of the occurrence immediately after Mr Holt's accident on 27th March, 1986.

The situation which has arisen in this case and the terms of the policy which I am considering are very close to the situation and to the terms of the policy considered by Gannon J. in *Gaelcrann Teoranta* v. *Payne*.[40] That, too, was a policy of insurance issued by a Lloyd's underwriter. In that case the arbitrator asked the court for its assistance and the question that arose related to the claims procedure clause of another Lloyd's policy which is virtually the same as the clause which I am considering. In that case the clause was:—

> "The assured shall give ... immediate notice in writing, with full particulars of the happening of any occurrence which could give rise to a claim under this insurance, or of the receipt by the assured of notice of any claim and of the institution of any proceedings against the assured."

The only difference between that clause and the one I am dealing with is that "and" is substituted for the final "or" in the instant case.

It is submitted on behalf of the defendant that I should reject the judgment of Gannon J. for the following reasons:—

It is submitted that the judgment of Gannon J. may have been correct in that the clause he was considering was considered as having imposed a disjunctive obligation on the assured to give notice in one or other of the circumstances outlined but that he was wrong in holding that these were alternative obligations. In fact, it is submitted that they were consecutive obligations. In this case it is submitted that I should construe the contract as imposing consecutive obligations on the assured. Alternatively, it is submitted that Gannon J. was wrong in holding that the obligations were disjunctive and that he should have held that "or" should be read as "and" and that they were conjunctive, and it is urged that I should so construe the contract in this case.

The judgment of Gannon J. was, if I may say so with respect, a very carefully and closely reasoned one and I have no difficulty in expressing my agreement with it. In my view the construction which Gannon J. put on the contract which he was considering was the correct one and the difference between the one which I have to construe and the one which he was construing is immaterial for the purposes of this case.

In my view the obligations that were imposed by this contract should be regarded as disjunctive ones. In my view it is correct to construe this contract as meaning that if the assured is aware of an accident or an occurrence which could give rise to a claim he is under an obligation to give immediate notice in writing of this claim, or on the receipt of notice of a claim he is also under an

---

[40] [1985] I.L.R.M. 109. See p.565 of this book

obligation to give notice, or on the receipt of notice of the institution of proceedings a further obligation will arise. It seems to me that the assured can give notice in writing in any of these events. I do not think that this produces an absurd result and I agree with the contention advanced on behalf of the plaintiff that a contract such as this must be strictly construed against the insurance company who had proffered the contract.

In these circumstances, if the insurance company wished the contract to have a meaning other than the meaning to which I have referred and wished to impose a stricter obligation than would otherwise be the case, the responsibility was on the insurance company to ensure that the clause was drafted in the way they so wished. In all the circumstances, therefore, I am of the view that the plaintiff's construction of the contract is the correct one. It is therefore unnecessary for me to consider the further arguments which were advanced. It was submitted on the plaintiff's behalf that this should not be regarded as a condition precedent and that I should consider the situation in the light of s. 39 of the Sale of Goods and Supply of Services Act, 1980, dealing with implied warranties in the supply of services. Furthermore, it was pointed out that it would be contrary to the proper construction of this contract to construe it in the way the defendant suggested it should be construed because of the very serious detriment that would result. Finally, it is submitted that the policy should not be construed as to conflict with public policy.

For these reasons, therefore, I hold that the plaintiff is entitled to the declaration sought.

[The defendant appealed to the Supreme Court against the judgment.... [I]n an *ex tempore* judgment the Chief Justice, Griffin and Hederman J.J. concurring, dismissed the appeal....]

CHAPTER 15

Miscellaneous

A. Discovery of Insurer's Documentation

A party to a dispute is entitled in particular circumstances to seek discovery of documentation in the possession of the other party to that dispute. Disputes involving an insurer are no different, whether that dispute involves an insured or a third party. All documentation in its possession must be disclosed. An insurer, like any other party to litigation, is entitled to claim privilege from disclosure in respect of documentation where, though that documentation comes into existence prior to the commencement of proceedings, it can be shown that the dominant reason for the documents coming into existence was the preparation for litigation apprehended or threatened.

In any such claim for privilege the individual facts of each case will be examined and the substantive grounds for claiming privilege carefully scrutinised. In *P.J. Carrigan Limited and Patrick J. Carrigan* v. *Norwich Union Fire Society Limited and Scottish Union and National Insurance Company (No. 1)* (1987) the insurer sought to claim privilege from discovery to its own insured in respect of a loss adjuster's report. The report had been commissioned specifically with the probability in mind of repudiating liability under the policy. The report had also been directed to the insurer's legal advisors for their advice. Mr Justice O'Hanlon confirmed its privileged nature.

In *Bernadette Davis* v. *St Michael's House* (1993) the insurer, while defending proceedings brought against its insured, claimed privilege in respect of statements, report forms, notes and some correspondence completed by the insured's personnel shortly after the incident giving rise to the proceedings, but well before the proceedings were instituted. Again the insurer was successful. Mr Justice Lynch held that, because this documentation only came into existence in apprehension and/or anticipation of the litigation, the claim for privilege was valid and discovery was refused.

P.J. Carrigan Limited and P.J. Carrigan & Norwich Union Fire Society Limited and Scottish Union and National Insurance Company Limited (No. 1)
[1987] I.R. 618
The High Court

O'HANLON J: In this case the plaintiffs claim against their insurers in respect of the destruction by fire of a dwellinghouse at Rathcore, Enfield, Co. Meath. The defendants have repudiated liability on a number of grounds, and an order for discovery of documents and cross-order have been made in the course of the proceedings. The plaintiffs are dissatisfied with the discovery made by the defendants and now apply for an order for further and better discovery, with particular reference to a report from Scully, [Tyrrell] & Co., loss adjusters, which was sought and obtained by the defendants prior to the institution of these proceedings. The defendants have disclosed the existence of this report but claim privilege in respect thereof.

The issue which I have to try is not unlike that which arose in the case of *Silver Hill Duckling* v. *Minister for Agriculture*[1] and accordingly I do not consider it necessary in the present case to review again the authorities which were referred to in that decision. I adhere to the view expressed by me in the judgment in that case that privilege from disclosure may be claimed by a party to litigation in respect of a document which has come into existence prior to the commencement of proceedings, where it can be shown that the dominant purpose for the document coming into existence in the first place was the purpose of preparing for litigation then apprehended or threatened. (Cf. — A. *Crompton Ltd.* v. *Customs and Excise;*[2] *Waugh* v. *British Railways Board.*[3])

The fire which occurred in the plaintiff's premises broke out on the 22nd May, 1981. Notification was given to the insurers on or about the 5th June, 1981, that a claim was being made under the policy. The insurers immediately sought a report from the loss adjusters, Messrs. Scully, [Tyrrell] and Co., and received a report dated the 8th June, 1981, headed "Privileged Private and Confidential for the attention of Legal Advisers only". Subsequent follow-up reports were also furnished, headed "Privileged for the attention of Legal Advisers".

In the course of an affidavit dated 6th June, 1987, sworn by Ronald McKenna, a senior official of the first defendant, on behalf of that defendant, he deposes that the probability of litigation was already contemplated by the defendants at the time they received the report from Messrs Scully, [Tyrrell] and Co., having regard to a number of suspicious circumstances which are enumerated in his affidavit. Accordingly, he says that Scully, [Tyrrell] and Co., were instructed to provide a report to be provided to Good and Murray Smith and Co., solicitors for the insurers and that as early as the 11th June, 1981, the said solicitors had given preliminary advices "consistent with

---

[1] [1987] I.R. 289.
[2] [1974] A.C. 405.
[3] [1980] A.C. 521.

defending any apprehended proceedings". The date of the first letter from the plaintiffs' solicitors was given as the 21st October, 1981, but the plenary summons did not issue until the 4th February, 1983.

I am satisfied on the evidence which has been adduced on behalf of the defendants in this case that the possibility of repudiating liability under the policy was a very real factor in their thinking from the time the claim to be indemnified was made by the plaintiffs, and that when commissioning a report from Scully, [Tyrrell] and Co., they were concerned to obtain not merely an evaluation of the claim in terms of financial loss, but also whatever expert advice could be given as to the circumstances in which the fire broke out. They already viewed the claim with some suspicion and wished to know whether any evidence available at the scene of the fire suggested that their suspicions were well-founded. In other words, they were, even at that early stage, contemplating the possibility of a showdown with the plaintiffs, in which they, the defendants, might well decide to repudiate liability under the policy, and the plaintiffs in turn would then have to decide whether they were prepared to embark on litigation to enforce their claims under the policy.

While no litigation was threatened at the time the report was commissioned I am satisfied that it was apprehended, in the thinking of the defendants, and that this apprehension constituted a dominant purpose in looking for the report. In these circumstances I am of opinion that the document is privileged and I propose to refuse the application for further and better discovery.

Bernadette Davis (a person of unsound mind not so found) suing by her mother and next friend Sarah Davis *v.* St Michael's House
Unreported, 25 November 1993
The High Court

LYNCH J: What came before me for decision on Friday the 5th of November 1993 was an application on behalf of the Plaintiff for further and better discovery of documents in relation to which the Defendants claim privilege on the grounds that they are communications of a confidential nature made in apprehension and/or anticipation of litigation and in particular this action.

This action is one for damages for alleged negligence on the part of the Defendants, their servants or agents as a result of which the Plaintiff is alleged to have fallen on the 24th of January 1986 in the Defendants' school and suffered injury to her left femur.

The Plaintiff was born on the 10th of January 1968 and was therefore 16 years old at the date of the accident and is now approaching 26 years of age. Unfortunately the Plaintiff is mentally handicapped, functioning at the mental level of a child of about 6 years and she also suffers from grand mal epilepsy since about the age of 6 years. She is not therefore in a position to give evidence relating to the matters in question in this action herself.

In the fall it is alleged in the Statement of Claim that the Plaintiff suffered a fracture of the lower end of the left femur: that open reduction was performed under general anaesthetic achieving a very satisfactory and stable position: that she was discharged from hospital in the 8th of April 1986 and that thereafter the satisfactory result of the operation continued and she was well but that she will have a permanent operation scar on her left thigh. In an Affidavit to ground an application to have the above named Sarah Davis added as next friend of the Plaintiff, a medical report dated the 28th of February 1990 was exhibited which states:—

> "This lady has come under my care in the past year only. She developed grand mal epilepsy when she was 6 years old and from this developed mental retardation. As far as I am aware her mental age is approx. 6 years. Her mother has to do most of the normal skills of living for her except feeding her. She is now toilet trained.
>
> She also had a smaller sized left foot from birth thus requiring two different sized shoes. Since her accident she has a lift on her left shoe because of shortening of the leg."

There is no mention of the shortening of the leg in the Statement of Claim but perhaps this is an oversight. Without in any way criticising the bringing of these proceedings, I mentioned to Counsel for the Plaintiff in the course of the argument that I find it hard to see how this litigation, even if successful, can be of any significant benefit to the Plaintiff as the level of damages (there being no special damages of any significance) would in my view not exceed the £15,000 jurisdiction of the Circuit Court as at the date of issue of the Plenary Summons on the 21st of January 1989 and if the action fails it could give rise to a very substantial liability for costs.

The documents in respect of which privilege is claimed by the Defendants and challenged on behalf of the Plaintiff are set out in paragraph 4 of the Affidavit sworn to ground the application for further and better discovery as follows:—

" 1. Statement of Bernard Green dated 24th January 1986.
  2. The accident report form part 1 and part 2.
  3. The notes on Niamh Patten's recall of the incident dated 14th April 1986.
  4. Statement dated April 1987 and initialled P.J. O'M.
  5. Letter dated 26th May 1987 Mr Paul Ledwidge to Mr Paul O'Mahony."

In a replying Affidavit sworn by Mr Ledwidge it is stated as follows:

" 4. The Defendant is insured against claims brought in respect of personal injury loss and damage alleged to have been suffered at the Defendants' premises under a policy held with the Church and General Insurance Company Plc. and I beg to refer to a copy of that policy upon which marked with the letter A I have endorsed my name prior to the swearing hereof.
  5. Under the terms of the policy (Clause 5 (a)) the Defendant is obliged to notify the insurer of all accidents that occur so as to enable the insurer to carry out such investigations as it may require for the purpose of assessing if liability attaches to the insurer under the policy. In addition to completing an accident report form the Defendant frequently obtained written statements from any witnesses to any accident and I confirm that the statements are obtained with a view to assessing the Defendant's position in relation to any claim that might arise as a result of the accident.

6. The accident report form and the statements obtained in relation to each accident come into being in contemplation of possible proceedings or threatened proceedings. Where proceedings actually issue the Defendant is often required to obtain more detailed statements in particular from expert witnesses.
7. I further confirm that the statements obtained in this case were obtained for the purposes of assessing the Defendant's position in the event of a claim being made resulting from the accident."

Counsel for the Plaintiff submitted that it must be shown by the Defendants that the dominant purpose of the coming into being of the documents was in anticipation of litigation and that this was not shown and he referred to the case of *Silver Hill Duckling Limited and Others* v. *Minister for Agriculture.*[4]

Counsel for the Defendants submitted that the documents came into being to meet an apprehended or anticipated claim against the Defendants and he relied on the case of *Alfred Crompton Amusement Machines Ltd* v. *Commissioners of Customs and Excise.*[5]

In order to decide this matter I have to ask myself what can be the purpose of getting the statements and reports in question? Once the Plaintiff was returned to the care of her parents and thence to appropriate hospitals the only purpose of such statements and reports can be to ensure that there is an accurate record of what happened from as many persons who may know something about it is as possible so that in the event of a claim:

1. The insurers will be forewarned and forearmed therewith for submission to their legal advisors, they having the usual right under Condition 5 (b) of the Policy to take over the defence of any proceedings against the Defendants, and
2. Witnesses will have a contemporary record of the events by reference to which they may be able to refresh their memories many years later, not overlooking the fact that it is now almost eight years since the accident, the subject matter of this action, occurred.

I am of the view that the dominant purpose for which the documents in question in this case came into being was in apprehension and/or anticipation of litigation and that the claim of privilege is therefore valid and the Plaintiff's Motion must be refused. This is not to say of course that the Plaintiff's advisers are not entitled to seek to interview the persons named as having made statements to the Defendants provided that such persons are willing and consent to such an interview.

---

[4] [1987] I.R. 289 and [1987] I.L.R.M. 516.
[5] [1972] 2 All E.R. 353.

B. Landlord's Duty to Insure

It is the standard practice in modern property leases for the landlord to retain full control over the arranging of building insurance on the property leased, and to include a term in the lease with his tenant that the tenant reimburse him all of, or a proportion of, the premium paid. In *Sepes Establishment Limited* v. *K.S.K. Enterprises Limited* (1993) the tenant disputed the landlord's entitlement to seek reimbursement on the basis that the method of valuation used by the landlord and on which the premium was calculated was incorrect. It further alleged that as similar insurances to those arranged by the landlord could be obtained cheaper elsewhere, the landlord had not taken sufficient care and had failed in its obligations to it.

Mr Justice O'Hanlon accepted that the method of valuation and reinstatement costings prepared by the landlord and its advisors, and on which the premium was based, were correct. In addition he held that once a landlord acted in a bona fide manner and was guided by suitable experts the landlord would be regarded as having satisfactorily discharged any duties so owned to the tenant. He held that the tenant who sought to challenge the landlord's actions in such circumstances undertook a very heavy onus of proof. An onus of proof, he believed, which had not been discharged by the tenant in the case before him.

Sepes Establishment Limited *v.* K.S.K. Enterprises Limited
[1993] 2 I.R. 225
The High Court

O'HANLON J: This case concerns a dispute between the plaintiff, as lessor of the premises situate at 4/5 Westmoreland Street in the City of Dublin and the defendant as lessee of the greater part of the said premises, under the terms of a lease dated the 25th August, 1978, made between the plaintiff and the defendant, as to the amount payable by the defendant to the plaintiff under the defendant's covenant to reimburse the lessor in respect of the cost of insuring the demised premises.

The amount claimed by the plaintiff in respect of the calendar year 1990 is a sum of £21,084.02. A payment of £4,950 was made by the defendant before proceedings were commenced, and the defendant is also entitled to credit for a further sum of £4,612.50 paid after the proceedings commenced (the two payments totalling £9,562.50), leaving the amount in dispute between the parties at £11,521.52. The plaintiff also claims interest under the terms of the lease in accordance with a clause providing for payment of interest in the event of late payment in respect of any amount found due under the relevant clause in the lease.

The lease was for a term of 38 years from the 1st July, 1978, the defendant by virtue of Clause 1 (e):—

"YIELDING AND PAYING the following rents:

(e) by way of further rent a yearly sum equal to 80% of the sum or sums which the lessor shall from time to time pay by way of premiums (including any increased premium payable by reason of any act or omission of the Lessee) for keeping the building insured against loss or damage by fire and such other risks under the Lessor's covenant in that behalf hereinafter contained the said further rent to be paid once a year on demand which said rents shall be paid clear of all deductions ... AND in the event of the said payments remaining unpaid for a period of 14 days from the due dates thereof the Lessee shall pay to the Lessor interest at the rate or rates charged in the Irish Banks from time to time on advances in the A Category but not below £12 per cent per annum and calculated according to the custom of bankers."

Clause 2 of the lease contains the defendant's covenants and provides as follows in para. 10 thereof:—

"Not to carry on or permit or suffer to be carried on upon the demised premises any user trade or occupation or to do permit or suffer any other thing which may make void or voidable any policy for insurance of the building against the special risks and loss or damage by fire or whereby the rate of premium thereon may be increased and to repay to the Lessor all sums paid by the Lessor by way of increased premium on the building and all expenses incurred by the Lessor in or about any renewal of such policy or policies rendered necessary by a breach of this covenant and all such payments shall be made payable and become due to the Lessor one week after the Lessor or the Lessor's agents notify the Lessee of the amount of the said payment."

The plaintiff's covenants under the lease include the following:—

(1) To insure and keep insured the building (except as to glass insurance for which provision is made in Clause 25 hereof) against loss or damage by fire and such other risks as the Lessor shall deem desirable or expedient in some insurance office or with underwriters of repute (a summary of insured risks and the name of the insurers to be supplied to the Lessee on request) and in case of destruction of or damage to the demised premises or any part thereof from any cause covered by such insurance as to make the same unfit for occupation and use to lay out all monies received in respect of such insurance (other than for loss of rent architects' and surveyors' fees and demolition and clearance expenses) in rebuilding and reinstating the same as soon as reasonably practicable...."

The current dispute between the plaintiff and the defendant arises under the following headings:—

1. The defendant, having been asked to pay the sum of £21,084.02 in respect of charges for the year commencing 1st January, 1990, contended that the figure claimed was much too high, and sought advice from a firm of insurance brokers who claimed to have secured a quotation for £15,969.61 plus 3% government levy from a duly authorised and reputable insurer.

2. The parties were not in agreement as to the area of the demised premises nor as to the user of the different sections of the premises, both of which factors were material in the calculation of the insurance premium payable.

3. The defendant contended that the insurance charges for which it was liable should not include insurance to cover demolition charges and professional fees in the event of destruction of damage by fire, loss of rent, public liability, or cost of prospective inflation.

4. While the insurance charges on the entire premises were loaded by reason of the nature of the business carried on by the defendant (being that of an amusement arcade) about one-fifth of the entire area was, in fact, demised to two other tenants (International Travel Bureau and Air Canada), and the defendant claimed, in reliance on the express terms of Clause 1 (e) as recited above, that it was only liable to pay 80% of all insurance charges, *including* any act or omission of the lessee. The plaintiff claimed that the entire of such increased charges on the entire building should properly be payable by the defendant whose user of the major part of the demised premises was the cause which attracted the enhanced premium on the entire.

The dispute was the subject of protracted and, at times, acrimonious correspondence between the solicitors representing the two parties for much of the year, 1990. On behalf of the defendant it was contended that the insurance charges were calculated on the basis of a floor area of 27,172 square feet, whereas the correct floor area (according to the defendant's calculations) was 22,098 square feet, resulting in an unjustifiable enhancement of the insurance charges by 23%.

The plaintiff responded to this charge by commissioning a new survey of the premises and to this end the overall insurance situation was reviewed on behalf of the plaintiff by their insurance brokers, O'Leary Insurance (Dublin) Ltd., by Lisney & Co., auctioneers and valuers, by P.C. O'Grady & Co., architects and by Patrick O'Donoghue, quantity surveyor. A similar exercise was carried out on behalf of the defendant by Insurance Facilities Ltd., insurance brokers, by McCarthy & Co., engineers, by Wm. Long & Partners, quantity surveyors and by Toplis Hume, loss adjusters.

The Lisney report (prepared on behalf of the plaintiff) which became available in May, 1990, took an external floor area of 27,172 square feet (gross) and a figure for cost of reinstatement, including demolition and site clearance, and professional fees at 15% (together with V.A.T. on the various charges), totalling in all £3,444,100.

The defendant, on the advice available to it, claimed that the floor area to be used for the purpose of the calculations should be 22,102 square feet, and the reinstatement cost £1,785,400, and a payment was made by the defendant's solicitors on this basis.

The premises obviously present considerable and unusual difficulty in the matter of measuring up the area involved for reinstatement purposes. They comprise not merely a substantial building fronting on to Westmoreland Street (from which the official address of the premises is derived), but a series of linked buildings to the rear of the main building enclosed on all sides by other third party buildings. In the result, Lisney & Co. had to report separately on different sections ranging from Block 1, comprising a four-storey over basement building fronting on to Westmoreland Street; Block 2a, a single-storey over basement construction linking the front building with substantial buildings giving access eventually to Parliament Row at the rear; Block 3, an older three-storey building: Block 3a, a two-storey structure similar in construction to Block 3; Block 4, a two-story structure; Block 4a, 4b, two and part three-storey building incorporating a lift shaft, and finally, Block 5 another two-storey building at the rear, at the furthest point removed from Westmoreland Street.

I am puzzled by the fact that the total policy premium put forward by the plaintiff's insurance brokers, O'Leary Insurances (Dublin) Ltd., to the plaintiff in December, 1989, in respect of the calendar year 1990, and by the plaintiff's solicitors to the defendant, was £22,163.04, of which £21,668.54 was sought from the defendant as the appropriate contribution to be made by the defendant, by letter of 2nd January, 1990, whereas when the reinstatement cost forecast had been revised upwards from £2,620,750 to £3,444,000 with effect from the 15th May, 1990, involving an additional premium of £5,690.80, the ultimate figure claimed against the defendant still remained as low as the sum of £21,084.02 (the figure referred to in the summary summons). I have also been unable to reconcile the figure of £21,668.54 claimed in the letter of 2nd January, 1990, as the defendant's apportioned liability in respect of insurance for 1990, with the renewal notice from Hibernian Insurance Co Ltd which was put in evidence and which referred to a sum insured of £2,620,750, and a premium of £16,303.62 falling due on the 1st January, 1990.

However, as the present claim no longer appears to be based on the figures referred to in that letter of the 2nd January, 1990, but on the revised assessment of areas and reinstatement costs which emerged in mid-1990 after the defendant had challenged the reliability of the first figures put forward, it does not appear necessary to unravel the earlier tangle as well.

Lisney & Co.'s representative, Mr Raymond Ward, stated that he carried out his calculations of the areas involved in the several buildings which made up the premises to be insured, using the "Measuring Practice Guidance Notes" published as a guide for surveyors and valuers by the Irish Auctioneers and Valuers Institute, the Incorporated Society of Valuers and Auctioneers (Republic of Ireland branch), and the Society of Chartered Surveyors in the Republic of Ireland.

This publication, which was produced in evidence, recommends measurement on the basis of the gross external area of a building when the purpose of the measurement is to provide a valuation and deal with letting and rating of modern industrial property, and also when the purpose of the exercise is to carry out a building cost estimation.

Measurements having been provided according to this formula, Patrick O'Donoghue, a quantity surveyor, examined the exterior of the premises in 1991 and his estimate of the square footage involved was 3% lower than Lisney & Co.'s figure. Taking the cost of reinstatement block by block he arrived at an overall figure of £3,410,000 as of November, 1991, and relating his estimate back to May, 1990, he considered that the figure might be 5% to 6% less (or about £200,000) as of that time.

In cross-examination he said that it would not be his custom to prepare a "bill of quantities" if assessing costs of reinstatement for insurance purposes, but only if actual rebuilding were taking place.

Mr Ward of Lisney & Co. concurred in this view and said that the cost involved in having a "bill of quantities" prepared would be three or four times the cost of measuring the areas involved and assessing the cost of reinstatement by conventional means. He described as "extraordinarily complicated" the method apparently adopted by the defendant's advisers, of carrying out a survey showing net internal measurements and adding on the thickness of the exterior walls of all the different buildings involved.

John O'Grady, an architect, provided a report for the plaintiff in February, 1990, to establish the external area and arrived at a figure of 27,351 square feet, having remeasured and having produced three sets of figures. He considered the figure put forward for reinstatement based on that gross external area, of £3.44m, was reasonable. He said that when a dispute arose about the figures for the area involved he verified his own figures again.

For the defendant, William Long, a quantity surveyor, instructed by the firm of Toplis Hume, loss adjusters, gave evidence of making a survey of the buildings in April, 1991, and of preparing a "bill of quantities" for reinstatement purposes which was put in evidence. The overall figure produced was £1,983,262.08. He disagreed with the approach adopted by the expert witnesses for the plaintiff, but conceded that the method favoured by him would be much more costly, and that he had not previously carried out a valuation for insurance purposes on a property of such magnitude and cost.

His figures for reinstatement cost did not include professional fees for architects or engineers.

The case for the defendant in resisting the plaintiff's claim is based largely on the submission that a lessor in the position of the plaintiff cannot simply insure and present a bill to be paid by the lessee, but owes a duty to the lessee not to impose an unnecessarily heavy burden on the lessee if more reasonable terms can be obtained by greater effort on the part of the lessor and must not, in any event, insure on a grossly inflated basis and seek to throw the whole burden of doing so on to the tenant.

In *Bander Property Holdings Ltd.* v. *J.S. Darwen (Successors) Ltd.*,[6] Roskill J. held that in the ordinary case where the lessor is to insure and the lessee is to refund the amount paid, there is no implied term that the lessor must insure in such a manner as not to place an unnecessarily heavy burden on the lessee. Accordingly, in that case, where the lessor claimed reimbursement of the amount paid and the lessee was able to produce a quotation for a significantly lower premium, each quotation coming from a firm of Lloyd's brokers, it was held that the lessee was not entitled to confine his liability to the smaller of the two sums. Roskill J. said at page 307:—

> "It is axiomatic that a court will not imply a term which has not been expressed merely because, had the parties thought of the possibility of expressing that term, it would have been reasonable for them to have done so. Before a term which has not been expressed can be implied it has got to

---

[6] [1968] 2 All E.R. 305.

be shown not only that it would be reasonable to make that implication, but that it is necessary in order to make the contract work that such a term should be implied. It has sometimes been expressed as 'necessary for the business efficacy of the contract'; and it is against that well-known and established principle that I approach the determination of the crucial question in this case."

In *Gleniffer Finance Corporation Ltd.* v. *Bamar Wood & Products Ltd.,*[7] the amount payable by the lessee under the insurance clause in a lease was again the subject of dispute, the lessor having insured against the cost of reinstatement, projecting it into the future to the date by which reinstatement could reasonably have been expected to be completed, while the lessee contended that it should be the cost as at the date when the annual renewal premium was paid.

Once again the decision went in favour of the lessor, Forbes J. deciding that the lease was to be construed as a whole in accordance with commercial good sense and that the "full cost of reinstatement" must have been intended by the parties to cover the cost that might properly be expected to be incurred at the time when the reinstatement took place.

He also referred to *dicta* in the case of *Finchbourne Ltd.* v. *Rodrigues,*[8] which are relevant in the circumstances of the present case.

In that case the Court of Appeal was dealing with charges which could be recovered by a lessor against a lessee and Cairns L.J. made the following comments at pp. 586–587:—

> "Is there an implication that the costs claimed are to be 'fair and reasonable'? It is contended that no such implication is necessary to give business efficacy to the contract.... Taking the strictest of tests on that matter, I am of the opinion that such an implication must be made here. It cannot be supposed that the plaintiffs were entitled to be as extravagant as they chose in the standards of repair, the appointment of porters etc. Counsel for the plaintiffs said that there would come a point without any implied term where the costs might be so outlandish as not to come within the description of the seventh schedule [to the lease] at all. In my opinion, the parties cannot have intended that the landlords should have an unfettered discretion to adopt the highest conceivable standard and to charge the tenant with it."

The other view that was canvassed in argument before Forbes J in *Gleniffer Finance Corporation Ltd.* v. *Bamar Wood & Products Ltd.*[9] was that the landlord's duty to insure was only one which he was obliged to carry out in a *bona fide* manner and that there was not an additional onus on him to show that his power to insure had been exercised in a fair and reasonable manner.

My own conclusion would be that if a lessee can establish that a lessor has clearly gone wrong in an important respect when effecting the insurance cover for which the lessee is ultimately to be liable, some scope must be

---

[7] (1978) 37 P. & C.R. 208.
[8] [1976] 3 All E.R. 581.
[9] (1978) 37 P.& C.R. 208.

allowed for the lessee to dispute the amount with which he is being charged.

However, if the lessor is clearly acting in a *bona fide* manner (as was the plaintiff in the present case, in my opinion), and is guided by persons who are presumed to be experts in the field whether as insurance brokers, valuers, engineers, architects, quantity surveyors and the like, I consider that a lessee challenging the figures put forward undertakes a very heavy onus of proof in seeking to establish that the figures charged are not fair or reasonable. I would respectfully agree with the decision of Roskill J. in *Bandar Property Holdings Ltd.* v. *J.S. Darwen (Successors) Ltd.*[10] that it is not sufficient to show that a quotation for a somewhat smaller figure can be obtained from another source.

Nor do I consider that a lessor should be put to the exceptionally high cost of having a "bill of quantities" prepared for the purpose of estimating the cost of reinstatement for insurance purposes, and I am further satisfied that the "Measuring Practice Guidance Notes" adopted by the two auctioneers' associations and the Society of Chartered Surveyors provide a useful and reasonable guide for estimation of building costs and for the other purposes referred to in this handbook.

I accept the evidence given by the expert witnesses called on behalf of the plaintiff in preference to that of the defendant's witnesses in relation to areas and costs of reinstatement and I am influenced in doing so by the fact that Mr Ward of Lisney & Co. in the month of August, 1990, offered to participate with the defendant's engineers in a joint remeasurement of the premises which, he said, "with the benefit of work already done should not take us more than 1 to 2 hours to complete". This offer was rejected out of hand, partly on the ground of the expense involved, yet the defendant in the following year, embarked on the huge expense of having a full "bill of quantities" prepared as though the premises had been destroyed and were about to be reinstated.

I find that the plaintiff is entitled to recover in respect of the various types of insurance cover referred to in the claim on the basis of the estimated floor areas and reinstatement costs put forward on behalf of the plaintiff, and the rates of insurance applicable to the premises having regard to the business carried on therein by the defendant.

This leaves for consideration the vexed question of whether the defendant is liable for the full amount of the excess attributable to the user, trade or occupation of the defendant, as suggested by clause 2.10 of the lease (referring to the lessee's covenants) or for only 80% of such excess, as can be inferred from Clause 1 (e) of the lease, dealing with the rent payable by the lessee (as set out in the opening part of the present judgment).

On the face of it, the two clauses are mutually contradictory and inconsistent, and following the customary rule of construing an agreement, where doubt arises, *contra proferentem,* (as I am urged to do by Mr Ralston for the defendant), the lower figure should be adopted in preference to the higher.

I feel, however, that a different approach may be necessary. The opening clause deals with the rent to be payable by the lessee and refers to the

---

[10] [1968] 2 All E.R. 305.

payment of the insurance premiums (including any increased premium payable by reason of any act or omission of the lessee) as a sum payable by the lessee "by way of further rent", in respect of which the lessee must pay 80% of the total for the entire building.

Failure to pay any sum payable by way of rent under the said clause (which term "rent" would include sums payable for insurance) within 14 days from the due date, was to give rise to a liability to pay interest on any amount outstanding at not less than 12% *per annum* until payment.

The lessee's covenant in Clause 2.10 carried an obligation to pay the full amount of the excess premium, but contained no similar provision for payment of interest in the event of non-payment when the amount fell due.

I am of opinion that the lease, although badly drafted in some respects, took effect to impose a dual obligation on the lessee — under the earlier provision to pay by way of rent 80% of the full insurance premium on the entire property, including any higher rate of premium brought about by the lessee's user of the demised property, and secondly, an obligation arising under the lessee's covenants in the lease to pay the full amount of the excess, the smaller liability being subsumed in the greater.

I conclude by giving judgment in favour of the plaintiff against the defendant for the sum of £11,521.42, together with interest thereon at the rate prescribed under the provisions of the Courts Act, 1981, from the 5th September, 1990, until payment.

C. Employer's Duty to Insure

Unlike Great Britain there is no statutory obligation in Ireland on employers to arrange valid employers' liability insurance to ensure that a source of compensation exists should an employee be injured in actionable circumstances at work. In *Daniel Sweeney* v. *Denis Duggan* (1991) the injured Plaintiff sought to lift the corporate veil and sue the managing director and principal of the company that employed him on the basis that he had failed in his duty to him as an employee by not ensuring proper employers' liability insurance was in place, thereby depriving him of his ability to enforce an award of damages obtained when his employing company proved to be insolvent. Mr Justice Barron refused to lift the corporate veil, but more importantly he held that such a general duty on the employer to protect the economic well being of his employees did not exist and in the absence of statutory authority he was not prepared to impose a duty at Common Law on an employer to provide such employer's liability insurance.

Daniel Sweeney *v.* Denis Duggan
[1991] 2 I.R. 274
The High Court

BARRON J: The plaintiff was until the accident which gave rise to the present proceedings a drilling machine operator employed by Kenmare Limework Ltd. at its quarry at Caher, Kenmare, County Kerry. He had been employed by the company for some ten years before his accident. Before that he had worked in other quarries. He had a take-home pay of approximately £100 a week. On the day of the accident he was drilling when the drill stuck. In his efforts to free the drill he caught his knee on a rock and found himself caught under the drill for approximately an hour. He was ultimately released by another driver who heard his cries. This accident occurred on the 18th February, 1984. He subsequently commenced proceedings against the company which were defended. The quarry continued in operation until the winter of 1984. It closed then and re-opened in March, 1985. Thereafter it remained open until November, 1986, when it closed for good. He himself was taken back after his accident and remained at work until the quarry closed. A creditor's voluntary liquidation commenced in August, 1987, after which date the defence to the action ceased. It came on for hearing in October, 1987. The plaintiff obtained judgment for the sum of £20,866 and costs. No part of this judgment has been paid to the plaintiff though it appears that in the liquidation of the company he will receive as a preferential creditor approximately 15% of his claim.

At the date of the plaintiff's accident the quarry employed four people. One of these was the defendant who was the quarry manager for the purposes of s. 23 of the Mines and Quarries Act, 1965. The company had an issued share capital of £18,999 of which all but one pound was in the beneficial ownership of the defendant. The remaining share was owned by the defendant's wife. The liquidator gave evidence as to the circumstances of the company. He was unable to give a proper picture of the state of the company at the date of the accident since there had been a fire in July, 1985, in which its records as of that date had been destroyed. In August, 1987, when the company went into liquidation it had a deficiency of £73,000. Its records and accounts were well kept. Its difficulties arose from the nature of its business. It produced lime for use by farmers. This business depended upon subsidies. These however were terminated with consequential loss of customers for the company. All statutory payments had been made on behalf of the plaintiff and the plaintiff's state benefits were in order.

The plaintiff's claim is for loss of the judgment which he obtained in October, 1987. The manner in which the claim is pleaded is set out in the following paragraphs contained in the statement of claim:—

"5.A At all material times the defendant was the designated sole manager of the said quarry under s. 23 of the Mines and Quarries Act, 1965, and thereby owed a special duty of care to the plaintiff.

5.B At all material times the company was experiencing financial difficulties such that would warrant a reasonable person, fully acquainted with its financial position, to be apprehensive that an award of substantial damages against it in a personal injuries action in respect of a serious injury brought by one of its employees, would not be met in full or in substantial part from the assets of the company.

6. At all material times the plaintiff was engaged in a dangerous and/or unsafe occupation and it was reasonably foreseeable by the defendant, the effective owner and operator of the said quarry business, that employees therein, and in particular the plaintiff, in the course of their employment would sustain personal injuries and would suffer loss and damage in respect of which the said business would be found liable to pay compensation as was the fact, as aforesaid.

7. In the circumstance at all material times the defendant had a duty of care to employees in the said business, and in particular to the plaintiff, and/or it was an express or an implied term of the plaintiff's employment contract that, by reason of the defendant being the controller and the effective owner of the business in the name of Kenmare Limeworks Ltd. aforesaid, and accordingly as the person primarily and solely responsible for its proper conduct, management and operation, to take reasonable steps so as to ensure that the said business would be capable of paying compensation to such employees, and in particular to the plaintiff, particularly by means of an appropriate policy of insurance for such personal injuries, loss and damage as might be suffered by such employees, and in particular the plaintiff in an accident at work as aforesaid.

8.A Further and in the alternative the defendant has impliedly undertaken to ensure or impliedly warranted that any damages which the plaintiff might be awarded against the company in respect of personal injuries he sustained in and or arising out of his employment would be met by the company either from the proceeds of an appropriate employer's liability insurance policy or otherwise.

8.B Further and in the alternative in the circumstances the defendant was under a duty to warn the plaintiff that the company did not have employer's liability insurance and that, in the light of the company's financial position at the time, there was a distinct possibility that any injuries the plaintiff might suffer in the quarry would not be compensated in full or substantially from the assets of the company.

9.   Further or in the alternative at all material times in the circumstances as aforesaid the defendant had a duty under the Constitution to safeguard the plaintiff's bodily integrity in and about his employment and by reason of the aforesaid to ensure that any bodily injuries suffered by the plaintiff arising out of or in the course of his employment as aforesaid would be duly compensated by or on behalf of the defendant."

The defence as pleaded is a traverse. There is also a plea that the plaintiff's claim is barred by reason of the provisions of s. 11, sub-s. 2 (b) of the Statute of Limitations, 1957. The plaintiff's claim is a claim for the amount of the lost judgment. There is no plea that the personal injuries sustained by the plaintiff which gave rise to the judgment were caused by the negligence or breach of statutory duty of either his employer, the company, or the defendant. The defence being a traverse, there is no plea that the plaintiff is not entitled to succeed in the absence of proof of negligence or breach of statutory duty. However the case as presented by the parties did not raise that issue specifically and I do not propose to found my judgment in any part on that basis.

Counsel for the plaintiff based his claim upon four special factors which he submitted imposed the duties which he was seeking to establish. These are:

(1) that the defendant was quarry manager;
(2) that the company was in severe financial difficulties;
(3) that the defendant was in fact the owner and manager of the company; and
(4) that the plaintiff's employment was extra hazardous.

Counsel for the plaintiff put particular emphasis on the fact that the plaintiff's claim was for a purely economic loss and sought to establish both foreseeability and proximity on the part of the defendant. The defendant did not contest many of his submissions. Essentially the difference between them was whether or not there could be a duty to insure arising out of a contract of employment.

In *Ward* v. *McMaster*[11] the Supreme Court considered the nature of a duty owed by a local authority to a borrower from that authority and whether or not that borrower could rely upon implied representations arising from the nature of the transaction. The plaintiff had applied to Louth County Council pursuant to the provisions of the Housing Acts for a loan to purchase a house within its administrative area. In accordance with the provisions of the relevant statutory scheme the Council obtained a report as to the value of the house but not one as to its structural condition. The loan was made and after the plaintiffs had completed the purchase with the aid of the loan, it was found that the house contained so many structural defects, most of which were concealed, that it was not habitable. It was accepted that the plaintiffs

---

[11] [1988] I.R. 337.

could not reasonably have been expected to have obtained their own structural survey but were entitled to assume since they had been granted a loan that the Council would have obtained a report that the house was structurally sound.

The court had to consider whether or not in those circumstances a duty of care was owed by the Council to the plaintiffs. They held that such duty was owed. In considering the test to be applied to establish a duty of care, McCarthy J. at p. 347 accepted the test as laid down by Lord Wilberforce in *Anns* v. *Merton London Borough Council*[12] at pp. 751 and 752, as follows:—

> "[T]he position has now been reached that in order to establish that a duty of care arises in a particular situation, it is not necessary to bring the facts of that situation within those of previous situations where a duty of care has been held to exist. Rather the question has to be approached in two stages. First one has to ask whether, as between the alleged wrongdoer and the person who has suffered damage there is a sufficient relationship of proximity or neighbourhood such that, in the reasonable contemplation of the former, carelessness on his part may be likely to cause damage to the latter — in which case a *prima facie* duty of care arises. Secondly, if the first question is answered affirmatively, it is necessary to consider whether there are any considerations which ought to be negative, or to reduce or limit the scope of the duty of the class of person to whom it is owed or the damages to which a breach of it may give rise...."

Having considered later English authorities, McCarthy J. rejected any variation of this test and said at p. 349:—

> "I prefer to express the duty as arising from the proximity of the parties, the foreseeability of the damage, and the absence of any compelling exemption based upon public policy. I do not, in any fashion, seek to exclude the latter consideration, although I confess that such a consideration must be a very powerful one if it is to be used to deny an injured party his right to redress at the expense of the person or body that injured him."

Having found that there existed both proximity and reasonable foreseeability, McCarthy J. concluded as follows at pp. 351 and 352:—

> "These two considerations are both involved in the first leg of the *Anns* principle. I do not understand it to be argued that there are considerations which ought to negative or to reduce or limit the scope of duty or the class of person to whom it is owed or the damages to which a breach of it may give rise, within the second leg of the observations of Lord Wilberforce. It follows, in my view, without entering into the question of whether or not it is 'just and reasonable' to impose the duty, that the duty arose from the proximity of the parties, the injury caused was reasonably foreseeable, the breach was established, and the first plaintiff was entitled to succeed."

---

[12] [1978] A.C. 728.

In two recent English cases *Reid* v. *Rush and Tompkins Group plc*[13] and *Van Oppen* v. *Clerk to the Bedford Charity Trustees*[14] the courts had to consider the extent of the duty of care owed by a master to a servant and by a school master to a pupil respectively. Both cases had to consider whether masters had in the particular circumstances of those cases to effect personal accident insurance to cover injury to their servant and pupil respectively.

In *Reid* v. *Rush and Tompkins Group plc*,[15] the plaintiff had been employed by the defendant in Ethiopia, a country in which there was no adequate provision to compensate those injured in road traffic accidents. While acting in the course of his employment, the plaintiff was involved in a road traffic accident in Ethiopia and sustained severe personal injury. He was unable to recover compensation. He sued his employer for damages for negligence. It was claimed that it was an implied term of his contract of employment that the employer should have taken out appropriate insurance cover to protect him against this loss or alternatively to warn him so that he could take out such insurance for himself. His action failed. Although the facts of that case differ substantially from those in the present case, the bases of the claims are essentially the same. The case was pleaded upon the basis of an implied term of the contract of employment as well as in tort. The latter duty was claimed to be a duty to take "all reasonable steps which were necessary, in the light of any special risks arising from his working in Ethiopia, properly to protect the economic welfare of the plaintiff whilst he was acting in the course of his employment, and, therefore, in particular either to provide the appropriate insurance cover or to inform the plaintiff of the special risk and advise the plaintiff himself to obtain that cover." Several reasons are set out in the judgment of Ralph Gibson L.J. in support of the court's decision. At p. 221 he said:—

> "If a servant is to have a claim in tort against his employer in respect of economic loss it must be based upon some special factor in the circumstances or in the relationship between them which justifies the extension of the scope of the duty to cover such a claim or upon a separate principle of the law of tort which imposes such a duty."

At p. 230 he said:—

> "As to the duty to provide personal accident insurance at the expense of the defendant for the plaintiff, it is in my judgment impossible to hold that the scope of the duty in tort could extend so far. The legislation has not in general extended even the duty of compulsory employer's liability insurance in respect of employment out of this country. It has not been suggested that the master is required to provide personal accident insurance in those cases where in this country his servant is exposed to the risk of suffering injury in the course of his employment through the fault of a third party who cannot pay. The common law cannot in my judgment devise such a duty which the

---

[13] [1990] 1 W.L.R. 212.
[14] [1990] 1 W.L.R. 235.
[15] [1990] 1 W.L.R. 212.

legislature has not thought fit to impose and it could not be just or reasonable for the court to impose it."

Again at p. 231 he said:—

"To impose the duty alleged in this case would be contrary, in my judgment, to the accepted principles of our law relating to the general duty of a master to his servant.

I have had much difficulty in concluding that a general duty at common law upon a master to take care for the protection of this servant's physical well being cannot be extended by decision of the courts to include protection for the financial well being of his servant in special circumstances where the foreseeable financial loss arises from foreseeable physical injury suffered in the course of the employment and the duty claimed would extend only to a warning of a special risk. If this view be right the only way in which an employer's general duty of care — and I emphasise that I am referring only to the general duty of care which arises out of the relationship — will be capable of extension to cover financial loss will be by legislation, or by a contractual term, express or implied on the particular facts, or by a term which the court is able to say must be implied by law."

In Van Oppen v. Clerk to the Bedford Charity Trustees,[16] a schoolboy had sustained severe spinal injuries during a rugby game at his school. In proceedings against the school for negligence, one of the issues raised was whether or not the school had a duty to insure its pupils against accidental injury. In his judgment at p. 251 Balcombe L.J. regarded the plaintiff's case as depending upon the existence of "either (a) a duty to have regard to the economic welfare of its pupils arising from the relationship of school and pupil; or (b) a duty arising from an assumption by the school of specific responsibility in relation to personal accident insurance."

He accepted an analysis of recent English cases on the law of negligence undertaken by Bingham L.J. In *Caparo Industries plc v. Dickman*[17] as showing that three requirements are necessary to establish a duty of care, viz.:

"(1) Foreseeability of harm;
(2) Proximity;
(3) That it must be just and reasonable to impose it."

He then considered two further recent English cases, *Banque Keyser Ullmann S.A. v. Skandia (UK) Insurance Co. Ltd.*[18] and *Reid v. Rush and Tompkins Group plc*[19] and said at pp. 259 and 260:—

"From these last two cases I derive the following principles, which are explanatory of, and a gloss upon, the general principles referred to in *Caparo Industries Plc v. Dickman.*[20]

---

[16] [1990] 1 W.L.R. 235.
[17] [1989] Q.B. 653.
[18] [1989] 3 W.L.R. 25.
[19] [1990] 1 W.L.R. 212.
[20] [1989] Q.B.653.

(1) A pure omission, consisting of a failure to speak or act, by A resulting in economic loss to B, can give rise to a liability in negligence by A to B, provided there has on the facts been a voluntary assumption of responsibility by A, and there has been reliance on that assumption by B.

(2) Exceptionally, in some cases of pure economic loss the Court may be prepared to find the existence of a duty of care and to treat the defendant in law as having assumed a responsibility or duty to the plaintiff which is capable of giving rise to a claim for damages for such loss. Although the point is not altogether free from doubt, for the purposes of this appeal I am prepared to assume that this duty of care not to cause economic loss can exist in the exceptional case.

(3) An existing relationship between the parties which may give rise to a duty of care by one party for the physical well-being and safety of the other (e.g. master and servant), does not of itself mean that there is sufficient proximity between the parties to justify finding the existence of a duty of care not to cause economic loss.

(4) Whether a duty of care should be held to exist in a particular case must in the last resort be a question of policy to be decided by the court by reference to the principles to be deduced from the decided cases."

In his judgment Croom-Johnson L.J. dealt with the plaintiff's claim that it was necessary to establish the three ingredients to which I have already referred. Dealing with proximity he said at p.266:—

"In the present case there was unquestionably a proximity between Bedford School and the pupil. The school has never contended that it does not owe a duty of care to each of its pupils. The only question is, what was the scope of that duty to the plaintiff? This is clearly not the kind of case where proximity can be regarded as a synonym for duty of care."

At p. 267 he said:—

"The alleged duty was put as a high as a duty on the school to take reasonable care to prevent economic loss by the pupils. Presumably that would mean economic loss, however caused, by every pupil, and would indeed be an open-ended commitment on the part of the school going much wider than any duty owed by a parent to a child. No such duty exists."

I have referred to these two cases in considerable detail since great reliance was placed upon them by counsel. However it seems to me that they must be of very limited authority. The two tier test enunciated by Lord Wilberforce in *Anns* v. *Merton London Borough Council*[21] has no longer the authority in England which it had. The authorities differentiate between pure economic loss and other forms of loss. The statutory provisions in England are different, *e.g.,* there is compulsory statutory employers' liability insurance for employees in respect of loss arising out of and in the course of their employment in Great Britain. The fair and reasonable element necessary to establish a duty of care is one which McCarthy J. in *Ward* v. *McMaster*[22]

---

[21] [1978] A.C. 728.
[22] [1988] I.R. 337.

treated with reservation. Also *Van Oppen* v. *The Clerk to the Bedford Charity Trustees*[23] was argued in the context of the acceptance by the parties that there was no general duty in English law to insure, even against negligence: see the judgment of Balcombe L.J. at page 250.

Applying the principles enunciated in *Ward* v. *McMaster*,[24] it is necessary to consider three elements:—

(1) Proximity;
(2) Foreseeability;
(3) Public Policy.

The nature of the loss is not material. Liability in negligence extends to both personal injury and economic loss suffered by reason of the defendant's wrong: see the passage from the judgment of Henchy J. In *Siney* v. *Corporation of Dublin*[25] cited in the judgment of McCarthy J. in *Ward* v. *McMaster*[26] at page 349.

Proximity must mean the existence of a duty of care such that if the person owing the duty is careless there is likelihood that damage will be caused to the person to whom it is owed. If proximity is to arise whenever loss to another can be foreseen then it would seem that foreseeability would alone be the substantial test. In *Ward* v. *McMaster*[27] the relationship between the parties was not of itself sufficient to satisfy the test of proximity. It was held that there were special circumstances which gave rise to the duty of care in the particular case. Henchy J. said at p. 342:—

> "It is necessary for him [the plaintiff] to show that the relationship between him and the Council was one of proximity or neighbourhood which cast a duty on the Council to ensure that, regardless of anything left undone by the plaintiff, he would not end up as the mortgagor of a house which was not a good security for the amount of the loan. A paternalist or protective duty of that kind would not normally be imposed on a mortgagee in favour of the mortgagor, but the plaintiff was in a special position."

In the present case foreseeability of loss is accepted and in my view correctly. However it is submitted that there is no duty at common law of the nature for which the plaintiff contends. Counsel for the defendant referred to various statutory provisions which might not otherwise have been necessary. Section 285, sub-s. 2 (g) of the Companies Act, 1963, gives, preferential rights to an employee where there is no insurance. The Mines and Quarries Act, 1965, does not include any obligation to insure. Motor insurance is a statutory code. There is no statutory insurance provided for in the Safety in Industry Acts, 1955–1980. The obligations contained in these Acts are limited to the protection of the safety and well-being of the employee. The P.R.S.I. code is aimed to protect employees. It was necessary to introduce compulsory

---

[23] [1990] 1 W.L.R. 235.
[24] [1988] I.R. 337.
[25] [1980] I.R. 400.
[26] [1988] I.R. 337.
[27] *Ibid.*

employers' liability insurance in England by statute.

Counsel for the plaintiff recognised the need to establish these special circumstances. He accepted that not all employers would have a duty insure. He submitted that the defendant is liable because he is in reality the company and also because he had been appointed quarry manager. Neither of these matters is a ground for imposing liability on the defendant personally. He is in law a different person from the company and there are no circumstances from which it could be inferred that the company was a sham or should be treated as an instrument of fraud. Undoubtedly, as quarry manager the defendant was personally liable for breach of any of the statutory duties imposed upon the holder of that office. But such duties relate only to safety. There is no statutory duty of the type which the plaintiff seeks to establish.

The further basis of the plaintiff's case is that the work upon which the plaintiff was engaged was extra hazardous and that the defendant knew that the financial state of the company was such that it could not meet an award of damages for personal injuries. The evidence of the dangerous nature of the employment was not very compelling. Obviously, quarrying is a dangerous employment; there would not be special legislation relating to it if it was not. The plaintiff was unable to adduce evidence relating to the financial status of the company at the date when it ought to have insured, if such was its duty. The test would not be its financial position at the date of the judgment but its reasonably perceived financial position on the date of the accident. It was a small company; its affairs were in order and its business failed because of outside circumstances which arose subsequently. In my view, the plaintiff has not established what he has set out to establish in this regard.

The danger to the plaintiff was not as extreme as the plaintiff contends. Even if such a duty can be imposed this was not a case in which it should be. The plaintiff's case extends also to the existence of an obligation to warn the employee. In my view, this duty also can arise only where there are special circumstances. The plaintiff relied upon an implied term in his contract of employment. Even if such term existed, it cannot be imposed upon the defendant since he had no contract with the plaintiff.

The reality of the plaintiff's claim is that the defendant was the person in control of the company. He can certainly have no greater liability than that of the company itself. However it does seem to me that perhaps this claim should be answered by saying that to allow it as against the defendant would in effect be depriving the defendant of his protection under company law and to nullify all the essential principles of that law. It would not be a claim which could lie in any circumstances where the employer was an individual.

Finally, it seems to me that the existence of a duty upon a master to have regard for the safety and well-being of his servant cannot be extended in the absence of special circumstances, if at all, to a duty of a different kind, *e.g.,* to have regard for his economic well-being. I would adopt the reasons given by Ralph Gibson L.J. In the passages from his judgment in *Reid* v. *Rush and Tompkins Group plc*[28] to which I have already referred. If a duty to provide

---

[28] [1990] 1 W.L.R. 212.

employers' liability insurance is to be imposed, then it seems to me that it is a matter solely for the Oireachtas.

The plaintiff's last submission is to rely upon Article 40, s.3, sub-s. 2 of the Constitution which is:—

> "The State shall, in particular, by its laws protect as best it may from unjust attack and, in the case of injustice done, vindicate the life, person, good name, and property rights of every citizen."

In my view there is nothing in that provision to assist him. It gives him no more than a guarantee of a just law of negligence, which in the circumstances exists.

If I am wrong in the view which I have taken as to the existence of duty to insure then it is necessary to consider the defence that the plaintiff's claim would in any event be statute barred.

Section 11, sub-s. 2(b) is as follows:—

> "An action claiming damages for negligence, nuisance or breach of duty ... where the damages by the plaintiff for the negligence, nuisance or breach of duty consist of or include damages in respect of personal injuries to any person, shall not be brought after the expiration of three years from the date on which the cause of action accrued."

In *Ackbar* v. *C.F. Green and Co. Ltd.*,[29] there was a claim against insurance brokers for failure to take out particular insurance as a result of which the plaintiff was unable to recover damages from an insurer for personal injuries sustained by him. It was held that the action against the brokers did not "consist of or include damages in respect of personal injuries to any person." At p.588 Croom-Johnson J. said as follows:—

> "In the end if one asks the question here 'What is this action all about?' one gets the answer that it is about an alleged breach of contract by the defendants, as a result of which the plaintiff lost the chance or right to recover his loss either from the driver or from his own insurers. I do not think that the damages sought in this action consist of or include damages in respect of personal injuries. Those damages, which might have been recovered heretofore, are only the measure of the damages now claimed. Accordingly, I find that the proviso has no application and that the period of limitation is six years in this case."

Croom-Johnson J. referred also to *McGahie* v. *Union of Shop Distributors and Allied Workers*[30] with approval. In that case, there was a claim by the plaintiff which arose out of a failure by the defendants to commence proceedings on her behalf within the three year limitation period for some personal injuries actions. The relevant Statute of Limitations was worded in similar fashion to the English equivalent section to s. 11, sub-s. 2 (b) of the 1957 Act. It was held that the loss sustained was not a loss due to personal injury but was a loss caused by the lapse of the plaintiff's right to sue her employers.

---

[29] [1975] Q.B. 582.
[30] [1966] S.L.T. 74.

These two cases appear to conflict with *Paterson* v. *Chadwick*[31] which was referred to in the judgment of Croom-Johnson J. In that case, the plaintiffs had taken an action against their former solicitors for negligence for failure to issue proceedings in time in an action for personal injuries. Discovery was sought of hospital records. It was argued that it could only be ordered in relation to a claim in respect of personal injuries. It was held that since proof of the nature and extent of the personal injuries was an essential element in the claim, discovery should be ordered.

The facts in this case are not identical to those in *Ackbar* v. *C.F. Green and Co. Ltd.*[32] The cause of action lies in tort and not in contract. However, it can be said that the damages which are recoverable against the company are only the measure of damages against the defendant. The fact that the judgment has already been given against the company is not material since the cause of action against the defendant would have been complete at the date of the injury since the probability of loss through lack of insurance would have existed as from that date. I cannot hold however that this particular type of claim, where the manager or owner of a business is being sued, differs in substance from a claim against the business itself. Both are equally actions where the damage claimed consist of or include damages in respect of personal injuries. In these circumstances I consider that the claim would in any event have been statute barred.

For these several reasons the plaintiff is not entitled to succeed.

---

[31] [1974] 1 W.L.R. 890.
[32] [1975] Q.B. 582.

D. Mandatory Injunction to Direct Payment to Insured

In normal circumstances an insured's challenge of an insurer's refusal to provide indemnity to meet a given claim against it takes the form of the insured instituting proceedings seeking a declaratory Order that it is justifiably entitled to such indemnity. Such is indeed what occurred in the case of *Capemel Limited, and Others* v. *Roger H. Lister (No. 2)* (1989) but further proceedings were then brought when the insured sought mandatory interlocutory injunctive relief requesting that the court direct immediate payment of moneys to the insured, representing the amount of a settlement reached by the insured with the Plaintiff suing it. Mr Justice Costello who had made the original decision in the insured's favour regarding indemnity, recognising the somewhat unique circumstances of the case, in that that original decision of his had been appealed to the Supreme Court and the insured being in imminent danger of being wound up by Plaintiff felt that the merits of the case entitled him to relax the normally very strict rules and principles applied by the courts when faced with such an application for mandatory relief. He allowed the application, made the Order directing payment and put a stay on that Order so as to allow the original matter of indemnity to be dealt with in the meantime by the Supreme Court.

Capemel Limited, Charles Roche, Ellen Roche, William Roche, David Roche, Cathal Roche and Geroid Roche v. Roger H. Lister (No. 2)
[1989] I.R. 323
The High Court

COSTELLO J: This is a very unusual situation. It arises from the following facts:—

On 27th February, 1986, the first plaintiff, Capemel Ltd., entered into a contract of insurance with a syndicate of Lloyd's Underwriters of which the leading underwriter is the defendant in these proceedings. The policy of insurance covered employer's liability and not long after it was entered into an employee of Capemel Ltd., Mr John Holt, was injured in an accident whilst in its employment.

Mr Holt instituted proceedings against Capemel Ltd. and the underwriting syndicate repudiated liability on foot of the policy. The repudiation resulted in proceedings which I heard and on 28th April 1989,[33] in which I decided that the repudiation was not justified and I made a declaratory order declaring that the underwriting syndicate were obliged to make good any

---

[33] See p.573 of this book.

claim which Mr Holt might have arising from the accident.

It so happened, and I was informed at the time, that the proceedings taken by Mr Holt were pending in the High Court and were shortly to be heard. In fact, it now transpires that on 2nd May, 1989, the case was listed and some discussions took place concerning a possible settlement of it, that is to say, discussions between the first plaintiff and the representative of the Lloyd's underwriters. It is said that these discussions were without prejudice and that it is improper to refer to them so I will make no further reference to them beyond referring to the fact that they took place.

On 5th May, 1989, Mr Holt's action was settled. The evidence before me is that it was a prudent and proper settlement. The evidence before me at the moment, which is uncontradicted, is that this settlement was arrived at on counsel's advice.

At the hearing before me of the earlier proceedings I was informed that the view of Capemel Limited was that the claim made by Mr Holt was a valid one and so I proceed on the basis that the settlement of Mr Holt's claim is reasonable in all the circumstances.

I also have evidence that there is a threat to wind up the first plaintiff, and I accept that there is a reasonable apprehension that the threat will be carried out. I was informed at the hearing, and I accept the evidence on the motion before me today, that the first plaintiff is unable to pay the settlement which it reached with Mr Holt and that it is unable to pay the debt which I must hold is properly payable by it to Mr Holt. In these circumstances the first plaintiff will go into liquidation unless the defendant makes good the liability which I have decided it has under its policy of insurance.

That is the situation that exists at the present time subject to one very important further development: The defendant has appealed my decision to the Supreme Court, as, of course, it is entitled to do. It is entitled to claim that the decision of this court was a wrong one and it is entitled to ask the Supreme Court to hold that it is not liable to indemnify the first plaintiff in respect of the damages which it agreed to pay to Mr Holt.

The remedy which the first plaintiff sought in the earlier proceedings was one of declaratory relief and I granted a declaratory order. Had I been requested to make an order that the defendant pay any damages properly payable to Mr Holt, I am quite satisfied that I would have made such an order. And I am quite satisfied, although it is not stated in the order, that liberty to apply is inherent in the situation that existed in the other proceedings; that had the other proceedings been re-entered I would have made an order pursuant to the view I had taken of the parties' liabilities directing the defendant to pay a sum of money. In view of the settlement and in view of the uncontradicted evidence that the settlement was a reasonable one, I would have ordered the defendant to pay a specific sum of money to the first plaintiff.

That is not what happened. What has happened instead is that a new set of proceedings has been instituted and in these proceedings the plaintiffs claim interlocutory relief. Because of the special circumstances of this case I do not think I should approach the claim for interlocutory relief on the basis on which the court normally approaches a claim for interlocutory relief, particularly the very stringent principles on which the court would give interlocutory relief of a mandatory sort.

There are two things I can do and I do not think it matters very much which it is. I can treat today's application as an application to re-enter the original proceedings and make an order on the original proceedings. Alternatively, I can make an order on the interlocutory application in these proceedings. I think it is more appropriate to make the order on the interlocutory motion because there is already an appeal pending on foot of the first action. But I think it would be wrong to approach the matter on the basis that I must be limited to the very strict rules in relation to mandatory relief. I must do what is best in the circumstances of this case. In the circumstances I think I would have made an order in the first set of proceedings directing payment and putting a stay on it and I propose to do the same on this interlocutory motion: to make an order directing payment, even though in the normal circumstances such an order would not be granted.

To my mind the justice of this case involves the court directing the defendants to make payment but putting a stay on the order so that the matter can be brought before the Supreme Court at the earliest possible opportunity should the defendant decide to go on with the appeal. If an order directing payment is not made, the first plaintiff is likely to go into liquidation. On the other hand, if I make an order directing payment and put no stay on it and do not permit the defendant to bring the matter to the Supreme Court so that the Supreme Court can deal with it earlier, if possible, than would normally be the case, the situation would be that the defendant may have been directed to make a payment which subsequently he may be unable to recover should he win on appeal in the first action.

In these circumstances, I think the justice of the case requires that an order be made on the present motion and that a stay be put on it for a limited period of, I suggest, four weeks. If an appeal is then taken against the question of the stay, the matter can be further considered by the Supreme Court in the light of the situation which they then have before them

I propose, therefore, to make an order directing that the sum of money reached by way of settlement of the proceedings be paid to the first plaintiff, Capemel Limited, and I propose to put a stay on that order for four weeks.

The actual terms of the order will be the payment of £65,000 together with a further sum for the costs of John Holt when they have been taxed or otherwise ascertained.

I am making no order in relation to the claim for the names of the underwriters.

[Reporter's Note: The defendant appealed to the Supreme Court against the judgment and order of Costello J. The Supreme Court in an *extempore* judgment dismissed the appeal and affirmed the High Court Order save regarding costs.]

E. Appointment of Insurer's Solicitor

Virtually all modern policies of liability insurance contain provisions entitling the insurer to deal as it pleases, and in its absolute discretion, with claims against its insured, and in respect of which indemnity is provided by the relevant policy. One of the most important aspects of how an insurer deals with such claims is the appointment of its own solicitor, to ensure that the claims are handled in a manner it has both control over and confidence in.

Usually by the time a decision has to be made as to the appointment of a solicitor, the insurer has fully investigated the nature and circumstances of the claim being made and is in a position to make an informed decision on the provision of indemnity. Sometimes, however, it is only after the insurer's own solicitor has been appointed and come formally on record that an insurer is in a position to reach a decision on indemnity. If it is decided that indemnity will not be provided, it is necessary for the solicitor appointed to apply to Court to come formally off record. Such an application was the subject of the recent case of *Sean O'Fearail* v. *Colm McManus* (1994) in which the solicitor appointed by the insurer of the Defendant so applied to come off record. The Supreme Court, exercising its discretion, allowed the solicitor's application so to come off record. In so doing, it was, however, critical of the practice of insurers' solicitors being appointed at a time prior to proper investigation being undertaken as to circumstances of the case against the insured. The insurer was penalised by being ordered to pay the costs of all parties to the application. The Court further emphasised that the mere coming off record of the solicitor had no bearing whatsoever on the substantive issue between the insurer and the insured as to the validity of the refusal of the insurer to provide indemnity.

Sean O'Fearail *v.* Colm McManus
[1994] I.L.R.M. 81
The Supreme Court

O'FLAHERTY J (EGAN AND DENHAM JJ CONCURRING): This is a case that has taken a rather bizarre twist. It began with a plenary summons that was issued by the plaintiff in which there was a claim for damages for the wrongful assault and battery of the plaintiff by the defendant on 23 February 1990 at Rock Road, Blackrock, Co. Dublin.

In the statement of claim it is pleaded that the plaintiff was cycling along Rock Road, in the direction of Dublin, when the defendant committed an unlawful assault and battery on him by dragging him and causing him to fall from his bicycle whereby he suffered severe personal injuries, loss and damage.

It will be clear that the essential plea in the case was one of assault and battery.

Nonetheless the insurance company, that is the insurance company who were indemnifying the defendant in respect of his driving of the car, instructed Mr John O'Brien, solicitor, to take up the matter on their behalf and he duly delivered a defence on 5 February. Then in due course the insurance company took the view that this incident was not covered by the policy of insurance that they had issued and that they should no longer be seen to be an insurance company who would indemnify the defendant in respect of this occurrence and therefore, in effect, Mr O'Brien found himself without instructions to act for the defendant and thought the appropriate thing to do would be to come off record.

The relevant rule obviously gives the courts a wide discretion. It is contained in O.7, r. 3 of the Rules of the Superior Courts 1986 and it gives a solicitor on record the entitlement to apply to the court for an order declaring that the solicitor has ceased to be the solicitor acting for the relevant party to the proceedings and the court may order accordingly.

The matter came before the High Court (Johnson J.) on 15 November 1993. He set forth the broad background to the case that I have already given and then he went on to say:

> In my view this application should be refused. This is not a case in which there is any suggestion of fraud or impropriety on the part of the defendant. While I have every sympathy for Mr O'Brien I take the view that, as officers of the courts, solicitors should be slow to take any steps in proceedings until such time as they are satisfied that their instructions are as complete as is possible. In the instant case the insurance company's instructions to Mr O'Brien were not as complete as they might have been had a proper investigation of the circumstances surrounding the case been undertaken in the first place.
>
> In my view insurance companies should conduct their investigations in as thorough going a manner as possible prior to instructing solicitors to act rather than, as seems to be the case here, instructing solicitors to act, then undertaking their investigations.

I, for my part, would endorse every word of that part of the judgment. Nevertheless, I have to come to grips with the reality of the situation as it is now, which is, that the insurance company is saying that it is not going to indemnify the defendant in respect of this occurrence and even if Mr O'Brien is kept on record it is not going to foot the bill – if there is an award made. That is as I understand Mr Comyn SC's submission to us.

I make no comment as to whether that repudiation is justified or that if it is henceforth put before some process of arbitration or other decision-making body that will be upheld and justified. I will make no judgment at all on that; I simply recount the situation as it is now presented to us. Counsel for the defendant, in his very able argument, has sought to say that the insurance company should not be entitled to repudiate and that it would follow from that that Mr O'Brien should stay in the case. That I think, with respect to his argument, is to reverse the manner in which things must now proceed.

The present situation, as it has unfolded before us, is that the insurance company, rightly or wrongly, has repudiated. It says that it does not want Mr O'Brien to act any longer and I think in those circumstances it would be a forced form of liaison to say to Mr O'Brien that he should continue to act for this defendant and I would in the circumstances allow him to come off record and to that extent I would reverse the order of the learned High Court judge. I would do so, however, on condition that the costs both in the High Court and of this hearing will be paid, not by Mr O'Brien, but by the insurance company concerned and I would look for Mr Comyn's undertaking in that regard that the insurance company will discharge the costs of all parties.

Index